D1452528

EVELYN WAUGH: THE CRITICAL HERITAGE

THE CRITICAL HERITAGE SERIES

GENERAL EDITOR: B. C. SOUTHAM, M.A., B.LITT. (OXON.)
Formerly Department of English, Westfield College, University of London

For a list of books in the series see the back end paper

EVELYN WAUGH

THE CRITICAL HERITAGE

Edited by
MARTIN STANNARD
Lecturer in English Literature
University of Leicester

ROUTLEDGE & KEGAN PAUL
LONDON, BOSTON, MELBOURNE AND HENLEY

First published in 1984
by Routledge & Kegan Paul plc

39 Store Street, London WC1E 7DD, England

9 Park Street, Boston, Mass. 02108, USA

464 St Kilda Road, Melbourne,
Victoria 3004, Australia, and

Broadway House, Newtown Road,
Henley-on-Thames, Oxon RG9 1EN, England

Printed in Great Britain by
⎮Redwood Burn Ltd

Compilation, introduction, notes, bibliography and index
© *Martin Stannard 1984*

Library of Congress Cataloging in Publication Data

Evelyn Waugh, the critical heritage.
(The critical heritage series)
Bibliography: p.
Includes index.
1. Waugh, Evelyn, 1903–1966—Criticism and interpre-
tation—Addresses, essays, lectures. I. Stannard,
Martin, 1947–. II. Series.
PR6045.A97Z683 1984   823'.912   83–21172

British Library CIP data available

ISBN 0–7100–9548–1

General Editor's Preface

The reception given to a writer by his contemporaries and near-contemporaries is evidence of considerable value to the student of literature. On one side we learn a great deal about the state of criticism at large and in particular about the development of critical attitudes towards a single writer; at the same time, through private comments in letters, journals or marginalia, we gain an insight upon the tastes and literary thought of individual readers of the period. Evidence of this kind helps us to understand the writer's historical situation, the nature of his immediate reading-public, and his response to these pressures.

The separate volumes in the *Critical Heritage Series* present a record of this early criticism. Clearly, for many of the highly productive and lengthily reviewed nineteenth- and twentieth-century writers, there exists an enormous body of material; and in these cases the volume editors have made a selection of the most important views, significant for their intrinsic critical worth or for their representative quality— perhaps even registering incomprehension!

For earlier writers, notably pre-eighteenth century, the materials are much scarcer and the historical period has been extended, sometimes far beyond the writer's lifetime, in order to show the inception and growth of critical views which were initially slow to appear.

In each volume the documents are headed by an Introduction, discussing the material assembled and relating the early stages of the author's reception to what we have come to identify as the critical tradition. The volumes will make available much material which would otherwise be difficult of access and it is hoped that the modern reader will be thereby helped towards an informed understanding of the ways in which literature has been read and judged.

B.C.S.

To My Mother

Contents

Preface

The reviews are generally ordered chronologically in each
section. Where several items appeared on the same day these
are in alphabetical order of the author's surname, unsigned
notices following these. Notices dated only by the month
come last of all, again wherever possible in alphabetical
order of the author's surname.

In trying to maintain chronology I have found it necessary to split two long essays which offered a book-by-book
account between the various sections. Nigel Dennis's
Evelyn Waugh: The Pillar of Anchorage House, 'Partisan
Review', 28 July 1943, 350-61, and Rose Macaulay's The Best
and the Worst II. Evelyn Waugh, 'Horizon', December 1946,
360-76 appear as Nos 84, 89, 92 and Nos 20, 30, 56, 63, 71,
79, 93, 101 respectively.

In the Introduction, reviews quoted but not included in
the book are indicated by full references in parentheses.
For the ease of the British reader at least, I have cited
quotations from the Penguin editions of the novels rather
than the expensive Uniform Edition. For the travel books
and biographies, page references are to the first edition.
Place of publication is London unless otherwise indicated.

Acknowledgments

I should like to thank the following: Mr Mark Amory, Dr
Robin Biswas, Professor Philip Collins, Mr Philip Dodd,
Dr Helen Evans, Mr Roger Fallon (for compiling the index),
the Leverhulme Trust (for my three years as Leverhulme
Research Fellow in English Literature at the University of
Edinburgh) and Ms Moragh Reid. I should also like to thank
the office staff of the Department of English, University
of Leicester, and the staffs of the following libraries for
their patient assistance: the Bodleian, the British Library,
Edinburgh University Library, Leicester University Library,
and the National Library of Scotland.

It has not always proved possible to locate the owners
of copyright material. However, all possible care has been
taken to trace ownership of the selections printed and to
make full acknowledgment for their use. For permission to
reprint, and for answering queries, thanks are due to the
following: Sir Harold Acton for No. 5; Kingsley Amis for
Nos 149 and 171; Associated Newspapers Group Ltd for No.
15, from the 'Evening News'; John Bayley and John Grigg
for No. 123; 'The Bell' for Nos 102, 103, 104 and 105;
Bernard Bergonzi for Nos 57 and 172; Malcolm Bradbury for
No. 184; Brigid Brophy for Nos 58 and 75; Anthony Burgess
for No. 188; Jonathan Cape Ltd for No. 58, from 'Don't
Never Forget' by Brigid Brophy; the 'Catholic Herald' for
No. 68; 'Cherwell' for Nos 2, 14 and 35; The Christian
Science Publishing Society for No. 49, from the 'Christian
Science Monitor'; Rosica Colin Ltd on behalf of the Estate
of Richard Aldington for No. 27 (© Madame Catharine Guil-
laume); Collins Publishers for No. 143, from 'Evelyn
Waugh. A Biography' by Christopher Sykes; 'Cosmopolitan'
for No. 187; the 'Daily Express' for Nos 34, 41 and 90;
the 'Daily Telegraph' for Nos 40, 78, 118, 125, 197 and
198; George Dangerfield for No. 88; 'Encounter' for Nos
109, 165 and 188; the 'Evening Standard' for Nos 13 and
25; Farrar, Straus and Giroux, Inc., for Nos 65 and 99,

first published in the 'New Yorker', reprinted by permission of Farrar, Straus and Giroux, Inc., from Splendors
and Miseries of Evelyn Waugh, from 'Classics and Commercials' by Edmund Wilson (Copyright 1950 by Edmund Wilson.
Copyright reviewed © 1978 by Elena Wilson); Graham Greene
for Nos 60 and 162; the 'Guardian' for Nos 1, 81, 94 and
146 from the 'Manchester Guardian' and Nos 172 and 194
from the 'Guardian'; Sir Rupert Hart-Davis as literary
executor of William Plomer for Nos 53 and 183; the Estate
of L.P. Hartley for No. 24; A.M. Heath & Company Ltd on
behalf of the Estate of the late Jocelyn Brooke for No.
181, and on behalf of the Estate of George Orwell for No.
114; Hodder & Stoughton for No. 43, from 'The Bookman';
I.H.T. Corporation for No. 10, Thomas Craven's review of
'Rossetti', 'New York Herald Tribune', 2 September 1928
(© I.H.T. Corporation), for No. 110, Thomas Sugrue's
review of 'When the Going was Good', 'New York Herald
Tribune Weekly Book Review', 5 January 1947 (© I.H.T.
Corporation), for No. 128, Gouverneur Paulding's review
of 'Helena', 'New York Herald Tribune Weekly Book Review',
22 October 1950 (© I.H.T. Corporation), and for No. 144,
Frank O'Connor's review of 'Tactical Exercise', 'New York
Herald Tribune Weekly Book Review', 7 November 1954 (©
I.H.T. Corporation), all used by permission; Stanley
Kauffmann for No. 186 (Copyright 1964 Harrison-Blaine Inc.
Reprinted by permission of the author); Frank Kermode for
No. 109; Philip Larkin for No. 194; the Editor of the
'Leicestershire Tatler' for No. 22, from 'Bystander'; the
Estate of Mrs G.A. Wyndham Lewis and the Wyndham Lewis
Memorial Trust for No. 196, from Wyndham Lewis, 'The Doom
of Youth' (Copyright © 1981 by the Estate of Mrs G.A.
Wyndham Lewis by permission of the Wyndham Lewis Memorial
Trust); 'London Magazine' for No. 163; Dr Dermod MacCarthy
for Nos 61 and 121; 'The Month' for Nos 130 and 152; 'The
Nation' (New York) for No. 178; 'New Blackfriars' for
No. 57, from 'Blackfriars'; 'The New Republic' for No. 151
by Curtis Bradford (© 1955, The New Republic. Inc.); the
'New Statesman' for Nos 6 and 8 from the 'Nation and
Athenaeum' and Nos 16, 26, 33, 54, 59, 69, 73, 87, 97,
122, 127, 133, 155, 157, 168, 173, 182 and 185 from the
'New Statesman'; 'The New Yorker' for No. 135 (Reprinted
by permission; © 1952, 1980 The New Yorker Magazine Inc.);
'The New York Times' for Nos 9, 18, 29, 38, 50, 64, 82, 98,
114, 150, 158, 164 and 177 (© 1928, 1929, 1930, 1932, 1934,
1939, 1945, 1946, 1949, 1955, 1958, 1960, 1962 by The New
York Times Company. Reprinted by permission); Nigel Nicolson for No. 80; 'The Observer' for Nos 4, 12, 32, 126,
156, 162 and 176; 'Partisan Review' for Nos 84, 89 and 92
(© 'Partisan Review', Vol. 10, No. 4, 1943, pp. 350-61),

for No. 136 (© 'Partisan Review', Vol. 19, No. 6, 1952)
and for No. 179 (© 'Partisan Review', Vol. 29, No. 3,
1962); A.D. Peters & Co. Ltd for published and unpublished
material by Evelyn Waugh, for No. 3, from 'My Brother
Evelyn' by Alec Waugh, for Nos 20, 30, 56, 63, 71, 79, 93
and 101 by Rose Macaulay, from 'Horizon', December 1946,
and for No. 42 by Eric Linklater, all reprinted by permission of A.D. Peters & Co. Ltd; David Pryce-Jones for No.
107; 'Punch' for No. 193; Peter Quennell for Nos 6, 7, 54
and 59; Deborah Rogers Ltd on behalf of the Estate of
Cyril Connolly for No. 116, reprinted from 'Horizon', 1948;
Alan Sillitoe for No. 170; the 'Spectator' for Nos 23, 39,
48, 53, 67, 76, 86, 96, 108, 111, 149, 153, 166, 171, 180,
184 and 195; Dr E.C. Stopp for No. 130; Christopher Sykes
for Nos 143 and 147; the Editor of 'The Tablet' for Nos
44, 45, 52, 72, 139, 142, 161, 167 and 174; 'Time Magazine'
Weekly News Magazine for No. 100 from 'Life' and Nos 117,
129, 134 and 159 from 'Time' (© Time Inc.); the 'Times
Literary Supplement' for Nos 36, 47, 51, 66, 70, 74, 85,
91, 95, 112, 120, 138, 141, 154, 160, 189, 190 and 191;
Times Newspapers Ltd for Nos 21 and 131 from 'The Times'
and Nos 113, 121, 132, 140, 148, 169 and 175 from the
'Sunday Times'; the late Alec Waugh for No. 187; Auberon
Waugh for published and unpublished material by Evelyn
Waugh (reprinted by permission of A.D. Peters & Co. Ltd);
the late Dame Rebecca West for Nos 11, 28 and 37; Angus
Wilson for Nos 165 and 191.

Abbreviations

ALO	Evelyn Waugh, 'A Little Order. A Selection from His Journalism', ed. Donat Gallagher (Eyre Methuen, 1977)
ALS, nd	Autograph letter, signed, no date
B & B	'Books and Bookmen'
DE	'Daily Express'
DH	'Daily Herald'
'Diaries'	'The Diaries of Evelyn Waugh', ed. Michael Davie (Weidenfeld & Nicolson, 1976)
DM	'Daily Mail'
DT	'Daily Telegraph'
DR	'Dublin Review'
EN	'Evening News'
GKW	'G.K.'s Weekly'
HRC	The Evelyn Waugh Archive, Humanities Research Center, University of Texas at Austin
'Letters'	'The Letters of Evelyn Waugh', ed. Mark Amory (Weidenfeld & Nicolson, 1980)
L & L	'Life and Letters'
MG	'Manchester Guardian'
NR	'New Republic'
NS	'New Statesman'
NYHT	'New York Herald Tribune'
NYHTBR	'New York Herald Tribune Book Review'
NY	'New Yorker'
SD	'Sunday Dispatch'
SR	'Saturday Review'
ST	'Sunday Times'
Sykes	Christopher Sykes, 'Evelyn Waugh. A Biography' (Collins, 1975)
T & T	'Time and Tide'
TLS	'Times Literary Supplement'
TC	'Twentieth Century'
'Writers'	Julian Jebb's interview with Waugh printed as

Evelyn Waugh in 'Writers at Work' (Secker &
Warburg, 1968), pp. 105-14

Introduction

'Evelyn Waugh...,' the 'Sunday Express' once remarked, 'was quite simply exceedingly unpleasant' (Graham Lord, 28 September 1975, 6). This view of his character is not uncommon, especially since the first appearance of sections from the 'Diaries' in the 'Observer Magazine' (1973). Christopher Sykes's 'official' biography (1975) did little to rectify the impression. Despite his loyal attempt to stitch up a suit of virtue for his subject the bile still, apparently, spilled through the seams. Waugh's enemies saw in the book what they had always suspected: he had been pompous, snobbish, sadistic; there was something of the Fascist and the philistine about him. The 'Letters' (1980) offered more ammunition. 'It is impossible to imagine getting a letter from Evelyn Waugh,' wrote Philip Larkin, 'unless it were of the "Mr Waugh deeply regrets that he is unable to do what is so kindly proposed" sort. In the first place, one would have to have a nursery nickname and be a member of White's, a Roman Catholic, a high-born lady or an Old Etonian novelist' (No. 194). In an age of egalitarianism, Waugh has often seemed a redundant elitist.

The reader will find several instances of displeasure at Waugh's ostensible political and social attitudes in the post-war reviews. But he will, perhaps, be surprised that their number is not greater. In fact, the mythology of Waugh's ogreish temperament was something largely constructed, with his help, through the popular press. Certainly, he was a right-wing Catholic apologist who sincerely lamented what he saw as the rape of European culture. The real Mr Waugh, however, would never stand up before the microphone or camera. There was always a melodramatic disguise, a parodied prejudice, to defend his privacy. Two such masks are ruthlessly analysed in his fictional self-portrait, 'The Ordeal of Gilbert Pinfold' (1957), as the 'eccentric don' and 'testy colonel'. But while the reviewers of the

1

private papers seem often to have confused these personae
with the real thing (see No. 192), few have attacked the
novels on these grounds. Many simply stand bemused and
often delighted before works whose artistry endears to them
a world which they believe never to have existed. Even his
literary antagonists (Philip Toynbee, Donat O'Donnell and
Kingsley Amis, for instance) cannot help but admire his
technical facility and comedic gifts. Graham Greene's opinion that 'Evelyn Waugh was the greatest novelist of my
generation' (headnote, No. 60) is often echoed. George
Orwell grudgingly recorded in his notebook that 'Waugh is
about as good a novelist as one can be (as novelists go
today) while holding untenable opinions'.(1) We will
return to the notion of 'untenable opinions' later but it
is as well to remind ourselves at the outset that, despite
the acrimony surrounding the publication of his personal
records, Waugh's impressive list of admirers includes many
prominent figures of modern British fiction and criticism:
Muriel Spark, Anthony Burgess, Angus Wilson, Anthony Powell,
Henry Green, Frank Kermode, Malcolm Bradbury and David
Lodge.

The primary object of this volume, in keeping with
others in the series, is to collect a representative
sample of contemporary reviews. The principal editorial
problem, however, arises from the fact that in discussing
Waugh's work reviewers found it difficult to escape discussion of his personality. Waugh was often directly responsible for this. In 'Labels' (1930) he wrote:

> one of the arts of successful authorship is preventing
> the reading public from forgetting one's name in between
> the times when they are reading one's books.... Now, even
> if you are very industrious, you cannot rely on writing
> more than two books a year.... So you have to spend half
> your leisure in writing articles for the papers; the edi-
> tors buy these because people read your books, and people
> read your books because they see your articles in the
> papers.... The rest of your leisure you have to spend in
> doing things which other people will think interesting.
> (pp. 9-10)

In the early days Waugh made good use of his friends who
wrote gossip columns (Tom Driberg, Patrick Balfour) and
reviews (Peter Quennell, Peter Fleming, Cyril Connolly,
Douglas Woodruff). It was common practice to try to direct
one's work towards reviewers likely to be sympathetic.
Even Orwell, who loathed the log-rolling of contemporary
criticism, indulged in this. But there are two aspects of
Waugh's 'Labels' statement which neatly exemplify the

editorial problems involved in providing a selection here
which might adequately suggest to the reader the effect he
had upon his contemporary audience. First, there is the
tongue-in-cheek bravado of disclaiming serious intention;
and second, there is the brutal definition of the mechanics of contemporary literary success. He both made light of
his talents and exploited the media. As he said in 1946:

> I have never, until quite lately, enjoyed writing. I am
> lazy and it is intensely hard work. I wanted to be a man
> of the world and I took to writing as I might have taken
> to archaeology or diplomacy or any other profession as
> a means of coming to terms with the world. (No. 100)

Waugh's public image was enigmatic and his artistic
approach baffling. To balance the selection, then, I have
also provided reviews of later editions, some edited essays
and, in the Miscellaneous section, three brief glimpses of
him in various 'roles'. Waugh was a public figure despite
his craving for privacy and it is in that context that we
should read the criticism. I have, therefore, included
Waugh's (and others') replies to certain notices as these
formed an essential part of the critical debate and often
conditioned later responses to his work. Controversy
surrounded not only his 'untenable ideas' but also his
artistic licence and historical scholarship. Arguments
raged over 'Black Mischief' (Nos 44-6), 'Edmund Campion'
(Nos 61, 62, 65) and 'Waugh in Abyssinia' (Nos 69, 71) and
there was an angry debate over 'Brideshead Revisited'
involving Edmund Wilson (No. 99).

It would be superfluous here to give a detailed biographical account of Waugh's career. The publication of his
biography and private papers, and the continuing popular
appeal of his novels (all are still in print in Penguin),
have meant that the details of his life and work are perhaps the best known of any modern writer. Suffice it to
say, then, that he was born in 1903, the son of Arthur
Waugh, literary critic and Managing Director of Chapman &
Hall, and the brother of Alec Waugh, the novelist; that he
was educated at Lancing College and Hertford College,
Oxford, leaving university without a degree but with
copious debts; that he attempted in turn and unsuccessfully
to become a painter, a printer and a carpenter and finally,
in need of money (and respectable status) to marry the
Hon. Evelyn Gardner, wrote a biography of Rossetti (1928)
and his first novel, 'Decline and Fall' (1928); that she
deserted him for another man (an experience which left an
indelible impression) and shortly afterwards (September
1930) Waugh was received into the Catholic Church; that he

travelled widely in Africa, South America and Mexico during
the 1930s, married again in 1937 and settled down to the
seclusion of country house life in the West Country, broken
only by a period of active service during the war and
occasional forays to London and trips abroad. He died in
1966. (More details can be gleaned from the reviews of 'A
Little Learning' (1964) and those of the biography,
journalism, 'Diaries' and 'Letters'.)

It is all too easy to impose on this framework clear
stages of literary 'development'. The obvious structure
would read something like: (a) 'The Balance' - 'Labels'
(1926-30; early, dilettante, pre-Catholic work);
(b) 'Remote People' - 'Robbery Under Law' (1931-9; light,
ingenious comic novels, with an undercurrent of serious
social commentary; right-wing Catholic apologist in biographical and travel writing); (c) 'Brideshead Revisited' -
'A Little Learning' (1945-64; the entrenched Catholic
apologist in both fiction and non-fiction, offering in his
novels a study of the operation of Divine Grace and a
blanket denunciation of the Age of the Common Man). This,
of course, will not do. The assumption behind it is that
Waugh only became a 'serious' artist with 'Brideshead'.
Several reviewers of that novel, for instance, saw him as
a lightweight social satirist whose ability to control his
material collapsed under the strain of attempting a more
complex moral structure. But, whatever our views of that
novel, the fact remains that for more than a decade he had
been a sophisticated aesthetician and a scrupulous techni-
cian. Despite his jaunty self-effacement he had been a
'serious' writer since 1929 when he was completing 'Vile
Bodies'.

Waugh considered himself a craftsman, a cabinet-maker of
fiction who belonged to no recognizable school of the
avant-garde. Little sympathy was spared for the 'conversation and biology' (2) of Huxley, the inchoate effusions
of Lawrence, the didactic optimism of Wells or the linguistic experiments of Joyce and Gertrude Stein. All, he
believed, suffered from subjectivity; all had failed to cut
the umbilical cord between themselves and their work. His
early literary heroes were Lewis Carroll, Firbank, T.S.
Eliot, Hemingway, Henry Green and Ivy Compton-Burnett.
Clarity, concision, the use of the 'refrain' (recurrent
image) rather than the statement, a sense of fantasy and of
the self-supporting reality of a work of art beyond and
above the 'issues' involved - these were the tenets of his
aesthetic faith, reiterated in odd, quiet corners of his
journalism during the 1930s. On a specific, technical level
he was interested in developing these themes through dialogue (particularly slang; see headnote to No. 196) with a

minimum of authorial intrusion. The artist should, in his
view, clarify and make exact those nebulous ideas thrown
up by experience; it was not his business to preach or to
confess. His trade, like the priest's, was concerned with
elucidation and communication, the formulation of order
from chaos. 'That is what makes story telling such an
absorbing task,' he wrote in 1946, 'the attempt to reduce
to order the anarchic raw materials of life' (No. 100).
Henry James's novels were the great (temporal) solace of
his later life.

Few reviewers, however, detected this subtlety of
approach in the early work. His failure to offer an essentially heroic vision of man, his refusal to stop laughing
at the absurdity and cruelty of human behaviour, often
led him to be classed with Saki and P.G. Wodehouse. In
fact, his early novels (1930-8) represent a 'serious'
Catholic apologetic by negative suggestion. The world
depicted is the humanist *reductio ad absurdum*, life without (or, at least, in ignorance of) God, a point missed by
most contemporary critics including Ernest Oldmeadow, the
Editor of the Catholic 'Tablet' (No. 44).

'Brideshead' was a positive statement of the same reaction. Edmund Wilson's approach to it was typical of many;
he saw Waugh as a delightful entertainer but, he said,
when he 'abandons his comic convention' and attempts 'a
"serious" novel, in the conventional sense', deserting
'two-dimensional caricature', he falls headlong into
'mere romantic fantasy' (No. 99). The justifiable argument
against the book's rampant snobbery (put rather more convincingly by Donat O'Donnell (No. 102) and Rose Macaulay
(No. 101)) becomes confused with technical discussion and
the spectre of Waugh's public personality stalks heavily
about, sometimes distorting critical evaluation.

I would suggest that there are five main groups of
reviewers: 'Georgian' *littérateurs*, Waugh's generation of
Oxbridge literary men, the Catholic intelligentsia, the
hacks, and those novelists and academics who have given
serious, detailed attention to Waugh's work. Some critics,
of course, would have a place in more than one group.
Christopher Sykes and Graham Greene, for instance, could
be included in both the second and the third. But in an
important sense their reviews are more usefully placed in
the third as the defence of a co-religionist.

The first category, then, would include those older,
established 'men of letters' who ruled the London literary
reviews during the early part of Waugh's career: for
instance, Arnold Bennett, Frank Swinnerton, J.C. Squire and
Gerald Gould. Waugh's father was a similar figure. The
1920s saw the disappearance of the professional 'man of

letters' whose complacent, easy-going clubland was under
attack by 1928. There is a whimsical, reflective and subjective approach in their reception of 'Rossetti': generous, paternal, but with an air of authority which often
allows them to illustrate their own opinions rather than to
review the book. The TLS piece (10 May 1928, 341-2) to
which Rebecca West refers in her letter (No. 11) largely
ignored Waugh's handling of the issues. Their reviews of
the novels are fairly represented by Arnold Bennett's
pieces (Nos 13 and 25). 'Decline and Fall' was warmly
received but the more aggressively 'modern' 'Vile Bodies'
seemed to them too brittle, often poorly constructed and
in bad taste.

The second group - the new Oxbridge 'generation' - would
comprehend Harold Acton, Peter Quennell, Alan Pryce-Jones,
Cyril Connolly, Maurice Bowra, Anthony Powell, Henry Green,
Harold Nicolson, Philip Toynbee, John Betjeman and W.H.
Auden. There is no common political affiliation here,
Pryce-Jones, Bowra, Powell, Betjeman and Acton 'tending' to
the right, the others to the left. There is, however, the
connection that all, with the exception of Auden, at
various stages moved in Waugh's circle of friends and many
shared his pugnacious, more businesslike approach to the
arts. These were among the men (ironically, along with
I.A. Richards and Leavis in Cambridge with whom they had
little in common) largely responsible for storming the
citadels of the *littérateurs*. They loved the pre-war fiction but were divided (largely by their political leanings) over 'Brideshead' and the work which followed.

The 'Catholic intelligentsia' would include Christopher
Hollis, Douglas Woodruff, Christopher Sykes, F.J. Stopp,
Graham Greene, Anthony Burgess and several 'literary'
priests: Fr Martindale, Mgr Ronald Knox and Illtud Evans.
These, while sometimes finding Waugh's social prejudice
after the Second World War too strong, shared his mystical
approach which ultimately abjured rationalist argument.
After Ernest Oldmeadow's attacks in the 'Tablet' (one hesi-
tates to include him among the 'intelligentsia'), the
Catholic press was usually delighted with Waugh's work (see
headnote, No. 44). With the publication of 'Brideshead'
Waugh was similarly praised by rigorously academic French
critics who had taken up Graham Greene as a writer in the
Mauriac tradition. (3) The distinction made here between
the Catholic and 'academic' criticism would not perhaps
have been necessary in France (see Mr Sykes's comments,
p. 36 below).

The 'hacks' worked for the popular newspapers or society
magazines. The standard of criticism was generally low.
These were the people who often confused Waugh's life with

his work and who delighted in the 'Diaries' as excellent
'copy'. In the early days they picked up the slang of 'Vile
Bodies' and bandied it about gleefully, delighting in the
rich comedy of the novels and largely ignoring their serious undertones. Ralph Straus, for instance, rather hopelessly remarks of 'Vile Bodies': 'The trouble is to know
what to say about it. You cannot be given an outline of
the plot for the simple reason that there is none' (No.
22). He was voicing the inadequacy of many to cope with
the transparency of Waugh's technique. They knew that it
worked but not how or why. Nevertheless, his fame relied
heavily upon their enthusiastic vagueness in the columns
of the daily papers. After the war, and especially after
the Nancy Spain libel suit (see No. 197), a note of acrimony began to creep into some of their articles and
reviews. Waugh had, after all, been openly lampooning the
yellow press since 'Scoop' in 1938.

The final classification would group together two radi-
cally opposed factions, admirers and dissenters. First,
there are those (few in number) who have successfully
attempted an objective appraisal of Waugh's work based on
aesthetic rather than political or religious argument:
Rebecca West, David Lodge, Frank Kermode, Malcolm Bradbury,
Nigel Dennis and Angus Wilson, for instance. These approach
the work with the sort of critical sophistication Waugh
himself brought to Firbank in his 1929 essay reprinted in
Donat Gallagher's 'A Little Order' (1978). Lightness of
touch is not equated with a lightweight mind; Waugh's innovation of literary form is given due credit. His novels are
compared on stylistic grounds with Hemingway's and the
'waste land' imagery of futility is seen, as it should be,
in the context of Eliot's notions about the decay of Western culture and the fundamental importance of 'tradition'.
The serious opposition is represented by Edmund Wilson,
Kingsley Amis, Donat O'Donnell, Simon Raven and Rose Macaulay, all of whom (with the exception of O'Donnell, apparently) admired the early fiction and deserted Waugh after
'Brideshead'. These objected to what they saw as a sneering, 'romantic' class-consciousness which devalued Waugh's
artistic objectivity.

So much, then, for the primary object of this book. The
ultimate aim, however, must be to provide an account of the
vacillations of an author's reputation. With Waugh the
curve of this graph is far from clear. For, despite the
serious reservations expressed by several influential critics, Waugh's work was continuously popular from the publication of his first novel. Of Pinfold he wrote that he 'had
been tenderly reared and, as a writer, welcomed and over-
rewarded early. It was his modesty which needed protection

and for this purpose, but without design, he gradually assumed the character of burlesque' (Penguin, p. 15). We need, then, to distinguish between 'popularity' (i.e. large sales) and 'prestige'. Up to and including 'Put Out More Flags' (1942) Waugh's fiction had few serious assailants. The only powerful attacks, and plainly foolish ones, came from Oldmeadow in 1932 and 1934 (Nos 44 and 52). Waugh's novels were mainly savoured as well-wrought black comedy. A few saw more serious elements, a few found them trivial or in bad taste. Largely, though, it was accepted that Waugh had carved out a style and a vision peculiar to himself for outrageously funny, pungent, serio-comic burlesque. His non-fiction after 1930 was another matter. Here his right-wing Catholic prejudices were openly on display and 'Edmund Campion' (1935), 'Waugh in Abyssinia' (1936) and 'Robbery Under Law' (1939) all initiated controversy.

With 'Brideshead' (1945) Waugh's 'political' and religious views entered undisguised into his fiction. Its publication largely damaged his 'prestige', with Edmund Wilson, Donat O'Donnell and Rose Macaulay fiercely attacking its romantic snobbery. The book seemed to present an elitist Catholic vision, fundamentally uncharitable, aligning Waugh's faith with the aristocracy against the partially educated and unkillable children of the Lower Orders, epitomized by the ranker officer, Hooper. Despite Waugh's ostensible delight at having 'shaken off one of the American critics' (Wilson) (No. 100), he later regretted the novel's subjective sensual luxuriance and completely revised it in 1959 (No. 106). He did not, however, regret the introduction of the mystical element and in 1946 stated that in future his books would have two things to make them unpopular: 'a pre-occupation with style and the attempt to represent man more fully, which, to me, means only one thing, man in his relation to God' (No. 100).

The stylistic and thematic intentions were perfectly sincere. The reference to unpopularity, though, emphasizes the need for a division in his case between 'popularity' and 'prestige'. The bad reviews of 'Brideshead' set the tone of antagonism for much of the left-wing or liberal-humanist criticism of later work. Nevertheless, the novel became a world best-seller and he conquered the American market convincingly for the first time. Suddenly, from being a smart and well-to-do author of fashionable, distinctly 'English' novels which appealed in the USA only to a coterie, he was transformed into an international celebrity. Hollywood sought the film rights of 'Brideshead' and many similar lucrative proposals were made,

even for the early work. (Waugh turned nearly all the
scripts down on the grounds of their aesthetic barbarity.
The whole business of becoming the object of 'fan mail'
he found profoundly repugnant, although he did not object
to the financial security such fame promised.) Retreating
to protect his 'modesty' (No. 184) behind the masks of
burlesque, Waugh continuously baffled those unsympathetic
critics who wanted to adopt the 'psychological' approach
and actively encouraged the 'biographical fallacy'.

It is after 'Brideshead' then, that the reviewers divide
into camps: those like Edmund Wilson, Kingsley Amis and,
later, Simon Raven who found Waugh's implicit 'political'
position facile or pernicious, and those who could disregard or applaud this element and still see his novels as
accurate social commentary. As a bridge between these
views Bernard Bergonzi and Frank Kermode (Nos 172 and 109)
offer the notion of Waugh's concern with aristocratic
values as a structural myth which it is largely irrelevant
to oppose or support. They see it more as a Jamesian
'point of view' allowing 'saturation' in an internally
consistent moral vision (No. 109). One might add that
Waugh's belief in the reality of the 'supernatural' is a
fundamental concept rarely considered by critics who might
be perfectly happy with it from the pen of Milton or
Blake. This theme is discussed below, pp. 42 and 43, and by
F.J. Stopp in No. 130.

Two 'graph curves', then, would be necessary to chart
Waugh's reputation, the first for sales and the second for
serious critical esteem. The first would demonstrate a
shaky start with 'Rossetti', climbing a little with 'Decline
and Fall', rising steeply with 'Vile Bodies' and levelling
off between 1930 and 1942. With 'Brideshead' it would
rocket to a new peak which could not be maintained because
Waugh interspersed his subsequent novels with a biography
and small, select editions of minor works. Despite this,
however, and the curiosities of 'Helena' (1950) and 'Pinfold' (1957), the public eagerly read everything, no matter
how slight, and still does. (For figures concerning first
edition sales see No. 197.)

The second curve would start high with 'Rossetti' and
continue to rise steadily to 'Brideshead'. Here it would
level out or perhaps drop a little until the last volume of
the trilogy (1961). Critics were evenly divided over the
merit of most of the post-war fiction with the exception of
'The Loved One' (jubilantly received by most) which
returned to his earlier manner and contained no overt
Catholic apologetic. 'Unconditional Surrender' did much to
re-establish his prestige as a major writer with the more
unsympathetic element. Certainly it reclaimed Cyril

Connolly as a devotee after his moderate reviews of the
trilogy's first two volumes.

Interesting anomalies appear in this development.
'Punch' and the 'New Yorker', magazines whose reputation
relies to a considerable extent on smart anarchic humour,
paid little attention to Waugh's work throughout most of
his career. His early books were noted only briefly. Similarly, a major organ of critical opinion in Britain, the
TLS, rarely credited Waugh with the literary status
accorded him by his peers. Another (gratifying) peculiarity
is that we do not find a simple division of opinion between
'right-wing' and 'left-wing' papers which we might suspect
to have been the case. The 'New Statesman' was a largely
consistent admirer as was its American counterpart, 'New
Republic'.

Certain attitudes are, however, predictable. Of the
major literary journals, Leavis's 'Scrutiny' offered nothing but a passing remark on two occasions, 'Essays in
Criticism' was at first dubious but later came to accept
Waugh as an important author, and Connolly's 'Horizon'
held him in high esteem. 'Encounter' was consistently
generous in its appreciation. Numerous, now defunct, serious literary magazines existed during Waugh's early and
middle career- 'Life and Letters', the 'London Mercury',
the 'Cornhill' - and all valued him highly. Waugh, as has
been said, had friends at court working for many papers;
Peter Quennell, for instance (with whom he had a stormy
relationship), wrote for the 'New Statesman' and 'Life and
Letters' and edited the 'Cornhill'. Peter Fleming and
Derek Verschoyle were literary editors of the 'Spectator'
and many of Waugh's cronies wrote for the latter. Even in
the early days he knew Viola Garvin, Literary Editor of the
'Observer', and several men running the Oxford undergraduate press. Cyril Connolly appears in these pages writing for 'Horizon' and the 'Sunday Times'.

Good books of criticism on (or including pieces on)
Waugh have been rare. A list of the better ones is included
in the bibliography, the more stimulating of which are by
Frederick Stopp, Sean O'Faolain, Terry Eagleton and
Malcolm Bradbury. As a straightforward critical survey Dr
Stopp's book (now out of print) is by far the most sensible, accurate and thorough although it was published in
1958 before the last volume of the trilogy and 'A Little
Learning'. Christopher Sykes's biography, despite its
faults, is the only substantial work based on research into
the private life and papers of the novelist. A much
slighter 'picture book' anthology was compiled by David
Pryce-Jones in 1973, 'Evelyn Waugh and his World', but it
contains some useful reminiscences and two interesting

essays by David Lodge and Malcolm Bradbury.

It is the Americans who have engaged most earnestly in
literary research on Waugh although he is gaining in popularity with British doctoral candidates every year. Several
of the American theses have been rewritten as books, the
best of which (not, unfortunately, a great compliment) is
James Carens's 'The Satiric Art of Evelyn Waugh'. Three
American scholars and a German provided the immensely valuable and extensive 'Checklist of Primary and Secondary
Material' (1972). This is often inaccurate in detail but
contains a mine of material for scholars. The year 1981 saw
the publication of Robert Murray Davis's fascinating and
extensive catalogue of the Waugh archive at the Humanities
Research Center, University of Texas at Austin.

Given the divergence between 'popularity' and 'prestige'
and the complications which arise from this in any attempt
to generalize about the development of Waugh's reputation,
I have avoided a detailed schematic introduction and settled for a book-by-book account. It is only fair, after
all, to treat each work as an entity.

THE BALANCE (1926)

The excerpt from Alec Waugh's book (No. 3) explains how
his younger brother came to write this, his first substantial piece of published fiction. Waugh had produced other,
lighter stories while at Oxford for the undergraduate
papers, the 'Cherwell' and the 'Isis', but his artistic
fame at the university relied then on his work as an illustrator. The 'Diaries' reveal that shortly before this
Waugh had attempted a novel, 'The Temple at Thatch'. (This
was destroyed after Harold Acton's 'chilling' assessment,
Waugh tells us in 'A Little Learning'.) Several entries describe the composition of The Balance, which occupied
Waugh from May to August 1925. (Alec Waugh appears to have
dated it wrongly in saying 'Early in 1926'; cf. 'Diaries',
26 August 1925, p. 218.) It is an interesting piece, experimenting boldly with avant-garde linguistic techniques.
The characters in the first section are involved in a film
watched by others who periodically interrupt. Contributors
to the volume in which the story was published include
William Gerhardi, Gertrude Stein and Somerset Maugham. It
was a considerable achievement for Waugh to be noticed
among such established writers. Reviews, however, failed
entirely to grasp the serious intention of the story. As
Waugh remarked in the 'Diaries': 'A very silly review in
the "Manchester Guardian" this morning commends my contribution to "Georgian Stories" but for the most futile

reasons.'(4) The review mentioned is No. 1.

It should also be noted that Waugh's early work was warmly received by the Oxford student papers which were often edited in the late 1920s by his friends (John Betjeman, for example). His woodcuts for column headings in both the 'Isis' and 'Cherwell' continued to appear for over a decade after he had gone down and his reputation as an iconoclast lived on among the undergraduate community.

'ROSSETTI' (1928)

Waugh wrote 'Rossetti' on a commission from Duckworth's secured for him by Anthony Powell who was then on the editorial staff. The Pre-Raphaelites had exerted a powerful fascination since Waugh's schooldays and he came to appreciate their interdisciplinary approach as painters, scribes, writers, printers and craftsmen eschewing individual indulgence for the reputation of the 'shop'. Rossetti, in particular, intrigued him and it is arguable that Waugh saw much of himself in this erratic bohemian. Writing the book, however, was particularly hard work (the manuscript concludes with 'The End. Thank God') as it closed an aimless period in Waugh's life during which he had been an art student, a schoolmaster and, for six weeks, a journalist. It did not involve original research but Waugh scoured the major authorities (particularly Holman Hunt's 'Pre-Raphaelitism and the Pre-Raphaelite Brotherhood').

Ten years earlier Lytton Strachey had shocked and delighted the public with his 'Eminent Victorians'. The aggressive 'objectivity' of that work set a style for more feeble imitators, and reviewers in the late 1920s were especially sensitive to stylistic experiment in biography. Several expressed delight that Waugh had not fallen into the 'tawdry facetiousness' of the '[Philip] Guedalla school' ('Cherwell', 16 June 1928, 187-8). These writers, in imitating the lighter side of Strachey's informality, ended by providing what Roy Campbell describes as 'the most perfect instrument that has yet been invented to enable the mediocre to patronize the great' (No. 8). Waugh in fact begins by discussing with such confidence the complex problems involved in the presentation of biographical material that he effectively forestalls criticism on these grounds.

The book was, in general, warmly received. Reviewers appreciated his 'acute perception of that feeling for purely pictorial values' (SR, 21 April 1928, 499-500) and

his grasp of the practical techniques of painting. They
liked even more the way Waugh 'confounds the modern school
of art criticism' (L&L, July 1928, 141-2) and 'with admirable lucidity, defining his terms precisely', translates
'the technical jargon of the fashionable aesthetic doctors
into language within the grasp of the general reader'
(No. 10). The 'school' attacked was that of Roger Fry,
Clive Bell and Hubert Waley whose Bloomsbury doctrine
of 'significant form' was used as a justification of
abstract art. Waugh found it interesting but inadequate to
comprehend such rogue-elephant figures as Rossetti in any
Great Tradition of graphic art. At this stage, though, he
was not the adversary of abstract art that he was to become and talks with admiration of 'the pellucid excellen-
cies of Picasso'. In 1928 he had no intention of becoming
a professional novelist and the 'Diaries' suggest that he
had begun 'Decline and Fall' while writing 'Rossetti', as
light relief from the ardours of biography.

The common complaint, and a perfectly fair one, concerns
the 'inadequate notice of Rossetti's poetry' (No. 4). He
was far more interested in the painting and knew relatively
little about the literary output. Waugh had no ear for
music and, although well-read in English poetry thanks
largely to his father's influence, had no genuine enthusiasm for verse.

'Rossetti', Waugh remarked in an interview with Julian
Jebb in 1962, was 'hurried and bad' ('Writers', p. 108).
Despite its *succès d'estime* it ran only to a reprint in
1935 in Duckworth's Georgian Library and later in life,
when reissuing the novels in the Uniform Edition, he would
not allow it to be republished. Waugh, however, was perhaps overstating the case. Duckworth's at last reissued it
in 1975, along with 'Labels', to coincide with the appearance of Christopher Sykes's long-awaited biography. John
Bryson, who wrote an introduction and corrected certain
errors, still found it well-written and provocative and
Orwell, reading it for the first time late in life for an
essay on Waugh (never completed), was surprised by its
quality. It contains distinct faults (the aesthetic argument is far from the lucid exposition admired by the contemporary reviewers and Waugh was well aware of this) but
it remains a vivid, well-written account and a remarkable
achievement for only six months' work.

'DECLINE AND FALL' (1928)

Waugh noted in 1957 that a review by Arnold Bennett in the
'Evening Standard' 'was believed to sell an edition in 24

hours. The claim was exaggerated as I learned to my disappointment when he kindly noticed my first novel. The ensuing demand was, I think, something between 200 and 300'
(No. 197). Although it sold many more copies than this,
running eventually to six hard-back editions of approximately 2,000 copies each by 1931, this book, like 'Rossetti', failed to make much money in 1928. It did, however,
establish his reputation as a bright young author and
bring in commissions for articles.

'Decline and Fall' was universally applauded as light
comedy of a high order. Gerald Gould, the influential
'Observer' critic, noted that 'he is an important addition
to the ranks of those dear and necessary creatures – the
writers who can make us laugh' (No. 12). Arnold Bennett
went further: '"Decline and Fall" is an uncompromising
and brilliantly malicious satire, which in my opinion comes
near to being quite first-rate' (No. 13). The 'mixture of
fantasy and reality' (Peter Fleming, 'Isis', 17 October
1928, 11), the creation of 'a really comic character' in
Captain Grimes (No. 15), the sheer exuberance and 'Love of
life', the 'natural and sparkling' dialogue (No. 16) all
exerted an immediate appeal. 'A reviewer has few epithets
of praise at his command', the young Cyril Connolly concluded, 'owing to the high mortality in the vocabulary of
appreciation, but of "Decline and Fall" he can say that
though not a great book, it is a funny book, and the only
one that, professionally, he has ever read twice' (No. 16).

It was of course, mildly scandalous in its subject-
matter. Originally intended for Duckworth's, the publishers
of 'Rossetti', it was refused by them, amid complicated
circumstances (5) on the grounds of its indelicacy. Waugh
then reluctantly submitted it to his father's firm, Chapman
& Hall, who published it (with substantial cuts) on condition that Waugh preface the volume with an Author's Note
disclaiming lubricious intent. Nevertheless, the 'bland
destructive brilliance' (No. 20) of Waugh's treatment of
homosexual schoolmasters, loss of religious faith, white
slaving, extra-marital sex, liberal social reform and
theological training is quite blatantly subversive and it
was the range and penetration of his scattered shot which
allowed such wide appeal. Undergraduates saw it in the
'Zuleika Dobson' tradition of 'Oxford novels' (Fleming,
'Isis'); tough young critics saw it as a blistering, light-
hearted satire of the contemporary world in the vein of
Ronald Firbank or Norman Douglas (No. 20); Bright Young
Things (as they always do) saw it as a novel about them
(Lady Eleanor Smith, SD, 23 September 1928, 4, and Ralph
Straus, 'Bystander', 21 November 1928, v). In this
case, they were all correct. Even the last group, seeing it

as a *roman à clef*, forced Waugh and his publishers to alter
two names. 'Martin Gaythorn-Brodie' and 'Kevin Saunderson'
were clearly portraits of Eddie Gaythorne Hardy and Gavin
Henderson. In the second impression they became 'Miles
Malpractice' and 'Lord Parakeet'. The photographer who
drives about in 'an electric brougham' (Smith, SD) was
distinguishable as Cecil Beaton, and Jack Spire as J.C.
Squire (see headnote to No. 4), but these, like the outrageous 'Chez Otteline' sign in one of Waugh's illustrations, remained unchanged.

A moderate *scandale* was precisely what Waugh wanted. He
needed to make money with this book in order to support his
new wife and he courted publicity. From this time his name
rarely left the gossip columns. Patrick Balfour (later,
Lord Kinross), writing much of Lady Eleanor Smith's
'Sunday Dispatch' column, kept the social activities of
'he-Evelyn' and 'she-Evelyn' constantly before the public.
But Waugh still did not want to be a novelist. Just before
leaving with his wife for the Mediterranean cruise which
was to provide the subject for 'Labels' he told Balfour:
'I am really going to concentrate on my drawing during the
voyage. I hope I can bring back enough sketches to hold an
Exhibition in June, and, if it is successful, abandon
writing for painting.'(6)

The few months before the voyage were perhaps the happiest period of Waugh's life. But it was a happiness marred
slightly by the melancholy spectacle of his Oxford friend
and mentor, Harold Acton, failing where he had succeeded.
Acton's novel, 'Humdrum', had been published contempora-
neously and reviewed by many alongside 'Decline and Fall'.
Waugh's novel was dedicated 'in homage and affection' to
him. 'Mr Waugh owes no homage to Mr Acton as a novelist,'
J.B. Priestley stated, 'for the latter's story is a poor
thing, showing us nothing but a vast social superiority to
everybody and everything' (No. 15). Much had been expected
of this former 'star' of undergraduate literary life, not
the least by Waugh himself. It was intensely embarrassing
for both that reviewers chose Waugh's work as a standard by
which to condemn his friend's.

'VILE BODIES' (1930)

'Vile Bodies' was an instant success and secured Waugh's
position as a prominent young writer although more reviewers expressed displeasure than with 'Decline and Fall'.
Ralph Straus began his eulogy with 'Adjectives fail me....
It is a masterpiece of inconsequence' (No. 22);

V.S. Pritchett admitted: 'I laughed until I was driven out
of the room' (No. 23). But Arnold Bennett was disappointed
(No. 25) and Frank Swinnerton found it 'bogus' (EN 7 February 1930, 8). The critics were quick to notice the
change in tone in this 'hectic piece of savage satire'
(No. 23) which offered an altogether darker vision: 'he
has scratched, as with a diamond, savagely upon a pane of
expensive glass, a biting caricature of the Bright Young
People' (A.C.E.M., 'Cherwell', 1 February 1930, 31-2).
Most liked it although the more staid found the experimental structure and apparent cynicism little to their taste.
     The element of bitterness in the novel (despite Mr
Sykes's assertions) (7) undoubtedly reflects the depression
he felt at his first wife's desertion in mid-1929. He
remarked to Julian Jebb:

> I was in the middle of 'Vile Bodies' when she left me.
> It was a bad book, I think, not so carefully constructed
> as the first. Separate scenes tended to go on far too
> long.... It was secondhand too. I cribbed much of the
> scene at the customs from Firbank. I popularised a
> fashionable language like the beatnik writers today
> [1962], and the book caught on. (8)

Writing to Henry Yorke during that desperate period when
he was trying to force himself back to work a few months
after the catastrophe, he described the problems of composition: 'It has been infinitely difficult and is certainly
the last time I shall try to make a book about sophisticated people. It all seems to shrivel up and rot internally
and I am relying on a sort of cumulative futility for any
effect it might have.'(9) These two aspects - the amusing
Mayfair slang and the 'cumulative futility' of the characters' lives - were discussed at length by the reviewers.
     Some of them, intoxicated with amusement at Waugh's com-
pound, bathetic adjectives, imitated them in describing the
book: 'the love-making ... in the first chapter', said
S.P.B. Mais, 'is just "sick-making"' (DT, 17 January 1930,
15). There are references,' Gerald Gould concludes,
' - well, my dear, too shy-making' ('Observer', 2 February
1930, 8). More sensible linguistic criticism came from
Rebecca West who suggested that Waugh's use of 'monosyllabic conversations' was as 'technically astonishing as the
dialogues in ... Hemingway's "Farewell to Arms"'(No. 28).
Few, however, had the perception to realize that 'Vile
Bodies' was a technical experiment following the tradition
of those writers Waugh admired - not only Hemingway but
Firbank and Gerhardi. Most concentrated on its humour and
its social satire, and were baffled by the form of the

work. Edward Shanks saw it less as a novel than as 'a
review between covers'. Concentrating on the attack on
the 'world of intellect and fashion' with 'small pebbles
of wit', he notes the Gerhardi connection but suggests
that 'What is lacking in Mr. Waugh at present is any
capacity for design' (No. 26). Arnold Bennett felt that
'the lack of a well-laid plot has resulted in a large number of pages which demand a certain obstinate and sustained
effort of will for their perusal' (No. 25). Perhaps the
most interesting aspect of Bennett's and St John Ervine's
(DT, 30 January 1930, 6) pieces, however, is that they
compare Waugh's book unfavourably with his brother's 'The
Coloured Countries', a travelogue published at the same
time. Alec Waugh, they considered, had the weightier, more
sympathetic, mind. The 'New York Times' suggested that
'Vile Bodies' might be termed 'needlessly nasty, decadent,
superficial and arrogantly, even offensively sophisticated'
and thought Waugh had borrowed much from Douglas, Arlen
and Huxley (No. 29).

Analysing the social satire, L.P. Hartley, Richard
Aldington and Rebecca West (Nos 24, 27 and 28) offer more
penetrating remarks. All were aware that, beneath the
humour, Waugh wished to suggest that we 'are dancing on a
volcano' (No. 24). It was a book 'based on complete despair' (No. 27), which Miss West saw as 'a further stage
in the contemporary literature of disillusionment' which
started with 'The Waste Land' (No. 28). Later (1946),
Rose Macaulay suggested that the society depicted is
characterized by pervasive philistinism, divorced from
'intellectuality, culture, artistic or literary sensibility' (No. 30).

By the time the Uniform Edition was published in 1965,
'Vile Bodies' was firmly established in the canon of
Waugh's work. Waugh expressed distaste for it in his preface but reviewers still delighted in its brittle humour
and 'mannered ruthlessness' (John Davenport, 'Spectator',
7 May 1965, 607). It has not died with the age it documents like Arlen's 'The Green Hat' but survives for new
readers both as a mordant, fantastical satire on hedonism
and as a work of 'historical interest' (Davenport,
'Spectator').

'LABELS' (1930)

'Labels' is a fascinating 'period piece' in that it was
written after the breakdown of Waugh's marriage and concerns the period of his honeymoon cruise. It is the only
complete work written between the separation and his

conversion to Catholicism. The American title, significantly, was 'A Bachelor Abroad' and Waugh overcame the
difficulty of describing this delicate period by inventing
a fictional honeymoon couple, Geoffrey and Juliet, whose
intimacy he purported to find embarrassing. The couple
seem to represent a portrait of he-Evelyn and she-Evelyn
as they *were*, the implication being that he had now out-
grown that softly romantic, boyish phase and become more
a 'man of the world'.

Most reviewers liked it as 'piquant, entertaining and
... pleasantly outspoken' (Ralph Straus, 'Bystander',
1 October 1930, 48). Harold Nicolson detected a distinctly
modern, 'post-war' consciousness, seeing Waugh as the
leading literary representative of this. 'He has all the
scepticism of ... Huxley and none of his despair' (No. 34),
an opinion reiterated by Hobhouse (No. 35). Waugh's
'impertinence' and blatant self-advertisement were emphasized by his cocksure indulgence in the cardinal sin of
literary journalism: he reviewed his own book in the
'Graphic' (No. 31).

Serious attention was paid to his ancillary discussion
of the Englishman's 'sense of period' (No. 34) and the
aesthetic discussion of the Tutankhamen relics and Gaudí's
Catalan art nouveau architecture (Nos 34 and 33). With the
exception of Edgar Holt, the critics were intrigued by
Waugh's ingenuity in making an entertaining spectacle of a
tourist route. Edgar Holt, however, found the book devoid
of 'original thought or material', a 'farago of longitude
and platitude' ('Bookman', November 1930, 140).

It sold well for a travel book, running to at least two
editions. When excerpts from it were reprinted in 'When the
Going was Good' (1946), many of the passages expressing
that post-war consciousness and nearly all the illuminating,
facetious asides were cut by Waugh. The full text was reprinted by Duckworth's in 1975 with an enthusiastic introduction by Kingsley Amis.

'REMOTE PEOPLE' (1931)

'Remote People' documents Waugh's first visit to Abyssinia
in 1930. He was 'The Times' correspondent covering the
coronation of Haile Selassie and continued his journey at
his own expense down through Rhodesia to South Africa.

It received a mixed reception but no notices which, like
Holt's on 'Labels', were wholly damning. Some expressed
intense enthusiasm. Frank Swinnerton thought that 'the
sincerity of this book, its candour and originality, the
quality of its perception, and the engrossing interest of

its narrative, cause me to regard it as the best book of
travel I have read for years' (EN, 30 October 1931, 11).
Peter Fleming saw it as 'the very best possible sort of
book about this journey' (No. 39). But the 'Observer',
after praising it, noted that Waugh's knowledge of local
affairs 'is necessarily external and trivial.... It follows
that the "political" parts are the least readable' (22
November 1931, 5). Rebecca West was disappointed after her
delight in the novels and 'Labels'. 'Remote People', she
considered, was 'well beneath his proper form' and she
compared it unfavourably with Norman Douglas's 'Summer
Islands' (No. 37). The 'New York Times Book Review' was
impressed by Waugh's ability to describe this 'pilgrimage
of ennui' in amusing fashion but detected racial and anti-
American prejudice (No. 38).

'BLACK MISCHIEF' (1932)

Reviews of this novel varied enormously. L.A.G. Strong
thought that 'Mr Waugh's note deepens in this brilliant
book' and found it 'amazingly well-written' and entirely
original ('Spectator', 1 October 1932, 420). Howard
Marshall also noted the increased seriousness and saw it
as 'a transitional stage in his work' (No. 40). Eric Linklater, like Rose Macaulay on 'Vile Bodies', saw it in the
'Waste Land' tradition of Eliot alongside Bates, Nicolson
and Muir: 'The manner in which Mr Waugh controls his widely
varied matter is admirable. His narrative is swift and
picturesque, and his cutting ... is masterly. "Black Mischief" ... shows an all-round growth of strength' (No. 42).
    The 'New Statesman' suggested comparison with Saki but
found the work largely distasteful (October 1932, 380).
James Agate thought it would be 'deemed wildly funny by
the intelligentsia' but found little sense in this 'yarn'
(No. 41). The TLS, ostentatiously yawning, thought it an
'extravaganza written largely about, and presumably for,
the bright young people' which was 'insubstantial for its
length' (13 October 1932, 736). Geoffrey West thought the
Book Society might have done better for its October choice
of the Book of the Month and saw the novel as another
'absurd' exercise in the tradition of Firbank's 'vapid
fatuities' (No. 43).
    Adverse criticism rarely bothered Waugh. The Book
Society selection ensured wide circulation and his novels
after 'Vile Bodies' always sold well whatever the critics
said. In this instance, however, one reviewer deeply
offended him. Ernest Oldmeadow with his remarks and then
his review in the 'Tablet' provoked a literary controversy

in the pages of that sober Catholic periodical. As Editor
and Book Critic he noted that a novel by Waugh had appeared
but refused to name either its title or publisher as it was
'a disgrace to anybody professing the Catholic name'. Waugh
was travelling in British Guiana at the time but his
friends defended his good faith and artistry in a vigorous
open letter. Oldmeadow responded with monumental super-
ciliousness by suggesting that publication of their letter
'must lower more than one of the signatories in public
esteem'. In the same piece (No. 44) he then reviewed
'Black Mischief' in a fashion which must have made him a
laughing stock among intelligent Catholics. It was clearly
intended as the final word in this unsavoury debate, offering a bald statement of what he saw as the novel's obvious
moral lapses. But still the arguments ran on week by week
under the title of A Recent Novel. In the end, Oldmeadow
found it necessary to reply yet again and at even greater
length by summarizing the entire discourse (No. 45).

On his return, Waugh was embarrassed and outraged. He
immediately wrote an Open Letter to H.E. the Cardinal
Archbishop of Westminster (set up in print and dated May
1933, but never published until included in the 'Letters',
1980) replying to the accusations and suggesting that Oldmeadow be sacked.

No American reviews are included because none could be
found which offered anything more than an account of the
plot.

'NINETY-TWO DAYS' (1934)

This is Waugh's account of his travels in British Guiana
and Brazil during 1932. It was his most adventurous excursion, partly in unmapped country (where he almost lost his
life), and the one on which he met the religious maniac,
Mr Christie, 'up-country'. Christie was to form a partial
model for the character of Mr Todd in 'A Handful of Dust'
(1934), the lunatic who imprisons Tony Last in the Brazilian jungle.

The book was generally liked. V.S. Pritchett saw it as
'a deep improvement on "Labels" and the book on Abyssinia
["Remote People"] in which farce and satire had become
farouche in order to conceal a sentimental malaise'. He
thought Waugh was emerging from a Noël Cowardly phase and
exchanging his 'sophistication for a pleasing collection of
sympathies, prejudices, fusses, worries and patient determinations' (No. 49). The 'New Statesman' also disparagingly
noted 'Labels'' adoption of 'the manner of Noël Coward' and
was pleased to see a more mature Waugh 'less sentimentally

savage', depending less on 'that querulous little stock of
sophistication and smartness' (17 March 1934, 420, 422).
Gilbert Armitage likened Waugh to Godfrey Winn as a
representative of Youth (cf. No. 196) and to Jane Austen
as a novelist. Eventually, he expresses admiration for
the '*absence* of prejudice' in 'Ninety-Two Days'; Waugh
is seen as 'the "pure" observer' ('Bookman', May 1934,12).
Blair Niles in the 'New York Times Book Review' was perhaps the most enthusiastic, linking Waugh's name with D.H.
Lawrence, Douglas and Tomlinson as one of an elite who
'had led the way back to high standards in travel writing'.
Niles saw it as a welcome relief from 'the distortion of
truth and the tawdry self-exploitation of the travel books
of the recent degenerate era' (No. 50).

'A HANDFUL OF DUST' (1934)

This novel is now widely regarded as Waugh's masterpiece.
One might expect there to have been a plethora of jubilant
contemporary criticism but, strangely, this was not the
case. Most praised it but the extraordinary power of the
work and its superiority to Waugh's earlier fiction was not
widely recognized. The rather sad little collection
included here does little justice to such a novel. Of the
contemporary reviewers, only Peter Quennell and William
Plomer would rank as 'critics'. Where were the rest of
Waugh's powerful literary backers? The enigma is perhaps
partly explained by the fact that 'A Handful of Dust' was
first published in five monthly instalments in 'Harper's
Bazaar' in both Britain and America) with a different ending
in which Tony returned from Brazil. Had the story become too
well known before the novel was published? Certainly it did
not burst upon an eager public as had the earlier works.
    The first edition appeared in September 1934. Waugh's
trip to British Guiana had left him short of money and
1933-5 was a period of unusually intense literary activity.
After grinding out 'Ninety-Two Days' in the winter of 1933
he wrote some stories to raise money quickly. Then he was
free to write a novel which included the South American
background. His story, The Man Who Liked Dickens, had been
written at Boa Vista, Brazil, and posted home for publication and, as he explained much later in Fan-Fare, he had
become intrigued by the theme and 'wanted to discover how
the prisoner got there' (No. 100). The novel, he noted,
'began at the end', and the manuscript actually includes a
typescript copy of much of this story with small alterations (Last was 'Henty' and Mr Todd 'McMaster').
    He was pleased with the book. A note originally enclosed

with Tom Driberg's copy reads:

> Here is my new novel. I hope you will like it. I think
> it is better than the others. At any rate the frontis-
> piece might amuse you. I instructed the architect to
> design the worst possible eighteen-sixty [Gothic] and I
> think he has done well.(10)

The frontispiece was of Hetton Abbey and Waugh's *leit-
motif* of 'English Gothic' was something which the contemporary reviewers unfortunately ignored. 'Unfortunately'
because it was clearly seen by Waugh as a fundamental
structural device. As he says in his letter to Henry Yorke:
'The scheme was a Gothic man in the hands of savages...'
(No. 55). But it was more subtle than this for the 'Gothic'
of Tony Last's world of 'arrested development' is distinctly second-rate. One sentence deleted from the manuscript describes Hetton as 'a huge building conceived in
the late generation of the Gothic revival when the movement had lost its fantasy and become structurally logical
and stodgy'.(11) Not until Professor Kermode published his
essay Mr. Waugh's Cities in 1960 (No. 109) did the architectural imagery and Waugh's notion of 'the Catholic City'
receive serious critical attention.

Peter Quennell thought it 'the most mature and the best
written novel that Mr. Waugh has yet produced' (No. 54) and
criticized Oldmeadow's review which had continued the campaign of vilification in the 'Tablet' (No. 52). But neither
Quennell nor Plomer does much to help us understand the
book, concentrating their attention on stylistic concerns:
Waugh's 'economical method', the realism of his apparently
'far-fetched' scenes (No. 53). James Agate, having complained about Waugh's last two books, exudes enthusiasm but
does little more than reveal himself as a prey to sentimentality (DE, 6 September 1934, 6). The TLS once again
expressed a certain weariness mixed this time with admiration for the novel's technical expertise: 'Whether his
study of futility is worth doing - and doing at such
length - is a matter of opinion; but there can be nothing
but praise for his consistency of outlook' (No. 51). Twelve
years later, Rose Macaulay described it as 'a social novel
about adultery, treachery, betrayal, tragic and sordid
desolation'. But even she, while acknowledging it as 'a
brilliant and terrifying *tour de force*' found it 'up to a
point more ordinary' than 'Black Mischief'. 'A Handful of
Dust', she says, 'seems to reach the climax of Mr. Waugh's
view of life as the meaningless jigging of barbarous nit-
wits. Pleasure, sympathetic or ironic, in their absurdities
has vanished: disgust has set in' (No. 56).

Yet when the Uniform Edition appeared in 1964, Professor
Bergonzi could remark that 'After thirty years, "A Handful
of Dust" remains in the first rank of Mr Waugh's novels'
(No. 57). Brigid Brophy, reviewing the same edition, terms
it 'a major work in the canon. It is the most open of
Waugh's books about having a tragic intention' (No. 58).
Miss Brophy, as an authority on Firbank, is perhaps the
subtlest of the literary journalists. Her use of the term
'baroque conceit' reflects Waugh's own phraseology in his
letter to Henry Yorke: 'I think I agree that the Todd
episode is fantastic. It is a "conceit" in the Webster
manner' (No. 55).

The most enthusiastic and stimulating comments of contemporary 'critics' appear in Waugh's private correspondence (see Sykes, pp. 141-3). Desmond MacCarthy, Hilaire
Belloc, Rebecca West, Lord David Cecil and Maurice Baring
all expressed unreserved admiration. J.B. Priestley and
Henry Yorke, however, had complaints. Priestley did not
think it a better book than the others (although it had 'a
bitter force beyond anything that appeared in the others')
and felt that 'the people in the book are altogether too
light weight'. Yorke's objections centred on his disappointment at the unreality of 'the Demerara trip'.
Waugh's reply (No. 55) is equally intriguing and demonstrates the seriousness with which he approached the design
and social commentary of his book.

There was, of course, a strong, if oblique, element of
autobiography in it. This was the first time he had
explored in detail the delicate subject of a wife's
desertion and his pain and disgust at such infidelity
spills over from his experience into the novel. It was a
particularly frustrating period in Waugh's emotional life.
Although divorced, his Church still considered him
married. Effectively he was isolated by his faith, prevented by what he believed to be true from developing a
supportive sexual relationship with another woman. He was
not chaste but casual encounters only irritated his wounded
self-esteem, emphasizing solitude. 'A Handful of Dust' was
written at a time when Waugh was sensing this frustration
intensely. He was deeply in love with Teresa Jungman, a
Catholic confidante who was devoted to him as a friend
but refused to enter into an affair. She is the 'Teresa'
the diary records Waugh's having left as the boat set sail
for British Guiana. (In the manuscript the frustrated
shipboard 'romance' with Therese was originally with 'Ber-
nadette'.) The glamorous public image of a boisterous and
brilliant adventurer was a long way from the sad, déraciné
figure, homeless and loveless despite many 'friends', who
really only wanted one thing: a safe Catholic marriage.

Whether or not these contingent factors are thought
relevant, recent criticism seems to agree that the novel
displays increased emotional intensity which sets it apart
from the ingenious fantasy of Waugh's other pre-war fiction.
Angus Wilson thinks that 'throughout "A Handful of Dust"
... we have moved beyond the realm of great talent into
that of genius' (No. 191).

'EDMUND CAMPION' (1935)

This biography of the Jesuit martyr was Waugh's first work
of overt Catholic apologetics. After completing 'A Handful
of Dust' he travelled with Alexander Glen and others to
Spitzbergen, above the Arctic Circle, a bleak and depressing experience for Waugh. He returned in August 1934 and
by October was at work on 'Campion'.

Mr Sykes's biography deals briefly (pp. 145-9 and 151-2)
with the book, noting Waugh's debt to Fr D'Arcy (then
Master of Campion Hall, Oxford) and the dubious nature of
some historical generalizations. He reviews it from the
standpoint of a contemporary Catholic, praising its literary facility, but he fails to note, first, the amount of
research Waugh put into the book and, second, that Waugh's
concept of Campion was as much that of artist as theologian.

On the first point the contemporary reviewers were
gnerally more perceptive. Fr Martindale noted that it was
clear Waugh 'had studied seriously' (GKW, 19 September
1935, 450-1). Despite Waugh's disclaimer that 'This book
makes no claim to all that is known, still less all that
diligent research might discover, about the life of
Edmund Campion', it was clear to most historians (including
Peter Quennell, No. 59) that Waugh had examined most available authorities. His correspondence confirms this and also
his concern with the smallest detail. At one stage he wrote
to Penelope Betjeman asking to stay at her house so that he
might conveniently visit the grange where Campion had been
arrested. Rose Macaulay's accusation in 1946 that Waugh had
not read the relevant State Papers and correspondence had
been refuted by the author at the time of publication in
answer to similar criticisms from another quarter (No. 62).
As Mr Quennell noted, however, 'the Catholic point of view
underlies every paragraph' (No. 59) and it was Waugh's
interpretation of the evidence, inverting the traditionally
'heroic' vision of the Elizabethan and Jacobean periods,
which provoked controversy. J.A. Kensit, on behalf of the
Protestant Truth Society, reacted violently to an enthusiastic radio review by Desmond MacCarthy and this initiated
a debate lasting several weeks in the pages of the 'Listener'

(see No. 61). Waugh replied to the accusations at some
length in the letter reproduced as No. 62.

The second point, that of Waugh's view of Campion as an
artist-figure, was scarcely picked up by anyone. Many
offered the sort of observation made by Graham Greene:
'Mr. Waugh's study is a model of what a short biography
should be. Sensitive and vivid, it catches the curious note
of gaiety and gallantry ... of an adventure' (No. 60). But
none articulated the fact that the book is more novel than
biography in places and that it throws an interesting light
on the relationship which Waugh saw between aesthetics and
religion. Oxford is described as emerging from the Middle
Ages 'into the spacious, luminous world of Catholic humanism' (p. 13). With the Reformation the Church, which while
'in undisputed authority ... could afford to wink at a
little speculative fancy in her philosophers, a pagan exuberance of taste in her artists', was now 'driven to defend
the basis and essential structure of her faith' (p. 14).
This is, surely, the fundamental concern of the book. The
thesis propounded is that, thanks to Campion and his fellows, Catholicism remained 'something historically and
continuously English, seeking to recover only what had been
taken from it by theft' (p. 54).

The Protestant aggressors are depicted as dull-witted
barbarians, sacking Duke Humphrey's library, smashing the
great reredos of All Souls, lying, informing, reduced to
inflicting torture where they were found intellectually
deficient in debate. The Catholics are sincere, zealous and
cultured men. Campion's 'The History of Ireland' is taken
as a demonstration that 'had ... [he] ... continued in the
life he was then planning for himself, he would, almost
certainly, have come down in history as one of the great
masters of English prose' (pp. 37-8).

There can be no doubt that 'Campion' was an extremely
important book to Waugh. He looked to it to re-establish
his integrity in Catholic circles at a time when
Oldmeadow's vendetta in the 'Tablet' continued unabated.
Oldmeadow had reviewed 'A Handful of Dust' harshly (No.
52) and refused to notice 'Campion'. He even went so far
as to 'protest' against the 'Daily Mail's' 'choice of
correspondent to send messages from Addis Ababa'.(12) It
was possibly the first book to which Waugh was wholly
committed. During his next visit to Abyssinia he wrote to
Katharine Asquith (Lady Horner): 'I am very excited about
the reception of "Campion". Just like a spinster with a
first novel.'(13) Later he wrote to Henry Yorke:

I am very pleased about the [Hawthornden] prize
because personally it takes the taste of the 'Daily

> Mail' out of my tongue and generally, which you won't
> sympathise with, because I am glad that a prize of that
> kind should go to a specifically Catholic book.(14)

Clearly, and this the reviewers missed entirely, Waugh
suggests in the biography an analogue with the situation
of all Catholics since the Reformation. Its attitudes are
essentially those expressed in a newspaper article explaining his 'conversion to Rome' in 1930: 'Civilization ...
has not in itself the power of survival. It came into
being through Christianity, and without it has no significance or power to command allegiance.'(15) 'Christianity',
of course, meant only 'Catholicism' for Waugh. Civilization
and faith were seen as interdependent.

Thanks to the Hawthornden and the generally warm reception of 'Campion' by Catholics and Protestants alike, the
book sold well. A new edition was eventually printed for
American circulation in 1946 to capitalize on the success
of 'Brideshead'. Edmund Wilson reviewed this sceptically,
antagonism having already been established between himself
and Waugh over 'Brideshead' and other issues (headnote,
No. 65). 'Mr. Waugh's version of history ...', he suggests,
'is, in its main lines, more or less in the vein of "1066
and All That". Catholicism was a Good Thing and Protestantism was a Bad Thing' (No. 65). But other Americans were
more generous. Richard Sullivan wondered 'if this excellent
little study of the Elizabethan priest did not ... foreshadow the profound eschatological concerns which much
later the author was to exhibit in his fiction' (No. 64)
and 'Time' thought it done 'skilfully and with full respect' (1 July 1946, 39). The year 1962 saw a handsome
third edition incorporating revisions. The 'Tablet' col-
lated the texts of this and the 1935 version and concluded
that the changes were 'very slight, being the result of
scrupulous care rather than further research' (7 April
1962, 332), and David Rogers wrote to correct some bibliographical errors in this assessment (5 May 1962, 42).

SHORT STORIES: 'MR LOVEDAY' ETC. (1936); 'WORK SUSPENDED
AND OTHER STORIES' ETC. (1949); 'TACTICAL EXERCISE' (1954)

Most of Waugh's short stories were written in the 1930s and
the three hard back volumes largely reproduce the same
material. It is sensible to deal with them here under a
single heading, although in this book the reviews appear
in their correct chronological order. 'Mr Loveday' included
the following: Mr Loveday's Little Outing, By Special
Request (alternative serial ending to 'A Handful of Dust'),

Cruise, Period Piece, On Guard, Incident in Azania, Out of
Depth, Excursion in Reality, Love in the Slump, Bella
Fleace Gave a Party and Winner Takes All. 'Work Suspended
and Other Stories Written Before the Second World War'
obviously adds Waugh's unfinished novel (first published
in full in 1942) to the list but also deletes Love in the
Slump, including instead An Englishman's Home. 'Tactical
Exercise', the second American edition of stories (the
first appearing simultaneously with the 1936 volume), reprints all of this adding a piece of Waugh's juvenilia
'The Curse of the Horse Race' and 'Love Among the Ruins'.
   Almost invariably Waugh wrote his short stories for
magazines like 'Vogue', 'Harper's Bazaar' and 'Nash's Pall
Mall' as a means of raising money quickly. Sometimes,
however, they represented a pre-publication glimpse of a
section of a forthcoming novel. 'Harper's Bazaar', for
instance, printed Waugh's The Hire-Purchase Marriage as a
short story (December 1929, 22-3, 98, 101) and it appeared
shortly afterwards as Chapter Five of 'Vile Bodies'. Such
'extracts' were excluded from Waugh's selection in these
volumes.
   There can be little doubt as to Waugh's attitude to all
these pieces excepting 'Work Suspended' and 'Love Among the
Ruins'. They were not conceived, as were the novels, with
serious artistic intent. The stories were seen as well-
wrought entertainments, amusing, occasionally suggestive of
serious themes, but essentially lighthearted. Usually, they
represent the working out of a 'conceit' for comic effect.
Their reviewers accepted them as such, often over-praising
them as ingenious 'miniatures'. James Agate, for instance,
saw Winner Takes All as 'a tiny masterpiece of suave,
polished and cruel irony' (DE, 2 July 1936, 8). Roger
Pippett, aware that the first volume 'will not prove ...
one of its author's major works', still appreciated its
sophisticated belligerence and found Waugh's 'imitators'
'thin' satirists by comparison (DH, 2 July 1936, 17). The
TLS apparently preferred the stories to the novels:

> He has the wit and the sense of style to hold the floor
> unsupported by his subject when the short, sharp shock
> is but twenty pages away, whereas when he expands
> themes of no more general significance to 300 pages his
> nonentities may fail with the reader to sustain the
> burden of the deferred catastrophe. (No. 66)

Maurice Bowra, however, was unreserved in his praise.
'Mr. Waugh,' he wrote, 'like Mr Maugham, succeeds at every
kind of writing he attempts.... He manages the short story
with the confident touch of an accomplished master' (No. 67).

Reviewers of the second volume (1949) concentrated on
'Work Suspended'. They knew most of the stories, and the
unfinished novel was making its first appearance since the
1942 limited edition. The American critics of 'Tactical
Exercise', however, saw the book in the context of Waugh's
huge surge in popularity with 'Brideshead' (1945) and the
subsequent parody of American material values in 'The Loved
One' (1948). 'Helena' (1950) and the first volume of the
war trilogy, 'Men at Arms' (1952), had also appeared.
Waugh was established as a serious novelist of ambiguous
political and distinct religious affiliations. Most of the
stories seemed either slight by comparison or revealed a
fundamental insincerity and snobbery in the entire *opus*.
'A coterie loved him seventeen years', wrote Donald Barr in
the 'New York Times Book Review',

> for being a heartless and light-minded satirist of the
> ruling classes. In 1945, the general public discovered
> that he was a snobbish and sentimental bigot who hated
> the common people, and they at once made him a best-
> seller.... The three abiding qualities of Mr Waugh are
> his barbarousness, his charity and his snobbery....
> (17 October 1954, 6, 36)

Frank O'Connor, the Irish short-story writer, considered
that

> The short story was never a form in which Mr Waugh
> excelled. Apart from Work Suspended, the rest of the
> book consists of tales rather than stories, and the
> rigidity of the formula almost suggests that the author
> had taken a correspondence course in story-telling.
> (No. 144)

Louis Coxe thought that 'satire' like Waugh's, 'without a
moral centre is not satire but at best the protracted
sneer' (No. 145), clearly oblivious of the fact that Waugh
had disowned the title of satirist in Fan-Fare (1946,
No. 100).

'Waugh in Abyssinia' (1936)

This book documents Waugh's life as a war correspondent and
his brief flirtation with Italian Fascism as an alternative
political system. He had travelled to Abyssinia in 1935 to
report on the Italian invasion for the pro-Mussolini
'Daily Mail' and then returned in 1936 to examine the
effects of the newly established government. The

enthusiasm with which he greeted this disgusted many
writers. Rose Macaulay dubbed the book 'a Fascist tract'
ten years later (No. 71) and when it first appeared David
Garnett complained of the biased omissions: 'He does not
tell us', he wrote, 'how many of [the natives] that "most
amiable and sensible man", Graziani, is hanging and shooting every day' (No. 69). The TLS complained of Waugh's
apparent ignorance of Abyssinia's complex customs, faith,
traditions (No. 74) and Donald Attwater in the 'Dublin
Review' similarly noted his 'sneering references to what he
does not understand' (January-June 1937, 174-5). The
right-wing and Catholic papers were, however, generally
more sympathetic to Waugh's use of his experience as political and religious propaganda. The 'Tablet', for example,
stated without qualification that 'Mr Waugh describes the
deadly and hopeless system which the dominant Abyssinians
imposed on the areas they conquered. They represented
Imperialism devoid of a single redeeming element' (14
November 1936, 674).

The book, then, is ultimately a justification of the
redeeming elements of Italian imperialism. Waugh argues
that the invaders represent order, culture and Catholicism.
During the period 1935-9 it may fairly be said that Waugh
toyed dangerously and often foolishly with the political
implications of his faith and that this indulgence in politics was something he later regretted. Corresponding with
his agent in 1937 (during the composition of 'Scoop') he
proposed writing a guide book to 'the most interesting
parts of Europe.... Ideology - part Belloc belief in the
permanence of Roman conquest, part anti-pacifist. I see a
very good book indeed on this subject'.(16) But it was
never written. The enthusiasm of this brief period as a
pugnacious, militarist Catholic apologist did not outlast
the Second World War. After that, military action appeared
corrupt and often cowardly. Editing his travel writings in
'When the Going was Good' (1946) he dropped the controver-
sial, pro-Fascist, concluding chapter about The Road, the
symbol of Roman civilization and religion made manifest.

Waugh's ostensible 'political' position during this
period is easily misinterpreted. His interest in the Italian invasion was principally the result of his aesthetic
and religious predilections rather than political ones. He
was more interested in the symbolic significance of the
events than in their intrinsic complexity. In 1938 he
wrote: 'Those of us who can afford to think without proclaiming ourselves "intellectuals", do not want or expect
a Fascist regime.'(17) He always despised Hitler. It was
the culture represented by the Italians, and the chance
for Catholicism to regain lost territories, which appealed

in his weaker moments. Ultimately his argument was abstract and theological.

'SCOOP' (1938)

The reviewers of 'Scoop' were uniformly delighted with this extravaganza demolishing the pretentions of the popular press. In the same essay which had condemned 'Waugh in Abyssinia' as a 'Fascist tract' Rose Macaulay remarked: 'With it Mr. Waugh re-entered his peculiar world; it was a relief to those of us who had begun to fear that we were losing him, that the wit was being slain by the propagandist and the partisan' (No. 79). This feeling was expressed by many. Here was Waugh back in his old form. 'I like Mr. Waugh best', wrote Desmond Shawe-Taylor, 'when he remains within his own territory, which I take to be the circles radiating outwards - not too far - from the lunch-table of Lady Metroland' (No. 73).

This limitation, however, to a form he knew he could execute with professional ease, was beginning to prove irksome to Waugh. He was, like John Plant in 'Work Suspended', reaching a 'climacteric' in his career as a novelist. He described 'Scoop' to his agent as 'light and excellent' but he was all the time thirsting for a new fictional approach which could include the dimension of 'supernatural' reality. 'Work Suspended' (written 1939) marks the first tentative step towards a fuller prose style but the transition was only completed with 'Brideshead'. (I have written an essay on this transformation, Work Suspended: Waugh's Climacteric, 'Essays in Criticism', October 1978, 302-20.) 'Scoop' was to prove almost the last in that sequence of anarchic 'fantasies' which had so endeared Waugh to his large British audience and American coterie. Only 'The Loved One' (1948) and 'Basil Seal Rides Again' (1963) were to revert to the earlier style.

Reviewing the Uniform Edition in 1964 Brigid Brophy remarked that '"Scoop" has always struck me as a mere, though entertaining, after-flutter of the fine imaginative flight which had produced "Black Mischief"' (No. 58). However, as a satire on journalism, indeed on the mass media in general, it remains a pungent and relevant document. The underlying notion of the absurdity of the rationalist viewpoint, implicit in the concept of a newspaper, that disparate events may be reported as reflecting an understandable 'whole', is another rendering of a continuous theme in Waugh's fiction. The world is not, he suggests, as Lucas Dockery or Seth would suppose, a composite of discernible facts; without the dimension of 'spiritual' experience, human behaviour is seen to be unreasonable (see Fan-Fare, No. 100).

Waugh, however, made no claim for the potential philosophical complexity of this work. In a 'memo' turning down a film scenario of the book in 1957 he wrote:

> This novel is a light satire on modern journalism, not a schoolboy's adventure story of plot, counterplot, capture and escape. Such incidents as provoke this misconception are extraneous to the main theme which is to expose the pretensions of foreign correspondents, popularised in countless novels, plays, autobiographies and films, to be heroes, statesmen and diplomats.(HRC)

'ROBBERY UNDER LAW' (1939)

While writing 'Scoop', Mr Sykes notes, Waugh was approached by 'Clive Pearson, the younger son of Lord Cowdray, acting as a representative of the extensive Pearson commercial interests in Central America' (p. 181). Pearson's family had lost considerable assets through the expropriation of foreign holdings in Mexico by the socialist regime led by General Cardenas. The idea was that Waugh should travel to Mexico at the Pearsons' expense and write a book defending their case. He agreed and, after finishing 'Scoop', travelled with his second wife, Laura, in July 1938, returning in October of the same year.

The brevity of the visit underlines the inescapable faults of the book. Waugh takes it upon himself to write an overtly political tract about a country of which he has little more than a tourist's knowledge. This was a different matter entirely from the literary use he made of his experience in Abyssinia, a country of which he had acquired considerable knowledge between 1930 and 1936. He came and left as a 'Conservative' (No. 84); his preconceptions preclude the objectivity demonstrated by Graham Greene's Mexican book 'The Lawless Roads', published a year earlier. Some reviewers condemned Waugh on these grounds. Harold Nicolson, a former admirer, described the work as 'a short but dull book.... He cannot forgive the Mexicans for having confiscated the large estates' (No. 80). 'Mr Waugh's professional intuition', said the TLS, '...is handicapped by the prejudices with which he approached the country' (1 July 1939, 382). Gerald Vann disliked the ease with which Waugh passed judgment on 'the goodness or badness, the success or failure, of men's rationalizations of their desires', despite Waugh's ingenuity in depicting the political situation as 'the writing on our own wall' (No. 83).

But a surprising number found the book convincing.
William Gower for the conservative 'Spectator' saw it as
'very brilliant, sad though its story is' (21 July 1939,
103). The liberal 'Manchester Guardian' was equally sympathetic: 'His book is admirably written, and few could have
set out more ably this view of Mexico' (No. 81). R.L. Martin, offering an American view which perhaps reflects a
certain nervousness as to the proximity of this socialist
revolution was deeply impressed by 'the calm logic' of
Waugh's argument (No. 82). By the time the American edition
had been published, of course, five months later, the
Second World War had been declared.

In later years Waugh clearly regretted this somewhat
hysterical document. He omitted it entirely from 'When the
Going was Good', saying in the Preface that he was 'content to leave [it] in oblivion, for it dealt little with
travel and much with political questions.... So let it lie
in its own dust'. It has not, however, been forgotten.
Anthony Quinton, reviewing the 'Letters' in 1980 was
clamouring for its republication ('Listener', 4 September
1980, 307-8).

'PUT OUT MORE FLAGS' (1942)

This novel, like 'Work Suspended', marks a transitional
stage in Waugh's career. It was written on a troop-ship
returning from South Africa (No. 100) and deals with the
period of the Phoney War or, as Waugh puts it: 'The Great
Bore War', 'that odd, dead period before the Churchillian
renaissance' (Dedicatory Letter to Major Randolph Churchill,
Penguin, p. 7). Unlike his earlier fiction, it is locked
firmly to a specific historical period and is, in one
sense, an historical novel. Waugh, of course, thought it
'historical' in more ways than one. The characters
described, some still from the circle of Lady Metroland, he
considered to be 'a race of ghosts' (Dedicatory Letter).
They no longer existed and his attitude to their (final)
'disappearance' is ambivalent. For the most part, though,
he was glad to see the back of the woolly-minded, liberal-
pacifist, rural-and-pansy-aesthetic sets he lampoons. Waugh
was at the height of his enthusiasm for the heroic possibilities of the war, the enemy was 'at last plain in view,
huge and hateful, all disguise cast off'.(18) And the
'enemy' was not only the military opponent. Here we see the
fifth column of the weak-minded and decadent whose subtle
subversion is itself undermined by the ruthlessness of the
irrepressible Basil Seal.

The reviewers were generally enthusiastic although Kate

O'Brien felt that they were too close to the historical
situation and its blunders, the country plunged as it was
in the darker days of the war, to appreciate facetious
'group-presentations of the inept' (No. 86). Most others,
however, found it a brilliant affair and noted a new
seriousness in Waugh's tone. 'Time' remarked that 'he has
become one of the most deadly serious moralists of his
generation' (25 May 1942, 90-1) and Alan Pryce-Jones
likened the 'logic' of his world-view to that of Kafka
(No. 87). Pryce-Jones may also lay claim to being one of
the earlier literary journalists (he was, after all, a
friend) to detect the 'Romantic' in Waugh, a word much
used later to describe the retrospective analysis of
'Brideshead' and the war trilogy. Even the left-wing 'New
Republic' found itself complimenting Waugh on successfully,
if only 'for a moment', engaging the reader's attention and
interest in the 'embarrassing' collection of 'frozen pretty
boys and exhausted glamour girls' (Dunstan Thompson, NR,
13 July 1942, 60-1).

Waugh, then, was beginning to claim respect as a 'serious' novelist at last although none of the contemporary
reviews noted the shift in prose style, moving gradually
away from the flickering images and cinematic 'cutting' of
the earlier work, towards the more 'conventional' novel of
detailed description and character analysis. A year later,
Nigel Dennis wrote an excellent essay centring on 'Put Out
More Flags', largely reprinted as No. 89. In this he also
takes note of the fragment of 'Work Suspended' published
in 'Horizon' in 1941 as My Father's House and assesses
Waugh's position as a social critic in comparison with the
left-wing writers (Auden and Isherwood were overtly satirized in the novel as Parsnip and Pimpernell) of 'New
Signatures'.

Today, the novel appears less important. Few would now
agree with those who considered it Waugh's finest achievement of the period 1928-42. Although still entertaining,
the specific contemporary relevance perhaps leaves it with
the flavour of a 'period piece' relying for its maximum
effect upon a detailed knowledge of events beyond the text.

'WORK SUSPENDED' (1942)

The publishing history of this piece is complex. Briefly,
Waugh wrote most of it in 1939 and then abandoned composi-
tion on being called up for the Marines in December. In
November 1941 Cyril Connolly published the first part as
My Father's House in 'Horizon' (see No. 92). Late in 1942
a Limited Edition of 500 copies of the complete work

(i.e. both parts) was printed by Chapman's. The first
notices here (Nos 90 and 91) are of that limited edition.
Few reviewed it. It was first brought before a wider audience with the appearance of 'Work Suspended and Other
Stories' (1949) although the Americans did not see it until
'Tactical Exercise' (1954) again included it in a collection of short stories. The 1949 and 1954 texts correspond
but both are substantially different from the 1942 limited
edition. Waugh, for instance, has added the Post-Script to
the later version and altered those names and dates which
located the story earlier in the 1930s than its ultimate
'date' of 1939. The later text, of course, is the one read
now, first published by Penguin Books in 1951. (A detailed
analysis of the revisions and their significance is included in my piece in 'Essays in Criticism', see p. 30 above.)
   For reviews of 'Work Suspended', then, the reader should
also look ahead in this volume to the 1949 and 1954 editions of short stories and remember that the text described
there is not that which baffled the TLS critic in No. 91.
In 1949 the issues seemed clearer. 'Brideshead' and 'The
Loved One' provided a perspective within which to interpret
the action of a 'narrative hanging between the death of an
old world ... and a new world viewed with displeasure'
(No. 26). In 1954 the generally unsympathetic Donald Barr
noted that it 'makes the transition to the later manner.
The "psychology" there is more copious and explicit, with
traces of the very firm, very explicit treatment of love,
marriage and adultery as questions in moral theology'
(NYTBR, 17 October 1954, 6, 36). The misunderstanding about
'adultery' here is implicitly repeated on the cover of the
current Penguin volume, which describes the hero as 'seeking inspiration through a highly illicit love affair with
his best friend's heavily-pregnant wife'. It is a 'love
affair' but there is no question of adultery as it is taken
for granted by Waugh that the pregnancy suspends sexual
relations.(19)
   The misreading is not surprising. No reviewer attempts
a detailed thematic discussion. 'Work Suspended' is a complex and suggestive work with large areas of oblique semi-
autobiographical reference. As I argue in my essay, it is
perhaps only possible to analyse it in detail in the context of Waugh's biography. The 1942 text was a more overtly
'personal' document which the later revisions have successfully disguised and objectified.

'BRIDESHEAD REVISITED' (1945)

'Brideshead' was written while Waugh was on leave from the

army during 1944 and the corrections were finished while he
was on active service with a military mission in Yugoslavia.
The 'Diaries' for the latter period reveal entertaining
encounters with Randolph Churchill (with whom Waugh was
once quartered), son of Sir Winston, the Prime Minister.
Waugh used the connection to post his page proofs back to
Chapman's via 10 Downing Street, and this extreme caution
about their safe arrival reflects his unusual attitude to
this book. In his letters home it is often referred to as
his 'M.O.' (Magnum Opus), his great fictional work of
Catholic apologetics. He was intensely concerned about its
theology and the quality of its prose style. In both areas
he was experimenting, writing openly about 'the workings of
the divine purpose in a pagan world' (No. 95, n. 1) in the
fuller, more evocative style first attempted, then abandoned, in 1939 with 'Work Suspended'. Indeed, the complexity of the novel's publishing history demonstrates that
Waugh's concern did not end with the correction of those
proofs. He first had a hundred paper-bound copies circulated among friends, and emended certain passages before
the book's appearance in the 1945 first edition. Then, in
1959, he completely revised the work, adding a Preface,
dividing the original two 'books' into three, and pruning
the romantic exuberance of the original.In the Preface
(dated 1960) he remarks that 'the book is infused with a
kind of gluttony, for food and wine, for the splendours of
the recent past, and for rhetorical and ornamental language, which now with a full stomach I find distasteful'
(No. 106). It must be remembered that reviews which date
from before 1960 are of the 1945 text.

The privately circulated edition was greeted enthusiastically by Graham Greene, Desmond MacCarthy and John Betjeman, whose letters of congraulation Waugh kept (see Sykes,
p. 248). Henry Yorke ('Green') and Mr Sykes were the only
'literary' friends to express reservations. Yorke admitted
that the theme

> was not easy for me. As you can imagine my heart was in
> my mouth all through the death bed scene, hoping against
> hope that the old man would not give way, that is take
> the course he eventually did. But I don't know when you
> have written more powerfully and with such command as
> you have done here. The suspense is superb. (Sykes,
> p. 251)

Mr Sykes felt that the 'theme of Charles Ryder, ... and his
love for Julia failed throughout' but that, overall, it was
a masterpiece. In his biography he notes:

The book had a boldness and originality of theme less
easy to discern now than when it first came out. Not
since the time of Robert Hugh Benson and his brother,
Arthur Benson, over thirty years before, had novelists
of high ambition taken Christian religion as the main
subject of a fiction to be treated without scepticism.
There had grown up a literary convention whereby religious faith was only referred to in a novel, if at all,
as a detail of the background or of character-sketching,
or as the object of ridicule or attack, but never
treated with implied or explicit respect. (Maurice
Baring is an exception.) ... If Evelyn had been a
French writer he could have written a French equivalent
of 'Brideshead' ... within a living tradition. As an
English novelist he was exploring neglected territory....
Since 1944 several writers including Graham Greene have
attempted serious, unsceptical treatment of orthodox
Christian religion in novels, notably Iris Murdoch
among Anglicans in 'The Bell'. I think they all owe
rather more to the example of Evelyn's novel than is
commonly recognized. (pp. 248-9)

Apart from J.D. Beresford's extraordinary complaint that
Waugh's themes were 'adultery, perversion, and drunkenness'
(No. 94), the early British reviews of the first public
edition (June 1945) expressed cautious pleasure. They were
rather confused by Waugh's new, three-dimensional approach,
his first overtly 'serious' novel. The TLS, perhaps being
wise after the event, noted that in the early work 'the
moralist or religious morality was almost always to be
discovered looking over his shoulder' (No. 95).
V.C. Clinton-Baddeley applauded its wit and claimed that
though 'the book has a powerful religious purpose it has
no shadow of Catholic exclusiveness' (No. 96). Comparisons
were made with Mauriac (No. 97) and, when it appeared in
America six months later, Edmund Wilson's was the only
dissenting voice in a chorus of praise. John Hutchens
concluded his piece in the influential 'New York Times
Book Review' by stating that 'Brideshead' was 'Mr. Waugh's
finest achievement' (No. 98). Waugh's reputation in
America had ensured a small but steady sale of his writings
to a few thousand devotees (see No. 117). Suddenly, he
found himself in the 'best-seller' lists there with a
massively increased public and sheafs of 'fan mail'. The
latter phenomenon he dealt with through a typically mischievous open letter to 'Life' entitled Fan-Fare in 1946
(No. 100) and this offers a useful résumé of the novel's
American success story as well as an answer to Edmund
Wilson.

Wilson's argument ran firmly in the opposite direction
to Baddeley's. It was precisely the Catholic 'exclusiveness' of the novel which wedged itself in his critical
nose. He, like other reviewers, admired the Oxford sections,
the flavour of which 'seen now from the bleak, shrivelled
'forties ... has taken on a remoteness and pathos'. But the
book as a whole was 'a bitter blow' to him after his
delight in the early novels. It degenerates, he suggests,
into 'mere romantic fantasy' and the writing of the early
chapters, 'felicitous, unobtrusive, exact', 'runs to dispiriting cliches' and 'stock characters'. At the very root
of his objections lies his disgust at what he terms
Waugh's 'beglamoured snobbery', his 'cult of the high
nobility' in a 'Catholic tract'. Wilson noted an absence
of the brutal truths of the anarchic earlier work; 'something essential has been left out ... and the religion
that is invoked to correct it seems more like an exorcistic
rite than a force of regeneration' (No. 99).

With time to reflect, other serious critics echoed these
comments and expanded upon them. Rose Macaulay in 'Horizon',
while not denying the importance of 'divine purpose',
objected to the idea that Waugh seemed to 'equate the
divine purpose, the tremendous fact of God at work in the
universe, with obedient membership of a church' (No. 101).
It was Donat O'Donnell in the 'Bell', however, who took the
argument a stage further by noting that 'one of the secrets
of Mr. Waugh's comic genius was his keen interest in
humiliation'. If we laugh, he suggests, we are a party to
prejudice. 'Mr. Edmund Wilson ... condemned the snobbery of
"Brideshead" ... but he had swallowed with delight the
snobbery implicit in the earlier novels.... Snobbery was
quite acceptable as an attitude: the critic objected only
when it was formulated as a doctrine.' Mr O'Donnell
attempts to elucidate the confusion caused by this inadequate, sentimental 'attitude' in Waugh's theology and
politics. His phrase, 'neo-Jacobitism', was taken up by
critics, particularly Kingsley Amis, as suggesting this
brand of wistful romanticism. But it was his remark - 'In
Mr. Waugh's theology, the love of money is not only not the
root of all evil, it is a preliminary form of the love of
God' - which provoked the considerable debate in the 'Bell'
to which Waugh himself contributed (Nos 102-5).

The reviewers of the 1960 revised edition came to it
(or returned to it) with the knowledge that 'Brideshead'
had marked a turning point in Waugh's career. In the
interim, 'Helena', 'Men at Arms' and 'Pinfold' had
appeared and Waugh was now firmly established as one of
the masters of contemporary fiction whose work demanded
attention from leading academic critics like Frank Kermode

(No. 109). An interesting account of the revisions
appeared in the TLS (16 September 1960, 594) but, the
reviewer suggests, even these do not rectify the essential
weakness, that marriage of theology and class-consciousness, which condemns Hooper.

Argument about the book's quality has continued. Orwell
remarked in a letter to Julian Symons in 1948 that 'Unlike
a lot a people, I thought "Brideshead" ... was very good,
in spite of hideous faults on the surface'(20) and this
reflects the general approach adopted in recent years.
Malcolm Bradbury sees Waugh's main subject in the novel as
'the instability of the world, the failure of human aspiration, the impermanence of any human edifice, the omni-
presence of suffering'. (21) James Carens, after praising
the book, remarks that 'it must be said, the revised
edition is not a success. Although Waugh did curb some of
the excesses of the original, he did not obliterate its
grosser qualities'.(22)

'WHEN THE GOING WAS GOOD' (1946)

This was Waugh's edited anthology of his pre-war travel
writings. Long excerpts are included from 'Labels',
'Remote People', 'Ninety-Two Days' and 'Waugh in Abyssinia'. As mentioned above (p. 32), he omitted 'Robbery
Under Law' on the grounds that it was a book concerned
more with politics than with travel.

'SCOTT-KING'S MODERN EUROPE' (1947)

'Scott-King' first appeared as a slim hard-back and was
later included in Penguin Books' 'Work Suspended and
Other Stories' (1967). The first American edition appeared
in 1949. It is 'hardly more than a short story expanded
just enough for book form' ('Time', 21 February 1949, 48,
50), a remark echoed by many reviewers disappointed at its
brevity. Only the 'Tablet' praised it warmly. The TLS
found the central character 'admirable' but refused to
commit itself to an opinion as to the book's overall
value. Illtud Evans seemed to voice the general feeling
(still current, surely) that it 'is a novelist's fair
copy: skilful, slight, an extended note in the margin'
('Blackfriars', February 1948, 107). The book's pretentions to political commentary were attacked by George
Orwell: 'In the Europe of the last fifty years', he said,
'the diehard, know-nothing attitude symbolized by Scott-
King has helped to bring about the very conditions that

Mr. Waugh is satirizing' (No. 114). Christopher Sykes was
out of step with current critical thinking when he
described it in his biography as 'a masterly minor work'
(p. 299) and his description of the book's genesis and
themes (pp. 295-9) is rather wayward. The experience on
which Waugh based his fiction was a trip to Spain, as
Douglas Woodruff's guest, to attend a conference of international lawyers. According to Woodruff, the abuses of
hospitality recorded by Mr Sykes did not occur. It was
simply dull. The extravagant insults of the fiction were
entirely the product of Waugh's imagination and this, perhaps, explains its weakness. Whereas in the African
novels the satirical overstatement had grown out of
experience, here it is a more vacuous form of prejudice.

Waugh, however, thought it 'good' ('Diaries', p. 690).
He was disappointed to find it reviewed in the 'Sunday
Times' by John Russell 'after Desmond [MacCarthy] had
expressed unqualified pleasure in it. The standard of
modern reviewing is lamentably low' ('Diaries', p. 692).
The latter remark was certainly justified in this case.
What *did* the critics mean by 'ironic and glacial ease'
(No. 113), 'the barbed smile of the satirist' (Robin
King, 'Spectator', 9 January 19428, 58), 'There is a
dreadful point ... about ... Waugh's latest story' and
'the resources of modern civilization are not ... baffled'
('Tablet', 24 January 1946, 58)?

'THE LOVED ONE' (1948)

This novel appeared originally as a single issue (February
1948, vol. VII, no. 98) of Cyril Connolly's 'Horizon'.
Waugh was negotiating with Connolly and putting the final
touches to the manuscript when 'Scott-King' was published
late in 1947. The first edition, however, had the unusual
distinction of being published in America (July 1948)
before being presented to the British market three months
later. The reasons for this were purely commercial. The
American edition was, in fact, delayed pending an investigation into possibly libellous material. Waugh's letters
to his agent, A.D. Peters, during the period 1947-8 make
interesting reading. Peters disliked it, advising against
US publication, and Waugh, unwilling to offend his custo-
mers, was (in September 1947) content not to have it appear
in the USA. The 'New Yorker' refused it. But for the Americans, of course, 'The Loved One' was the long-awaited
successor to 'Brideshead'. It was sure to be widely
reviewed and, because of its lurid parody of the intrinsic
sentimentality he saw in their civilization, sure to

provoke comparison and controversy. The 'cruelty' of
Waugh's vision became a commonplace of criticism on both
sides of the Atlantic. The book seemed to many to place
Waugh in the tradition of acerbic satirists typified by
Swift.

The latter point was first made by Connolly in his
Introduction where he distinguished between the 'satirist'
and the 'humorist' and aligned Waugh with Swift and Donne:

> Mr. Waugh ... is exposed to the two prevailing gusts
> of middle-age; rage and nostalgia. In 'Brideshead' the
> nostalgia was uncontrolled, in 'Scott-King' ... there
> was perhaps a little too much anger. In 'The Loved
> One' both are invisible, and it is, in my opinion, one
> of the most perfect short novels of the last ten years
> and the most complete of his creations.... (No. 116)

The American reaction was perhaps surprising. Waugh had
forecast 'ructions' (No. 116) but the only overtly unfavourable notices came later from the British. 'Time' found
faults (in the dialogue and 'the intricate inanities of
Whispering Glades') but was generally enthusiastic,
devoting six columns to a review and a survey of Waugh's
career (No. 17). The more radical 'New Republic' considered it 'strong medicine' but, technically, 'nearly faultless' and 'as satire ... an act of devastation, an angry,
important, moral effort that does not fail' (No. 119).
Waugh's view of Americans in the novel suggests an innate,
puritanical mirthlessness which allows them to take seriously a world of substitute values. They are eminently
shockable, complacently ignorant of their own vulnerability
and corruption. Perhaps, in anticipating a *scandale*, he had
underestimated the Americans' ability to laugh at themselves.

Most British reviewers were delighted. Even that famous
Americophile Alistair Cooke could remark: 'The writing is
matchless, the mood finished and serene' (MG, 19 November
1948, 3). The TLS gave extensive coverage and for the first
time placed Waugh in the front rank of those distinguished
writers offering an alternative to the liberal humanism of
novelists like E.M. Forster. His apparent return to a more
allusive, 'two-dimensional' style suggested (wrongly) to
their critic that Waugh had 'finally accepted his métier'
and in so doing had provided 'a satire, witty and macabre,
ominous and polished, which strikes straight at the heart
of the contemporary problem' (No. 120). Desmond MacCarthy,
a friend, pointed to the implicit metaphysic behind the
work. He saw the novel as

a ruthless exposure of a silly optimistic trend in
modern civilization which takes for granted that the
consolations of religion can be enjoyed without belief
in them, ... and seeks to persuade us that there is
nothing really tragic in the predicament of man. (No.
121)

This, surely, although rather feebly expressed, was precisely Waugh's intention; ultimately his satire aimed to
establish theological rather than 'sociological' truths.
The notion of 'tragedy' indicated by the subtitle ('An
Anglo-American Tragedy') was largely ignored. But the
comi-tragic power of the book demanded respect. 'Scrutiny',
F.R. Leavis's Cambridge quarterly dedicated to the serious
and exact study of serious and exact literature, had consistently ignored Waugh's work. Waugh, equally, had lam-
basted the Cambridge school of 'state-trained literary
critics' in his reviews. 'The Loved One' was the only novel
discussed in any detail by the Leavisites when it was
defended, in passing, against an attack by Edmund Wilson
(no. 124).
    Apart from Wilson's, the only unfavourable notices came
from R.D. Smith (NS) and John Bayley. Mrs Smith thought
that Waugh exacted 'nothing from the uncritical reader out
for a laugh ... and, most serious of all, he exacts too
little from himself, an established writer of high talent'
(No. 122). It had all, she thought, been done better by
Aldous Huxley, Sinclair Lewis and S.J. Perelman. Few would
agree with her now but many would still side with Professor
Bayley (No. 123). His objection is to the novel as a form
of didacticism and he sees Waugh and Greene as one facet
of a contemporary trend in fiction towards the establishment of isolated camps defending prejudices - Catholic or
Communist/existentialist. He dislikes the notion that
'Fiction approaches theosophy'. Ironically, Waugh would
have agreed wholeheartedly with this as an aesthetic principle. A work of art, he thought, should be self-supporting, internally coherent and reliant upon no external
political or philosophical 'system' to sustain it. His
reviews constantly criticize the 'symbolism' of authors
offering empty didactic allegory. This trend he lampoons
in 'Work Suspended' through the character of Roger
Symmonds who writes a play in which all 'the characters
are economic types, not individuals, and as long as they
look and speak like individuals it's bad art' (Penguin,
p. 134).
    In 1957, analysing his own writing through the persona
of Gilbert Pinfold, he noted that:

those who sought to detect cosmic significance in Mr
Pinfold's work, to relate it to fashions in philosophy,
social predicaments or psychological tensions, were
baffled by his frank, curt replies to their question-
naires... He regarded his books as objects which he had
made, things quite external to himself to be used and
judged by others. (Penguin, p. 9)

Waugh, then, took pains to 'exclude' himself from his work,
and, to be fair, it would be difficult to detect in 'The
Loved One' that Waugh was a Catholic. 'Brideshead',
'Helena' and 'Sword of Honour' are a different matter.
Waugh's defence would have been that although these are
explicitly 'Catholic' novels they do not proselytize. No
attempt is made to convert the reader to the author's
belief. Professor Bayley's argument, however, suggests
that this belief is a form of prejudice and here Waugh and
the ungodly begin to talk in a different language. For
Waugh, Catholicism represented the absolute truth, not just
an alternative idealism. Supernatural reality revealed
through his religion superseded the rational analysis of
natural phenomena. To have suggested to Waugh that his
faith was a matter of opinion would have been akin to suggesting to Orwell that the working classes did not exist.

'HELENA' (1950)

In this, Waugh's only historical novel in the strict sense
of the term, the public were presented with a second explicitly apologetic work of Catholic fiction. Waugh offers
a 'legend' (R.D. Charques , 'Spectator', 13 October 1950,
388) which is both an historical reconstruction and a metaphor for contemporary political and religious conflicts:
'his British generals', wrote Gouverneur Paulding, 'were
to [regard] Italians [as] Hitler-like Fascist "cads"'
(no. 128). The dust-cover stated that 'Technically this is
the most ambitious work of a writer who is devoted to the
niceties of his trade' (quoted in No. 130), a remark which
must have surprised the contemporary reviewers and continues to amaze critics. To the end Waugh maintained that,
of his own work, it was the book he liked best because,
quite simply, it was the best written and concerned the
most interesting subject.
    Most reviewers, however, recorded a similar verdict to
R.D. Charques's: 'This is a lightly devotional, decorative,
frequently entertaining, but not very substantial work of
fiction' ('Spectator', 13 October 1950). The TLS felt that
Waugh had taken on too much for the scope of 'a single,

comparatively brief fable' (13 October 1950, 641). The
'Angela Brazil accent' (TLS, 13 October 1950) of the
heroine and her general appearance as 'one of [Waugh's]
favourite vices in the way of characterisation - the clear-
eyed, clean-limbed, daughter of Diana, with a niche in
Debrett' (No. 127), was found both entertaining and limited
as a fictional device. 'Waugh's converts', suggests John
Raymond, 'generally get to Heaven the back way, through
having had the right kind of Nanny' (No. 127). 'Time'
expressed a general feeling that 'Campion', 'Brideshead'
and now this were unfortunate aberrations from Waugh's
first-class talent for contemporary satire, a largely un-
successful attempt to 'clear the satiric brambles out of
his literary field, and to plant in their stead the herb
of grace' (No. 129). Hardly anyone touched on the spiritual
implications of Helena's quest for the True Cross. Clearly
Waugh is at pains to emphasize the physical reality of this
'lump of wood' and thus to relate the crucifixion to a specific time and place in history. Once again we are returned
to the theme discussed in the section on 'The Loved One':
the supernatural as the real.
    F.J. Stopp was one of the few to take this proposition
seriously as a basis for criticism. His essay, Grace in
Reins, is reproduced in an edited version as No. 130. 'The
alleged incongruity [in Waugh's fiction]', he wrote,

> is in fact a congruity, that between the supernatural
> and the natural.... For Mr. Waugh ... any book about
> St. Helena ... must show the intimate fusion of the
> historical and the personal in a unique act in time,
> and the no less intimate consonance of the supernatural
> and the natural which made this act a miraculous and
> saintly one.

'MEN AT ARMS' (1952)

Advertised as the first volume of a trilogy, 'Men at
Arms' had a mixed reception. John Raymond considered that
'however much below form, any new novel from [Waugh's] pen
is bound to add immeasurably to the gaiety of his own
nation' (No. 133) and Ronald Knox, a friend, compared it
favourably with the 'Iliad' as war fiction ('Month', October 1952, 236-8). Cyril Connolly, however, had reservations. Waugh, he felt, failed to 'build up relationships
between his military characters' and he saw it as 'a
chronicle rather than a novel', often reminiscent of
Kipling, Ian Hay and P.G. Wodehouse (No. 132). The
Kipling/Waugh connection was also emphasized by Raymond,

not as in Connolly's pejorative comparison, but with
enthusiasm for both: 'Their great gifts spring from a
common fountain-head of anger' (No. 133).

However, it was not so much Waugh's 'anger' as his more
placid approach that struck many. 'Because [Guy] is in
love, Mr Waugh is gentler than usual,' said Tangye Lean
('Spectator', 12 September 1952, 342). Raymond also
remarked that 'On the whole "Men at Arms" is good-tempered
Waugh - and therefore Waugh at his second best' (No. 133).
'Time' preferred the more sober approach: 'If his trilogy
continues as well as it has begun, it will be the best
British novel of World War II' (No. 134). But several
American reviews offered the harshest remarks: 'Newsweek'
found it 'uneven' (20 October 1952, 126, 128) and a feebler
version of Madox Ford's 'Parade's End'; Joseph Frank felt
that this presented the sad spectacle of a 'satirist who
has fallen in love with his subject' (No. 137), and Delmore
Schwartz found it tedious and snobbish: 'If one had no
other information on the subject, the beginning of ... "Men
At Arms" would convince one that the ... War occurred solely
to rescue Englishmen from boredom and decadence' (No. 136).

'THE HOLY PLACES' (1952)

This little book contained two essays: St Helena, Empress
(noted by Stopp, No. 130) and The Defence of The Holy
Places. It was printed as a bibliographers', collectors'
item by the Queen Anne Press: a limited edition in red
buckram and, for friends, fifty signed copies in red niger
morocco. The first essay was published before 'Helena' and
reprinted here to bulk out the slim volume. The subjects of
both pieces, however, were intimately connected. The second
resulted from a trip Waugh had made to Jerusalem at the
expense of 'Life' magazine. Christopher Sykes, later to be
his biographer, had accompanied him. Waugh was paid to
provide his 'impressions' and suggested that 'the United
Nations should honour its undertaking to internationalize
Jerusalem and should itself see to the urgent task of
repairing the Holy Sepulchre' (No. 138).

Reviews were few and generous, although the TLS felt
that 'Mr Waugh's history is at times oversimplified and a
little facile' (No. 138).

'LOVE AMONG THE RUINS' (1953)

Few would surely disagree with Christopher Sykes's assessment of this work as 'the least book of Evelyn's maturity'.

As Mr Sykes points out, Waugh himself thought it 'a bit of
nonsense ... hastily finished & injudiciously published'
(No. 143). There is little evidence, however, of the harshness both noted in contemporary reviews. The TLS, with its
unerring lack of discrimination, gave over two columns of
jubilant praise for a work which was (again) seen as a
return to Waugh's earlier manner (No. 141). Cyril Connolly
derived 'delight and pleasure' from it but summed up a
general feeling in saying that it was 'a waste of his time
- though not of ours' (No. 140). As a history of the future
it was inevitably compared unfavourably with 'Brave New
World', 'Nineteen Eighty-Four' and even C.S. Lewis's 'That
Hideous Strength'. All enjoyed the jokes but most found its
'plausibility' (H.D. Zimon, DT, 29 May 1953, 8) implausible.

'OFFICERS AND GENTLEMEN' (1955)

Opinions were again divided over this book, although most
reviewers were in agreement as to the technical brilliance
of Waugh's prose style. Confusion arose partly from the
unexpected announcement on the dust-jacket that this would
complete the work begun with 'Men at Arms'. There was, then,
to be no trilogy although Waugh promised to continue writi-
ing about the same set of characters (NY, 9 July 1955,
50-1). Some saw this change of plan reflected in weaknesses
in the novel's structure. 'The book ends with such a tangle
of loose threads', wrote Geoffrey Moore, 'that it is difficult to agree with Mr. Waugh that it and "Men At Arms"
"form a whole"' (No. 150). Cyril Connolly was 'disappointed' with it because he found the characters 'too superficial to sustain the structure' (No. 148) and Kingsley
Amis (who clearly had not read his dust-jacket carefully)
looked only half optimistically to 'the continuation of
this saga' to pull together the 'discursive and episodic'
elements of the narrative (No. 149). Amis, in company with
many others since 1945, found 'A Handful of Dust' Waugh's
best and 'Brideshead' his worst book and lamented the decline
of comic ferocity in the post-war works. The opposite view
is taken by Norman Shrapnel in suggesting, perhaps more
subtly, that 'Disorganisation is more than merely a subject
for his fierce brand of farce; it is an expression of
spiritual perversity' (No. 146).
    From 'Brideshead' onwards, as has been said, the critics
tended to belong to one of two camps - those who could
accept Waugh's Catholic apologetics and those who found
them a gross aesthetic intrusion. 'The Times' remarked
that 'For some ... Guy Crouchback will be a sympathetic
type; others may find him a rather boring snob' (30 June

1955, 13) and this proved to be the case. Nevertheless, Amis admitted that 'a great deal of the baronial wrought-iron, on which one was always barking one's shins at Brideshead, has been torn down' (No. 149) and Curtis Bradford in the left-wing 'New Republic' could say that 'His Catholic apologetics are so quiet, so undemanding that the non-Catholic reader is quite willing to accept them' (No. 151).

The tenets of Edmund Wilson's and Donat O'Donnell's arguments about 'Brideshead', however, still formed the parameters of many critiques - the implicit snobbery, the 'sentimental' attachment to 'tradition'. Waugh could not easily shake off his earlier reputations as an anarchic wit and the sneering 'romantic' Catholic. Reviewers would, for instance, select sections of 'Officers and Gentlemen' - the 'progressive novelists' fighting the fire at Turtle's Club, the Cretan debacle - and decide that the mixture of these two elements from former styles (the burlesque and the 'serious' social comment) were 'too discordant for unity' (Maurice Richardson, NS, 9 July 1955, 50-51). Few accepted that Waugh had succeeded in transforming these elements into a new style and persisted in looking for 'the right serio-comic touch' (Richardson, NS). Christopher Sykes recognized the difficulty but rejected the conclusion:

> Of these audacities the most hazardous is the way the story opens in farce, and then sets out in the spirit of farce towards the horrors and tragedy of battle and defeat.... A primary rule of style is broken: farce is mixed with comedy, with tragi-comedy, and even with tragedy. Well, the only question worth asking is whether this matters. It does not matter a bit. The result is abundantly successful. (No. 147)

Amis, of course, felt that it did matter; Bradford (No. 151) agreed with Sykes.

'THE ORDEAL OF GILBERT PINFOLD' (1957)

In the 'Face to Face' interview with John Freeman Waugh admitted that he had suffered exactly the same hallucinations as those described in this novel (see No. 198). Indeed, the dust-jacket notes had already implied this. Of all his fiction, it is the piece most directly drawn from his life ('Work Suspended' coming a close 'second'). The text describes this as 'a hamper to be unpacked of fresh, rich experience - perishable goods' (quotation, No. 154),

recalling the penultimate paragraph of 'The Loved One':
'[Dennis] was carrying back ... the artist's load, a great,
shapeless chunk of experience; bearing it home to his
ancient and comfortless shore; to work on it hard and
long.... For that moment of vision a lifetime is often too
short' (Penguin, p. 127). Waugh had openly admitted to the
autobiographical basis of 'Pinfold' within two months of
publication. No apology was ever offered for this bout of
temporary insanity. He relished it as a curiosity and
would regale his friends with the story of his voyage in
even funnier and more fantastical terms than the fiction.

His public explanation was purely physiological: an
unfortunate mixture of drink and sleeping draughts. There
can be no doubt, however, that this temporary insanity dis-
turbed him deeply and that 'Pinfold' was a form of exor-
cism. In his review of the 'Diaries' Graham Greene records
a conversation with Waugh from this period: 'I had asked
him why there was no indication on the dust-wrapper of
'Officers & Gentlemen' that a third volume of the trilogy
was to come. He said, "I'm not sure that I'll be able to
write it. I may go off my head again, and this time permanently"' (B&B, October 1976, 19-21).

An excellent account of the circumstances has been provided by Frances Donaldson in her book 'Evelyn Waugh.
Portrait of a Country Neighbour' (Weidenfeld & Nicolson,
1967), pp. 54-70.

The reviewers, of course, were not slow to note the
Waugh-Pinfold correspondence. Donat O'Donnell found the
objective cruelty of Waugh's comic vision 'embarrassing'
when turned to self-examination (No. 152), and the TLS
printed a quietly savage piece, trying to cut Waugh's
talent down to size:

> It is time people stopped treating Mr. Waugh as a
> failed Mauriac. He is a lightweight who has suffered
> from being bracketed with completely different writers
> like Mr. Graham Greene.... Like Sheridan or Fitzgerald
> or Max Beerbohm, [he] has a freak talent and is entitled
> to be judged on what he writes without any attempt to
> relate him to trends or other writers or anything else.
> (No. 154)

This notion of Waugh as an amusing writer of squibs or
romantic religious melodrama was something we might have
expected O'Donnell or Philip Toynbee to reiterate. Neither
had been great admirers of his earlier work and both found
this book unsatisfactory. Their dissatisfaction, however,
seemed to spring more from the fact that Waugh was still
capable of shocking them with both style and subject-

matter. Mr Toynbee was puzzled by the suggestion that
Waugh was horrified by 'colonels, public school men, upper-
class thugs, anti-Semites, Fascists and bullies - just the
kind of people, in fact, to whom [he] has sometimes seemed
to be a little over-indulgent' (No. 156). The remark neatly
demonstrates how dangerous it is to draw parallels between
an author's characters and his beliefs. Pinfold-Waugh
clearly stated that his works were 'quite external to himself' and the only partial exception to this was 'Brideshead', a book which he regretted publishing in its original
form and massively revised.

Of those who welcomed the novel, John Raymond was the
most generous: 'To read anything he writes has always been,
for this reviewer, an almost physical pleasure'. The excursion into yet another literary style was greeted by him
with delight: 'It is possible to predict a new novel by ...
Greene say, a new Compton Burnett, a Henry Green even, in a
way that it is impossible ... [with] ... Waugh' (No. 155).
Douglas Woodruff found that it 'succeeds remarkably' while
being naively puzzled as to why a man 'should invent unreal-
ities about himself' ('Tablet', 20 July 1957, 60); 'Time',
lamenting that it was not 'up to the level of the early-
vintage Waugh', still recommended it highly as 'probably
the most off-beat novel of the season, and certainly
Waugh's strangest' (12 August 1957, 58).

Like 'Decline and Fall', 'Black Mischief', 'Campion' and
'Brideshead' before it, 'Pinfold' spawned controversy. J.B.
Priestley, an admirer of the early work, wrote a piece of
amateur psycho-analysis for the 'New Statesman' based on the
book. He suggested that the insanity described was the
result of Waugh's attempt to combine two incompatible
roles: those of artist and Catholic country gentleman.
The hallucination scenes he found 'rather crude and
tedious' because the author had become 'bogged down somewhere between reality and invention' (No. 157). Waugh's
reply (significantly, in the conservative 'Spectator') was
hilarious and devastating (13 September 1957, 328-9;
reprinted ALO, pp. 136-9). Even 'The Times' noted the dispute and rebuked both for meddling in 'politics and
sociology'. They should stick, suggests this anonymous
writer, to the business of story-telling and their 'inevitable function' of helping ' to cheer us all up' (14 September 1957, 7).

The book is not now regarded as a major work in the
canon but is used rather as a piece of fictional autobiography to illustrate Waugh's aesthetic precepts and his
opinion of his career and domestic life. This fails to do
it justice although it has to be admitted that Waugh's
self-analysis is disarmingly accurate. The ease with which

it translated into a successful radio play testifies to
the quality of the novel's structure and dialogue (see
'The Times', 8 June 1960, 16). Anthony Powell believes it
to be one of Waugh's most interesting works. B.S. Johnson,
the avant-garde novelist, later experimented with the mixture of autobiography and fiction and Muriel Spark in the
same year wrote 'The Comforters' on a similar theme of
persecution by disembodied voices. Angus Wilson likened
'Pinfold' to Kafka (No. 165). The technical innovation it
represented is worthy of more serious critical attention.
Waugh, however, never followed it up. He described it as
'a light novel' and considered it merely as an account of
an extraordinary sequence of events in which 'the reason
remains strenuously active but the information on which it
acts is delusory' (quoted in No. 155). The phrasing here
is significant. However we interpret the novel, it is
surely another parable, based on the assumption of the
reality of the supernatural, challenging the humanist
belief in the controlling power of reason. Man's multiple
failures to rationalize the universe, despite the threatening nightmare of madness, are a constant source of delight
to him. In a curious fashion they substantiate his religious faith. He was perennially drawn by the 'rich glint of
lunacy' which he had seen in the eye of Aimée Thanatogenos
('The Loved One'). Perhaps this is what was implicit in
the 'moment of vision' Dennis Barlow, like Pinfold, was
granted.

'THE WORLD OF EVEYLN WAUGH' (1958)

This is the only anthology of Waugh's fiction so far
printed: it was edited by Charles J. Rolo and published
only in America. The 'New York Herald Tribune' described
it as

> A collection sampling the rich treasury of ... Waugh's
> work, containing short stories, the complete text of
> 'The Loved One' and excerpts from eight other novels,
> including the entire second part of 'Brideshead'....
> Mr Rolo's introduction furnishes both critical and bio-
> graphical information. (25 May 1958, 13)

While of no intrinsic value, this collection received two
interesting reviews which help to define American critical
attitudes to Waugh. The 'New York Times' described him as
a literary leader of the 'professional children' attacking
'the uplifters' in an 'over-reasonable society' (No. 158).
'Time' compared Waugh with Aldous Huxley, speaking of them

approvingly as 'two wondrously articulate Fools [who] were
wiser than the lugubrious Lear of the tottering old order'
(No. 159).

'RONALD KNOX' (1959)

Ronald Knox, the distinguished Catholic priest, was Waugh's
close friend. The enormous labour of writing this biography
was not something Waugh anticipated with relish; scholarly
research did not come easily to him. But it had been the
specific wish of Mgr Knox that if a biography had to be written (and this was, given his fame as a theologian, writer
and convert, inevitable) then he would prefer Waugh to do
it. Knox was often seen as a modern Newman. His great work
was a new translation of the Bible but he was also a *littérateur* - a humorist, essayist, detective story writer -
with a *penchant* for upper-class life. The latter characteristic did not endear him to many (Graham Greene, for
example) but Waugh found in him a sympathetic nature. The
biography, as with the earlier 'Rossetti' and 'Campion',
reveals as much about Waugh as it does about his subject.
    The reviews, in this instance, largely speak for them-
selves and little additional commentary is required. Mgr
Gordon Wheeler (DR, Winter 1959-60, 346-52) corrected
Waugh's interpretation of certain facts and noted his failure to examine others. In particular, he objected to Cardinal Bourne's being made the villain of the piece. This was
surely a result of personal antagonism on Waugh's part.
Bourne had been the patron of Oldmeadow and had implicitly
supported his attacks on 'Black Mischief' and 'A Handful of
Dust' in the 'Tablet'. To Waugh (although not, says
Wheeler, to Knox), Bourne was the epitome of philistinism.
    The reception was surprisingly favourable for this
overtly apologetic work (in one sense a modern version of
'Campion'). The TLS regarded it as 'an extremely good biography' (No. 160) and this was the opinion of the majority.
Characteristically, Graham Greene relished the lurid portrayal of villainy showing 'Knox meeting the meanness, jealousies and misunderstandings of the hierarchy'. He disliked the world Knox represented but generously remarked
that 'it is Mr Waugh's very great achievement that he holds
the interest even of the unsympathetic' (No. 162). Muriel
Spark (TC, January 1960, 601), Maurice Bowra (No. 163) and
John Betjeman (NY, 23 April 1960, 174-7) all joined the
chorus of congratulation. Only Angus Wilson found himself
unable to praise the book 'that for all its competence and
high intention, seems to me dull, at times, even empty'
(No. 165). He had waited years for a chance to record his

sincere admiration for Waugh's writings. He had also a debt
of honour to pay off for Waugh's muscular defence of 'Hemlock and After' (see No. 165, n. 1). But now that the
chance had at last presented itself he could in all honesty
only regard the biography as little more than a 'dismal'
act of piety.

'A TOURIST IN AFRICA' (1960)

Few would now disagree that of all Waugh's travel books
this is the slightest. It was, in fact, the only post-war
excursion into that literary form so heavily used by him
before 1939. The reviews note the inevitable change. The
lightness of touch, the inexhaustible curiosity, the
delight in the fantastic and the grotesque which sustained
those works collected in 'When the Going was Good' had now
disappeared. 'This is Waugh, once again, of the Middle-Late
Mood:' wrote Basil Davidson, 'more in sorrow, for the most
part, than in wit' (No. 168). '"A Tourist In Africa"',
Cyril Connolly remarked, 'is quite the thinnest piece of
book-making which Mr. Waugh has undertaken and must be
viewed in relation to the labours on Father Ronald Knox
which preceded it' (No. 169). Certainly, Waugh regarded his
trip as something of a holiday. The book was written to pay
for his passage.
    Waugh was by this time, however, firmly established as a
senior figure in English letters. In a period of rather low
literary achievement anything from his pen merited careful
attention and Dan Jacobson and Alan Sillitoe both dealt
with the book seriously, the first seeing it as a fascinating offshoot of that 'nostalgia' which had coloured Waugh's
fiction (No. 166), the second objecting to 'that curious,
falsely attractive sense of tolerance of a caste-bound
mind' (No. 170). A professor of African law found it 'well-
balanced and objective' (No. 167) while Davidson,
another expert on African affairs, discovered numerous
elementary historical errors (No. 168).
    In retrospect, Davidson would appear to have been
closer to the truth. Observation in this quietly humorous,
prejudiced manner relies on generalization and Waugh had
been out of close touch with events in Africa since the
1930s. As a serious political statement it is, like
'Mexico', largely negligible. As an entertainment, however, it has something to recommend it: 'not seldom foolish; and yet enough for a book that will be read and
liked,' wrote Davidson (No. 168). He was wrong. The
travel book as a *genre* was no longer popular. 'A Tourist
in Africa' was remaindered and gathered dust on booksellers'

shelves until the early 1970s when, at last, collectors began to seek it out.

'UNCONDITIONAL SURRENDER' (1961)

Apart from the freakish 'Pinfold', by 1961 Waugh had not
published a full-length work of fiction for six years. In
1955 the 'trilogy' had apparently been abandoned. Now he
announced that his earlier statement 'was not quite candid.
I knew that a third volume was needed' (quoted in No. 175).
This proved to be his last novel although he lived for
another five years. Perhaps he felt that with this he had
said everything he had wanted to say. There is an air of
finality about it, of resignation, which the reviewers
often remarked upon (Anthony Quinton, T&T, 26 October
1961, 1801-2).
    Distinct critical camps were again established with
the familiar arguments for and against Waugh's vision of
the war and the world. Amis and Toynbee attacked him
on the grounds that his literary realism was subverted by
prejudice. Crouchback's motto is, according to the first,
'It's all right when I do it' (No. 171): according to the
second, 'The man who knows a good brandy is a *better* man
that the man who does not' (No. 176). They treated the work
as a moral statement and, quite apart from the technical
facility of the writing, found it essentially pernicious.
In 1962 the American writers Joseph Heller and Gore Vidal
took much the same line but in gentler prose (Nos 178 and
177). Heller disliked Crouchback and attributed motives
to him other than those acknowledged in the text; the hero
is not seen as 'innocent' but by turns stupid and
apathetic. Vidal, while finding that the 'trilogy has
much to recommend it' feared that Waugh had dropped the
mask of the satirist for the indulgent daydreams of the
romantic, forsaking, unlike Juvenal ('his great precursor'), 'the sins of the dreadful, usable present'. Simon
Raven, in 1964, largely retracted his favourable contemporary review on the grounds that the social commentary
of the trilogy was too simplistic and often simply inaccurate (No. 180).
    There was one notable exception from this list: Cyril
Connolly. He still had certain reservations about those
caricatures which the 'biliousness of Mr. Waugh's gaze'
rendered 'dreary' (No. 175). But he had decisively transferred to the opposite camp with this review which stated
that, on re-reading all three volumes, 'the cumulative
effect is most impressive, and it seems to me unquestionably the finest novel to have come out of the war'. He even

described 'Officers and Gentlemen' as 'a magnificent novel', largely reversing his earlier complaints (No. 148). The Catholic intelligentsia also applauded it warmly. Bernard Bergonzi noted that 'the whole work now looks a substantial achievement, and one which may alter our total picture of Mr Waugh's writings' (No. 172). Christopher Derrick saw the inevitable complaints about 'snobbery and romanticism' as emphasizing 'Waugh's own present position, an *avant-garde* position, a very serious and responsible one in the front rank of the contemporary movement' (No. 174). This was an interesting paradox. Waugh's refusal to believe in conventional heroism, Progress or rationalism, allowed Derrick to label the ostensible avant-garde as 'reactionaries'.

With his notice, V.S. Pritchett introduced a little more subtlety into this rancorous taking of sides. The left wing and the Catholics had their own prejudices and often attacked or defended according to preconceptions beyond the text. Pritchett suggested that 'To object to his snobbery is as futile as objecting to cricket, for every summer the damn game comes round again whether you like it or not' (No. 173). Social exclusivism, in other words, exists as a perennial part of the British consciousness. It won't disappear if ignored and Waugh is entitled to write about it, even to share in it, as an objective observer. There is no reason for us to be affronted by it except when it is 'violent'. The point at which 'Waugh's High Romance becomes vulgar sentimentality' is when he distorts a description of snobbery to imply moral failing, even criminal tendency, in the lower classes.

A discussion of Waugh's use of 'class' forms the central theme of Frank Kermode's piece in which he groups Waugh with Powell, Snow and Richard Hughes, seeing all as novelists obsessed with this theme. Waugh, he concludes, is

> a writer of very great talent ... who has got into his books a whole self-subsistent vision. That this is to some implausible, to some repulsive, may matter only in the very long run; perhaps the aristocratic myth, however extreme and bizarre, corresponds to a society which, seen under this aspect, offers possibilities for what [Henry] James called 'saturation'.... (No. 179)

Professor Kermode, then, suggests that we take the argument beyond personal political or religious prejudice and regard the value structure offered as a literary device capable of extensive exploration within its own terms of reference.

One might add that these are largely the same terms, the

same assumptions, implicit in the work of Fielding, Pope
and Smollett and the modern reader is not prevented from
appreciating the bite of their satire because he no longer
shares their view of an hierarchical society. Most satirists appear anarchic and are at heart deeply conservative.
Crouchback's is a world in which 'quantitative judgements
don't apply' and the only reality is symbolized by the
Church (parodied by the surrogate cross of the Sword of
Stalingrad). To talk of the worldly attitudes expressed in
the novel as anything other than 'mythical' is in Waugh's
own terms a nonsense. As one reviewer remarked, the trilogy deliberately darkens in tone as it progresses and the
progression marks Guy's gradual loss of faith in rational
answers and class assumptions. Upper and lower classes are
alike condemned. Only the faith survives. Ultimately this
is a mystical work and the reviewers who complained about
the drabness of its ineffectual hero surely miss the point.
Professor Kermode's idea, that we should regard the social
attitudes expressed by this 'hero' as a structural myth,
leads, perhaps, to a more fruitful line of inquiry based
on aesthetics rather than political or religious partizan-
ship. Professor Bergonzi had already hinted at this in
1961:

> To anyone brought up as a Catholic Mr Waugh's image of
> Catholicism is, to say the least, peculiar; and the
> same thing may well be true of his picture of the gentry.
> But that is beside the point; it is enough that Mr
> Waugh has found the myth creatively valuable. (No. 172)

'BASIL SEAL RIDES AGAIN' (1963)

In his dedication Waugh described this, his last piece of
published fiction, as 'a senile attempt to recapture the
manner of my youth'. It is not much more than that, as the
reviews suggest: competent, amusing, slight and now republished in Penguin's 'Work Suspended and Other Stories'.
V.S. Pritchett (No. 182) turned out a superbly amusing
account of this little book, disingenuously distressed, as
were others, by the displacement of Basil Seal from his
realm of eternal youth in 'Black Mischief' and 'Put Out
More Flags'. The TLS was alone in offering harsh criticism
of it as a 'nasty little book' (14 November 1963, 921). The
strongest impression to percolate through from the other
reviews is that of massive respect for Waugh's mastery of
English prose. As pure entertainment this was a draught of
vintage in the wastelands of experimental or didactic fiction (No. 181).

'A LITTLE LEARNING' (1964)

The manuscripts in the University of Texas suggest that
Waugh was unusually conscientious in writing this, the
first volume of his autobiography. Several drafts of certain sections exist which demonstrate massive revisions.
From this evidence alone, it could be argued that he had
worked harder on this than on any book since 'Brideshead'.
We can only guess at the difficulties he clearly encountered in producing a satisfactory autobiography. But one
problem must, surely, have arisen immediately: what he
calls in 'Work Suspended' 'the problem of privacy'. It has
been noted that Waugh protected his private life with a
series of public masks. For the most part, 'Pinfold'
represented an objective analysis of the personae he
adopted. 'Mr Pinfold', he wrote, 'gave nothing away' and
neither did Waugh. He strongly objected to the 'presumption' of psycho-analysis in novels and biographies and
was equally critical of those who poured their souls upon
the public's carpet. It was not only undignified but inaccurate, subjective. He found himself now needing to
reveal more of his personal affairs than ever before and
had to devise a format which would deflect the Freudians
and at the same time tell the truth. The result, most
agreed, was brilliantly successful. We are accurately informed of the details of his early life and his own analysis of the importance of crucial relationships is so per-
ceptively self-critical that there is very little left for
the 'interpreters' to do.

  Certain minor distortions are concealed by the rhetoric.
The relationship with his father and brother was perhaps
more awkward than he suggests. His Protestant forebears are
played down (the Rev. Alexander Waugh, for example, clearly
being a considerable celebrity in his day) while the link
with Lord Cockburn is emphasized. The degradations and
homosexual affairs at Oxford are largely omitted in favour
of a 'Brideshead' version of the period. Generally there
is an unacknowledged favouritism for his mother's side of
the family which Freudians would doubtless attribute to his
greater affection for her. But these are small points. The
general picture is exact and uncompromising. He does not
spare the reader embarrassing quotations from his Lancing
diaries or deny the despair and futility of his life early
in that particularly bleak and shiftless period 1924-8. As
though to demonstrate his absolute honesty he concludes
with an account of attempted suicide. No one, not even his
brother, had known of this shameful episode. It was a
particularly brave admission for a Catholic. The classic-
ally precise use of language, ornately archaic at times,

reflects a pervasive irony. Waugh succeeds in maintaining
his privacy (as Graham Greene does in 'Ways of Escape') by
treating his younger self as another character. There is a
cool and humorous detachment about this work which was
much appreciated by reviewers. This was, in one sense,
Basil Seal quietly riding again round those strange tracks
of his childhood and adolescence now lost for ever but to
memory.

'A Little Learning' was Waugh's last book. He made
several stabs at beginning a second volume. A few heavily
corrected sheets entitled 'A Little Hope' are filed in
Texas as the only evidence of this attempt. They deal
kindly with his relationship with his brother during the
brief period in 1925 when they were both living in London.
But somehow he could not make progress with it. Perhaps the
further he moved through chronology the closer the older
and younger self approached and the more awkward became the
'problem of privacy'. One thing seems certain. The most
important single event he would have needed to describe in
the next volume was the desertion of his first wife, Evelyn
Gardner, in 1929. To the end he found the incident painfully embarrassing. The wound of that affront to his dignity never completely healed. Its discomfort is, surely,
reflected in his novels by a long line of attractive,
faithless wives from Agatha Runcible to Virginia Troy.
Perhaps he could not trust himself to be objective about
she-Evelyn. Perhaps, as a Catholic public figure, he did
not wish to degrade himself and his family by recalling
the incident. Scarcely more than 500 words were written in
the two years between 'A Little Learning' and his death in
1966.

Most reviewers were delighted by the book; 'one ends it',
wrote Plomer, 'with an appetite for its continuation' (No.
183). 'It is a compliment', said Stanley Kauffmann, 'to
this (presumably) least interesting part to say that it
does nothing to diminish eagerness for the rest' (No. 186).
Inevitably, reviewers of these memoirs reflect on their own
lives during the period covered by the book (1903-25). In
this respect Plomer, Pritchett (No. 185) and Alec Waugh
(No. 187) are particularly interesting, setting Waugh's
record in the context of their own experiences. In a piece
too long to be reprinted here, Auden also adds Leonard
Woolf's autobiography to his three-cornered discussion of
'period' (NY, 3 April 1965, 159-92; reprinted in 'Forewords
and Afterwords'). Malcolm Bradbury begins his piece with a
useful résumé of critical approaches to Waugh's fiction and
continues with an analysis of its major thematic concerns
and 'conflicts'. He considers the autobiography as an
account of 'the culture out of which these conflicts

emerged' (No. 184). Anthony Burgess notes the contrast in
literary styles between Waugh *père* and *fils*, the latter's
'comic-stoic mock-Augustan' prose reflecting a character
who refuses to 'repine' but who nevertheless is describing
a period often clouded by 'loneliness and dejection' (No.
188).

Those who complained tended to concentrate on this
'deep undercurrent of melancholy' (Malcolm Muggeridge,
'Esquire', February 1965, 56) which appeared to them to
be faintly absurd. Only 'The Economist' felt the book to be
a failure: 'Mr Waugh writes throughout', it remarked,

> with a simplicity that is extremely effective. It does
> not, however, reveal as much as it promises to do. Mr
> Waugh has faithfully displayed the mechanisms - heredity,
> environment, education ... - that went to the making of
> the boy and so of the man; it is the spirit that informs
> the mechanism that is missing. (12 December 1964, 1031)

Despite the largely favourable reception, 'A Little
Learning' sold badly. Waugh's last book, like 'A Tourist
in Africa', was remaindered and stayed out of print until
Sidgwick and Jackson produced a paperback (with rather too
many misprints) in 1973. Penguin Books re-printed it at last
in 1983.

'SWORD OF HONOUR' (1965)

Waugh's last 'fictional work' was the recension of his trilogy to a single volume of approximately 800 pages. The
reviewers had already stated their opinions of the thematic
concerns but the book still merited notice. The TLS gave a
detailed account of the revisions (No. 189) and Anthony
Burgess, while not writing specifically on Waugh, produced
an interesting article placing him in the tradition of
Huxley, Greene, Isherwood, Golding and Spark as a writer
concerned with 'mystical' experience (TLS, 3 March 1966,
153-4).

It should be noted that the three volumes currently
issued by Penguin Books are reprints of the original texts
and do not include Waugh's revisions. The recension is now
only available in the hardback Uniform Edition.

CHRISTOPHER SYKES'S BIOGRAPHY (1975), 'DIARIES' (1976),
'A LITTLE ORDER' (1978), 'LETTERS' (1980)

The publication of Christopher Sykes's 'Evelyn Waugh. A

Biography' (Collins, 1975) was a major event in 'Waugh
scholarship'. It was an 'official' biography (although he
prefers not to use this term) and represented the first
substantial collation of previously unpublished material.
My opinion of it is stated in 'Essays in Criticism' (April
1976, 182-8). Suffice it to say that it did little to endear the public to Waugh. He apparently died leaving an
impression of himself as a clever but bigoted writer of
black comedy and Catholic propaganda. And despite Mr
Sykes's loyal portrait, his friend still appears as a
difficult and often unpleasant character. Waugh's eldest
son and literary executor, Auberon Waugh, was not pleased
(B&B October, 1975, 410-11) although many others of Waugh's
friends felt it to be an excellent book. Angus Wilson's
long TLS review is ultimately unfavourable and offers a
perceptive assessment of Waugh's career (No. 191).
    Hard upon the biography followed the 'Diaries', edited
by Michael Davie (Weidenfeld & Nicolson, 1976) which, if
anything, depressed an already low estimate of Waugh's
character. I reprint my own review (No. 192) to save space
here. The critical response was, if anything, a little
hypocritical. Publication of edited excerpts from the
'Diaries' in 1973 had whetted the readers' appetite for
outrageous gossip by omitting names (to avoid libel action)
and the hardback edition sold so well that it went into
soft covers shortly afterwards. Frederick Raphael's piece
Portrait of the Artist as a Bad Man (ST, 5 September 1976,
27) reflected a violent distaste for Waugh's personality
which appears to have coloured his appreciation of him as
a serious artist. No one gave Mr Davie due credit for a
massive work of scholarship and several, including Graham
Greene (B&B, October 1976, 19-21), complained about slov-
enly editing, and in particular the great length of the
book. My piece is a reaction to the general reception which
I thought to be unfair both to editor and subject.
    'A Little Order' (Eyre Methuen, 1978) was Donat
Gallagher's edition of Waugh's journalism. Due to various
difficulties with his publisher the book was not what Dr
Gallagher had intended but ended up as a slim 'coffee
table' volume, again unlikely to impress critics with the
essential seriousness of Waugh's artistic concerns. It is
interesting to note that the publishers could not be persuaded to allow more than 60,000 words because they
believed only a handful of devotees would bother with it.
Nevertheless it was generally well received, even allowing
for the insult to Dr Gallagher that his 'editorial matter
is usefully informative, but written as if in mud with a
cleft stick' (Jonathan Raban, NS, 23-30 December 1977,
902-4). Paul Johnson noted that the volume 'testifies to

the almost insatiable demand for [Waugh's] work' and
reflects a widely held view that, even in Grub Street,
Waugh 'was the great prose master of the age' (No. 193).
   'The Letters of Evelyn Waugh', edited by Mark Amory
(Weidenfeld & Nicolson, 1980), was again subject to the
sort of reluctant admiration offered to the 'Diaries'.
Philip Larkin was clearly appalled by what he saw as the
lack of 'charity' in many of these epistles (No. 194) but
most found another, more pleasant, aspect of Waugh's
character here. 'Seldom, if ever,' said Anthony Quinton,
'can the task of reviewing a book of more than six hundred pages ... have taken the form of such unqualified
self-indulgence' ('Listener', 4 September 1980, 12).
Reviews were becoming more sympathetic to what Christopher
Sykes termed Waugh's 'sleepless sense of farce'. As
Auberon Waugh had remarked, 'Any biographer or critic who
fails to spot this one characteristic and bring it into
prominence, and ... there have been hundreds, misses if
not the whole point of the person he is discussing at any
rate the only context in which those less endearing characteristics ... can usefully be discussed' (B&B, October
1975, 7-9). It is this 'context' which reviewers of the
'Letters' began to explore. A résumé of several notices is
offered in the opening paragraph of No. 195 although
Jonathan Raban's piece (ST, 7 September 1980, 28) is not
as unsympathetic as Mr Wheatcroft suggests.
   Most agreed with Phillip Parrish's comment that 'the
abiding impression the letters leave behind is not one of
malice but of love' (DM, 4 September 1980, 7), love for his
faith, his family and friends, love of human vitality but
not, unfortunately in his later years, of his own life. We
are introduced to the extraordinary spectacle of Waugh
describing himself as an 'elderly buffer' at the age of
thirty-two (Raban, ST).
   Anthony Quinton noted that there 'is little about writing here' but that does not mean that Waugh did not discuss
aesthetic concerns earnestly in many letters. It is perhaps
unfortunate that Mark Amory, able to use only a fifth of
the material available to him, tends to omit some epistles
on the ground that they are less entertaining. Waugh did
not only write to the rich and famous. Long letters on
literary technique were dispatched to aspiring writers whom
he thought promising. The correspondence with his agent,
A.D. Peters, is massive and amusing with its jocular, workmanlike approach to the business of writing and publishing.
(Résumés of these letters from Waugh appear in Section E
of Professor Davis's Texas catalogue.) It seems that there
is never space to include enough of Waugh's serious artistic statements to establish him once for all as a

sophisticated aesthetician. The book is scrupulously
edited with copious and often droll footnotes but the basic
selection of letters slightly distorts the truth.

MISCELLANEOUS

This section of the book is intended to give the reader a
glimpse of Waugh's public image. As Philip Toynbee said,
'In his life-time Evelyn Waugh was news' ('Observer', 7
September 1980, 28). The result of this is described by
Jonathan Raban: 'It has become harder and harder to read
Waugh's novels without finding them being elbowed off the
table by the importunate character of Waugh himself'
(ST, 7 September 1980, 42). Here are two press reports of
Waugh's activities at different stages in his career and
an excerpt from Wyndham Lewis's 'The Doom of Youth' (No.
196). The latter sees Waugh in the 1930s as the arbiter of
the Bright Young Things (a role which he had in fact abandoned more than two years earlier). The court case (1957)
recorded in the 'Telegraph' (No. 197) illustrates many
things: his attitude to writing and his sales, his contempt for intrusive journalists in general and the Beaverbrook press in particular, his dilatory sport in the
largely monotonous later years of scanning the papers for
libellous remarks in the hope (here successful) of out-
witting the Inland Revenue by securing a tax-free settlement. The incident involving Lord Noel-Buxton and Nancy
Spain is now legend (see ALO, pp. 133-6, for Waugh's
account of this) and even the dry legal report conveys
that tincture of riotous fantasy with which Waugh coloured
the drabbest events. In the dock, as in the television
studio (No. 198), he is dead pan, well-dressed, giving
nothing away, up to and beyond all the tricks of his
inquisitor.

NOTES

1 George Orwell, 'Collected Essays, Journalism and
  Letters', ed. Sonia Orwell and Ian Angus, vol. IV,
  1945-50 (Harmondsworth, Penguin, 1970), p. 576.
2 'Diaries', p. 297.
3 H.A. Mason noted in 'Scrutiny': 'Occasionally this sense
  of possessing superior equipment has led French critics
  to rediscover or "revalue" English authors. Waugh and
  Greene, it appears, have been enjoying a vogue in France.'
  (A Note on Contemporary 'Philosophical' Literary Criticism in France, 'Scrutiny', vol. XVI, March 1949, 53.)

4 'Diaries', 30 October 1926, p. 268.
5 See Anthony Powell, 'Messengers of Day' (Heinemann, 1979), pp. 102-5. Waugh's business correspondence with Duckworth's at this time was with Mr Powell. The original title, one of these letters notes, was to have been 'Untoward Incidents'.
6 Evelyn Waugh as Artist, 'Daily Sketch', 30 January 1929, 5.
7 Sykes, p. 98.
8 'Writers', pp. 108-9.
9 'Letters', p. 39.
10 'Letters', p. 88.
11 The description was cut, surely, not because Waugh had changed his mind, but because of its overt didacticism; it tells the reader what to think rather than allowing the book's images to speak for themselves. Hetton still recognizably demonstrates the faults of late Gothic and the letter to Driberg supports the idea that it was Waugh's consistent intention to suggest an inferior form of a (Spanish Catholic) ideal.
12 Ernest Oldmeadow, 'Tablet', 12 October 1935, 451.
13 Unpublished letter, n.d., to 'Catherine' (*sic*) from Addis Ababa.
14 Unpublished letter, n.d., no address, to Henry Yorke (probably written early 1936).
15 Evelyn Waugh, Converted to Rome, 'Daily Express', 20 October 1930, 10.
16 Unpublished letter to A.D. Peters, 26 January 1938, from Pixton Park, Dulverton (HRC).
17 Evelyn Waugh, 'New Statesman', 5 March 1938, 365-6.
18 Evelyn Waugh, 'Men at Arms' (1952), Penguin, p. 12.
19 Cf. 'Work Suspended' (Penguin), p. 163: 'deprived of sex, as women are, by its fulfilment...'.
20 George Orwell, 'Collected Essays, Journalism and Letters', vol. IV, p. 496.
21 Malcolm Bradbury, 'Evelyn Waugh', Writers and Critics series (Oliver & Boyd, 1964), p. 86.
22 James Carens, 'The Satiric Art of Evelyn Waugh' (Seattle and London, University of Washington Press, 1966), p. 110.

The Balance in 'Georgian Stories 1926'

1926

1. R.B.L., 'MANCHESTER GUARDIAN'

29 October 1926, 7

Here are the eighteen stories chosen for the 1926 volume of
'Georgian Stories'. All but one of them are good and three
of them are brilliant, and yet, somehow, the book as a
whole does not come off, for there is neither unity of
theme nor manner to give cohesion to the fragmentary parts.
So many authors, be they ever so admirable in themselves,
together make an awkward job, and the average reader will
feel vaguely dissatisfied with the book as a whole, even
though he will certainly enjoy many stories in it. All the
authors are well known, and some of them, Mr Aldous Huxley
and Mr Somerset Maugham, for instance, are famous. But the
chief honours are carried off by Mr Liam O'Flaherty in his
subtle and finely written story, The Tent; by Mr Evelyn
Waugh, who pillories the stupidity of the average film
story by telling one and affixing to it the logical and
absurd prologue and epilogue; and by Mr Geoffrey Moss in
his terrible study of Koekritz, chief constable in an
occupied German city after the war....

2. M.A.S., 'CHERWELL'

13 November 1926, 155

That modern literary form, the short story, has been
thought by some - perhaps after reading the 'Strand'

magazine - to be in a decline. Certainly it is of all forms
the easiest to criticise; in a book the trees may be
obscured by the wood, but in a story the flaw is as evident
as the cleavage in a crystal. But if you wish to be reassured read these stories: if you are short of a Christmas present, buy the book.

We in Oxford, in our usual perverse way, will perhaps
want to start at the end where Evelyn Waugh, writes of
Oxford - and of a 'blind'.

> ... he had stumbled to the window and leant there with
> the cold air in his face and the steady moisture of the
> rain fighting with the drumming of blood in his head.
> Gradually, as he stood there motionless, nausea had
> come upon him; he had fought it back, his whole will
> struggling in the effort; it had come again; his drunken
> senses relaxed their resistance and with complete aban-
> donment of purpose and restraint, he vomited into the
> yard below.

This is something that rings true; that recalls personal
experience....

3.   ALEC WAUGH ON THE BALANCE

1967

Alexander Raban Waugh (1898-1981), was the elder brother of
Evelyn. He was a prolific popular novelist, biographer and
writer of travel books and memoirs, author of 'The Loom of
Youth' (1917), 'Kept' (1925), 'Hot Countries' (1930),
'Island in the Sun' (1956), 'The Early Years of Alec
Waugh' (1962), 'My Brother Evelyn and Other Profiles'
(1967) and 'The Fatal Gift' (1973). The last two volumes go
some way towards explaining the complex relationship with
his brother which was rarely intimate but consistently
loyal. They saw little of each other as adults except for a
brief period in the 1920s. Both, of course, spent much of
their time travelling abroad.

From 'My Brother Evelyn and Other Profiles' (Cassell,
1967), p. 179.

... Early in 1926 he wrote a long *avant-garde* short story,
The Balance which I included in 'Georgian Stories 1926', of

which I was the editor. Several writers - G.B. Stern in
particular - recognized its originality, and Michael
Sadleir asked him to contribute to his symposium the 'New
Decameron'. I have not read The Balance for forty years.
Evelyn did not think it worth including in 'Mr Loveday's
Little Outing'. But I hope that it will appear in the even-
tual canon of his writings. It gives me pleasure to be able
to boast that I was his first editor....(1)

Note

1   The British Library Catalogue and several critics mis-
    takenly attribute the editorship of this volume (printed
    as 'A. Waugh') to Arthur Waugh (see p. 3).

'Rossetti, His Life and Works'

1928

4. J.C. SQUIRE, 'OBSERVER'

29 April 1928, 6

Sir John Collings Squire (1884-1958) was a poet, essayist,
short story writer, parodist and anthologist; he was author
of 'Collected Parodies' (1921), 'Poems in One Volume'
(1926), 'Outside Eden' (1933) and his autobiography 'The
Honeysuckle and the Bee' (1937). Squire was a leading figure in the literary world of 'Georgian' London, moving from
his post as Acting Editor of the 'New Statesman' in 1918 to
found the 'London Mercury' of which he remained Editor
until 1933. Waugh found Squire's brand of cricketing, beer-
drinking, well-brushed literary man rather tedious. There
is a thinly veiled satirical portrait of him in 'Decline
and Fall' as Jack Spire, the littérateur and preservation-
ist. (Squire ran a campaign in the 'Mercury' for the preservation of ancient buildings.)

It is, perhaps, hardly fair to say that the reputation of
Dante Gabriel Rossetti (whose centenary arrives next month)
has waned during the last generation. So far as I am aware,
nobody of any consequence has arisen to say that he was a
worthless painter and a bad poet; he has not even been (as
Tennyson for a time was) a favourite target of the idiots
who draw attention to themselves by sneering at anything
which their fathers admired, and thus prepare the way for
later reactions. Rossetti has never been widely depricia-
ted; he has merely faded out of notice. The centenary
ritual, in his connection, should be particularly useful.
  What a vogue it was! In his lifetime he was, except to
the Pre-Raphaelite circle, first and foremost a painter.

His 'Poems' in 1870 made a deep, but not a very wide, impression; it was not until the late 'nineties and early nineteen-hundreds (he had died in 1882) that he really became popular. He then became popular with a vengeance. I remember it well, because I grew up in the middle of it. Twenty-five years ago I was an undergraduate, and the Rossetti 'boom' was in full swing. Not the extraordinary, but the ordinary, young man had his walls covered with brown reproductions of Rossetti's yearning ladies....

Mr Evelyn Waugh's book has a double interest, because he himself is a member of the youngest generation of authors who have grown up since the War and never knew Rossetti as what an American has recently called 'the schoolmarm's god'. The modern Old Masters of his youth were probably Gauguin, Cézanne, and Van Gogh; he comes fresh to the work of criticism, having no overnight orgie of Pre-Raphaelite succulence to cause a morning revulsion. The result is an extremely sensible and readable book.

Mr. Waugh writes with terse elegance and unobtrusive wit. He has a good eye for humours of detail and presents them without unnecessary fuss, as in his account of Rossetti's father:

> He was born in 1783 of very humble parentage. His father, Nicolo, was blacksmith at Vasto, in the Abruzzi (or, as one of Rossetti's biographers prefers, 'connected with the iron trade of that city').

As a biographical summary, extracting the essence of the great library of Pre-Raphaelite memoirs, the book is excellent. We are presented with a clear narrative of the early struggles of the Pre-Raphaelites, of their gradual triumph, of Rossetti's long and tragic love-story, of his gradual collapse after his wife's death: with adequate, but not excessive, disquisitions on the traditional controversies about 'the Fleshly School of Poetry' and Rossetti's exhumation of the manuscript poems which he had passionately interred with his wife. Elizabeth [Siddal] herself is well-drawn (there are interesting quotations from her poems), and several of the subordinate figures (notably Ruskin) are well suggested. The last years of chloral, drink, and fierce suspicion are described with unusual candour, though not morbidly. It is evident, however, that Mr Waugh's principal interest lies in Rossetti's work as a painter.

This is admirably described and interestingly discussed: That Rossetti was a limited and peculiar painter is evident. His work (like that of Burne-Jones) is mainly in one mood: painted in an ecstasy of fleshly mysticism.... His pictures are precise equivalents of the most emotional and slowly musical of his poems. Grant their monotony; there remains their power. And this is where Mr Waugh is troubled. According, he says, to the modern canons of art (he adds, surprisingly, that 'there is probably less nonsense talked about art than ever before') Rossetti cannot be a painter at all. He never concentrated on 'the necessary relations of forms in space' or realised that he must not paint women because he thought them beautiful; he was a thoroughly literary artist, with his personal emotions burning in every selected theme. And yet Mr Waugh admires his pictures.

He does not solve his problem of theory. Problems of aesthetic theory have a habit of not being solved. But it is gratifying to find him at the end sighing for an hour of Hieronymus Bosch, or even Frith. It is all very well to abuse anecdotal painting in order to get rid of the worst Academicians; but you end by ruling out Wilkie, Hogarth, and half the Dutch. It is all very well to revolt against prettiness; but it is depressing if this results in the studied avoidance by artists of anything in the least agreeable to look at. There must be something wrong with theories which are filling the world with deformed nudes and groups of fruit which are painted simply because their shapes are rather geometrical. Art as a branch of physical science has no room for Rossetti.

The principal defect of Mr Waugh's book is its inadequate notice of Rossetti's poetry. It is not merely that Mr Waugh is more interested in the painting, but that he seems not at all to realise how good in its way much of the poetry is. It is symptomatic that he does not so much [as] mention one of the two best of all Rossetti's poems, that majestic dirge, 'The Burden of Nineveh'. Rossetti was a master of the verbal adagio and the 'dying fall'; he wrote some very fine love-poetry; his verbal pictures of landscape [are] of an exquisite accuracy; and sometimes he suddenly deserted his embroidered and archaic style for a precise and poignant simplicity. Posterity may ultimately think him a greater poet than painter.

5.   HAROLD ACTON, LETTER FROM 8 WARWICK SQUARE

1 May 1928

Sir Harold Acton (b. 1904) is a poet, novelist, translator, art connoisseur, historian and autobiographer. He

was a leading figure in the Eton Society of the Arts
(which included Henry Green (Yorke) and Anthony Powell),
then of the 'aesthetic' set at Oxford where he became a
close friend and mentor of Waugh (1922-4). He wrote
'Aquarium' (poems, 1923) , 'Cornelian' (1928), 'Humdrum'
(novel, 1928), 'The Last Medici' (1932) and 'Memoirs of an
Aesthete' (1948).

Dear Evelyn,
   What [?] a delight to hear from you. I wondered where
you were....
   I can now say that I have read and honestly enjoyed your
'Rossetti'. Your maturity of mind alarms and terrifies me,
it is so tremendously able and considered. Peter Quennell
did his best in his own peculiar delicate way, to prejudice
me before I read the book: he said it might have been made
so infinitely more amusing, but I myself am glad you did
not fall a victim to that vulgar temptation. You would have
been accused of a thousand things - imitating Strachey, or
even ... Guedalla!(1) As it is you have written in your own
genuine and agreeable style, and dealt quietly and elo-
quently with your subject. You could not expect me to agree
with some of your opinions of his [Rossetti's] painting,
but all the same I was continually interested and liked it
all the better for that. I see that J.C. Squire has done
his duty for once and given you a good review. All my con-
gratulations. I am sure it will get the success it deserves,
and it must have been hard work writing.
   I am quite sad when I think of the utter miscarriage of
my poems - ironically 'Cornelian' has been selling.
   Of course nothing would please me better than your dedication of your novel (2) to myself. I long to read it.
When shall I see it?...

Yours ever,
Harold.

Notes

1   Philip Guedalla, popular biographer.
2   'Decline and Fall'. Waugh dedicated the novel to him
    'in homage and affection'.

6.   PETER QUENNELL, 'NEW STATESMAN'

12 May 1928, 160-1

Peter Quennell (b. 1905), poet, biographer, critic, historian and literary editor, was Editor of the 'Cornhill Magazine', 1944-51, and 'History Today' 1951-79. He is author
of 'Poems' (1926), 'Baudelaire and the Symbolists' (1929),
'Byron: The Years of Fame' (1935), etc., and two autobiographical works, 'The Marble Foot' (1976) and 'The Wanton
Chase' (1980). Mr Quennell arrived in Oxford from Berk-
hamsted School (where he was a friend and contemporary of
Graham Greene) with a high reputation as a young poet and
represented the only serious challenge to Harold Acton's
authority (among undergraduates) in aesthetics (they
edited 'Oxford Poetry 1924' together). Waugh and he were
close friends at university; but in later years Waugh
snubbed him. The reasons for this unusual breach of loyalty
are unclear. It would seem, however, that this review at
least precipitated the deterioration of their relationship.
Mr Quennell's letter (No. 7) suggests that both Waugh and
Evelyn Gardner were outraged by the apparently cool reception of 'Rossetti' here; they looked to their friends for
support.

There are many periods, further removed in time, which are
much closer to us in sympathy than the days of the Pre-
Raphaelite Brotherhood. In those earlier periods we have
discovered, or think we have discovered, fresh virtues;
their outstanding virtues were exactly those which our
personal and intellectual life most conspicuously lacks.
The memory of them persists like the memory of some
delightful and irrecoverable island, a delightful memory,
it is true, but no integral part of our heritage. The
vices of their method, besides, emerge in rather pitiful
relief, viewed by the cruel light of modern aesthetics.
Aware of those deficiencies, a new biographer has undertaken Rossetti's defence. And herein, perhaps, lies the
chief weakness of the monograph; we could have spared Mr
Waugh's lengthly analysis of Rossetti's pictures, as
against a detailed and elaborate representation of the
entire group. Rossetti is exalted at the expense of his
contemporaries. We need a collective, not a single portrait. The conduct of the pre-Raphaelite adventure, its
enthusiasm and impetus, is, on the whole, more entertaining
than its actual results.
  For enthusiasm was their primary characteristic, and

Mr. Waugh seems to have approached his subject with something of a kindred alacrity and zeal. Flippancy he abhors; anecdote, especially when the anecdote is scandalous, he shows a commendable anxiety to avoid. His treatment is consequently a little sparse and curtailed. Half the colour of the movement is implicit in their nicknames, their slang, their hurriedly scrawled letters and reported snatches of conversation....

7. PETER QUENNELL, LETTER FROM 189 HIGH HOLBORN, W.

14 May 1928

You too, Evelyn dear? Well I know from experience how useless it is to defend oneself on such occasions. The choice was between a short detailed review and an article on Rossetti, with a short reference to the author of the book. Of the two I had always [?] imagined that an article did most good. Certainly I didn't mean my reference to be unkindly: it still doesn't read unkindly to me; I will try and find out what other people think. Meanwhile, let us avoid anything so silly as a definite *quarrel*, and content ourselves with being, perhaps, a little frigid and surprised at the mention of each other's name. Though even that, I very much hope, won't last for ever. I am sad to think that the other Evelyn (1) should [?] be in a white heat of indignation. Give [my] love to her.

Love,
Peter.

Note

1 The Hon. Evelyn Gardner whom Waugh married in June 1928.

8. ROY CAMPBELL, 'NATION AND ATHENAEUM'

19 May 1928, 212

Roy Campbell (1902-57), filibustering South African expatriate poet, critic, translator, traveller and 'man of

action', was converted to Roman Catholicism during the
Spanish Civil War. He was author of 'The Wayzgoose' (1928),
'Adamastor' (1930), 'Flowering Rifle' (1939) and 'Light on
a Dark Horse. An Autobiography 1901-1935' (1951). Campbell
was an aggressive aesthete in the style of Pound or Wyndham
Lewis. His 'Who's Who' entry for 1948 includes: 'Won the
steer-throwing of Provence 1932 and 1933.' He was killed in
a road accident in Portugal. Waugh later reviewed
'Adamastor' favourably ('Graphic', 7 June 1930, 543).

When the next generation comes to revalue the standards of
the present one, it is possible that they will react
against us as violently as we have done against the
Victorians. As we ridicule the Victorians for their
prudishness and hypocrisy, so our children may come to
regard our ostentations of frankness as a rather feeble
apology for our flabby sensuality, and ourselves as a
generation of harmlessly undiscriminating old fogeys who
were as sheepish about our few virtues and enthusiasms as
the Victorians were about their vices. The sex-socialism of
this period, with its genteel and fashionable ramifications
of inversion, will perhaps be regarded as an earnest
attempt to keep in step with the Feminist Movement and all
those other progressive institutions of to-day which concern themselves with the rights, the liberty, the brotherhood, and the enlightenment of mankind. In comparing our
promiscuity and frankness with that of the eighteenth century they will not fail to notice the peculiar absence of
zest or enjoyment in its pleasures, and the lack of intellectual and physical vitality, which distinguish the present generation. Such a revaluation is not inconceivable,
and it is possible that those of us who survive to witness
it may one day be exasperated to see our own children
raising many of the fallen Victorian idols from their present degradation to an eminence far above our own idols of
the present day. All this should be borne in mind in dealing with such a figure as Rossetti - a subject so dangerously well-suited to the traditions of modern biography,
especially in its attitude to Victorians. The tradition of
modern biography is to search for incompatibilities: to
adopt a tone of indulgent irony towards one's subject: and
to rely on a slick, slightly epigrammatical, journalistic
style to carry it off. At its supreme moments it provokes
one to a mischievous titter at the absurdity of some great
man like Wordsworth or Goethe. It is the most perfect
instrument that has yet been invented to enable the mediocre to patronize the great.
    Rossetti, as a personality, if not as a poet or a

painter, is certainly a major Victorian: and like most of
his contemporaries he appears to us as a galaxy of incompatibilities. He was simultaneously a sensualist and a
prude, an idealist and a commercialist. Such a mixture of
pomposities, affectations, and unconscious contradictions
would seem an irresistible subject for the more obvious
forms of modern biography. But Mr. Waugh has achieved a
rare distinction for a contemporary biographer - he has
succeeded in *not* patronizing his subject, though he makes
no attempt to whitewash him. He is fully alive to the
comic aspects of his subject, but does not make this a
pretext for adopting a superior tone. The result is that,
however we may disagree with Mr. Waugh's literary and
artistic estimations, he has produced a life of Rossetti
which is both lively and reliable. Mr. Waugh has a very
exalted idea of Rossetti as a painter and attaches more
importance to his painting than to his poetry. Everything
he says about Rossetti's paintings is true enough, but
whether it constitutes any reason to regard Rossetti as
a very fine painter is another matter. To say that such-
and-such a picture is like 'a golden, dim dream' is all
very well - but so are scenes from 'Hassan' and 'Salome'.
Rossetti's was an age which appreciated dimness and
dreaminess for their own sake - and we are rightly suspi-
cious of them to-day. Rossetti, as a painter, was singularly unambitious: he painted with one eye on the market
and seems to have been quite frank about it: he took no
pains to perfect himself as a craftsman: and he seldom
experimented further than was financially expedient. It
satisfied both his public and himself to go on repeating
his dim, voluptuous visions.

In his poetry Rossetti was far less automatic. He wrote
his poems privately - without any hints from the market.
The sonnets in 'The House of Life,' in spite of their many
affectations of mediaevalism, are remarkably fine. From
the rest of the Pre-Raphaelites, Rossetti's character distinguishes itself through its intactness and its pride.
He was the Mussolini of the group. Swinburne was perhaps a
much better poet than Rossetti, but there is something a
little ignoble about this Victorian iconoclast, with his
roses and raptures, his benevolent keeper and his daily
ration of a bottle of Bass. There is something, if not
ignoble, at least unlikable about 'Topsy' Morris with his
toadying hero-worship of Rossetti, his extreme jocularity,
and his meaningless practical jokes. Why is it that excessive facetiousness and geniality always make one suspi-
cious? Rossetti seems to have sized up the Brotherhood very
well. He was under no illusions about them. Ruskin he
tolerated because he was financially useful, but he paid no

attention to his advice or his criticisms. Ridiculous as
Rossetti was in his occult experiments, his fantastic collection of animals, his burial of his poems, and other
eccentricities, there was something in his temperament
which compels respect; and we have only to read this 'Life'
to feel something of the magnetism which drew round him
such incongruous admirers as Whistler, Ruskin, and even,
in the end, the idiotic Buchanan.

9. HERBERT L. MATTHEWS, 'NEW YORK TIMES BOOK REVIEW'

24 June 1928, 5, 29

Herbert Lionel Matthews (b. 1900) was, between 1922 and
1967, in turn reporter, Foreign Editor and War Correspondent for the 'New York Times'. He was author of 'Eye-
witness in Abyssinia' (1937), 'The Education of a Correspondent' (1946), 'The Yoke and the Arrows' (on the Spanish
Civil War, 1956) and 'Revolution in Cuba' (1975). As a
correspondent in Abyssinia in 1935 he may well have met
Waugh who was covering the hostilities for the 'Daily Mail'.

The glamour that surrounded Rossetti's name is now dissi-
pated by the not too sympathetic blasts of modern biographical technique. It is just a century since Gabriel was
born into the exotic atmosphere of the Rossetti home. He
never recovered from that exoticism during his life, and
the aura was so strong even after his death that it has
taken us nearly fifty years to see the man as he was.
     The time is exactly right for this biography by Mr.
Waugh. Most of the contemporaries have passed away, leaving
their copious and adequate accounts of Rossetti's life. The
list is imposing: William Rossetti, Holman-Hunt, William
Bell Scott, Watts-Dunton, Treffrey Dunn, Ford Madox Brown,
Ruskin, Morris, Swinburne, and last, but not least, one who
is still with us - Sir Hall Caine.
     Each one gave his side of the picture with the personal
bias his nature and place in Rossetti's life may have
prompted. Now is the time for posterity to have its
fling.... Mr. Waugh is not very decisive in his answer. He
has his own very definite and very intelligent ideas on the
subject, but he is a rarely impartial critic, and seldom
yields to the temptation of making generalities. Piece by
piece Rossetti is presented to us, the good and bad

together, and we may make up our own minds at the end. The problem is stated, but the solution is left to the reader.

It is Rossetti the painter, rather than the poet, whom Mr. Waugh gives us. In the course of his biography he demonstrates a knowledge of painting and an independent understanding of its principles which is evidence of a critical talent one would hope to see extended to wider fields in future books. And the whole is written with a zest, a cynical humor and a gift of characterization which makes absorbing reading from beginning to end. A better picture of this 'turgid and perverse genius' has surely never before been written, nor have the once sacrosanct Pre-Raphaelite Brotherhood and the later movement ever been set so neatly in their proper places. It can be done, now that art criticism has become a fairly scientific study, and a properly detached viewpoint can be taken.

That Rossetti regarded himself primarily as a painter is well known. 'If any man has poetry in him,' he once said, 'he should paint, for it has all been said, written, and they have scarcely begun to paint it.'

His life was bitterly tragic. One cannot help thinking of that other, even more tragic figure of nineteenth century painting, Vincent Van Gogh. The problem is stated at the beginning of his book by Mr. Waugh:

> As one follows the story of his life one leaves behind the benign genius of Theodore Watts-Dunton's 'Alwyn' and finds the baffled and very tragic figure of an artist born into an age devoid of artistic standards; a man of the South, sensual, indolent and richly versatile, exiled in the narrow, scrambling, specialised life of a Northern city; a mystic without the discipline or consolation of the Church; a life between the rocks and the high road, like the scrub of a Southern hillside, sombre, aromatic and impenetrable.

There is no need to retell a life history so well known as Rossetti's. So far as it had any guidance from manhood onward, three women play the leading parts - Elizabeth Siddal, his wife, that rare and exotic bloom, which withered early and died; the unspeakable Mrs. Schott, as gross and sensual and earthly as the other was delicate, cold and spirituelle; and the sane, motherly, Jane Morris.

Each has been immortalized in dozens of pictures, some very good, some very bad indeed, and all come in for their due meed of praise or blame from Mr. Waugh. To the biographer, Rossetti's eventual claim to distinction as a painter will rest upon his water colors, but he does

manage to become very enthusiastic over some of the oil
paintings....

The time has come, with all due respects to the biographer, to speak of Rossetti the poet. However justified
Mr. Waugh may be in stressing the relatively greater
importance of his subject as an artist, Rossetti has played
too important a part in English literature to be dismissed
with justice as cursorily as he is in this book. His contribution may not have been as great as certain of his
gigantic contemporaries, but it was distinctive, and earned
him a permanent and undisputed niche in the poetical Hall
of Fame.

Mr. Waugh does give due place in his biography to the
volume of poetry published in 1870, but he is chiefly concerned with the furore it created. His opinion of the dis-
interment of 'The House of Life' is interesting. It will be
remembered that Rossetti, in a fit of mystic hysteria,
placed the manuscript against the cheek of his dead wife
in the coffin, and it was buried with her.

> There is no reason why one should look upon the grave
> as more sacred than the dung-heap [writes Mr. Waugh].
> The point is that Rossetti did so look upon it and it is
> his reluctance to comply, coupled with his compliance,
> that clearly indicates a real degradation in his charac-
> ter. In burying the poems, he was, according to his
> lights, performing a sacramental act, and in digging
> them up he violated that sacrament, and one can discern
> no motive for this violation other than frank, dis-
> agreeable vanity.

Some new light, although not much, is thrown on the
publication of that excitedly discussed book in Mr. Oswald
Doughty's carefully edited 'Letters of Dante Gabriel
Rossetti to His Publisher, F.S. Ellis'. These letters have
never previously been published. They reveal beyond question how much Rossetti feared the possibility of adverse
criticism in general, and that of Buchanan in particular,
and how carefully he laid his plans in advance to obtain
the timely support of his friends....

By way of conclusion one can do no better than to quote
the last paragraph of Mr. Waugh's biography:

> There was fatally lacking in him that *essential rec-
> titude* that underlies the serenity of all really great
> art. All his brooding about magic and suicide are symp-
> tomatic not so much of genius as of mediocrity. There
> is a spiritual inadequacy, a sense of ill-organization
> about all that he did. But if he were merely a

psychopathic case and nothing more, there would be no
problem and no need for a book about him. The problem is
that here and there in his life he seems, without ever
feeling it, to have transcended this inadequacy in a
fashion that admits of no glib explanation. Just as the
broken arch at Glastonbury Abbey is, in its ruin, so
much more moving than it can ever have been when it
stood whole and part of a great building, so Rossetti's
art, at fitful moments, flames into the exquisite beauty
of 'Beata Beatrix'. It is the sort of problem that
modern esthetics does not seem capable of coping with.
It has been the object of this book to state, though,
alas! not to solve, this problem.

10. THOMAS CRAVEN, 'NEW YORK HERALD TRIBUNE'

2 September 1928, xii

Thomas Craven (1889-1969), American art critic and biographer, was author of 'Paint' (1923), 'Men of Art' (1931),
'Modern Art' (1934) and 'The Story of Painting' (1943).

'Unfortunately,' writes Mr. Waugh at the beginning of his
study, 'there is singularly little fun to be got out of
Rossetti.' Perhaps this explains the cold squeamishness and
ironic disapproval with which he recounts the unsavory
habits of the master of the Pre-Raphaelites. It is not
often that a biographer chooses a subject whose personality
disgusts him, and is at such pains to get his facts in
order, to present them truthfully, and to estimate artistic
performances for what they are worth, without allowing his
prejudices to override his critical judgment. The excuse
for the book is Mr. Waugh's faith in Rossetti's art. He
believes that modern aesthetic science, in restricting the
appeal of painting to a single pure and isolated emotion
provoked exclusively by certain combinations of plastic
forms, has by no means discovered the mysterious vital
factor common to all works of art, and that Rossetti's
painting cannot be ruled out of court by any such arbitrary
scheme of reasoning. He supports his contention with admirable lucidity, defining his terms precisely, and translat-
ing the technical jargon of the fashionable aesthetic doctors into a language within the grasp of the general reader. The biographical passages are equally well written and
with no concessions whatever to the sensational methods in

vogue at the moment. Though he dwells too insistently on
the darker aspects of Rossetti's life, he does so with a
specific purpose; he does not stoop to the practices of
contemporary biographers who take a famous man, strip him
of everything that raises him above his fellows, gather
together every filthy anecdote and smelly idiosyncracy, and
then ask us to accept the distortion as an authentic portrait, a *humanization*, as they are pleased to call it. Mr.
Waugh's point of view is essentially critical, and as such,
carefully reasoned out and, for the most part, sound. 'It
is not so much that as a man Rossetti was a bad man,' he
concludes, ' - mere lawless wickedness has frequently been
a concomitant of the highest genius - but there was fatally
lacking in him that *essential rectitude* that underlies the
serenity of all really great art.'

It is not hard to understand why Rossetti is offensive
to Mr. Waugh. He was offensive to the Victorians, and if
such a man should appear in modern New York he would be
regarded by most Americans as intolerable....

In short, as a man, he lived as he pleased, a condition
which all men covet and few attain; as an artist, he
painted as he pleased, an ideal to which all artists
aspire and very few even approximate. In him the spiritual
and the sensual reposed in perfect harmony. That he loved
Elizabeth Siddal with a great and spiritual passion his
worst enemies would not deny - that is, until they discovered his numerous intrigues with other women....

In the esteem of artists, Rossetti's pictures have
passed into oblivion. Mr Waugh admits that most of the
paintings are artistically negligible, but makes a few
exceptions, notably the 'Beata Beatrix,' concerning which
he says, 'It is, perhaps, the most purely spiritual and
devotional work of European art since the fall of the
Byzantine Empire.' Lest we should doubt the seriousness of
this incredible statement, he adds at once that it is
offered as a considered judgment and not as an ecstatic
outburst. If, by the fall of the Byzantine Empire, he
means the capture of Constantinople by the Turks and not
the decline of Byzantine art, half of his remark is safe
enough; strictly speaking, there has been no purely devotional work in European art since the overthrow of the
Eastern capital. His definition of the spiritual leaves no
room for doubts. 'There are manifestations of the human
spirit that transcend the materials in which they are discernible; this picture is one of them, and it cannot be
dealt with by the workaday machinery of technical valua-
tion, however high-sounding the phrase and however little
understood.'

It is strange that Rossetti, a master of poetic form,

should have had such a confused and paltry sense of pictorial design. He had a certain gift for linear rhythms –
even Mr. Waugh concedes this, in spite of his horror of
aesthetic valuations, and contrives four meaningless dia-
grams to prove the point – but [Rossetti's] work, as a
whole, is ill organized. He attempted to make pictures by
the sheer intensity of his convictions, without tradition,
formal knowledge or guidance of any sort. A great artist
might conceivably triumph over the banalities of a sterile
age: Rembrandt did it, but only by means of gigantic
labor. Rossetti was notoriously slothful....

11. REBECCA WEST, LETTER TO WAUGH

n.d. (probably June–September 1928)

Dame Rebecca West (1892–1983), novelist, journalist and
critic, had by 1928 gained a reputation as one of the
sharpest minds of literary London. She wrote 'Henry James'
(1916), 'The Return of the Soldier' (1918), 'The Judge'
(1918), 'The Strange Necessity' (1928), 'Harriet Hume'
(1929), 'Black Lamb and Grey Falcon' (two vols, 1942), 'The
Meaning of Treason' (1949) and 'The Birds Fall Down' (1966).
Waugh pasted this letter which was sent from 80 Onslow
Gardens, London, SW7, into the back of the 'Rossetti'
manuscript. They were to meet not long after when he gained
fame as a novelist. Dame Rebecca was one of the very few
critics (Rose Macaulay was another) who understood the
stylistic innovations (deriving from Firbank) with which
Waugh was experimenting in his early fiction and who saw
the connection between these and a vision of contemporary
society typified for a generation by Eliot's 'The Waste
Land'; see No. 28.

Dear Mr Waugh,
    May I tell you how much I liked 'Rossetti'? – to say
nothing of the incidental entertainment of your letter to
the 'Times Lit. Sup.', which was a model of how one might
behave to that swollen-headed Parish Magazine.(1) I can't
tell you whether I most admire your presentation of the
aesthetic matters relevant to the P.R.B. or the kind of
writing that makes you pull off things like that subtle and
amusing and illuminating 'Brown [?] disapproved of the
whole business.' I hope you will go on being so much more

intelligent and amusing than most people in such a useful
form. By the way, has it ever struck you how thoroughly
doped the Victorians were? Not only Rossetti - but Elizabeth Barrett Browning, George Eliot and Harriet Martineau
were all given doses of opium and laudanum by their doctors
over long periods of time which must have made them complete dope-fiends.

I hope you won't think this letter an uncalled-for
approach - but I've been ill with 'flu and its sequels
and I've read dozens of books which bored me so and yours
so emphatically didn't that I'm full of gratitude.

Yours sincerely,
Rebecca West

Note

1 Waugh's amusing letter replying to the TLS review (10
   May 1928, 341-2) was published on 17 May 1928, 379 (cf.
   'Letters', p. 28). The reviewer had referred to him
   throughout as 'Miss Waugh'.

'Decline and Fall'

1928 (US edition, 1929)

12.   GERALD GOULD, 'OBSERVER'

23 September 1928, 8

Gerald Gould (1885-1936), poet, critic and journalist, was author of 'The Happy Tree' (1919), 'Collected Poems' (1929), and 'Refuge from Nightmare and Other Essays' (1933).

...Mr. Evelyn Waugh says defiantly, in capital letters, that his 'novelette' is meant to be funny. The claim is just, the defiance unnecessary - 'Decline and Fall' *is* funny, richly and roaringly funny. Its hero is a master in a school, is involved in the White Slave Traffic, and is sent to prison. The fun goes off after the school part; for sexual degradation and penal systems are in themselves repugnant to the idea of light treatment; wit may be used on them, as Voltaire used it in 'Candide,' but it must be the savage wit that reveals and exposes. And Mr. Waugh is anything but savage. He has an exquisite ingenuousness of manner combined with a searching ingenuity of method; he is a critic of life, whose weapon is the joke disguised as the simple statement; he is an important addition to the ranks of those dear and necessary creatures - the writers who can make us laugh. Over the first half of his book I have laughed consumedly: I hope you will do the same!

13.   ARNOLD BENNETT, 'EVENING STANDARD'

11 October 1928, 5

Arnold Bennett (1867-1931) was a novelist, playwright and
the high priest of the London critics in 1928. He was
author of 'Anna of the Five Towns' (1902), 'The Old Wives'
Tale' (1908), 'Clayhanger' (1910), 'The Love Match' (1922)
and 'Riceyman Steps' (1923).

...The season so far as it had proceeded strikes me as
unusually distinguished. Aldous Huxley, the most destructive force in the younger fiction, and a tonic, hostile
and audacious witness of the age, has appeared at full
length.(1) 'Anonymous' (whose identity is amply revealed
by internal evidence) has issued an autobiographical novel,
'Memoirs of a Fox-hunting Man,' of real importance. Written
with a certain sporting negligence of composition, it has
much originality and much beauty, and is certainly right
past the comprehension of nineteen M.F.H.'s out of twenty.
    Many honest open-air fellows who buy this first prose
work of Siegfried Sassoon's on its title will assuredly
want their money back.
    A genuinely new humorist has presented himself in the
person of Evelyn Waugh, whose 'Decline and Fall' is an
uncompromising and brilliantly malicious satire, which in
my opinion comes near to being quite first-rate - especially in its third part dealing with the prison system.
I say without reserve that this novel delighted me....

Note

1   Aldous Huxley, 'Point Counter Point' (1928).

14.   J.M.S.G., 'CHERWELL'

20 October 1928, 24

Arnold Bennett considers that this is probably the wittiest
and most amusing book of the year.(1) Admittedly, Mr
Bennett's judgment does not pass everywhere as an infallible oracle, but I feel that in this case most people will

be disposed to agree with him. Even such a hackneyed
theme as a 'Bollinger' club dinner he makes amusing, and
other more promising themes he makes outrageously amusing.
Did I say 'outrageously?' That is the right word. There is
a steady stream running through the book of salacious
innuendoes, which seem perpetually about to break out into
something which one would not expect to see in print. Time
and again one frowns and says to oneself, 'We'll soon be
finding the work of the censor.' But I don't believe one
ever does:(2) his delicacy is supreme, and innuendo it
remains.

But 'Gawd, - what laughs!' There are so many good things
- the scholastic agents 'Church and Gargoyle' - who class
schools into first-rate school, very good school, good
school, and school ('frankly, "school" is pretty bad'), the
Sports at Llanabba (*status of school: school*), the prison, Capt. Grimes the public school man, and above all
Potts the theological scholar of Scone. I cannot resist
quoting one of Mr. Potts' letters:

Dear Pennyfather,
...Stiggins is reading a paper to the O.S.C.U. on 'Sex
Repression and Religious Experience.' Everyone expects
a row, because you know how keen Walton is on the mystical element, which I think Stiggins is inclined to dis-
count.

Yours,
Arthur Potts.

P.S. - There is a most interesting article in the
'Educational Review' on the new methods that are being
tried at Innesborough High School to induce co-
ordination of the senses. They put small objects into
the children's mouths and make them draw the shapes in
red chalk. Have you tried this with your boys? I must
say I envy you your opportunities.
Are your colleagues enlightened?

Perfect! The author says firmly in the short introduction that it is meant to be funny. It is funny - the
funniest book I can remember reading.

Notes

1 Incorrect; cf. No. 13.
2 'Decline and Fall' was quite heavily censored by Chapman
   & Hall after it had been refused by Duckworth's on the
   grounds of indecency. In the original manuscript, for

instance, Captain Grimes is clearly involved in a homosexual relationship with the boy Clutterbuck.

15.   J.B. PRIESTLEY, 'EVENING NEWS'

2 November 1928, 11

John Boynton Priestley (b. 1894), the prolific novelist,
playwright, critic, biographer and librettist, is author
of 'The Good Companions' (1929), 'Angel Pavement' (1930),
'I Have Been Here Before' (1939), 'The Linden Tree' (1947),
'The Edwardians' (1970) and his autobiography 'Instead of
the Trees' (1977). Waugh returned Mr Priestley's critical
generosity here with an enthusiastic notice for 'Angel
Pavement' ('Graphic', 16 August 1930, 280). But as No. 157
shows, certain fundamental disagreements emerged later as
Mr Priestley became associated with socialism and vaguely
Bergsonian 'time flux' theories.

The English specimen of good light-weight fiction is
'Decline and Fall' by Evelyn Waugh, son of Arthur and
brother of Alec. The story is a frank absurdity, and the
second and wilder half of it is not so good as the first.
But Mr. Waugh has done something very difficult to do, he
has created a really comic character. This is Captain
Grimes. I congratulate him heartily on Captain Grimes, the
man who is always being kicked out of jobs. ('This looks
like the first end of term I've seen for two years,' he
says), who trades for ever on having been to a public
school for a year or two, who is perpetually 'In the
soup, old man' and 'having binges' and remains a vague
and cheerful bounder to the end.
    Mr. Waugh has a real sense of humour, and I strongly
advise him to try his hand next at a genuine humorous
novel, something nearer to life and far more satisfying
than these light satirical pieces that everybody is doing.
Incidentally, his book is dedicated 'In homage' to Mr.
Harold Acton, author of 'Humdrum.' Mr. Waugh owes no
homage to Mr. Acton as a novelist, for the latter's story
is a poor thing, showing us nothing but a vast social
superiority to everybody and everything. I have always
heard that Mr. Acton is one of the brightest of our young
wits, but 'Humdrum' seems to me really tedious. Perhaps
his title was too much for him.

16.   CYRIL CONNOLLY, 'NEW STATESMAN'

3 November 1928, 126

Cyril Connolly (1903-74), was a critic, novelist, parodist
and writer of *pensées*. He was founder of 'Horizon' in
1939 and was Editor, 1939-50; Literary Editor of the
'Observer', 1942-3; and weekly contributor to the 'Sunday
Times' later in life. He wrote 'The Rock Pool' (1935),
'Enemies of Promise' (1938), 'The Unquiet Grave' (under
the pseudonym 'Palinurus', 1944-5) and 'The Condemned
Playground' (1944). 'Horizon' rapidly became the most
prestigious London literary magazine of its day, publishing not only criticism but much original work, including
reproductions of painting and sculpture. As Editor,
Connolly saw himself as the defendant of culture, and
particularly the British avant-garde, during the privation
of the war years. His relationship with Waugh was uneasy.
Waugh certainly regarded him as an unusual talent in literary criticism, outshining his drab or feeble-minded competitors. Connolly, he considered, raised the form to an
art as opposed to those immersed either in subjectivity or
the new Leavisite pedantry. But, although Connolly was
brilliant, he had failed in his greatest ambition: to be a
creative artist. He longed for the approval of those who
had succeeded, Huxley and Waugh, for example. Knowing this,
and realizing Connolly's admiration for his work, Waugh
tended to exploit his advantage and enjoyed playing the
'tease' and intellectual bully. He reviewed 'Enemies of
Promise' with great scorn ('Tablet', 3 December 1938, 743-
4) yet not long after allowed Connolly the scoop of the
first printing of My Father's House (first chapter of 'Work
Suspended', November 1941, 329-41). Later he offered an
even greater compliment, giving the first printing of 'The
Loved One' to 'Horizon' gratis upon the sole condition
that it appear as a single issue (February 1948, 76-159).
But the truth is that Waugh had a deep-seated distrust for
Connolly's vaguely left-wing modernism. In 1971 the critic
visited the Waugh archive (University of Texas at Austin)
and asked to see copies of his own books in Waugh's library. The staff attempted to dissuade him but were eventually obliged to produce a copy of 'The Unquiet Grave'. It
had been sent to Waugh during a period of intense boredom
and frustration on active service in Yugoslavia at the end
of the war. Throughout, the book is viciously annotated and
'corrected' and its author addressed as 'Paddy'. Connolly
recorded his feelings about the incident in Apotheosis at
Austin, ST, 6 June 1971.

In 1928, of course, none of this acidity had crept into their friendship. Both were young and ambitious literary prodigies, eager to make their way in the world of letters. Connolly's Eton and Oxford background caused them to have many friends and social engagements in common and, although his judgment need not be questioned, we might suspect some degree of 'log-rolling' here.

...'Humdrum' falls rather flat ... As a satire, 'Decline and Fall' seems to possess every virtue which it lacks. In a way 'Humdrum' is a true picture of modern life, but its very truth gives it a kind of woodenness, for all the characters are types and hence incapable of behaving unlike themselves. Now, in any character that is alive, and not a type, contradictions are right and proper, and where red-faced colonels are made to talk of a woman as 'devilish distanggay' in inverted commas, we know that the author is taking a short cut to caricature without any knowledge or observation of what such people would really say. 'Humdrum' reads like a painstaking attempt to satirise modern life by a Chinaman who has been reading 'Punch', and the result is a catalogue of offences in the style of Becker's 'Gallus' or a second-rate Roman satirist in a third-rate modern crib....

'Decline and Fall' is not a satire, but a farce. The author's object is to write something funny, and he has certainly succeeded. Here there is a love of life, and consequently a real understanding of it. The timid clergy-man who has doubts is so obviously a timid clergyman that it is entirely permissible for him to get drunk and brow-beat the Welsh aristocracy. The humour throughout is of that subtle metallic kind which, more than anything else, seems a product of this generation. A delicious cynicism runs through the book, from the moment when the hero, stripped of his clothes by some drunken undergraduates, is sent down from Oxford for indecent behaviour. He goes as master to a school where his colleagues have all suffered the same fate, and where the boys have all reached the knowledge, the poise, and the weariness of 'Mona Lisa'. From there he becomes a tutor, and called in, like all tutors, for the purpose of squaring the family circle, he goes through the classic process of getting engaged to his pupil's mother. On his wedding-day he finds himself in prison, and when he is released, he is able to go unas-sumingly back to Oxford, and resume his theological studies as before. School life, high life, and prison are the three stages, and each is exquisitely comic and plausible. The essence of the book is the charm of the incorrigible. All

the characters are hopelessly past reformation. When Paul
goes to prison it is natural that all his colleagues should
be there to greet him, too. In a book in which everyone is
dishonest and delightful, only the virtuous hero is really
punished, like those mythical people who are said to be
charged by tailors for the suits of those who will not pay.
Though much of the book is improbable the scenes ring true.
Llanabba School is a real school, and the prison is more
convincing than the usual idea of a prison, especially the
gem of the convict's hymn. The author possesses the comic
spirit. All his characters are alive, the dialogue is
natural and sparkling, there are some amusing drawings,
and no epigrams, and one cannot but be grateful to a
writer who for once sets out purely to amuse the reader and
succeeds so well. A reviewer has few epithets of praise at
his command, owing to the high mortality in the vocabulary
of appreciation, but of 'Decline and Fall' he can say that
though not a great book, it is a funny book, and the only
one that, professionally, he has ever read twice.

17. UNSIGNED REVIEW, 'LIFE AND LETTERS'

December 1928, 624-5

'Decline and Fall' contains true satire on such verities of
modern society as the power of money and the anaemia of
schoolmastering. True satire implies a latent philosophy of
life, which is not less genuine because it is wittily or
fantastically expressed. In this it differs from the purely
preposterous, as popularized by Mr. Aldous Huxley. Unfortunately, Mr. Waugh's penetration is occasionally sidetracked
by personal dislike, which results in a note of over-
emphasis with its inartistically exact portrayal of unpleasant superficialities, in order to shock the suburbs.
But the general tenor of the book is wholly refreshing: it
intends to be funny; and it produces, in fact, a degree of
laughter which is embarrassingly physical under the hostile
silence of a crowded railway carriage. The author, moreover, is an artist of considerable talent. And his illustrations thus achieve a delightful concert with the matter
of the book.
      At the beginning of the year, Mr. Waugh contributed, in
a life of Rossetti, a definite addition to the history of
English aesthetics. Thus, at the age of twenty-three,(1)
he is presented in two entirely different lights. And there

is no doubt that his inevitable success as a writer will
result from much the same fusion of satirical exploitation
of weakness, with technical ability, to illustrate morality, as made Hogarth a painter. His future hangs on a
choice of subjects admitting of this combination.

Note

1   Waugh was twenty-five on 28 October 1928.

18.   UNSIGNED REVIEW, 'NEW YORK TIMES BOOK REVIEW'

7 April 1929, 6

'Decline and Fall' is a satirical cross-section of very
English society. The book was, in fact, originally conceived for the British public, but, although much of its
humor is insular in its appeal, there are large sections
that make very amusing universal reading. The exaggerated
realism and mock sophistication of the style are excel-
lently adapted to the story of the vicissitudes of Paul
Pennyfeather, a poor but sincere theological student who
was 'sent down' for no fault of his own. His consequent
and highly unfortunate adventures bring him into contact
with the school system, high and low society, the smart
set, the new art movement and the penal system, and
return him a sadder and wiser young man to the halls of his
college.
    To be sure there is not a great deal in the book that is
startlingly original. Most of the characters have been met
before, many times, but they are presented so amusingly
that there is a certain joy of recognition in encountering
Mrs. Beste Chetwynde and her colored friend Chokie who
thinks religion 'is just divine,' or Sir Wilfred Lucas-
Dockery, Governor of Blackstone Gaol, who 'came to the
conclusion many years ago that all crime is due to the
repressed desire for esthetic expression.' The illustrations, line drawings by the author, are also amusing,
particularly one of the tea party at Llanabba Castle, which
is quite reminiscent of Mr. Lear.

19.   T.S. MATTHEWS, 'NEW REPUBLIC'

17 April 1929, 259

Thomas Stanley Matthews (b. 1901), novelist, poet and
journalist, was Associate Editor of the 'New Republic' in
1929, and Editor of 'Time' 1949-53, and is the author of
'To the Gallows I Must Go' (1931), 'The Sugar Pill' (1958)
and 'Jacks or Better' (1977).

Where was Mr. Acton's fairy godmother when he named his
novel 'Humdrum'? This unconscious self-criticism is more
severe than any that is likely to be inflicted on him by
a conscienceless reviewer. We can only agree; the book,
though brilliantly intended, is actually boring.... As a
novelist, Mr. Acton is not only precious, but world-weary.
Life, as he knows it, is apparently 'Humdrum'. But perhaps
he has still more disillusioning years ahead of him.

 'Decline and Fall,' whose author is a contemporary,
friend, and apparently admirer of Mr. Acton's, is quite
out of 'Humdrum's' class. It is that all-too-rare phenomenon, a good nonsense novel. Its author has had the happy
inspiration to take nothing seriously, and least of all
himself. The result is a book which makes more sense than
most. Paul Pennyfeather, the simple-minded hero, is study-
ing at Oxford for holy orders, when he unfortunately runs
into the members of an aristocratic club, full of drink
and the English sense of humor, is promptly 'debagged'
(removed from his trousers), and as promptly expelled by
the college authorities for disgraceful behavior. His
subsequent adventures include school-teaching at a far from
model institution; a love-affair with a beautiful lady who
turns out to be in Mrs. Warren's profession, though on a
grand and South American scale; and prison, to which he is
very properly consigned for being mixed up in the shady
business. Through all these changes and chances he keeps
his simple-minded rectitude. Mr. Waugh makes us snicker
oftener than he makes us laugh, but it is not his fault
that he was born an Englishman.

20.   ROSE MACAULAY, 'HORIZON'

December 1946, 360-2

Dame Rose Macaulay (1881-1958) was a novelist, poet and cri-
tic; she was author of 'Dangerous Ages' (1921), 'Staying with
Relations' (1930), 'John Milton' (1933) and 'The Towers of
Trebizond' (1956). This is part of a long essay entitled
Eveyln Waugh, dealing with Waugh's career, book by book,
up to 'Brideshead'. Her remarks on some of these works
appear in the relevant sections of this volume: 'Vile
Bodies', 'A Handful of Dust', 'Edmund Campion', 'Scoop',
'Work Suspended' and 'Brideshead'.

Most novelists set themselves to explore the world, or some
corner of the world, in which they believe themselves to
live; they weave their dreams, imaginations and tales
within their apprehensions of the life they perceive about
them, composing variations on the theme. Other writers step
aside, turn an oblique glance on the world they know,
reject it, and, half deliberate, half instinctive, compose
one of their own making, a world within a world, in which
they can move and invent with greater felicity, sureness
and ease. Among the world-creators of our time Evelyn Waugh
is the most entertaining, and perhaps the most gifted. The
world he invented and decorated with extravagant *jeux
d'esprit* is a comic world. In it he moves with the blandest
security and ease; from within its circumference he can
utter any commentary on life, create and manipulate any
beings who inhabit there. Brilliantly equipped to direct
the radiant and fantastic circus he has called into being,
he can stand within it cracking his whip while his creatures leap through his paper hoops with the most engaging
levity, the gravest fantastic capers. His command of
verbal style is adept and skilled, his characters amirably
irresponsible, his wit unfailing. Like Anthony Blanche in
'Brideshead Revisited', he does more than entertain,
'transfiguring the party, shedding a vivid, false light
of eccentricity upon everyone', so that prosaic people
seem to become creatures of his fantasy.
     What would occur should he step out of his delightful
baroque circus tent into a solid actual world (if indeed
any world is this) was not a question which used to trouble
the reader, who accepted his unique contribution as a
priceless gift. It would seem that he has now stepped out
of it; and the airs beyond the ropes breathe on us with
something less of rarity, with a lusher, less sharp and

exhilarating taste. It must be the desire of his most
ardent devotees that he should speedily retrace his steps.

He did not begin with the circus. His first published
works were a brief and competent essay on the Pre-
Raphaelites (1) (at the age of twenty-three) and (at
twenty-five) a life of Rossetti, an able, scholarly and
entertaining study, which, if it reveals nothing new about
its fascinating, over-written hero or his friends, gives on
them an intelligent and sympathetic slant. A serious work of
interpretation and history, it did nothing to prepare the
way for 'Decline and Fall', which broke on the English
literary scene the following year. Sub-titled 'an illustrated novelette', it was, the author explained in a note,
not meant to be shocking but funny. A redundant note:
'Decline and Fall' is funny from first to last. Its bland,
destructive brilliance lights up a world of comic happenings through which people move with the lunatic logic and
inconsequence imparted to them by their creator's ironic
vision of mankind. Though it was apparent that a bright
particular star had risen in the fictional firmament, that
firmament was not empty of stars that twinkled a little
similarly, with something of the same bland and gay insouciance. But 'Decline and Fall' carried the subversive
approach further, enlarging the bounds of erratic nonsense.
It opens at Oxford, with a riotous meeting of the Bollinger
Club. 'A shriller note could now be heard rising from Sir
Alastair's rooms; any who have heard that sound will shrink
at the recollection of it; it is the sound of the English
county families baying for broken glass....'

The detachment is complete. (The scene may profitably be
compared with the Oxford scenes, more nostalgically and
naturalistically handled, in 'Brideshead Revisited'.) In the
ensuing romp, the Bollinger bloods break up pianos, smash
china, throw pictures into water-jugs, tear up sheets and
destroy manuscripts, and debag Paul Pennyfeather, the
innocuous and luckless hero of this tale, a quiet young man
from Lancing (2) who is reading for holy orders; he is sent
down for running trouserless across the quad. 'I expect
you'll be becoming a schoolmaster, sir,' the college porter
says to him. 'That's what most of the gentlemen does, sir,
that gets sent down for indecent behaviour.'

That is, in fact, what Paul does; he gets a post in a
private school, perhaps the only attractive private school
in modern fiction, and continues his innocent and disastrous downward career. The school staff, and in particular
the headmaster and his assistant Captain Grimes, are superb
figures of comedy; the climate is that of an inspired
lunatic asylum, the conversations extremely and cease-
lessly funny. The story is gaily, grimly and totally

amoral; its vicissitudes catastrophically logical; its
ingenuous hero the victim of the most shocking turpitudes
and betrayals. He is landed in prison, helped out of it by
intriguing friends, and ends officially dead and resuming
life in disguise, a quiet Oxford ordinand once more. The
book is, apart from the sparkle of its wit and its baroque
detail, an excellent and coherent story. It moves from
start to finish with experienced ease. It has, I believe,
been found vulgar by some critics: but it moves in a sphere
where vulgarity, refinement and morality do not apply, the
sphere of irreverent and essentially anarchic fantasy. The
world, one might say, of Ronald Firbank, of Norman Douglas,
perhaps of the brothers Marx. But it reflected none of
these; it was a genuinely original comic work....

Notes

1 'P.R.B. An Essay on the Pre-Raphaelite Brotherhood
   1846-1854' (privately printed by Alastair Graham,
   1926). It was this essay which Anthony Powell used as
   evidence of Waugh's abilities to secure him the commission from Duckworth's to write 'Rossetti'. It is very
   rare and the fact of Miss Macaulay's having seen it
   suggests a keen personal interest in Waugh's work.
2 The text actually reads: 'a small public school of
   ecclesiastical temper on the South Downs'. Miss
   Macaulay's mistake again suggests knowledge of Waugh's
   background.

21. JOHN WILLETT, 'THE TIMES'

10 March 1966, 13

John Willett (b. 1917) is a critic, journalist and translator. He was Assistant Editor of the TLS, 1960-7, and became Planning Editor in 1969. He is author of 'The Theatre
of Bertolt Brecht' (1959) and 'Expressionism' (1970).

'Decline and Fall' was Evelyn Waugh's first novel, and it
appeared in 1928, a few weeks before its author's twenty-
fifth birthday. That spring 'The Times Literary Supplement'
had reviewed his biography of Rossetti on the rather unfortunate assumption that it was by a squeamish young lady.

Originally subtitled 'An Illustrated Novelette', with
drawings and a gay green-red-and-black jacket by Mr.
Waugh himself, the new book offered little inducement to
such mistakes. The publishers of 'Rossetti' found it too
shocking; even his father's firm Chapman and Hall asked
for minor amendments (expunged when they reset the book in
1962). It had not the success of his second novel, 'Vile
Bodies', but it sold some 3,000 copies in its first year
and had gone through four reprints and a 'pocket edition'
by the time Penguin, in 1937, issued it as their first
Waugh. Many readers, of all generations, find it his funniest work.

It is not hard to see why. For the book's dominant
theme - the theme, certainly, by which it is remembered -
is one peculiarly dear to the twentieth-century British
heart: the boy's boarding school. This institution could be
looked at in many ways, through eyes as various as those of
Stalky and Bunter and Young Woodley; Mr. Waugh's own elder
brother had exposed one of its major peculiarities, previously unrecorded, in 'The Loom of Youth'. But it had not
yet been satirized, nor had any author turned his attention to its submerged depths: the dimmer prep schools and
the odd fish that lurk there. Luckily, Mr. Waugh himself
had led a sheltered life in this respect, having been a
day-boy at an unusually tolerant prep school run by a
friend of his father. The revelations to which he was subjected in his own short spell as prep schoolmaster only
needed a slight push from the imagination to make a momen-
tous farce.

One of these revelations, so the first instalment of his
autobiography tells us, was Captain Grimes. There are not
many very durable characters in the modern English novel,
let alone immortals, like Don Juan or Jeeves, but Grimes
is now part of our heritage; his language and values, his
reflections on the public schools and the honour of the
regiment, are marvellous glimpses of a suppressed rich
underworld of English life. As a result he is the mainstay
of the novel, even though the space given him hardly suggests it. The other clowns are all good - the headmaster
and his ghastly daughters, Philbrick the demon butler, the
melancholy Mr. Prendergast - but there is only one memorable episode in which Grimes does not take part: the con-
victs in chapel making their gory *ad hoc* adaptation of
hymns A. & M.

There are enough touches of genius to colour our judgment, but they are spread very unevely and there are
sizable bald patches, particularly in the second section of
the book. To some extent this comes from the novel's pattern. The school staff have to be brought together in

prison so as to stress the similarity of the two regimes;
and this means that the school has to be abandoned in all
its glory midway through the novel, which tails off badly
during the 50 pages needed to get the hero arrested for
white-slaving and never quite recovers. But it is also a
regrettable fact that this hero is so much the innocent
victim as to become blankly uninteresting - there is an
awkward passage where the author seems to apologize for
this - while the fabulous Mrs. Beste Chetwynde who manipu-
lates him is a bore. She dominates the second of the book's
three parts and gives a fatal stamp of spuriousness to
whatever depends on her in the third: the hero's escape
from prison, his meditations on the relativity of honour.

    There are interesting anticipations here of the author's
later writings. Honour, much more subtly handled, is the
theme of his war trilogy; the deity from the machine reappears in other books as Mr. Baldwin and Mrs Stich [in
'Scoop' (1938)]; the demolished King's Thursday is the
first of a long line of great houses that stand for the
crumbling of the old order. He gratuitously butchers Prendergast like so many of his characters; Grimes he never
revives; only Mrs. Beste-Chetwynde and her crew pass into
the corpus. He makes comedy along the tight-rope of his
prejudices: against modern architecture (with Silenus as
his dummy Gropius),(1) against the Welsh, against well-
intentioned social reformers, against coloured people's
claims to culture (though he ridicules other kinds of
racialist gossip). Now and again he falls off.

    You still laugh. Few living writers, indeed, are so
good to reread as Mr. Waugh; his dialogue was even then
masterly, his sense of ridicule astonishingly modern. For
all its imperfections the book has the germ of life. Yet
this is not quite how the majority of critics now see it,
for ever since the excesses of 'Brideshead Revisited' it
has been fashionable to speak of the satirical novels of
his twenties as if they set a standard by which the rest
of his work must be judged and found largely wanting. To
my mind this is total nonsense. Put against 'The Ordeal of
Gilbert Pinfold' and the 'Sword of Honour' trilogy, with
their far greater insight and control, 'Decline and Fall'
looks what it is: *juvenilia*. It is no good trying to beat
his late works with a stick that breaks in the middle.

Note

1   Walter Gropius (1883-1969) was a leading designer of
    'functionalist' twentieth-century architecture.

'Vile Bodies'

1930

22. RALPH STRAUS, 'BYSTANDER'

15 January 1930, 140

Ralph Straus (1882-1950) was a novelist, biographer and
journalist, and author of 'The Scandalous Mr Waldo' (1909),
'Married Alive' (1925) and 'Dickens: A Portrait in Pencil'
(1928). Straus's reviews are typical of many in the lighter
journals which later became infatuated with the catch-
phrases of 'Vile Bodies'. Straus wrote a long review of
'Decline and Fall' for the 'Bystander' (a 'society' magazine) in this vein (31 October 1928, 260), crammed with
fulsome praise and plot recapitulation.

Adjectives fail me, for I have just finished reading 'Vile
Bodies' by Evelyn Waugh. I was prepared to be disappointed.
I thought: 'he can't improve on "Decline and Fall"; he
can't even repeat it.' But he has. I assure you that 'Vile
Bodies' is one of the drollest and most entertaining
affairs that ever strayed into print. It is a masterpiece
of inconsequence. It has irony and the right amount of
malice. It is as free from sentimentalism as a five-
shilling watch is from gold. And its improprieties are so
deliciously subtle that I confidently expect even the late
Home Secretary (1) to succumb to its blandishments.
    The trouble is to know what to say about it. You cannot
be given an outline of the plot, for the simple reason that
there is none. Mr. Waugh merely takes a look a little way
ahead, and proceeds to show us the Brighter Young Folk of
those days, largely depending for his information, of
course, on the gossip-writers of the time. (These, by the
way, are almost invariably young peers of the realm,

regrettably without realms of their own.) And these folk
are really very bright indeed. Moreover, the struggle for
Brightness has become so intense that they are constantly
being killed off in their efforts to obtain it - good copy
for Mr. Gossip, but a little unfortunate for them....

Now I am quite prepared to be told by one or two soured
Edwardians that the whole thing is a bit of dangerous nonsense. I am even prepared to be told that it is not what
they call really funny at all. And it is certainly the
fact that the most appalling suggestions are constantly
being made. But they are made in the charmingest fashion,
and for my part I cannot conceive of a droller or more cunning or more subtly ironical commentary on the juvenile
absurdities of to-day. It seems to me that in Mr. Evelyn
Waugh we have a humorist who has little, if anything, in
common with the older school. He sails along gaily by himself, allowing his ship to steer its own wild course. It
is all utterly fantastic, and yet it is - very nearly -
life as the popular Press would have us believe it to be.

There is this, too, to be said about his book. You can
open it up anywhere, and instantly find yourself absorbed
in its eccentrics. For myself, I confess that on coming to
the end I re-read the earlier chapters - with increased
enjoyment. I wanted to renew acquaintance with one or two
of the unfortunates who had fallen on the way. They are
all such excellent company. Mr. Waugh, moreover, does not
depend on any particular trick for his effects. His prose
is perfectly simple, and yet it is quite distinctive. I
can say with truth that I have rarely been sorrier to reach
the last page of a novel.

Note

1 The confiscation of Adam's book by customs officials is
   probably a satirical dig at Sir William Joynson Hicks's
   enforcement of the Defence of the Realm Act. Hicks
   (later Viscount Brentford and known in the popular press
   as 'Jix') was an evangelist and teetotaller. As a vigi-
   lant Conservative Home Secretary (1924-9) in the
   administration toppled by Attlee he became something of
   a figure of fun to Waugh's more anarchic contemporaries.

23.   V.S. PRITCHETT, 'SPECTATOR'

18 January 1930, 99

Sir Victor Sawdon Pritchett (b. 1900) is a novelist, critic,
biographer, short story writer and sometime Director of the
'New Statesman'. He is the author of 'Nothing Like Leather'
(1935), 'Dead Man Leading' (1937), 'The Living Novel' .
(1946), 'Why do I Write?' (with Graham Greene and Elizabeth
Bowen, 1948), his autobiography 'A Cab at the Door' (1968)
and 'Balzac' (1973).

Mr. Evelyn Waugh has written in 'Vile Bodies' a hectic
piece of savage satire. The time is in the future when the
Bright Young People have become so riotously bright that
even Society gossip writers are driven to suicide. Here is
a mad world where an American revivalist and her delicious,
but slightly fallen angels whirl round together with film-
struck Colonels, Peers on the Yellow Press, dirt-track
racers, bewildered Prime Ministers, like a collection of
catherine wheels which have gone off on their own account
before their time. I laughed until I was driven out of
the room. Unfortunately Mr. Waugh has felt obliged to moral-
ize occasionally; amid the wild masque of satire, it is a
vice to announce in a stage whisper:

> The truth is that like so many young people of their
> age and class, Adam and Nina were suffering from being
> sophisticated about sex before they were at all widely
> experienced.

Oh, wise young judge! There is a plotting Jesuit who
might have been sacrified, too, because of his wisdom; and
I am not sure about the rector and a lot of the garrulous
people who infest the main line to Aylesbury; or about the
final world catastrophe which is Mr. Waugh's judgment upon
his revels.

24.   L.P. HARTLEY, 'SATURDAY REVIEW'

25 January 1930, 115

Leslie Poles Hartley (1895-1973), novelist and critic, was

the author of 'The Shrimp and the Anemone' (1944), 'The
Sixth Heaven' (1946), 'Eustace and Hilda' (1947, the three
published as a trilogy), 'The Go-Between' (1953) and 'The
Hireling' (1957).

This charge ['that heroes ... are too aquiescent in frustration to win our sympathy'], at least, cannot be levelled
against Mr. Waugh's 'Vile Bodies,' whose chief characteristic is mobility and their chief virtue enterprise. While a
cocktail remains to be drunk and a sensation to be tried
they never say die. Even in the next war (a brief scene
... which brings the story to a close) they are still
making love and getting fun out of life. If we read this
high-spirited book between the lines, and look its gift-
horse, humour, in the mouth, we may find that the ground is
not really solid beneath our feet; we are dancing on a
volcano, carousing on the edge of a precipice; that Mr.
Waugh is not the happy humorist he seems, and that the
ability of his characters to respond to life is only the
ability of the drunkard to laugh in his cups or of the
lunatic to be diverted by his delusions. But perish the
thought! Let us believe that Mr. Waugh's natural impulse
to gaiety is as important as his intellectual conviction
(if he holds it) that his gaiety is ill-founded. He is a
satirist, no doubt, but not a sceptic, for he believes,
and proves, that amusement can be derived from the most
unpromising material, from people, that is, whose one
occupation in life is the quest for amusement, people
who give and attend parties:

> ...Masked parties, Savage parties, Victorian parties,
> Greek parties, Wild West parties, Russian parties,
> parties where one had to dress as somebody else, almost
> naked parties in St. John's Wood, parties in flats and
> studios and houses and ships and hotels and night clubs,
> in windmills and swimming baths, tea-parties at school
> where one ate muffins and meringues and tinned crab,
> parties at Oxford where one drank brown sherry and
> smoked Turkish cigarettes, dull dances in London and
> comic dances in Scotland and disgusting dances in
> Paris - all that succession and repetition of human-
> ity.... Those vile bodies....

For a moment the hero, contemplating these varied
gatherings, feels a surfeit, but only for a moment. As for
Mr. Waugh, he delights in the succession and repetition of
humanity; it feeds his omnivorous comic spirit. 'Posterity
will laugh,' a distinguished contemporary poet bitterly

observed, 'when it reads about the age in which I have had
to live.' I have sometimes doubted whether it will; but if
(as might easily happen) it has Mr. Waugh's book to turn
to, it may have its laugh after all.

25.   ARNOLD BENNETT, 'EVENING STANDARD'

39 January 1930, 9

Like most professional humorists, I rarely laugh, even at
what I think is funny. There are two sorts of humour, the
sort that makes you laugh audibly, and the sort that makes
you laugh subterraneanly and noiselessly somewhere down in
your solar plexus. Some people hold that the second is better than the first. I am not of this opinion. I would give
the two sorts equal marks. And the first or loud sort holds
a clear advantage over the second in that it has a positive
ameliorating influence on the bodily health....

Have we any humorists now who can divert the whole town
as Barry Pain (1) did, and W.W. Jacobs(2) and Pett Ridge(3)
in their heyday? We have, at any rate, one - P.G. Wodehouse, who has beneficially influenced my health on various
occasions and agitated my solar plexus on hundreds of
occasions. We have other admirable humorists - A.P. Herbert,
for instance, creator of Topsy - but they have not yet
gained the popular prestige of their elders.

We have also a few very young humorists, of whom the
chief in my view is Evelyn Waugh. Mr. Waugh's first novel,
'Decline and Fall,' provoked in me laughter of both sorts.
Lord Brentford (4) might not have unreservedly approved it.
But it was really brilliantly funny about once a page. His
new novel, 'Vile Bodies,' is less successful. It has a few
satirical sallies of the first order of merit, but the
lack of a well-laid plot has resulted in a large number of
pages which demand a certain obstinate and sustained effort
of will for their perusal. Mr. Waugh's subject is the silly
set, more commonly known as the smart set - social, pseudo-
artistic, pseudo-literary, and genuinely alcoholic; the set
which is always trying to run away from the shadow of its
own fundamental stupidity. An easy subject. None of the
satire in the book is unjust, but some of it is extremely,
wildly farcical, and bits of it would not induce laughter
in Lord Brentford. I began 'Vile Bodies' with great expectations, and found hard times in the middle of it.

Evelyn Waugh has a brother, Alec. More correctly, Alec

Waugh has a brother, Evelyn: for Alec began first, and
probably has more to say. I think that Alec Waugh's 'The
Loom of Youth' was a pretty fine book for a youth of 17 or
18, better than for instance Disraeli's 'Vivian Grey,'
written at about the same age. The author of 'The Loom of
Youth' is weightier than his cadet. His new book, 'The
Coloured Countries' ... is full of the discernments and
the preoccupations of a weighty mind....

Notes

1   Barry Pain (1864-1928) was an author of humorous novels
    and stories about London cockney and suburban charac-
    ters, e.g. 'Eliza' (1900).
2   W.W. Jacobs (1863-1943), a family friend of the Waugh's,
    was famous for short stories about cockneys and long-
    shoremen.
3   Pett Ridge, another similar writer, was also a play-
    wright, author of 'London Please. Four Cockney Plays'
    (1925).
4   Sir William Joynson Hicks; see No. 22, n. 1.

26.   E[DWARD] S[HANKS], 'NEW STATESMAN'

8 February 1930, 572

Edward Shanks (1892-1953) was a 'Georgian' poet, critic
and journalist. He was chief leader-writer of the 'Evening
Standard', 1928-35 and author of 'Collected Poems' (1926)
and 'Rudyard Kipling' (1939). Shanks was another of the
middle-aged *littérateurs* controlling the review columns in
the late 1920s and early 1930s (see headnote to No. 4 and
Introduction, pp. 5-6).

The modern world of intellect and fashion is having a bad
time just now. Mr. Waugh pelts it with small pebbles of
wit on one side, while Miss Sharp (1) smiles it out of
existence on the other. But it must not be understood that
there is any resemblance between these two authors. Miss
Sharp has written a novel, Mr. Waugh what must be called
rather a revue, between covers. He does not lack even a
female chorus, which we meet on his second page. It consists of the 'angels,' whom Mrs. Melrose Ape, the woman
evangelist, carries about with her on her evangelising

tours. On their appearance Mr. Waugh falls at once into
his stride:

> 'Chastity didn't feel well, Mrs. Ape. She went
> below.'
> 'That girl's more trouble than she's worth. Whenever
> there's any packing to be done, Chastity doesn't feel
> well. Are all the rest here - Humility, Prudence,
> Divine Discontent, Mercy, Justice and Creative Endea-
> vour?'
> 'Creative Endeavour lost her wings, Mrs. Ape. She got
> talking to a gentleman in the train.... Oh, there she
> is.'
> 'Got 'em?' asked Mrs. Ape.
> Too breathless to speak, Creative Endeavour nodded.
> (Each of the angels carried her wings in a little black
> box like a violin case.)
> 'Right,' said Mrs. Ape, 'and just you hold on to 'em
> tight and not so much talking to gentlemen in trains.
> You're angels, not a panto, see?'

With this we are off among the topicalities, through which
Mr. Waugh ranges with the keen acquisitive eye of a magpie
for anything glittering or oddly shaped. Among the things
he picks out are the determination of the Home Office to
prevent obscene literature from entering England, the members of the Peerage who earn their livings as sneak-
guests, dirt-track racing and the making of a film about
John Wesley in the grounds of a country-house. These are
made to succeed one another with a snap and variety that
many a revue-producer might envy.

But, like the scenes of most revues, they vary in merit.
The film, for example, in which Wesley and Whitefield are
provoked to a duel by their rivalry for the favours of
Selina, Countess of Huntingdon, is rather an old joke. So
too is the story of the gossip-writer who fills his space,
and offends no one, by means of the invention of quite
imaginary social characters. Mr. Waugh, I think, belongs to
the school of Mr. William Gerhardi,(2) whose most successful manner is not the easiest thing in the world to imitate, as has been proved by Mr. Gerhardi's own failure to
imitate it. The method of the unexpected (and it is on
unexpectedness that the comic power of both these writers
depends) is very difficult to keep going and there is
nothing more fatal to its total effect than a recurrent
impression that the author is merely filling in time until
he shall next find something striking to say. What is
lacking in Mr. Waugh at present is any capacity for
design. He makes one feel what he has light-heartedly

flung a handful of dried peas into the face of the world -
and that some of the peas are soft. Unity of idea is not a
bad starting point even for a comic writer, and until he
learns how to start with it Mr. Waugh will continue partially to waste a good deal of quite brilliant material.
He will also continue to waver uncertainly between one
tone and another. Thus after a deliberately farcical (and
otherwise somewhat surprising) account of the sexual
adventures of two of his persons he solemnly adds: 'The
truth is that like so many people of their age and class,
Adam and Nina were suffering from being sophisticated about
sex before they were at all widely experienced.'

Notes

1 Margery Sharp's 'Rhododendron Pie' (Chatto & Windus,
   1930) was reviewed in the same column.
2 Waugh openly acknowledged his debt to Gerhardie (sic) in
   a letter to him from Piers Court, dated 10 May 1949.
   He thanked Gerhardie for remarks made about his work on
   the radio and added: 'As no doubt you recognized I
   learned a great deal of my trade from your own novels'
   (HRC).

27.   RICHARD ALDINGTON, 'SUNDAY REFEREE'

9 February 1930, 6

Richard Aldington (1892-1962), a prolific novelist, bio-
grapher, poet, critic, translator and historian, was a
friend of D.H. Lawrence and Roy Campbell (see headnote to
No. 8). He was author of 'Images Old and New' (1915),
'Voltaire' (1926), 'Death of a Hero' (1929), 'Lawrence of
Arabia' (1955), 'Portrait of a Genius, but ... the Life of
D.H. Lawrence' (1950), 'Selected Critical Writings 1928-
1960' (ed. Alistair Kershaw, 1970).

It has always seemed to me very unfair to review a book on
the evidence of the publisher's blurb and quotations from
other reviews, even when, as frequently happens, both have
been written by the author himself. I see one reviewer
claims that Mr. Waugh is 'roaringly funny,' while the
blurb says his new book is 'a tragedy in which comic relief

overwhelmingly predominates.' Personally, I see nothing to
roar about in a book which seems to be based on complete
despair. Of course, Mr. Waugh is very high-spirited and
does his best to be amusing (often, in fact, succeeds), but
I find his discouragement infectious. Nor can I find anything particularly tragic in the fates of such futile
people.

Which only goes to show how completely one generation is
a mystery to another.

Probably nothing is sillier than for a reviewer to try
to make deductions about such abstractions as 'the new
generation' and 'the present state of English life,' even
from a book so brilliant, shrewd, and witty as 'Vile
Bodies.' After all, Mr. Waugh has simply written another
regionalist novel about the more harum-scarum youthful
members of a small village called Mayfair and its hangers-
on. And what they do and think would not be of the
slightest importance to anybody if it were not for British
snobbery. To which Mr. Waugh most definitely appeals, even
when he is honestly satirising it. Here we have the inner-
dope, so to speak. We mustn't, like the ingenuous Ginger,
say 'Real top-holers,' but 'How too bogus.' Which is an
immense advance.

Speaking of the erotic doings of two of his characters
Mr. Waugh says:

'The truth is that, like so many people of their age and
class, Adam and Nina were suffering from being sophisticated about sex before they were at all widely experienced.'
'Widely' is good, considering they knew nothing at all.
And again on the subject of attitude to life generally:
'My private schoolmaster used to say "If a thing's worth
doing at all, it's worth doing well." My Church has taught
that in different words for several centuries. But these
young people have got hold of the other end of the stick,
and for all we know it may be the right one. They say 'If a
thing's not worth doing well, it's not worth doing at all.'

Heaven knows I feel sympathetic to the 'younger generation' - i.e., those who were under eighteen when the glad-
some maroons boomed out the information that Truth, Justice,
Right, and Democracy had triumphed on the Western Front.
The schoolboys were growing up under the apparently certain
menace that they, too, would be roped in for the slaughter;
the schoolgirls, I suppose, were to see them cheerfully
off. And then it was all cancelled. We, at least, had seen
something, been something, done something. But they
couldn't do anything or be anything. They were ushered
into life during one of the meanest and most fraudulent
decades staining the annals of history. And it's still
going on - forgery, fraudulent bankruptcy, false banknotes,

intensive commercial warfare, lying conferences to deceive
the nations' demand for peace.... No; I don't think we
can blame the 'Young.' I certainly should not, even if they
were all as silly and futile as the *fantoches* in Mr.
Waugh's satire. 'Vile Bodies' ends up with another European War, in which everybody is more or less wiped out.
Personally, I should imagine the kind of impotent futility
described by Mr. Waugh would be more likely to end in an
internal collapse. His novel is surprisingly like some of
those which appeared just before 1789 in France....

But, no doubt, all this is being far too serious. And,
which is worse, it is possibly rather stupid. After all,
Mr. Waugh is chiefly trying to amuse us, not to analyse the
woes of an age, and he succeeds in being amusing. It was
certainly time we had a little fresh blood in the effete
stock of our professional humorists. There is no fate more
awful than that of having to be funny to order, or even
of having to be funny too long. (In fact, I think 'Vile
Bodies' would be more fun if it were not so continuously
humorous.) Is there any type of writing more local and
temporary than the humorous? Are you 'convulsed' by Mr.
Will Rogers,(1) as the Continental papers say the guests
at a dinner were? Wit is a very different matter - Voltaire
and Congreve are as brilliant now as in the eighteenth century, but humour fades like the autumn leaves. And that is
why it is necessary to enjoy it immediately. I have insinu-
ated that 'Vile Bodies' is local in place; it is also local
in time. If you don't read it now you'll be too late. And
it is certainly good enough not to miss.

The virtue of wit lies in felicity and truth; of humour,
in a kind of exaggeration. The humour of over-statement is
called 'rich' or 'hearty'; the humour of under-statement is
called 'dry.' (Irony is a very different thing.) Humour is
chiefly attractive to schoolboys - undergrown, grown, and
overgrown. Mr. Evelyn Waugh has a good deal of wit, but he
also has a lot of humour. Possibly I am inventing distinctions for my own convenience, but it seems to me that his
portrait of Ginger, the brainless idiot, is chiefly witty,
whereas his much fuller portrait of Colonel Blount, the
eccentric and solitary squire, is chiefly humorous. I read
in a periodical (2) an excerpt from this novel containing
the visit of Adam to Colonel Blount, and I felt pained for
Mr. Waugh. The scene is undoubtedly better when read in its
setting, but the 'humour' makes it sadly exaggerated and
still a bit painful. This is a pity, because the eccentric
squire is undoubtedly a 'character' in modern English life.
I suppose the real reason that Colonel Blount seems so exaggerated and unreal is that he is copied direct from life
- a most dangerous thing to do, because such characters

always appear false.

Mr. Waugh is at his best when he is presenting his bright young people and their favoured sports and haunts. His description of Lottie and her hotel is excellent, and I like his dismal-rackety parties. I also like his parodies of social journalism. Parodies of journalism, by the way, are becoming quite an accepted form of comic relief in novels. To the best of my knowledge, the custom began with Mr. Joyce's 'Ulysses,' which contains one of the best headlines I ever read. The Professor says to Stephen Dedalus that he is like Antisthenes, a pupil of Gorgias, who took the prize of beauty from Helen of Troy and gave it to Penelope. Whereupon Joyce flashes up the divine head-line: 'Sophist Wallops Haughty Helen on Proboscis - Spartans Gnash Molars - Ithacans Vow Pen is Champ.' Mr. Osbert Sitwell has a real genius for such parodies - I put him easily second, for there are some excellent passages of the kind in 'Before the Bombardment.' So Mr. Waugh comes only third, but still he is very amusing. And there is plenty of sting in his parody of social journalism. I particularly liked the 'fan' letter from the man with large ears who was a 'chub fuddler.' And I liked Mr. Waugh's portrait of the mysterious Jesuit. It was extremely shrewd of him to pick on that particular figure.

Above all, I like Mr. Waugh's unpretentiousness. There are so many people writing immortal works for posterity that it is very pleasant to find a writer of really superior gifts who is content to write about a little bit of his own time for his own time. And you never can tell - 'Candide' and 'Dr. Akakia' (3) were squibs.

Notes

1 Will Rogers was an American humorist and film star (1876-1936), and author of 'Rogerisms - What We Laugh At' (1920).
2 The Hire-Purchase Marriage, an Inconsequent Version of the Love-in-a-Cottage Myth, 'Harper's Bazaar' (London), December 1929, 22-3, 98, 101. This became Chapter Five of 'Vile Bodies'.
3 Voltaire, 'Diatribe du Docteur Akakia' (Rome, 1753). Aldington had recently translated some of Voltaire's work.

28.   REBECCA WEST, 'FORTNIGHTLY REVIEW'

February 1930, 273-4

It is not necessary, since such a short time has elapsed
since the publication of 'Decline and Fall', to say that
'Vile Bodies' is an extremely funny book. It may not contain any such endearing character as Grimes, but it deals
out situation after situation that is authentically comic.
Deals out is the right expression; for there is in Mr.
Waugh's apparently casual but actually intricate technique
some analogy to a card game. The smooth glossy pieces of
paste-board with their conventional design fall before
one: the scenes, some of them only a few lines long, by
which Mr. Waugh can evoke the atmosphere of a party
drearily held by the Bright Young People in a captive diri-
gible, or an evening at the Rectory when the Colonel has
fused the electric light by showing, unasked, his home-
made film, and the Rector and his wife finding themselves
faced by the prospect of spending Christmas week-end in
darkness, or any other focus of human passion. These sort
themselves out into suits. There are the spades, the souls
sad, however gay, doomed to destruction, however much they
wriggle with excess of vitality, such as the gossip-
writers ('At Archie Schwert's party the fifteenth Marquess
of Vanburgh, Earl Vanburgh de Brendon, Baron Brendon, Lord
of the Five Isles and Hereditary Grand Falconer to the
Kingdom of Connaught, said to the eighth Earl of Balcairn,
Viscount Erdinge, Baron Cairn of Balcairn, Red Knight of
Lancaster, Count of the Holy Roman Empire and Chenonceaux
Herald to the Duchy of Aquitaine, "Hullo," he said. "Isn't
this a repulsive party? What are you going to say about
it?" for they were both of them, as it happened, gossip-
writers for the daily papers') and the deplorable Miss
Runcible, who spins like a top at parties, at the motor-
race (quite a marvellous piece of reporting here), in the
nursing-home till she topples over into dementia and death.
There are the clubs, not so fatal as the spades, but still
low-priced and fatuous, such as the wastrels who sit and
drink with Lottie Crump in her frowsty Shepheard's Hotel,
and the drunken major whose appearances on occasions of public rejoicing give such a dreadful rhythm to the book. There
are the diamonds; nobody writing in English has more vividly
recorded the horrible magnificence of those whose success
stands for nothing honourable or valid than Mr. Waugh when
he writes of Lord Metroland, the Circumferences, Mr. Outrage,
Lord Monomark. There are the hearts, Adam and Nina, in any
other age than this inevitably the raw material for romance,

In the monosyllabic conversations of these two, brief as can-
ary cheep, Mr. Waugh has done something as technically astonishing as the dialogues in Mr. Ernest Hemingway's 'Farewell to
Arms', so cunningly does he persuade the barest formula to
carry a weight of intense emotion. There is a game played
between these suits, and in the game it is no use declaring
hearts. The spades and the clubs and the diamonds score all
over them. The book ends with the outbreak of another war,
which the author plainly welcomes as the only way of sweeping the cards off the table and beginning a fresh game, an
extremity of desperation which makes his work as touching
as it is amusing. 'Vile Bodies' has, indeed, apart from its
success in being really funny, a very considerable value as
a further stage in the contemporary literature of disillusionment. That may be said to have started with T.S.
Eliot's 'The Waste Land'. Although that work had a supreme
emotional effect it was not easy to guess what Mr. Eliot
was disillusioned with, and why. He specifically referred
his disillusionment to a contemporary state of discontent
but did nothing to establish the connection, and a scrutiny
of his work suggested that what he was suffering from was
an eternally recurrent condition, to which he was attaching
undue importance because of a false identification. He had
mistaken the malaise that comes on most artists before they
create for the whole of his creative experience, and had
restricted both his subject material and his treatment to
its limitations. This mistake was able to survive and even
put on intellectual airs, because Mr. Eliot pointed for
evidence that his was a mood of universal importance to
this generation's distaste for life. Then came Mr. Aldous
Huxley, whose contribution to the literature of disillusionment left no doubt whatsoever as to what he was disillusioned with, and why. Human beings were, it seemed,
equally apelike in their lives and their excretions; highest and lowest were remarkably alike. A scrutiny of his
work suggested that Mr. Huxley was a person of acute insight who (inspired by the researches of certain psycho-
logists) had looked into the human mind and had been
shocked by certain regressive forces therein; and had, in
the artist's desire to share his experiences, been tempted
into fabricating a universe in which these forces were
represented as being much more dominant and less censored
than they are. But for this vision of the universe he too
gained credence by pointing to this generation's distaste
for life, and claiming that they felt it because they saw
with his eyes. Now Mr. Evelyn Waugh comes along to define
this distaste, and it rather knocks on the head these
attempts to capitalize it. Young people, he tells us, are
disgusted with the world because it is full of those who

drink too much and think too little. One is willing to con-
cede that the world is full of such, and that their proceedings are loathsome; but one must argue against the
assumption that this is anything new. The world that is
described by Arthur Binstead in 'Gals Gossip' and 'The
Pink 'Un and the Pelican'(1) is every whit as unpleasing
as anything Mr. Waugh can find in his surroundings. The
only new thing about the overdrinking and underthinking
world is that clever young people insist on establishing a
connection with it; that Adam, as well as the drunken major,
are to be found with Lottie Crump in Shepheard's Hotel. And
this itself admits of an easy explanation. After the war
the world of ideas was in a state of unsightly ruin for a
time. The overdrinking and underthinking world, ruin being
its *status quo*, was unaltered, and therefore had the cheerfulness of use and wont. It was natural that the younger
generation should for a time prefer the latter to the
former. The exuberance of Mr. Waugh's work, its indomitable
creativeness, is the best proof that the movement is over.

Note

1   The works of Arthur Binstead were reissued in two
    volumes in 1927, the two quoted having first appeared in
    1899 and 1898. He wrote scandalous 'sporting' reminis-
    cences of low high life.

29.   UNSIGNED REVIEW, 'NEW YORK TIMES BOOK REVIEW'

23 March 1930, 7, 20

The various perturbed elders who made such vociferous
outcry when the younger generation started to make public
- via numerous novels - its gay-hearted private lives, will
give thanks, surely - after reading this series of episodes - that they were not born in England. For in England,
they will discover, there was a younger generation that
really was a younger generation. At least if Mr. Evelyn
Waugh can be believed! As in his widely-applauded 'Decline
and Fall,' so now in 'Vile Bodies' he has set down the
antics of a group of youngsters so madly and unmorally
irresponsible that beside them Scott Fitzgerald's most
defiant characters are staid and conservative.
    The book, so the publishers inform us, is satire. It

seems, rather, a dizzy nightmare. One of those weird
nighttime dream productions in which everything gives the
impression of being fiercely logical, until - to your disillusion - you start to tell about it. The author prefaces
it with two quotations from 'Alice in Wonderland,' and it
has at least this in common with Mr. Lewis Carroll's
immortal fairy tale: everything in it is very nearly
utterly impossible; everything in it seems absolutely
true....

The book could be called needlessly nasty, decadent,
superficial, and arrogantly, even offensively sophisticated. It is not even brilliantly original, for Mr. Waugh
is decidedly indebted to Norman Douglas, Michael Arlen
and Aldous Huxley. Yet it certainly is funny and that,
surely, is enough to say for it. The larger part of modern
satire makes you smile, and smile only faintly. 'Vile
Bodies' may shock you, but it will make you laugh.

30. ROSE MACAULAY, 'HORIZON'

December 1946, 362-5

...['Decline and Fall'] was followed next year by 'Vile
Bodies', a novel more crowded, less classic and clear-cut
in plot, more dispersed in interest, more of a revue show.
Disappointing at first reading to some who had looked for
another 'Decline and Fall', it proved a dazzling kaleido-
scope of brightest Mayfair, brilliantly fantasticated.
'The action of the book', says the Author's Note, 'is laid
in the near future, when existing social tendencies have
become more marked.... I have assumed a certain speeding
up of legal procedure and daily journalism.' Social life,
too, is sped up; the parties, the racket, the vices, the
chatter, the jokes. Here and there Firbank (1) takes a hand;
as in the dialogue between the two old *mondaines* on the
channel crossing. But Mr. Waugh has not Firbank's butter-
fly irresponsibility; he is never silly; he knows what he
is about; his imagination is at once more constructive and
destructive. The giddy whirl of 'Vile Bodies' snatches up
in its dance at least a dozen separate groups of people,
each with their own story, as in a ballet where groups
perform in different corners of the stage, sometimes crossing one another's orbits, entangling one another's courses,
flung together and lurching apart like heavenly bodies on
the run. The mass effect of unsteady, extravagant fantasy

and sick and squalid reaction is breath-taking. The moralist has looked in; the smell of dust and ashes hangs on the circus air; irony has become less bland, the death's head grins among the roses. Every now and then Mr. Waugh extricates himself from his tale and becomes a commentator, pointing a social moral, with 'Oh, bright young people', or 'You see, that was the kind of party Archie Schwert's party was'. When 'Vile Bodies' was dramatized,(2) a chorus of draped figures came on between acts and made lament. This damaged the play. But the comments in the book, though out of keeping, are too infrequent to damage it; it pursues its course, kaleidoscopic, various, irresistibly funny. Its wit seldom flags; situations and persons are flung on the scene with lavish extravagance; a more parsimonious or cautious novelist might have reflected that he was using up in this one book material for a dozen. As before, he has for *jeune premier* and fortune's football an ingenuous and luckless youth, see-sawed up and down by fate, roguery, and his own folly. He saunters tranquilly among sudden fortunes and catastrophes, love, loss, customs officers, dud cheques, drunken majors who welsh, young women as debonair and luckless as himself. He has no more moral sense than anyone else in the book, but a rather appealing innocence. We leave him on the battle-field, grasping in his pocket a Huxdane-Halley bomb for the dissemination of leprosy germs among the foe.

Moral scruples nowhere intrude in 'Vile Bodies'. That is, no one has them except the author himself, who shows occasional signs; we discern them, apart from explicit comment, in the book's structure. Agatha Runcible, whirling to her fatal crash in a fantastic motor race, then dying among cocktails and chattering friends, and finally buried with only one of her gay companions at the funeral (the others did not bother to go, or were too uneasily alarmed at such a grim intruder on their revels as death), is a figure perhaps more menacing and exemplary than the Bright Young Person she seems; Mr. Waugh might, with a little less of artistic control, have emphasized this aspect of her, given her in her last moments a spiritual malaise more explicit and profound than her delirium of racing cars. She dies in a nightmare of skidding wheels and crazy speed, crying *Faster, Faster*. Symbolic, but admirable in its reticent realism. Would the later Waugh, the Waugh of 'Brideshead', have been equal to this, or would he have floundered the girl into remorse, bewildered terror of death, change of heart, perhaps introducing Father Rothschild, the priest, into her last hour? There is no such concession here: Agatha dies as she has lived, in a hectic spin.

It is noticeable that none of these people, young or

older, has any interest in art, literature, drama, music,
or world affairs. They are amiable nit-wits. True, one of
them has apparently had abroad with him some books on
architecture, economics and history, and the 'Purgatorio';
but really only to give the Dover customs officer opportunity for cracks. 'French, eh?' he says of Dante. 'I guessed
as much, and pretty dirty too, I shouldn't wonder.' And,
'Particularly against books the Home Secretary is. If we
can't stamp out literature in the country, we can at least
stop its being brought in from outside. That's what he said
the other day in Parliament, and I says Hear hear....'

A pretty scene; but one cannot believe that the traveller had ever read the books. None of the vile bodies reads
anything, except the gossip columns in the papers, for
which they also write. A critic has said lately in these
pages that genuine tragedy at a low level of mentality is
a contradiction in terms, and attempts to create it produce
an impression of impertinence and moral chaos. I do not
myself find this altogether true; one can think of tra-
gedies that befell low mentalities, in Dickens, George
Eliot, E.M. Forster, and elsewhere. But if it were true,
there could be no tragedy in 'Decline and Fall' or in
'Vile Bodies', where the intellectual sensibility of the
characters is as low as their moral and spiritual apprehension. Indeed, it is lower. It is not out of the question
that the young (and old) barbarians should 'get religion';
there is a moment at a party when under the hypnotic influence of a troupe of evangelists, Lady Metroland's worldly
guests quiver on the verge of self-abandonment to religious
hysteria.

'But suddenly on the silence vibrant with self-accusa-
tion broke the organ voice of England, the hunting-cry of
the *ancien régime*. Lady Circumference gave a resounding
snort of disapproval. "What a damned impudent woman," she
said. Adam and Nina began to giggle....'

It had been, perhaps, a close thing. The catching of the
Bright Young People by any exciting religious movement,
whether Aimée Macpherson's Angels, or Mr. Buchman's life-
changers, or a branch of an historic church, is always a
possibility round the corner. What is not round any corner
for them is their conversion to intellectuality, culture,
artistic or literary sensibility. Sublimely uneducated,
gaily philistine, blandly barbarian, agreeably funny, they
reel through the book with the maximum of wit on the part
of their creator, the minimum of intelligence on their own.
Not for a moment does the brilliance falter or the pace
slacken. More truly comic situations, the extravagance of
their conception balancing the unemotional economy of
their setting forth, are to be found in few novels. As a

whole, 'Vile Bodies' cannot compete with the more close-
knit 'Decline and Fall', but the bits and pieces are as
funny, the general effect as glittering. 'Decline and Fall'
approaches more nearly to the bland shimmer of 'South
Wind',(3) that great amoral novel whose ripe intellectual
humour none of its contemporaries or successors can emu-
late. In 'South Wind' is true ironic detachment; its author
surveys the world with the amused derision of a learned
elderly satyr looking on at humanity's capers from his
private brake, mocking, philosophic and undisturbed.
Norman Douglas deals with all ranks and kinds of person,
from peasant to prince; Evelyn Waugh in 'Vile Bodies' (more
than in 'Decline and Fall', which includes a fantastic
scholastic world) concerns himself almost entirely with the
rich of Mayfair. Though some of them think themselves poor,
they always have money for parties of pleasure. The professional middle classes, who live by their wits, not on
inherited capital, and therefore with enforced economy, do
not really engage his attention. He is amused and a little
beglamoured by the gay and idle rich: too much so, for his
wit can play with peculiar excellence on such small beer as
seedy journalists, dingy schoolmasters, and shady adventurers....

Notes

1 Ronald Firbank was certainly a partial model for Waugh
   when he was developing his early style. Harold Acton
   (see headnote to No. 5) probably introduced Waugh to his
   work at Oxford. In an interview with Julian Jebb in
   1962 Waugh said of 'Vile Bodies': 'It was a bad book ...
   not so carefully constructed as the first ['Decline']....
   It was secondhand too. I cribbed much of the scene at
   the customs from Firbank' ['Writers', pp. 108-9].
2 'Vile Bodies, a Play in Twelve Episodes', adapted by H.
   Dennis Bradley (Chapman & Hall, 1931). Twelve performances were given at the Arts Theatre Club, London,
   during October 1931.
3 Norman Douglas, 'South Wind' (Secker & Warburg, 1917).
   Rebecca West compares Waugh unfavourably with Douglas
   in No. 37.

'Labels'

1930 (US title: 'A Bachelor Abroad', 1930)

31.   EVELYN WAUGH, 'GRAPHIC'

4 October 1930, 25

The book that interests me most this week is a new travel
book issued by Duckworth's under the title of 'Labels'.
My interest in it comes less from any outstanding merits it
may possess, than from the fact that I wrote it myself. I
suppose that it is improper to review one's own work under
one's own name at any great length; I will therefore content myself with saying that it is the account of a journey
I made eighteen months ago round the Mediterranean sea-
board.

   The places I visited are for the most part the ones that
everyone else in the world has gone to, too - Monte Carlo,
Naples, Cairo, Constantinople, Athens, Seville and so on -
but quite amusing things seemed to happen to me in most of
them, and I think it conceivable that some readers will
enjoy comparing their own impressions and experiences with
mine. There are some photographs of the work of a very
amusing architect called Gaudí in Barcelona, and there is
an accurate and full description of the night life in Port
Said.(1)

Note

1 Deliberately misleading. He discovers that Port Said is
   rather dull, despite its reputation.

32. UNSIGNED REVIEW, 'OBSERVER'

12 October 1930, 7

It would be difficult to imagine a more devastating exposure of the fatuity of modern travel than Mr. Evelyn
Waugh's Mediterranean journal. Merely turning over his
pages we suffer all the fatigue, ennui, and disgust of
being transported from one disappointment to another by
contrivances whose luxury seems as vain as the pleasures
to which they profess to carry us. For let us be candid,
European travel has become as tiresome and unnecessary as
toothache. It has been too much - one cannot say too well -
organised by semi- or demisemi-occidentalised people,
whose avarice, officiousness, and incompetence are enough
to make any sensitive excursionist as splenetic as Smel-
fungus himself.
    'All the best places are on the beaten track,' said the
perspicacious American; 'that's why the track is beaten.'
Yet beating a beaten track is an exercise even more dispiriting than flogging a dead horse; and Mr. Waugh's
adventures excite not so much the surprise of the innocent
as the reminiscent compassion of the fellow-sufferer. Our
natural impatience with pioneers and their trail-blazing
exploits must be at least partly due to our envy at their
discovery of a fresh experience. But there is nothing fresh
about the Mediterranean; its staleness is so penetrating
that even a writer with Mr. Waugh's alert eye and lively
fancy can do little but acknowledge the triumphs of platitude and confess himself as beaten as his track.
    ...It is a heartening sight to see Mr. Waugh bravely
registering a thrill at the spectacle of the Pyramids,
which he loyally equates in interest with the Prince of
Wales, and bringing all his period-sense to bear on the
enormities of Catalan *art nouveau*.
    It is the period-sense, incidentally, that saves the
modern traveller. Unless he can summon up spirit enough
to laugh at a private joke, he is lost indeed. A Frenchman,
walking with Henry James in the neighbourhood of Rye, is
reported to have exploded in the middle of a perfectly
featureless field and to have gasped between his paroxysms
of mirth: 'si vous saviez ... comme ces petits coins
d'Angleterre m'amusent....' There is nothing more delicious
than these private apocalypses; but one sometimes wonders
whether it is worth while to endure so much on the off
chance of being vouchsafed one.

33. UNSIGNED REVIEW, 'NEW STATESMAN'

18 October 1930, 58, 60

...Mr. Waugh booked a passage on the M.Y. Stella Polaris
and did the round trip.... This book is a description of
his travels with comments on hotels, local extortionists
and fellow-passengers, and exhaustive surveys of the
aesthetic and worldly pleasures to be obtained at every
port at which the Stella called. As was to be expected
from the author of 'Decline and Fall', the book is
extremely witty and entertaining; and it is only occasionally dull when the author turns from his gay, holiday
observation of people and places to a serious consideration
of the aesthetic beauties which even tourists on luxury
launches are unable to avoid in the Mediterranean. Mr.
Waugh's talent more easily allows him to write of the
affairs of the world than of the mind. Besides its engaging
style and amusing matter, the book is full of information
for tourists who have money to spend. The author is a sensible traveller and, like Baedeker, quite independent.
   But 'Labels' will be read more for the ability with
which the author depicts the different types which constitute modern travellers, and for the wit with which he
invests the age-long encounters of beggars, bawds and
dragomans with the helpless tourist, than for its value as
a straightforward guide-book. The average traveller goes
second class, by rail, and stays at pensions. He is
advised not to study Mr. Waugh's list of hotels, restau-
rants and night clubs too closely - until he draws a number in the Calcutta Sweep.
   When the author reached Barcelona he discovered Gaudí.
Gaudí is responsible for the reports which travellers
bring home of this town. 'Barcelona,' they whisper in awed
tones, 'is a modern town. It has a new kind of architecture. It is very beautiful.' Mr. Waugh devotes nine pages
and seven excellent photographs to a discussion of Gaudí's
architecture. He describes it as 'tiffany bathroom'; and a
Gaudí cottage (of which there is a good photograph) does,
in effect, bear a striking resemblance to Hansel and
Gretel's sugar-candy cottage, with the sugar-icing roof
slopped on hastily and left to harden in rich curves. It
is not clear whether Mr. Waugh likes or dislikes Gaudí. But
he is certainly fascinated by him. And if he should ever
write a monograph on his art (which he threatens to do) he
must visit the Zoo at Madrid which belongs to the same
school, and is either the work of Gaudí himself or that of
a devoted pupil. One would like to think that the master

had found recognition outside his native Catalonia. With
'Labels,' Mr. Waugh has definitely established his reputation as a minor critic and master of modern manners and a
very amusing and intelligent writer.

34.   HAROLD NICOLSON, 'DAILY EXPRESS'

3 October 1930, 8

Sir Harold Nicolson (1886-1968) was a diplomat, diarist,
historian, critic and biographer. He was author of 'Tennyson' (1923), 'Swinburne' (1926), 'The English Sense of
Humour' (1947), 'King George V' (1952) and three volumes of
diaries and letters (edited by his son, Nigel, in 1966,
1967 and 1968). He was married to Vita Sackville-West, the
novelist (1892-1962), and was a close friend of Virginia
Woolf. This is a rare example of 'Bloomsbury' taking note
of Waugh's work.

It was, I admit, with some relief that I turned from the
sinister implications of General Spears' war commentary(1)
to the post-war flippancies of Mr. Evelyn Waugh.
     Admirers of 'Decline and Fall' or 'Vile Bodies' may be
slightly disappointed with Mr. Waugh's 'Labels.' I agree
that it is not quite so good as 'Decline and Fall,' but I
find it much better than 'Vile Bodies.' For Mr. Waugh,
conveyed languorously in the yacht Stella Polaris, has for
once had a little time to think. And it is a great pleasure
to me to read what Mr. Waugh thinks.
     His mind is more than inquisitive; it is acquisitive.
When Mr. Waugh reaches Cairo and visits the Tutankhamen
relics he immediately wants to know more; he wants, moreover, to be instructed how to feel. He wants Mr. Roger
Fry.(2) I find his engaging modesty attractive.
     It would have been so easy for him to decry the Tutan-
khamen relics as 'too dreadfully Lalique for words':(3) it
would have been equally easy for him to keep to his paean
thereof, but, being disconcerted by these bright relics of
a forgotten age, hesitating whether they be art or merely
craft, he has the good manners to admit his uncertainty.
Which shows us that even Mr. Waugh, alas! is growing up.
     If I were asked who best represents the post-war spirit
I should reply unhesitatingly, 'Evelyn Waugh.' He has all
the scepticism of Aldous Huxley and none of his despair.

He shares Mr. Huxley's suspicion that the leaves are
barren, but he has a cheery feeling that barren leaves may
be just as amusing as the pregnant variety. And in this I
am with him all the time.

Then I find Mr. Waugh funny. His are the sort of jokes
that make me laugh. Take this, for instance, as a description of his first landing in Gibraltar:

> An English policeman, with helmet, whistle, trun-
> cheon, and rolled macintosh cape, was on duty at the
> landing stage. I think this man pleased the English
> passengers more than anything they had seen on their
> travels. 'It makes one feel so safe inside,' said one
> of the ladies; but I cannot for the life of me think
> what she meant by that.

I should recommend, also, his encounter with the guide
at Naples and with the old-Etonian Greek at Galata. There
is much intelligence behind Mr. Waugh's flippancy. His
analysis of Eton-Oxford culture, his definition of the
'sense of period,' is something more than an easy gibe.

I do not agree with him that all a gentleman of England
extracts from his education is a sense of period. I should
suggest that it is a sense of proportion; but I am grateful
to Mr. Waugh for giving me the idea (which I hope subsequently to make some use of), and I trust that his book
will sell enough copies to make him take a further yachting
trip, but not enough copies to lead him to the Toteninsel
of Corfu.(4)

Notes

1 Brigadier-General E.L. Spears's 'Liaison' (Heinemann,
   1930) was reviewed in the same column.
2 'It would be interesting if some publisher or public
   body would send out Mr. Roger Fry or some other cultured
   and articulate critic to write a review of these works
   from a purely aesthetic attitude. It seemed to me to be
   a collection which ought to form a necessary part of
   every artistic education' ('Labels', p. 109; cut from
   'When the Going was Good', 1946)
3 René Lalique (1860-1945), was an art nouveau jewellery
   designer who later designed elaborate, mass-produced
   moulded glassware. It was the latter which Waugh disliked as an aspect of 'sham modernity' (p. 19).
4 Waugh suggested that it would be pleasant to sell enough
   copies of 'Labels' to be able to retire to Corfu,
   typical of his self-advertisement throughout the book.

35.   C[HRISTOPHER] B. H[OBHOUSE], 'CHERWELL'

8 November 1930, 101

Christopher Hobhouse (1910-40), barrister and writer, was
killed on active service during the war. He wrote 'Fox'
(biography of Charles James Fox, 1934), '1851 and the
Crystal Palace' (1937) and 'Oxford as It Was and Is Today'
(1939). Harold Nicolson's biographical note to the paperback edition 'Fox' (John Murray, 1964) provides further
details.

Since Aldous Huxley emerged just after the War as the
embodiment of the critical and analytical spirit of the
early twenties, and summarized his impressions of a tour
round the world in terms of elephant-dung and bits of
marble;(1) no writer quite so representative of his own day
has appeared as Evelyn Waugh. Not even A.P. Herbert, with
his passionate sincerity and his infinite capacity for
indignation, is quite so true a mirror of a world which
has regained some sense of values, though it is not yet
quite sure *which*. It is not for me to illustrate my point
by referring to Mr. Waugh's religion; but his conversion to
Rome (2) must at least have convinced the less intelligent
readers of his earlier books that they had missed the point
of what they imagined to be a purely facetious form of
literature. The difference between Aldous Huxley and
Evelyn Waugh is that the former is predisposed to laugh at
absolutely everything, that he reduces everything - even
things be cares for - to their component parts (a treatment
as easy as it is effective); while the latter only makes
fun of those things which lack a sense of proportion.
Aldous Huxley thought he was inaugurating a new Age of
Reason: but he only lasted a decade.
   If anything is wanting to prove that Evelyn Waugh's
latest book must be read, and read with appreciation, I
will add:

(a) That it deals with an extremely interesting cruise
    round the Mediterranean;
(b) That it is exceedingly amusing; and
(c) That it is written in beautiful prose.

Notes

1   A reference to Huxley's 'Jesting Pilate' (Chatto &

Windus, 1926).
2 Waugh was receiving 'instruction' while correcting the proofs of 'Labels' and clearly it contained a certain levity, particularly on religious subjects, which he regretted. An Author's Note was added: 'So far as this book contains any serious opinions, they are those of the dates with which it deals, eighteen months ago. Since then my views on several subjects, and particularly on Roman Catholicism, have developed and changed in many ways.'

'Remote People'

1931 (US title: 'They were Still Dancing', 1932)

36. UNSIGNED REVIEW, 'TIMES LITERARY SUPPLEMENT'

5 November 1931, 864

This book is the story of a trip to Africa. The author left
England in October, 1930, for Abyssinia to attend, as a
newspaper correspondent the coronation of the Emperor of
Ethiopia.(1) After the ceremony he went to Zanzibar by way
of Aden, where he stayed longer than do the majority of
globe trotters. From Zanzibar he proceeded to Kenya Colony
with the intention of crossing the continent westwards to
Boma - an intention which he abandoned at Elizabethville on
realizing the discomforts of travel in Belgian territory.
From Elizabethville he made south through Rhodesia to Cape
Town, whence he sailed for Southampton. The trip took him
about five months.

The track covered by Mr. Waugh has been so thoroughly
bewritten in recent years that it is not to be expected of
him that he can add to what is common knowledge about the
places he passed through. He is under the further handicap
that his manner is not suited to his matter. As a writer it
appears to be his bent to express his disillusionment *ex
cathedra*, and what he has to write about is little more
than what is visible from the seat of a public conveyance.
Africa eludes him. He uses his literary experience to
compensate for these disadvantages - dwelling on the eccentricities of an American professor with whom he visited a
monastery near Addis Ababa and on the crotchets of Custom
House officials. But it is such as these, together with
acquaintances made in local clubs and his hosts at cocktail
parties and elsewhere, who are the most closely studied of
his 'remote people.' He has the technical skill to make

them dance to his tune in fictitious dialogue; but he does
not make them interesting. It would be odd if he did; for
the state of mind that he records most frequently is lack
of interest. A river journey had no attraction for him -
'I had a cabin to myself and I fought boredom, and to some
extent overcame it, by the desperate expedient of writing -
it was there, in fact, that I ground out the first two
chapters of this book.'

The reader would guess without this confession that the
book was ground out. But Mr. Waugh has the qualities of his
defects. He has failed to supply the answer to his rhetorical question 'How to recapture, how retail, the crazy
enchantment of those Ethiopian days?' but in his account of
the Abyssinian coronation he does convey 'the irregularity
of the proceedings, their unpunctuality and their occasional failure.' He is never led by romantic fervour to
falsify the facts, and what he writes of political conditions is the truth so far as he knows it. He hits off the
British contribution to Zanzibar in the phrase: 'Instead of
the cultured, rather decadent aristocracy of the Oman
Arabs, we have given them [the Islanders] a 'caste of just,
soap-loving young men with public school blazers. And these
young men have made the place safe for the Indians.' A
little later he gives several carefully written pages to an
impartial summary of the relations between the white and
coloured races in Kenya.

Note

1 For 'The Times'.

37. REBECCA WEST, 'DAILY TELEGRAPH'

4 December 1931, 18

[Norman Douglas's 'Summer Islands'] should be given to
anybody who loves Italy south of Rome; and it should be
given, one may humbly suggest, to Mr. Evelyn Waugh in order
that he may see how to do it. There is no doubt at all that
Mr. Waugh is one of the first half-dozen among young English writers; his book on Rossetti and his two novels have
proved that to any reasonable person. But 'Remote People,'
like his previous travel book 'Labels,' is well beneath his
proper form.

This is odd, because he takes abroad a mind which is
well-furnished, discriminating, and sensitive to beauty
and the humorous; and it springs from something fundamentally wrong in his conception of a travel book. He has here
almost ideal material, in the coronation of the Emperor of
Ethiopia in Abyssinia, and he has had an eye for the peculiar charm of its mingled magnificence and ramshackledom.
But here, and in his description of his subsequent travels,
he makes the mistake of treating events, not according to
the importance that is theirs in relation to other events
in the generally apprehended system of events, but according to the time they took in his itinerary, and their
immediate effect on his nerves.

Relentlessly we are told such things as that 'I stayed
on until Sunday afternoon, resting that night at Haramaya
and reaching the station, after a tiring but eventful ride,
at mid-day on Sunday.' He forgets that even when a writer
is describing the unpleasant he must not neglect his primary duty to please; and Mr. Norman Douglas demonstrates
how that can be done in his denunciations of Mediterranean
fish and the Ischian hen considered as articles of food,
which are full of the beautiful sinister jollity of a
Breughel.

Furthermore, Mr. Waugh has failed to observe that it is
an iron law of literature that the minute one begins to
describe how one has been bored one becomes a bore onself.
And he has an epilogue which is a naughty fuss about nothing. He relates therein how, on the night of his return, he
went to a night-club, and found it intolerable to the
senses and far less civilised than Africa. Quite so, but
why did he go to the night-club? The vast majority of
human beings avoid such painful experiences with the greatest of ease. Is he enamoured of a female saxophonist? Or
is he taken by his friends? And if so, why does an intelligent person have friends with such unintelligent habits?

It is regrettable that a genuine talent should present
itself in a predicament as bogus as the worst type of
Victorian smugness, or Burne-Jonesian melancholy, or any of
the shams of the past which Mr. Waugh would recognise with
half an eye.

But, all the same, 'Remote People' is as often as not
quite gorgeous reading, and has passages remarkable for
their good sense.

And Mr. Waugh has still his exquisite eye for character,
and power of conveying it by fragments of dialogue.

'Remote People' is well worth reading....

38.   UNSIGNED REVIEW, 'NEW YORK TIMES BOOK REVIEW'

3 January 1932, 8

Mr. Waugh, like a bored Roman of the late imperial days,
set forth in the Fall of 1930 to attend the coronation of
the present Emperor of Abyssinia, and incidentally to
observe the queer doings of several of the non-British
races of Northeastern Africa. He was not a traveler of the
Stevensonian stripe, to whom every change of scenery is a
delight and every new face a thrill. On the whole, he did
not much enjoy his trip or much approve of what he saw. He
notes soon after landing in Abyssinia that 'no one volun-
tarily stays long in Djibouti,' and the same thing turns
out to be true of Addis Ababa of Harar of Zanzibar, where
it was too hot; of Kigoma, of Kabolo and of several places
that the traveler reaches by going inland from Mombasa to
Victoria Nyanza, thence to Lake Tanganyika and thence up
the Congo. Mr. Waugh did like Aden pretty well and he did
like Kenya, where charming British settlers are trying to
live the life of a country gentleman as it is no longer
possible to do in England.

But boredom and a fairly constant dissatisfaction with
the way Africa does things characterized almost every stage
of Mr. Waugh's hopelessly unsentimental journey. However,
it may be said that his own boredom does not inspire a like
sentiment in the reader. He manages, indeed, rather skill-
fully to make the reader believe that he himself would have
had a fine time had he been in Mr. Waugh's shoes. Mr. Waugh
saw the coronation - and thought the diplomats on the stage
looked like the people 'in crowded second-class railway
carriages, at dawn, between Avignon and Marseilles.' He
visited the ancient monastery at Debra Lebanos - and carried away sad memories of honey full of 'bits of stick and
mud, bird dung, dead bees and grubs,' of annoying insects
and of the cold night wind. He found himself stranded at
Dirre-Dowa, waiting for a train which was due in a day or
two, and writes:

> I am constitutionally a martyr to boredom, but never
> in Europe have I been so desperately and degradingly
> bored as I was during the next four days. They were as
> black and timeless as Damnation; a handful of fine
> ashes thrown into the eyes, a blanket over the face, a
> mass of soft clay knee deep.

His pilgrimage of ennui finally ends when he takes a
train from Elizabethville, on the upper Congo, which lands

him, after six days on a train 'with little to relieve the
monotony,' in 'the hideous city' of Cape Town. From there
he returned to England by steamer and had an unpleasant
evening in a stuffy supper restaurant, where waiters
'elbowed their way in and out muttering abuse in each
other's ears,' then brought the wrong wine and spilled it
as they set it down. 'Just watch London knock spots off
the Dark Continent,' he savagely comments.

An American might complain because the only two American characters Mr. Waugh noticed were, or seemed to him,
exceedingly foolish and disagreeable. An African, an
Indian or any other of the races which do not belong to
the best clubs might see prejudice in the ironic assumption that 'there may be something valuable behind the
indefensible and inexplicable assumption of superiority by
the Anglo-Saxon race.' But when one has done impeaching
Mr. Waugh's attitudes and manners one has to admit that he
has done all that can rightly be expected of a writer of
travels - he has made a highly interesting book.

39.   PETER FLEMING, 'SPECTATOR'

23 January 1932, 118

Peter Fleming (1907-71) was a traveller and writer who
become Waugh's friend during the 1930s. He was author of
'Brazilian Adventure' (1933, to which Waugh was partially
endebted for certain themes in 'A Handful of Dust', 1934),
'News from Tartary' (1936) and 'The Sixth Column' (1951).
As a reviewer for the undergraduate Oxford press in the late
1920s, Fleming must have been aware of Waugh's reputation
as a leading figure in the university's journalism four
years earlier. The 'Isis' and the 'Cherwell' still used
many of Waugh's wood-block column headings. In 1932 Fleming
could be of use to Waugh as Literary Editor of the 'Spectator'. His brother, Ian, wrote the James Bond novels and
Ian's wife, Anne, was to become one of Waugh's confidantes.

The position of the returned traveller is nowadays a delicate one. There was a time when he had only to put pen to
paper to increase (if he was a truthful man) the sum of
human knowledge, to stimulate (if he was not) the flights
of human imagination. It mattered little which he did.

Illusion was then almost as good a currency as fact; when
Sir John Mandeville (1) threw dust in our eyes it was gold
dust. But things are different now. To anxiety lest you
should be proved a liar is added the terror that you may
be thought a bore. Your readers want the truth about the
places you have seen; but they do not want the whole truth
(for they can look up the rainfall, the principal exports,
and the religious history in the 'Encyclopaedia Britan-
nica'; nor, as yet, does their thirst for information rage
so platonically that they demand nothing but the truth.
Success demands so nice a blend of the subjective and the
objective that it is small wonder that the good travel
book is as rare as ever it was, while the bad is very much
rarer.

Mr. Evelyn Waugh ... has written the very best possible
sort of book about this journey. He is extremely witty. He
observes with insight and, where his curiosity is touched,
enquires with discrimination. The traveller is too often
only an eye-witness, too seldom an interpreter. Mr. Waugh
gives frequent proofs (never more convincingly than in his
assessments of Aden and Kenya) that he has this gift of
interpretation, this power to substantiate impressions and
correlate experiences, which is to-day the only real justification for writing a travel book. His manner is honest,
subjective, and therefore - if for no other reason -
delightful. All records of travel might be described as
discomfort recollected in tranquillity, and we distrust
those writers on whose work the discomfort, whether physical or otherwise, has been allowed to leave no traces
because it was not on a spectacular scale. Their sensibili-
ties seem unnaturally alert. Were hunger, fatigue, or boredom never at hand to modulate the calculated and quivering
exuberance of their raptures? Did beauty or grandeur never
find them unresponsive? Apparently not. They stand out as
supermen. They leave us cold. For a journey is coloured as
much by one's moods as by one's experiences, and Mr. Waugh
recognizes this. He is not ashamed to admit to boredom,
and describes it exquisitely.

He is at his best in Ethiopia. For the atmosphere of
the coronation with 'its peculiar flavour of galvanized
and translated reality,' he can find no parallel outside
'Alice in Wonderland.' He recaptures its extravagance with
a restraint which has in it a touch of incredulity, almost
of stupefaction; on a scene so fantastic the known laws of
comedy no longer held good. But the book would be delightful throughout if it had nothing to recommend it save Mr.
Waugh's prose; for this has something of the uncompromising strength, the disdainful cadences, the power of dis-
paraging without comment which marks that of his fellow-

satirist, Mr. Maugham.

Note

1   Supposed author of a book of travels, the 'Voiage of Sir
    John Maundevile'; in fact a forgery (dating from the
    mid-fourteenth century) being a compilation.

'Black Mischief'

1932

40. HOWARD MARSHALL, 'DAILY TELEGRAPH'

4 October 1932, 16

Here, I thought, looking at the uninteresting jacket of
'Black Mischief,' Mr. Evelyn Waugh's new novel - here at
least is something amusing. I could light my pipe and
stretch my feet to the fire, and prepare to be entertained.

Mr. Waugh did not fail me. He was entertaining; he was
modern; he told a story swiftly and competently.

For all that, I closed his book a little uneasily.
Something is happening to Mr. Waugh. It seems to me that
he grows a trifle weary of the cap and bells; in the words
of one of his own characters, 'I've a tiny fear that he is
going to turn serious on us.'

The truth of the matter is that all satirists are
serious at heart. They may destroy, but they also long to
construct. Mr. Waugh has had his fling at the follies of
the age, and now, unless I am much mistaken, he is searching for something to put in their place.

'Black Mischief,' therefore, represents a transitional
stage in his work, and there is an air of uncertainty
about it which we did not find in his previous novels.

I should not like to imply that it misses the mark. To
my mind it falters here and there, but we are not likely to
have a more satisfactory novel of its kind during the
autumn publishing season...

41.   JAMES AGATE, 'DAILY EXPRESS'

6 October 1932, 6

James Agate (1887-1947) was an essayist, novelist, prolific drama, film and literary critic for the London press,
and author of 'Responsibility: A Novel' (1919), numerous
books of essays on the theatre and nine volumes of autobiography, 'Ego' (1935) to 'Ego 9' (issued posthumously,
1948).

'I'm sure it's all very fine and grand, but it doesn't make
much sense to a stay-at-home like me,' says a character towards the end of this book. Them's my sentiments exactly -
at which statement all the intelligentsia will wave pale
hands of protest.

This book is an extravaganza ... and I take the point of
the yarn to be the extreme incivility of the uncivilised
nigger and the even worse manners of the civil servants
sent out to look after him.

A good deal of the satire is heavy-handed. The old
empress could not make up her mind about a steam-roller:-

> The Metropolitan Archbishop (who was working with the
> American attaché on a half commission basis), supported
> a very magnificent engine named Pennsylvania Monarch:
> the Prince Consort, whose personal allowance was com-
> promised by any public extravagance, headed a party in
> favour of the more modest Kentucky Midget.

And there is a familiar ring about -

> For the last four days Basil had been on a racket.
> He had woken up an hour ago on the sofa of a totally
> strange flat. There was a gramophone playing. A lady
> in a dressing jacket sat in an armchair by the gas
> fire, eating sardines from the tin with a shoe horn. An
> unknown man in shirtsleeves was shaving, the glass
> propped on the chimney-piece.

I assume that Mr. Waugh's plan was to think of an island
of cannibals to whose vile bodies he could add Lottie
Crump's clientèle out of an earlier novel. The book will be
deemed wildly funny by the intelligentsia, and there is
always the chance that it is too clever for me.

42.   ERIC LINKLATER, 'LISTENER'

19 October 1932, 576

Eric Linklater (1899-1974) was a Scottish novelist, playwright, biographer and critic. He was author of 'Poet's
Pub' (1929), 'Juan in America' (1931), 'Private Angelo'
(1946), 'Edinburgh' (1960) and his autobiography 'Fanfare
for a Tin Hat' (1970).

Readers of 'The Waste Land' will remember the picture of
Mr. T.S. Eliot angling in the dull canal 'on a winter
evening behind the gas-house' and playing his fish in the
cold certainty that they will be dead before he lands
them - almost indifferent, indeed, whether it is a fish or
an old boot that he has on his line. And on all four of
these novels lies a shadow that may well be the twilight
greyness of Mr. Eliot's gas-house; the several waters upon
which these four distinguished novelists (1) cast their
bait are like Mr. Eliot's canal in so far as they are without any confident current; and the fish that are hooked -
though large and handsome fish - are pretty well filleted.
The pessimism that pervades this week's reading is, however, a very distinguished pessimism, and charmingly varied
in its presentation. Mr. Bates pursues despair with melancholy beauty and autumnal grandeur. Mr. Waugh is the smiler
with the knife - though a moment ago he was only a fisher-
man - and dissects his vile bodies with murderous gaiety.
Mr. Muir is also surgical in his interest, exploring the
cerebral and emotional interiors of his unhappy subjects
with the grave concern of the scientist, not with the bedside manner of one who says, 'You will be much better in
another hundred pages'. And Mr. Nicolson, pressing political disillusionment into the service of comedy, up-ends a
British Cabinet for a most nursery inspection of its
frailty, spanks it with the urbanity of a diplomat and the
swift vigour of M. Borotra, and sends it back to the Front
Bench without any supper.
     Perhaps Mr. Nicolson's novel is the most disturbing of
the four, at any rate to the devout reader of newspapers
and the faithful who frequent places where they vote. Mr.
Waugh is so abominably subversive as to mock the idea of
progress, especially in such manifestations as might be
expected to promote, by a One Year's Plan, the adoption
of modern organisation and habits of life in the negroid
Empire of Azania; but Mr. Waugh, by living rather on the
plane of Restoration Comedy, permits his readers, if they

prefer it, to take his criticism simply as a good joke.
Mr. Nicolson, however, gives such a persuasive air of verisimilitude to his narrative - real people come in and go
out of it, the political atmosphere is true to the last
mote in the air - that one is almost persuaded to believe
that statesmen do really swing by their tails and pick up
a protocol as though it were a peanut.... [Mr. Bates] is
essentially a poet, who can see with a poet's eye such
things as the snow clinging to the storm side of apple
trees, gathering its whiteness on the rain-green trunks;
and tell with a poet's pen such matters as old Mortimer's
death in the yellow lake of a cowslip field.

We are far from this kind of beauty in 'Black Mischief'.
I hardly think that Mr. Waugh has Mr. Bates' consoling
belief that the land is all right, even though its inhabitants are undesirable. Certainly the land with which he is
presently occupied ... inspires neither confidence nor
comfort. But Mr. Waugh has wit, and that is a species of
gallantry that may defeat even the foulest circumstance.
One may despair about the people of whom he writes, but
he himself is an exhilarating spectacle.

In 'Black Mischief' he has enormously enlarged his stage.
He has added Seth to his gallery ... of fatuous young
people and Welsh musicians. He has impressed warfare and
conscribed hairy adventure. In Mr. Youkoumian he has created a charming figure of comic villany, and in the cannibals who eat poor Prudence he has contrived not only an
excellent novelty in the way of dramatic exits, but a
thoughtful contribution to the problem of disposing of the
unproductive surplus of our population. The manner in
which Mr. Waugh controls his widely varied matter is
admirable. His narrative is swift and picturesque, and
his cutting - if one may borrow a Hollywood term - is
masterly. 'Black Mischief', indeed, shows an all-round
growth of strength.

Note

1 H.E. Bates's 'The Fallow Land', Harold Nicolson's
   'Public Faces' and Edwin Muir's 'Poor Tom' were also
   reviewed.

43.   GEOFFREY WEST, 'BOOKMAN'

November 1932, 135

Geoffrey West (pseudonym of Geoffrey Harry Wells, b. 1900),
biographer and bibliographer (of Shaw and H.G. Wells), was
author of 'Annie Besant' (1927), 'Six Brilliant English
Women' (1930) and 'Charles Darwin' (1938).

When is a form not a form? The answer might be: when it is
a novel. Beyond dispute the novel is the most vigorous and
vital of contemporary art-forms, yet sometimes one is
forced to wonder, regarding its total field and individual
fruits, whether it can be regarded as a form any longer.
Opening its arms ever wider in its ambition to embrace all
life within its scope, it seems to have taken the attitude,
to have suffered the fate, of a thing crucified - by its
own intentions. Almost anything may call itself a novel,
and almost everything does, from Lionel Britton's 'Hunger
and Love' to Lawrence's 'The Rainbow,' from 'William Clissold'(1) to 'Kristin Lavransdatter.'(2) The reviewer of
novels must be an avaricious man - not of money indeed but
of sensation, able to respond to every wind that blows,
to forget his own personal theories of the novel and
attend without prepossession to *novels*. Even when they
turn out not to be novels at all, but short stories or
autobiography, he must not shy at them.
    'Black Mischief' was selected by the Book Society as
its October Book of the Month. With all respect to Mr.
Evelyn Waugh, the Society might have looked further and
found better. Mr. Waugh still seems to suffer from his
early illusion that the vapid fatuities of Ronald Firbank
are funny, and in this as in his earlier books he mounte-
Firbanks all too readily, to his own delight perhaps, but
the reader's tedium. This story of the modernisation of an
African island empire by the One Year Plan of a progressive
Emperor, Oxford-educated (which is a nasty knock for
Oxford), starts badly, and I confess I should have given it
up long before page 120, where the fun really begins, had I
not been paid to persevere. The Emperor's instructions to
his Minister of Modernisation are typical of the humour:

    Do you realise the magnitude of the fixed stars? They
    are immense. I have read a book which says that the mind
    boggles at their distances. I did not know that word -
    boggles. I am immediately founding an Institute for
    Astronomical Research. I must have Professors. Cable

for them to Europe. Get me tip-top professors, the best procurable.

Mr. Waugh gets his laughs mainly from such detail, from speeches at native functions and from the relations of the Foreign Legations. It is all totally absurd....

Notes

1   H.G. Wells, 'The World of William Clissold' (1926).
2   By Sigrid Undset (1882-1949), Norwegian novelist and devout Catholic convert. 'Kristin Lavransdatter' (1929) was a trilogy bringing together 'The Garland' (1923), 'The Mistress of Husaby' (1925) and 'The Cross' (1927).

44.   ERNEST OLDMEADOW, EDITORIAL, 'TABLET'

21 January 1933, 85

Ernest Oldmeadow (1867-1949) was editor of the 'Tablet' from 1923 to 1936, a journalist, novelist, and writer of books on food and the standard biography 'Francis, Cardinal Bourne' (vol. 1, 1940; vol. 2, 1944). On 7 January 1933 Oldmeadow had launched a campaign of vilification against Waugh's novels. Here and in the next piece he is attempting to defend his position against the criticisms of Waugh's Catholic friends. Oldmeadow was eventually replaced as Editor by a younger man, Waugh's friend Douglas Woodruff (see headnote to No. 139), in 1936. From that time Waugh's books were generally applauded by the magazine.

Sir, - In a paragraph in your issue of January 7 you say of Mr. Evelyn Waugh that 'his latest novel would be a disgrace to anybody professing the Catholic name.' You refer to 'outrageous lapses in those who are, or are supposed to be, our co-religionists,' with evident reference to Mr. Waugh. We think these sentences exceed the bounds of legitimate criticism and are in fact an imputation of bad faith. In writing, we wish only to express our great regret at their being published and our regard for Mr. Waugh.

M.C. D'ARCY, S.J.   BEDE JARRETT, O.P.
T.F. BURNS.   D.B. WYNDHAM LEWIS.

CLONMORE.   C.C. MARTINDALE, S.J.
LETITIA FAIRFIELD.   R.H.J. STEUART, S.J.
ERIC GILL.   ALGAR THOROLD.
CHRISTOPHER HOLLIS.   DOUGLAS WOODRUFF.
January 10, 1933.

Foreseeing that its publication must lower more than one
of the signatories in public esteem, we have printed the
above letter with sorrow; but we cannot refuse a little
space to twelve writers, most of whom have long been
respected by Catholics.

Two statements of ours are comdemned by the remonstrants. We said - and still say - that Mr. Evelyn Waugh's
latest novel 'would be a disgrace to anyone professing the
Catholic name,' and that it is disfigured by 'outrageous
lapses.'

Ours being a paper which is received into thousands of
houses whose heads trust us to print nothing vile, we are
debarred from fully proving our case by extended extracts.
But, in these special circumstances, we must ask our
readers' indulgence for a minimum of quotation.

The novel in question is about an imaginary island in
the Indian Ocean, ruled by a black Emperor. Prudence,
daughter of the British Minister at the Emperor's court,
goes up to the unsavoury room (the soapy water unemptied)
of Basil, a man she hardly knows, and, after saying 'You
might have shaved' and 'Please help with my boots', stays
till there is 'a banging on the door.' In the end, Basil,
at a cannibal feast, unwittingly helps to eat the body of
Prudence 'stewed to pulp amid peppers and aromatic roots.'
In working out this foul invention, Mr. Waugh gives us
disgusting passages. We are introduced to a young couple
dining in bed, with 'a bull terrier and a chow flirting on
their feet.' The young wife suddenly calls out 'Oh God,
he's made a mess again'; and Basil exclaims 'How dirty the
bed is.' These nasty details are not necessary to the story.
A dozen silly pages are devoted to a Birth Control Pageant,
announced by posters which flaunt all over the island 'a
detailed drawing of some up-to-date contraceptive apparatus.' The Emperor 're-names the site of the Anglican
Cathedral "Place Marie Stopes."' Two humane ladies are
ridiculed; in one place so indelicately that the passage
cannot be described by us. There is a comic description of
a Nestorian monastery with a venerated cross 'which had
fallen from heaven quite unexpectedly during Good Friday
luncheon, some years back.' If the twelve signatories of
the above protest find nothing wrong with 'during Good
Friday luncheon' we cannot help them.

On learning that Mr. Waugh's novel was being widely

circulated as the Book Society's Book of the Month, the
'Tablet's' Catholic duty became clear. Having again and
again denounced immodesty and irreverence in non-Catholic
novelists, who have no fixed Christian principles to guide
them, we should have been hypocrites if we had not applied
to Mr. Waugh's book the words which we re-apply to it now.
It is a disgrace to a professing Catholic and its lapses
are outrageous. As for the remonstrants' *ad hoc* status,
not one of them has ever sent us a helpful word to fortify
us in our defence of clean literature and our campaigns
against immodesty. 'Regard for Mr Waugh' has roused them
at last; but their protest is unaccompanied by even the
faintest expression of 'regard' for the Catholic standards
of decency which have indisputably been outraged.

Lest the letters 'S.J.' in the remonstrance should hurt
the English prestige of the great Ignatius family, we beg
readers of this note to read also the beautiful Call to
Prayer on behalf of Catholic authors which is transcribed
on our 'Et Caetera' page. The writer (a Jesuit, whose
name we do not know), hits the nail roundly on the head
when he speaks of authors 'whose writings make their
fellow-Catholics wish either that they did not write, or
were not known as Catholics.' Finding Mr. Evelyn Waugh in
that category, the 'Tablet' has put confiding readers on
their guard against him. At the same time we respectfully
and sincerely obey our Cardinal Archbishop's wish that,
during this month of January, Catholics shall pray that
authors be clearly on the side of the angels.

One point more. We did not go out and buy this novel.
It was sent to The 'Tablet,' a known Catholic paper, for
our opinion; and our opinion has been delivered. The
'Tablet' has said its say about the book; the remonstrants
have said their say about the 'Tablet'; and we must now
leave others to decide whether disgrace rests upon ourselves or upon our censors.

45.   ERNEST OLDMEADOW, EDITORIAL, 'TABLET'

18 February 1933, 213-15

Among Letters to the Editor in this week's 'Tablet' is one
from the Very Rev. Dom Benedict Steuart, O.S.B., Prior of
Prinknash, challenging us to say 'where exactly lies the
"scandal" and "disgrace"' in a now notorious affair. With
confidence, though with distaste, we take up the gage.

A.   In the year 1930, it was noised (*le mot juste*) that
Mr. Evelyn Waugh, a novelist, had become a Catholic. Who
instructed and received him we do not know,(1) but, as
this young author had some indelicate writings to his
name, it is inconceivable that his ghostly counsellor did
not tell the neophyte what is expected from a Catholic in
the making of novels. Moreover, Mr. Waugh is literate and
must be presumed to have acquainted himself with what the
Church teaches and requires in a matter so vital to him as
the exercise of his own profession.
B.   Persons who heard of this conversion took it for
granted that the convert would play the game. Among the
letters (all originals) in the 'Tablet's' dossier is one
from a friend of Mr. Waugh's, who wrote:

> He became a Catholic knowing that it would be neces-
> sary for him to modify his literary manner, and so prob-
> ably to lessen his income.

'And so thought All of Us.' Our loyal and generous Catholic
folk concluded that it would be their duty and privilege to
spend their seven-and-sixpences on the works of a writer
who was making sacrifices for Catholic standards of modesty.
C.   The convert, as if to signalize the Catholicization
of his pen, sat down, in 1931, to write a novel and dated
it from Stonyhurst, the great Jesuit school.
D.   There is a Book Society, which has been reproached
for not including a fair proportion of works by Catholic
authors in its Books of the Month. In the winter of 1932,
enemies of the Church began saying, with malicious glee,
'Here is a Catholic Book of the Month for you at last.'
E.   This Book of the Month, dated from Stonyhurst and
signed by an author whose conversion had been widely and
loudly bruited, turned out to be a work both disgraceful
and scandalous. It abounds in coarse and sometimes disgusting passages, and its climax is nauseating. Nowhere in
its three hundred pages is the reader's mind lifted to
anything noble. Of the very many characters, hardly one is
other than contemptible or ridiculous. Religion and Altru-
ism are extensively mentioned; but invariably in a spirit
of cynicism and, in some places, offensively. There may be
books in which sordidness of detail does not overwhelm
the spirituality of the pervading idea; but Mr. Waugh's
is not one of them. On his dunghill no lily blooms.
F.   The above-mentioned colophon, showing that the book
was begun at Stonyhurst, shows also that its author was at
work upon it for eight months. Thus his act was no momentary lapse, such as might happen to any of us. For two-
thirds of a year, Mr. Waugh was intent on elaborating a

work outrageous not only to Catholic but to ordinary standards of modesty. Here lie scandal and disgrace, calling
for disavowal and reproof.

G. To the 'Tablet,' well-known to be what is called 'a
religious weekly', a copy of the book in question was sent
by the publishers for the 'Tablet's' opinion.

H. On many occasions the 'Tablet' has rebuked coarse-
ness in non-Catholic novelists and has not been afraid to
take the legal risks involved in warning the public not to
buy or borrow the works of certain authors. To scold non-
Catholics (and, in some cases, non-Christians) for immodesty and to condone such immodesty in a professing
Catholic would have been cowardice and hypocrisy - a
scandal and a disgrace on our part.

I. See B., above. Thousands of Catholic heads of
families and other Superiors look to the 'Tablet' to protect their homes from books which are scandalous and disgraceful.

J. On January 7, 1933, the 'Tablet' published the
following paragraph:

> A year or two ago, paragraphs appeared in various
> newspapers announcing that Mr. Evelyn Waugh, a novelist,
> had been received into the Church. Whether Mr. Waugh
> still considers himself a Catholic, the 'Tablet' does
> not know; but, in case he is so regarded by booksellers,
> librarians, and novel-readers in general, we hereby
> state that his latest novel would be a disgrace to
> anybody professing the Catholic name. We refuse to print
> its title or to mention its publishers. Indeed, this
> paragraph is not to be read as a review. We are mention-
> ing Mr. Evelyn Waugh's work only because it would not
> be fair on the 'Tablet's part to condemn coarseness and
> foulness in non-Catholic writers while glossing over
> equally outrageous lapses in those who are, or are sup-
> posed to be, our co-religionists. One of the worst fea-
> tures of this nasty business is that Mr. Evelyn Waugh
> has enough satirical wit and invention to write an
> attractive novel without following vile fashions or
> without setting new fashions which are viler still.

To every word of the above warning the 'Tablet' adheres.

K. Not until the above paragraph appeared did Mr.
Waugh's twelve Catholic friends (who are all writers, and
might have been expected to dissociate themselves and the
Catholic body from this outrage) show any sign of life.
Here, it seems to us, are scandal and disgrace.

L. Within three days of the 'Tablet's' caveat appearing
in print, the aforesaid twelve friends of Mr. Waugh had

completed and posted the following protest.... [See No. 44
above.] Scandal and disgrace, in our opinion, attach to the
above joint letter; because (i) while pontifically censur-
ing a Catholic Editor who has discharged a painful duty, it
does not contain one word of disapprobation for the vile
work which has caused the trouble; (ii) its last six words
are a deliberate and public testimonial to the wrong-doer
and a coat of whitewash for him; (iii) in it, the names of
priests are higgledy-piggledy with the names of laymen of
whom some had already caused uneasiness by their treatment
of immodesty in art and literature; and (iv) having acted
collectively against the repute of the 'Tablet' by a joint
Note which has been eagerly pounced upon by enemies of the
Church, they have bolted, leaving only a sniper or two
behind.

   M.   The Remonstrants' assertion that the 'Tablet' has
'in fact, imputed bad faith to Mr. Waugh' is untrue. But,
as it is within our knowledge that some of the Twelve
persist in this false declaration, we will dispose of it,
here and now.

   When young Mr. X. (who was elected some years ago to the
safe Conservative seat of X-borough) is found to be voting,
speaking and writing against his Party, the journalists of
that Party naturally ask where Mr. X. stands, and they warn
unwary listeners to his speeches and readers of his
articles that a riddle exists. But, when they do so, nobody
turns savagely upon those journalists and cries, 'This is
shameful! You are imputing bad faith to our friend X.'
Certain of the Twelve are saying that the 'Tablet' accuses
Mr. Waugh of being 'a sham Catholic,' whose conversion was
not sincere. There is disgrace in so misrepresenting our
words; just as there would be disgrace in saying that a
journalist who asks, 'Does Mr. X still regard himself as a
Conservative?' has made the grave charge that Mr. X cheated
the electors of X-borough some years ago, and grabbed the
seat by shamming to be a Conservative.

   Many converts come into the Church; and a few go out
again.... The 'Tablet' has certainly not committed the
enormous insolence of pretending to un-church Mr. Waugh;
but we have asked a reasonable *a fructibus eorum cogno-
scetis eos* question. Even among our Divine Master's
followers there were some who found His words and ways too
hard. Demas, loving this world's toys and joys, forsook St.
Paul. The Catholic public is entitled to know where Mr.
Waugh stands. If he be indeed with us (as we hope and pray
he is), why does he write like those who are against us,
and what reparation will be made?

   N.   As it is our task to locate the sandal and disgrace,
we will frankly disclose an interrogatory on our procedure

which is pointedly administered to us by Mr. H. Walter, of
Beckenham, who has written to us as follows:

> You rightly call the letter with twelve signatories
> a scandal; but need it have been?
> I feel sure that at least the Jesuit and Dominican
> signatories, and probably some of the others, had not
> themselves carefully read the novel in question. It was,
> no doubt, extremely unwise to write such a letter if
> they have not; but an indiscretion need not be made a
> public scandal.
> I take leave to doubt if you made sure that they were
> fully aware of what they were defending before publish-
> ing their letter. If you did not, on whom does the scan-
> dal rest? But if you did make sure, then I apologise for
> writing this letter before it is in the post.

Not only to Mr. Walter, but to any others who may have
feared that we uncharitably allowed the Twelve to 'walk
into it' with their four-and-twenty feet, we hereby make a
self-exculpatory statement. On receiving the Remonstrance
through a signatory, Mr. Burns (whose name and status we
do not find in the 'Catholic Who's Who,' or in the bigger
'Who's Who',(2) we wrote, within a few minutes, requesting
that the Remonstrance be 'slightly extended' to include a
'declaration that the signatories, each and all, have read,
in its entirety, the book to which the letter refers.' By
the same post, we asked Father Martindale (who, although a
signatory, had separately rebuked us in the harshest terms)
whether he (and some other priests mentioned) had read the
book. He replied that he was 'in no way obliged' to answer
us; and he used this enigmatic sentence:

> I may say - without giving you any grounds for
> remarking publicly or privately on what I say - that
> some had read it, and some had not.

Mr. Burns haughtily told us that it is 'not the function of an Editor to edit the letters in his correspondence
columns'; and his final reply, an inexplicably angry one,
delivered to us this bewildering ultimatum:

> I am presented with the anomolous (sic) vision of the
> Editor of a 'Catholic' weekly making a stand for
> 'morality' against a very varied and not in all parts
> negligable [sic] section of 'Catholic' opinion, clerical
> and lay. But what is the Editor going to do about it?

The spelling in the above extract is Mr. Burns' own; and

so are the inscrutable inverted commas.

Having wasted a whole week trying to protect the Twelve from their own folly, we printed their unjust censure upon ourselves and their untimely proclamation of regard for Mr. Waugh, together with a rejoinder which necessarily became *fortiter in re*. The good Prior of Prinknash blames us for the rejoinder's length. Ought we to have bowed meekly to a Twelve so little 'judicial' that they refused to admit their obligation to know what manner of book was the origin of the trouble?

O.   The Prior's dislike of our 'pontifical' style is taken by us in good part. It is our pride to be outspoken and unequivocal in these days, when the usually splendid solidarity of English Catholics is ever so slightly dinted and rifted by a very few Modernists (in Aesthetics, not Faith), whose feminine terror of being behind the latest fashions in Literature, Painting and Sculpture has momentarily led them astray. We bear no hostility to those of the Twelve who have more than once acted with hostility against the 'Tablet.' Our campaign for clean books and sane art, and for the observance of the Sovereign Pontiff's *Mortalium animos*, will go on; because we are content to be dubbed 'pontifical' a thousand times, even by Priors, so long as the humblest Catholic can never say that we blame immodesty in Protestants, and gloss it over in those whose standards ought to be far higher, seeing that they profess the Catholic name.

P.   Although nearly six weeks have passed since the Remonstrance was penned, not one of the signatories has qualified his 'regard for Mr. Waugh' by condemning the novel's foulness, or even by deploring its allusion to a Cross which fell from heaven 'during Good Friday luncheon.' In this instance we do not say merely that 'we think' scandal and disgrace are here. We say bluntly that there is a scandal and a disgrace.

R.   We are pontifical in the sense that we conscientiously and fearlessly labour to further the teachings of the Sovereign Pontiff. Therefore, we have caused a new translation to be made of the Instructions of the Holy Office on immodest books. It will be found on page 200.

Notes

1   Waugh was instructed and then received by the Very Rev. Martin D'Arcy, S.J. (1888-1976), on 29 September 1930. Fr D'Arcy, of course, was one of the signatories of the letter of protest.
2   Tom Burns, publisher; he was Waugh's contact at Longman,

Green & Co. through whom Waugh published 'Waugh in
Abyssinia' (1936); later he was a founder of Burns,
Oates & Co., the Catholic publishers.

46.   EVELYN WAUGH, LETTER TO TOM DRIBERG

September 1934

This gives the text of Waugh's reply to Oldmeadow reproduced in Driberg's William Hickey column, DE, 11 September
1934. The letter was sent from 14A Hampstead Lane, Highgate, London.

Biographical details about Tom Driberg appear in the
headnote to No. 90.

Enclosed statement re. Meadow. If you think it worth printing to be used as it stands, fully, or not at all.

Evelyn

TEXT
Two aspects of 'Tablet' article

a) an unfavourable criticism
b) a moral lecture

The first is completely justifiable. A copy of my novel was
sent to the 'Tablet' for review and the editor is therefore
entitled to give his opinion of its literary quality in any
terms he thinks suitable.

In the second aspect he is in the position of a valet
masquerading in his master's clothes.

Long employment by a prince of the Church has tempted
him to ape his superiors, and, naturally enough, he gives
an uncouth and impudent performance.

'Ninety-Two Days'

1934

47. UNSIGNED REVIEW, 'TIMES LITERARY SUPPLEMENT'

15 March 1934, 178

It is perhaps not an accident that the title of this travel-
book suggests a penal sentence of three months, but it
would have been more illuminating if it had indicated that
they were spent for the most part in the interior of
British Guiana. In choosing that little-bewritten country
for his subject Mr Waugh has shown the bent, otherwise
associated with him, for taking his own line. Apart from
being thus novel in his theme, he is to be credited with
two other qualifications for holding the attention with a
travel-book - a type of book which when the compiler has no
gift for selection may be as wearisome as an auctioneer's
catalogue of a forced sale. In the first place Mr Waugh
writes extremely well. It is not only that his sentences
express without strain his exact meaning, but that they
also conform in their tone to the consistent attitude of
mind which is the second of his qualifications. This attitude invests him with personality, and renders his epithets
and so forth a reliable medium for exchange into the
reader's own mental currency. It is not exactly one of
denigration, for the lapses of men and the contrariety of
things are noted rather than condemned. There is something
in it of the French 'horreur d'être dupe' and 'horreur
d'être plat'. No one is permitted to humbug Mr Waugh. Least
of all himself. He records in their place, as part of the
day's impressions incidents that go to show that he is not
very clever with a horse, at distributing his kit, at finding his way, at foreseeing obstacles; if it becomes difficult to go where he proposed, he goes somewhere else. He
nowhere presents himself as the complete backwoodsman.

141

Indeed, the reader may well be puzzled to understand
why Mr. Waugh, whose spiritual home is, he infers, Bath,
should have betaken himself to Guiana. For it inheres in
that attitude of his that there shall be no silly nonsense
about the pleasures of primitive existence. A time comes
when the club pessimist gets a laugh when he makes his
moan; and in this book the reader comes to reckon that Mr
Waugh is not playing his part adequately unless he produces some phrase such as 'Depression deepened'; 'As depressing a time as I have known in adult life'; 'Monotonous
vegetable walls on either bank'; 'It would be tedious to
record...'; 'I was to grow to hate it' [a river]; 'But
there were only two more days to Bon Success, where I
should be leaving all three of them'; 'At last that day,
like all others, came to an end'; 'My enthusiasm had
already cooled considerably...'; 'The mist of frustration
still hung about us'; 'Our camp was the least attractive
we had yet made', &c., &c.. To express the distance of Mr
Waugh from those who are said to write with a gusto of
appreciation we want some such word as 'disgusto' for his
colic welcome for the asperities (his word) of travelling
in Guiana.
      It was necessary to dwell at length on what we have
called his 'attitude'; because Mr Waugh, who adopts it
deliberately, defends it in a long and entertaining passage on the delights - real and so-called - of travelling
in the back [sic] blocks. The former, according to him, are
'incommunicable'; the others he 'debunks'. He recognizes
only two pleasures obtainable in Guiana but not - by him -
in Europe. One was washing after a long journey; the other
reading. (It may be just the attitude prescribed for books,
but we have to take it from him that it is ten years since
he read any 'for the mere pleasure of the process.') Then
he adds a third, and with it indicates what, with all his
gifts of style and wit, he lacks as a writer about travel.
He tells us that he began to make 'a compass traverse of
the route' but gave it up as too difficult: 'While it
lasted, however, the practice made me observant of the
country as I had not been before and heightened my enjoyment of the change of scenery.' There we have it! His eyes
are turned inwards; he is not an instinctive observer; it
is only by a definite intellectual effort or as the reaction to some direct physical stimulus that he distinguishes
among the objects presented to his vision. Of insects what
he records - repeatedly - is that they bite. He has little
to say of animals and birds. It is not an accident that the
varied trees of Guiana exhibited themselves to him as
'monotonous vegetable walls'. On the other hand, among many
passages that one would gladly quote for the felicity in

description are two of the flower-crowned forest wall in certain effects of light.

Starting from Georgetown, Mr. Waugh made his way south-wards to Boa Vista in Brazil, returning by a more westerly route which allowed him, or rather compelled him, to see the famous Kaieteur Falls. Famous falls, of course, were forbidden ground, his attitude being what it was, but hav-ing seen them he makes them serve his own talent in yet another admirable passage of description. Accompanied by servants engaged locally he travelled on horseback, by boat, and now and again on foot. At times he was the guest of settlers or priests; at times he slept in dilapidated huts found on a cattle trail. He must have penetrated some 350 miles into the interior before relinquishing his plan to reach Manaos by river.

48. PETER FLEMING, 'SPECTATOR"

23 March 1934, 474, 476

On the dust-wrapper Mr. Waugh confronts us with a prismatic compass and an air of determination. He needed both. His ninety-two days were spent between Georgetown in British Guiana and Boa Vista on the Rio Branco, over the Brazilian border. The distance is less than four hundred miles, but the going was bad, the living was hard, and Mr. Waugh was for a great part of the time alone save for one or two un-reliable servants. He endured considerable discomforts and some privations, and these he reports in detail and with irony.

It is the book's weakness - though not the author's fault - that there was very little else to report. The territory he traversed is known only to a handful of Euro-peans and Americans; and after reading Mr. Waugh's book this seems a very natural and proper state of affairs. The Brazilian savannah is a monotonous desolation, and on the British side of the frontier the country is neither developed nor likely to be developed. From the traveller's point of view it has the disadvantage of being inadequately mapped without boasting the compensatory cachet of virgin territory. Similarly, the Aboriginal Indians are in that half-baked state between savagery and civilisation which substitutes only a veneer of incongruity for whatever charms or terrors they may once have had.

Mr. Waugh met with an alarming number of vicissitudes

but they were not of a sensational kind, and that transparent honesty which is one of his most attractive qualities as a travel-writer prevents the author from pretending that they were. Though the book is far from being dull
- the digressions especially are often brilliant - it is
as nearly dull as anything Mr. Waugh can write: which
means, I would point out, low marks for tedium.

His original purpose of journeying down the Rio Branco
to Manaos on the Amazon had to be abandoned because he was
refused accommodation on the launch. But this purpose was
in itself too arbitrary and aimless - it meant too little
to the traveller - to supply the reader with continuity of
interest. That element of suspense which to a certain extent enlivens all narratives of human endeavour is lacking,
and not even Mr. Waugh, in those forbidding wastes, can
substitute for it the alternative charm of the picaresque
flâneur.

The best thing in the book is the encounter with Mr.
Christie, a religious gentleman of some eccentricity....
Here experience came up to scratch and gave the author
material which he knows how to use better than anyone else.
For the rest, 'it is by crawling on the face of it that one
learns a country,' remarks Mr. Waugh with great justice and
the reader who follows the ups and downs of his journey
will get a vivid impression of that 'mist of frustration'
which usually dominates travel in the less civilised parts
of Latin America.

That the book is well written goes without saying. All
the same, I doubt whether a man can be said to be either
'of unpredictable descent' or 'on an inscrutable errand'.
As for the photographs, they may, as the publishers claim,
'be of great anthropological interest'; but not to anthro-
pologists.

49. V.S. PRITCHETT, 'CHRISTIAN SCIENCE MONITOR'

25 April 1934, 10

'I always know the character of any visitors by the visions
I have of them,' said the negroid Mr. Christie, whom Mr.
Waugh met up-country during his 92-day journey through
British Guiana. 'Sometimes I see a pig or a jackal; often a
ravaging tiger.' In what form, Mr Waugh naturally asked,
had *he* appeared? And Mr. Christie politely replied, 'As a
sweetly toned harmonium.'

Well, sweet is hardly the word for the writings of Mr.
Waugh. He is distinctly an acid writer. 'Harmonium' is unkind as a definition of a satirist whose early manner was
saxophonic; but I am coming to the conclusion that the
eccentric Mr. Christie was not far wrong. Scratch the
surface of much sophistication and there is revealed a
great deal of carefully repressed harmonium underneath. As
for Mr. Christie's 'sweetly toned' - this book is a deep
improvement on 'Labels' and the book on Abyssinia in which
farce and satire had become *farouche* in order to conceal a
sentimental *malaise*. One gets the impression that Mr. Waugh
was angry not with Africa but with himself, that he longed
to like something but was too 'tied up' to do so; and
although he was preëminent as an 'amusing' writer, one felt
the sort of embarrassment that comes when Mr. Noel Coward,
for example, is under the delusion that he is exposing the
evils of Society with a capital 'S'.

In '92 Days' Mr. Evelyn Waugh appears to be emerging
from this phase. He matures. He even likes one or two
people. And ennui is giving place to patient observation.
He is slowly exchanging his little stock of sophistication
for a pleasing collection of sympathies, prejudices,
fusses, worries and patient determinations. The satirist
still conducts him to 'borderline cultures' where grotesque contrasts in development make vivid and obvious
material, but that is natural and legitimate for his talent, although the choice is a further example of the
traveler seeking abroad that which has conditioned him at
home.

His course lay from Georgetown - a name to evoke romantic and delusive Irish pictures - inland through bush and
savannah to the mission at Bon Success and on to Boa Vista,
in Brazil. He hoped to get down to Manoas on the Amazon by
boat, but he was obliged to give up the plan. Boa Vista -
another name of false evocations - was the farthest south
and the low-water mark of Mr. Waugh's melancholy; he
returned to Georgetown by another route. Except for a few
ranchers, diamond prospectors and missionaries, the white
man is a rare visitor inland, and Mr. Waugh found himself
confined to the company of Yeppo, his honest guide; Sinclair, the trouble-maker, but indispensable cook, and the
conversation of a whole string of melancholy and almost
sublime eccentrics. British Guiana, like all those places
where the spaces are wide and open, is enlivened by the
declamations of white and near-white men who may be strong
but are rarely silent.

Travelling rough increased Mr. Waugh's respect for
scenery and in his subdued fashion - for the influence of
the obligation to 'debunk' travel is strong in him - he

gives a lucid and fascinating picture of places and people.
He was not impressed by the nobility of the savage; on the
other hand he protests that missionaries are not to blame
for clothing natives against their will. Imitation of the
white man is stronger, he thinks, than the missionary. He
also disagrees with those who say the white man has corrupted the native by the introduction of alcohol. The
native tribes he came across made primitive liquors of
their own.

Altogether, although his interests had been aroused by
his many diverting experiences, he was glad when his journey was over. And with a parting dig at the anthropologist,
he was glad to forget the brown-paper taste of *farine*, and
the shoe-leather flavor of *tasso*, the staple diet, and to
return to Bath. Then from this eighteen-century security,
he could reflect with dry humor on the interesting un-
pleasantness and bizarre confusion of the world.

50. BLAIR NILES, 'NEW YORK TIMES BOOK REVIEW'

27 May 1934, 12

Evelyn Waugh's 'Ninety-Two Days' won me in its first chapter; in spite of a prejudice established by the frontispiece of the author clad in shorts; in spite also of the
photographic illustrations which are of the snapshot
variety, and badly reproduced, with often two unrelated
pictures appearing on the same page. Such a format suggests
the banal mediocre type of travel book that is so easy to
write and so painful to read

But all this was forgotten in the pleasure of Mr.
Waugh's book. For some time there have been, here and
there, symptoms that we are emerging from the distortion of
truth and the tawdry self-exploitation of the travel books
of the recent degenerate era, and returning to the fine
tradition of such books as Doughty's 'Arabia Deserta' and
Stephens's 'Incidents of Travel in Central America.' D.H.
Lawrence, Norman Douglas and Tomlinson led the way back to
high standards in travel literature. And now comes Evelyn
Waugh. His book is a simple, straightforward record of a
journey into British Guiana and part of Brazil. It is told
with integrity, charm and humor. It even bears reading
aloud, and that is a test which not many books survive. I
happen to know the British Guiana 'bush,' but if that were
not the case I should still feel, after reading 'Ninety-Two

Days,' that I had personally experienced Mr. Waugh's adventures there. And that is the essential quality in such a book.

Early in the volume Mr. Waugh explains his attitude toward travel:

When any one hears that a writer is going to do anything unusual, such as going to British Guiana, the invariable comment is, 'I suppose you are going to collect material for a book.' And since no one but a prig can take the trouble to be always explaining his motives, it is convenient to answer 'Yes' and leave it at that. But the truth is that self-respecting writers do not 'collect material' for their books, or, rather, they do it all the time in living their lives.

One does not travel, any more than one falls in love, to collect material. It is simply part of one's life. Some writers have a devotion for rural England; they settle in Sussex, identifying themselves with the village, the farm and the hedgerow, and inevitably they write about it; others move into high society; for myself and many better than me, there is a fascination in distant and barbarous places, and particularly in the borderlands of conflicting cultures and states of development, where ideas uprooted from their traditions become oddly changed in transportation. It is there that I find the experiences vivid enough to demand translation into literary form.

It is interesting that many of our best travel writers - D.H. Lawrence, H.M. Tomlinson, Norman Douglas, W.H. Hudson - have also been writers of fiction, and it seems to me significant that integrity is a striking characteristic of these authors who are novelists as well as travel writers. As their fiction has the vitality to stand on its own feet, so their non-fiction never descends to misrepresentation of fact. To this, as it were ambidextrous class of writers Evelyn Waugh and his brother Alec belong. In 'Ninety-Two Days' Evelyn Waugh tells us that

Alec also is fond of traveling. Like me, poor fish, he lives by writing books, so on one of our rare but agreeable meetings we made a compact each to keep off the other's territory. With a papal gesture Alec made me a present of the whole of Africa and a good share of Asia, in return for the Polynesian Islands, North America and the West Indies.

Out of respect to this fraternal pact, Evelyn Waugh

mentions only incidentally the islands which he visits en
route to British Guiana, and from Georgetown he hurries
the reader almost at once into the interior, taking him by
way of the Berbice River as far as Takama, and eventually
across the Brazilian frontier.

Of this journey Mr. Waugh writes divertingly of the
difficulties of getting from place to place; adding that
'it is by crawling on the face of it that one learns a
country; by the problems of transportation that its geo-
graphy becomes a reality and its inhabitants real people.'
He possesses the gift of conveying to the reader the
flavor of his travel experience.

'A Handful of Dust'

1934

51. UNSIGNED REVIEW, 'TIMES LITERARY SUPPLEMENT'

6 September 1934, 602

'Nadir' - Place or time of greatest depression, &c. We have
the authority of the dictionary for this; and the labour of
looking it out represents a small tribute to the precision
with which Mr. Evelyn Waugh expresses himself. For 'climax'
- at any rate until it has been looked out - is associated
with climbing; and while we need a word for the terminal
point to which in 'A Handful of Dust' he inexorably progresses, there would be, in any suggestion of ascent, an
insensitiveness to the effect aimed at and produced.
Whether his study of futility is worth doing - and doing at
such length - is a matter of opinion; but there can be
nothing but praise for his consistency of outlook and for
the grasp of purpose which rejects not only all details
that might conflict with it, but any word that might be
used by a shocked or sympathetic observer.

He has set out to tell us of the extinction of feeble
Tony Last; and when he has finished it would be a job to
find a trace of him. Not that any reader will be moved to
undertake it; for though Mr. Waugh, confronted with the
alternative of appearing to administer poetic justice, has
drawn his victim as a decent fellow - at any rate by comparison with his associates - Tony is so incapable of helping himself that he is not worth helping. Tony is living
feudally, as it pleases him to think, at Hetton Abbey with
his wife, Brenda, and an heir to his cherished property in
his boy John. Lest it be thought that with an abbey Mr.
Waugh has blundered into allowing him an impressive setting, we quote from his guide-book that this abbey 'was
entirely rebuilt in 1864 in the Gothic style and is now

devoid of interest.' The internal decorations of the abbey
are by Mr. Waugh, who has had the bedrooms named 'Yseult,'
'Elaine,' &c. Unknown to Tony, Brenda is having an affair
with a professional sponger. Passion? Certainly not; not
even jolly old appetite. Hear Brenda: 'He's second rate
and a snob ... but he's never had a proper affair with
anyone decent ... he's got to be taught a whole lot of
things. That's part of his attraction.' John went to his
first meet. They failed to find. A bungling woman lost
control of her horse. It kicked, and killed John. What
with Brenda's greed and Tony's clumsiness in providing
evidence the arranged divorce is a fiasco. Tony is persuaded to join a Dr. Messinger in an exploring expedition.
They set out from Georgetown. In Brazil or somewhere they
are deserted by their porters. Dr. Messinger goes out of
the story 'over the Falls'; and, with really handsome
Falls to be had anywhere about, the niggardly Mr. Waugh
allows him only a ten-feet drop. Fever-stricken Tony is
found by an illiterate poly-caste who lives alone in bush
from which Tony cannot escape unaided. Tony is held prisoner to read Dickens aloud to his captor. He is there
still.

52.   ERNEST OLDMEADOW, EDITORIAL, 'TABLET'

8 September 1934, 300

As we counsel our friends to spend no money and no time in
acquiring and reading the book before us, we had better
explain why it is receiving a lengthy review. Last year, a
novel from the same pen evoked a sequel which gave pain to
Catholics. A reproof to the author from our unimportant
selves was amplified from a quarter so authoritative that
his co-religionists reasonably hoped to find Mr. Waugh
turning over a completely new leaf. He has not done so.
His 1934 novel, although it is disfigured by coarse expressions, is free from the gross indecency and irreverence
which made its forerunner abominable; but the forerunner
has not been scratched by its owner. On the contrary, all
unwithdrawn, unrevised and unrepented, it is loudly
advertised on a whole page at the end of the new work.
  Sincerely did we trust that Mr. Waugh's 1934 novel would
be such as we could praise. Our heart sank, however, when
we found clasped round our review-copy, like a bar sinister,
a paper band with the inscription 'Recommended by the Book

Society.' As this cliquish Society is always delivering
judgments, it is salutary that it should be told what is
thought of it by many persons whose taste and skill in
appreciating and producing literature are perhaps not less
than its own. Taken year in and year out, the Book
Society's recommendations are a deplorable aiding and
abetting of the men and women who have rapidly succeeded
in fouling English literature. So we also have a Recom-
mendation; namely that, unless and until a wholesome
change takes place, the words 'Recommended by the Book
Society' shall be regarded as what the Ministry of Agriculture calls a Notification of an Infected Area. Now and
again, those readers who act upon our advice may miss a
clean and good book; but they will have the satisfaction
of knowing that their money has not encouraged frequent
lewdness and baseness.

We return to 'A Handful of Dust.' Like its immediate
forerunner, it aims primarily at entertainment; an aim of
which we in nowise complain. The entertainment is satirical;
and with satirical entertainment, when it is well done, we
are hugely pleased. But 'A Handful of Dust' is not well
done. The author has not made a clear choice between tragi-
comedy and farce. Such names as 'Lord Monomark,' 'Mr.
Graceful,' and 'Polly Cockpurse' are out of the key of this
composition. So is the whole business of 'Mr. Tendril,'
Vicar of Hetton, which our Anglican friends may justly
resent. The fun with Mr. Tendril, who had been a chaplain
in India, consists in making him forget that he is back in
England. Although the period of 'A Handful of Dust' is
1933-34, Mr. Tendril, who is 'reckoned the best preacher
for many miles around,' still speaks of Queen Victoria as
regnant - 'our Gracious Queen Empress' - and on Christmas
Day, when the congregation are 'coughing into their muff-
lers and chafing their chilblains under their woollen
gloves,' he condoles with his hearers on having to spend
Christmas thousands of miles from home amidst 'the un-
comprehending stares of the subjugated, though no doubt
grateful, heathen' and on having for companions 'the raven-
ing tiger and the exotic camel, the furtive jackal and the
ponderous elephant.' In a mainly realistic novel of contemporary smartness and actuality, such farce or burlesque
suggests a 'ponderous elephant' dancing. A question and
answer in the House of Commons as given by Mr. Waugh are
equally removed from authentic satire.

Bungling indecision is, however, so common among novelists that its evidence on Mr. Waugh's pages would not, by
itself, justify us in deploring his book, which certainly
contains some witty pages. The trouble is that this author
has once more laboriously led up to a brutal finale. In

last year's book the lover (if so sweet a name can be given
to the low amorist in question) found at the end of the
story that he had unwittingly helped some cannibals to eat
the body of the English girl with whom he had had the most
intimate relations. The climax of 'A Handful of Dust' is
less disgusting, but it is sedulously and diabolically
cruel. Tony Last, a young squire who is almost the only un-
selfish and non-rotten person in the book, goes exploring
in Brazil (or British Guiana), so as to forget his terrible
griefs and wrongs. Tony's only son has just been killed in
the hunting-field; and his adored young wife, Brenda, has
run away with a dull sponger and cad who is not even in
love with her. The story closes with the unclean little
cheat Brenda happily married to a rich young M.P., who had
been Tony's best friend, while Hetton Abbey, the family
seat for which Tony had made heavy sacrifices, is the
setting, on the very last page, for the doings of new
owners. A monolith cenotaph in the Abbey grounds is a
memorial to the lost Tony. But here comes the vileness.
Tony is not dead. He is the prisoner of a monomaniac (half
English, half Indian) in the depths of a tropical forest,
where he is compelled - more farce here - to read the whole
works of Dickens aloud, again and again, from a set of
tattered, ant-eaten volumes. The frustration of his attempt
at escape is one of the cruellest passages ever invented by
a novelist. So Brenda is a bigamist; and Tony's cousins
(frugal and worthy people) are in wrongful possession of
the Abbey. For all we know, Tony (who is only half his
gaoler's age, and is a pure-bred Englishman) will get home
again, and his cousins will go back to their impecuniosity,
while Brenda will have to rearrange her promiscuity.

   In the days of his happiness at the Abbey, Tony sometimes read the lessons in church. Yet when 'Mr. Tendril,'
the vicar, called on him after the death of the little heir
in the hunting-field, Tony's complaint of the 'awful' and
'very painful' interview was that 'the last thing one wants
to talk about at a time like this is religion.' Throughout
the book English Society is viewed as godless, while Religion, as the great Anglican Bishop Butler said, is treated
as if it is no longer even matter for inquiry. Mr. Waugh
satirizes this 'Society' with its women who pay five
guineas each to have their fortunes told from the soles of
their feet instead of from the palms of their hands, and
so on; but we are sorry to say that any contempt he may
have for the cadgers and gluttons and adulteresses is
obscured by the snobbery - this harsh word is the only
word for it - with which he fondly contemplates them.

   The pity of it is that Mr. Waugh is misusing his indubitable talent. He can achieve expansions of beautiful

prose, as in Tony's dream of the buried Amazonian City. If he wants to taste true happiness, he will make a clean Franciscan cut with the past. He will stop the reprinting of every ignoble book of which he controls the copyright, and will show the world that a writer of genuine talent is not dependent upon malodorousness for his drawing-power. So acting, he may lose the recommendations of the Book Society; but he will some day hear a 'Well done!' from a Voice of more consequence. We do not, however, indulge any strong hope that this appeal of ours will work the wonder. Will not Mr. Waugh's Catholic friends come to the rescue? A year or two ago they rushed into print with a declaration of their 'regard for Mr. Waugh.'(1) Let them show that the regard is sincere. They might begin by presenting him with an illuminated 'text' for his writing-table - the text in which St. Paul says: 'Whatsoever things are true, whatsoever modest, whatsoever just, whatsoever holy, whatsoever lovely, whatsoever of good report, if there be any virtue, if any praise of discipline, think on these things.'

Note

1 Cf. No. 44 above.

53. WILLIAM PLOMER, 'SPECTATOR'

14 September 1934, 374

William Plomer (1903-73) was a South African poet, novelist, librettist (for Benjamin Britten's 'Gloriana') and biographer. He was author of 'Cecil Rhodes' (1933), 'Kilvert's Diary' (three vols, 1938, 1939, 1940), his autobiography 'Double Lives' (1943), 'Museum Pieces' (1952) and 'Collected Poems' (1960).

Mr. Evelyn Waugh seems to be moved chiefly by a kind of fascinated disgust, and the irritation which this useful emotion sets up in him has caused him to produce another of his cultivated pearls. He takes the title of his new book from 'The Waste Land' - 'I will show you fear in a handful of dust.' The fear chiefly exhibited by his characters seems to be the fear of living anything like what

used to be called a God-fearing life. The story, which
deals largely with what might once have been called 'the
sins of society,' is neatly contrived and adroitly written,
with a neatness that is perhaps French rather than English, and it catches exactly certain of the rhythms of
contemporary life. There is no waste, no whimsy and no
padding; the book holds the attention throughout and is of
exactly the right length. I think it would be a mistake to
regard Mr. Waugh's more surprising situations as farcical
or far-fetched; they are on the whole extremely realistic,
and charged with the irony that belongs to the commonplace
but is not always perceived. His large and well-earned
public will lose no time in discovering the plot for themselves: it is enough to say here that it concerns the
victimization of a 'commonplace, romantic English squire'
who suddenly discovers that he is living in a world bereft
of order.

> It was as though the whole reasonable and decent con-
> stitution of things, the sum of all he had experienced
> or learned to expect, were an inconspicuous, inconsider-
> able object mislaid somewhere on the dressing table; no
> outrageous circumstance in which he found himself, no
> new, mad thing brought to his notice, could add a jot to
> the all-encompassing chaos that shrieked about his ears.

Mr. Waugh has such an economical method of showing up the
fool in his folly that he does not allow himself scope for
elaborate characterization, and his virtuous hero remains
a little vague, but his method might well be studied by
some of his untidier contemporaries....

54.   PETER QUENNELL, 'NEW STATESMAN'

15 September 1934, 329

For some time - ever since the publication of 'Black Mischief' - Mr. Evelyn Waugh's admirers have been asking themselves just how long he would be able to preserve the
exquisite comic equilibrium that distinguished 'Vile
Bodies' and 'Decline and Fall.' Solemnity showed signs of
creeping in. No one who has studied Mr. Waugh's novels
with a close and sympathetic eye can have failed to
recognise that he is at bottom a profoundly pensive -
indeed, an extremely serious and, at moments, a melancholy

and disenchanted - character; but though one did not
grudge him the expression of what is, perhaps, after all,
his real literary temperament, one could not help feeling
that these intervals of solemnity, when the satirist gave
way to the Catholic moralist, detracted from the charm of
otherwise extravagant and light-hearted stories; in short,
that his serious passages were out of tune. Thus, I looked
forward with apprehension to his next novel. It is pleasant
to record that any fears I may have harboured - fears
somewhat intensified as I noticed the title and observed
the quotation from Mr. T.S. Eliot that adorns the title
page - proved completely baseless; for 'A Handful of Dust,'
if not the most exhilarating, is certainly the most mature
and the best written novel that Mr. Waugh has yet produced.
Here tragedy and comedy are interdependent. It is true that
the reader of 'A Handful of Dust,' unlike the reader of
'Decline and Fall,' no longer interrupts his reading to put
down the book and laugh aloud. On the other hand, he is
kept lightly, skilfully and continuously amused throughout
the entire volume, and smiles and is subtly horrified at
the same instant. In essence, the harrowing is often farcical; and there is a touch of tragedy in many comic situations

The story is equally painful and hilarious. Mr Waugh
handles his *dramatis personae* with a masterly and dispassionate deftness; and only in one episode does there
seem to be a slight softening of his attitude, a failure
of that tone of acerbity which suits him so well. I am
thinking of the passages which Mr. Waugh devotes to Tony
Last's little son and his relationship with his nurse and
parents and with the groom who teaches him to ride. Itself,
the episode is not calculated to shock a sensitive and unsentimental reader; but, given the rest of the narrative,
I feel that Mr. Waugh might have done better to harden his
heart. Elsewhere, the beauty of his method is its complete
heartlessness. Tony Last is a good creature, fond of his
wife, of his little boy - presently killed in a hunting
accident - and of Hetton, the large, hideous Victorian-
Gothic mansion, which he spends his whole income to keep
up, but so foolish as almost to deserve the cuckoldom
which which his trust and affection are eventually requited.
Brenda, his wife, is a charming sham. There was no particular reason why she should fall in love with John Beaver, a
young man who passes his mornings by the telephone, hoping
for the eleventh-hour invitation that sometimes material-
ises; and this very lack of motive makes her infatuation,
as described - or implied - by Mr. Waugh, appear all the
more plausible. To Brenda, her *cicisbeo* is 'my Mr. Beaver,'
'poor Mr. Beaver'; and yet when the news is broken to her

of the little boy's death she experiences an immense relief
when she understands that it is her son - John Andrew - and
not her lover - plain John - who has been killed.

> She sat down on a hard little Empire chair against the
> wall, perfectly still with her hands folded in her lap.
> like a small well-brought-up child introduced into a
> room full of grown-ups. She said, 'Tell me what hap-
> pened. Why do you know about it first?'
>   'I've been down at Hetton since the week-end.'
>   'Hetton?'
>   'Don't you remember? John was going hunting to-day.'
>   She frowned, not at once taking in what he was saying.
> 'John ... John Andrew ... I ... Oh thank God....' Then
> she burst into tears.
>   She wept helplessly, turning round in the chair and
> pressing her forehead against its gilt back.

The tragedy of their love affair was its utter emptiness; Mr. Waugh's treatment of this episode is all the
more convincing because he tells us so little about the
lovers and, except by implication, does not attempt to
analyse the nature of 'poor Mr. Beaver's' physical and
emotional appeal. The love affair is scarcely a love
affair in the genuine sense; Brenda and her paramour seem
to be engaged in some absurd, rather destructive and
vaguely improper game, egged on by the gossip of their
acquaintances, stimulated - as far as Mr. Beaver is concerned - by the knowledge that such an affair adds
immensely to his social prestige, and by Brenda's belief
that she is recapturing her lost girlhood. Their friendship flickers out, as it was bound to do. How odd, then,
that the editor of a Catholic paper should charge the
book with being 'sedulously and diabolically cruel,'
'vile,' 'malodorous,' and generally quite unfit for the
bookshelves of a chaste and self-respecting Papist!(1)
Cruel 'A Handful of Dust' certainly is; a more 'moral'
book - though Mr. Waugh is too intelligent a novelist to
append any explicit moral message - has seldom come my
way. I rise from Mr. Waugh's new novel as from a reading
of one of the sterner and more uncompromising Fathers,
convinced that human life is a chaos of inclinations and
appetites, and that few appetites are strong enough to be
worth gratifying. Strange to add, I am also amused and
enlivened; but it is not the novelist's fault that he is
a brilliantly diverting storyteller.
    Mr. Waugh's narrative method is economical. His por-
traits - notably those of John Beaver and of his mother,
the indefatigable Mrs. Beaver, who lives by the practice

of that bizarre modern craft known as 'interior decoration' - are dashed in with a few savage, affectionately feline strokes. Mr. Waugh does not waste his own, or the reader's time.

Note

1   Cf. No. 52 above.

55.   EVELYN WAUGH, LETTER TO HENRY YORKE (GREEN)

September 1934

Waugh replies here to Yorke's letter quoted in the Introduction. The letter was sent from 14A Hampstead Lane, Highgate, London.

Dear Henry,
   Very many thanks for your letter of criticism.
   You must remember that to me the savages come into the category of 'people one has met and may at any moment meet again.' I think they appear fake to you largely because you don't really believe they exist. The reason they didn't take the stores was not honesty in any Sunday school sense. I think it is that they couldn't do two things at once. Going home meant going complete with their own belongings - an act of theft, though not at all repugnant, would have been a different kind of action - and they were impelled by the mechanical mouse (1) simply to go home.
   I think I agree that the Todd episode is fantastic. It is a 'conceit' in the Webster manner - wishing to bring Tony to a sad end I made it an elaborate & improbable one. I think too the sentimental episode with Therese in the ship is probably a mistake. But the Amazon stuff had to be there. The scheme was a Gothic man in the hands of savages - first Mrs Beaver etc. then the real ones, finally the silver foxes at Hetton. All that quest for a city seems to me justifiable symbolism.

Best love to you both
Evelyn

Note

1   'Letters', p. 88, prints '[motive]' here, but 'mouse'
    reads more sensibly; the savages are frightened by
    Dr Messinger's mechanical mouse.

56.   ROSE MACAULAY, 'HORIZON'

December 1946, 367

...'A Handful of Dust' ... seems up to a point more ordinary [than 'Black Mischief'], for it deals with real life:
it is a social novel about adultery, treachery, betrayal,
tragic and sordid desolation. The gaiety has gone, and
much of the wit. The characters seem to lack motive and
awareness. The theme is the destruction of a simple, dull
and honest bore by his wife, a cad without heart or affections; the social scene is one of dreary squalor and unkindness. Gone is the sparkle of 'Vile Bodies'; it is
replaced by a neat, crisp, jabbing bitterness and the
tragedy of meaningless, silly lusts. Grim events succeed
each other; wit is not lacking in their narration, but it
has become angry and adult. The last section of the book,
however, gives the tragedy a new and wholly original
baroque twist; the dull and ill-used hero, born to be betrayed, is left the victim of a fate contrived with devilish ingenuity, and will pass the rest of his life a slave,
reading Dickens aloud to his master in an Amazonian
jungle; a brilliant and terrifying *tour de force*. Later,
the author wrote an alternative ending, of a more ordinary,
cynical type; more probable, less remarkable, it has a
closer coherence with the rest of the book. 'A Handful of
Dust' seems to reach the climax of Mr. Waugh's view of
life as the meaningless jigging of barbarous nit-wits.
Pleasure, sympathetic or ironic, in their absurdities has
vanished: disgust has set in....

57.   BERNARD BERGONZI, 'BLACKFRIARS'

July-August 1964, 349-50

Bernard Bergonzi (b. 1929), poet and critic, is Professor
of English Literature at the University of Warwick. He is
author of 'Descartes and the Animals. Poems 1948-1954'
(1954), 'The Early H.G. Wells' (1961), 'Heroes' Twilight'
(1965), 'The Situation of the Novel' (1970) and 'T.S.
Eliot' (1972).

After thirty years 'A Handful of Dust' remains in the first
rank of Mr. Waugh's novels: a chilling blend of the farcical, the tragic and the macabre. It is the first of his
essays in 'serious' fiction, and in its treatment of the
doomed Gothic hero - not yet a Catholic hero - it points
forward to such ambitious later novels as 'Brideshead
Revisited' and, in particular, the 'Sword of Honour' trilogy where Guy Crouchback, a more complex and developed
version of Tony Last in the early novel (both have
appropriately suggestive surnames), realises the insuffi-
ciency of the gentlemanly ideal and is stripped of his
romantic illusions. This new edition of 'A Handful of
Dust' is supplied with an 'Alternative Ending', and Mr.
Waugh explains in an introductory note how it came to be
written; it appears that the harrowing penultimate chapter
of the novel called Du Côté de Chez Todd, in which Tony
ends his days having to read Dickens to Mr Todd in the
Brazilian jungle, was written first and originally published as a short story.(1) An American magazine (2)
wished to serialize the novel but was unable, no doubt for
copyright reasons, to reprint Du Côté de Chez Todd: to
accommodate it, Mr Waugh wrote the alternative ending
which is now reprinted.(3) The novel in that version was a
much slighter but a more homogeneous story; the whole
South American episode was dropped, and in the alternative
ending Tony Last returns to England having merely idly
cruised for a few months:

> It had been an uneventful excursion. Not for Tony were
> the ardours of serious travel, desert or jungle, moun-
> tains or pampas; he had no inclination to kill big
> game or survey unmapped tributaries. He had left England
> because, in the circumstances, it seemed the correct
> procedure, a convention hallowed in fiction and history
> by generations of disillusioned husbands. He had put
> himself in the hands of a travel agency and for lazy

months had pottered from island to island in the West
Indies, lunching at Government Houses, drinking
swizzles on club verandahs, achieving an easy popularity at Captains' tables; he had played deck quoits
and ping-pong, had danced on deck and driven with new
acquaintances on well-laid roads amid tropical vegeta-
tion. Now he was home again. He had thought less and
less of Brenda during the passing weeks.

In this version, Tony returns to Hetton and Brenda, who
by now has been abandoned by John Beaver. They settle down
to a flat loveless life, trying to pick up the threads of
their former existence. The novel ends on a mute ambiguous
note, with Brenda expecting a baby and Tony clandestinely
keeping on their flat in London, though pretending to
Brenda that he has let it. This version of the novel
centres the interest much more squarely on Brenda and Tony
as a couple, and less on Tony as a doomed romantic; it becomes a fairly conventional story of the failure of a
marriage in fashionable society, and the full implications
of Tony's Gothic aspirations are not brought out. In the
definitive version, incorporating Tony's South American
expedition and his search for the 'City', Mr Waugh achieved
a far greater imaginative power, and, in Tony's ultimate
fate, a horrifying originality. Nevertheless, it is interesting to see the alternative version, though the interest
is rather more bibliographical than critical.

Notes

1   The Man Who Liked Dickens, 'Nash's Pall Mall Magazine',
    November 1933, 18-21, 80, 82-3.
2   'Harper's Bazaar' (New York), five monthly instalments,
    June-October 1934.
3   By Special Request, first reprinted in 'Mr Loveday's
    Little Outing and Other Sad Stories' (1936).

58.   BRIGID BROPHY, 'NEW STATESMAN'

25 September 1964, 450

Brigid Brophy (b. 1929), novelist, playwright, biographer
and critic, is the author of 'Hackenfeller's Ape' (1953),
'Flesh' (1962), 'In Transit' (1969) and 'Prancing Novelist'

(a biography of Ronald Firbank, 1973).

In literary calendars 1945 is marked as the year Waugh
ended. It was the year of 'Brideshead Revisited'. To be
precise, Waugh made one further appearance - in 1948, with
'The Loved One'. After that it was clear he had been
conclusively eaten by his successor, Mr Evelyn Waugh,
English novelist, officer (ret.) and gentleman. Mr Waugh
writes a prose as fluent, lovely and lacking in intellectual content as a weeping willow: Waugh had written - and,
almost as much as written, *omitted* - in fragments and
ellipses, like a fiercer Firbank. Mr Waugh has still only
to give what 'Brideshead' calls 'a twitch upon the thread',
and he twitches tears into your eyes - but they are the
weeping-willow tears of a sentimental sensibility: Waugh
could appal your imagination. Mr Waugh, after stating that
'Brideshead,' in contrast to the first novel by Waugh, was
'*not* meant to be funny', declared its 'general theme' to
be 'romantic and eschatological': the really extraordinary
thing is that precisely the same is true of the general
theme of Waugh's novels.

Two of those, dating respectively from 1938 and 1934,
have now been republished in hard covers. 'Scoop' has
always struck me as a mere, though entertaining, after-
flutter of the fine imaginative flight which had produced
'Black Mischief'; it is a 'Black Mischief' without the
great Seal set on it, and starting from a springboard of
mistaken identity which is not quite bouncy enough to get
the invention into the air. But 'A Handful of Dust' is a
major work in the canon. It is the most open of Waugh's
books about having a tragic intention (even though it is
'The Loved One' which is subtitled a tragedy), and this
makes it Waugh's equivalent to 'The Flower Beneath the
Foot' ('Vile Bodies' being his 'Pirelli').(1) The characters
break the classical rules for tragedy by being in themselves shallow and vulgar-minded. But the essential advantage of the fragmentary method is to put perspectives round
the characters beyond their, or conceivably the author's,
vision. The irony and poetry echo in, so to speak, the
interstices of the narrative. For all the vulgarity of its
characters' values, the book is not a vulgar tragedy. The
adultery of Lady Brenda Last and her parasite John Beaver
catches a particular cold lust in action - in the very
action of cold-sweating; theirs is a sado-masochistic
relation which is expressed and enjoyed in social terms, in
the actual mental vocabulary of snobbism. At the moment
(one of the miracles of English fiction) where Brenda is
told that John has been killed and takes the John concerned

to be her lover instead of her small son, the plot-making
has plunged into contrivance: yet it is the poetic contrivance of a baroque conceit, and the plunge is not into sentimentality but into the moving and nauseating depths of
authentic bad taste.

The holes in Waugh's narrative, unlike those of Firbank,
who often drops stitches through sheer giggling inattention,
compose into a deliberate vista pointing in a single relentless direction. Like the thoughts of his Father Rothschild during the Channel crossing,(2) Waugh's imagination
works towards the Four Last Things. This the preface to the
new edition emphasises by recording that the ultimate doom
of Tony Last, the horrific perpetual motion in which he re-
reads Dickens aloud to Mr Todd in the jungle to all eter-
nities, was the first part of the book to be conceived. It
was published on its own as a short story, so when the
whole book was serialised an alternative ending had to be
written. It is printed now 'as a curiosity'; it is deft but
falls flat, because it falls short of the Last Day.

As a matter of fact, the eschatology of Waugh's imagination, like that of Catholic doctrine, distinguishes between
a Particular and a General Last Judgement - which gives
Waugh's characteristic form a climax and then a coda. In
'A Handful of Dust', Tony's particular doom is followed by
the general devastation of his beloved, neo-feudal domain by
middle-class heirs - a bourgeois sack of a fake-Gothic Rome.
In 'Vile Bodies', Agatha Runcible is immolated in her perpetual motion, as she continues in hallucination round and
round the motor-racing track; and then comes general
destruction on 'the biggest battlefield in the history of
the world' - an end-of-the world landscape imagined by a
funny Signorelli. There are three, perhaps four, novelists
now practising who write like angels. Only Waugh could
write like a baroque cherub - a baroque cherub on a funerary monument, forever ushering in the 'Dies Irae'.

Notes

1   Ronald Firbank, 'The Flower Beneath the Foot' (1923) and
    'Concerning the Eccentricities of Cardinal Pirelli'
    (1926).
2   In 'Vile Bodies'.

'Edmund Campion'

1935

59. PETER QUENNELL, 'NEW STATESMAN'

28 September 1935, 422, 424

'Edmund Campion' far outshines its neighbours.(1) Carried
away by the popularity of his recent novels, we are apt to
forget that Mr. Evelyn Waugh once produced a distinguished
volume on Dante Gabriel Rossetti, and that, like all good
writers, he is many-sided. In 'Edmund Campion' he turns
Catholic apologist. But it is not necessary to be a Catholic to enjoy the qualities of his intelligence as they
appear in his dry, witty, well-modulated yet exceedingly
effective - and, at times, exceedingly destructive - prose
style. The Catholic point of view underlies every paragraph. There are sentences, it is true - as on page 65
where, having previously described Pope Pius V as a saint
of the first order, he remarks blithely that, under Pius,
'a drove of harlots' had been 'turned loose on the campagna
to be massacred by bandits' - which may put the reader's
sympathy to a severe strain, and may cause him to wonder
at the surprising effects of faith. Yet the book is so well
written and so full of life that we accept the bias as an
incidental part of the author's narrative.

Certainly Campion himself emerges as a gallant figure.
Having distinguished himself before the Queen when she
visited Oxford and secured the patronage of Leicester, the
royal favourite, the young man might have counted on a
brilliant worldly destiny. But religious doubts and
scruples soon invaded his mind. He left Oxford, left England, and, via Dublin, where he began 'The History of Ireland' from which Mr. Waugh has extracted several delightful
pages, found his way to the loneliness and prviation of
religious exile in Douai, Prague and Rome. His biographer

makes the most of the dispassionate fortitude with which
Campion embraced a career that could only end in the rack-
ings, hanging and disembowelment that were reserved by
every religious sect of the period - including, of course,
the Catholic - for believers bold and misguided enough to
dispute its doctrinal claims. He died, as he had meant to
die, at Tyburn.... Mr. Waugh has drawn a brilliant and
convincing portrait of his hero; but he has also embel-
lished his narrative with a variety of vivacious minor
portraits, some eulogistic, some satirical, all sharply
designed. Here and there, we notice the influence of Lytton
Strachey; otherwise, Mr. Waugh's method is entirely his
own.

Note

1   Also reviewed are Günther Birkenfield's 'Augustus',
    translated by Winifred Ray (Constable 1935); Sulamith
    Ish-Kishor's 'Magnificent Hadrian' (Gollancz, 1935); and
    Evarts S. Scudder's 'Mirabeau' (Barker, 1935).

60.   GRAHAM GREENE, 'SPECTATOR'

1 November 1935, 734, 736

Graham Greene (b. 1904), novelist, playwright and critic,
is author of 'Stamboul Train' (1932), 'Brighton Rock'
(1938), 'The Power and the Glory' (1940), 'The Heart of the
Matter' (1948), 'The Quiet American' (1955), 'The Potting
Shed' (1957), 'The Honorary Consul' (1973) and 'The Human
Factor' (1978). Waugh and he became close friends when
both contributed to 'Night and Day', a short-lived arts
magazine edited by Mr Greene during 1937. In 1940-42 he
was Literary Editor of the 'Spectator'. Each valued the
other's assessment of his work highly. In a letter commenting on 'The Times' obituary Mr Greene wrote:

Evelyn Waugh was the greatest novelist of my generation.... We were deeply divided politically, we were
divided even in our conception of the same church, and
there were times when certain popular journalists tried
to push us into ... a confrontation, but [he] had an
unshakeable loyalty to his friends, even if he may have
detested their opinions and sometimes their actions.

> One could never depend on him for an easy approval or
> a warm, weak complaisance, but when one felt the need
> he was always there. ('The Times', 15 April 1966, 15)

The age of Marlowe and Drake, to which the formal courtesy
of poets has attached the name of a clever, unscrupulous
woman, would have lacked the finest expression of the
human spirit without the Douai martyrs. If we are to be
fair to Drake's character and courage, we need a sense of
historical relativity: even our appreciation of Marlowe's
poetry demands a knowledge of his position in time. But the
characters of Campion and Southwell have the qualities of
absoluteness; they can be appreciated fairly from the point
of view of any age or any faith. This does not mean that
Mr. Waugh's personal knowledge of the atmosphere which sur-
rounds a convert to Catholicism, as Campion was, and the
high contemporary standard of M. Janelle's (1) scholarship
may not add immensely to the value of their biographies.

The two books are written from superficially different
points of view. Mr. Waugh is chiefly concerned with Campion's sanctity, Mr. Janelle with Southwell's scholarship.
But in these extraordinarily complete, fused characters
the two things merge. They came to England as missionaries
of their faith; but in quite an academic sense they were
graduates of Douai, representatives of the old learning.
It was the scholarship of centuries that moved in a hang-
man's hand, when an eye-witness observed the leap of
Southwell's torn-out heart; when the spot of blood from
Campion's entrails splashed Henry Walpole's coat, so that
the course of the young man's life changed towards Tyburn,
a Latin tradition was reinforced as well as a Catholic one,
a continuity of culture which enabled, a century later,
the greatest Catholic poet to translate Virgil.... (2)

Mr. Waugh's study is a model of what a short biography
should be. Sensitive and vivid, it catches the curious
note of gaiety and gallantry (Campion in his 'brag'
addressed to the Queen's Council spoke of the priests'
determination 'never to give you over, but either to win
you to heaven, or to die upon your pikes') of an adventure
which, in spite of the inevitable end at Tyburn, was never
sombre. The graduates from Douai crossed the Channel to
martyrdom with the same enthusiasm, the same rather childish release of spirits in practical jokes, as recruits in
the first months of the War. The similarity ends at the
Channel ports. For these recruits there were no leave
trains. They had simply to stay in the line till death,
and of the few, like Parsons, who escaped, not one wrote
an 'All Quiet' in disgust and self-pity. For Campion just

as much as for Southwell faith and learning were at one.
If they belonged to a Faith which took little account of
human pain, their honours course in martyrdom at Douai
had included a study of the Stoics.

Notes

1   Pierre Janelle's 'Robert Southwell the Writer' (Sheed
    & Ward, 1935) is also reviewed.
2   John Dryden (1631-1700), 'The Works of Virgil, trans-
    lated into English Verse' (1697, undertaken 1693).

61.   J.A. KENSIT AND DESMOND MacCARTHY, 'LISTENER'

30 January 1936, 221-2

John Alfred Kensit (1881-1939?) was author of several pamphlets for the Protestant Truth Society. These documents
tended to suggest that there was an element of Roman
Catholic subversion in world affairs.
    Sir Desmond MacCarthy (1877-1952) was a distinguished
literary journalist and critic. He was author of 'The Court
Theatre 1904-1907' (1907), 'Criticism' (1932), 'Leslie
Stephen; (1937) and 'Shaw' (1951), and Editor of 'Eye
Witness' and 'Life and Letters'. During the 1940s and
1950s MacCarthy was a strong supporter of Waugh's work in
the columns of the 'Sunday Times'.

The United Protestant Council has instructed me on their
behalf to lodge a protest with the B.B.C. concerning the
review by Mr. Desmond MacCarthy of the life of Edmund
Campion. The Council feels that something ought to be said
to counter the suggestion that Edmund Campion was a kind
of injured innocent who was not righteously executed under
the laws of the Realm. It seemed obvious to us that your
reviewer was not aware of the recently recovered Vatican
documents at the Public Record Office, and that his com-
mendation of the book in question would have been modified
had he been acquainted with the plain national evidence,
for we presume that the function of a B.B.C. reviewer
would be to advise listeners whether a book professing to
be biography is reliable or deficient - and particularly
so in the case of famous figures in English history. Our
contention is that Evelyn Waugh's book has merely served up

afresh the discredited Jesuit history of Campion. May we
therefore ask you to give publicity to the following
evidence?

On February 18, 1580, two months to a day before the
Jesuits Campion and Parsons left Rome to start the Jesuit
mission in England, Pope Gregory XIII, the Duke of Flor-
ence, and the King of Spain signed a Treaty to invade
England with an army of 35,000 men. (See Venetian State
Papers, pages 650-1.) Queen Elizabeth's Secret Service
secured a copy of this Treaty a fortnight later. Campion
and Parsons landed in England about June 14, 1580. Campion
was arrested during the following year, convicted and
executed December 1, 1581. Father Pollen, S.J., gives to
us the following document, dated November 6, 1581, as his
own translation:

> Allen, Morton, Ely, Parsons, Campion*, Bosgrave*,
> Ford*, Cottam*, Filby, Colleton, Richardson, Sherwin*,
> Kirby*, Johnson*, Richton, Bryant*, John Hart, Oscliffe,
> Shert*, Orton, conspired on March 31st, 1580, in Rome,
> and on the last of April at Rheims (and at other times
> and places), to depose and kill the Queen, etc., to
> cause war, slaughter and insurrection, to change
> religion and government, to call in foreign enemies.
> For which purposes on the 20th May and at other
> times, in Rome and in other places, they excited inva-
> sion of the realm, and agreed then and on the last of
> May at Rheims that nineteen of their number should come
> to England to excite rebellion and subvert religion,
> and that on the 1st of June these nineteen, comforted
> by the rest, started from Rheims on their traitorous
> purpose. All those in court pleaded 'Not Guilty'. (Coram
> Rege Roll, K.B. 27/1279.2. P.R.O.)

The further evidence against Campion is extensive, and
this Council will be happy to supply it to any enquirer.
We may summarise it by mentioning the fact that Pope
Gregory XIII gave sanction to the plot against Elizabeth
by the Jesuits Parsons and Campion, and that the letter
from the Papal Nuncio, Bishop Sega at Madrid, to the
Cardinal of Como, the Pope's Prime Minister, was only
discovered in the Vatican in 1886. There is a copy of this
letter in Italian from the Vatican Archives, deposited in
the Public Record Office and marked: 'TRA. 9/77 Roman
Transcripts'. Similarly the document is there to be found
showing how Gregory XIII sanctioned the assassination of
Queen Elizabeth, and these were the plots which incrimi-
nated Campion.

According to the Jesuit records published by Father

Pollen, S.J., in the 'Month', January to June, 1902, there
were only *two* Jesuit priests in England in 1580 - Campion
and Parsons. Father Pollen says, concerning the Nuncio
Sega's letter: 'Parsons and Campion seem to be meant'.
This settles the long disputed question as to whether
Campion was involved in the conspiracy to dethrone or
murder Queen Elizabeth.

We trust we have indicated sufficiently the strength of
the Protestant objection to the white-washing of Campion.
Our conviction is your reviewer did not know of the documents we draw attention to.

London, E.C.4   J.A. KENSIT
            Acting Hon. Secretary, United Protestant Council

*We have sent Mr. Kensit's letter to Mr. Desmond MacCarthy,
who replies:*

In my brief comments on Mr. Evelyn Waugh's 'Life of Campion, S.J.', to which the above letter refers, I spoke of
Campion as a brave, saintly young man who suffered death
and torture in the cause of his religion; and I praised Mr.
Waugh for using well the evidence confirming that view of
his character. There is plenty of it.

I am far from being a specialist on the reign of Elizabeth, and the Vatican documents mentioned above were unknown to me then. But I possessed what is common knowledge: that during the first dozen years of her reign
Roman Catholics were only fined, but that after the Pope
excommunicated the Queen and commanded her Catholic subjects to abjure their allegiance (1570), persecution of
them became drastic. Everybody knows that the object of
Papal foreign policy from that date onward was to attempt
to bring England back into the Catholic fold, by fostering
devotion to the old Faith, by encouraging sedition, and
ultimately by conquest (the Armada). All English Catholics after 1570 were therefore in the position of French
aristocrats in revolutionary France after the Allies prepared to invade it. They were mistrusted as citizens whose
interests and sympathies must be divided, and whose intentions might even be hostile. In both cases, there were
many executions of men who had never conspired against
their government, though they detested it. The object of
the Jesuit mission was primarily religious, to help those
priests and Catholics who were striving to keep the old
Faith alive, and to prevent the squires of England
slipping towards acquiescence in the new ritual. But as
its success might have involved revolution and the de-
thronement of the Queen, the Crown hunted them down and
hanged them as *traitors* (about 120 of them), while their
co-religionists, who were numerous, naturally regarded them
as martyrs.

The position of the Catholic Church today with regard to these men is, I understand, to distinguish between those of them whose aim was to foment plots against the Queen or to prepare a revolt in case of foreign invasion, and those who strove religiously to keep Catholicism alive. Only the latter can be regarded as having suffered martyrdom for their Faith. The question at issue between me and the spokesman of the United Protestant Council is whether or not Campion is rightly included among them. Did he come to England to plot the murder of Elizabeth? I took the view that he was not that sort of man. It is a view shared by historians of repute. Professor George Trevelyan, who is not a historian of Catholic temper, let alone convictions, says: 'Of the two most noted leaders of the Jesuit mission in England, Campion, who cared more for religion than politics, was unfortunately caught and hanged, while the indubitable traitor, Parsons, escaped abroad to work for a Spanish invasion' ('History of England', page 363). Note the 'unfortunately', implying that Campion's torture and execution were a miscarriage of justice. 'The Cambridge Modern History's' comment (Vol. III, page 287) says that the government 'brought him with several of his companions to the gallows on the charge of a treasonable plot of which they were manifestly innocent'. 'The Cambridge Modern History' is an unemotional, documented survey, in which each period has been treated by an acknowledged authority on it; you can hardly expect a scholar to be more emphatic than that.

My view of Campion's case was not, therefore, without backing of weight. Indeed, a B.B.C. critic, not himself a researcher, could hardly run counter to it; while, after reading Campion's life, I was more convinced than ever myself that he was *not* the sort of man to plot murder. Nor is the evidence, new to me, and now brought forward, conclusive. The quotation of the document dated November 6, 1581, is not 'evidence', but a restatement of the indictment, the justice of which is precisely what is in question.

Moreover, Mr. Kensit's references to Gregory XIII's offer of absolution to anyone compassing the death of the Queen and to the letter of Bishop Sega (Record Office 9/77, Roman Transcripts) are misleading. The public might suppose from his words, 'Gregory XIII gave sanction to the plot against Elizabeth *by the Jesuits, Parsons and Campion*', that this document mentions them. It does not. It is merely a general offer of absolution to anyone who 'sends her out of the world with the pious intention of doing God service'; and it continues: 'And so if those English nobles decide actually to undertake so glorious a work, your lordship can assure them that they do not commit any sin'. While the letter of Bishop Sega, to which the Pope's letter is a reply, runs as follows: 'Among other things Humphrey Ely tells me, one is a great secret of some Island (English) nobleman and of the Jesuit Fathers themselves. It was that the said nobles are determined to try to kill the Queen with their own hands if they are assured, at least verbally, by His Holiness that in doing so they would not fall into sin'. Now, only two Jesuit fathers (there may have been more) are *known* (according to Father Pollen, S.J.) to have been in England at that date, Parsons and Campion. But all this document indicates is a probability that Campion was aware of plots among the Catholic nobles to kill the Queen. Even without that letter, I should have supposed him likely to be aware of what many Protestants in England had an inkling. But this letter in itself is no proof whatever that he was concerned in a plot; and at his trial, apparently, no satisfactory evidence of that was forthcoming. At least the legal-minded Protestant historian, Hallam, was shocked when he read it: 'The prosecution was as unfairly conducted and supported by as slender evidence as any, perhaps, that can be found in our books' ('Constitutional History', Vol I, page 143), which, as those who have read our old trials know, is saying a good deal. The complicity of the Pope is, of course, proved up to the hilt. It always has been known that the Papal policy was to stir up sedition in England and attack from without. But the complicity of Campion is not proved. His character and career point rather to his having been one of those missionaries whose aim was to foster devotion to the old Faith, and who, therefore, may be said to have suffered martyrdom for his religion.

I am glad, however, that any talk of mine should have roused controversy. This is an age of discussion and it is chiefly to the Reformation that we owe it. What I resent is not Mr. Kensit's endeavour to prove what I said untrue, but his writing first to the Director-General, suggesting that I was an unfit person to review historical or biographical books for the B.B.C., because I had not known (apparently) of certain Vatican documents, and expressed views inconsistent with the conclusions drawn from them by the United Protestant Council on an exceedingly moot point. My chief objection to the Catholic Church has always been that in the past she had done her best to muzzle those who disagreed with her, and this seemed hardly in harmony with the better side of the Protestant tradition. Something most important is at stake. If listeners cannot tolerate hearing any wireless comment with which they disagree, either the Talks Department will find itself in the

predicament of a chameleon on a tartan plaid, or have to
confine itself to a dribble of drab, non-committal commentary on stone-cold topics: - worse.
London, W.1.   DESMOND MacCARTHY

(With reference to the concluding paragraph in Mr. Desmond MacCarthy's letter, this refers to a passage in the
original letter from the United Protestant Council signed
by Mr. J.A. Kensit and dated December 12, 1935. This
letter was not written for publication, but we feel it
necessary to say that the B.B.C. does not put on the passage in question the construction which Mr. MacCarthy puts
upon it in his letter. The passage referred to, which we
have now obtained Mr. Kensit's persmission to quote, runs
as follows: 'The Council respectfully suggest to you that
in future no reviewers should be employed by the B.B.C. to
review historical and biographical works on historical
characters, who have not an up-to-date knowledge of the
Vatican documents (or transcripts) and other State papers
at the Public Record Office'. - EDITOR, THE 'LISTENER')

Note

1 [Kensit's note] The men whose names are starred were
   actually executed. Allen, Ely, Morton and Parsons were
   not tried as they fled to the Continent and remained
   there for the rest of their lives. The dates are those
   of the indictments. Writs concerning Campion are also
   on the Controllment Roll. (Ref. K.B. 29/217. Num. 24
   and 25, P.R.O.)

62.   EVELYN WAUGH, 'LISTENER'

26 February 1936, 410-11

Waugh is referring here to Kensit's second letter to the
'Listener' (12 February 1936, 318-19) in which he ampli-
fied what he saw as the 'facts' of the Campion story.
Following this there were three more letters, two from Fr
Hicks, then Historiographer of the English Province,
defending Waugh's account (4 March 1936, 457-8, and 1
April 1936, 642) and another from Kensit (18 March 1936,
552-3) hammering home the views of the United Protestant
Council. The Editor then closed the correspondence but

Kensit did not let the matter rest. Under the imprint of
the Protestant Truth Society he produced a lengthly pamphlet entitled 'The Campion-Parsons Invasion Plot' (May
1937) reprinting the entire correspondence.

I have never (except with singular lack of success in the
Final Schools at Oxford) sought reputation as a historical
scholar; if I did so, I do not think the fact of Mr. Kensit's opposition would seriously imperil it; I do not care
a hoot that Mr. Kensit thinks my life of Edmund Campion a
'second-hand hearsay romance of the novelist'. But it *is*
important that readers of the 'Listener', who lack the
time and inclination for historical reading, should be left
with the impression that new, damning evidence against
Campion has lately come to light, reversing the judgment of
previous history, and fouling a name which all of my Faith
and countless others, who know the true marks of heroism
and sanctity, hold in the highest honour.

  If Mr. Kensit had had the patience to read my little
book attentively, he would have found the topics he
raises discussed in some detail; he would also have found
listed in the bibliography the work upon which he mainly
relies - Professor Meyer's 'The English Catholics under
Queen Elizabeth'. I knew all about the Cardinal of Como -
Nuncio Sega correspondence. I did not mention it because it
seemed to me irrelevant to the subject about which I was
writing. Professor Meyer himself, summing up the case
against Campion, says: 'The attempt to prove conspiracy had
failed entirely, and was bound to fail because the conspiracy had no existence'. Professor Pollard, reviewing the
work, supported this view. These are first-class historians, non-Catholics, fully informed of the most recent documents. It is not surprising that Mr. Kensit came to a different conclusion, but it must be made clear that the
division is not one between historians who wrote prior to
the publication of the Sega correspondence and those who
wrote after it, but between the United Protestant Council
and the massed wisdom and knowledge of European scholarship.

  Of course there were English Catholics in Elizabeth's
reign who saw in revolution and assassination the only
cure for their ills. I constantly referred to them in my
book. Elizabeth's legislation left the Catholics with the
choice of three positions - apostasy, conspiracy or sacrifice. There was no place for legitimate opposition under
the Tudors. The reason that we love Campion was that his
teaching and example showed the way of sacrifice.

  I cannot rewrite my book in the form of a letter.

I, too, was working from the 'State Trials' used by Mr.
Kensit. Anyone who reads that account with an open mind
must realise not only that the charges were unproved, but
that they were made in bad faith. Mr. Kensit slaps them
down on the table as though the very fact of their having
been made proved their truth. He assumes what he has to
prove when he talks about 'Campion's Oath forms'. Personally, I think it very doubtful if they ever existed at
all. What is certain is that no connection was ever established between them and Campion. They were not found in
'his lodgings', as Mr. Kensit states. Campion had no lodgings; he was constantly on the move. They were not found in
his saddle-bags. The most that his accusers dared say was
that they were found in houses where Campion had visited.
Mr. Kensit has taken on himself the task of amplifying the
evidence which even the perjurers and *agents provocateurs*
of Cecil and Walsingham shrank from avowing.

Humphrey Ely was barely, if at all, known to Campion.
He was a bitter opponent of Parsons and the Society of
Jesus. Campion and Parsons were *not* 'inseparable companions'. They had not met before Campion was called to Rome
for his journey to England; on the road to Rheims they
seemed to have had little contact; they travelled to
England separately and during their joint mission spent
only a few days in one another's company.

At Lyford, in the sermon quoted, Campion was preaching
to a congregation consisting mainly of pious old ladies.
Does Mr. Kensit really think he was exhorting them to
armed rebellion and assassination?

There were certainly two other Jesuits in England at
the same time as Campion and Parsons; they are named in
my book. I am forced to the conclusion that Mr. Kensit has
not read it and that his rage is aroused, not that an inaccurate work should be unjustly commended, but that any
book by a Catholic about a Catholic should be mentioned at
all by anyone anywhere.

What a funny man he must be.

63.   ROSE MACAULAY, 'HORIZON'

December 1946, 368-70

What has ... gone from his view is detachment. In ['Edmund
Campion'] he is no longer objective: he has come down on a
side. In art so naturally ironic and detached as his, this
is a serious loss; it undermines his best gifts. And it

was unlucky that the first of his partisan, side-taking
books should have been a work of history, where objective-
ness and truth to fact should be a *sine qua non*. In
'Edmund Campion' there is too little of both, though there
is interest, brilliance, imagination, and sympathetic
interpretation. But it is like a barrister's brief, omitting all that does not support his case. It would seem
scarcely credible, for instance, that any one should undertake a serious life of Campion without familiarity with the
State Papers of the time, the letters that passed between
Madrid, the Vatican, the Spanish ambassador in London,
Cardinal Allen of Douai, Father Parsons, Dr. Nicholas
Sanders, and the others of the 'Spanish party' among the
English Catholics (which included nearly all the prominent
Jesuits abroad). Yet Mr. Waugh shows no signs throughout
his book (or in his lists of references) of having read
these, or of familiarity with the unceasing plots,
intrigues and correspondence that went on about 'the enterprise of England', the plots to invade Britain, murder or
depose Elizabeth, and set Philip of Spain on the English
throne. The Spanish ambassador wrote continually of his
hope to see his Majesty in speedy possession of his realm,
that heresy might be extirpated and the Faith restored.
English Catholics were absolved from their allegiance, and
those who obeyed the Queen's laws put under sentence of
anathema by a Bull whose provocative folly caused even
Philip and Alva to protest; for, said Philip, 'it will
drive the queen and her friends to oppress and persecute
the few good Catholics who remain in England'. The English
exiles were in perpetual intrigue - 'traitors who gape
daily for the death of the queen', as an agent wrote home.
Madrid and Rome financed and equipped one fruitless invasion expedition after another. Yet Mr. Waugh can write
almost as if Catholic plots were an invention of Cecil's.
Campion was, indeed, an innocent non-political missionary;
but Parsons, his chief colleague in the mission, was
steeped, like Dr. Allen, in conspiracy. As an earlier biographer of Campion observes, though Campion himself disapproved of the papal policy, and laboured merely to make
every Englishman a Catholic, his friends wished to make
every Catholic a conspirator. Allen wrote to the Pope that
English Catholics were already conspirators, and would
welcome Catholic invaders of any nation, since they detested their own government more than any foreign prince, and
would all join the Pope's army if it landed, and help to
depose 'this Jezebel'. Such views were an exile's pipe-
dream, of a kind familiar in history: their answer was the
English Catholic resistance to the Armada, when nearly all
Allen's fifth column let him down. But even the innocent

Campion's mission was not, as has been pointed out by historians, purely spiritual; indeed, how could it be, since Catholics were contending for more than their lives? There are other indications of bias (that natural but deadly poison to historians) than the glossing over of the political side of these heroic expeditions. That fanatical religious idealist, Pope Pius V, with his notorious record as Grand Inquisitor, his incitement to murder and war, his rejoicing over the massacre of the Huguenots, is described as a saint; this is surely to debase the currency of words. Then Mr. Waugh's excessive hostility to the Anglican Church leads him too often into inaccuracies, as when he calls it 'the crazy, fashionable Calvinism' (ignoring the incessant war waged against it after the Elizabethan settlement by Calvinists and other Puritans) and repeats several times that it had no sacraments. What he of course means is that, in the eyes of his Church, Anglican sacraments were not valid; but, from the way he puts it, one might not gather that the deluded Anglicans believed that they were, or that they were taught that they 'verily and indeed received the body and blood of Christ' in communion. After all, the Prayer Book was mainly translated (as Milton was to complain bitterly) from Catholic missals, though mutilated; it earned the undying hatred of the Puritan party, who were persecuted under Elizabeth with cruel severity. But Mr. Waugh dislikes this wary *via media* so much that he relegates it to the outer darkness of the Protestant left wing. To dislike the deplorable outrages of the Reformation, and many aspects of the whole business, is natural enough; indeed, it is rather hard not to; but to take ecclesiastical sides is, to a style such as Mr. Waugh's, part of whose charm is in ironic objectivity and detachment, fatal. Partisanship should be left to thunderers; one cannot have it both ways, and something must be sacrificed to individual style.

Though 'Campion' is a very readable and often moving book, and its brave and touching story beautifully told, greater accuracy and balance would have given it a finer urbane polish; as it is, it remains a little one-sided and shrill, and strengthens one's view that its author betrays his gifts when he deserts his own idiom and convention....

64.   RICHARD SULLIVAN, 'NEW YORK TIMES BOOK REVIEW'

7 July 1946, 6

Richard Sullivan (b. 1908), novelist, playwright and short-
story-writer, is the author of 'Our Lady's Tumbler' (1940),
'First Citizen' (1948), 'The Fresh and Open Sky and Other
Stories' (1950), '311 Congress Court' (1953) and 'The Three
Kings' (1956).

The story of this book may be summed up very simply as that
of a man tracked down and killed because of his religion.
More specifically, it is that of a priest put to violent
death for ministering to men of his own country and of his
own faith. The charge against him is, of course, ostentatiously political. According to the hunters he is guilty
of treason. Under the sad and constant confusion to which
human motives may be subjected, this man's purely spiritual
activities are interpreted, with considerable difficulty,
as antagonistic to the State. And so all the familiar
machinery of paid informers, perjurers, a prejudiced court
and the private application of torture goes into operation.
The State puts the man briskly through the travesty of a
formal trial and thus with a solemn show of legality seeks
to justify in advance the sentence which it is infamously
determined to impose upon him.
     Thus the story is, in the abstract, a timeless and a
changeless one, although in the concrete it has permitted
innumerable variations of name, place and condition. The
drama of the human being caught in the conflict between
obligations of conscience on the one side and obligations
to the State on the other goes back in literature at least
as far as 'Antigone.' In the real experience which is the
base of all literature it no doubt goes back even further.
And no one can doubt that it makes contemporary drama.
(Graham Greene - in that magnificent novel lately reissued
under the title, 'The Power and the Glory' - recorded his
fictional version of the material, using one set of recent
circumstances and involving imagined characters.)
     Mr. Waugh, working not in fiction, but in this factual
study of the Elizabethan Jesuit and scholar, Edmund Campion
(which was first published in England eleven years ago),
prefaces his new American edition with the explicit reminder that 'in fragments and whispers we get news of other
saints in the prison camps of eastern and southeastern
Europe, of cruelty and degradation more frightful than
anything in Tudor England and of the same pure light

shining in the darkness, uncomprehended. The hunted,
trapped, murdered priest is amongst us again, and the voice
of Campion comes to us across the centuries as though he
were walking at our side.'

It is a strangely intimate, strangely clear voice, that
of Campion, as rendered in this little book. Not at all the
strident or harsh tone of the fanatic, never the insistent
sanctimoniousness of the zealot, anything but the holy
murmuring of the conventionalized martyr - it is merely the
charming, companionable, intelligent voice of a gracious
man. The sort of man, indeed, who would be embarrassed at
any mention, let alone praise, of his own almost incredible
heroism. A quiet but spectacular man, very gentle and
strong, very manlike.

For above all, it is the manliness, the humanity of
Campion which shows through most impressively in this
rendering. From his early days at Oxford, where he served
prominently in the academic functions which celebrated the
visit of Queen Elizabeth, to the day fifteen years later
when, at Tyburn, under sentence of the same Queen's Lord
Chief Justice, he was hanged, mutilated, beheaded and
quartered, Campion remains wonderfully and beautifully a
human being, warm, vital and real. Waugh does not present
him in anything like a posed portrait. Reading, one feels
the personality grow and change - he is first the entranc-
ing scholar, occupied chiefly with maintaining in a turbulent age his own intellectual serenity. He is then the
uncertain exile, groping in the spiritual confusion of the
time for his own soul; he becomes the quiet Jesuit,
obedient to his mission to teach for years at Prague; and
then he is all at once, in a brief glory, one of the
priests smuggled from the Continent into England, to preach
there the Old Faith to the recusant Catholic population, in
secrecy and under peril.

So far as substance is concerned there is probably nothing at all new in this treatment. The facts were known
before; they are here diligently and accurately reassembled;
and the author disavows any claim to either original or
searching scholarship. Yet there is genuine illumination in,
say, such a piece of full analysis as Waugh devotes to the
four conferences, the public disputations in which Campion,
as prisoner, denied all means of preparation and subjected
to impossible controls, valiantly justified his position,
both religious and political, against a battery of opponents. And there is great richness in the discussion and
inclusion of the famous 'Brag' - the 'statement of aims'
which at Thomas Pounde's suggestion Campion wrote soon
after his arrival in England and which, though it was
intended simply to anticipate and dispose of the charges

which might later be leveled against him, actually turned
in its wide underground circulation into a triumphant mani-
festo of his mission.

Throughout Waugh's whole compact little book there is
such a right choice of detail from the abundant material,
such consistent understanding and insight, such a true
distribution of emphasis, such remarkable interpretation
both of people and of period, that in a very real way this
work becomes, not merely a craftsmanlike reorganization of
the data but a fresh and creative revelation of the subject.

The characterization of Campion - and that of his fellow-
Jesuit, Parsons, and of the professional priest-hunter,
George Eliot, of Elizabeth herself, and Cecil and Leicester,
each of whom played some part in the drama - suggests not
so much Waugh the novelist as Waugh the accomplished man of
letters. Indeed, in this work in general there is nothing
of the manner of fiction except the practiced skill, the
firm control of the medium.

Readers familiar only with Waugh's satirical novels may
indeed be startled by his 'Edmund Campion' (as some of them
were recently startled by his 'Brideshead Revisited'), for
this is grave work, hardly to be believed of the author of
'Vile Bodies' or 'Decline and Fall.' In quite another way
'Brideshead Revisited' will, of course, find here, despite
the serious religious concern which that novel and this
study have in common, a natural and complete difference in
method, approach and tone.

It is possible, however, for those who recall the
author's full range to speculate - pleasantly if uncertainly - on the place which 'Edmund Campion' may hold in
his general progression as a writer. From mischievous,
engaging, often formidable but always minor satires, Waugh
has lately turned, in his fiction, to a major theme; the
question of his full success in handling this major theme
need not be again debated here; but it is possible to
wonder if, eleven years ago, on the initial publication
of 'Edmund Campion,' the break to come was not prefigured -
if this excellent little study of the Elizabethan priest
did not, queerly yet strictly, foreshadow the profound
eschatological concerns which much later the author was to
exhibit in his fiction.

65.   EDMUND WILSON, 'NEW YORKER'

13 July 1946, 81

Edmund Wilson (1895-1972) was an American novelist, poet
and playwright, but he is primarily remembered as a literary critic and political historian. He was Associate Editor
of the 'New Republic', 1926-32, and book reviewer for the
'New Yorker', 1944-8. He was author of 'I Thought of Daisy'
(1929), 'Poet's Farewell' (1929), 'Axel's Castle' (1931),
'This Room and This Gin and These Sandwiches' (1937), 'The
Triple Thinkers' (1938), 'To the Finland Station' (1940),
'The Wound and the Bow' (1941), 'Classics and Commercials'
(1950), 'A Piece of My Mind' (1956) and 'Prelude' (1967).
   Wilson's writings reached a wide public who trusted his
judgment. He had warmly praised the early novels in 'Never
Apologise, Never Explain': The Art of Evelyn Waugh (NY, 4
March 1944). To lose Wilson's approval as Waugh did with
'Brideshead' (No. 99) might have represented a serious
blow to both reputation and income. But Waugh cared little
for his opinions as he explained in Fan-Fare (No. 100).
Perhaps not so strangely, it was the radical sentimentality
condemned by Wilson and others that caused the novel to
become a best-seller on both sides of the Atlantic. The
intensity of Wilson's displeasure with 'Brideshead' (and,
of course, with this second edition of 'Campion' which followed on the heels of that book's success) was undoubtedly
exacerbated by an unfortunate meeting with Waugh in April
1945. At a dinner party given by Cyril Connolly Waugh
deliberately goaded Wilson on the subject of his book of
stories, 'Memoirs of Hecate County', which had been refused
by his publishers on the grounds of obscenity, and concluded by suggesting that he publish in Cairo. See Sykes, pp.
284-7.

When Evelyn Waugh was converted to Catholicism by the
Jesuit Father D'Arcy, he wrote, as a tribute to D'Arcy and
in celebration of the rebuilding of Campion Hall, the
Jesuit college at Oxford, a short biography of Edmund Campion, the Elizabethan Jesuit martyr. This book, which first
appeared in 1935, has now been republished by Little,
Brown. The story is quite soberly and simply told - with no
attempt to create historical atmosphere - and it is not uninteresting to read. Campion is very impressive in the
utterances which Mr. Waugh quotes. A man of intellectual
distinction, exalted religious vocations, and great moral
and physical courage, he was the victim, after the suppression of Catholicism in England, of one of those

political frameups which, though not carried out on the
same enormous scale or engineered with the same efficiency
as those of our own day, were already a feature of the
struggle between Catholicism and Protestantism.

Mr. Waugh's version of history, however, is, in its
main lines, more or less in the vein of '1066 and All
That.' Catholicism was a Good Thing and Protestantism was
a Bad Thing, and that is all that needs to be said about
it. The book is chiefly valuable for providing a glimpse
of Mr. Waugh's general view of modern England. The triumph
of Protestantism under Elizabeth meant, he writes, that the
country was 'secure, independent, insular; the course of
her history lay plain ahead: competitive nationalism, competitive industrialism, competitive imperialism, the looms
and coal mines and counting houses, the joint stock companies and the cantonments; the power and the weakness of
great possessions.' For him, Protestantism is not merely
one of the phases of the rise of the middle class; it is
the cause of all the phenomena mentioned above. And, in
recounting this incident in the history of the great period
of religious intolerance, he continually insists on the
cruelties of the Protestant persecution of Catholics but
passes lightly over any instance - such as the St. Bartho-
lomew Day's massacre - of the horrors committed by Catholics against Protestants. If we had no source but Mr.
Waugh, we might assume that the Society of Jesus had always
consisted solely of pure-hearted servants of God and that
no racks had been operated or faggots lit by the followers
of St. Ignatius de Loyola.

'Mr Loveday's Little Outing and Other Sad Stories'

1936

66. UNSIGNED REVIEW, 'TIMES LITERARY SUPPLEMENT'

4 July 1936, 561-2

This collection of short stories is, we are informed, the
first of its kind to be published by Mr. Waugh. They are
not sad stories of the deaths of kings, for Mr. Waugh is
not constrained to introduce eminence in any form to suggest catastrophe. On the contrary he eschews it. The sadness resides in this - that somebody is sold; if the reader
chooses to sympathize with the somebody, that is his
affair; Mr. Waugh has done nothing to encourage him; his
responsibility is at an end when the sell has been completed. The stories are magazine stories if magazine
stories are stories in which character is subordinated to
situation. But they are not magazine stories if magazine
stories are stories which involve the great passions. With
Mr. Waugh what is involved is of no account except to
people who are of no account; his skill lies in construct-
ing his situation out of these nothings.

The medium of the short story lends itself to that consciousness of futility which it is laid upon him to express. He has the wit and the sense of style to hold the
floor unsupported by his subject when the short sharp
shock is but twenty pages away, whereas when he expands
themes of no more general significance to 300 pages his
nonentities may fail with the reader to sustain the burden
of the deferred catastrophe. And the more so that if all
is vanity it is incongruous to take so much pains to say
it. For though Mr. Waugh's style is at the opposite pole
from the laboured, we cannot believe that he just threw off
his economical phrases and descending scales. These are

vehicles for his own bitterness - to be dwelt on for their
virtuosity; but they would be obtrusive if he had conferred
on the people to whom they are applied any vitality of
their own.
   One pair may be taken as generally representative:-

   The marriage of Tom Watch and Angela Trench-
   Troubridge was, perhaps, as unimportant an event as has
   occurred within living memory. No feature was lacking in
   the previous histories of the two young people, in their
   engagement or their wedding, that could make them completely typical of all that was most unremarkable in
   modern social conditions.

If we qualify 'modern social conditions' with 'as conceived by Mr. Waugh' it has to be granted him that he has
constructed for his two young people a honeymoon trip that
justifies the apparently barren exordium and yet contains
a surprise.
   In the majority of the eleven short stories the interest
does not lie in the surprise of the climax - for we can
foresee its nature - but in the detachment and austerity
with which the inevitable ineptitude is formulated. Given
a lunatic whose life since he was certified for killing a
chance-met girl on a bicycle has been such a model of tact-
ful kindness that he is allowed an outing when at last he
asks for it, we guess what the lunatic will do. Given a
big property and a hard-up Waughian man who must inherit it
if the wife of the owner continues childless, we know what
the Waughian man will do.

67. C.M. BOWRA, 'SPECTATOR'

10 July 1936, 70

Sir Cecil Maurice Bowra (1898-1971) was a celebrated
Fellow and later Warden of Wadham College, Oxford, and
Professor of Poetry, 1946-51. Although he was a Classics
scholar, his interests stretched to cover contemporary
literature and he was particularly keen to promote his
coterie of undergraduates who included at one time Anthony
Powell and John Betjeman. He wrote 'Tradition and Design in
The Iliad' (1930), 'The Heritage of Symbolism' (1943) and
'The Romantic Imagination' (1950). Waugh became friends
with him after publishing 'Decline and Fall' but he was

always mildly resentful that 'Maurice' had not noticed his
talent earlier.

Mr. Waugh, like Mr. Maugham, succeeds at every kind of
writing he attempts. Fresh from winning the Hawthornden
Prize with a biography of a persecuted priest, he now
publishes his first book of short stories. Most of them
have appeared in magazines, and though the criminal lunatic in the first has had his name changed from Cruttwell
to Loveday,(1) they do not seem to be much altered. But
Mr. Waugh's devoted readers do not all read magazines, and
it is excellent to have these examples of his great
talent collected. He manages the short story with the confident touch of an accomplished master, and it is interesting to see how he impresses his own personality and literary method on it. These stories, like Mr. Waugh's novels
are created out of his own bitter experience. They belong
to that special kind of comedy, which he has invented,
where failure, frustration, guilt, persecution-mania,
sorrow and death become ludicrous. It is impossible not to
laugh at what he writes, and equally impossible not to feel
that it is all extremely painful and tragic. These stories
may lack some of Mr. Waugh's more sustained flights of
fancy, because there is no room for prolonged nightmares
like Tony Last's journey through the jungle or for lyrical
flights like Sir Samson Courtenay in his bath. But his
essential qualities are in them, as the words 'Sad Stories'
in the title show.

The stories are not dated, but they show different levels of skill, and a historical critic might deduce a chronology from the degree of independence shown in each. Out
of Depth, for instance, is a failure, an attempt on the
macabre which suggests unfavourable comparisons with so
oddly assorted a pair as H.G. Wells and R.H. Benson, and
even has echoes of R.A. Knox. By Special Request is an
alternative ending to 'A Handful of Dust.' Those who are
haunted by the thought of Tony endlessly reading Dickens
aloud in the Brazilian forest may turn with hope to it.
But they will not be comforted. Tony comes back to Brenda,
and life at Hetton is resumed, but the dream is shattered
and the happy ending is squalid and depressing. Incident
in Azania too, is a kind of sequel to 'Black Mischief.'
In it Mr Waugh depicts the limited suburban life of the
country after it has passed under Anglo-French control and
tells a delightful story of a girl whose tastes were not
so conventional as the small English circle at first
thought.

The real creations of the book are those stories in

which Mr. Waugh exploits his special taste for ironical
turns of events and tells how something that looked full
of promise turns out for the worst. The kind and apparently
sane inmate of an asylum is released and at once strangles
a young woman on a bicycle; a young man, going to the colonies, gives to his betrothed a dog who is so faithful in
dealing with admirers that eventually he condemns her to
spinsterhood by biting off her one attraction, her nose;
an old Irish lady decides to give a magnificent party in
her decaying house, but nobody comes to it because she has
not sent out the invitations. In this peculiar art of
exploiting disappointment and failure Mr. Waugh is truly
himself, and those who admire his novels will find here
something very much to their taste. And this admirable
irony is placed with all Mr. Waugh's skill in a setting
which is always vivid, amusing, and constructed with consummate economy. Nothing could be better than the decaying
Irish house in Bella Fleace gave a Party or the garrulous,
busy, mad peer in Mr. Loveday's Little Outing. The world of
Mr. Waugh's imagination is intensely alive, because every
item in it has been chosen with a perfect literary tact and
unfailing sense of its place in the complete structure. It
may not be everybody's world, but it has its own laws, and
its own indubitable charm. Is it too much to ask of Mr.
Waugh that he will abandon biography to lesser men and give
us more novels and more short stories like these?

Note

1   Waugh had a long-standing feud with C.R.M.F. Cruttwell,
    Dean and Senior History Tutor of Hertford College,
    Oxford. It began with Cruttwell's displeasure with
    Waugh's laziness as an undergraduate and continued
    through the 1930s with the novelist giving his old
    tutor's name to a series of ludicrous minor fictional
    characters. Bowra shared Waugh's aversion for Cruttwell
    (nominally, at least, his colleague) and is advertising
    the poor man's discomfiture here.

'Waugh in Abyssinia'

1936

68. MICHAEL DE LA BEDOYERE, 'CATHOLIC HERALD'

31 October 1936, 3

Count Michael de la Bedoyere (1900-73) was Editor of the
'Catholic Herald', 1934-62, and 'Search Newsletter', 1962-8,
and author of 'Christianity in the Market Place' (1943),
'The Life of Baron Von Hügel' (1951), and 'The Meddlesome
Friar' (1958).

In recognising Italian sovereignty over Abyssinia Germany
has led the way for the other great powers to follow suit at
their convenience and the convenience of their subjects'
moral feelings.

It is therefore an interesting moment to read Evelyn
Waugh's approval of the Italian occupation, expressed in
the following words:

> Rome will bring to Abyssinia the inestimable gifts of
> fine workmanship and clear judgment - the two determin-
> ing qualities of the human spirit, by which alone, under
> God, man grows and flourishes.

In 'Waugh in Abyssinia' Evelyn Waugh recounts his experiences as a war correspondent and the impressions he
obtained from a second journey to Abyssinia under the
Italian occupation.

The fine workmanship and clear judgment of which he so
highly approves are very conspicuous in this survey of the
whole affair. Survey is not the right word, for it denotes
precisely the abstract, distant view with which the world,
and Britain in particular, approached the problem. Waugh's

method has been to reach clear judgment through his own
concrete, unbiassed, workmanlike experience.

There is no attempt here to answer the moral and legal
arguments of the League - a hopeless task for, given the
League premises and the alleged facts on which its reasoning was based, there is no answer - but, instead, to bring
home to the reader the fact that the League was thinking of
something quite different from the Abyssinian situation as
it really was.

Scholastic ethicians have a phrase 'change of matter' to
which they have recourse when they wish to show that
apparent breaches of the Natural Law are not breaches at
all. Whatever it may really stand for, it seems to apply
here. There was a change of matter as between the League's
argument and the Italian argument.

Without ever saying so in so many words, for Waugh is
too good a writer ever to plead, he leaves the reader certain of the fact that there never was such a thing as
Abyssinia: a sovereign State, in the way the League understands the term and in view of which the League machinery
was thought out.

Abyssinia, materially and spiritually, stood for
slovenliness and confusion, the exact opposites of what
Waugh considers the two determining qualities of the human
spirit. Not only was its political system the merest
veneer covering a barbaric anarchy - in itself not necessarily a bad thing - but its achievement was shoddy, inert,
sub-human, destined to wither.

Waugh - and this is the importance of his book - is not
taking as his standard the achievement of what we call
civilisation; he is taking the eternal standard of the
human spirit.

Abyssinia was shoddy compared with other barbaric tribes,
the Middle-ages, England, quite as much as with the Fascist
ideal of Italy.

He never defends Italy's action, but makes the reader
appreciate how aware Italy was, through constant troubles
and close contact of the shoddiness of Abyssinia, how
impossible it was for her to see this country in the light
in which the well-intentioned but abstract moralists of the
League persuaded themselves to regard her.

That the greater part of Abyssinia lay within Italy's
legitimate sphere of influence had been internationally
recognised and, had Menelik's (1) Empire broken up earlier
in the century, as was expected, Italy would have automatically stepped in. Disappointed in her colonial ambitions at the peace treaty, Italy tried one way after

another to come to an understanding with the country that
lay beyond her African colonies even to the extent of
sponsoring her entry into the League.

By that immense mistake Italy put Abyssinia under the
protection of the world, but Abyssinia itself was not capable of rising to the status of a member of that international society of nations. She remained the same impossible, barbarous, provoking hopeless neighbour. It was
evident that she had within her no seeds of new life, but
must sooner or later come under the domination of an
imported civilisation. Italians - and any honest observer
- could not doubt that Italy was destined by history and
position to be Abyssinia's reformer.

Returning after the war to the conquered country, Evelyn
Waugh is able to support by observation his belief that
Italy's aims were genuinely of higher moral value not only
than anything which Abyssinia herself could boast, but than
the imperialism of other countries.

> It was a new thing in East Africa ... to see white
> men hard at work on simple manual labour; the portent of
> a new type of conquest. To the other imperial races it
> was slightly shocking. To the Abyssinians it was in-
> comprehensible. To them the fruit of victory is leisure.
> They fought their wars against neighbouring tribes, won
> them as the Italians had done, through superior arms and
> organisation, and from then onwards settled back to a
> life of ease. The idea of conquering a country in order
> to work there, of treating an empire as a place to which
> things must be brought, to be fertilised and cultivated
> and embellished instead of as a place from which things
> could be taken, to be denuded and depopulated; to labour
> like a slave instead of sprawling idle like a master -
> was something wholly outside their range of thought. It
> is the principle of the Italian occupation. It is some-
> thing new in Africa; something, indeed, that has not
> been seen anywhere outside the United States for two
> hundred years.

In fairness to Mr. Waugh it must again be emphasised
that this summary of a small portion of a beautifully written and delightfully amusing account of his experiences as
a war correspondent in the oddest of wars is absolutely
unrepresentative of the book.

The work can scarcely be laid down once it is begun just
because the author never argues; he leaves one with an
impressive representation of the truth carved with delicate
workmanship out of the unwieldy and formless mass which
most Europeans have been content to take to their hearts

and decorate with their own excellent but most unsuitable
designs.

The author may be inaccurate here and there; he may have
over-emphasised one aspect at the expense of another; but
the unbiassed reader will come away convinced that the
forty nations (or whatever the number of sanctionist
countries were) could after all be largely wrong.

Note

1   The emperor from whom Haile Selassie (Ras Tafari) took
over in 1930.

69.   DAVID GARNETT, 'NEW STATESMAN'

7 November 1936, 735.

David Garnett (1892-1981), son of the critic Edward Garnett,
was a novelist, biographer, literary editor and critic. He
wrote 'Lady into Fox' (1922), 'The Sailor's Return'
(1925), 'Pocahontas' (1933) and two volumes of autobiography, 'The Golden Echo' (1953) and 'The Flowers of the
Forest' (1955). He was editor of 'The Letters of T.E.
Lawrence' (1938). Garnett's pacifist/agnostic Fabian up-
bringing (cf. his novel 'No Love', 1929) naturally made
him antagonistic to what he saw as Waugh's Catholic
imperialism in this book.

I cannot recommend anyone with a queasy stomach to follow
my example and read and compare 'Waugh in Abyssinia ...
and 'Desert Encounter' by Knud Holmboe....
Evelyn Waugh is the opposite of Holmboe in every possible respect. Waugh knows that a writer's business in
life is to please and to amuse, that books are only ano-
dynes to make life easy. He has been three times to
Abyssinia, which he has shown us to be a wonderfully barbaric joke of a place and not unnaturally he has come to
hate the Abyssinians.

The essence of the offence was that the Abyssinians,
in spite of being by any possible standard an inferior

race, persisted in behaving as superiors; it was not
that they were hostile, but contemptuous. The white man,
accustomed to other parts of Africa, was disgusted to
find the first-class carriages on the railway usurped
by local dignitaries: he found himself subject to officials and villanous-looking men-at-arms whose language
he did not know, who showed him no sort of preference
on account of his colour, and had not the smallest
reluctance to using force on him if he became truculent.

'Usurped' is good. So might a Japanese feel about hunting
men in first-class carriages in Leicestershire. Mr. Waugh
explains that when Italy, in spite of British oppositions,
secured Abyssinia membership of the League of Nations it
'corresponded exactly to the present of ammunition to
Menelik in 1893; the Italians had armed the Abyssinians
against themselves.' But it does not cross his mind that
the covenant of the League of Nations was a binding
document or that Italy was bound in honour to observe it,
and that the only hope for the other countries was to take
action against the aggressor, and that now that they have
failed, the fate of Abyssinia is likely to be theirs. His
book is not really about the war, but about the absurdities
which attend the life of a war correspondent who has to
dish up hearsay or invent lies. Like most of us, he likes
the Italian character and Italian chianti and Italian culture and this must be his reason for writing enthusiastically of the Italian conquest which is:

> the expansion of a race, not a military movement like
> the French occupation of Morocco ... not a capitalistic
> movement like the British occupation of the South Afri-
> can goldfields. It is being attended by the spread of
> order and decency, education and medicine in a dis-
> graceful place, but it is not primarily a humane move-
> ment....

After the Italian occupation he revisited Addis and: 'It
was a revelation to me to see how little damage a bomb
does,' and 'at no time was gas or yperite very effective as a lethal weapon. Nor was it primarily used as
such,' but rather 'to sterilise the bush.' Mr. Waugh says
little about the Italian habit of persistently bombing
Red Cross units, the nature of which, as every pilot knows,
could not possibly have been mistaken from the air, and he
rhapsodises rather unduly over the spectacle of seeing
Italians, white men, working at the building of a road.

After all, there must be a division of labour, and the
Eritreans were doing the fighting. However, Addis is very
much the same, only 'the taxis had disappeared from the
streets. So had the natives.' He does not tell us how many
of them that 'most amiable and sensible man,' Graziani, is
hanging and shooting every day.

70.   UNSIGNED REVIEW, 'TIMES LITERARY SUPPLEMENT'

7 November 1936, 900

Abyssinia seems, in a strange way, to have transmitted
something of her character to most of the writers who in
the past two years have tried to portray her people or elucidate her problems. For Abyssinia is a country of
extremes, of parched and burning deserts, of cold and wind-
swept uplands. There is indeed the middle zone, the temperate *woina dega*; but few writers have been content to dwell
in it, and those few have also been content to write of
trivialities, of journalistic bickerings, cafés and alien
adventurers - in fact, of anything but the real Abyssinia.
    Remembering 'Black Mischief' and reading Mr. Waugh's
presumably punning title, one might expect to find him
among the dwellers in the *woina dega*, though standing head
and shoulders above his neighbours for the distinction of
his writing and his wit. There one does indeed find him in
the middle portion of his book, making great play with the
Deutsches Haus,(1) Le Perroquet and Le Select,(2) his
comic-opera spies and oddly assorted colleagues of the
Press. But in his more serious mood - and the book is in
the main a serious one - he joins the ranks of the extrem-
ists, becoming a most bitter critic of the old regime with
hardly a kind word to spare for Abyssinian morals, men or
manners; and a most confirmed adherent of the Italian idea.
    Mr. Waugh is of course entitled to his opinions; but
when he broadcasts them to an audience which, in its inevitable ignorance, is bound to be receptive he should, perhaps, temper his judgment with a little generosity. Take,
for instance, the Jeunesse Ethiopienne, that band of young
men with a smattering - and some with very much more than a
smattering - of European education whom the Emperor gathered round him and on whom Mr. Waugh empties the vials of
his scorn. They wore black or yellow boots, and sometimes
whiteish collars. They were callow, superficial and often

ridiculous. In the transition stage between the ancient and
the modern they had perhaps lost some of the virtue of the
one and acquired but little from the other. Children in
progress, they could not and did not think with the mind of
a sophisticated adult. But they were the tentacles stretched out by Ethiopia to civilization, and they did at least
learn to speak its language. Yet Mr. Waugh, who judges them
and their more barbarous brothers so unsparingly, does not
seem to have taken the trouble to learn theirs, or to give
more than the most casual study to their customs, faith or
traditions.

More than once he trips over this ignorance. He cites
the strength of the escort which accompanied the Boundary
Commission to Walwal - 'far in excess of any normal protective escort ... this extraordinary force' - as an
instance of folly and provocation. Yet the size of an
Abyssinian escort is almost invariably governed not by
protective needs but by the importance of its chief; and
that of the Commissioners who visited the south-western
frontier without provoking protest or comment was nearer
800 than the 600 which he finds so excessive. Again, he
writes with suspicion of the long conversation between the
chief of police at Harar and his companion's servant, which
when translated purported to deal with nothing more than a
cold and inquiries after his health. Perhaps his suspicions
were justified; but on a visit of politeness it is rare
for a conversation to touch on anything but health and the
weather, and the more polite the visitor the longer the
inquiry. On political history, to which he devotes the best
chapter in the book, Mr. Waugh stands on firmer ground,
and here the reader may be left to find any tendency to
bias for himself. But, whether bias be found or not, this
is a remarkably interesting and admirable example of the
art of lucid compression.

In the last chapter of his book Mr. Waugh ceases to be a
critic and becomes an enthusiast. Returning to Abyssinia,
he revisited Harar and found a contented populace. At
Addis Ababa he was most favourably impressed by General
Graziani. True, he was driven home from dinner with a
machine-gun on the box, but concluded that though there
was some discomfort, there was little real danger in the
situation of the Italians. And, homeward bound, he traversed the completed section of the Great Trunk Road which
will one day span Abyssinia from north to south. There is
something deeply stirring in the spectacle of a great road
driving slowly and relentlessly across a country which for
untold ages has defied the efforts of man to tame it. No
wonder Mr. Waugh is moved to enthusiasm. In it he sees the
promise of order, fertility and peace. Some may think that

its foundations were laid in arrogance and dishonour; but
all will hope that it will serve the purpose which Mr.
Waugh, cynic turned idealist, foretells.

Notes

1   The pension where Waugh stayed in Addis Ababa in com-
    pany with (Sir) William Deedes, Patrick Balfour (the
    late Lord Kinross) and Stewart Emeny representing,
    respectively, the 'Morning Post', 'Evening Standard'
    and 'News Chronicle'.
2   Two nightclubs in Addis.

71.   ROSE MACAULAY, 'HORIZON'

December 1946, 370

'Campion' is ... mellowness itself compared with 'Waugh in
Abyssinia' ... a blast of triumph over the Italian conquest of that land. Mr. Waugh went to Abyssinia to write
of its subjugation for 'the only London paper that seemed
to be taking a realistic view of the situation',(1) and
to blow a scornful trumpet against the 'whinney of the non-
conformist conscience' which had protested against the
assault - the same whinney from the same conscience that
protested against the Nazis, and is protesting now,
though more faintly, against the enslavement of eastern
Europe. Mr. Waugh disagreed with this whinney. He found
that the Italians had spread order, decency and civilization, that yperite was pretty harmless, though the Abyssinians were 'bored and exasperated with a weapon to
which they could make no effective return', that Graziani
was a most agreeable man, that along the new Italian roads
'will pass the eagles of ancient Rome, as they came to our
savage ancestors in France and Britain and Germany', and
that 'the new régime is going to succeed'. He completely
failed to grasp the idea behind the League sanctions
applied to Italy for its aggression against another League
State, and calls the British protests 'peevish and impoli-
tic remonstrance'.
    An odd and rather unchivalrous book. What is its motive?
Preference for Italians over Abyssinians? That we most of
us share; it should not, but perhaps does, affect the
issue. Dislike of black populations? He shows no such

dislike in 'Remote People', 'Black Mischief', or 'Scoop'.
Support of a policy endorsed by the Italian clergy. Very
probably. Dislike of the League of Nations? Again, likely
enough. Or merely sympathy with the big battalions? If it
were that, Mr. Waugh should now be crying up the Russian
domination, and he is not. This book must be pronounced a
Fascist tract....

Note

1   'Daily Mail'.

'Scoop'

1938

72.   RUPERT CROFT-COOKE, 'TABLET'

7 May 1938, 606

Rupert Croft-Cooke (1904-79) was a novelist, playwright,
biographer and writer of books on travel, food and wine,
the circus and gipsies. He wrote 'God in Ruins' (1936),
'Kingdom Come' (1937), 'Seven Thunders' (1956) and 'The
Green Green Grass' (1977).

This book of Mr. Evelyn Waugh's was, in a sense, inevitable. Sooner or later, one felt, he would turn his eye on
the Press, and his eye, like that of 'She',(1) in another
African novel, blasts and withers whoever falls under its
glance. His satire has always been unclouded by mercy,
unspoilt by sentimentality. Schools, Bright Young Things,
and Diplomats have already gone down before it, and now
Press Lords and Pressmen alike are shattered. Without
invective, without passion, without a smirk, he coolly
demolishes their fortresses, and one sees the great
Megalopolitan building, 'numbers 700-853 Fleet Street,'
totter and fall under the machine-gun fire of his wit.
    It is all superb entertainment, from the moment in
which William Boot, who wrote the Lush Places column for
the 'Daily Beast' ('Feather footed through the plashy
fen passes the questing vole') is sent by mistake to
report a civil war in the negro State of Ishmaelia, right
down to the banquet which Lord Copper gives to another
Boot in mistake for him, after a third Boot, by mistake,
has been knighted. There are cold-blooded ironies, such as
one remembers in 'Black Mischief', and coloured gentlemen
like General Gollancz Jackson, and all the topsy-turvy

absurdities which, in Mr. Waugh's novels, make hard if
cruel sense. One cannot say that it is better than his
previous books, but then one does not need to say that.
The world is mad, Mr. Waugh seems to remark calmly, and
one is grateful that this satirist, while moving through
the Bedlam he sees about him, keeps his head.

Note

1   Sir Henry Rider Haggard (1856-1925), 'She' (1887).

73.   DESMOND SHAWE-TAYLOR, 'NEW STATESMAN'

7 May 1938, 795

Desmond Shawe-Taylor (b. 1907), Music Critic of the 'Sunday
Times' since 1958, is author of 'Covent Garden' (1948) and
editor of Joseph Maunsell Hone's 'Life of George Moore'
(1936) and (with Edward Sackville-West, Waugh's friend)
'The Record Guide' (1951).

'Scoop' is exceedingly amusing: the sort of book a reviewer
gets back to after lunch with no sense of duty, but with
the certain expectation of continued pleasure. Just as I
like best those pantomimes which stick to the five or six
classic stories, so I like Mr. Waugh best when he remains
within his own territory, which I take to be the circles
radiating outwards - not too far - from the lunch-table of
Lady Metroland. 'Scoop' opens with a brilliant addition to
the Metroland circus, a Cabinet Minister's wife called Mrs.
Stitch, a woman of equal beauty and vitality. Her bedroom
levée is like a combination, reflected in a modishly distorting mirror, of von Hoffmansthal's Marschallin (1) and
Ruth Draper's Italian-learning New Yorker;(2) she simultaneously discusses accounts, signs cheques, dictates over
the telephone the costumes for a charity ball, and directs
the painting of ruined castles on the ceiling by an elegant
young man on a step ladder. Meanwhile her daughter, an
eight-year-old prodigy, construes Virgil at the foot of the
bed ('munera, darling, like tumtiddy; always a short "a"
in neuter plurals'), and the maid reads out the clues of
the morning crossword. At lunch with Lady Metroland she
recommends a young literary protégé, John Boot, as war

correspondent to Lord Copper, the bewildered but flattered proprietor of the 'Daily Beast.' The 'Beast' runs a fragrant little country corner called Lush Places, contributed twice a week by a distant relative of Mrs. Stitch's protégé; inevitably muddle sets in, and it is the rural, and not the urban, Mr. Boot who is sent out to report the impending civil war in Ishmaelia.

Ishmaelia is a republic in the North-East of Africa; and, of course, Mr. Waugh does not fail to people it with fantastic, irritating and diverting inhabitants. The whole country is run by the descendants and collaterals of a pious old Alabama dusky named Jackson, who had been appointed first President; thus the army is commanded by General Gollancz Jackson, and the principal hotel in Jacksonburg is owned by Mrs. Earl Russell Jackson. But all the ingenuity of the plot and the variety of the decorations cannot dispel a feeling that the author is here getting a little too tangled up with realism; why, he even allows William Boot (who, both in London and Ishmaelia, is really no more than an Alice in Wonderland) to have a love affair. In Metroland-Copper circles he can keep realism at precisely the distance that suits his talent - namely, at arm's length. On the whole it is a relief to get back to a world where Lord Copper gives a knighthood to the Boot that should have gone, but didn't and a dinner of welcome to yet another Boot, who comes, like all the rural Boots, from Boot Magna Hall. Boot Magna is an exceedingly dilapidated counterpart of Mr. Wodehouse's Blandings Castle; in Colonel Blount of 'Vile Bodies' there were traces of a Wodehouse strain in Mr. Waugh, and how marked it has now become may be observed in the account of Mr. Salter's cross-country walk to and arrival at Boot Magna Hall:

> No sound broke the peace of the evening save, in the elms that stood cumbrously on every side, the crying of the rooks and, not unlike it but nearer at hand, directly it seemed over Mr. Salter's head, a strong baritone decanting irregular snatches of sacred music. 'In thy courts no more are needed, sun by day nor moon by night,' sang Uncle Theodore blithely, stepping into his evening trousers.

'Decanting' might be the Master himself.

Notes

1   Hugo von Hofmannsthal (1874-1929), an Austrian playwright and poet, was librettist for Richard Strauss's

operas, e.g. 'Der Rosenkavalier'.
2   American monologuist (1884-1956). Waugh comments on her
    entertainment in his 'Diaries' (10 June 1930, p. 314):
    'A brilliant artist if she was satirical but always sen-
    timental and sympathetic at heart.' He would not have
    been pleased with the comparison.

74.   UNSIGNED REVIEW, 'TIMES LITERARY SUPPLEMENT'

7 May 1938, 313

In his new novel Mr. Waugh's ribald wit spurts in a brisk
uninterrupted flow upon the caprices of sensational journalism. He is ingenious, satirical, extremely funny, as indeed
is his habit, alive to the danger of forgetting to be funny
and newly possessed of an assortment of jokes ranging in
subject from the habits of the great crested grebe to the
cleft stick in which a veteran war correspondent forwarded
his dispatches. Like his previous novels, 'Scoop' is
entertaining reading all through, with more than a single
good laugh or chuckle to the page.
    It all began with the crisis in Ishmaelia, a country of
which Mr. Waugh has a low opinion. There was a successful
but rather lovelorn young novelist named John Courtenay
Boot, who had thought of going out to Ishmaelia as a newspaper correspondent. Mrs. Algernon Stitch was obviously
Boot's man. Her husband was in the Cabinet, she was fascinating even with her face encased in clay at eleven in the
morning, and Lord Copper, the proprietor of the 'Daily
Beast', held no terrors for her. This was remarkable in
the circumstances, since Lord Copper, who had sixteen peers
on his staff and special typewriters whose keys made no
more sound than the drumming of a bishop's fingertips on an
upholsered *prie-Dieu*, was the sort of man who believed in
strong mutually antagonistic governments everywhere. Still,
the Stitch Service had a deserved reputation for infalli-
bility, and Lord Copper pressed the button on his desk.
Alas! - or fortunately - there was a William Boot who did
a weekly nature article for the 'Beast', a diffident and
inoffensive fellow in Somerset. What more natural than that
William should be sent to North-East Africa, all but buried
beneath mountains of equipment that might stir the envy of
a film company going on location in the Arctic?
    The narrative becomes a little inconsequential now and
then and the pace flags, but Mr. Waugh's farcical invention

and his deft verbal witticisms flow together in a steady
stream. The sketches of some of the horde of correspondents
assembled in Jacksonburg before hostilities actually break
out are amusingly unkind, and the nomadic Kätchen, who provides a love interest that is distinctly airy even in the
altitudes of Jacksonburg, has a fetching chatter. It was
only to be expected that William, after an interval of
phlegmatic calm, during which the 'Beast' rained anguished
cables upon him, should rouse himself to a proper appreciation of his opportunities. But William, it must be con-
fessed, is an extravagant type even for this cautionary
tale of the large-circulation Press; he is too much the
simpleton, too facile an instrument for satire, and it was
fitting that the knighthood so easily procured at Lord
Copper's request should go to the other Boot and not to
this. Mr. Waugh's story is a trifle too deliberately concocted, and less criticism than usual is implied in his
gleeful ridicule. Still, a bundle of cleft sticks has its
uses.

75. JOHN BROPHY, 'DAILY TELEGRAPH'

13 May 1938, 6

John Brophy (1899-1965), novelist and anthologist, was the
father of Brigid Brophy (see headnote to No. 58). He was
author of 'The Bitter End' (1928), 'Waterfront' (1934),
'Green Ladies' (1940) and 'Body and Soul' (1947).

The news is good, for Mr. Evelyn Waugh continues his ribald,
fantastic and unpredictable way. This time he turns on the
newspaper world, and, as a hard-working novelist who has
lately seen much money and fame cornered by war correspondents turned author, let me confess that I enjoyed nothing
in 'Scoop' more than those interludes in which we glimpse
Mr. Wenlock Jakes tapping out fatuous passages from his
forthcoming reminiscences for which he is to receive an
advance of 20,000 dollars.
   'Scoop' is about the Boots, three of them. One is a
novelist in need of money - Mr. Waugh never disdains realism in its due place. A society hostess uses her influence
with the newspaper proprietor, Lord Copper, to secure for
this John Boot the post of special correspondent in Ishmaelia, where civil war is expected to break out.

Lord Copper's staff have never heard of his highbrow novelist (more grim realism!), and when they discover that the man who sends in Nature Notes from the depths of the country is a William Boot, they promptly pack him off to Ishmaelia.

As special correspondent, William Boot flowers in amateurish innocence. He arrives with a collapsible canoe and cleft sticks - to carry messages! He has to have his job explained to him by a colleague, and radio, at 26s a word, press reports like this: 'Please don't worry, quite safe and well, in fact rather enjoying things, weather improving, will cable again if there is any news, yours Boot.'

He sees the other correspondents troop off to a town that does not exist, and luck gives him his 'scoop', for if Ishmaelia is to have no war, it gets a revolution. Returning home to fame, he prefers retirement, and so is impersonated by the third Boot, who winds up the story with a glorious burlesque banquet.

Mr. Waugh is not a satirist, for indignation founded on some belief is necessary to satire, and I have never been able from his books to discover what Mr. Waugh believes in. His job is to provide laughter, and how well he does it.

76.   DEREK VERSCHOYLE, 'SPECTATOR'

13 May 1938, 886

Derek Verschoyle (1911-73), Wing Commander RAFO, was a diplomat, publisher and poet, but was best known as a literary journalist (he was Editor of the 'Spectator', taking over from Peter Fleming; see headnote to No. 39). He was author of 'XXX Poems' (1931) and editor of 'The English Novelists' (1936). Verschoyle was one of Waugh's pupils at Arnold House, Denbighshire, in 1925-6, the school which formed a partial model for Llanabba Castle in 'Decline and Fall', and remembered their time together with affection and respect.

Mr. Waugh has had his eye on the Press since (at the latest) 1930, the year of 'Vile Bodies' and the birth of the 'Excess'. In eight years his Fleet Street has changed little. There is of course some new blood in the monde, Lord Monomark appears to have retired, the 'Excess' (one assumes) has ceased publication or subsists obscurely on dwindling sales, for Lord Copper now crows upon his hill

and supremacy is disputed between the 'Daily Brute' and the
'Daily Beast'. But the principles upon which Fleet Street
conducts its affairs remains unchanged. In 'Scoop', as in
'Vile Bodies', and almost as in life, it is a Wonderland in
which the extravagant or the idiotic is also the inevitable. Mr. Waugh fixes on the fantastic place an eye unlit
by surprise and undimmed by pity, and with the utmost com-
posure announces to the world what that superhumanly discerning eye detects.

It detects a number, much too large to be catalogued, of
highly entertaining things - the mortification of William
Boot, who contributes to the 'Beast' a nature column...;
Ishmaelia, congested with war correspondents and administered with benevolent inefficiency by a ruling family
named Jackson, of whom President Rathbone Jackson, General
Gollancz Jackson, Messrs. Garnett, Huxley and Mander Jackson, and Mrs. Earl Russell Jackson are the most taking and
among the most important; Mrs. Stitch, a fetching and
resourceful recruit to Lady Metroland's troupe, who evades
the inconvenience of traffic blocks by driving her diminu-
tive car along the pavement; Lord Copper, the victim of
such sudden enthusiasms as appoint trick cyclists to edit
Sporting Pages, and the members of Lord Copper's staff,
shooed from post to post in the Megalopolitan building ...
in obedience to Lord Copper's policy of keeping his subordinates alert by changes of occupation; the Boot family,
of Boot Magna Hall. The Boot family is the particular triumph of this book. It is all, from the first page to the
much too soon reached last, magnificent entertainment; but
the Boot *ménage*, from Uncle Theodore, with his complementary passions for sacred music and feline prowlings after
dark, to the bevy of retainers reclining about Boot Magna
Hall in varying degrees of invalid retirement, reveals an
inventive power which it is little exaggeration to call
that of genius.

What makes Mr. Waugh's novels so much superior as
entertainment to any other fiction written today? His
inventive talent, his intelligence, the flexibility of
his prose contribute; but more important than these is his
gift, so desirable in a satirist and so rare, of never losing either head or temper while engaged in the work of
demolition. The world he seems to regard as an asylum, but
he walks through it with calm and distinguishes the eccentricities and unpleasant habits of the inmates without
surprise, sentiment, or resentment. Almost all his contemporaries could take lessons from him in technique. His
books are so easy to read that it is possible to overlook
how intricately they are organised. They are exactly of the
length and of the form which their subject requires; there

is never a word wasted or an emphasis misplaced. I do not
think that 'Scoop', as a whole, is as good as some of Mr.
Waugh's other books, but that is merely because I find
Europe a more effective background to his characters than
the other continents. But it is none the less an enchanting
book, which like everything written by Mr. Waugh can be
reread with pleasure as often as the whim takes one....

77.   UNSIGNED REVIEW, 'SATURDAY REVIEW'

14 May 1938, 313

Mr. Evelyn Waugh gives his fanciful humour full rein in
'Scoop', in which we have a cast of incredibly fantastic
creatures invented for the purpose of satirising the
methods of modern sensational journalism. It is an impossible table, but exceedingly amusing; a gay extravaganza
that trips along merrily from Mayfair and Fleet-street to
Ishmaelia and then back again to London. A brilliant and
sparkling display of entertaining nonsense.

78.   'PETERBOROUGH', 'DAILY TELEGRAPH'

2 June 1938, 14

Mr. Evelyn Waugh, in his entertaining new novel 'Scoop,'
which I have been late off the mark in reading, is anxious
to point out that the African war it describes should not
be confused with the Abyssinian campaign. In this he was
himself a newspaper correspondent.

I imagine, nevertheless, that most readers have recognised the late Sir Percival Phillips in Sir Jocelyn Hitchcock, the famous journalist who figures in the book.

It is true that while Mr. Waugh carefully gives Hitchcock a white moustache, Phillips was clean-shaven. But,
with one important reservation, the portrait is unmistake-
able. Mr. Waugh even makes Hitchcock ascribe his success to
a habit of 'getting up earlier than the other fellow.'

It was in these very words that Phillips himself explained the one great 'scoop' of the Abyssinian war. This
was his own.

At this point Mr. Waugh does less than justice to his
distinguished original. He makes Hitchcock return home
early in the war.

This leaves the 'scoop' of the title to be obtained by
the novel's incompetent hero.

Actually, as will be well remembered, Phillips's famous
message from Addis Ababa to the 'Daily Telegraph' revealing the Rickett concession was not only the war's biggest
scoop but one of the greatest in modern journalism.

79.   ROSE MACAULAY, 'HORIZON'

December 1946, 370-1

...This gay fantasy ... (also about Abyssinia) is extremely
funny, entirely good-tempered, and of considerable brilliance. If any one in it is a Roman Catholic or a Protestant, Mr. Waugh does not mention it; religion does not
throw its fatal apple of discord among the dramatis personae; every one gets fair treatment, every one is ridiculous, and the whole scene of delicious absurdity. With it
Mr. Waugh re-entered his peculiar world; it was a relief to
those of us who had begun to fear that we were losing him,
that the wit was being slain by the propagandist and the
partisan. 'Scoop' carries an ingenious plot, and a crackling of jokes only a little less good than those of
'Decline and Fall'; it is a completely light-hearted jeu
d'esprit, in which the journalistic and tourist experience
gained in Abyssinia is again brilliantly used....

'Robbery Under Law: The Mexican Object-Lesson'

1939 (US title: 'Mexico: An Object Lesson', 1939)

80. HAROLD NICOLSON, 'DAILY TELEGRAPH'

30 June 1939, 9

Mr. Evelyn Waugh has written a short but dull book upon
Mexico. He adopts towards that lovely but misgoverned
country the Catholic, the Conservative, the Phalangist,
point of view. He cannot forgive the Mexicans for having
seized the oil industry, for having dispossessed the
Church. His book, as he himself admits, is a collection of
'notes on anarchy.'

He is not in the least interested in the fauna or flora
of the country even as he is bored by its dramatic scenery.
'There are,' he says, 'more thorns, than roses everywhere
in Mexico.' 'The pervading atmosphere,' he says again,
'ranges from vexation to despair.' And from this atmosphere
Mr Waugh has caught, 'that peculiar mirthlessness that
characterises the Mexican Indian.' His account of the oil
controversy, as of the relations between Mexico and the
United States, is as jejune as any blue book. 'It is,'
explains Mr. Waugh, 'a common complaint against Catholics
that they intrude their religion into every discussion,
postulating a Church question in matters which seem to
have no theological connection.' Mr. Graham Greene, whose
recent book on Mexico (1) was equally biassed, might have
adduced a similar excuse. It is an excuse with which any
reasonable man must sympathise.

I agree with Mr. Waugh that the Mexican Government's
treatment of the Church is one of the greatest crimes, and
therefore one of the greatest errors, in history; I can
understand his wrath.

Anger, however, unless it be completely uncontrolled,
makes a dull book. Mr. Waugh compresses his lips so tightly

that he becomes almost inaudible. At moments (as when he
discusses the diplomacy of Mr. Josephus Daniels) some of
his old gay sparkle appears. But for the rest his account
of what might have been a happy journey is veiled, as the
cone of Popocateptl was veiled, in sad clouds of disgust.

Note

1   'The Lawless Roads' (Longmans, 1939) which Waugh
    reviewed in the 'Spectator' (10 March 1939, 414).

81.   A.W.J., 'MANCHESTER GUARDIAN'

28 July 1939, 7

Mexico is one of those countries that emerged from feudal-
ism late. The change is not complete, any more than in the
parent country of Spain. It has been governed disgrace-
fully. Its rulers now pursue liberal ideals – peasant
ownership of land, educational reform – through mists of
self-interest and ideologies imported from Europe. Mr.
Waugh proclaims himself a Conservative. He believes that
man's chances 'of happiness and virtue, here, remain more
or less constant through the centuries, are not much
affected by the political and economic conditions in which
he lives' – in other words, that no revolution is worth
the trouble. This contempt for change and political forms
does not prevent him from lambasting the present Mexican
Government for all he is worth. He sets out the case
against the spoliation of the foreign oil interests with
the greatest zest. He is of course, a Catholic, and he
wields the sword of apologetic with fine grace. The persecution of the Church in Mexico is a hideous taint upon
its Government. But does Mr. Waugh not see that this can be
man's brutal criticism of a Church which, as in Russia,
made no attempt to move with the times, that had become
identified with a system, and allied itself with the
perishable social forms of this world? Mr. Waugh recounts
his experiences in Mexico with great agreeableness. His
book is admirably written, and few could have set out more
ably this view of Mexico, a view which is open to argument
but deserves to be understood.

82. R.L. MARTIN, 'NEW YORK TIMES BOOK REVIEW'

19 November 1939, 9, 19

Robert Lee Martin, American academic, is the author of
Mexican Prospects, 'Yale Review' (Spring 1936), 511-36.

Evelyn Waugh warns the reader that he went to Mexico a
conservative and came away a conservative. Such candor from
a writer on Mexico is exceptional. When it is combined with
a lively critical faculty and superior skill in handling
the English language, you have something new in political
travelogues. Mr. Waugh's outspoken account of what he saw
and heard below the Rio Grande during the Summer of 1938
is, in its way, a landmark in American publishing history.
For of the many explanatory volumes about Mexico printed
here since 1935 this is the first to tell what a conservative thinks of President Cardenas's recent experiments in
agriculture, industry and education.

It is no accident, perhaps, that such a book should have
been written by a Britisher and published originally in
England. The absence of diplomatic relations between Mexico
and Great Britain may have encouraged Mr. Waugh to greater
freedom of speech than any American author with similar
views on Mexico has so far found it practical to employ. In
the United States the Good Neighbor Policy appears inadvertently to have operated in favor of the literary supporters
of the Cardenas administration. Whether or not, therefore,
one agrees with Mr. Waugh, it must be admitted that he has
performed a liberal public service in helping to redress
the balance between Right-Wing and Left-Wing opinions on
Mexico.

Mr. Waugh's conservatism is a philosophy in itself, as
broad as the British Empire and apparently quite free from
petty partisan considerations. Discounting the claim to
'contemporary significance' which today makes Mexico a
place of pilgrimage for so many hopeful ideologues, he
adopts the long view - so long a view, in fact, that it
stirs uneasy memories of the fall of Babylon or Rome.
Mexico, as Mr. Waugh sees her, is a country that has been
progressively and persistently ruining herself, with only
a few breathing-spells, ever since 1810.

Instead of moving forward, as the United States has done
in the past century, Mr. Waugh finds that Mexico has actually declined culturally and economically from the position
she enjoyed around 1800. She appears to him a land grown
shabby and gone to seed, obliged to import not only food

supplies but fully 80 per cent of her manufactured articles
from abroad - and unable to pay for either. Her agricul-
tural production is at the lowest ebb in history; her
industry is operating in such a way as to benefit no one
except a few politicians; her finances are chaotic and
largely non-existent. Litigation is so constant a feature
of Mexican life that initiative is throttled. Strikes,
says Mr. Waugh, 'are a topic of general discussion, like
the weather in England, and like it, the habitual excuse
for any failure of plans.'

In spite of many potent speeches about democracy, which
have won for Cardenas the voluble support of a 'Left Book
Club' minority in England, Mr. Waugh finds government in
Mexico to be autocratic and education state-propagandist,
with teachers politically appointed. The church, he points
out, has been driven into the catacombs, after being
deprived not only of all its property but of the most
elementary civil rights; and the social services which it
once performed have not been replaced by other agencies to
any conspicuous degree. In short, it appears to him the
people have sacrificed their social and political liberties
without receiving any returns in the shape of internal
security or prestige abroad.

For the time being, Mr. Waugh opines, Mexico survives
largely as a sad example of the chaos-from-within which
threatens to extinguish civilization all over the world
today. An alarming note, to be sure, but one whose implications no thoughtful person may be quite prepared to
ignore nowadays. It is all the more disturbing because,
as Mr. Waugh remarks, there has been no lack in Mexico of
'what are generally referred to as "enlightened ideas."'
Almost every unhappy figure from Iturbide to Cardenas who
has appeared as a leader of the country has spoken in the
phrases of contemporary advanced thought. The country has
known, in form at least, Napoleonic Masonic monarchy,
liberal-representative democracy, German enlightened-
constitutional monarchy, international individualist-
capitalism, socialism, dictatorship of the proletariat,
and it seems probable it will shortly develop a species of
Hitlerism. Concerning the precise shape of things to come.
Mr. Waugh drops at least one interesting hint:

> There is a heresy in the Nazi party that is con-
> demned - but rather leniently punished - under the
> title of National Bolshevism, a combination of the
> race-myth with the destruction of private property that
> seems peculiarly apt for importation into Mexico. And
> the trade routes for its importation are already
> established.

Stripped of all phrases what is happening in Mexico now
is not, he believes, particularly new. For him the rosy
claims of the current liberators only mask their addition
to an 'old Mexican precedent that has proved disastrous
again and again but remains ineradicable in Mexican states-
manship, of progress through theft.' He notes little difference between the nineteenth century confiscations legislated by Juarez and the twentieth century expropriations
legislated by Cardenas - except a slight difference in the
vocabulary of their authors. In both cases he remarks with
some surprise on the benevolent attitude shown by the
United States, and infers among other things that a small
but influential group of independent capitalists in this
country has an interest in the marketing of expropriated
Mexican oil. In the long run, he wonders if the United
States, unconsciously pursuing its 'manifest destiny,' will
not be found to have urged Mexico tolerantly down the road
to ruin and thereby made final absorption by this country
inevitable.

The picture of unrelieved gloom below the border which
Mr. Waugh presents may come as a shock to many Americans
who have enjoyed pleasant holidays in Mexico. No less
shocking, perhaps, will be his strictures on United States
policy in Mexico, which are probably the sharpest printed
in English since Francisco Bulnes (1) took President Wilson
to task. There is no question this book will provoke indignation in some quarters and wry amusement in others; but it
can scarcely be overlooked. Soberly conceived and wittily
executed in the best tradition of the familiar essay, it is
one of those astringent volumes which appear every now and
then as an antidote to complacency, sweetness and light.

The evident sincerity of the author, the high quality
of his literary talent and the calm logic with which he
pursues his theme entitle him to a hearing in this country.
Possibly the sole concession he makes to diplomacy is in
refraining from suggesting any immediate solution for current British troubles in Mexico. In discussing Mexico's
past and present, and in dismissing her future as one
vast, disturbing question-mark, he has produced passages
which rank as first-rate literature.

The fascination of Mexico lies in the stimulus it
gives to the imagination. Anything may happen there;
almost everything has happened there; it has seen every
extreme of human nature, good, bad and ridiculous. It
has, in a way, the position toward Europe that Africa
had to the Romans; a source of novelty - 'Always something new out of Africa' - but also a distorting mirror
in which objects are reflected in perverse and threatening forms. The Romans sent their great men to Africa;

they went to seed and became despots and voluptuaries;
they sent their ideas and the Africans turned them into
engimas and paradoxes; the precise statements of Roman
law and faith became equivocal in the African mirage;
and when the barbarians came Africa was the first to go;
her canals silted up, her buildings fell, the sand swept
in from the desert over her fields.

Note

1   Francisco Bulnes was a Mexican political historian
(1853-1924) who wrote 'The Whole Truth about Mexico:
President Wilson's Responsibility', translated by Dora
Scott (New York, M. Bulnes Book Co., 1916).

83.   G[ERALD] V[ANN], 'DUBLIN REVIEW'

June-December 1939, 433-5

[Graham Greene's 'The Lawless Roads'] is no ordinary
travel-book. Quite apart from the interest of the events
themselves - the perils by water, the perils by land, the
perils by air - the skill with which the book is written
makes it memorable; and what emerges so clearly, and is of
such value is the effect of physical upon spiritual atmosphere in general, and the characters of those with whom
the author came in contact, whether Spaniards, Indians, or
lost men of other nations, in particular. The mixture of
religion and superstition, of deep fervour and of apathy;
the presence alike of priests of the heroic mould of Father
Pro, and of sacerdotal gold-diggers cashing in on the situation; the anti-God exhibitions and the piety of Indians
robbed of God; these and other contrasts are vividly
drawn....
    Mr. Waugh pursues a different purpose. For him, Mexico
is the writing on our own wall; he discusses its history
and its present condition with an eye to pointing the moral.
He has marshalled his facts with care and thoroughness; his
apologia for the Church is convincing, his exegesis of the
attack on the *hacienda* system, and of the oil expropriations, cleverly done. But one cannot help feeling that
there is a certain *simplisme* here. How, indeed, should it
be otherwise? For a few months' acquaintance and study may
be sufficient to acquire a sound knowledge of the

externals, the facts; and that is the time when it is
dangerous to make judgements. It is easy to pass judgement
on the goodness or badness, the success or failure, of
men's rationalizations of their desires; it is very much
harder to understand those desires themselves, especially
where one is concerned with a people whose habits of mind
and whose background are so different from one's own. What
does the superficial marxist terminology correspond to in
the soul of Mexicans? - that is the real question. Mr.
Waugh tells us that he went to Mexico a Conservative, with
all the preconceptions of his political theory (and there
are elements in his version of that theory which are a
trifle surprising) firmly established; and he thinks it
humbug to suppose that he could judge of what he saw
except through the spectacles of these preconceptions. That
no doubt is true; but it does not seem to have occurred to
him that there are different levels of thought and cona-
tion, and that it is not the most apparent which are the
most interesting or the most important, or that a superficial dishonesty of the most glaring type is sometimes
compatible with a deeper honesty, or that the behaviour
even of politicians such as he describes is conceivably
more to be explained sometimes by stupidity and ignorance
than by unrelieved wickedness.

84.   NIGEL DENNIS, 'PARTISAN REVIEW'

28 July 1943, 356-7

Nigel Dennis (b. 1912), American novelist and critic, is
author of 'Boys and Girls Come Out to Play' (1949) and
'Cards of Identity' (1955).

The friendly Alun Lewis, writing recently in the 'New
Statesman', opposed himself to critics who considered Waugh
a reactionary. 'Romantic' he believed to be the proper
description. But in the years before the war, Waugh's
'romanticism' flowed smoothly into a contemporary main-
stream of which so-called romanticism was no more than
tributary. Visiting Ethiopia at the time of Mussolini's
invasion, he wrote enthusiastically of the caliber of the
invading armies, and condemned Englishmen who failed to
see in this new colonial regime 'inestimable gifts of fine
workmanship and clear judgment' ('Waugh in Abyssinia').

A trip to Mexico shortly before the war led him to write
'Robber Under the Law' - more discreetly titled in good-
neighborly America, 'Mexico, An Object Lesson'. This violent diatribe of a converted Catholic was more than an
indignant protest against the humbling of the Catholic
church under the Cardenas government. It was also an intricate defense of unromantic General Franco. But perhaps
most tragic to Waugh was the awful fate of Mexico's huge
estates. 'My father's house' (1) had been virtually
destroyed; the fate of the English manorial holdings was
here in evidence on a huge scale. With bitter anger, Waugh
demanded more 'discipline' of the *peon* (2) and inevitably
saw Mexico's poverty as resulting from the country's lack
of a landed gentry.

It was then that he published his unromantic Conservative Creed:

> I believe that man is, by nature, an exile...; that
> his chances of happiness and virtue ... generally speak-
> ing, are not much affected by the political and economic
> conditions in which he lives;...that the intellectual
> communists of today have personal, irrelevant grounds
> for their antagonism to society, which they are trying
> to exploit. I believe ... that there is no form of
> government ordained from God as being better than any
> other; that the anarchic elements in society are so
> strong that it is a wholetime task to keep the peace. I
> believe the inequalities of wealth and position are
> inevitable and that it is therefore meaningless to dis-
> cuss the advantages of their elimination; that men
> naturally arrange themselves in a system of classes;
> that such a system is necessary for any form of co-
> operative work.... I do not think that British prosper-
> ity must necessarily be inimical to anyone else, but if,
> on occasions, it is, I want Britain to prosper and not
> her rivals.... I believe that Art is a natural function
> of man; it so happens that most of the greatest art has
> appeared under systems of tyranny, but I do not think
> it has a connection with any particular system, least
> of all with representative government, as nowadays in
> England, America and France it seems popular to believe;
> artists have always spent some of their spare time in
> flattering the governments under whom they live, so it
> is natural that, at the moment, English, American and
> French artists should be volubly democratic.

It must have seemed to him that the ceiling of the whole
world was descending in blocks and splinters on the sagging
roof of the paternal home. At least, on leaving Ethiopia,

he had been able to view with pride the efforts of British
gentlemen to live like squires in Kenya. But all Mexico
could give him was the hardly surprising 'trust' of members of the Catholic laity, some 'good company in the Ritz
bar', and 'a bottle of magnificent claret in Mexico City'.
To return to an England on the verge of war under that
epitome of unknightly rule, Neville Chamberlain, must have
been the last straw. A world in which radicals were still
vociferous, disjointed negresses still in vogue, playboys
making their last bids, and the young squires held in
their tents by industrialists in black coats – this was
surely England's lowest decline from Waugh's high standard
of glory.

When Tory salvation came in the form of the Churchill
government, Waugh recognized it instantly. Returning from
the Middle East he wrote 'Put Out More Flags'....

Notes

1   The original title of the first part of 'Work Sus-
    pended'; see headnote to No. 16.
2   Peasant.

'Put Out More Flags'

1942

85. UNSIGNED REVIEW, 'TIMES LITERARY SUPPLEMENT'

21 March 1942, 137

For the elucidation of his title Mr. Waugh provides a
quotation from a Chinese sage, '...a drunk military man
should order gallons and put out more flags in order to
increase his military splendour.' The period of which he is
writing is that of the present war; the people are rogues
or inept - people such as in the years after the last war
were drawn by authors dubbed young intellectuals, to the
weakening, as some think, of the nation's faith in itself
and with general disruptive effects from which its enemies
are now profiting. In fact, in its rendering of those to
whom the nation has to look for orders and guidance this
book would be mischievous, but that it is unlikely to
impress readers whose value to the community would be
reduced by accepting its implications.

Neither in the pathological vagaries of the characters
nor in the chaos in which they have their being is there
any thread of development to hold the attention of those
insensitive to Mr. Waugh's virtuosity with words and
artistry in imbroglio; while to appreciate them is to
assume with him that all else is of small account. Indeed,
though the publishers have found in the book 'a picture of
English life painted with precision and brilliance,' we
think that Mr. Waugh might admit to some affinity with one
Ambrose Silk of whom he writes that he

> lived in and for conversation: he rejoiced in the whole
> intricate art of it - the timing and striking the
> proper juxtaposition of narrative and comment, the
> bursts of spontaneous parody, the allusion one would

recognize and one would not, the changes of alliance,
the betrayals.... Why, he wondered, do real intellectuals always prefer the company of rakes to that of their
fellows? Basil is a Philistine and a crook ... and yet,
thought Ambrose, I hunger for his company.

If in his vision of his fellow-creatures Mr. Waugh is
limited to their defects, it is the more comprehensive for
being unobscured by political prejudice. The relish with
which a left-winger will savour his upper classes will be
damped by his refugee children. They are loathsome. Indeed,
it is these children who yield the most coherent and successful example of his art. When the ingenious Basil found
them billeted on the house where he was staying he pushed
them over to his neighbours, to whom he presented himself
as 'district billeting officer,' and then he levied blackmail to remove them. (We forget if he held the authority he
claimed, and to look it up conscientiously would be to be
out of touch with Mr. Waugh.) Anyhow Basil tried it on with
a Mr. Todhunter, who turned out to be the billeting officer
of the district! Retribution? Nothing so commonplace from
Mr. Waugh. The profitable racket explained to him, Mr. Todhunter bought the children at five pounds a leg.

86. KATE O'BRIEN, 'SPECTATOR'

3 April 1942, 336

Kate O'Brien (1897-1974) was an Irish playwright and
novelist who lived in London and Spain. She was author of
'The Distinguished Villa' (1926), 'Without My Cloak' (1931)
and 'Presentation Parlour' (1963). Her work often described
the Irish bourgeoisie and its religious conflicts.

Mr. Evelyn Waugh has an agreeable way of making his reader
feel that he writes as easily as people are said to fall
off logs. His manner is vigorous, and unblushingly free of
affectation or hesitation; it is clear that he could fool
along indefinitely with any of his chosen sets of characters without the least need for economy in farce or jibe,
his harlequin humour being extremely fertile and his own
confidence in it complete. The danger for these qualities
is a lack of shape, an ultimate vague sense of aimlessness
and a good deal of jolt as we are bounced along. But if on

the whole the entertainment is good enough such menaces will not worry us very much, and usually with this author it is good enough.

With 'Put Out More Flags,' however, some readers may feel that Mr. Waugh has been unlucky in his timing. We are still so near the Great Bore War of '39-40, and now so much more than ever worried by the consequences of all the error and fooling that it represented, that inconsequential mockery of it is not exactly what we want; and in any case perhaps at present we are a bit off group-presentations of the inept, the immoral, the egocentric - however lightheartedly set out. For our hearts are not light, and somehow they are not lightened by witty reminder of recent inanities, either our own or our friends'. Still, for the tough, here again are Mr. Waugh's smart sillies, going at the war as inconsequentially, selfishly, absurdly and, in a few cases, as sentimentally as we might expect. Basil Seal is here, propped up through his schemings by his mother, his sister and his rich mistress, the bogus Mrs. Lyne, who talks, we are assured but not convinced, 'like an intelligent man,' and who takes to drink in a big way, for no very potent reason. Basil runs a small blackmail racket with three horrible evacuee children for pawns, and though this idea gives Mr. Waugh scope for amusing incidental stuff, it is not in itself very convincing, nor are the three children credibly written. There are some elaborate bits of fun inside the Ministry of Information and the War Office, and in the bedrooms, bars and studios frequented by the two Evelyn Waugh sets, the smart and the intellectual. And there is a new character, a whining pansy called Ambrose Silk, who has an absurd adventure. Basil himself, as a great and awkward concession, actually attempts a lighthearted change of heart in the second last page. Except for this the book runs true enough to its author's form, and often raises a good laugh....

87.   ALAN PRYCE-JONES, 'NEW STATESMAN'

11 April 1942, 245-6

Alan Pryce-Jones (b. 1908) is a literary journalist, biographer, librettist and poet; he was Editor of the 'Times Literary Supplement', 1948-59, and book critic for the 'New York Herald Tribune', 1963-6. He is author of 'The Spring Journey' (1931), 'Beethoven' (1933) and 'Twenty-

Seven Poems' (1935). Mr Pryce-Jones was one of Waugh's
social circle during the late 1920s and 1930s.

It would be interesting to know what Mr. Waugh's large public makes of him; also, for that matter, to know for certain what Mr. Waugh makes of his large public. A vitupera-
tive young man, using the unpopular weapons of economy,
proportion, an eager brilliance inventive but well controlled, possessing a social sense which is dead-accurate
but fundamentally without humour - it is not in these
terms that one draws the normal outline of a popular novelist. Besides, he writes about people who are, in two
senses, real. They are never hypothecated or bowdlerized
to suit public sentiment, and often, despite the usual dis-
claimers, they contain ingenious portraits, built up in the
manner of a *collage* from appropriate fragments of old
friends. Thus according to the rules his novels ought to be
limited to a public of those in the know. They should be
left out on the table in appreciative flats or stuffed into
the gas-masks of highbrow sergeants. Instead of which they
sell like hot cakes.

It is worth while considering why. Evelyn Waugh is one
of our rare male novelists to write as an adult, and he is
flattering enough to postulate an adult, sophisticated
audience. The early novels were written from this simple
position. They made no personal statement, they hid their
healthy dislikes under his elegance, his beautiful timing
for each invention. But since 'A Handful of Dust' appeared
the author himself has been taking shape behind his creations, and in this latest book his position is quite clearly
defined. Catholic; good. There isn't much danger of such a
peppery individualist sharing the general conformity (burgundy, the Pyrenees, invective, pub-life, Pantagruel)
among lay English converts; although one may regret that
the Fr. Rothschild S.J. of 1930 will not be revived. Solitary; also good. He can modulate his spleen without previous commitments. Romantic; a superficial view might write
off this aspect of him as plain reactionary. Unrelenting;
the frustrations and punishments which occur in each novel
share the logic of Kafka. And very grown up.

His popularity, it is to be supposed, depends chiefly on
this last characteristic. There is an audience ready to be
quelled by the spectacle of a sophistication which does not
trouble to wink, a knowledge of the world which can traffic
in the dodges of three iniquitous continents, and an assumption of equal familiarity with the apparently not dissimilar
climates - at least during the timeless epoch of 'Vile
Bodies' - of Downing Street and the stews.

The more discriminating, while they laugh, make a minor reservation, however. Doesn't Mr. Waugh overdo it a little? Aren't the great ramshackle houses now too finely observed? Don't the casual details ring too carefully true? One cannot imagine any of these young men, shameless as they are in the conduct of life, doing up the bottom button of their waistcoat; and is not each overtone of adultery – in not somewhere obvious like Berkeley Square but a knowing by-street, say Montpellier Walk - recorded with rather too modish an air? This is a fault of taste which may be inseparable from the novelist's intention. English novelists are generally soft hearted and their sense of social values is rarely acute. Evelyn Waugh, within his chosen limits, applies a hard head to those values; where he fails it is from too facile a cynicism in face of the present day; too indulgent an eye for any idiosyncrasy that evokes an age in which the ordinary citizen was more likely to be a boor than a cad.

This reservation does not, however, affect the pleasure to be got from his negative side. 'Put Out More Flags' is to be praised without any reserve so long as the author is at the attack, direct or implicit. The best of the book shows that his commando has little to teach him in the technique of the sharp destructive raid. The Connolly passages, for example, stand among the modern show-pieces of brilliance and economy of means; and each prim recital of military behaviour, from battalion exercise to death in action, emphasises again what we already knew; that Mr. Waugh has a unique gift for pinning down the occasionally memorable astonishment of plain truth. The plot does not matter; it imposes a vague pattern on selected instances of incompetence, lying, theft, graft, fornication, unkindness, ineptitude, snobbery, cowardice, drink and unnatural vice during the first year of the war. The English world is neatly, and to some extent justly, divided into those who get away with it and those who don't, by a judge who has a weakness for the former. A young man trickles through to page 255 with so unforced a gift for self-preservation that it is embarrassing to leave him a hero in the epilogue. There is an aesthete who is heavily raided at intervals, but without quite enough trouble being taken to present him as a credible target. There is a typical product of Mr. Waugh's romanticism - the totally sophisticated, intelligent, rich, ravishing woman of thirty 'dressed to inform rather than to attract,' who is drunk during most of the book. Amateurs of the earlier Waugh will complain that she is modelled rather too lazily on Lady Metroland before her second marriage. There is a first-rate statesman's widow, and there is a small collection of old friends still pertinaciously doing their stuff.

One more minor complaint. Lord Pastmaster - who has sobered down into rather a dull young man - is written off at thirty-three whereas he cannot be a day over twenty-eight. Those who read all the Waugh novels with the respectful attention they deserve notice these things.

88.   GEORGE DANGERFIELD, 'SATURDAY REVIEW'

30 May 1942, 7

George Dangerfield (b. 1904), a distinguished social historian, is author of 'Bengal Mutiny' (1933), 'The Strange Death of Liberal England' (1935), 'Victoria's Heir' (1941), 'The Era of Good Feelings' (1952) and 'The Damnable Question' (1976).

It is very tempting to 'discover' in Basil Seal, the protagonist of Evelyn Waugh's latest novel, a kinship with Clovis Sangrail. Perhaps Mr. Waugh is indebted to Saki, but it would not be wise for his reviewer to make too much of this. The difference between the two writers is far more interesting than any debt that the younger may - possibly - owe to the older. The charm of Saki lies in his abiding immaturity. He never grew up. His worldly style - like a crystal - encloses but does not conceal a vein of childish cruelty. Evelyn Waugh is not cruel in that sense nor irresponsible in that sense, though a superficial reading of this novel might lead one to believe that both words applied to it. He is writing about a society which has afforded him a great deal of amusement and which he heartily dislikes. He is eminently a mature artist. In all his novels - and I think that they are among the most original novels of our time - he has always sought to discover the *lacrimae rerum*; and we should not take him any the less seriously because he makes his discovery with a fleer.

'Put Out More Flags' comes less close to tragedy than do some of his earlier books, because the characters are no longer involved in a personal dilemma. The joke was always on them, but now they have no answer; and when they have no answer they cease to be persons. The world is at war in this novel, and - wriggle as they will - they can find no place for themselves in it. They are not persons any more, but just unhappy examples of a bad and silly society. They are out of date and therefore dead.

Thus Basil Seal, who is a predatory young man and a
professional outcast, finds that it is one thing to be an
outcast in a world of peace and quite another to be an
outcast in a world at war. Seriousness is his greatest
enemy, and, from the moment that war breaks out, it begins
to threaten him. For the first months, it is true, England
was still not very serious; and it was possible for Basil
to make his way. There was the Ministry of Information to
be approached with a scheme for annexing Liberia; and there
was money to be made by taking a trio of impossible evacués
from one country house to another and demanding a bribe
before removing them. Even Military Intelligence received
Basil for a while - long enough for him to lay false evidence against one of his oldest friends. It is all quite
hilarious and all rather horrible.

To allow these people to behave on their own terms, and
condemn themselves out of their own mouths, is a dangerous
procedure; the book may be - perhaps will be - deliberately misunderstood. In 'Put Out More Flags,' however, the
apparently heartless jesting reveals a bitter attack upon
the society which made Basil Seal possible in the first
place; upon false internationalism, official pomposity,
selfishness, blindness, greed, betrayal. It is all very
lightly done, but it should not be lightly construed. Just
at the end, though, there is a false note. Mr. Waugh has
Basil say: 'There's only one serious occupation for a chap
now, that's killing Germans.' It is quite impossible for
Basil to say this, because Basil is a state of mind not a
human being; he is, as Mr. Waugh writes in his Dedicatory
Letter, a 'ghost.' By the end of the book Mr. Waugh has
sucessfully consigned Basil to Limbo; and, by snatching
him back at the last moment, he ceases to be an artist
and becomes a sentimentalist. But this is a transitory
fault in a brilliant and telling book.

89. NIGEL DENNIS, 'PARTISAN REVIEW'

28 July 1943, 357-61

When Evelyn Waugh's last novel, 'Put Out More Flags',
appeared in the summer of 1942, the 'Retail Bookseller'
summed it up for the American trade:

     The Waugh type of cleverness is for a definite mar-
     ket, faithful but limited.

It was a precise tribute to England's foremost contemporary comic novelist. Here, far more than in England,
Waugh has tended to be a special taste established in the
first years of Depression and savored devotedly by a handful of people through ten years of proletarian novels,
monsters of historical romance, and dubious charts for
liberal futures. Uneasily reviewed in the line of duty,
this author of two incomparable period pieces ('Decline and
Fall', 'Vile Bodies') has received no serious recognition.
Woollcott (1) called Waugh the nearest thing to a genius
the English 30s had produced, and chose 'A Handful of Dust'
as the best English novel in 100 years. But Woollcott called
so many things so many things.

One of the problems has been what the 'Retail Bookseller'
blandly calls 'the Waugh type of cleverness'. The same
descriptive terms have been used for Waugh by intellectuals
who should know better. Waugh has been shrugged off on
grounds that are his most serious claim to distinction. The
nature of his best fiction; its fantastic gravity in the
face of the ridiculous, its levity over accepted forms of
seriousness, its high narrative flash-point accompanied by
one sleight of hand after another - these admirable gifts of
the satirical novelist have frightened even his admirers
into their hole-and-corner approval that family men whisper
behind their hands about prostitutes, but never admit to
their wives. So rubbed away in Waugh's finished work are
the pain and labor of the writing, that the artist is condemned as frivolous. He is frowned on for his dexterity
when, five characters in each hand, he can develop, in
smoothly interlocking conversations and exits and entries,
the reader's understanding of his people, their immediate
situation, and the theme of the novel. He is mistrusted
because he can pull anything from performing seals and
oranges to acute major materials out of an air of nonsense
at a second's notice, fit them perfectly into narrative-
place, and flick them out again with none of the second-
rate writer's passion for clutching his material. Time and
place are fixed with admirably brief descriptive passages,
only to be ignored and ridiculed by characters whose hand-
to-mouth thinking and behavior make a mockery of established
form.

If Waugh's unique combination of daring, control, and
side-glance exercises has caused him to be classed merely
with tight-rope walkers, his subject matter, attitude, and
choice of characters have been found equally damning. In a
period that has rejoiced in solemnly attributing the most
superficial accident to a basic historical condition, Waugh
has preferred to indicate how a minor accident can render
the important ridiculous. '[Basil] rejoiced, always, in the

spectacle of women at a disadvantage: thus he would watch, in the asparagus season, a dribble of melted butter on a [beautiful] woman's chin....' Where others have shown in a million ways the crushing effect of social forms on strug- gling individuals, Waugh, the lover of inanimate objects, has delighted in showing how valued material may be de- stroyed at a moment's whim by the wilful use of individual power. Candide is usually Waugh's central character - though his Candide may as easily be a house or a painting or a tradition as a man or a woman - and with the bland- ness of Goldsmith and the sophistication of Trollope he has liked to put rural innocence into the cruel hands of urban wise-guys, and to show, with sadistic pleasure, the helplessness of the intellectual confronted by the brute. Finally, in a period in which class tragedy superseded individual suffering, Waugh's sufferers and settings were stubbornly upper class. In the town it was Mayfair, in the country it was parkland; and the 'thirties were not a period which fostered aesthetic respect for both the young manhood of Studs Lonigan (2) *and* the offspring of the landed gentry and new rich. The drip of butter on the face of beauty was inconspicuous against the monstrous social background.

But the ultimate fault was Waugh's. In the twelve years following his conversion to Catholicism, he produced a series of novels, short stories and travel books in which his satire and outrageous burlesque of English society changed, as Dunstan Thompson has pointed out, (3) to kindly parody, of the kind 'Punch' delights in. He showed clearly that his rebelliousness was to be that of the palace revolutionary - limited by England's palace walls. Father Rothschild S.J., the motor-cycling Jesuit who pulled strings of Cabinet policy with priestly dexterity, rode off on his machine in a cloud of pity for young aris- tocrats and never re-appeared. Never again did the Evangel- ist, Mrs. Ape, and her 'angels' sing 'There Ain't No Flies on The Lamb of God.'... Gone [was] ... the extraordinary terror of the few terse lines in which a well-born daugh- ter, suddenly awaking to her fate, futilely begs her snob- bish mother to help her escape from a socially desirable marriage to a man she despises.(4) What Waugh wanted there- after was to use the palace inmates as subjects for tra- gedy, not satire; but when he tried in 'A Handful of Dust', he failed because the field was too shallow. The nearest he came to success was in the short extract of an unpublished novel, which appeared in 'Horizon' last year under the title My Father's House....(5)

To return [from Mexico] to an England on the verge of war under that epitome of unknightly rule, Neville

Chamberlain, must have been the last straw. A world in
which radicals were still vociferous, ... the young squires
held in their tents by industrialists in black coats - this
was surely England's lowest decline from Waugh's high standard of glory.

When Tory salvation came in the form of the Churchill
government, Waugh recognized it instantly. Returning from
the Middle East he wrote 'Put Out More Flags'. 'A new
spirit' was 'abroad in the land', and in dedicating his
work to the new Prime Minister's son, Major Randolph Churchill M.P., of the 4th Hussars, Waugh apologized for the
fact that he was not entirely contemporary in his approach.
'These pages,' he said, 'may not be altogether acceptable
to your ardent and sanguine nature. They deal, mostly with
a race of ghosts, the survivors of the world we both knew
ten years ago ... but where my imagination still fondly
lingers.... These characters are no longer contemporary in
sympathy; they were forgotten even before the war; but they
lived on delightfully in holes and corners.... Here they
are in that odd, dead period before the Churchillian
renaissance.'

Who are these neglected phantoms with a low standard of
living, from whom Waugh dissociates himself with such tolerant superiority? Most of them appear from Waugh's own
sleeve; they are his own literary creations invoked from
the pages of his own novels. And, despite the nostalgic
tone of Waugh's dedicatory words, we quickly find that
these ghosts are highly contemporary; that while some are
to be exorcised forever, others are to be reembodied into
active elements of the 'Churchillian renaissance.'

The old gentlemen are out. The doddering ghosts of aristocracy who spent their paternal vitality serving the
squirearchy - they are through and will haunt no more. Not
so the playboys. With Waugh's aid they do penance for their
wasted ghosthood, conquer their dissipation and are entered,
like gentlemanly *condottieri*, into the 'new spirit' of the
age. Readers of early Waugh may remember, for instance,
Alistair Digby-Vaine-Trumpington. Alistair was distinctly
a 'vile body'. But now, his wife Sonia tells us:

> ...he was a much odder character than anyone knows. You
> remember that man who used to dress as an Arab and then
> went into the Air Force as a private because he thought
> the British government had let the Arabs down?(6) ... I
> believe Alistair felt like that. You see he'd never done
> anything for the country.... I believe he thought that
> perhaps if he had done something perhaps there wouldn't
> have been any war.... He went into the ranks as a kind
> of penance.

As Alistair, saved from wraithhood by consorting with
the lowest type of soldier, kneels in confession, he must
note with some surprise that his literary creator has set
on their knees beside him a row of reformed rakes. There is
Sonia, bearing Alistair the child she could never conceive
in her ghostly period. There is Peter Pastmaster, who mixed
cocktails so expertly at the age of fourteen, and played
'Pop Goes the Weasel' on the school organ. There is Angela
Lyne, who took veronal under Chamberlain. There is even
Angela's future husband, Basil Seal of 'Black Mischief',
who carried self-interest to a sublime level of cruelty,
and, before Chamberlain was ousted, conducted a virtually
incestuous relationship with his sister while running a
blackmail scheme.... The menfolk of this group of peni-
tents are destined to join Waugh's own branch of the services, the Commandos - by Waugh's description a chummy sort
of war club for reformed gentlemen. 'Most of the war,' explains Peter Pastmaster, 'seems to consist of hanging
about. Let's at least hang about with our own friends.'

How well it has all worked out! These ghosts are ghosts
no more; they have come through the hail of Spanish Loyal-
ists, misguided intellectuals, decayed elder statesmen,
enemies of the true faith, and are now ready to set a glowing seal on their creator's choice of life; to ride out of
their English-Gothic castles - 20th century Knight Commandos going out to overthrow the ungentlemanly materialists
of Nazidom.

Keeping their place till they return are the gentle
Babbitts (7) of the landed gentry. How near they came to
ghosthood, those people of 'decent and temperate life' we
met ten years ago on the steps of Anchorage House! We saw
them then in the London season; in 'Put Out More Flags'
they are back in their country homes, as though having
caught the night train down. They are grooming 'the splendid surface' of their lawns and devoutly working in the
herbaceous borders; when 'ice stood thick on the lily ponds
... these good people fed the birds daily with crumbs from
the dining-room table and saw to it that no old person in
the village went short of coal.'

The fate of permanent ghosthood is reserved for another
group - England's younger intellectuals. These people have
never before been mentioned in a Waugh novel; but they are
Waugh's ghosts nonetheless, because the new signatures of
most of them have stood on the wall to haunt him throughout
his literary career. Now, the 'Churchillian renaissance'
has delivered them into his hands. The most opportunistic
playboys - the men who drove the Gothic squire to his death
in 'A Handful of Dust' - may rise to the occasion in a time
of crisis, but no radical is to be anything but a ghost

beside the 'new spirit'. In prose that varies from childish-
ness to a very high standard, Waugh throws his great capacity for savagery against the most thoughtful enemies of 'my
father's house'. With Auden and Isherwood he plays with the
happy cruelty of a slightly demented child, taunting them
with Spain, reminding them in New York of their past devotion to contemporary happenings, recalling, for comparison,
'Socrates marching to the sea with Xenophon ... Horace
singing the sweetness of dying for one's country'. And to
make sure the board is swept clean, Waugh rids England of
the esthete, shown in the person of Ambrose Silk, one of
Waugh's most able and cynical characterizations, combining
low birth, Jewish blood, homosexuality and cowardice with
decadent memories of Gertrude Stein, Cocteau and Diaghilev.
Face to face with the aristocratic Commando, Basil Seal,
Ambrose is utterly routed.

This is more than a parable of war. The conflict between
the esthete and the man of action is Waugh's own conflict.
For Ambrose, with his 'Yellow Book' dreams, embodies so
many of the anti-materialistic, esthetic elements that
Waugh himself has advanced, and consequently there are
moments in 'Put Out More Flags' when Ambrose is more
pitied than censured by his author. But the point is that
estheticism is not in future to be sullied by such as
Ambrose. In a typically Waugh scene we are shown Basil's
mistress picking the monogram off the departed Ambrose's
crepe-de-chine underwear, and replacing it with a 'B' for
Basil.

In 'Horizon', in a discussion of the sterility of 'Puritan'
poetry, Waugh presented his view of the proper function of
the contemporary poet. 'I think it is time,' he said:

> we made up our minds that poetry is one of the arts
> which has died in the last eighty years.... The men who
> write your 'poetry' seem to me to be trying to live on
> the prestige of a dead art. Shelley talked of poets as
> the legislators of the world, and they seem to have
> applied this to themselves without any justification at
> all.... Here we reach a deep cause of Puritanism - the
> poetic sense of responsibility. Let us tell the poets at
> once that no one need legislate who does not want to....
> All we ask of the poets is to sing.

'Horizon's' editor (8) rejects Waugh's charge that
poetry is dead. But he tells us that 'the sophisticated
intellectual poetry of the 'twenties is exhausted,' that
poetry was 'taken down a cul de sac to get away from the
Georgians'. The 'thirties gave it inadequate revival in

'academic socialism.' Now, 'we are waiting for a new romanticism to bring it back to life.' This will happen when
'the tide of events sweeps round the lonely stumps on which
our cormorants have been sitting and gives them a fishing
ground.' Meantime, editors must publish, among other
things, 'poems which reflect the lyrical influence of Lorca
rather than the intellectual one of Auden, Eliot or Rilke.'
Only the 'best work' of the best younger poets - Spender,
Empson, Thomas, Barker, Rodgers, Vernon Watkins, 'must be
encouraged.'

These remarks, so valuable if they had been made in the
30's, are worrying at the present moment. Just what do
they indicate? That the lyric poet, the domestic novelist
and the literary essayist are to supersede writers whose
only virtue is political propriety? Or, as seems more probable, that the editorial political narrowness of the '30's
must give way to a new narrowness? In exchange for Puritan-
ism we are to have, as Dali suggests, 'an individualistic
tradition ... Catholic, aristocratic, and probably monar-
chic'?

The 'Churchillian renaissance' is abroad in England.
Behind its dashing skirts sit the pre-war industrialists,
looking forward to the day when adventurous leadership will
give place again to the 1922 Committee, and the demands of
generals be as remote as reminiscent book reviews in the
'Times Literary Supplement'. The call to poets to cease
from legislating and to 'sing', is invariably made loudest
by men like Waugh, who cannot put pen to paper without
legislating. And before we give Auden a military funeral
and fire a volley into his grave, it will be well to look
back at the lessons of the 30's and not throw the value
out with the ignorance. The struggle to leave 'my father's
house' was no exercise in 'academic socialism', however
much it became inter-mixed with the sycophantic intolerance of fellow travellers. If, in the name of art and
'singing', the intellectual is to sit passively waiting
for the waters to bring him fish, the 'romantic revival' is
likely to be one-sided in the creels it fills. To fail to
appreciate the Waughs of literature was a crime of the
30's; to accept their dicta as a way of life will be the
crime of the 40's. In gloomier moments one pictures the
abashed intellectuals returning like prodigals to the halls
they abandoned, and singing as they polish their pedigrees.
Gothic texts will line the walls where 'New Signatures'
once hung. To the cheers of his tenantry the reformed rake
will return from the Commandos to take up his squireship
of 'English Gothic'.

Notes

1 Alexander Woollcott was the American writer and critic,
   to whom Waugh dedicated 'Work Suspended' (1942).
2 The Studs Lonigan novels were written by the American
   James T. Farrell.
3 NR, 13 July 1942, 60-1.
4 In 'Vile Bodies'; the incident occurs between Lady
   Ursula and her mother, the Duchess of Stayle (Penguin,
   pp. 135-6).
5 See headnote to No. 16 above.
6 T.E. Lawrence (Lawrence of Arabia).
7 I.e. the unambitious middle classes, after the epony-
   mous hero of Sinclair Lewis's novel, 'Babbit' (1922).
8 Cyril Connolly (see headnote to No. 16).

'Work Suspended'

1942

90. 'WILLIAM HICKEY' (TOM DRIBERG), 'DAILY EXPRESS'

1 January 1943, 2

Tom Driberg (Baron Bradwell) (1905-76), was a journalist
(inventor of the William Hickey column in the 'Express'),
writer, broadcaster and, from 1959, Labour M.P. for Barking. He wrote 'Beaverbrook' (1956), 'Guy Burgess' (1956),
'The Mystery of Moral Re-Armament' (1964) and his autobiography 'Ruling Passions' (published posthumously, 1977).
  Driberg and Waugh were friends at Lancing (1917-21) and
remained so to the end despite Driberg's left-wing politics
and flagrant homosexuality. As 'Dragoman' and 'William
Hickey' (1928-43) he provided Waugh with a great deal of
free publicity of which the following piece is a typical
example. Waugh was too well aware of the importance of keeping his name before the public in the gaps between the
publication of his novels not to take advantage of this.
Indeed, he encouraged it while openly lampooning the Beaverbrook press in his fiction (cf. his treatment of journalists in 'Vile Bodies' and 'Scoop').

Another fairly rare review-copy has come to me - a copy of
Captain Evelyn Waugh's unfinished novel 'Work Suspended,'
of which only 500 copies have been printed.
  The author (a contemporary of mine) has inscribed it
'Nous ne sommes pas heureux à notre âge.' (Roughly, 'We are
an unlucky generation.') He seems to look back more wist-
fully than I to the lost, careless, picturesque, unjust
world of our youth.
  Even this fragment is delightful to read. I am sure that
Waugh is an admirable Commando, but he was also an

admirable novelist, and it seems tragic that he could not
have completed this one further book before joining up -
tho' I think I understand the spiritual compulsion which
made such a delay and labour impossible for him.

91.   UNSIGNED REVIEW, 'TIMES LITERARY SUPPLEMENT'

23 January 1943, 41

This is a limited edition of a fragment of a novel of which
Mr. Waugh says that it cannot and will not be completed
because 'the world in which and for which it was designed
has ceased to exist', and of which he also says that, so
far as it went, 'this was my best writing.' The importance
of the occasion is perhaps not quite so apparent to the
reader. The fragment seems a little more urbane and
rounded in manner than usual and may reflect - it is hard
to tell - a more transparently serious intention, but at
any rate it mingles the usual unsmiling ribaldry and a
grave trick of comic fancy with familiar satire, a slightly
mystifying touch of social criticism and a deal of over-
prolonged metaphor. Chapter one describes how John Plant,
a deliberate young man who wrote detective fiction, left
Morocco after the death of his father, a painter of strong
and perverse temperament who produced facsimiles of the
masters of English portraiture, and returned to England. It
describes, too, a trying and foolish young man named
Atwater, who had driven his car into Mr. Plant, senior,
and killed him. Chapter two describes how John Plant fell
in love with Lucy, the wife of his writer friend, Roger,
who had turned Communist, and how Lucy, until her child was
born, accompanied him in quest of a house in the country.
And there the matter ends. Mr. Waugh is often amusing,
sometimes acute, at times pleasantly decorative and at
other times a trifle shrill with prejudice, but what else
this fragment is intended to convey there is no means of
knowing.

92.   NIGEL DENNIS, 'PARTISAN REVIEW'

28 July 1943, 352-6

Mr Dennis is commenting here on the first part of 'Work
Suspended', My Father's House, which appeared in 'Horizon'
in November 1941.

...Here was a brilliant study of a Victorian painter watching his world crumbling about him: his huge canvases
entitled 'Agag Before Samuel' and 'Feet of Clay' being
pushed off the market by Gauguin's 'disjointed negresses,'
his Victorian mansion becoming hemmed in by monster apartment houses panelled with green wood and infested with rats
and prostitutes, his social status undermined when the
politicians went into alliance 'with the slaves.' '"We [the
gentry] are extinct already, I am a Dodo," he used to
say.... "You, my poor son, are a petrified egg."'
   My Father's House. It is the most meaningful of all
Waugh's titles and, with its summons to lament the past, it
could stand as an invisible title to everything Waugh has
written. Houses, houses, houses - from the pages of
'Decline and Fall,' 'Vile Bodies,' 'A Handful of Dust,'
'Rossetti,' 'Put Out More Flags.' Mostly they have been
large country houses, often falling down or badly kept up.
Sometimes they have been raped by vile bodies who have
pulled them down and replaced them with modern horrors of
chromium and colored slats. Sometimes they have been the
individualistic creations of men like Rossetti and William
Morris with massive, blackened furniture and immense
appurtenances. Always the house has made the man; man has
not existed apart from his roof any more than the rat has
failed to swarm into the apartment house. And always the
house has been a way of life for Waugh, desirable or detes-
table. He has dwelt on its driveways and park, the iron
railings and stone walls that have stood between the house
and the slaves; the carpets, busts and old priest-holes;
the warm libraries where a dozing visitor is awoken by a
padding maid with an afternoon tea in a silver pot surrounded by scones, relish, toast and cherry jam. For fifteen years Waugh has sung the house, and with it the precious furnishings he finds suited to it - the paintings
that are not of disjointed negresses, the timbers that have
been seasoned in estate barns, the owners who cherish it
above themselves. And in this love of house, of continuous
domicile and individual roof, Waugh appears for the defense
in one of the most important struggles in English poetry

and letters of the last 20 years. My Father's House (it
would be 'my Mother's' to many) is the starting point of
England's recent literary past. It has shaped the intellectuals' outlook, their conduct, their England - indeed, the
literary history of the 'thirties can be written with the
house of childhood as its center.

The young men who have written English poetry for the
last ten years have been mostly the men of Waugh's class,
with gradations above and below. Their battle has been for
self-emancipation; freedom, not from riches or love of
grandeur but from the far more insidious influences of the
houses of their birth and education. What appeared in their
writings as a new faith in the proletariat and an enthusiasm for the urban under-privileged was, far more, an effort
to purge the author's own personality of its upper-class
preferences and trained acceptance of the old, rural order;
to bring the lagging instincts into line with the advancing
intellect. The bonds that held the heart in a setting of
lawns, trees, cool drawing rooms and soft-spoken family
friends were less evident but far more binding that the
parallel ties of the public school. The intellectual
pledged his new fidelity to the city, to the waste land
that must [be] recreated; he entered the woods only by chara-
banc. In 'New Signatures,'(1) the poets' first public
avowal of their determination to achieve self-conversion,
one finds the whole intimate and painful struggle with past
allegiances, phrased usually as an appeal to the non-
fighters rather than a lyric expression of the writers' own
dilemma. And the recurring center is 'my father's house'.
In Spender it was a warning to young men that

> It is too late now to stay in those houses your fathers
> built ...
> It is too late to stay in great houses where the ghosts
> are prisoned
> - those ladies like flies perfect in amber

In Day-Lewis it was the lament of a landed mother for
her son:

> Warm in my walled garden the flower grew first.
> Transplanted it ran wild on the estate.
> Why should it ever need a new sun?
> (...One day) He crossed the frontier and I did not
> follow:
> Returning, spoke another language.

The strain is clear, too, in Auden's most famous sonnet:

...Publish each healer that in city lives
Or country houses at the end of drives;
Harrow the house of the dead; look shining at
New styles of architecture, a change of heart.

There was at issue a literal walking out from the paternal halls; Auden's 'styles of architecture' were exactly
that as well as symbols of the old and new in living. And
in the new direction, there is clearly indicated the sharp
line that had emerged to divide the intellectuals of the
Left from such as Evelyn Waugh. Like these intellectuals
Waugh saw the ghosts in the old houses, the flies lovely
in amber; unlike them, he totally rejected the plea to
'advance to rebuild'. The ghosts must be materialized; or,
if that were impossible, they must be preserved as the best
available wraiths. In two brilliant satires ('Decline and
Fall,' 'Vile Bodies') he had said what he thought of people
who destroyed old houses; although his victims were of his
own class, to say the least, he had pilloried them because
they failed to see that their duty lay in preserving their
country homes rather than in hell-raising in Mayfair. He
had a clear idea of what England's house should look like,
of the people that should live in it, of the art that
should grace its walls. The people were to be the ones whom
Lady Circumference of 'Vile Bodies' found attending a
reception at Anchorage House, one of the last of London's
great town houses. They were not the bloated great, with
their dubiously-acquired fortunes and reverberating soap-
and-brewery titles. They were the relatively small fry:

> ...a great concourse of pious and honorable people
> (many of whom made the Anchorage House reception the
> one outing of the year), their womenfolk well gowned in
> rich and durable stuffs, their menfolk ablaze with
> orders; people who had represented their country in
> foreign places and sent their sons to die for her in
> battle, people of decent and temperate life, uncul-
> tured, unaffected, unembarrassed, unassuming, unambi-
> tious people, of independent judgment and marked eccen-
> tricities, kind people who cared for animals and the
> deserving poor, brave and rather unreasonable people,
> that fine phalanx of the passing order, approaching, as
> one day at the Last Trump they hoped to meet their
> Maker, with decorous and frank cordiality to shake Lady
> Anchorage by the hand at the top of her staircase.

We know at once who these ideal souls are: they are the
landed, and would-be landed, gentry of England, the ones to
whom 'father' made his pledge of fidelity, though he

professed to see them as dead as dodos, and their offspring
as petrified eggs. They are that rigid backbone of England's rural constituencies - the conservative squirearchy
(even when their houses are small) on whose paternalism the
existence of millions of rural Englishmen depends.

What of the art that these squires should cherish? Waugh
had chosen that in the first book he ever wrote: 'Rossetti:
His Life and Works.' His squire was to enliven his solidity
with Pre-Raphaelite dreams of knighthood. The Pre-Raphaelite
struggle against materialism - against the huge apartments
'my father' hated, and industrialized living - Waugh made
his own, ignoring Morris's socialism but accepting both the
aesthetic and moral visions of the Pre-Raphaelite conception of medievalism, and relishing 'the stimulus it gives
to one's restiveness in an era of complete stultification.'
His world was not in negroid primitivism, but in such
favorite paintings as Rossetti's 'Marriage of St. George,'
and he quoted approvingly James Smetham's description of
that odd hodge-podge of cluttered 'medieval' objects:

> One of the grandest things, like a golden, dim
> dream. Love 'credulous all gold', gold armour, a sense
> of secret enclosure in 'palace chambers far apart'; but
> quaint chambers in quaint palaces, where angels creep in
> through sliding panel doors, and stand behind rows of
> flowers, drumming on golden bells, with wings crimson
> and green....

'English Gothic' Waugh called it and, in 'A Handful of
Dust,' he lamented its passing, exiling the Squire who
tried to restore it to the jungles of Brazil - where he
perished by the fiendish torture of reading aloud to a
lonely maniac the novels of the industrialized Charles
Dickens....

Note

1 'New Signatures' (Leonard and Virginia Woolf, 1932) was
   the first of three important anthologies compiled by
   Michael Roberts (pseudonym of William Edward Roberts,
   1902-48), the poet, during the 1930s. The other two were
   'New Country' (1933) and 'The Faber Book of Modern Verse'
   (1936). The first two, and particularly Roberts's introduction to 'New Country', helped to establish the left-
   wing poets of the period - Auden, Spender, Day-Lewis,
   for instance - in the canon of contemporary literature,
   and justify political conscience and consciousness in
   art. Roberts defined this new awareness as 'social

communism', 'that extension of personality and consciousness which comes sometimes to a group of men when they
are working together for some common purpose'.

93. ROSE MACAULAY, 'HORIZON'

December 1946, 371

After it ['Put Out More Flags'] (published [in 1942] with a
preliminary note that it dealt with a world now dead and
would never be finished) came a perfectly serious fragment
of a novel called 'Work Suspended'. Mr. Waugh said that it
was his best writing up till then. He is right that it is
well written: he always (or nearly always) writes well. It
is carefully composed; it lacks the earlier sparkle; it
has a seriousness of tone that might or might not have been
fully justified by its theme as it developed: it did not
develop, so we cannot know. In spite of a fine and delicate
vein of comedy (the hero's artist father and the commercial
traveller who ran him down and killed him, are both charming figures of fun), there is a sobriety, almost a solemnity, of mood that foreshadows that of 'Brideshead'. Lucy,
the grave young heroine, is presented with restraint, and
with a new subtlety of emotion, composed and near-profound,
at times a little Jamesian in slant. The style is quiet and
full. That it was not finished one feels a loss. It was an
experiment, a study, abandoned, in a new *genre*; it seems,
fragment though it is, to have balance and perspective; and
the key is low; if ecstasy should develop, one does not
feel that it would necessarily be flamboyant. It might (or
possibly not) have justified its author as a straight novelist. But it shows the warning red - or perhaps only amber
- lights.

'Brideshead Revisited'

1945

94. J.D. BERESFORD, 'MANCHESTER GUARDIAN'

1 June 1945, 3

John Davys Beresford (1873-1947), biographer and prolific
popular novelist, was author of 'Jacob Stahl' (1911),
'H.G. Wells' (1915), 'God's Counterpoint' (1918) and 'The
Camberwell Miracle' (1933).

Mr. Evelyn Waugh is a highly gifted and imaginative writer,
but I must confess to a strong personal prejudice against
his choice of subjects. In 'Brideshead Revisited' he is
concerned with a titled Roman Catholic family of considerable wealth. The elder son is a religiously minded nonentity, the younger a man of great personal charm but a confirmed dipsomaniac, and the daughter who marries a divorced
Canadian in face of the opposition of her family, to whom
such a marriage would mean 'living in sin,' does not remain
faithful to him. In short, Mr. Waugh's principal themes are
adultery, perversion, and drunkenness, and while I could
not fail to admire the brilliance of his writing I greatly
disliked his story.

95. UNSIGNED REVIEW, 'TIMES LITERARY SUPPLEMENT'

2 June 1945, 257

In finding it necessary to warn the reader that 'Brides-

head Revisited' is 'not meant to be funny,' Mr. Evelyn
Waugh will surely have the reader's sympathy.(1) He has
seldom been a comic writer and nothing else, for the moralist or religious moralist was almost always to be discovered looking over his shoulder and casting a somewhat
chill shadow upon his buffoonery. Now Mr. Waugh is at some
pains to protest the high seriousness of his purpose. It is
'nothing less,' he writes, 'than an attempt to trace the
workings of the divine purpose in a pagan world, in the
lives of an English Catholic family, half-paganized themselves, in the world of 1923-1939.' Whether, in fact, he
gives the impression in the end of having traced the workings of the divine purpose with any marked clarity is
doubtful, but at least the permeating consciousness of a
Roman Catholic point of view is never in question. A sense
of personal destiny deriving from the acknowledgement of
his religious belief would seem to be strongly at work in
Mr. Waugh.

Needless to say, the book is often extremely amusing.
Mr. Waugh's humour is of several kinds - the ribald, the
oblique and sophisticated, the intellectually astringent -
and each is paraded with a careless and flowing ease. But
nowhere in the book does the humour stand alone, nowhere
does it suggest any sort of detachment or disinterestedness
of mind. The book, indeed, is not meant to be funny, as
Mr. Waugh puts it, because its comedy is always engulfed in
the last resort in the author's asseveration of Catholic
doctrine, in his sentiment of the aristocratic or oligar-
chic English past, in his feeling for whatever may be
thought to be a corrective for the idea of progress. Mr.
Waugh, that is, for all his apparent high spirits, is here
very much the Catholic apologist and romantically conservative preacher.

The story he tells pursues a rather winding course.
There is a prologue which introduces the narrator, Charles
Ryder, as an infantry commander in this war; at the end of
a long journey in darkness to a new camp in the south
Charles finds himself once more in the grounds of Brideshead Castle in Wiltshire. Back he goes in memory to the
beginning of his acquaintance with the Flyte family, the
beginning of his friendship at Oxford with Lord Sebastian,
the Marquis of Marchmain's younger son, the beginning of
his discovery of his soul's dependence upon the mercy of
God. The Oxford scenes, which make up a third or so of the
book, are very well done in their way, though it is a
rather lordly way. Charles is entranced from the first by
Sebastian, his epicure beauty, his gaiety, eccentricity of
spirit and knowledge of food and wine, and is beguiled at
the same time by the apparent mystery of Sebastian's family

and the family charm. From another undergraduate, the
horridly loquacious aesthete Anthony Blanche, sinister and
stammering, Charles learns something of the mystery - the
Marchmains live apart - but still not a great deal. Then
comes his first real visit to the domed and columned palace
at Brideshead, his first glimpse of Lady Marchmain and of
Julia, Sebastian's sister; and after that there is a visit
to Venice and to Lord Marchmain's palace there. So to the
issue presented in the first place by Sebastian's drunkenness.

In all this Mr. Waugh seems to be taking his time before
getting to grips with anything of moment. Sebastian's cultivated inconsequence is seldom without entertainment,
though it lacks a stamp of truth through being indulged in
too facile a manner; the trick of remoteness, at once
benign and malicious, of Charles's elderly father is
brought out to happier and more significant effect. But for
the rest it seems difficult to account for the weight of
emphasis laid upon Sebastian's inner being or to connect
his incipient dipsomania either with the paganism of English society or with an attempt to diagnose this paganism.
What exactly has Mr. Waugh in mind, one would like to know,
in making the perhaps too charming young man a dipsomaniac?
Is it no more than that, being himself an unsatisfactory
Roman Catholic, Sebastian lacked the will to resist drink?

The decorations of the tale, if one may say so, are
devised to better advantage than the theme which Mr. Waugh
announces. Even his prejudices, the small ones as well as
those not so small, carry from time to time an engaging
warmth or candour. Mr. Waugh seems to be convinced, for
instance, that there was less madness - mental disease -
among human beings when there was less talk of progress.
He has only scorn for the bathroom with chromium fittings
in place of the copper, mahogany-framed bath, brass lever,
coal fire and chintz armchair of an earlier and more oblig-
ing day. He realizes that 'it is possible for the rich to
sin by coveting the privileges of the poor.' His prepposses-
sions, as a matter of fact, where such things as wealth and
privilege are concerned, are of an unambiguously romantic
character.

With Sebastian removed from the foreground of the scene
the brilliant Julia comes into her own. She did not want a
royal marriage, although purer lineage or a more gracious
presence, as Mr. Waugh puts it, was far to seek, and
although also she outshone by far all the girls of her age.
By some means then, she consented to marry the rich, hard,
bouncing, vulgar Rex Mottram, M.P., and marry him she did
just after the family discovered he had already been
married and divorced. It was years after that Charles, now

an architectural painter and married to the shallow and
faithless Lady Celia, discovered his love for Julia. How
Charles and Julia became lovers during a storm at sea and
then, having contemplated matrimony, were parted finally by
a true apprehension of Catholic doctrine on the subject of
divorce provides hurried conclusion. Mr. Waugh has his
felicities of illustration and phrase, of course, but
seems in general to have had his style cramped by a too
obviously preconceived idea.

Note

1 Waugh's 'warning' appeared on the inside flap of the
   dust jacket:

   When I wrote my first novel sixteen years ago, my
   publishers advised me, and I readily agreed, to prefix the warning that it was 'meant to be funny.' The
   phrase proved a welcome gift to unsympathetic critics.
   Now, in a more sombre decade, I must provide them
   with another text, and, in honesty to the patrons who
   have supported me hitherto, state that 'Brideshead
   Revisited' is *not* meant to be funny. There are passages of buffoonery, but the general theme is at once
   romantic and eschatological. It is ambitious, perhaps
   intolerably presumptuous; nothing less than an
   attempt to trace the workings of the divine purpose
   in a pagan world, in the lives of an English Catholic
   family, half paganised themselves, in the world of
   1923-1939. The story will be uncongenial alike to
   those who look back on that pagan world with unalloyed
   affection, and to those who see it as transitory,
   insignificant and, already, hopefully passed. Whom
   then can I hope to please? Perhaps those who have the
   leisure to read a book word for word for the interest
   of the writer's use of language; perhaps those who
   look to the future with black forebodings and need
   more solid comfort than rosy memories. For the latter
   I have given my hero, and them, if they will allow
   me, a hope, not, indeed, that anything but disaster
   lies ahead, but that the human spirit, redeemed, can
   survive all disasters.

96.   V.C. CLINTON-BADDELEY, 'SPECTATOR'

8 June 1945, 532

Victor Clinton-Baddeley (1900-70), was a playwright, travel
writer, critic and novelist. He was author of 'Devon'
(1925), 'Alladin; or, Love Will Find Out a Way' (1931),
'The Split in the Cabinet' (1938), 'Sleeping Beauty' (1959)
and 'No Case for the Police' (1970). 'The Burlesque Tradition in the English Theatre' and 'To Study a Long Silence'
were published posthumously in 1971 and 1972 respectively.

'Brideshead Revisited' is a story of the years between the
wars. The prologue - a sketch of Army life in the present
war, embracing in a short space an astonishing amount of
satirical detail - is extremely important to the book, because it introduces a narrator who instantly lays hold on
the reader's affection. The 'I' of a story told in the
first person is sometimes an uncertain figure - merely a
part of the book's machinery. Captain Charles Ryder is a
sharply-drawn character, gentle, humorous, civilised,
entirely likeable. The story he has to tell is that of a
Catholic family's apostasies and repentances, and it is a
brilliant stroke of Mr. Waugh's to tell that story through
the mind of a non-Catholic.(1) Though the book has a
powerful religious purpose it has no shadow of Catholic
exclusiveness.
    A deplorable lot these Flytes seem to be when you first
meet them - the good ones as well as the bad. Lord Marchmain had deserted wife, family and home and had lived im-
properly in Italy for twenty years. Lady Marchmain, though
infinitely religious, was unsympathetic and unloved.
Brideshead, the heir, was a prejudiced bonehead; Sebastian,
the second son, a drunkard. Cordelia, the youngest, was a
good girl, but Lady Julia had cut herself off, not only by
marrying a divorced man but by subsequently living in sin
with Captain Ryder. But the Flytes had not been brought up
as Catholics for nothing. Lord Marchmain makes a just sufficient death-bed repentance; Sebastian ends up as a hanger-
on in a monastery in Africa; and Julia, after risking so
much for love, decides after all that she can not 'set up
a rival good to God's.' Charles Ryder is the loser, but he
has the wit and the love to understand why.
    'Brideshead Revisited' is a story of the voice of man's
conscience, and such a theme could only be expounded by a
master of character creation. Anything improbable, anything unreasonable, would have been disastrous. It is the

measure of Evelyn Waugh's success that every move in the untwisting of this tangle appears not merely probable but pre-ordained. As in all good novels the slender plot is created by the characters, and so careful is their development that it is long past the middle of the book before the reader can have any honest apprehension of the end. Much seems to surprise: yet all is prepared. Particularly good is the character development of Julia. Her swift determination to rebel and her slow determination to recant are both equally and inevitably right. Sebastian, who in the first part of the book appears to be the leading character, is less successful. The reader catches the author here attempting to shift some of the responsibility of creation on to the other characters of the story. Everyone is made to make repeated references to Sebastian's irresistible charm. But (except at the beginning) there is not much in his character, as deduced from his own behaviour, to suggest anything but the melancholic dipsomaniac, never a very entertaining character. But the theme (as the reader slowly recognises) is not the story of Sebastian, but the reclamation of the whole family, whose most important member is Julia. Her story is told to perfection.

Although the theme of 'Brideshead Revisited' is deeply serious, it is accompanied by a brighter wit and a more sudden laughter than you will find in any other novel of these last anxious years. There is an admirable comic portrait of Charles Ryder's father, and many welcome scenes, of which the most memorable are those at Oxford, a ghastly dinner conversation at the captain's table on a trans-atlantic liner, and Father Mowbray's patient attempts to instruct the infidel Rex in the rudiments of Christian belief.

In a word of warning on the dust wrapper Mr. Waugh has expressed the modest hope that the book may please 'those who have the leisure to read a book word by word for the interest of the writer's use of language.' The number should approach a multitude. It is his most ambitious novel and his best.

Note

1   The narrative is, of course, retrospective and the implication at the end of the novel is that Charles Ryder has become a Catholic. Thus, while the story is told through the consciousness of an intelligent agnostic, this view of the world is effectively an historical re-creation by a hero who has transcended it and come to see the workings of 'divine purpose' in the lives he describes.

97.   HENRY REED, 'NEW STATESMAN'

23 June 1945, 408-9

Henry Reed (b. 1914), poet, radio dramatist, journalist and
translator, is the author of 'A Map of Venice' (1946), 'The
Lessons of the War' (1970) and 'The Streets of Pompeii and
Other Plays for Radio' (1971).

Serious implications have been present often enough in Mr.
Evelyn Waugh's previous novels. The title of 'A Handful of
Dust' was significant; and certain excruciating moments in
that book, as when the mother hears of her little boy's
death, were threatening signs of a novelist whose powers
were not easily to be ignored. Those powers find full expression in 'Brideshead Revisited,' a novel flagrantly
defective at times in artistic sensibility, yet deeply
moving in its theme and its design. It is as well to describe Mr. Waugh's faults at once; they recur constantly,
both while one is reading him and while one is remembering
him. They radiate almost wholly from an overpowering snobbishness: 'How beautiful they are, the lordly ones,' might
well stand as an epigraph to Mr. Waugh's *oeuvre* so far. A
burden of respect for the peerage and for Eton, which those
who belong to the former, or who have been to the latter,
seem able lightly to discard, weighs heavily upon him; and
his satiric studies of the follies and cruelties of the
posh have always been remarkable for the fact that their
poshness has always seemed to the author more lovable than
their silliness has seemed outrageous. It is a kind of
snobbishness which finds one outlet in a special vulgarity
of its own. There are several scenes in 'Brideshead Revisited' where the narrator sets his own *savoir faire* against
that of the lower characters - the scene in the Parisian
restaurant with the colonial go-getter Rex, for example, or
the pages satirising the transatlantic liner - and emerges
as no less vulgar than his victims. It is as if a man
should repeatedly point out to one that his bottom waist-
coat-button is undone. This vulgarity goes very deep with
Mr. Waugh; and it is not surprising that in embarking on
his most serious novel he should show an addiction to the
purple.
    The subjects of 'Brideshead Revisited' are the inescap-
able watchfulness of God, and the contrast between the
Christian (for Mr. Waugh, the Roman Catholic) sinner, and
the other kind of sinner described in the cant term of our
day as 'pagan.' Boldly, Mr. Waugh writes throughout from

the point of view of the pagan, which he, a convert to
Roman Catholicism, has not forgotten; even more boldly he
puts some of the most devout of his Roman Catholics among
his least attractive characters. The book opens with a tale
of romantic friendship at Oxford in the years following the
first great war. Charles Ryder, the narrator, falls in love
with Lord Sebastian Flyte, the beautiful son of Lord Marchmain; Marchmain himself, once a Catholic convert, is now an
apostate; Sebastian is half-pagan. The Oxford passage,
comic and romantic, is the most brilliant part of the book;
nothing in the latter part approaches it, save the last few
pages of the story proper. The farce is of a high order;
the picture of the narrator's father is a masterpiece of
comedy; and the seeds of the later conflict are dextrously
sown.

Sebastian is tormented by his mother, whom he cannot
bear to be with. The mother is a mysterious and ambiguous
figure, but not dissatisfying to the reader on that account.
Sebastian's father has cut himself off from her and lives
in Venice with a mistress. Like Sebastian, he flees from
her, and it is perhaps not an over-interpretation to see
here a suggestion that she represents some of the absolute
exaction, difficult to face, of the Church. Symbolic or
not, she is, in the story itself, patient, wonderful, cunning and unbearable; Sebastian cannot keep Ryder to himself
and away from the family; and gradually he secedes from the
relationship into drunkenness and vagabondage. Ten years
later, Charles again meets Sebastian's sister, Julia,
unhappily married to the barbarian Rex. The family charm
works again, Charles falls in love with her, and is, in a
curious phrase, 'made free of her narrow loins' during a
gale in mid-Atlantic. For two years their love survives
happily; they are both about to be divorced in order to
marry each other, when Julia feels 'a twitch upon the
thread'; she is reminded that she is living in a state of
unchanging mortal sin, and cannot escape that consciousness; in the final pages, Charles is dismissed; we have
already learned that Sebastian, far away in Morocco, has
also felt the twitch upon the thread. The second part of
the book falls far below the first; not only because for
many pages we live in the dimensions of a gaudy novelette,
enlivened, if at all, by the author's testiness at other
people's bad taste, but because Julia is only a theme and
not a person, whereas Sebastian has been both. Julia is
alive only in her final speeches; and then simply because
what she says is alive.

Underneath all the disfigurements, and never for long
out of sight, there is in 'Brideshead Revisited' a fine and
brilliant book; its plan and a good deal of its execution

are masterly, and it haunts one for days after one has read
it. If one is reminded of François Mauriac (1) it is not
because Mr. Waugh's book is derivative, but for two other
reasons. One remembers how much M. Mauriac can take for
granted in his audience: Christian or agnostic, it knows
what Catholicism is about. Mr. Waugh is in the far more
difficult position of writing to an audience which in
general is without that knowledge; he acquits himself
convincingly, even to the pagan reader. Secondly, M. Mauriac reminds one of a lack in Mr. Waugh, for the great
French novelist has sympathy with, and love for, the actual
emotions of human beings. This sympathy and love are things
no novelist can get along without; they are things which
Mr. Waugh is still in the process of acquiring or re-
acquiring. A hard task; for they do not always survive
religious conversion.

Note

1   François Mauriac (1885-1970) was a French playwright,
    novelist and critic whose work is dominated by his
    Catholic faith. He was author of 'The Kiss of the Leper'
    (1922), 'Térèse Desqueyroux' (1927), 'Asmodé' (1938) and
    'Proust's Way' (1950).

98.   JOHN K. HUTCHENS, 'NEW YORK TIMES BOOK REVIEW'

30 December 1945, 1, 16

John Kennedy Hutchens (b. 1905), an American, was a journalist for the New York press from 1926; Assistant Editor of
the 'New York Times Book Review', 1944-6, and Editor,
1946-8. He is author of 'One Man's Montana' (1964) and
editor of 'The American Twenties' (1952).

'My theme,' says the narrator in Evelyn Waugh's latest, his
most carefully written and deeply felt novel, 'is memory,
that winged host.' And, with that, the brightly devastating
satirist of England's Twenties and Thirties moves from one
world to another and a larger one: from the lunacy of a
burlesqued Mayfair, very glib and funny and masking the
serious point in farce, to a world in which people credibly
think and feel. Whether 'Brideshead Revisited' is

technically as expert, of its kind, as 'Decline and Fall,'
'Vile Bodies' or 'A Handful of Dust' may be debatable. The
important point just now is that it is bigger and richer,
and that - to those of Mr. Waugh's admirers who might
recently have suspected he was exhausting a rather limited
field - it will almost certainly be his most interesting
book in ten years: more interesting in story and in style,
and not least in what it implies about its author and his
growth as an analyst and an artist.

For Mr. Waugh is very definitely an artist, with something like a genius for precision and clarity not sur-
passed by any novelist writing in English in his time. This
has been apparent from the very beginning of his career -
a career in which 'Brideshead Revisited' different in setting, tone and technique from all his earlier creative
work, is yet a logical development.

'Brideshead Revisited' has the depth and weight that are
found in a writer working in his prime, in the full powers
of an eager, good mind and a skilled hand, retaining the
best of what he has already learned. It tells an absorbing
story in imaginative terms. By indirection it summarizes
and comments upon a time and a society. It has an almost
romantic sense of wonder, together with the provocative,
personal point of view of a writer who sees life realisti-
cally. It is, in short, a large, inclusive novel with which
the 1946 season begins, a novel more fully realized than
any of the year now ending, whatever their other virtues.

Of the earlier Waugh, the moralist remains. For Mr.
Waugh is, of course, a moralist after his fashion, and always was; when you look even slightly beneath the hilarity
of those Mayfair studies, you see that he is performing the
satirist's ancient function: he is excoriating the morals
and standards of a society. Needless to say, he is too much
the artist - and too astute as an entertainer - ever to be
didactic; but inevitably it is there, the satirist's way
with absurdity, including what is absurd in empty tradition; the moralist's hatred of injustice and his unspoken
belief in the value of intelligence and simple decency.

Unless 'Brideshead Revisited' finds you a very new member of the Waugh public, you realized with his first novel
('Decline and Fall') that his equipment as a social satirist was just about perfect. In the first place, he obviously knew what he was talking about: this was reporting
at first-hand by one who had been in that world if not of
it. He wrote with a sharp thrust which smote a victim or
merely pinked him, as circumstances dictated. His style
was clean and fast. From one sentence to another you read
with a virtually sensuous delight in his gift for the
exact word, his remarkable use of a detail to summarize a

place or a person, his wonderful sense of the ridiculous.
The first two pages of 'Decline and Fall' told you that, at
the very least, a first-rank farceur had arrived.... If he
had not gone beyond this book, he would still be remembered
for the bright performance he gave in it....

The problem facing Mr. Waugh as a novelist was not one
that worried the American reading public in general. Until
now his books have never been best-sellers here, though one
would be put to it to say why. 'Vile Bodies' was widely
circulated in a couple of reprint editions. 'A Handful of
Dust' was blessed by Alexander Woollcott (1) and placed in
one of his popular 'Readers.' But the original American
editions sold little, and only a small circle of Waugh fans
could really have told you much about him, his works or
his career...

But even those to whom Mr. Waugh and his work were only
slightly familiar must have wondered what direction his
talent would take during the climactic war years since
'Put Our More Flags.' 'Brideshead Revisited' tells them, in
a fashion more mature and ultimately more satisfying than
even his admirers could confidently have predicted.

Here, again, is the post-World War I England, but in
very different focus; the story seen not through the eyes
of a Paul Pennyfeather or a William Boot ... but told in
the first person by a sensitive and intelligent observer,
one Charles Ryder, architectural painter, captain in the
British Army, looking back from middle-age at his youth.
In the scheme of 'Brideshead Revisited' that change in
focus is all-important, the frame in which the story is set
between prologue and epilogue lending it perspective and
narrative flexibility, the enchantment of experience recalled and sifted. The emotional tone and content of
'Brideshead Revisited' are accordingly heightened beyond
any Mr. Waugh has achieved before. He has elsewhere conveyed a muted poignance - the death of the boy in 'A Handful of Dust' and the ingenious, nightmarish conclusion of
the same book. In 'Brideshead Revisited' the emotion is
unwrapped, so to speak, and sent from the heart.

In the beginning it is gay enough - an affectionately
ironic picture of Oxford in 1923, the sunflower estheticism, plovers' eggs and getting drunk at luncheon, the
lively, small banter, the happy irresponsibility, ' Antic
Hay'....(2) Then, with the story's arrival at Brideshead
and its baroque castle, the tone changes to a somber hue as
the themes develop: the love story of Ryder and Sebastian's
sister Julia, of which Ryder's and Sebastian's friendship
had been a spiritual forerunner; the Church giving haven to
the soul-torn, drunken Sebastian and reclaiming Julia and
even the Byronic father who comes home at last from Italy
to die.

There is much of the earlier Waugh in this: the sharp
phrasing, the keen and often deadly use of detail, the
living speech, the scorn of vulgarity, the light summary
touch with minor characters.... What is quite new is a
leisure, a spaciousness of style and structure. One sentence and one paragraph after another, of reflection and
description, could have found no place in the staccato
atmosphere of his other works. By comparison with them,
this is as a full-bodied play to a deft vaudeville sketch.
Nowhere, for example, even in 'A Handful of Dust,' would
you have found Mr. Waugh letting himself go to the extent
of:

> This was the creature, neither child nor woman, that
> drove me through the dusk that summer evening,
> untroubled by love, taken aback by the power of her own
> beauty, hesitating on the steps of life; one who had
> suddenly found herself armed, unawares; the heroine of
> a fairy story turning over in her hands the magic ring;
> she had only to stroke it with her fingertips, and
> whisper the charmed word, for the earth to open at her
> feet....

There will be, quite certainly, no little discussion and
even controversy about the problem he poses, or rather the
conclusion he offers. Mr. Waugh, a Catholic, is also, politically, a Tory. As a writer, as a story-teller and an
artist, he insists on nothing. Of Catholicism as a factor
in the lives of the Marchmains he writes so objectively,
seeing it through the eyes of the non-Catholic narrator,
that it could actually be construed as the slightly sardonic report of an unbeliever confronted with (and baffled
by) 'an entirely different outlook on life.' What he is
saying in effect is that faith is a saving answer to anyone
who has it or had had it; which could scarcely be called
propaganda, though he will surely be charged with propaganda. It will be said, too, that his political conservatism is patent in his reluctant acceptance of social
change, and this will be true; the end of a Brideshead is
to him a matter for regret and misgiving, for he believes
in 'order' and the continuity of tradition. Above all, he
believes in responsibility, the absence of which in his own
class he has castigated so fiercely.
But those who disagree with him on religious or political grounds, or both, will have a time for themselves in
trying to prove that his beliefs have marred his literary
artistry. 'Brideshead Revisited' is Mr. Waugh's finest
achievement.

Notes

1   See No. 89, n. 1, above. The reference is to 'The Wooll-
    cott Reader' (New York, Viking Press, 1935), pp. 799-
    1008.
2   Aldous Huxley, 'Antic Hay' (1923).

99.   EDMUND WILSON, 'NEW YORKER'

5 January 1946, 71, 74

The new novel by Evelyn Waugh - 'Brideshead Revisited' -
has been a bitter blow to this reviewer. I have admired and
praised Mr. Waugh, and when I began reading 'Brideshead
Revisited,' I was excited at finding that he had broken
away from the comic vein for which he is famous and expanded into a new dimension. The new story - with its subtitle, 'The Sacred and Profane Memories of Captain Charles
Ryder' - is a 'serious' novel, in the conventional sense,
and the opening is invested with a poetry and staged with a
dramatic effectiveness which seem to promise much.... This
early section is all quite brilliant, partly in the manner
of the Waugh we know, partly with a new kind of glamour
that is closer to Scott Fitzgerald and Compton Mackenzie.
It is the period that these older writers celebrated, but
seen now from the bleak, shrivelled forties, so that everything - the freedom, the fun, the varied intoxications of
youth - has taken on a remoteness and pathos. The introduction of the hero to the Catholic family and the gradual
revelation of their queerness, their differences from
Protestant England, is brought off with accomplished art,
and through almost the whole of the first half of the book,
the habitual reader of Waugh is likely to tell himself that
his favorite has been fledged as a first-rank straight
novelist.
    But this enthusiasm is to be cruelly disappointed. What
happens when Evelyn Waugh abandons his comic convention -
as fundamental in his previous work as that of any Restoration dramatist - turns out to be more or less disastrous.
The writer, in this more normal world, no longer knows his
way: his deficiency in common sense here ceases to be an
asset and gets him into some embarrassing situations, and
his creative imagination, accustomed in his satirical fiction to work partly in two-dimensional caricature but now
called upon for passions and motives, supplies instead mere

romantic fantasy. The hero is to have an affair with the
married elder daughter of the house, and this is conducted
on a plane of banality - the woman is quite unreal - reminiscent of the full-dress adulteries of the period in the
early nineteen-hundreds when Galsworthy and other writers
were making people throb and weep with such fiction as
'The Dark Flower.'(1) And as the author's taste thus
fails him his excellent style goes to seed. The writing -
which, in the early chapters, is of Evelyn Waugh's best:
felicitous, unobtrusive, exact - here runs to such dispiriting clichés as 'Still the clouds gathered and did not
break' and 'So the year wore on and the secret of the
engagement spread from Julia's confidantes to their confidantes and so, like ripples on the water, in ever widening
circles.' The stock characters - the worldly nobleman, the
good old nurse - which have always been a feature of Waugh
and which are all right in a harlequinade, here simply become implausible and tiresome. The last scenes are extravagantly absurd, with an absurdity which would be worthy of
Waugh at his best if it were not - painful to say - meant
quite seriously. The worldly Lord Marchmain, when he left
his wife, repudiated his Catholic faith, and on his deathbed he sends the priest packing, but when the old man has
sunk lower, the priest is recalled. The family all kneel,
and Charles, who is present, kneels, too. Stoutly though he
has defended his Protestantism, his resistance breaks down
today. He prays that this time the old man will not reject
the final sacrament, and lo, Lord Marchmain makes the sign
of the cross! The peer, as he has drifted toward death, has
been soliloquizing at eloquent length: 'We were knights
then, barons since Agincourt, the larger honors came with
the Georges,' etc., etc., and the reader has an uncomfortable feeling that what has caused Mr. Waugh's hero to plump
on his knees is not, perhaps, the sign of the cross but the
prestige, in the person of Lord Marchmain, of one of the
oldest families in England.

For Waugh's snobbery, hitherto held in check by his
satirical point of view, has here emerged shameless and
rampant. His admiration for the qualities of the older
British families, as contrasted with modern upstarts, had
its value in his earlier novels, where the standards of
morals and taste are kept in the background and merely
implied. But here the upstarts are rather crudely overdone
and the aristocrats become terribly trashy, and his cult of
the high nobility is allowed to become so rapturous and
solemn that it finally gives the impression of being the
only real religion in the book.

Yet the novel is a Catholic tract. The Marchmain family,
in their various fashions, all yield, ultimately, to the

promptings of their faith and give witness to its enduring
virtue; the skeptical hero, long hostile and mocking,
eventually becomes converted; the old chapel is opened up
and put at the disposition of the troops, and a 'surprising
lot use it, too.' Now, this reviewer may perhaps be insen-
sible to some value the book will have for other readers,
since he is unsympathetic by conviction with the point of
view of the Catholic converts, but he finds it impossible
to feel that the author has conveyed in all this any genuine religious experience. In the earlier novels of Waugh
there was always a very important element of perverse, un-
regenerate self-will that, giving rise to confusion and
impudence, was a great asset for a comic writer. In his new
book, this theme is sounded explicitly, with an unaccustomed portentousness and rhetoric, at an early point in the
story, when he speaks of 'the hot spring of anarchy' that
'rose from deep furnaces where was no solid earth, and
burst into the sunlight - a rainbow in its cooling vapors
with a power the rocks could not repress,' and of course it
is this hot spring of anarchy, this reckless, unredeemed
humanity, that is supposed to be cooled and controlled by
the discipline of the Catholic faith. But, once he has come
to see this force as sin, Evelyn Waugh seems to be rather
afraid of it: he does not allow it really to raise its
head - boldly, outrageously, hilariously, or horribly - as
he has in his other books, and the result is that we miss
it extremely: something essential has been left out of
Waugh, and the religion that is invoked to correct it seems
more like an exorcistic rite than a force of regeneration.

There is, however, another subject in 'Brideshead
Revisited' - a subject which is incompletely developed but
which has far more reality than the religious one: the situation of Charles Ryder between the Brideshead family on
the one hand and his own family background on the other. The
young man has no mother and his only home is with a scholarly and self-centered father, who reduces life to something so dry, so withdrawn, so devoid of affection or color
that the boy is driven to look for a home in the family of
his Oxford friend and to idealize their charm and grace.
What is interesting to a non-Catholic reader are the origins and the evolution of the hero's beglamoured snobbery,
and the amusing and chilling picture of Charles's holidays
at home with his father is one of the very good things in
the book.

The comic parts of 'Brideshead Revisited' are as funny
as anything that the author has done, and the Catholic
characters are sometimes good, when they are being observed
as social types and get the same kind of relentless treatment as the characters in his satirical books. I do not

mean to suggest, however, that Mr. Waugh should revert to his
his earlier vein. He has been steadily broadening his art,
and when he next tries to be completely serious, he may
have learned how to avoid bathos.

In the meantime, I predict that 'Brideshead Revisited'
will prove to be the most successful, the only extremely
successful, book that Evelyn Waugh has written, and that it
will soon be up in the best-seller list somewhere between
'The Black Rose' (2) and 'The Manatee.'(3)

Notes

1   John Galsworthy (1867-1933), 'The Dark Flower' (1913).
2   Thomas Bertram Costain (b. 1885), 'The Black Rose'
    (1945).
3   Nancy Bruff (b. 1915), 'The Manatee' (1945).

100.   EVELYN WAUGH, 'LIFE' (INTERNATIONAL: CHICAGO)

8 April 1946, 53-4, 56, 58, 60

This article was Waugh's response to the enormous correspondence from American readers of 'Brideshead'. The
article was entitled Fan-Fare and has been reprinted in
'A Little Order' (1978), pp. 29-34.

Frequently, unobtrusively, in the last 17 years I have had
books published in the United States of America. No one
noticed them. A parcel would appear on my breakfast table
containing a familiar work with a strange wrapper and sometimes a strange title; an item would recur in my agent's
accounts: 'Unearned advance on American edition' and that
was the end of the matter. Now, unseasonably, like a shy
water-fowl who has hatched out a dragon's egg, I find that
I have written a 'best-seller.' 'Unseasonably,' because the
time has passed when the event brings any substantial
reward. In a civilized age this unexpected movement of
popularity would have endowed me with a competency for
life. But perhaps in a civilized age I should not be so
popular. As it is the politicians confiscate my earnings
and I am left with the correspondence.

This is something new to me, for Englishwomen do not
write letters to men they do not know; indeed they seldom

write letters to anyone nowadays; they are too hard-driven
at home. Even before the war English readers were seldom
seen or heard. It is true that there are facilities for
writers whose vanity so inclines them to join literary
associations, make speeches and even expose themselves to
view at public luncheons, but no one expects it of them or
respects them for it. Instead of the Liberty, Equality and
Fraternity of the Americas, Europe offers its artists
Liberty, Diversity and Privacy. Perhaps it is for this that
so many of the best American writers go abroad. But, as
Hitler observed, there are no islands in the modern world.
I have momentarily become an object of curiosity to Americans and I find that they believe that my friendship and
confidence are included in the price of my book....
    [During the pre-war] years and in the preposterous years
of the Second World War I collected enough experience to
last several lifetimes of novel writing. If you hear a
novelist say he needs to collect 'copy,' be sure he is no
good. Most of the great writers led very quiet lives; when,
like Cervantes, they were adventurous, it was not for professional reasons. When I gadded, among savages and
people of fashion and politicians and crazy generals, it
was because I enjoyed them. I have settled down now because
I ceased to enjoy them and because I have found a much more
abiding interest - the English language. My father, who was
a respected literary critic of his day, first imbued me
with the desire to learn this language, of which he had a
mastery. It is the most lavish and delicate which mankind
has ever known. It is in perpetual danger of extinction
and has survived so far by the combination of a high civilized society, where it was spoken and given its authority
and sanctity, with a thin line of devotees who made its
refinement and adornment their life's work. The first of
these is being destroyed; if the thing is to be saved it
will be by the second. I did not set out to be a writer.
My first ambition was to paint. I had little talent but I
enjoyed it as, I believe, many very bad writers enjoy
writing. I spent some time at an art school which was not
as wantonly wasted as it seemed then. Those hours with the
plaster casts taught me to enjoy architecture, just as the
hours with the Greek paradigms, now forgotten, taught me to
enjoy reading English. I have never, until quite lately,
enjoyed writing. I am lazy and it is intensely hard work. I
wanted to be a man of the world and I took to writing as I
might have taken to archaeology or diplomacy or any other
profession as a means of coming to terms with the world.
Now I see it as an end in itself. Most European writers
suffer a climacteric at the age of 40. Youthful volubility
carries them so far. After that they either become prophets

or hacks or esthetes. (American writers, I think, nearly all become hacks.) I am no prophet and, I hope, no hack.

That, I think, answers the second question so often put to me in the last few weeks: 'When can we expect another "Brideshead Revisited"?' Dear ladies, never. I can never hope to engage your attentions in quite the same way. I have already shaken off one of the American critics, Mr Edmund Wilson, who once professed a generous interest in me. He was outraged (quite legitimately by his standards) at finding God introduced into my story. I believe that you can only leave God out by making your characters pure abstractions. Countless admirable writers, perhaps some of the best in the world, succeed in this. Henry James was the last of them. The failure of modern novelists since and including James Joyce is one of presumption and exorbitance. They are not content with the artificial figures which hitherto passed so gracefully as men and women. They try to represent the whole human mind and soul and yet omit its determining character - that of being God's creature with a defined purpose.

So in my future books there will be two things to make them unpopular: a preoccupation with style and the attempt to represent man more fully, which, to me, means only one thing, man in his relation to God.

But before we part company there are other questions you ask which I will try to answer. A lady in Hempstead, N.Y. asks me whether I consider my characters 'typical.' No, Mrs. Schultz, I do not. It is horrible of you to ask. A novelist has no business with types; they are the property of economists and politicians and advertisers and the other professional bores of our period. The artist is interested only in individuals. The statesman who damned the age with the name 'the Century of the Common Man' neglected to notice the simple, historical fact that it is the artists, not the statesmen, who decide the character of a period. The Common Man does not exist. He is an abstraction invented by bores for bores. Even you, dear Mrs. Schultz, are an individual. Do not ask yourself, when you read a story, 'Is this the behaviour common to such and such an age group, income group, psychologically conditioned group?' but, 'Why did these particular people behave in this particular way?' Otherwise you are wasting your time in reading works of imagination at all.

There is another more intelligent question more often asked: 'Are your characters drawn from life?' In the broadest sense, of course, they are. None except one or two negligible minor figures is a portrait; all the major characters are the result of numberless diverse observations fusing in the imagination into a single whole. My

problem has been to distill comedy and sometimes tragedy
from the knockabout farce of people's outward behaviour.
Men and women as I see them would not be credible if they
were literally transcribed; for instance the international
journalists whom I met for a few delirious weeks in Addis
Ababa, some of whose abandoned acts I tried to introduce
into 'Scoop.' Or there is the character Captain Grimes in
'Decline and Fall.' I knew such a man. One of the more
absurd escapades of my youth, the result of a debt-
settlement conference with my father after which I undertook to make myself financially independent of him, was to
take a job as master at a private school. There I met a
man who made what has seemed to me the lapidary statement,
'This looks like being the first end of term I've seen,
old boy, for two years.' But had I written anything like a
full account of his iniquities, my publishers and I would
have been in the police court.

As for the major characters, I really have very little
control over them. I start them off with certain preconceived notions of what they will do and say in certain
circumstances but I constantly find them moving another
way. For example there was the heroine of 'Put Out More
Flags,' a Mrs. Lyne. I had no idea until halfway through
the book that she drank secretly. I could not understand
why she behaved so oddly. Then when she sat down suddenly
on the steps of the cinema I understood all and I had to
go back and introduce a series of empty bottles into her
flat. I was on board a troopship at the time. There is a
young destroyer commander who sat next to me at table who
can bear witness of this. He asked me one day at luncheon
how my book was going. I said, 'Badly. I can't understand
it at all' and then quite suddenly 'I know. Mrs. Lyne has
been drinking.'

'A Handful of Dust,' on the other hand, began at the
end. I had written a short story about a man trapped in the
jungle, ending his days reading Dickens aloud. The idea
came quite naturally from the experience of visiting a
lonely settler of that kind and reflecting how easily he
could hold me prisoner. Then, after the short story was
written and published, the idea kept working in my mind.
I wanted to discover how the prisoner got there, and
eventually the thing grew into a study of other sorts of
savage at home and the civilized man's helpless plight
among them.

People sometimes say to me, 'I met someone exactly like
a character out of one of your books.' I meet them everywhere, not by choice but luck. I believe the world is
populated by them. Before the war it was sometimes said
that I must move in a very peculiar circle. Then I joined

the army and served six years, mostly with regular soldiers who are reputed to be uniformly conventional. I found myself under the command and in the mess with one man of startling singularity after another. That is what makes story telling such an absorbing task, the attempt to reduce to order the anarchic raw materials of life.

That leads to another question: 'Are your books meant to be satirical?' No. Satire is a matter of period. It flourishes in a stable society and presupposes homogeneous moral standards - the early Roman Empire and 18th Century Europe. It is aimed at inconsistency and hypocrisy. It exposes polite cruelty and folly by exaggerating them. It seeks to produce shame. All this has no place in the Century of the Common Man where vice no longer pays lip service to virtue. The artist's only service to the disintegrated society of today is to create little independent systems of order of his own. I foresee in the dark age opening that the scribes may play the part of the monks after the first barbarian victories. They were not satirists.

A final question: 'Do you consider "Brideshead Revisited" your best book?' Yes. 'A Handful of Dust,' my favourite hitherto, dealt entirely with behaviour. It was humanist and contained all I had to say about humanism. 'Brideshead Revisited' is vastly more ambitious; perhaps less successful, but I am not deterred either by popular applause or critical blame from being rather proud of the attempt. In particular I am not the least worried about the charge of using clichés. I think to be oversensitive about clichés is like being oversensitive about table manners. It comes from keeping second-rate company. Professional reviewers read so many bad books in the course of duty that they get an unhealthy craving for arresting phrases. There are many occasions in writing when one needs an unobtrusive background to action, when the landscape *must* become conventionalized if the foreground is to have the right prominence. I do not believe that a serious writer has ever been shy of an expression because it has been used before. It is the writer of advertisements who is always straining to find bizarre epithets for commonplace objects.

Nor am I worried at the charge of snobbery. Class consciousness, particularly in England, has been so much inflamed nowadays that to mention a nobleman is like mentioning a prostitute 60 years ago. The new prudes say, 'No doubt such people do exist but we would sooner not hear about them.' I reserve the right to deal with the kind of people I know best.

One criticism does deeply discourage me: a postcard from a man (my sole male correspondent) in Alexandria, Va. He

says, 'Your "Brideshead Revisited" is a strange way to
show that Catholicism is an answer to anything. Seems more
like the kiss of Death.' I can only say: I am sorry Mr.
McClose, I did my best. I am not quite clear what you mean
by the 'kiss of Death' but I am sure it is gruesome. Is it
something to do with halitosis? If so I have failed indeed
and my characters have got wildly out of hand once more.

101.   ROSE MACAULAY, 'HORIZON'

December 1946, 372-6

...Between ['Work Suspended' (1942)] and writing 'Brideshead Revisited' (in 1944), Mr. Waugh underwent development.
The baroque became flamboyant; the style curved and
flowered; sentimentality at times cushioned it; a grave
lushness bloomed. Not continuously, but at intervals,
emotionalism, over-brimming the theme, swamped it. The era
of brilliant farce was over; the circus was deserted.
Irony and humour still remained; there are in 'Brideshead'
wit of character and some sharply drawn comic scenes; there
is also much subtly precise and intelligent writing; but it
flowers too often into an orchidaceous luxury of bloom that,
in a hitherto ironic wit, startles and disconcerts. Love,
the English aristocracy, and the Roman Catholic Church,
combine to liquefy a style that should be dry. Like 'Work
Suspended', the story is told in the first person; a mode
that affords opportunities too tempting for romantic soliloquy. The Oxford section is good, its characters excel-
lently suggested (rather than drawn), its atmosphere
authentic, its period the lavish 'twenties.... About the
Flytes there remains to the end something phoney: they
belong to a day-dream, to a grandiose world of elegance
and Palladian grace, a more than mortal ecstasy. Their
conversation is at times incredible; Julia's monologue
about her 'sin' on pages 251-3; Lord Marchmain's about his
ancestors on his deathbed; some other passages, which
flower up from naturalism like exotic purple plants in a
hot-house. Some of these purple passages concern love, some
a romantic memory, some sin, some religion, some food and
drink (which are treated with intense and almost mystical
earnestness; a good meal in a restaurant becomes a sacred
rite). Mr. Waugh has been charged with snobbishness. I
would rather call it self-indulgence in the pleasures of
adolescent surrender to glamour, whether to the glamour of

beauty, food, rank, love, church, society, or fine writings.... [Many] passages ... might have been pilloried in
bland ridicule in the earlier novels - in Lord Copper's
newspapers, for instance, along with the finny creatures
plashing their lush way through the reeds.(1)

It is part of the adolescent approach, too, to mistake a
part for the whole; this, I think, Mr. Waugh does in
'Brideshead', and it gives just the effect of triviality
which should have been avoided in a book alleged to be 'an
attempt to trace the workings of the divine purpose in a
pagan world'. No purpose can well have greater importance; no faith can be more worth asserting than that 'the
human spirit, redeemed, can survive all disasters'. But Mr.
Waugh seems to equate the divine purpose, the tremendous
fact of God at work in the universe, with obedient membership of a church; the human spirit, if redeemed, must
loyally conform to this church and its rules. But ... it
seems ... to reduce the formidable problems of the universe
and the human spirit to a level almost parochial. Divine
purpose, human redemption, must flow through channels
larger than those of any church; the impression is rather
of an attempt to pour the ocean into a stoup. The interest
in moral issues which, as has been lately said by a critic,
must in the end impose itself again on novelists, trans-
cends (even if it often includes) loyalty to a church: in
Mr. Waugh's novel, it is subordinate to and conditioned by
this. (Here he differs from that equally convinced Catholic
but greater and more sin-haunted moralist, Graham Greene.)

Not only does this concentration on a church narrow the
moral issues, but it seems to add a flavour of acrimony, a
kind of partisan contempt for other churches, about whose
members acid and uncivil remarks are made by persons in the
book, voicing, one would say, their author. It is the same
belligerent attitude as was shown in 'Campion', but with
less excuse, since Protestants and Catholics were in Campion's time at war, and enmity may be part of the period
approach. They are now at peace; and great civility and
respect are shown, at least in this country, towards
Catholics by Protestants. Mr. Waugh's answer would perhaps
be that other churches, being in schism, are unworthy of
civility in return.... Gone is the detachment, and with it
the bland, amused tolerance, of the early novels. Belief
meant for him hatred of misbelievers; no sympathetic effort
to understand their standpoint has been evident, still less
the urbane culture which recognizes human error to be dis-
tributed among all sections of opinion, including that to
which oneself belongs. This is the spirit that shows itself
intermittently, and to its detriment, through 'Brideshead
Revisited'.

Nevertheless, 'Brideshead' has remarkable qualities....
If Mr. Waugh would sternly root out the sentimentalities
and adolescent values which have, so deplorably as it seems
to many of us, coiled themselves about the enchanting comic
spirit which is his supreme asset as a writer, and return
to being the drily ironic narrator of the humours of his
world and of his lavish inventive fancy, he would thereby
increase his stature, he would be not a less but a more
serious and considerable figure in contemporary and future
letters. His genius and his reputation seem to stand at the
crossroads; his admirers can only hope that he will take
the right turning. It is possible that he may.

Note

1   A 'mis-quotation' from William Boot's Lush Places column
    in 'Scoop': 'Feather-footed through the plashy fens
    passes the questing vole...'.

102.   DONAT O'DONNELL, 'BELL'

December 1946, 38-49

Donat O'Donnell is the pseudonym of Conor Cruise O'Brien
(b. 1917), an Irish historian, critic and statesman. He was
UN representative in Katanga in 1961 and author of 'Maria
Cross' (1952), 'Parnell and His Party' (1957), 'Writers and
Politics' (1965) and 'Camus' (1969). He is ex-Minister of
Posts and Telegraphs and was formerly Executive Editor of
the 'Observer'.

Mr. Evelyn Waugh's seventh and latest novel, 'Brideshead
Revisited,' was fortunate in earning the approval both of
the reading public and of the theologians. In England, the
'Tablet' saw in it 'a great apologetic work in the larger
and more humane sense,' and in the United States, where it
sold over half a million copies, the critics of the leading
Catholic journals concurred in this judgment. One of them,
however - H.C. Gardiner in 'America,' 12th January, 1946 -
complained with justice that all the non-Catholic reviewers - including those who made it the Book of the Month
Club selection - had missed the religious point of the
book. It seems probable therefore that most of Mr. Waugh's

readers, in America at any rate, did not know that they were reading a great apologetic work, and that, if they paid any attention to the Catholicism of 'Brideshead Revisited' at all, they valued it as part of the general baronial decorations around a tale of love and high-life.

In this, of course, they were wrong, but their mistake was not entirely due to 'secularist' stupidity and indifference. 'Brideshead Revisited' is, in its author's words, 'an attempt to trace the divine purpose in a pagan world'; men and women try to escape from the love of God, to find human happiness, but God destroys their human hopes and brings them back with 'a twitch upon the thread.' This is the central theme, austere and theological, but obscured (for those whose approach to religion is different from Mr. Waugh's) by bulky memorials of devotion to other gods. These alien pieties, some of them hardly compatible with strict Catholicism, were perhaps for Mr. Waugh the forerunners of a more articulated faith - as, in 'Brideshead Revisited,' Sebastian Flyte's affection for a teddy-bear was the forerunner of a vocation. They appear in varying degrees and shapes in all his work, and now mingle with Catholicism in a highly personal system of belief and devotion, well worth analysis.

The main emotional constituent of Mr. Waugh's religion - using the term in a wide sense - is a deep English romanticism. His earliest work, 'Rossetti,' betrayed a pre-Raphaelite affinity; and his first 'serious' novel, 'A Handful of Dust,' deals with the injury inflicted by modern flippancy and shallowness on a romantic mind. The hero, Tony Last, lives in a great ramshackle country house of nineteenth century Gothic which he dearly loves, and which his wife's friends sneer at; his wife betrays him, and when he realizes the extent of her treachery his disillusionment shows us in a blinding flash his imaginative world:

'A whole Gothic world had come to grief ... there was now no armour glittering through the forest glades, no embroidered feet on the green sward; the cream and dappled unicorns had fled....'

We should of course be wary of too easily attributing similar fantasies to the author - although he takes his hero's side so bitterly as to mar what is in many ways his best novel - but it is significant that Captain Ryder, the hero of 'Brideshead Revisited,' lives in the same sort of climate. 'Hooper,' he says, referring to a member of the lower classes, 'was no romantic. He had not as a child ridden with Rupert's horse or sat among the camp-fires at Xanthus.... Hooper had wept often but never for Henry's speech on St. Crispin's day, nor for the epitaph at

Thermopylae. The history they taught him had had few
battles in it....' And Captain Ryder hoped to find 'that
low door in the wall ... which opened on an enclosed and
enchanted garden, which was somewhere, not overlooked by
any window, in the heart of that grey city.' This persis-
tence and intensity of youthful romanticism are remarkable,
so also is the fierce conviction that the romantic dream is
directly menaced by some element in modernity. Tony Last's
Gothic forest is withered by the cynicism of smart and up-
to-date people in London; Captain Ryder's enchanted garden
is trampled by the mechanized Hooper.

Closely allied with this romanticism is a nostalgia for
the period of extreme youth. Tony Last was an adult, but
his bedroom 'formed a gallery representative of every
phase of his adolescence....' The only card game he can
play is 'animal snap.'... Captain Ryder during part of his
undergraduate life with the beautiful and charming Sebastian Flyte felt that he was 'given a brief spell of what I
had never known, a happy childhood, and though its toys
were silk shirts and liqueurs and cigars, and its naughti-
ness high in the catalogue of grave sins, there was something of nursery freshness about us that fell little short
of the joy of innocence.' And amid all this he is conscious
of 'homesickness for nursery morality.' Sebastian himself
is described as being 'in love with his own childhood.' He
carries with him everywhere a teddy-bear called Aloysius,
which he occasionally threatens to spank. Mr. Waugh's preoccupation with youth even permeates his more or less
cynical comic novels ('Decline and Fall,' 'Vile Bodies,'
etc.). There is no display of emotion in these, nor much
analysis of states of mind, but sophisticated young people
play Happy Families ('Black Mischief') and a communist
journalist concentrates on working a toy train ('Scoop').
More important is the schoolboy delight in cruelty which
marks the earlier books especially, and gives an almost
hysterical tempo to their farce. One of the funniest
scenes in 'Decline and Fall' deals with the brutal murder
of an inoffensive old prison chaplain.... 'Vile Bodies' is
rich in unregarded death; ... the comedy of 'Black Mischief' is ingeniously designed to lead up to a gruesome
piece of cannibalism....

'In laughter,' according to Bergson 'we always find an
unavowed intention to humiliate and consequently to correct,
our neighbour.' One of the secrets of Mr. Waugh's comic
genius was his keen interest in humiliation. Basil Seal,
the adventurer-hero ('insolent, sulky and curiously childish') of 'Black Mischief' and 'Put Out More Flags,' 'rejoiced always, 'we are told, 'in the spectacle of women at
a disadvantage.' Mr. Waugh is a great exploiter of human

disadvantages, and his unscrupulous adolescent cruelty in
this is the common quality of his two most obvious characteristics: his humour and his snobbery. Two of his comic
novels, 'Black Mischief' and 'Scoop,' are largely based on
a sly appeal to the white man's sense of racial superiority; much of the best fun in 'Decline and Fall' comes from
the exploitation of the manners of Captain Grimes who,
although he claimed to be a public school man, was not
really a gentleman and did not often have a bath.... It can
be said indeed that if he were not a snob ... he could not
have written such funny books. This is an unpleasant fact;
it means that the countless liberal newstatesmanish people
who have laughed over these books share unconsciously these
prejudices. Mr. Edmund Wilson, in the 'New Yorker,' condemned the snobbery of 'Brideshead Revisited,' but he had
swallowed with delight the snobbery implicit in the earlier
novels, from 'Decline and Fall' to 'Scoop.' Snobbery was
quite acceptable as an attitude: the critic objected only
when it was formulated as a doctrine.

It is true that in his later books Mr. Waugh's snobbery
has taken on a different emphasis. As he becomes more serious, his veneration for the upper classes becomes more
marked than his contempt for his social inferiors. This
almost mystical veneration, entirely free from any taint of
morality, may be discerned in a slightly burlesque form in
his early books. Paul Pennyfeather ... forgave [Margot]
because he believed 'that there was in fact, and should be,
one law for her and another for himself, and that the
naïve little exertions of nineteenth-century Radicals were
essentially base and trivial and misdirected.' 'Decline and
Fall' was, of course, published before Mr. Waugh's conversion to Catholicism, which took place in 1930; no doubt he
would not now express his thought in the same way. But his
almost idolatrous reverence for birth and wealth has not
been destroyed by the Faith; on the contrary, 'Brideshead
Revisited' breathes from beginning to end a loving patience
with mortal sin among the aristocracy and an unchristian
petulance towards the minor foibles of the middle class.

As might be expected, Mr. Waugh's political outlook is
the expression of his social prejudices. In the introduction to his book on Mexico, 'Robbery under Law,' he has set
out his political creed in general terms.... Taking Abyssinia from its Emperor is 'inevitable' but taking Mexican oil
from British investors is plain robbery. So phrased the
argument appears dishonest, but Mr. Waugh's sincerity is
beyond all doubt. Indeed his conservatism is so intensely
emotional that he is a sort of Jacobite by anticipation.
In his imagination the class he loves is already oppressed;
the king has taken to the hills. Already in 'Decline and

Fall' Lady Circumference and her friends were 'feeling the
wind a bit'; in 'Vile Bodies,' the Bright Young People gad
around gallantly, touched by the fever of impending doom,
to be blasted in the final prophetic chapter by war and
inflation.... In the later works the shadow deepens
(brightened by the brief rally of the 'Churchillian renaissance,'* 1940-41) into the midnight of 'Brideshead
Revisited.' 'These men,' reflects Captain Ryder, contemplating the fate of some relatives of Lady Marchmain's,
'must die to make a world for Hooper; they were the abori-
gines, vermin by right of law, to be shot off at leisure
so that things might be safe for the travelling salesman
with his polygonal pince-nez, his fat wet handshake, his
grinning dentures.' The Prison Governor in 'Decline and
Fall' whose ideas on occupational therapy had such unfortunate consequences for the Chaplain is, in Mr. Waugh's eyes,
the typical reformer. He turns the full battery of his
satirical power against 'progressive' thinkers and workers,
for he sees them as working to hand over power to a slaver-
ing mob of criminals, communists and commercial travellers....

The Gothic dream, nostalgia for childhood, snobbery,
neo-Jacobitism - this whole complex of longings, fears and
prejudices, 'wistful, half-romantic, half-aesthetic,'(1) to
use a phrase of Mr. Waugh's, must be taken into account in
approaching the question of Mr. Waugh's Catholicism. In
Catholic countries Catholicism is not romantic, not invariably associated with big houses, or the fate of an aristocracy. The Bordeaux of M. Mauriac and the Cork of Mr. Frank
O'Connor are not Gothic cities nor objects of wistfulness.
But the Catholicism of Mr. Waugh, and of certain other
English converts, is hardly separable from a personal
romanticism and a class loyalty. Is Lord Marchmain's soul
more valuable than Hooper's? To say in so many words that
it was would be heresy, but 'Brideshead Revisited' almost
seems to imply that the wretched Hooper has no soul at all,
certainly nothing to compare with the genuine old landed
article. And 'Brideshead Revisited' is the most Catholic
of his novels. Mr. Waugh's religion, even before his conversion, abounded in consolation for the rich. That oblig-
ing and ubiquitous priest, Father Rothschild, S.J. (of
'Vile Bodies'), refuses to censure the goings on of the
Bright Young People.... The paradoxes of the wealthy Jesuit
are not perhaps intended to be taken very seriously, but
the same sort of spiritual consolation, this time with no
perceptible trace of irony, may be derived from 'Brideshead Revisited.' Lady Marchmain confesses that once she
thought it wrong 'to have so many beautiful things when
others had nothing,' but she overcame these scruples,

saying: 'The poor have always been the favourites of God
and his saints, but I believe that it is one of the special
achievements of Grace to sanctify the whole of life, riches
included.' In Mr. Waugh's theology, the love of money is
not only not the root of all evil, it is a preliminary form
of the love of God.

After the publication of 'Brideshead Revisited' in
America, a certain Mr. McClose, of Alexandria (Va.), wrote
a postcard to Mr. Waugh saying: 'Your 'Brideshead Revisited' is a strange way to show that Catholicism is an answer
to anything. Seems more like the kiss of Death to me.' Mr.
Waugh in an article in 'Life' (8th April, 1946) (2) dismisses this criticism with a sneer about halitosis. And yet
it is much more to the point than are the 'Tablet's' eulo-
gies. The deathbed conversion of Lord Marchmain is the
decisive crisis of the book; the death of an upper-class
and the death of all earthly hope are two of its principal
themes. The lovers are forced apart by a sense of sin; the
house is deserted; the family scattered; the only child
that is born is dead. Mr. Waugh's political forebodings
and the form of his private myths (of which a sense of
exile is the main constituent) make his Catholicism something that is, in earthly affairs, dark and defeatist,
alien to the bright aggressive Catholicism of the New World,
as well as to the workaday faith of the old Catholic countries. Out of all the tragedy, and justifying it, one good
is seen emerging - the conversion of the narrator. In
Brideshead chapel he has seen 'a beaten copper lamp of
deplorable design relit before the beaten doors of a
tabernacle,' and he rejoices; but when he leaves the
chapel, he leaves it empty of worshippers.

This rearguard Catholicism is not indeed 'an answer to
anything,' nor intended to be, any more than Tony Last's
Gothic city or Proust's rediscovered time is an answer to
anything....

And just as snobbery and adolescent cruelty gave edge
and tension to his early work, so now the intense romantic
and exclusive piety of his maturer years gives him strength
and eloquence. The clear focussing of remembered detail,
the loving reconstructions of youth, and the great extension of metaphor in 'Brideshead Revisited' all recall
Proust more than any living writer, and the texture of Mr.
Waugh's writing is both finer and stronger than is usual
in Proust.† Mr. Waugh has evidently read some Proust -
indeed in 'A Handful of Dust' he twice pays him the tribute
of misquotation - and there are passages in 'Brideshead
Revisited,' notably the opening of Book Two, that seem to
paraphrase 'Remembrance of Things Past.'(3) 'My theme is
memory,' says Mr. Waugh, 'that winged host that soared

about me one grey morning of war-time. These memories
which are my life - for we possess nothing certainly
except the past - were always with me. Like the pigeons of
St. Mark's, they were everywhere, under my feet singly, in
pairs.' He continues in this strain for much longer than I
can quote, and we recall Proust, whose theme was the same,
whose metaphors equally exuberant, and who developed his
theme from a recollection of feeling, under his feet, two
uneven paving-stones in the baptistery of St. Mark's.

The resemblance is neither accidental nor merely superficial and it has nothing to do with plagiarism. The outward lives of the two men are very different - one can
hardly imagine Proust in the Commandos - but their mental
worlds are, up to a point, surprisingly similar. Proust
was tenacious of childhood, with a feverishly romantic
mind capable of turning a common seaside town into an
enchanted city. This romantic sensitivity to names, and
perhaps also his social position (he belonged, like Mr.
Waugh, to the upper middle-class) led him to a veneration
for the aristocracy ... and it was in pursuit of [them]
that he entered the salons of the Faubourg St. Germain.
There he acquired a sense of social distinction as marked
as Mr. Waugh's, and much more delicate. So far the resemblance is striking, but there it ends. Proust never raised
a political or religious superstructure on these foundations.... He shows Parisian society decaying and breaking
up under the pressure of the war, but he writes as a spectator, even as a connoisseur, not as a partisan. More than
this, his mind is able at last to ... regard fashionable
snobberies as not different in kind from disputes on pre-
cedence among greengrocers' wives. Mr. Waugh has not yet
taken this decisive step. And Proust's religious experience, if we may call it so, is confined to the discrepancies of mortal life in time. He never took Mr. Waugh's
decisive step, from romanticism to the acceptance of
dogma.

The difference between the two men may be in part explained by their historical setting. Proust lived and
wrote at a time when the upper classes were menaced, but
not severely damaged. They had suffered an infusion from
the classes below, but their money was still safe enough....
He could therefore cultivate an easy and speculative
detachment. In our time, however, the upper-classes, even
in England, are not merely menaced; they have been gravely
damaged; ... they see ... their hold on their own masses
almost gone. Proustian detachment and sense of nuance tend
to perish in this atmosphere, and the wistful romantic
easily develops, as Mr. Waugh has done, into an embattled
Jacobite.

It would, however, be a simplification to insist too
much on the direct influence of economic history.... The
efforts of Proust's parents to 'harden' him were neither
consistent nor successful.... The young Waugh, on the contrary, was subjected to the discipline of an English public
school, and a religious one at that.(4) Captain Ryder
speaks sadly of 'the hard bachelordom of English adolescence, the premature dignity and authority of the school
system.' Mr. Waugh endured these things and emerged an
English gentleman, with slight symptoms of hysteria. Cream
and dappled unicorns have clearly no place at a public
school, and an interior life which includes such creatures
will feel itself menaced. If it does not die it will take
on a new intensity, becoming a fixed intolerant mythology.
Such is Mr. Waugh's private religion, on which he has
superimposed Catholicism, much as newly-converted pagans
are said to superimpose a Christian nomenclature on their
ancient cults of trees and thunder.

Notes

* This is a period reflected in 'Put Out More Flags.'
  A review of that novel in 'Partisan Review' (Summer
  1943) gave an interesting survey of Mr. Waugh's political development, but rather exaggerated its symptomatic
  importance for England. [No. 89 above.]

† This is not to imply that 'Brideshead Revisited,' as a
  totality, comes within measurable distance of Proust's
  tremendous achievement....

1 From 'Work Suspended' (1942):

   In youth we had pruned our aesthetic emotions hard
   back so that in many cases they had reverted to
   briar stock; we none of us wrote or read poetry, or,
   if we did, it was of a kind which left unsatisfied
   those wistful, half-romantic, half-aesthetic, peculiarly British longings which, in the past, used to
   find expression in so many slim lambskin volumes.
   When the poetic mood was on us we turned to buildings, and gave them the place which our fathers
   accorded to Nature....' (Penguin, pp. 145-6)

2 See No. 100 above.

3 Waugh always claimed that he had not read Proust until
  late in life but there is some evidence to suggest that
  he had dipped into 'A la Recherche' as a young man.
  Certainly his two friends, Anthony Powell and Henry
  Yorke ('Green'), were intrigued by the novel and spent

a great deal of time discussing it at Oxford. Several volumes of Proust, annotated by Waugh, are in his library, now kept in the HRC.

4 Lancing College, Sussex.

103. T.J. BARRINGTON, 'BELL'

February 1947, 58-63

The intelligence is knocked out so brilliantly in Donat O'Donnell's December article, The Pieties of Evelyn Waugh [No. 102], that it seems unsporting to suggest that some of the blows must have escaped the referee. Donat O'Donnell, like Waugh, is class-conscious - within limits, a modest fault....

'Black Mischief' we are told is 'largely based on a sly appeal to the white man's sense of racial superiority.'
... A coloured man, or an unprejudiced one, might be pardoned for believing ... that Waugh is being sly about the whites.... It is not disingenuous, then, to cite the book in support of the race snobbery theory without the warning that it could support the converse view?

I have no desire to dispute Donat O'Donnell's materialist interpretation of Waugh. I judge it only by the methods used in selling it to us, for even class-conscious writers might abide by the rules of argument.

[His] central argument is ... calculated to shake the boys on the pious papers, the 'Tablet,' 'America,' and the rest, who because of 'Brideshead Revisited' hailed Waugh as a great apologist of the Catholic Church. What a jolt to them to learn from Donat O'Donnell that Babbit failed to get the point of the book partly because Waugh's Catholicism, as illustrated in 'Brideshead Revisited,' is unorthodox! Why? Because it is 'mingled' with 'a highly personal system of belief and devotion' and is 'superimposed' on a 'fixed and intolerant mythology' which is Waugh's 'private religion.' In short, Waugh's Catholic apologetics do not click because Waugh is a heretic. It is obvious that any Catholic who practises a private religion is a heretic; but this heresy-hunt follows, oddly enough, the dialectical form: Waugh is, amongst other things, a snob; Waugh is a Catholic; Waugh's Catholicism is a kind of religious snobbery. The synthesis is intended to make unambiguous the charge of heresy - though Donat O'Donnell shrinks from actually joining the Holy Brotherhood.

As this has an ecclesiastical flavour perhaps we could
put the snob-Catholicism-religious snobbery argument in the
sanctified form of the syllogism; which shows that the
conclusion does not *necessarily* follow from the premises....
[He] does not argue that Waugh is simply a Catholic and a
snob, as many are; he asserts a 'mingling' of the two, and
his argument demands in Waugh's mind a necessary connexion
between them. The following passage is the only attempt to
argue this connexion: 'But the Catholicism of Mr. Waugh,
and of certain other English converts ... riches included."'
The reader who has some knowledge of the doctrine of Grace,
and some regard for logic, needs to be prepared for the
conclusion to all this:

> In Mr. Waugh's theology, the love of money is not
> only not the root of all evil, it is a preliminary form
> of the love of God.

That kind of reasoning leaves one gasping. One appreci-
ates that Donat O'Donnell does not like the rich, an
ancient and respectable dislike which many of us share....
Lady Marchmain knows the enormous evil latent in riches,
but she holds, with Waugh and the Catholic Church, that
God's grace can change that evil into good. Waugh's theology is unimpeachable on that score; but what can one
think of Donat O'Donnell's logic in imputing to Waugh the
nonsense that riches of themselves earn grace?
As well as this peculiar way of connecting Waugh's snobbery with Waugh's Catholicism, Donat O'Donnell makes certain assertions to that end. Take the reference, in the
passage I have quoted, to Hooper's soul as being somewhat
less valuable in Waugh's eyes than Lord Marchmain's 'genuine old landed article.' Donat O'Donnell rightly stresses
that it would be heresy for Waugh to imply - or even
'almost seem to imply' - any such thing. Indeed it would be
heresy to believe it without implying it at all. What evidence does Donat O'Donnell produce to show that Waugh tends
to believe it? Hooper's misfortune is not so much that he
was born poor but that he was apparently born without, and
did not acquire, a consciousness of God and of possessing
a soul. (Donat O'Donnell overplays the Hooper card: Ryder,
the unbeliever at, as it were, Marchmain's deathbed, is the
relevant person; but I confine myself to the article as it
is written.) Objectively, Hooper's soul and Marchmain's are
equally valuable; but subjectively there is a difference.
Apparently Hooper places little value on his soul, while to
Lord Marchmain's family, and ultimately to Lord Marchmain,
his soul, as he lies dying, is of supreme importance. The
assessment of subjective values proves merely that

Catholics sometimes find it necessary to value their souls, whereas unbelievers feel no such necessity. What have class loyalty, wealth and poverty to do with that? It is possibly a valid criticism of Waugh's social outlook that his Catholics are aristocrats - just as valid as the criticism that in his earlier books his dissolute young things belong to the upper classes; but this is no criticism of Waugh's Catholicism.

If Waugh is blind in loving lords, O'Donnell is blind in hating them. Look at this (italics mine):

> But his (Waugh's) almost idolatrous reverence for birth has not been *destroyed* by the Faith; *on the contrary*, 'Brideshead Revisited' breathes from beginning to end a loving patience with mortal sin among the aristocracy and an unchristian petulance towards the minor foibles of the middle class.

That is brilliantly said, but it is brilliantly wrong. (Note the words I have italicised: what is the contrary of destruction? Creation?) Lord Sebastian, for all his drunkenness and sexual perversion, probably saved his soul, not because God, in Waugh's theology, especially loves a lord, but because the lord occasionally loved God. Donat O'Donnell must be familiar with the timeworn antithesis between those who behave but don't believe, and those who believe but don't behave. Waugh is not to be damned for using that antithesis, even when he makes the rich to be believers and the poor to be behavers. (Most dialecticians would prefer it so.) Waugh's apologetic is plainly that the believers, no matter how badly they behave, or how rich they are, must sooner or later face the logic of their belief: one day God calls them to heel with 'a twitch upon the thread.'

It is patent that Donat O'Donnell's article fails to prove the existence in Waugh's mind of a necessary connexion between snobbery and Catholicism. To lead us to believe, then, on the evidence produced that there is implicit in 'Brideshead Revisited' an heretical private religion is to attempt to bamboozle us. Waugh's pieties have not been shown to have mingled with Catholicism to produce a private religion, 'a highly personal system of belief and devotion'. Apparently it is not only in America, to call on Donat O'Donnell's Jesuit source, that the commentators have missed the point of 'Brideshead Revisited.' Even in Ireland class-conscious criticism may on occasion be as blind, or as perverse, as '"secularist" stupidity and indifference'!

104.   DONAT O'DONNELL, 'BELL'

March 1947, 57-62

I wish to defend the opinions set out in my article The
Pieties of Evelyn Waugh [No. 102] against the attacks made
on them by Mr. T.J. Barrington in his interesting and
briskly argued letter in your February issue [No. 103].
   Mr. Barrington's main line of argument may be summarized as follows:

1. My article charged Mr. Waugh with holding a heretical
   private religion, consisting of a mixture of snobbery
   and Catholicism.
2. I did not prove that Mr. Waugh was a snob.
3. Even if he is a snob, I 'failed to prove' the existence
   in his mind of a necessary connection between snobbery
   and Catholicism.
4. Therefore my argument represents an attempt to 'bamboozle' the public.

   I shall try to answer these points *seriatim*:
   1. I had better clear the ground here by indicating certain assumptions underlying my criticism of Mr. Waugh (and
also, in the February 'Bell,' of that other eminent Catholic writer, Mr. Graham Greene). I have assumed that in the
mind of a convert to a religion there has existed, before
his conversion, a complex (I am not using the word in the
vulgar pseudo-Freudian sense) of ideas and emotions, principles and loyalties, which predisposed him towards that
religion. I am speaking here of course in strictly lay
terms and am far from attempting a complete 'explanation'
of conversion. Now these predispositions, although they
may lead in the end to complete acceptance of the dogmas
of a religion, are likely to point in the beginning to a
limited number of that religion's real or rumoured tenets,
or even to mere outward appearances, such as architecture
or ritual, or to fortuitous historical circumstances such
as the attractive manners and social traditions of a particular body of believers. The instructed acceptance of
the whole body of dogma will destroy the errors of the
original approach, but the initial predispositions are
likely to remain, and, if the convert writes a novel,
these predispositions will play a great part in shaping it,
since, in the composition of a work of art, emotional attitudes are at least as potent as intellectual convictions.
Furthermore, if he writes a novel with a deliberate intention of upholding the religion he has chosen, he will under

the domination of his predispositions, tend to stress the
aspects of that religion which first attracted him. If his
initial predisposing complex was strong and highly charged
with emotion - as was clearly the case with Mr. Waugh -
the stress will fall very heavily.(1) So heavily indeed
will it fall, that the novel may fail altogether to convey
a Catholic message to minds not in sympathy with the
writer's particular predispositions. This was, I think, the
case with 'Brideshead Revisited.' Also, and this is the
really important point, the stresses in 'Brideshead Revisited' fall so heavily on certain aspects of Catholic belief
to the exclusion of all others, that it is, in my opinion,
dangerous and confusing to call that novel (as the 'Tablet'
did) 'a great apologetic work in the larger and more humane
sense.' If a work of apologetics were as one-sided as
'Brideshead Revisited' it would be considered heretical,
since heresy consists, I believe, precisely in emphasising
a truth to the exclusion of other truths. But 'Brideshead
Revisited' is a work of fiction, and is not to be judged by
the same standards as an apologetic work. I did not therefore presume to charge its author with heresy. When I referred to 'bulky memorials of devotion to other gods,' to
'alien pieties' a 'private religion' and so on, I meant
what in this letter I call the 'predisposing complex' and
its effects. It seemed to me from reading Mr. Waugh's books
that in him that complex was so strong and fixed, and its
subsistence dominated his work to such an extent that these
terms were justified. I did not, as Mr. Barrington seems to
believe, charge Mr. Waugh with consciously holding and
practising a 'private religion.' I should like to under-
line, for Mr. Barrington, the following sentence from my
article: 'These alien pieties, some of them hardly compatible with strict Catholicism, were perhaps for Mr. Waugh
the forerunners of a more articulated faith - as, in
"Brideshead Revisited," Sebastian Flyte's affection for a
teddy-bear was the forerunner of a vocation.' I should have
added that even after Sebastian had become a lay-brother,
what one might call the teddy-bear side of his character
did not altogether disappear.

2. It is quite true that I did not (for reasons which I
shall discuss later) prove that Mr. Waugh is a snob, but I
think that one would need to be very innocent, or possess a
peculiar definition of snobbery, not to perceive the fact
for oneself. I take a snob as being one who despises his
social inferiors, and admires his social superiors, as
groups. In my article I gave a number of examples of Mr.
Waugh's contempt for his inferiors. I instanced, *inter
alia*, his jokes at the expense of coloured people ('Black
Mischief,' 'Scoop').... Mr. Barrington claims that the fun

... is impartial; Mr. Waugh is laughing equally at whites
and blacks (in 'Black Mischief').... He misses the point;
the amount of laughter may be equal, but the quality is
different. Mr. Waugh laughs at Basil Seal and various
Bright Young Things, but there is affection, nostalgia,
even admiration, in his laughter. Basil Seal may eat his
fiancée by accident, but his creator does not think any
the less of him for that. When Mr. Waugh turns, however,
to Seth, the black king with 'western' ideas, there is
somthing different, something brutal, about his laughter.
Clearly to him Seth is in himself a butt, a more sophisticated version of the chimpanzee-with-a-clay-pipe joke....
Mr. Barrington is very wide of the mark in believing that
the joke here is similar to that of letting out a mouse in
a girls' school. Letting out three monkeys in the Senate
would be more like it. No one laughs at a mouse, because a
mouse does not resemble a man. Mr. Waugh's evacuees are
grotesque half-animal beings whose parody of human behaviour and persecution of real though silly, human beings,
provide the fun. Wit is a sly, evasive thing, hard to pin
down and on these points, where no proof is possible, I can
only call on those who have read the texts to judge between
my view and Mr. Barrington's.... I notice ... that Mr. Barrington wisely makes no attempt to deny Mr. Waugh's veneration for his social superiors. There is therefore no need
for me to argue that part of the definition.

3. Mr. François Mauriac has stated that criticism of
living writers is 'impossible.' It is certainly impossible
if criticism means 'proving' the existence in a writer's
mind of the ideas and relationships of ideas which the
critic thinks he perceives in the writer's work. In writing
an article on Mr. Waugh I did not set out to prove anything
about his mind.... A critic should give his own conclusions, and indicate how he arrived at them, but these conclusions should not be held proven; they should simply
serve to indicate possible lines of approach to the work
criticised. If the lines of approach do not prove viable
the reader can, as Mr. Barrington does, reject the critic's
conclusions.

In my answer to Mr. Barrington's first point I gave a
general idea of the manner in which (I believe) extraneous
elements (such as snobbery) may mingle with Catholicism in
the work of a creative writer, especially a convert. In my
original article, in a discussion of this theme, I instanced Lady Marchmain's [remark and] made the comment, which
horrifies Mr. Barrington, that 'in Mr. Waugh's theology the
love of money is not only not the root of all evil, it is a
preliminary form of the love of God.' My point, of course,
was that Mr. Waugh, as a writer, takes the elements in

Catholicism that suit his 'predispositions' and leaves out
the others; the truth that the love of money is the root of
all evil, and many similar truths of Christianity, do not
suit him; the equally undeniable truth that grace can sanctify even riches does suit him. Incidentally Mr. Barrington
accuses me, on the strength of the passage quoted above,
of 'imputing to Waugh the nonsense that riches of themselves earn grace.' If he reads the passage again he will
see that I am imputing nothing of the sort. My meaning was
that Mr. Waugh seems to make the love of money, like Sebastian's love for his teddy-bear, or Captain Ryder's love of
Julia, a forerunner of the love of God.

I also ... compared Mr. Waugh's anxious interest in Lord
Marchmain's soul and in the souls of his other aristocratic
characters, with his apparently complete indifference about
the soul of Hooper. I mentioned that Mr. Waugh 'almost
seemed to imply that the wretched Hooper has no soul at
all.' This is not a very strong statement but Mr. Barrington challenges me to produce 'evidence' for even this
reference to a partial appearance of an implication. I can
only refer to what I mentioned before about the distribution of emphasis. 'Grace can sanctify the whole of life,
riches included,' but can it sanctify the whole of life,
Hooper included? It cannot apparently, for Mr. Waugh has
created a Hooper who has no part in any spiritual world.
Mr. Barrington says: 'Objectively, Hooper's soul and Marchmain's are equally valuable; but subjectively there is a
difference.' There is; but the subjective difference
resides, I think, in the mind of their creator Mr. Waugh
and not only (as Mr. Barrington ingeniously argues) in the
fictitious minds of the characters.

Mr. Barrington also takes exception to my statement that
Mr. Waugh's 'almost idolatrous reverence for birth has not
been destroyed by the Faith.' He italicizes destroyed,
and claims that my use of this word shows my 'blind hatred'
for lords. I rather like lords, although less than Mr.
Waugh does, and I have no idea what Mr. Barrington is driving at here. Surely it is a commonplace that Christianity
should destroy idolatrous reverence for anything, birth
included?

4. I must say that this charge rather pains me. I made
a quite honest attempt at an analysis of Mr. Waugh's ideas
and arrived at certain conclusions which Mr. Barrington
rejects. That is fair enough. But I think he is going a
little far when he argues that because I have 'failed to
prove my case,' I am 'attempting to bamboozle' the public
by 'leading us to believe' certain things about Mr. Waugh.
Does Mr. Barrington really think that whenever we are led

to believe something that has not been proved to us we are
being 'bamboozled'? I am sure that he does not think anything so Hooperish; he probably merely meant that I put my
case too strongly, and in that he may be right. All of us
are liable to the temptations of rhetoric.

Before I end, I should like to thank Mr. Barrington
('across the havoc of war' as Mr. Churchill used to say)
for the courteous tone which he maintained in his letter.
Politeness is too rare a thing in Irish controversy for it
to be allowed to pass unremarked.

Note

1   Cf. Waugh's 'Diaries': 'When I first came into the
    Church I was drawn, not by splendid ceremonies but by
    the spectacle of the priest as a craftsman. He had an
    important job to do which none but he was qualified for'
    (Easter, 1964, p. 792); also Waugh's article, Converted
    to Rome, (DE, 20 October 1930, 10) and his letter (No.
    105) which concludes the 'Bell' debate.

105.   EVELYN WAUGH, 'BELL'

July 1947, 77

I am most grateful for the attention given to my work in
your pages [Nos 102-4 above] and would not intrude in the
discussion but for the fear that a hasty reader might conceive the doubt, which your reviewer scrupulously refrains
from expressing, of the good faith of my conversion to
Catholicism.

I think perhaps your reviewer is right in calling me a
snob; that is to say I am happiest in the company of the
European upper-classes; but I do not think this preference
is necessarily an offence against Charity, still less
against Faith. I can assure you it had no influence on my
conversion. In England Catholicism is predominantly a religion of the poor. There is a handful of Catholic aristocratic families, but I knew none of them in 1930 when I
was received into the Church. My friends were fashionable
agnostics and the Faith I then accepted had none of the
extraneous glamour which your reviewer imputes to it.

Nor, I think, does this preference unduly influence my
writing. Besides Hooper there are two characters in

'Brideshead Revisited' whom I represent as worldly - Rex
Mottram, a millionaire, and Lady Celia Ryder, a lady of
high birth. Why did my reverence for money and rank not
sanctify those two?

106.   EVELYN WAUGH, PREFACE TO THE 1960 REVISED EDITION OF
'BRIDESHEAD REVISITED'

1959

This novel, which is here re-issued with many small additions and some substantial cuts, lost me such esteem as I
once enjoyed among my contemporaries and led me into an
unfamiliar world of fan-mail and press photographers. Its
theme - the operation of divine grace on a group of
diverse but closely connected characters - was perhaps
presumptuously large, but I make no apology for it. I am
less happy about its form, whose more glaring defects may
be blamed on the circumstances in which it was written.
   In December 1943 I had the good fortune when parachuting
to incur a minor injury which afforded me a rest from military service. This was extended by a sympathetic commanding
officer, who let me remain unemployed until June 1944 when
the book was finished. I wrote with a zest that was quite
strange to me and also with impatience to get back to the
war. It was a bleak period of present privation and
threatening disaster - the period of soya beans and Basic
English - and in consequence the book is infused with a
kind of gluttony, for food and wine, for the splendours of
the recent past, and for rhetorical and ornamental language,
which now with a full stomach I find distasteful. I have
modified the grosser passages but have not obliterated
them because they are an essential part of the book.
   I have been in two minds as to the treatment of Julia's
outburst about mortal sin and Lord Marchmain's dying soliloquy. These passages were never, of course, intended to
report words actually spoken. They belong to a different
way of writing from, say, the early scenes between
Charles and his father. I would not now introduce them into
a novel which elsewhere aims at verisimilitude. But I have
retained them here in something near their original form
because, like the Burgundy (misprinted in many editions)
and the moonlight they were essentially of the mood of
writing; also because many readers liked them, though that
is not a consideration of first importance.

It was impossible to foresee, in the spring of 1944,
the present cult of the English country house. It seemed
then that the ancestral seats which were our chief national
artistic achievement were doomed to decay and spoliation
like the monasteries in the sixteenth century. So I piled
it on rather, with passionate sincerity. Brideshead today
would be open to trippers, its treasures rearranged by
expert hands and the fabric better maintained than it was
by Lord Marchmain. And the English aristrocracy has maintained its identity to a degree that then seemed impossible. The advance of Hooper has been held up at several
points. Much of this book therefore is a panegyric preached
over an empty coffin. But it would be impossible to bring
it up to date without totally destroying it. It is offered
to a younger generation of readers as a souvenir of the
Second War rather than of the twenties or of the thirties,
with which it ostensibly deals.

107.   DAVID PRYCE-JONES, 'TIME AND TIDE'

23 July 1960, 863-4

David Pryce-Jones (b. 1936) is a novelist, critic, lecturer
and travel writer; the author of 'Owls and Satyrs' (1961),
'Graham Greene' (1963) and 'Running Away' (1971) and editor
of 'Evelyn Waugh and His World' (1973). He is the son of
Alan Pryce-Jones (see headnote to No. 87).
    This piece offended Waugh who lost no time in informing
its author of the fact. Later, Mr Pryce-Jones came to
regret writing the review, 'especially the infantile left-
ism in it'. He was Literary Editor of 'Time and Tide' in
1960.

It is unlikely that many a student's thesis will be written
comparing the new text of 'Brideshead Revisited' with the
old, contrary to the devoted forecast made in the blurb to
the new edition. The alterations are few and unimportant,
toning down hyperbole, concealing some architectural
references about Brideshead and spoiling a few jokes, as
for instance when Anthony Blanche is no longer described
'like the fine piece of cookery he was'.
    'Brideshead Revisited' may be taken as Evelyn Waugh's
magnum opus. It is the grand climax of his gifts as a
writer and his fullest exposition of his views of the world.

This novel in itself seems to epitomise the rest of his work, starting with brilliant levity, to end on a note of histrionic Catholicism. It is also the cleverest and most persuasive of all his novels, lacking the blatancy of 'Put Out More Flags' or 'Black Mischief', and it is thereby all the more outstanding as a work of art. Written during the war, it is deeply melancholic, casting a miasma, half-poetic and half-apologetic across the *fin de siècle* disintegration of the Marchmain family. This is as attractive as it is repulsive. Waugh is evoking the sense of decay to cast a dazzling spell with which to enlist our sympathy for the old order, our sorrow at the financial and moral collapse of the aristocracy, our fear of the triumph of sin.

Evelyn Waugh writes novels about people and therefore only inductively about what they represent. Ideas are secondary to him, as a writer he appears fundamentally disinterested in intellectual arguments or appraisals. 'Brideshead Revisited' is the nearest that he comes to an argument, for Charles Ryder whose memories Sacred and Profane they are, is not a Catholic (in either edition) and the new order is juxtaposed against the old, not purely as a laughing-stock, but as a historical fact. It is as if Mr Waugh had mistaken himself temporarily for Aldous Huxley.

For it is the old order that matters to Evelyn Waugh. He is a Burkian with a difference.... Like Burke, he sees a hierarchical society which tampering can only harm. Instinctively he prefers the menials, butlers and house-maids who know their station, to the middle classes, *petit bourgeois* who thrust forward on the heels of the great. As he says in the preface to the new edition of 'Brideshead Revisited', 'The advance of Hooper has been held up at several points.' Hooper, *petit bourgeois* second lieutenant, stands for Evelyn Waugh's view of the class struggle, and Mr Waugh does not like Hooper.

It is because his own intellectual position hardened almost as soon as he began to put pen to paper that Mr Waugh does not acknowledge intellectuals' alternatives. Points of view which should be taken seriously, even if then rejected, do not exist for Mr Waugh. He is dealing with a small section of society, a limited number of men and women who could only behave in the way he describes in their limited social circumstances, and whose behaviour is their only value. Mr Waugh justifies them for what they are, and if the reader still feels no kinship or warmth for these people, Mr Waugh is not going to explain them any further. All the characters of whom he writes with approval, the Marchmains, Basil Seal, Margot Metroland even Helena and Campion, are supposed to possess self-evident virtues. Not to approve is to have a chink in one's social armour, to be a poor, carping critic and kill-joy, or simply, and Mr Waugh must take some of the blame for the phrase, non-U.(1) Most writers have blind spots and Mr Waugh's is his total lack of imagination, not about situations, but about human beings. Mr Waugh is a social Philistine.

This means that his 'heroes and villains' have a Dickensian obviousness about them. Some of the 'heroes' like Basil Seal, Margot Metroland, Sebastian Flyte and Mrs Stitch are frankly anti-social. Others like Jock and Brenda of 'A Handful of Dust', or Sonia and Alastair and Peter Pastmaster are no more than props of a cosy upper class life, people who can be relied upon to drink black velvet in the bathroom and provide civilised chatter. It is for them all, of both categories, toughs or softies, that ease of life has been conceived and by them that it is rightly practised. The 'villains' have nothing melodramatic about them for they are so ludicrously parodied and caricatured. Easy targets are foreigners, negroes, socialists, academics, journalists, poets and social climbers; the long endlessly funny list; Potts and Pennyfeather, Professor Silenus, Parsnip and Pimpernell, Ambrose Silk, Corker, Seth and every negro in 'Scoop' and 'Black Mischief', Scott-King in his Modern Europe, Mr Joyboy and Aimée etc. We are made to squirm as Mr Waugh mercilessly and accurately exposes the weaknesses of them all, their comic transparency.

His essential view of society is indeed based upon a belief in the inherent superiority of one section at the expense of all others.

This attitude of superiority finds its corollary in Waugh's views about foreigners.... With this double attitude towards English values and the rest of the world, it might be wondered why in the disastrous political climate of the Thirties, Evelyn Waugh never took to political action, nor as far as I know, to pamphleteering.

The answer, I suspect, lies in Mr Waugh's conversion to Catholicism, which seems to have had the important effect of concentrating all his efforts on writing novels. His first two novels, 'Decline and Fall' and 'Vile Bodies', are to my mind his best, full of verve and satirical humour. But they are novels of the Disillusion, of the period when the Twenties were turning into the Thirties, and men began to sniff the air for dictators. Mr Waugh was converted in 1930 to the medieval, traditionalist Catholicism whose feudal image had been projected by Belloc and Chesterton. This sort of religion, more ritualistic and historical-mystical than thoughtful or doctrinal gave a core to Waugh's Disillusion. The collapse of moral

standards and of a society held up by these standards was a
theme for discussing the universality of sin and not a peg
for political action. Because Mr Waugh is a social Philistine he could take refuge from events in Catholicism. Had
it been otherwise, might 'Brideshead Revisited' have ended
with Julia redeeming Sebastian by both joining the Mosley
group?

If Catholicism saved Waugh from politics, it also
orientated his writing. Emphasising that he wrote as a
novelist, his three specifically Catholic exegetical books,
'Helena' (his own favourite), 'Campion' and the biography
of Monsignor Knox, are interpretations rather than works
of scholarship. These books extol the good old days which
came before the recurrent waves of crudely trampling reformers. Helena emerges as a glorified Lady Marchmain and
Campion as an elder Basil Seal. But, 'Brideshead Revisited'
apart, there is less Catholic content in his work than in,
say, Graham Greene.

As a matter of literature, his religion has merely
intensified Waugh's dislike of the human race, striving in
vain for its own salvation. The vanity of human effort,
the hopelessness of attaching importance to any individual
and the futility of happiness, except in terms of social
or personal advancement, are favourite themes of Mr.
Waugh's. They are also continuous, for Pennyfeather is not
that different from Gilbert Pinfold, sane in a mad world
or mad in a sane world, whichever it is, both are going to
survive on their feet. This is not an outlook that despises
the world for its dullness which is a projection of upper
class melancholia, but it is the dark knowledge that the
world is a godless, graceless place. It does not spring
from a conviction that nobody understands the true state
of things, and should be enlightened. It is Mr Evelyn
Waugh fighting for protection in a world of moral *laisser-
faire*, singing a song of hate.

It has its lighter side, of course, for Mr Waugh is a
real master of English prose. A comparison of 'Decline and
Fall' with 'Antic Hay' or 'Crome Yellow' leaves Huxley, his
closest competitor in the field, far behind.

But compare the same two authors when they write almost
the same book, Huxley's 'After Many a Summer', 1939, and
Waugh's 'The Loved One', 1948. Huxley used Hollywood life
to write about the fear of death and the desire for immortality on earth: it is an intellectual pseudo-scientific
satire, with many disagreeable throw-aways about human
nature. Waugh took the same Hollywood framework to mock the
Americans, to savage the idea of romance and love by por-
traying its hideous manifestation in a morgue, to observe
sadistically a worthless and aimless selection of cranks.

Sadism, cruelty, a horror of humanity and its emotions, the failure of mankind and irredeemable sin: we are back to the essential Waugh. And yet this Thirtyish doctrine of reaction and defeatism is so well put forward that the Penguin covers can present Waugh as the satirist *par excellence* of English ways, while announcing that in 1951 he joined the authors who have had ten of their books published simultaneously by Penguins in the uneasy company of Shaw, Wells and D.H. Lawrence.

Note

1 Waugh contributed to the 'U' and 'non-U' debate (concerning '"class indicators" in the differing modes of speech among English groups'; see Sykes, pp. 384-6) with his An Open Letter to Hon. Mrs. Peter Rodd [Nancy Mitford, his friend, the novelist] on a Very Serious Subject ('Encounter', December 1955, 11-17); reprinted in 'Noblesse Oblige', ed. Nancy Mitford (Hamish Hamilton, 1956).

108. JOHN COLEMAN, 'SPECTATOR'

29 July 1960, 187

For a man who, on his own confession, detests the lenses of publicity, an image of Mr. Waugh has registered with surprising clarity on the public retina. It is partly, of course, the urbanity with which he expresses illiberal, unfashionable opinions that has made his rare statements *in propria persona* so memorable. And it is precisely the scope and intensity of his rejection of the twentieth century - and of a good deal of the nineteenth, too, I should imagine - that has made him so pungent a present force. If Gilbert Harding can earn surcease from schoolmastering by gently grumbling, it is not hard to see how much more effective Mr. Waugh is likely to be, dealing out his acerbities on 'Face to Face.'(1) This is the latest, still vibrating image; and its fragmented, faddy, turbulent presence in certain of his books is surely their most tiresome feature.

For Mr. Waugh reigns undisturbed as the funniest of living English writers. He is also one of the most technically adroit. 'The Ordeal of Gilbert Pinfold,' that extraordinary experiment in semi-autobiography, opens thus:

> It may happen in the next hundred years that the
> English novelists of the present day will come to be
> valued as we now value the artists and craftsmen of the
> late eighteenth century. The originators, the exuberant
> men, are extinct and in their place subsists and
> modestly flourishes a generation notable for elegance
> and variety of contrivance.

It would be difficult to think of a novelist to whom the
pleasantly Augustan terms of that final phrase better
apply than to Mr. Waugh himself: he is, one suspects,
aware of this. 'Writing should be like clockwork', is another of his dicta and his own work, with its fine timing
and cunning intricacy of incident, supports the comparison
well enough.... There are already examples of the characteristic throw-away joke - young Tangent's amputated foot,
Mr. Prendergast's murder - that is to become a full-grown
element of later books.... Somewhere along the line that
runs from Harry Graham to Tom Lehrer Mr. Waugh purloined
something for art.

There seems, however, to be fairly general agreement
that the purest form of this art is to be found in the
earliest books. Certainly they contain few indications of
the author's presence, working as they do through swift,
Firbankian cutting from one dialogue-episode to the next.
They are harsh, exact farce; not satire. They play on the
surface of the emotions, never quite releasing them. Their
pace and poise, the sense they communicate of 'playing a
game,' debar the reader from complicity in the circumstances of stupidity, mutilation, and betrayal; in making
fun *out of* conventionally serious occasions, they give a
sort of dispensation from the everyday stress of reacting.
Pity and anger are in abeyance and laughter may come as
much from the sense of relief from these as from anything
else; for once the awful human exactions are not being
made. The point is worth taking at this length, if only
because hesitations creep in with Mr. Waugh's fourth novel,
'A Handful of Dust.' Tony Last may be presented as a creature of supine permissiveness in the best Pennyfeather tradition, but he is unusually well documented for a Waugh
hero, principally with forms of nostalgia - for his Gothic
country house and a roomful of childhood mementoes; some
sympathy seems to have been extended to his creation. The
torments to which he is subjected before he makes a break
for the jungle and an original doom, though decked out
with brilliancies of comedy, are so elaborated that one
carries away an uneasy sense of some principle of masochism

slithering just below the decorous surface.

There were occasions for doubt, then, about the art of Mr. Waugh some time before the appearance in 1945 of his most ambitious novel, 'Brideshead Revisited.' All the world might love a laugher, but there were those who had begun to ask themselves what exactly they were being invited to laugh at. While Mr. Waugh manipulated his figures of fantasy through upper-class situations, and for just so long as the conventions remained those of a game, there was no point in being incensed because he wasn't also purveying a 'criticism of life.' Anyone who looked for a larger pattern in 'Vile Bodies' or 'Scoop' would be deservedly disappointed. It is, after all, important not to expect from Mr. Waugh's comedies more than they engage to give. Pinfold was 'neither a scholar nor a regular soldier; the part for which he cast himself was a combination of eccentric don and testy colonel and he acted it strenuously.' Annoyance at certain quirky interpolations may lead one to miss much that is genuinely witty and finely conceived. But 'Brideshead Revisited,' now reissued with various alterations, was a different matter: an enormously wrought-upon novel of serious intent. In the author's own words, it 'lost me such esteem as I once enjoyed among my contemporaries,' and I am bound to say that it seems to me still (the sixty or so additions and excisions are in no way fundamental) a basically sapless piece of work, for all the audacities of structure, language and aim. The extent to which an author endorses the acts and beliefs of one of his characters is generally hard and hazardous to assess, but there is every indication here that Mr. Waugh wholeheartedly indulged himself, through the narrator Charles Ryder, in a kind of ornate justification of the desires on which his less attractive prejudices are based.

Note

1   Waugh was interviewed by John Freeman for the BBC TV series 'Face to Face'; recorded 18 June 1960 for transmission on 26 June 1960.

109.   FRANK KERMODE, 'ENCOUNTER'

November 1960, 63-6, 68-70

Frank Kermode (b. 1919), King Edward VII Professor of
English Literature and Fellow of King's College, Cambridge,
was co-editor of 'Encounter', 1966-7; Chairman of the
Poetry Book Society, 1968-76; and is author of 'Romantic
Image' (1957), 'The Sense of an Ending' (1967) and 'The
Genesis of Secrecy' (1979).

This well-known essay is entitled Mr Waugh's Cities.
Waugh loathed it and responded in the next issue ('Encounter', December 1960, 83): 'Your reviewer's theme has long
been tedious to me, but as it impugns my good faith as a
Catholic, it is right to answer. He imputes to me the
absurd and blasphemous opinion that divine grace is "confined" to the highest and lowest class. May I draw his
attention to a passage in a book which he appears to have
read with imperfect comprehension?' (Quotes '"*Odi profanum
vulgus et areo*" ... the See of Peter.' - from 'Helena',
p. 145 - a passage emphasizing the interdependence of all
social classes who could be 'one with the Empress Dowager
in the Mystical Body'.)

It is probably safe to assume that most readers of 'Brideshead Revisited'* know and care as much about Papist history
and theology as Charles Ryder did before he became intimate
with the Flytes; and although the novel contains a fair
amount of surprisingly overt instruction we are much more
likely to allow our reading of it to be corrupted by
ignorance than by an excessively curious attention to matters of doctrine. In fact this is true of Mr. Waugh's fiction as a whole; and one of the rewards of curiosity is a
clearer notion of the differences, as well as of the simi-
larities, between his most successful books.

At the end of 'Decline and Fall' (1928), Paul Pennyfeather, back at Scone after his sufferings on Egdon Heath,
notes with approval the condemnation of a second-century
Bithynian bishop who had denied the divinity of Christ and
the validity of the sacrament of Extreme Unction; a singularly dangerous heretic. A few moments later, however, he
turns his attention to an apparently more innocent sect:
'the ascetic Ebionites used to turn towards Jerusalem when
they prayed.... Quite right to suppress them.' They too
tended, for all the apparent harmlessness of their idiosyncrasy, to pervert fact with fantasy and truth with
opinion. More than twenty years later Mr. Waugh's Helena

ridicules theological fantasies concerning the composition
of the Cross (that it was compounded of every species of
wood so that the vegetable world could participate in the
act of redemption....) She is also offended by the untruths
and mythopoeic absurdities of her son Constantine. The
Cross she seeks and finds consists merely of large pieces
of wood. The Wandering Jew lets her have it free, foreseeing future business in relics. 'It's a stiff price,' says
Helena. She wanted none of that fantastic piety, only the
real routine baulks of timber used on a matter-of-fact historical occasion. 'Above the babble of her age and ours,'
comments the author, 'she makes one blunt assertion. And
there alone lies our Hope.'
    These passages illustrate what is static in Mr. Waugh's
expression of his religion. Religion as a man-made answer
to pressing human needs disgusts him.... The Church is concerned to preserve the truth, solid and palpable as a lump
of wood, from the rot of fantasy. It is entirely concerned
with fact. Hence it was quite right to suppress the fanciful Ebionites with the same severity as the intolerable
bishop; and the sentimental myth-making of Helena's scholars is dangerous because it tends to soften hard fact.

A number of such facts are at present ignored in our
society, which has apostatised to paganism. Yet they are
facts. Given the necessary instruction, the necessary
intellect, and the necessary grace, a man will be a Catholic. Mr. Waugh, paraphrasing Campion's Brag in his 'Life'
(1935) of the martyr does not even specify the third of
these necessities: 'he ... makes the claim, which lies at
the root of all Catholic apologetics, that the Faith is
absolutely satisfactory to the mind, enlisting all knowledge and all reason in its cause; that it is completely
compelling to any who give it an "indifferent and quiet
audience."' And the author has himself written that he was
admitted into the Church 'on firm intellectual conviction
but with little emotion.' As Mr. F.J. Stopp comments, in his
admirable 'Evelyn Waugh,'(1) it is also apparent that this
'firm intellectual conviction' relates 'not primarily to
the vanquishing of philosophical doubts about the existence
of God, or considerations of the nature of authority,' but
rather to 'a realisation of the undeniable historical presence and continuity of the Church.'
    Quod semper, quod ubique.... The English Reformation was
not only an attempt to break this historical continuity,
but a very insular movement. The Counter-Reformation, on
the other hand, was an affair of genuine vitality and
spirituality, universal in its scope; England was impoverished by its failure to participate. The consistency of

Mr. Waugh's opinions is indicated by his admiration for
Baroque art, the plastic expression of Tridentine Catholicism and a great European movement that left England almost
untouched. His version of English history at large is
simply but fairly stated in this way: after being Catholic
for nine hundred years, many English families, whether from
intellectual confusion or false prudence, apostasised in
the 16th century to schismatic institutions which were good
only in so far as they retained elements of the true worship. The consequence has been modern paganism (at a guess,
Mr. Waugh thinks of this as an atavism in degenerating
stock); the inevitable end is a restoration of the faith,
but the interim is ugly and tragic except in so far as it
is redeemed by the suffering of the martyrs and the
patience of the faithful. ('Have you ever thought,' asks
Helena, 'how awfully few martyrs there were, compared with
how many there ought to have been?') This conservatism is
of course reflected in the author's social opinions; the
upper classes are good in so far as they hold on to the
values and the properties cherished by their families.
Aristocracy, like the Church, fights a defensive action,
and that which it defends is, in the long run, a Catholic
structure. Very intelligent upper-class Englishmen are not
common in Waugh, and when they occur (Basil Seal is the
notable case) they are not intellectuals. Their brains have
nothing solid to work on; not being Catholics they are not
in a position to pursue the truth with any seriousness.
Yet if they preserve their families and their customs they
do as much as they can to maintain the link with those
'ancestors - all the ancient priests, bishops, and kings -
all that was once the glory of England, the island of
saints, and the most devoted child of the See of Peter.'
The words are Campion's.

This is the 'historical intransigence' that Ryder (in
the first edition of 'Brideshead Revisited') learnt to
admire. It is like Guyon smashing up the Bower of Bliss; a
great deal that might, to a less ruthless mind seem admirable, if mistaken, is pulled down without a regretful
glance. The age of Hooker (and Shakespeare) becomes merely
a good time for prospective martyrs to live in....

The extension of the frontier is not, however, the main
responsibility of the faithful in our time; it is
defence....

This, then, is what must be defended: the arts and
institutions of rational humanity and the clear reason-
ableness of the faith. Mr. Waugh is much concerned with the
clarity and openness of Catholic worship as an expression
of this. Here, from 'When the Going was Good,' is a passage
from an account of his attendance at a Mass of the

Ethiopian Church, 'secret and confused in character':

> I had sometimes thought it an odd thing that Western
> Christianity, alone of all the religions of the world,
> exposes its mysteries to every observer, but I was so
> accustomed to this openness that I had never before
> questioned whether it was an essential and natural fea-
> ture of the Christian system. Indeed, so saturated are
> we in this spirit that many people regard the growth of
> the Church as a process of elaboration - even obfusca-
> tion.... At Debra Labanos I suddenly saw the classic
> basilica and open altar as a great positive achievement,
> a triumph of light over darkness consciously accom-
> plished.... I saw the Church of the first century as a
> dark and hidden thing.... The pure nucleus of the truth
> lay in the minds of the people, encumbered with super-
> stitions, gross survivals of the paganism in which they
> had been brought up; hazy and obscene nonsense seeping
> through from the other esoteric cults of the Near East,
> magical infections from the conquered barbarian. And I
> began to see how these obscure sanctuaries had grown,
> with the clarity of Western reason, into the great open
> altars of Catholic Europe, where Mass is said in a flood
> of light, high in the sight of all....

Helena, we saw, was devoted to this openness, clarity,
commonsense; she is brusque and reasonable.... The Faith
may be driven back to the catacombs, but its agreement with
reason must never be obscured. Mr. Waugh perhaps took a
hint from Mr. Eliot in characterising the years between the
wars as a period during which pagan obscenities seeped in.
The Reformation opened the door to Madame Sosostris (2) to
a society in which rich women cut cards to see who shall go
first to have her fortune told by a foot-reader. The relig-
ions of darkness are the pagan intrusions; Catholic Christianity is light, order, life. 'The Loved One,' Mr. Waugh's
most perfect book (as 'Silas Marner' is more perfect than
'Middlemarch'), sketches a highly-developed religion of
darkness, in which art, love, language are totally corrupted and brought under the domination of death, as must happen when the offices of the Church are in every sphere
usurped.

   ...With the Donation of Constantine ('as for the old
Rome, it's yours') the secular became the holy Empire, the
Catholic City that the civilised must defend. Inside the
City are traditions of reason, clarity, beauty; outside,
obscene nonsense, the uncreating Word. Mr. Waugh is the
Augustine who, because he has a vision of this City,
detests Pelagius as a heretic and Apuleius as a sorcerer;

anathematises the humanitarian and the hot-gospeller.

Yet barbarism has its attractions. The 'atavistic callousness' of Lady Marchmain is only another form of that barbaric vitality which animates the upper classes even in decadence. 'Capital fellows *are* bounders' - if it were not so there would not be much fun in the early novels. Sometimes it seems that not to be corrupted is the shame, as with the dull Wykehamist of 'Brideshead Revisited', the chic, efficient corruption of Lady Metroland belongs inside, the depredations of Mrs. Beaver outside the pale. The moral distinctions are as bewildering as the semantics of *U* (3) or the social criteria which determine what is Pont Street and what is not. And they are, of course, employed without the least trace of Protestant assertiveness; to make them appear self-evident without mentioning them is one of the triumphant aspects of Mr. Waugh's early technique. One notices that the voices which tormented Mr. Pinfold puzzled him by missing out many of the accusations he would have made had he wished to torment himself. His mind worked much as it habitually did in composing his novels; the quality of the fantasies reminds one of Lord Tangent's death or the Christmas sermon in 'A Handful of Dust.' The vision of barbarism is a farcical one, and the fantasy has its own vitality; the truth exists, self-evident, isolated from all this nonsense, and there is no need to arrange a direct confrontation.

This co-existence of truth and fantasy is most beautifully sustained in 'A Handful of Dust,' surely Mr. Waugh's best book, and one of the most distinguished novels of the century. The great houses of England become by an easy transition types of the Catholic City, and in this book the threatened City is Hetton; it will not prove to be a continuing city. *No hinc habemus manentem civitatem* - the lament resounds in 'Brideshead.' Hetton is not beautiful; it was 'entirely rebuilt in 1864 in the Gothic style and is now devoid of interest,' says the guide-book. But Tony Last has the correct Betjemanic feelings for the battlements, the pitchpine minstrels' gallery, the bedrooms named from Malory. He is 'madly feudal,' which means he reads the lesson in church at Christmas and is thinking of having the fire lit in his pew. The nonsense that goes on in the church troubles nobody. Tony is a nice dull gentleman who knows vaguely that the defence of Hetton is the defence of everything the past has made valuable. He loses it because his wife takes up with a colourless rootless bore; Hetton and Tony are sacrificed, in the end, to a sterile affair in a London flat. The death of her son shows how far Brenda Last has departed from sanity and normality. There is a hideous divorce, a meaningless arrangement in

the middle of chaos. All this without comment; ennui,
sterility, cruelty represent themselves as farcically
funny. But the attempt of the lawyers to reduce him to the
point where he must give up Hetton rouses Tony, and he
breaks off the proceedings. Leaving England he goes in
search of another City; but there is no other City, and
this one is a fraud, like the Boa Vista of 'When the Going
was Good.' Tony was in search of something 'Gothic in
character, all vanes and pinnacles, gargoyles, battlements,
groining and tracery, pavilions and terraces, a trans-
figured Hetton.' He found the deathly Mr. Todd, and a
prison whose circular walls are the novels of Dickens.
Hetton becomes a silver-fox farm. Throughout this novel
the callousness of incident and the coldness of tone work
by suggesting the positive and rational declarations of the
Faith. Civility is the silent context of barbarism; truth
of fantasy. And Hetton, within the limits of Tony's understanding, is an emblem of the true City. Mr. Pinfold's mind
proliferates with infidel irrationality; this is useful,
provided the truth can be seen by its own light.

In 'Brideshead Revisited,' perhaps, it is not allowed to
do so. The great house as emblem of the City is enormously
developed, but opinion - or truth, if you are Catholic -
breaks into the text. The tone is less certain than that
of 'A Handful of Dust,' the prose slower, more explicit,
more like that of the 'Campion' biography than any of the
other novels; a slower prose, weighed with semi-colons.
Even in the making of the house itself fantasy has a smaller part than it had in Hetton. It has to be seen in the
historical perspective I have been sketching; the account
of Ryder - 'solid, purposeful, observant' no doubt, as an
artist should be, but not at the time of observing a Catholic - has to be put in order. 'Brideshead' is English ·
Baroque, but its stone came from an earlier castle. The
family was apostate until the marriage of the present
Marquis, reconciled to the Church on marriage (his wife,
he said, 'brought back my family to the faith of their
ancestors'). Lady Marchmain's family were old Catholic;
'from Elizabeth's reign till Victoria's they lived seques-
tered lives among their tenantry and kinsmen, sending their
sons to school abroad, often marrying there, inter-marrying,
if not, with a score of families like themselves, debarred
from all preferment, and learning, in those lost generations, lessons which could still be read in the lives of
the last three men of the house' - Lady Marchmain's
brothers, killed in 1914-18 'to make a world for Hooper.'
The Chapel at Brideshead is accordingly not in the style
of the house but in the art nouveau manner of the period
of Lord Marchmain's reconciliation, as if to symbolise the
delayed advent of toleration.

And their old religion sits just as uneasily upon the
house's occupants. Mr. Waugh is always emphatic that his
reasonable religion has nothing to do with making or keeping people in the ordinary sense happy. Lady Marchmain herself uneasily bears the sins of her family; Julia (descen-
dant of earlier, somewhat Arlenesque heroines) (4) drifts
into marriage with Rex Mottram, a sub-man with no sense of
reality (the scenes in which he dismisses it - when he is
under religious instruction with a view to his being
received into the Church - are the most amusing in the book
because Mr. Waugh is always at his cruel best with people
who cannot face reality), and is forced in the end to a
self-lacerating penance. Cordelia's life is, on any naturalist view, squandered in good works. Sebastian, gifted
with the power to attract love, attracts the love of God
and is hounded through alcoholism and pauperism into simple
holiness. Only Brideshead, the elder son, lives calmly and
unimaginatively with the truth; understanding even that
Sebastian's career, so wildly outside his own experience,
has in the end a purpose. They are all locked into a class,
these characters, and into the religion, which, by the
logic of Mr. Waugh's fiction, is in the long run inseparable from that class. Lord Marchmain makes his Byronic protest but dies in awkward splendour at Brideshead, finally
reconciled to the Church. Only in misery, it seems, will
the Faith be restored in the great families of England.

The death of Lord Marchmain is the climax of the process
by which Ryder returns to the Faith of his fathers, at the
end of which he can see his love for Sebastian and for
Julia as types and forerunners of this love of God. He
begins in deep ignorance. (In the first edition he complained that 'no one had ever suggested to me that these
quaint observances expressed a coherent philosophical system and intransigent historical claims.' Now he says, 'They
never suggested I should try to pray.... Later ... I have
come to accept claims which then ... I never troubled to
examine, and to accept the supernatural as the real.'
This shift of emphasis is an improvement, since Ryder's
intimacy with the Flytes may teach him something of 'the
operation of divine grace' but nothing directly about the
validity of the Church's historical claims.

Ryder learns certain associated lessons from the
Flytes. It is Sebastian who shows him that the beauty of
the City can be known only to the rich, that architecture
and wine, for example, are aspects of it. The scene of
Ryder's dinner with Mottram is a parable; the Burgundy is
a symbol of civility, 'a reminder that the world was an
older and better place than Rex knew, that mankind in its
long passion had learned another wisdom than his;' the

brandy is a test of man's truth and authenticity. Devoting
his life to such civilities, exempted by an infection of
the Flyte charm - as Blanche tells him - from the fate of
the classless artist, Ryder is already a Catholic in everything but religion. Mr. Waugh has done a little to reinforce this point in his revised text by re-writing the
passage describing the reunion of Ryder and his wife in New
York. His indifference and distaste are unchanged, but now
they make love with chill hygiene; a sham wasteland marriage, essentially terminable. But he too must lose everything; he loses Brideshead and Julia. So, in the end, all
these lives are broken, the war is on and Brideshead itself
a desolation (*quomodo sedet sola civitas*), defaced by
soldiers and housing Hooper. However, in the *art nouveau*
chapel the 'beaten-copper lamp of deplorable design' burns
anew. The saving of a soul may call for the ruin of a life;
the saving of the City for its desecration.

> Something quite remote from anything the builders
> intended has come out of their work, and out of the
> the fierce little human tragedy in which I played.

The desecration of the City as a mysterious means to its
restoration was the vision Mr. Waugh attributed to Pius V.
   Mr. Waugh says he has kept in certain details because
'they were essentially of the mood of writing; also because
many readers liked them, though that is not a consideration
of first importance.' I think it is possible to like these
details but to dislike other, perhaps more radical elements;
though this is doubtless even less important, since to name
them is to place oneself with the Hoopers. I mean that the
characters are sometimes repulsive, and it spoils this book,
as it doesn't the earlier work, to disagree with the author
on this point. It is, for example, such a surprise to learn
that Ryder is beautiful and beloved. Again there is Hooper,
in whose person we are to see an abstract of the stupidity
and vulgarity that beat upon the outer wall. The defenders
have made a wrong appreciation; their enemy is more dangerous, much cleverer, than Hooper. As soon as Mr. Waugh dis-
ciplines his fantasy to a more explicit statement of the
theme that has so long haunted him that theme is played
falsely; Hooper marks the degree of distortion.
   What we have in this book is the fullest statement of
this image of the City, powered by that historical intransigence that equates the English aristocratic with the
Catholic tradition; and very remarkable it is. But the
operation of divine grace seems to be confined to those who
say 'chimney-piece' and to the enviable poor. Hooper and
his brothers may be hard to bear, they may be ignorant of

the City, but it seems outrageous to damn them for their manners. One would like, no doubt, to keep the Faith, in all its aspects, uncontaminated; but Hoopers are not Ebionites, and the novelist, imitating the action of grace, is not an infallible church to suppress them. For all that one admires in 'Brideshead' - the City, the treatment of suffering, the useful and delightful Blanche, and Ryder's father - there is this difficulty, that intransigence when it gets into the texture of a novel breeds resistance; one fights rather than becomes absorbed. To suspend disbelief in these circumstances would be an act of sentimentality; a weakness not wholly unrelated to intransigence, and according to some discoverable in the text itself as well as in many readers.

Notes

* This edition is revised and has a Preface by the author.... The text is re-set. There is a surprising number of misprints, and some of them are bad ones, for example, p. 241, where 'I'm not sure,' should presumably read as formerly, 'I'm sure not.'

1 Frederick J. Stopp (see headnote to No. 130), 'Evelyn Waugh. Portrait of an Artist' (Chapman & Hall, 1958).
2 The fortune teller in the first section of T.S. Eliot's 'The Waste Land', The Burial of the Dead, ll. 43-59.
3 See No. 107, n. 1, above.
4 Michael Arlen created Iris Storm in his novel 'The Green Hat' (1924) and set the pattern for a certain kind of fictional heroine during the 1920s and 1930s - Hemingway's Brett Ashley ('Fiesta'), for example, and the long line of intelligent, careless, sexually liberated female protagonists in Waugh's work. Waugh remarked on the Arlen archetype in 'Unconditional Surrender' (Penguin, p. 200).

'When the Going was Good'

1946

110. THOMAS SUGRUE, 'NEW YORK HERALD TRIBUNE WEEKLY BOOK
REVIEW'

5 January 1947, 4

Thomas Sugrue (1907-53), American journalist and Catholic
writer, was a reporter for the 'New York Herald Tribune',
1931-4, and author of 'Such is the Kingdom' (1940), 'Star-
ling of the White House' (1946) and 'A Catholic Speaks his
Mind' (1952). Sugrue also contributed book reviews to the
'New York Times' and the 'Saturday Review of Literature'.

Between 1929 and 1935 Evelyn Waugh wrote four travel books
detailing his peregrinations in the Mediterranean countries, Abyssinia, Zanzibar, British Guiana, and Brazil.
From these volumes, now out of print, the author has selected what he considers worthy of re-issue, adding that 'My
own traveling days are over.... I rejoice that I went when
the going was good.' This latter opinion is a new one,
brought on by the present state of the world, whereby a
wanderer is more apt to be a displaced person or a melancholy soldier than a satirist on a holiday from the satur-
nalia which nourishes his art. While he was going Mr. Waugh
thought he was having a manly and a rugged time.

The book, of course, is not about Abyssinia or Zanzibar
or Brazil or Egypt or Palestine. It is about Mr. Waugh, who
reveals himself as very much the kind of person he ridicules so effectively in his novels. Another satirist, in
fact, might have found this Mr. Waugh an excellent subject,
and since every writer is both the father and the son of
his art that other satirist was Mr. Waugh himself. These
pieces, reportorial, superficial, hiding with a shimmering

surface the mental life underneath, are the raw material
of such novels as 'Black Mischief' and 'Scoop.' They are
also an exposition of Mr. Waugh, a self-portrait which
leaked unsuspected from the pen and left its image between
the lines. It is an excellent study of one of the genuine
character roles in history, a certain type of English
gentleman whom Chesterton described as being 'proud of
money and bad manners.' In a sense this type, as Mr. Waugh
has delineated it in his fiction, is above pride. It is, in
fact, above everything, which gives to all things observed
a somewhat diminished size.

Things all over the world, from the pyramids to the
Amazon jungle, diminish under Mr. Waugh's gaze as he goes
from site to saloon to safari in these memoirs. He is, in
the first place, not very much interested in passing on
information to his reader. He is writing about his travels
as a means of paying for them. But he is not very interested in the places he visits either, though this may be
due to a feeling that enthusiasm is bad taste. In this matter of taste American writers and reporters will be astounded to know that, having spent too much money staying at
Mena House, near Cairo, Mr. Waugh wrote to the two leading
hotels in Malta, stating that he was writing a travel book
and would give the hostelry a boost for free board and room.
Both accepted his offer and he went to what he considered
the better of the two establishments. After this incident,
it is amusing to find Mr. Waugh concerned about being
thought a tourist, he considered himself a traveler. It
never occured to him, apparently, that he was just a writer
working his way through a vacation.

Before judging these and other eccentricities of Mr.
Waugh the reporter and traveler too harshly it is well to
look at the frontispiece of the book, a color photograph of
Henry Lamb's portrait of Mr. Waugh, painted when the author
was twenty-six, in the flower of his travel years. One hand
holds a pipe to his mouth; the other grips a glass of ale.
Harvard sophomores sometimes look as daring and untried,
but not often.

The world has been so thoroughly tramped over, bombed,
sliced up, razed, raped and reported in the last seven
years that what description of it gets into 'When the Going
was Good' seems rather dull; the attitude of the times,
which Mr. Waugh considered worth preserving, is largely
Mr. Waugh's attitude, which still persists. There is no
great writing in these pages. There is just Mr. Waugh, a
fascinating fellow, well worth any one's consideration,
whether as a satirical genius or a type of Englishman
which in another generation may become extinct.

111.   PETER FLEMING, 'SPECTATOR'

24 January 1947, 116

'My own travelling days are over,' writes Mr. Waugh in his
preface, and the admission can hardly fail to sadden anyone
who reads this book ... for there is no doubt that Mr.
Waugh does this sort of thing extremely well. The books in
question dealt with the Mediterranean, Africa, British
Guiana and Abyssinia, where the author's experiences as a
war correspondent provided the scintillating material for
'Scoop'. Already a faint and rather agreeable patina of
period is discernible on this early work. If, in some
literary general-knowledge paper, competitors were asked,
'Who wrote, in what decade, of a night-club proprietress
"She seemed the least bogus person in Paris"?' a fair few
of them would score a right and left. And the mention of a
war correspondent representing the 'Morning Post' (1)
evokes, already, an irrevocably bygone atmosphere.
    Whether Mr. Waugh greatly enjoyed the journeys which, he
explains, he undertook like most of his contemporaries as a
matter of course is not clear; raptures are not in his line
and the general tone is one of sardonic resignation to discomforts and delays and the vagaries of foreigners. But the
reader - unless he demands either heroics or statistics -
will find in the narratives of this urbanely disgruntled
observer all the entertainment he could wish. The more fantastic his predicaments, the more bizarre his encounters,
the better Mr. Waugh describes them. His comment is capable
of a brilliant economy. At the Emperor of Abyssinia's coronation were 'two formidable ladies in knitted suits and
topees' who found the celebrations a profound disappointment. 'They were out for vice.... Prostitution and drug
traffic comprised their modest interests, and they were too
dense to find evidence of either.' The use of 'dense' well
illustrates the felicities of this author's style.
    Apart from its entertainment value, Mr. Waugh's account
of his experiences has some interest as what it is usual to
call a social document. More intelligent and (fortunately
for us) more articulate than most of his fellow travellers,
he is in some sense typical of a generation made footloose
by a combination of half-baked dissatisfaction and rather
aimless curiosity. 'Each book,' he found on re-reading
them, 'had a slightly grimmer air, as, year by year, the
shades of the prison house closed.' It is no coincidence
that his book opens in a bar and ends on a battlefield; and
it is even more inevitable - because he is such an admirable writer - that in between them the going is extremely
good.

Note

1   This was (Sir) William Deedes, then a cub reporter for
    the 'Post', now Editor of the 'Daily Telegraph'.

'Scott-King's Modern Europe'

1947 (US edition, 1949)

112. UNSIGNED REVIEW, 'TIMES LITERARY SUPPLEMENT'

20 December 1947, 657

Although all novelists inevitably show their personality
through their writing, the tendency of the last twenty
years has been for the author - within the range of his
book - to withdraw into a shell of comparative anonymity,
with the result that many relatively good contemporary
writers seem to speak with the voice of a group rather than
an individual. Mr. Evelyn Waugh stands notably apart from
this literary mood, and 'Scott-King's Modern Europe', a
story of about 24,000 words, concise, witty, making its
points with hammer-blows, shows the strength and weakness
of the extremely personal - almost cantankerous - position
he has taken up....

Mr. Waugh's character of Scott-King himself is admirable,
and his powers as a pamphleteer are keen, so that he surmounts a certain inconsistency that exists in his approach
at two levels - realistic and satirical; but even those who
share his loathing for the world of V.I.P.s, Priorities,
and jacks-in-office (excoriated with savage skill) must to
some extent regret that there is not more of the lighter,
naturalistic side, such as the treatment of head master,
boys and common-room of which there are glimpses at the
beginning and end of the book. This regret, it is true, is
merely a reassertion of Mr. Waugh's own point of view; and
he might legitimately argue that if it were not necessary
for someone to point out in no uncertain terms that politics and materialism are playing an increasingly damaging
part in the life of the individual, he could devote more
space to depicting surroundings like those of his hero,
who 'found a peculiar relish in contemplating the victories

292

of barbarism and positively rejoiced in his reduced station,
for he was of a type, unknown in the New World but quite
common in Europe, which is fascinated by obscurity and failure.' Anyway, as Scott-King himself would no doubt remark:

> *Cui dono lepidum novum libellum*
> *Arido modo pumice expolitum?* (1)

Note

1   'To whom am I to give my charming new little book,
    smoothed off only just now with the dry pumice?' These
    are the opening lines of Catullus (I, 1-2).

113.   JOHN RUSSELL, 'SUNDAY TIMES'

21 December 1947, 3

John Russell (b. 1919), art critic and book reviewer, has
been on the editorial staff of the 'Sunday Times' from 1946.
He is the author of 'G. Braque' (1959) and 'Seurat' (1965).

The early novels of Evelyn Waugh reveal, to readers of a
younger generation, a kind of life as strange to us as that
of the Tahitians once seemed to Captain Cook. An extinct
civilisation, it seems - Chinese in its formality, Paphian
in its promise of enjoyment, and English in the profusion
of its unwritten laws. All Melanesia could not show a
society more stiff with totem and taboo; but Mr. Waugh was
already an experienced traveller among primitive peoples,
and he could handle our native rites with ironic and
glacial ease.
    Time has embellished these four novels; they have, now
more than ever, the perpetuating virtue of style. As Mr.
Waugh did not then obtrude his own views about politics,
religion, personal relations and the Struggle Between The
Orders, it was not possible to discern that as a novelist
he had the gift of seeing through everybody except himself.
    More recent novels by this master of detached comedy
have disclosed a deutero-Waugh; and our original interlocu-
tor, who combined within himself the qualities of Horace,
Martial and Propertius, has often been shouted down by the
voice of an irritable and self-infatuated child. It was

difficult, after reading 'Brideshead Revisited', to
judge whether the admirations were really serious or
whether the creator of Mrs. Ape and Father Rothschild had
devised for himself a new vein of esoteric farce.

His new book, 'Scott-King's Modern Europe', is trifling
in size, and for the most part purely and mercifully comic
in intention. The middle-aged schoolmaster, harassed, perplexed and finally almost destroyed by the inhospitalities
of an unnamed totalitarian republic, is material that Mr.
Waugh can employ with unsurpassable zest and skill.

114.   GEORGE ORWELL, 'NEW YORK TIMES BOOK REVIEW'

20 February 1949, I, 25

George Orwell (pseudonym of Eric Blair, 1903-50) was a
left-wing novelist, essayist, journalist and political
commentator. He wrote 'Down and Out in Paris and London'
(1933), 'The Road to Wigan Pier' (1937), 'Homage to Catalonia' (1938), 'Animal Farm' (1945) and 'Nineteen Eighty-
Four' (1949).

Mr. Evelyn Waugh's recent book, 'The Loved One,' was an
attack, and by no means a good-natured attack, on American
civilization, but in 'Scott-King's Modern Europe' he shows
himself willing to handle his native Continent with at
least equal rudeness. America worships corpses but Europe
mass-produces them, is what he seems to be saying. The two
books are indeed in some sense complementary to one another,
though 'Scott-King's Modern Europe' is less obviously brilliant than the other.

The book has a general resemblance to 'Candide,' and is
perhaps even intended to be a modern counterpart of
'Candide,' with the significant difference that the hero is
middle-aged at the start. Nowadays, it is implied, only the
middle-aged have scruples or ideals; the young are born
hard-boiled. Scott-King, age about 43, 'slightly bald and
slightly corpulent,' is senior classics master at Granchester, a respectable but not fashionable public school. A
dusty, unhonored figure, a praiser of the past, a lover of
exact scholarship, he fights a steadily losing battle
against what he regards as the debasement of modern education.

'Dim,' we are told, is the epithet that describes him.

His hobby is the study of a poet even dimmer than himself, a certain Bellorius, who flourished in the seventeenth century in what was then a province of the Habsburg Empire and is now the independent republic of Neutralia.

In an evil hour Scott-King receives an invitation to visit Neutralia, which is celebrating the tercentenary of the death of Bellorius. It is the wet summer of 1946 - a summer of austerity - and Scott-King envisions garlicky meals and flasks of red wine. He succumbs to the invitation, although half aware that it is probably a swindle of some kind.

At this point any experienced reader of Waugh's works would predict unpleasant adventures for Scott-King and he would be right. Neutralia, a compound of Yugoslavia and Greece, is ruled over by a 'Marshal,' and there is the usual police espionage, banditry, ceremonial banquets and speeches about Youth and Progress. The commemoration of Bellorius is in fact an imposture. Its object is to trap the visitors into endorsing the Marshal's regime. They fall for the trap and later learn that this stamps them everywhere as 'Fascist Beasts.' Thereafter Neutralia's hospitality ends abruptly.

Some of the visitors are killed and the others stranded, unable to get out of the country. Airplanes are reserved for VIP's, and to leave Neutralia any other way entails weeks and months of besieging embassies and consulates. After adventures which Mr. Waugh suppresses because they are too painful for a work of light fiction, Scott-King ends up stark naked in a camp for illegal Jewish immigrants in Palestine.

Back at Granchester, amid the notched desks and the draughty corridors, the headmaster informs him sadly that the number of classical scholars is falling off and suggests that he shall combine his teaching of the classics with something a little more up-to-date:

'Parents are not interested in producing the "complete man" any more. They want to qualify their boys for jobs in the modern world. You can hardly blame them, can you?'

'Oh, yes,' said Scott-King, 'I can and do.'

Later he adds: 'I think it would be very wicked indeed to do anything to fit a boy for the modern world.' And when the headmaster objects that this is a short-sighted view, Scott-King retorts, 'I think it the most long-sighted view it is possible to take.'

This last statement, it should be noted, is intended seriously. The book is very short, hardly longer than a short story, and it is written with the utmost lightness, but it has a definite political meaning. The modern world, we are meant to infer, is so unmistakably crazy, so certain to smash itself to pieces in the near future, that to attempt to understand it or come to terms with it is simply a purposeless self-corruption. In the chaos that is shortly coming, a few moral principles that one can cling to, and perhaps even a few half-remembered odes of Horace or choruses from Euripides, will be more useful than what is now called 'enlightenment.'

There is something to be said for this point of view, and and yet one must always regard with suspicion the claim that ignorance is, or can be, an advantage. In the Europe of the last fifty years the diehard, know-nothing attitude symbolized by Scott-King, has helped to bring about the very conditions that Mr. Waugh is satirizing. Revolutions happen in authoritarian countries, not in liberal ones, and Mr. Waugh's failure to see the implications of this fact not only narrows his political vision but also robs his story of part of its point.

His standpoint, or Scott-King's, is that of a Conservative - that is to say, a person who disbelieves in progress and refuses to differentiate between one version of progress and another - and his lack of interest in his opponents induces, unavoidably, a certain perfunctoriness. It was a mistake, for instance, to present Neutralia as a dictatorship of the Right while giving it most of the stigmata of a dictatorship of the Left. 'There is nothing to choose between communism and fascism,' Mr. Waugh seems to be saying; but these two creeds, though they have much in common, are not the same, and can only be made to appear the same by leaving out a good deal. Again, Mr. Waugh's portraits of scheming Neutralian officials would have been more telling if he were not too contemptuous of the kind of state that calls itself a 'people's democracy' to find out in detail how it works.

This is an extremely readable book, but it lacks the touch of affection that political satire ought to have. One can accept Scott-King's estimate of the modern world, and perhaps even agree with him that a classical education is the best prophylactic against insanity, and yet still feel that he could fight the modern world more effectively if he would occasionally turn aside to read a sixpenny pamphlet on Marxism.

115.   JOHN WOODBURN, 'NEW REPUBLIC'

21 March 1949, 23-4

This pony novel by the *enfant terrible* of contemporary
English letters made its first appearance more than a year
ago, under the title 'A Sojourn in Neutralia', in Hearst's
'Cosmopolitan', a publication not notorious for the astrin-
gency of its satire. Now that it has been put between
boards and has resumed its own name, 'Scott-King's Modern
Europe' seems rather less impressive than it did under
gloss. In a setting of prefabricated fiction and puréed
articles, Evelyn Waugh, even noticeably off his stride,
had at least the distinction of egregiousness, like a
celebrity with a hangover at a women's-club luncheon.

   In this new, or perhaps I should say current, story,
Waugh directs his satire at the totalitarian state, an
aspect of modern Europe which Waugh, as an individualist
and a conservative Catholic, views with a special loathing.
Such a subject clearly offers rich opportunities to a satirical gift as great as his, and I admit that my disappointment in these eighty-nine skimped and slapdash pages was in
direct proportion to my expectations.

   Scott-King is a scholarly middle-aged master at a typical English public school, where for twenty years, against
the increasing emphasis upon science and economics, he has
tended the flame of the classics. He suffers from two of
the diseases of our time: world-guilt and world-pain, but
endures them with a kind of hypochondria. He is both
appalled and fascinated by the decadence of the modern
world, and finds a masochistic stimulation in surveying
the spread of barbarism, as he takes a perverse comfort in
the climate of his own obscurity and failure.

   In this frame of mind he discovers a kinship and
exquisite communication in the work of Bellorius, a dim,
forgotten, seventeenth-century poet who had written a long
Utopian poem and had died without recognition in what was
once 'a happy kingdom of the Habsburg Empire' and is now,
in 1946, the dictator-state of Neutralia.... Although Waugh
informs us that the Republic of Neutralia is 'imaginary
and composite and represents no existing state', [his
description] can serve as a handy reference catalogue for
almost any one of the several European countries now in the
Russian sphere of influence.

   It was [on the schoolmaster's arrival there] that I
began to have the impression that Evelyn Waugh was doing a
libretto for Bobby Clark. Perhaps so relaxed and inspired a
comedian could make something out of the fact that Scott-

King's place card at a formal dinner read 'Scotch-Kink',
that Whitemaid got tight and made an incomprehensible
speech, that he was later discovered in a hotel bedroom
with a voluptuous lady athlete clad in a bath towel, and
that Scott-King suffered a prolonged attack of hiccoughs
during that dinner. I did not find it very funny and am
still at a loss as to its relevance.

The rest of the story is a staggering pyramid of frustrations: the delegates are tricked into laying a wreath
before a statue of the current dictator instead of the
tomb of Bellorius; two of them disappear mysteriously,
supposedly at the hands of the rebels in the hills; there
is some witty dialogue in which Waugh flashes into his old
form, and some which is not so witty, depending, as in
'Scotch-Kink', upon mispronunciation and language difficulties. Gradually the skeins of red tape entwine about Scott-
King until he approaches mummification ... [until] he is
smuggled out by the underground....

...One feels that Waugh wrote this as he went along,
without much care, to get it done and over with. On page
eighty-six nearly at the end of the book, he seems to have
wandered without realizing it into an area of tragedy he
had not intended. When Scott-King finds himself on the boat
bearing displaced Jews to the then forbidden Palestine,
Waugh brings himself up abruptly. It struck me that there
was embarrassment and apology in the paragraph which begins:
'This is the story of a summer holiday: a light tale. It
treats, at the worst, with solid discomfort and intellectual doubt. It would be inappropriate to speak here of those
depths of the human spirit, the agony and despair, of the
next few days of Scott-King's life.' It seemed inappropriate in a 'light tale', 'the story of a summer holiday' -
a story keyed pretty generally to the guffaw - to introduce that tragic predicament at all.

It is, I suppose, impertinent, but I cannot help specu-
lating as to what pressures caused Evelyn Waugh to do so
little with this theme, when there was so much awaiting his
hand. If there were pressures, and certainly they are
understandable in Waugh's Modern Europe, then, as a satirist of consistently high performance, it would seem that
he was taking the most shortsighted view it is possible to
take.

'The Loved One'

1948

116. CYRIL CONNOLLY, 'HORIZON'

February 1948, 76-7

This was Connolly's Introduction to the first printing of 'The Loved One' as a single issue of 'Horizon'.

This month (than which we hope 1948 will yield none more depressing) we let our readers in for a treat - a sneak pre-view! Why have they been chosen to receive this smooth, all-star performance? The answer is partly given by Mr. Waugh himself: 'I anticipated ructions,' he writes, 'and one reason for my seeking publication in "Horizon" was the confidence that its readers were tough stuff.' The ructions can be reduced to two. From some of our English readers a protest at the unseemly preoccupation with the cadaver, from some of our American ones an additional indignation at the unflattering portraits of their fellow-countrymen. The age-old defence-plea of 'artistic license' covers both. Mr. Waugh continues: 'The ideas I had in mind were: 1. Quite predominantly, over-excitement with the scene [the cemeteries of Southern California]. 2. The Anglo-American impasse - "never the twain shall meet". 3. There is no such thing as an "American". They are all exiles uprooted, transplanted and doomed to sterility. The ancestral gods they have abjured get them in the end. 4. The European raiders who come for the spoils and if they are lucky make for home with them. 5. *Memento mori*.' Now if we talk of the 'Anglo-Californian impasse' and say there is no such thing as a Southern Californian, there is nothing in Mr. Waugh's phrasing with which many Americans would not agree. Mr. Waugh, in fact, has written a Swiftian satire on the

burial customs of Southern California, and his irony need
not be taken to reflect on America as a whole. But since
Southern California is one of the most American places,
with a society some ten years ahead of the rest of the
country in a materialist sense, its burial customs are
extremely important, for they reveal in all their empty
enormity the American conception of death and the elaborate
effort made by those who most worship comfort, beauty and
life to euphemize that stark object which is of all the
most ill-favoured and unreassuring. In its attitude to
death, and to death's stand-in, failure, Mr. Waugh exposes
a materialist society at its weakest spot, as would Swift
or Donne were they alive today.

I mention Swift and Donne because Evelyn Waugh has affi-
nities with them rather than with the humorists to which
he is so often compared. A 'humorist' is a being in a state
of flux at a moment when the courage to laugh at life has
not yet been undermined by its horrors; in fact, he is
young, and so will either cease to be a humorist or become
the dreariest of hacks, a professional funny man. Mr. Waugh
is not young and he is exposed to the two prevailing gusts
of middle-age; rage and nostalgia. In 'Brideshead' the nostalgia was uncontrolled, in 'Scott-King's Modern Europe'
there was perhaps a little too much anger. In 'The Loved
One' both are invisible, and it is, in my opinion, one of
the most perfect short novels of the last ten years and the
most complete of his creations, a story cast in a kind of
light but immensely strong aluminium alloy, like the one-
piece chassis of a racing car. Lurking at the centre are
the immense motives of love and death, our two most felt
experiences, and receding away from the central theme are
ranged dualisms of humorous contrast, the Megalo Studios
and the British Cricket Club, the pets and the Loved Ones,
the Delphic Oracle and Mr. Slump. It is not a question of
whether Mr. Waugh has or has not returned to his earlier
manner or recaptured his ancient insouciance. This fierce,
luminous, passionate love-story is only incidentally witty.
It is *dans le vrai*. And at a time when most of us lie pro-
strate with winter-gloom, out comes this beautifully constructed, irresistible and haunting affair, this crisp cos
lettuce. Fortunate guinea-pigs, go to!

117.   UNSIGNED REVIEW, 'TIME'

12 July 1948, 40-2, 44

'Of course, parts of "Brideshead" are wicked, really
wicked. But does one have the feeling that Evelyn Waugh
himself is wicked _enough_?'
  In a dingy Manhattan bar, some members of the Waugh
cult were measuring out their lives with swizzle sticks.
They had been badly shaken by 'Brideshead Revisited.'
Unlike Waugh's earlier novels, its irony had not been
outrageously funny, and the typical Waugh mood, bright,
pardlike and impermeable, had been clouded by a sweat of
nostalgic and religious dither. Worse still, 'Brideshead'
was the first of Waugh's novels to become a U.S. best-
seller. His fans had reluctantly winked at the fact that he
is a conservative and a Roman Catholic convert. But popular? No literary cult can tolerate popularity in its prey.
The boys were preparing to dump Evelyn.
  'I know what you mean, Eustace - is Evelyn _depraved_
enough so that, as an artist, he can make the _spiritual_
leap from malice to malignance?'
  'After all, if he is ever to mature as a satirist, he
must stop tickling the public's toes, and start cutting its
throats.'
  'Instead of simply _festering_, as in "Brideshead," like
an old, old staphylococcus, my dear, in a _duodenal_ ulcer.'
  'I am afraid poor Evelyn has begun to take the problem
of evil seriously.'
  'How very tiresome.'
  Last week Novelist Waugh was tickling toes and cutting
throats again. 'The Loved One,' his first novel published
in the U.S. since 'Brideshead,' was in the eager hands of
U.S. readers, most of whom did not know whether to gasp,
hoot or holler at the uncomfortable feeling that they had
been smudged with soot from a crematory. The title was
Waugh's creamy trade name for a corpse. A tale of love and
suicide among the morticians of a cemetery that physically
resembles Hollywood's fabulous Forest Lawn, 'The Loved
One' was either Novelist Waugh's most funereal horse laugh
or a retch of glacial rage at two of America's most
cherished deceits - its effort to prettify death and to
vulgarize love, and hence escape the impact of both.
Intellectuals were bitterly divided over Waugh's intention.
But the book, which was richly laced with the fun of
embalming fluid, might well become a bestseller.
  Last year Metro-Goldwyn Mayer offered Waugh $150,000 for
the film rights to 'Brideshead.' It was a situation worthy

of a Waugh novel. It is explained, according to Waugh, by
the fact that none of the top studio brass had ever read
the book. When Waugh demanded 'full Molotov veto rights'
over the script, the deal fell through.

Waugh's Hollywood trip was not wasted. He was fascinated by the ritual for disguising death which is big business in Southern California. Waugh spent every day that he
could get away prying into the fatuous, sumptuous necro-
polis of Forest Lawn. The result was 'The Loved One.'

It was first published in 'Horizon'. Editor Cyril Connolly devoted the entire February issue of the highbrow
British literary monthly to Waugh's short novel. This
smart devotion paid off. 'Horizon' for February was sold
out in a week.

'The Loved One' is by no means the subtle and cold-
blooded rage at the perversion of death and love which
some subtle and raging people suppose it to be. It is
Evelyn Waugh caught between laughter and vomiting. The
story of the patriotic pretensions and fussy snobbishness
of the British film colony is grade A Waugh. Less artful is
the travelogue of the intricate inanities of Whispering
Glades, from the voice of a nightingale piped through the
grounds and mortuary buildings to the Lake Isle of Innis-
free, complete with nine rows of beans and beeless bee-
hives with electric buzzers (burial plots $1,000). Most
amusing is the love of Mr. Joyboy, the senior mortician,
and Miss Aimée Thanatogenos, his assistant, uttered in an
American idiom which Author Waugh has not entirely mas-
tered. Their passion, unrolling between the refrigerators
and the crematory, is alternately hot & cold. They play
games of hearts & flowers with the corpses. When the lovers
tiffed, the corpses looked 'woebegone and reproachful.'
When love ran smoothly, they 'grinned with triumph.'

The failure of this funerary passion, the intrusion of
an Englishman named Dennis, who works in a neighbouring
cat & dog cemetery, the Happier Hunting Ground, and Miss
Thanatogenos' love-death, are the burden of 'The Loved
One.'...

118.   'PETERBOROUGH', 'DAILY TELEGRAPH'

14 July 1948, 4

Publication of Evelyn Waugh's newest book, 'The Loved One,'
is being treated as an event in America. It is not yet on
sale here.

The news magazine 'Time' in its current issue gives six
columns to the book and Waugh's career. The fact that his
latest satire is set in America may have something to do
with it.

During a visit to Hollywood a year ago - of which some
impressions appeared on this page - Evelyn Waugh was
fascinated by the fabulous cemetery, Forest Lawn. 'The
Loved One' (euphemism for corpse) is his version of the way
in which death is made beautiful and very expensive on the
West Coast.

Waugh's admirers who feared after reading his last major
effort, 'Brideshead Revisited', that he had lost his power
to be shocking may, from all accounts, take fresh heart.

119.   JOHN WOODBURN, 'NEW REPUBLIC'

26 July 1948, 24

This cold-blooded little novel made its first appearance
five months ago in ... 'Horizon,' and almost immediately
aroused clashing comment. Waugh himself has anticipated
this reaction in a nervous prefatory note to the American
edition, called A Warning, in which he says, in part: 'This
is a purely fanciful tale, a little nightmare produced by
the unaccustomed high living of a brief visit to Hollywood.... This is a nightmare and in parts, perhaps, somewhat gruesome. The squeamish should return their copies to
the library or the bookstore unread.'

I do not know of anyone who has returned his copy of the
February issue of 'Horizon' to the newsstand, read or
unread, but it may well have happened, for 'The Loved One'
is very strong medicine.

I do know several people of rugged intellectual con-
stitution who considered 'The Loved One' affronting and
outrageous, and seemed genuinely shocked and sickened by
its preoccupation with cosmeticized cadavers, with the
obscene mechanics involved in the temporary preservation of
the lifeless human body, and the hypocrisy and relentless
commercialization of the rituals of American burial, California style. All of them have the common knowledge of
Hollywood and California and the undertaking business, and
none of them, it seemed to me, got Waugh's point.

At the risk of being called morbid or necrophiliac, I
wish to say that, while I understand their horror and distaste, I do not agree that 'The Loved One' is outrageous,

unforgivable, or in any way a flower of evil. I think it is
a good book, a very good book, and further proof of Evelyn
Waugh's unerring marksmanship, this time with a dum-dum
bullet. I had long ago been shocked and revolted by the
cause of Evelyn Waugh's brilliant, ruthless reaction, and
was not, like these friends of mine, affronted by its
effect, a revulsion superbly articulated in satire. I have
lived in California, and while there once attended a small,
informal party at which, out of ten people, I was the only
one who was not an undertaker or an undertaker's wife.
After the third highball they talked shop. I mention this
only to explain why 'The Loved One' did not make a wholly
fresh impact upon me, and why its satire did not strike me
as being at all times removed from reality.

...Evelyn Waugh has handled his repulsive, fractious
material with unfaltering suavity, using dualisms in
humorous contrast: the Megalo Studios and the Cricket Club;
the pets and the Loved Ones; and the exquisitely repellent
atmosphere of the Happier Hunting Grounds and Whispering
Glades.

As a piece of writing it is nearly faultless; as satire
it is an act of devastation, an angry, important, moral
effort that does not fail. 'The Loved One' is not outrageous but outraged; sickened but not sickening; its
macabre humor is the shocked, protective laughter of the
civilized man confronted with the unassimilable horror
that permits no other means of rejection.

120.   UNSIGNED REVIEW, 'TIMES LITERARY SUPPLEMENT'

20 November 1948, 652

In this age of materialism, dominated by the principles of
Marx, Freud or Henry Ford, dissident writers have taken
refuge either in a well-bred irony derived from James or
more recently in religion. The growing strength of the new
school of Roman Catholic writers, of whom Mr. Evelyn Waugh
must be claimed as one, suggests that the humanism of Mr.
Forster and his followers has proved an inadequate weapon
against the attacks of the Philistines, armed as they now
are with both philosophy and science. The time has come
again for the transcendental answer. Yet faith is apt nowadays to be private and esoteric. The suspicion is always
with us that writers have taken to religion not because
they have discovered truth but because they dislike the

world as they find it. If 'Brideshead Revisited', Mr.
Waugh's only explicitly Catholic novel, or his hero-
worshipping life of Edmund Campion were the only basis for
a judgment, we might extend this suspicion to him. These
works reveal a nostalgia in the one case, a romanticism in
the other, which promote a certain scepticism. But Mr.
Waugh is the author of a series of satires so impregnated
with religious rage that we are compelled to a belief in
his religious attitude. It is a negative approach with a
positive result. Mr. Waugh upbraids the materialists with
creative passion.

This is a period which cries out for the robust ridicule
of a Swift. Yet it is one singularly poor in satirists.
Mr. Aldous Huxley, who once looked like being the scourge
of his contemporaries, has declined into a false *nirvana*
inspired by a too personal disgust. His fastidiousness has
been the death of him. Mr. Waugh alone seems to possess the
wit, gusto and detached fury which are the marks of the
true satirist. Yet he has been more usually regarded as a
melancholy clown, witty, despairing and damned, or as the
accomplished cad of contemporary fiction. That there is
something of the cad in Mr. Waugh he would be the last to
deny. Basil Seal is obviously a favourite and congenial
character. But his caddishness is that of Jeremiah, Swift
or anyone else ill-bred enough to describe an unpleasant
character in unpleasant terms. He does sometimes glorify
his rakes - he did this to an altogether unseemly extent in
'Put Out More Flags', where the bright young people were
whitewashed out of existence - but it is always at the
expense of the truly vile bodies who respond to life in a
purely automatic way. The adventurous sinner at least has
vitality. He may yet be plucked from the burning. It is the
codgers, young or old, pursuing the same dreary round of
business or pleasure, who are irretrievably damned. This is
a perfectly orthodox religious position and one which might
have reassured those who found Mr. Waugh's Roman Catholicism inconsistent with his ribaldry....

...The suspicion that he was softening in middle age,
that he was giving way to nostalgia and regret, was para-
doxically furthered by the appearance of 'Scott-King's
Modern Europe', a neat if rather arid little comment on
modern civilization which was marred by an excess of
irritability. Once the personal grievance obtrudes the
satirist is lost. There was more than a suggestion of the
disgruntled clubman about this sally. Such doubts and misgivings, however, are stilled by the appearance of 'The
Loved One', Mr. Waugh's latest, most mature and most awe-
inspiring satire. Here we have, in a short piece of corus-
cating brilliance, the most devastating and explicit attack

which he has so far launched on the enemies of the spirit.
...Mr. Waugh has gone to the country where man has
achieved his greatest material triumphs in order to expose
the hollowness of the pretensions of modern civilization as
a whole. In choosing the extravagant funeral rites of the
Californian tribe as the target of his wit, he has wished
to expose the prevailing attitude to death as a fatal weakness in the contemporary conduct of life. All that we have
achieved so far, he suggests, is a precarious bodily comfort. Our denial of the spirit, with its accompaniments of
distaste for failure and horror of the idea of death,
punishes us here and now, whatever our view of the here-
after. In its extremist form the materialism of modern
society has already succeeded in destroying imagination,
the finite expression of the spiritual aspect of man. As a
result, we have robots instead of people, vile bodies
indistinguishable from the corpses we so elaborately
embalm. What is shocking in this gruesome little tale is
not the preoccupation with corpses but the fact that the
live characters are virtually indistinguishable from the
dead.

Mr. Waugh proceeds by means of a series of contrasting
scenes, each an aspect of an over-riding failure. From the
melancholy compound with its cricket club and old school
ties where the Englishmen whose Hollywood contracts have
not been renewed cosset their fading prestige with evening
whiskies we pass to the lunatic bustle of the Megalopolitan
studios where inanity receives the highest rewards that
wealth can offer. In both *milieux* it is the Hollywood standard which counts. Failure is disreputable. When it can no
longer be avoided it must be euphemized. Established by
choice among the casualties, the young Englishman, Dennis
Barlow (a more creative Basil Seal), has decided to abandon
the career of script-writer for that of pets' mortician....
It is the suicide of a friend, one of the Hollywood failures, which leads him to that far more gorgeous establishment, Whispering Glades, where human bodies are subjected
to the most exquisite and recondite processes of the morticians' art. In this fantastic temple the euphemization of
death, the worst kind of social failure, reaches its
highest pitch. Whispering Glades is the ultimate expression
of mankind's superstition and fear....

But alas for Dennis, for love, for Anglo-American relations, there exists in this monument to artifice a beautiful maiden, a decadent from Greece who does not conform to
the type of American womanhood. Aimée, the cosmetician of
the Orchid Room, who is virtually engaged to Mr. Joyboy, is
destined to be the sacrifice which materialism requires
from time to time from its devotees. Dennis, charmed by her

apparent deviation from the norm, makes the mistake of
yielding to a human impulse in a mechanical world. Now
Mr. Waugh introduces the theme of love as well as death.
Both these major experiences are to be shown as equally
debased by our present method of living.

Aimée, bewildered by a new and rather distasteful
experience - she has after all been conditioned in America
- consults the Guru Brahmin, the Oracle of the place, who
is in real life a certain Mr. Slump of the local newspaper.
Ought she to marry Mr. Joyboy, whom she respects and
admires, or Mr. Barlow, who inspires in her unethical
feelings? Mr. Slump, the reader knows, is a drunken journalist. But to Aimée he is the mysterious voice of dimly
remembered gods. The oracle's American instinct is of
course in favour of Mr. Joyboy, the personification of
respectability and success. But it is not until Aimée discovers at one stroke that Dennis is menially employed at
the Happier Hunting Grounds and that all the love poems he
has been sending her come out of the 'Oxford Book of English Verse' that she finally betrays what we may tenta-
tively call her heart. Dennis, she realizes, is un-Ameri-
can, immoral, dangerous, alive. Mr. Joyboy must be her fate.
Even then Mr. Slump has to be invoked for a last judgment.
The oracle, more drunk than usual, off-handedly advises her
to take the High Jump.

Thus it is that Aimée's corpse is found in Mr. Joyboy's
workroom. Thus it is that Dennis finds himself on his last
night in Hollywood pounding up the pelvis of his beloved
and raking out her ashes in the pets' crematorium. He is
at once relieving Mr. Joyboy of an embarrassment and
divesting himself of his superfluous heart. He is to return
with the spoils of experience to England, where, like the
Ancient Mariner, he will unfold a traveller's tale.

Here in this hint of Coleridge we have the clue to Mr.
Waugh's vocation. He is to warn, to startle and affright
the Wedding Guests. It is as an Old Testament prophet
exposing our festering sores, as a flayer of society that
he excels. 'The Loved One' perhaps indicates that he has
finally accepted his métier. At any rate, he has given us
a satire, witty and macabre, ominous and polished, which
strikes straight at the heart of the contemporary problem.

121.   DESMOND MacCARTHY, 'SUNDAY TIMES'

21 November 1948, 3

'The Loved One', published only a few days ago, is already
widely known. The number of 'Horizon' in which it appeared,
complete, some months ago, was soon sold out, and copies of
it passed rapidly from hand to hand. 'What did you think of
it?' 'Wasn't it devastating?' 'Wasn't it horribly amusing?'
'Did you enjoy it?' 'What didn't you like about it?' Such
were the questions which those lucky enough to get hold of
copies of that issue of 'Horizon' kept asking each other....
    Do not suppose because 'The Loved One' is ... described
[in the publisher's blurb] as 'a nightmare' that there is
anything dream-like or terrifying about the details and
events presented. On the contrary, they are described and
narrated with cold matter-of-factness. And there lies the
power of the book; its effectiveness in exposing fatuous
insensibility and commercialised sympathy for the bereaved.
The book is a ruthless exposure of a silly optimistic trend
in modern civilisation which takes for granted that the
consolations of religion can be enjoyed without belief in
them, its symbols and associations remain beautiful when
they have ceased to mean anything; and seeks to persuade us
that there is nothing really tragic in the predicament of
man.
    If you dislike and despise such a point of view; if it
seems to rob life of real beauty without dignifying death;
if it strikes you as the last insult to poor humanity to
try to rob it of its crown of thorns; then this book will
give you also, as it gave me, keen satisfaction. You will
then perceive also that the cynical harshness of the poet,
which is the counterfoil to the mechanical tenderness of
the ludicrous master-mortician, was an essential element in
producing the ultimate effect. A reader who has not grasped
that might complain that hate-directed satire is too unkind. If such a thought does cross his mind, let him recall
the thick-skinned humbugging smugness against which it is
in this case directed.
    Mr. Evelyn Waugh is an original writer; possibly others
may be able to find a pedigree for his work - I cannot. I
cannot point confidently to a predecessor from whom he
derived his own peculiar mixture of fantasticality and
realism. He is also a remarkably good writer; and like his
older contemporary, Somerset Maugham, he has gone on
patiently learning how to write even better, till he has
acquired a masterly precision both in description and in
brief dialogue. When 'Scott-King's Modern Europe' came out

last year, having read it with relish straight through, I
found myself starting again, and re-read it with equal, if
not more, pleasure and satisfaction. There lies the difference between well-written fiction and powerful, interesting fiction which is not well-written: you cannot re-
read the latter until you have more or less forgotten it.
I take for granted that what is well written is more likely
to live, because its merits are instantly noticeable and
may prove even greater than at first sight.

He has an eye which pounces on whatever is widely significant in what is extravagantly unique. In that sense he is
a caricaturist, but at his best he does not strike you as
being one. When he began - I am thinking particularly of
that admirable extravaganza 'Decline and Fall' - there was
something Puckish in his satire.... Recently, though there
may be still passages in his work feather-light, his satire
has taken on a definitely misanthropic tinge more reminiscent of Swift, though his contempt is not based on loathing for the animal in man, but for human humbug - most
recently, for the pretentious silly arrogance of people who
think they will get along best by ignoring the experience
of those who lived before them. Beneath satire of any
depth there always lies, in addition to a sense of humour
and an eye for glaring incongruities, a tragic conception
of life. It is that which makes 'The Loved One' not only a
macabre farce but a significant criticism of life.

I regret the illustrations: this is not a work that
requires illustration, and the spirit informing these
pattern-pictures is so much feebler and less vivid than
that which animates the text that I would rather they did
not accompany it. Mr. Stuart Boyle was set a hopeless task.

122. R.D. SMITH, 'NEW STATESMAN'

11 December 1948, 528-9

Mrs R.D. Smith (pseudonym: Olivia Manning, d. 1980), was a
novelist, short story writer and journalist; she was author
of 'The Wind Changes' (1938), The Balkan Trilogy ('The
Great Fortune' (1960), 'The Spoilt City' (1962), 'Friends
and Heroes' (1965)) and 'The Battle Lost and Won' (1978).

English poets were proving uncertain guides in the
labyrinth of Californian courtship ... nearly all were

too casual, too despondent, too ceremonious, or too
exacting.

I would say just that of Mr. Waugh on his conducted tour
of Californian cemeteries, if I didn't feel that 'exacting'
is what he isn't. He exacts nothing from the uncritical
reader out for a laugh; he exacts nothing from devotees
who interpret misanthropy as idealism, or dislike of modern
civilisation as moral indignation; and, most serious of all,
he exacts too little from himself, an established writer of
high talent.

'The Loved One' in certain scenes recalls the comic
genius of 'Decline and Fall' and 'Vile Bodies'. 'My memory's
very bad for live faces'; 'Dog that is born of bitch hath
but a short time to live'; 'Your little Arthur is thinking
of you in Heaven to-day, and wagging his tail'; lines like
these are funny, even outside their contexts. His prodi-
gious gift for evoking macabre yet fascinating horror by
apparently simple means has never been more strikingly displayed.... The plot is ingeniously and vividly worked out,
but the work as a whole is uneven, in planning, execution
and feeling. Hollywood, funeral hypocrisy, and the ad-man's
domain of nutbergers, Jungle Venom perfume, and peaches
without stones are themes that have been well worked over
before, more effectively indeed, by Mr. Aldous Huxley, Mr.
Sinclair Lewis, and by various hands in the 'New Yorker',
notably Mr. S.J. Perelman. Here, the satire on the English
Cricket Club at Hollywood is disproportionately long and
mechanical. Though Sir Francis, the Georgian poet laid off
by Megalopolitan, who hangs himself by his braces, speaks
individually, his knightly colleague Sir Ambrose wears his
Eton Rambler tie and I Zingari ribbon in no more personal
way than the Western Brothers. Mr. Waugh at his best would
have recreated this hackneyed type; here it lies on the
page lifeless as a Man of Distinction advertisement.

The reporting of the animal cemetery, the Happier Hunting Grounds, and of the human, Whispering Glades, is exact,
and terrible; but when invented characters move into the
documentary scene, they dispel the horror, and force on us
the question of taste. Mr. Joyboy, the master mortician,
might possibly make us accept without uneasiness his tale
of love amid the formaldehyde and the farded corpses,
because he is a creature existing outside life, in the
sphere of fantasy or farce. Even so, we are not convinced.
... And Aimée Thanatogenos, we cannot take for a minute.
The author uses her to engage our pity; we are intended to
believe in her as a human being; on her he lavishes 'fine
writing' to stir our feelings. And through this insistence
we are driven to notice, despite the intended defensive

irony of the following passage, a vulgarity apparent in
the sentence rhythms, and the way the words are used to
touch off an expected response.

Aimée, while working away at her employment as make-up
girl to a Loved One:

> re-read the poem she had received from Dennis:
>   Her little hands are soft and when
>   I see her fingers move,
>   I know in very truth that men
>   Have died for less than love.
> A single tear ran down Aimée's cheek and fell on the
> smiling waxy mask below her. She put the manuscript into
> the pocket of her linen smock and her little soft hands
> began to move over the dead face.

This is a cheapened form of 'Sweeney' cross-cutting from
the nightingales' singing to the dishonoured shroud: (1)
moreover it is only a particular instance of a general tendency to milk every situation, to overwork the dying
fall.... The appeal to our feelings is at the level of some
of the copy-writers Mr. Waugh elsewhere satirises. Even
more damning than these lapses is the character of the hero,
Dennis, the poet, pet-incinerator, quack clergyman, and
general intellectual spiv, who is presented as the moral
fixed-point from which the surrounding slough of vulgarity
is surveyed, and condemned. Unfortunately, Dennis is un-
stable, immoral, dishonest and, in the literary sense,
phoney. Even his woman he chooses because she

> was unique, not indefinably: the appropriate distin-
> guishing epithet leapt to Dennis's mind: sole Eve in a
> bustling, hygienic Eden, this girl was decadent ... she
> was what Dennis had vainly sought during a lonely year
> of exile.

His phoneyness is even more clearly shown by his attitude to art. He reads popular anthologies as 'a drug,
specific big magic' and this, we are supposed to believe,
because 'artists are by nature versatile and precise.' On
seeing his hanging friend's distorted face he feels 'pleasantly exhilarated and full of curiosity' *because* this is
'the kind of thing to be expected in the world he knew'
(which has given him six literary prizes and a cushy job as
Air Priority Officer).

The terrible vulgarity which Mr. Waugh, by implication,
is attacking is 'necessary to him', alerting his literary
sense 'like a hunting hound'.

It was not thus that one day he would write what had
to be written, not here that the spirit would be
appeased, which now more faintly pressed its mysterious
claim. Rhythms from the anthologies moved softly through
his mind.

What was moving with soft pace through Mr. Waugh's mind was
not, in this case, the anthologies, but The Master, (2) and
the current 'correct' view of how great artists live and
work.

We are told that Dennis is 'a young man of sensibility
not of sentiment,' a statement contradicted by his every
thought and action. We feel a similar contradiction between
what Mr. Waugh intends us to understand are his values, and
what the feel and texture of his writing reveal. Satire
requires less erratic values than Mr. Waugh's style and
characters suggest; like Swift in 'A Modest Proposal', the
writer must hate life steadily and hate it whole.

Notes

1 A reference to the character Sweeney in T.S. Eliot's
   poetry (e.g. 'Sweeney Among the Nightingales'), the
   epitome of the poet's vision of coarsened, slightly
   decadent bourgeois malaise.
2 Henry James?

123. JOHN BAYLEY, 'NATIONAL REVIEW'

February 1949, 232-5

John Bayley (b. 1925), Warton Professor of English Literature and Fellow of St Catherine's College, Oxford, is a
novelist and critic, and the husband of Iris Murdoch. He
is author of 'In Another Country' (1954), 'The Romantic
Survival' (1956), and 'An Essay on Hardy' (1978).

'The Loved One' and 'The Heart of the Matter' have made a
great impression recently. The two books have much in common. Both Evelyn Waugh and Graham Greene are writers who
use their Catholicism as a weapon and a probe; they explore
vice and anarchy from a definite standpoint. In 'The Heart
of the Matter' a single person, the West African police

official Scobie, is drowned in a morass of individual feuds: in 'The Loved One' a whole society is indicted, the California whose standard of living has culminated in a refusal to admit the horror of death. Neither book is impassive and self-explanatory; both claim a knowledge of something better, whether it is simply the belief that human beings are capable of living together in happiness and understanding, or the conviction that the Catholic and European tradition about death is right and that the Californian conspiracy about it is wrong.

In 'The Heart of the Matter' there is a Portuguese sea-captain, a fat, ignoble creature, who becomes beautiful at the moment when he discovers that the police-official, a fellow-Catholic, has not reported him for spying. His sudden nobility is moving and coherent, it does not jar in the least, but it is not a literary necessity; it is the work of a partisan, and of an author who is obsessed with the need for human virtue and determined to find it in the Catholic attitude. Similarly, in 'The Loved One', the way of life of the girl mortician's Greek forebears is described with nostalgia and made to appear rich and dignified. The point is the same; the author's insistence that something very much better exists somewhere. The stories are of Hell, but they contain a belief in Heaven.

'The Loved One' is slight, but the light-weight masterpiece is a feature of the present day. We have a cult of the unemphatic, the real stuff rolled up in a thriller or a satire, which is a relief after those massive explanatory works of the 'twenties and 'thirties - Mann's 'Zauberberg', for example. The deeper change, however, is between books like Waugh's and Greene's and the attitude of most other fiction since Henry James. The day of the novelist who explored life from the standpoint of a fixed idea seems to have come again. For a novelist to-day it is almost an unfair advantage to be a Catholic or Existentialist or Communist, just as it was an advantage to Richardson to be a fanatical believer in social morality and for Sir Philip Sidney to be a Puritan. 'Pamela' and 'The Arcadia' are buttressed and supported by the beliefs of their authors: inside those beliefs the fancy had freeplay. Since then the novel has discovered the dangers of freedom, of groping in the limbo of self-consciousness. For Richardson and Sidney the purpose was, not to set out hopefully, but to arrive at the goal as well and as beneficially as possible. As beneficially, for they were out to edify as Greene and Waugh are out to edify. 'The Heart of the Matter' is mediaeval because there is nothing meaningless in it; every detail, however sordid, has its place in the act of creation, in the pattern that keeps

the stars from wrong. It is a drastic solution of the
dilemma into which the thoughtful novel was falling, the
dilemma of one thing being neither more nor less relevant
than another.

For the logical consequence of Henry James's attempt
at impartial complication is the work of Faulkner and
Hemingway, just as - (at least in the eyes of Graham
Greene and his fellow-Catholics) - the logical consequence
of Luther was the chaos of the Anabaptist movement. Communism, promiscuity, whisky, hunting, fire-arms, Mantegna,
bravery, rotting corpses - Hemingway offers them all to us
with the same remorseless and bewildering enthusiasm. At
first this confused feeding seems lifelike and stimulating,
but very soon we give up in despair. Boundless despair,
handled with a kind of gusto, is the atmosphere of the
American novel. Its first richness and promise were like
that of the Elizabethan theatre; a consciousness of libera-
tion and of infinite possibility. Both were godless; at
once optimistic and disillusioned, on the verge of anarchy
and finally engulfed by it. Shakespeare, the justification
of the English Renaissance, is a mediaeval scrap-heap acres
high and wide, and glittering with dismembered relics. But
richness is not all. Though there is a lot to look at for
the tourist in Main Street, there are no values, there is
no alternative to Babbitt. 'Why, this is Hell, nor are we
out of it.'

The French Existentialist writers have canalised this
anarchy into a creed strictly comparable to that of Waugh
and Greene. In either case the policy is deliberate and
brings in a quick dividend - the relief and respect of
the reader who finds that the book has a message. French
Catholic and Existentialist novels alike are oracular,
they have the weight of a pronouncement. Fiction approaches
theosophy. The English novelists who continued in the
inter-war years to note with quiet ability what went on
seem rather lost when compared with the portentous Sartre
or Mauriac. (1) The skill of a writer like Patrick Hamilton
(2) was certainly as great; his London is pitilessly
accurate but quite unpretentious, so unpretentious that it
is forgotten at the moment, while the Catholics and Exis-
tentialists are on the flood-tide of popularity.

Perhaps this is why Waugh and Greene write about
California and West Africa in their latest moral fantasies.
The landscape is unfamiliar, and the author can pick out
what he wishes to give the reader and what he thinks will
produce the desired impression. But the reader has an
instinct for probability even when he knows nothing of the
writer's subject, and it is here that the didactic novel
falls down. We cannot really believe either in Greene's

West Africa or in Waugh's California; they do not become
part of us as the Russia of Chekhov and Tolstoy is part of
us, because we are under constant supervision by a party
guide. In 19th century Russia we are not. There we find
ourselves at one moment talking to a tramp on the banks
of the Neva, then in a workman's home where the tempera-
ture never rises above freezing; and just as we are thinking that something ought to be done and that the rich
behave abominably, we stroll into the prince's ball-room
and at once forget our indignation in the pure pleasure of
being among these happy innocent people and watching a girl
at her first dance.

In West Africa and California it is very different.
Nothing is concealed from us by our bitter and intelligent
companion - (in Russia we had none; only letters of introduction) - but we feel that our contacts were interviewed
beforehand and told what they should say. We never see anyone enjoying themselves, because the point of our trip is
to remind us that no facilities for happiness existed
there, and we remain at the end rebelliously convinced that
even a film-operative, mortuary-attendant or colonial
policeman is a happier and more dignified being in his work
and amusement than our guide would wish us to think.

For the characters in these two books are frankly manipulated, and on the whole it is the great writers who con-
trive the least manipulation. Karénin (3) is finished after
his wife has left him; he might be expected to drop nearly
out of sight, but in fact he continues almost tiresomely to
engage our attention. His dabbling in spiritualism is a
kind of embarrassment to the author and a drag on the book;
he is a true victim. In 'Le Journal d'un Curé de Campagne',
(4) on the other hand, the priest is given a horrifying
disease to die of, and so is detached artificially from his
tragedy. The three suicides in 'The Loved One' and 'The
Heart of the Matter' are all equally arbitrary. As a
martyr Karénin is by far the most independent and profound.

The conclusion seems to be that the novel with a purpose may be less revealing, less truth-telling than the
plain tale. We have a tradition of non-party fiction; it
would be a pity if the Catholics and Communists were to
have it all their own way in this country as in literary
Europe. Let us hope that Evelyn Waugh and Graham Greene
will not be taken too seriously and will not attract too
many disciples.

Notes

1   François Mauriac; see No. 97, n. 1.

2   Patrick Hamilton (1904-62), actor turned playwright and
    novelist, was author of 'Rope' (1929) and 'Gas Light'
    (1938).
3   In Tolstoy's 'Anna Karenina'.
4   Waugh reviewed Georges Bernanos's 'Diary of a Country
    Priest' very favourably in 'Night and Day', 28 October
    1937, 24; it was first published in Paris in 1936.

124.   JOHN FARRELLY, 'SCRUTINY'

XXIII, Winter 1951-2, 233

This is part of a review of Edmund Wilson's 'Classics and
Commercials' (W.H. Allen, 1951) which contains two sections
on Waugh: 'Never Apologise, Never Explain': The Art of Evelyn
Waugh (pp. 140-6) and Splendours and Miseries of Evelyn
Waugh (pp. 298-305). It represents the only time 'Scrutiny'
discussed Waugh's work in any detail. The magazine, edited
by F.R. Leavis whose 'Cambridge school' of 'practical
criticism' Waugh persistenly attacked in his own reviews,
never reviewed a Waugh novel. It is significant, surely,
that this brief allusion to 'The Loved One' creeps in only
in the context of a discussion of one of Waugh's literary
antagonists.

...Mr. Wilson is occasionally handicapped by what can be
most suggestively termed his cranks. His anglophobia is an
instance. Another is implied in his naïve and invidious
reference to 'the obedient Catholic [who] swallows the
priest's doctrine'. But these cranks can be more serious,
and then 'handicapped' is scarcely the description of Mr.
Wilson's limitations: *disqualified*, rather. In a note,
printed in this volume, on Mr. Evelyn Waugh's 'The Loved
One', Mr. Wilson has this to say on the author's satire of
'those de luxe California cemeteries that attempt to render
death less unpleasant by exploiting all the resources of
landscape-gardening and Hollywood mummery. To the non-
religious reader ... the patrons and proprietors of Whispering Glades [the cemetery in the book] seem more sensible
and less absurd than the priest-guided Evelyn Waugh. What
the former are trying to do is, after all, merely to gloss
over physical death with smooth lawns and soothing rites;
but, for the Catholic, the fact of death is not to be faced
at all: he is solaced with the fantasy of another world in

which everyone who has died in the flesh is somehow supposed to be still alive and in which it is supposed to be
possible to help souls advance themselves by buying candles
to burn in churches. The trappings invented for this other
world by imaginative believers in the Christian myth ...
beat anything concocted by Whispering Glades'. It is true
that Mr. Waugh is a convert to the Roman Catholic Church,
but he doesn't find it necessary in his book to invoke
dogma or to appeal to any specific religious belief to condemn a morbid preoccupation with physical dissolution in
death. It is Mr. Waugh's point that this vulgarization of
death by grotesque mortuary art and the magic of cosmetics
parallels a shrivelled and vulgar attitude to *life*. If Mr.
Wilson finds the attitude to life implicit in Whispering
Glades more congenial than that explicit in the traditional
'Christian myth', that should prove 'disturbing', as I said
above.... Rather, 'depressing' would be the more sympathetic term.

'Work Suspended and Other Stories Written Before the Second World War'

1949 (no US edition)

125. UNSIGNED REVIEW, 'DAILY TELEGRAPH'

25 March 1949, 3

Evelyn Waugh's unfinished novel, 'Work Suspended' originally written in 1941 and published in 1943 (1) is reissued
with eight short stories which were written before the war.
Included are that macabre trifle, Mr. Loveday's Little
Outing, an amusing satire in Excursion in Reality, showing
that the ways of film magnates have changed little in 15
years, and Winner Takes All, which exhibits so amusingly
the importance of being born the elder son. Mr. Waugh may
have revised 'Work Suspended', but even now the war is
over he is disinclined to finish it. It is a good tale as
it stands, leaving the reader, as before, with the birth of
Lucy's baby in 1939. The date is significant - the end of
an epoch. The threads are broken. We shall never know what
happened to John and Lucy and the others.

Note

1 Incorrect; written in 1939 and published in 1942.

126. EDWARD CRANKSHAW, 'OBSERVER'

27 March 1949, 3

Edward Crankshaw (b. 1909), critic, translator and writer

of several books on Russia, is the author of 'Joseph Conrad'
(1936), 'Russia and Britain' (1944), 'Gestapo, Instrument
of Tyranny' (1956) and 'Tolstoy: The Making of a Novelist'
(1974).

The title-piece is a long story printed in a limited edition
in 1942. There are seven other short stories written in the
thirties, all but one of which have appeared elsewhere; and
between them these offer a fairly complete cross-section of
a formidable talent. It gives us abounding satire of all
kinds: the high-spirited absurdity of Cruise; the vindictive venom of Winner Takes All; the pitiless macabre of
Mr. Loveday's Little Outing; the reckless, possessed hilarity of Excursion into [sic] Reality.

But in two of the shorter stories and in Work Suspended
itself, restless and merciless lampooning gives way to
something quieter. The most obvious and immediate charm of
Mr. Waugh in a subdued frame of mind is the beauty of his
writing. It is always present but as a rule the antics of
his puppets interpose their violence between the reader
and the chaste propriety of the most disciplined of contemporary stylists.

In these three stories the mind can attend to words. It
can also wonder what Mr. Waugh is really up to. For here,
with the stillness, is the chance for Mr. Waugh's better
self to operate. He amuses constantly, because you cannot
keep a good wit down; but he suggests as well the aspect of
a man beginning to doubt whether fire and fury are enough.
Bella Fleace Gives a Party, for example, is remarkable for
an attempt to let things seen speak for themselves, presumably in the faint hope that there may be something to be
said for what they say.

'Work Suspended' carries this attitude of hopeful inquiry one stage further. Very much an affair of symbols,
the narrative hanging between the death of an old world
rejected with sentimental contempt and a new world viewed
with displeasure, it seems also to indicate a conscious
attempt to give birth to a new Waugh who shall know pity
and compassion. Let us see what really *is*, he seems to say;
let us not lash and deride. Because if only we listen
attentively we may catch a deeper chord of meaning.

We listen in vain, as, later, we listened in 'Brideshead Revisited' when Mr. Waugh positively banged the
strings about to make them sound some sort of a tune. But
the record of this strange experience is beautifully done.

'Helena'

1950

127. JOHN RAYMOND, 'NEW STATESMAN'

21 October 1950, 374

John Raymond (b. 1923) is a journalist, critic and historian; he is author of 'The Baldwin Age' (1960), 'The Doge of
Dover and Other Essays' (1960) and 'Simeon in Court' (1968).

Though he has long been recognised as our best contemporary
satirist, Mr. Waugh is at heart a romantic. For him the
Catholic Church, on the secular plane at least, is not
merely Professor Toynbee's (1) bulwark, the spiritual successor to the legions in the task of warding off the Eastern assault: it is also the whole leaven in the lump of
Christian history - St. Mark's galleys, Roland's horn at
Roncevalles, the lances of Acre and the smoke of Lepanto.
It is therefore not surprising that when he takes time off
from savaging the lesser breeds or depicting the tribal
mores of California, Waugh should prefer to leave the heart
of the matter to others and concentrate on the trimmings
instead.

His new novel is a quasi-historical *sortie* in the style
of Maugham's 'Catalina' (though a good deal wittier) on
the subject of Helena, saint and dowager, whose discovery
of the true cross became one of the great medieval legends
of the Christian Church. The author eschews history in favour of the tradition ('invented', wrote Gibbon, 'in the
darkness of monasteries'), that Constantine's mother was an
Essex princess. This gives him the opportunity to surrender
to one of his favourite vices in the way of characterisation - the clear-eyed, clean-limbed, daughter of Diana,
with a niche in Debrett and an ultimate refuge in the Great

Good Place. Waugh's heroines, even when, as in the case of Brenda in 'A Handful of Dust', they have betrayed the County, remain like Miss Mitford's 'Hons', (2) sheathed in a strange primary virtue engendered by prayers in the gas-lit nursery and long, golden afternoons spent in the pad-dock. While Graham Greene's characters make the frontal approach to Catholicism - undergoing the betrayal on the pier or the Pascalian agony in the shrubbery - Waugh's con-verts generally get to Heaven the back way, through having had the right kind of Nanny. In a non-Catholic writer, such a scheme of salvation would look dangerously like predes-tination.

The reader who feels that Waugh's Roman empress is only an atavistic manifestation of Lady Seal, is bound to find 'Helena' disappointing. Waugh has done nothing in this book that he has not done as well or better elsewhere. It goes without saying that 'Helena' is amusing, shapely and well-written, and it also contains some extremely witty inci-dents: the Empress Fausta's description of the Council of Nicaea, for example, is Anatole France of the best 'Ile des Pingouins' vintage. Nevertheless, one cannot help feeling that Waugh has been pulling his punches in this book. A Christian saint and empress is not perhaps the most suit-able theme for a satirist who is irrevocably on the side of the angels.

Notes

1 Arnold Toynbee (1889-1975), an historian and social reformer, was author of the massive 'Study of History' (1934-61).
2 I.e. the aristocratic characters in Nancy Mitford's fiction.

128. GOUVERNEUR PAULDING, 'NEW YORK HERALD TRIBUNE BOOK REVIEW'

22 October 1950, 6

When one is born British, no matter how long one has been dead, there is always the chance that some British writer, looking through the nation's inexhaustible gallery of unusual characters, will come upon one's name and provide it once again with body, spirit and speech. Most of us are

convinced that human character does not greatly change
throughout the ages, but the British conviction that British character never changes at all furnishes a tool sharper
than any generalization for endowing the dead with life -
so long as the dead are British.

Helena, mother of Constantine the Great, was British: at
least there is no proof to the contrary. Toward the end of
her life she traveled to Jerusalem and discovered the True
Cross. Then, for long centuries, she stood immobilized and
hieratic there in that one scene of the 'Invention' - pic-
tured by the Italian painters - a figure remembered for
that one act, that single discovery. For centuries no one
has wondered how and why this English maid, this daughter
of King Cole 'the merry old soul' of Colchester, ever came
to Palestine or by what strange paths of destiny or chance.

Now, in 'Helena,' with his customary brilliant writing
more carefully handled than ever before and with a deeper,
gentler humanity than he has ever shown in previous work,
Evelyn Waugh tells her story. Fundamentally it is a story
that has often been told: that of the English girl who
marries abroad and discovers that her husband (Constantius) is really and irremediably a 'foreigner' and that
her son (Constantine the Great) is even more of a foreigner
- that is to say some one who would not even think of riding a horse for the simple pleasure of riding. These
ladies' adventures generally are most disillusioning.

When the scene is placed far enough back in time the
opportunities for jokes, anachronisms and satire are
limitless. Mr. Waugh, as one would expect, misses none of
them: his British generals were to [regard] Italians [as]
Hitler-like Fascist 'cads'; the 'Army wives' of the Imperial forces chatter away about promotions as if they were
Allied wives in the Berlin of the recent Air Lift. The
worldly philosopher lectures to them when they can find
nothing better with which to fill the long afternoons of
garrison town life. Like Hitler with his horoscopic advis-
ors, Constantine calls in witches for consultation. One of
these hears music 'wailing in the *bistro* where the jazz
disc spun,' transmits her message of warning in what, presumably, are supposed to be jazz rhythms, but Mr. Waugh,
whose ear for dialogue is so good, has never been able to
reproduce American speech.

In 'Helena,' the play of words, and the fireworks, the
exquisite descriptions of landscapes, and even the finished
portraits of the heroine, her husband and her son, are
always subordinate to the author's broad vision of the
mixed anguish and hope with which the world of Constantine's times was filled. With remarkable economy and selec-
tivity, Mr. Waugh has managed to get all of this immense

drama into the brief episodes of this short novel. The
great system of antiquity was breaking down but it was not
among the pagans that there was any feeling of anguish; the
old world was too tired to care what happened. And now the
Christians who had lived so long in hiding were coming out
into the open - and on that side there was hope indeed but
anguish too. A Resistance movement is always anguished when
it becomes official. So here we see Constantine making that
famous 'Donation' of Rome to the Christians which was to
have so fateful an effect on Christianity's future. And
here we have Helena a convert now, with her simple,
straightforward desire to discover and give to the Christian world this material reminder of Christ's passage on
earth, the wood of the cross on which he suffered. She
orders churches to be built over the Holy Places, Macarius,
the local bishop, knows that you can cover things with
marble to honor them, but when they are covered you cannot
see them any more. When Helena finally got the True Cross
and the nails, she gave the nails to her son the Emperor.
Constantine 'was delighted with his nails.' He stuck one in
his hat.

129. UNSIGNED REVIEW, 'TIME'

23 October 1950, 44

Britain's old King Coel, a Roman puppet of the 3rd Century,
may have been a merry old soul, but his daughter Helena was
a sober young gentlewoman. She made a proper marriage to
the Roman Emperor Constantius Chlorus, and bore him a son
who became Constantine the Great. After Constantine had
accepted Christianity, the Empress Dowager Helena - by that
time a doughty dame of 80 or so - undertook the arduous
pilgrimage to Jerusalem. While there, she discovered in an
abandoned cistern two baulks of timber which a great part
of the Christian world has ever since accepted as the
pieces of the True Cross of Christ.*

Or so Evelyn Waugh, picking his way through facts and
legends, tells Helena's story.† Satirist Waugh has put away
his satire this time. The religious theme of 'Helena' runs
close to the ruling passion of Waugh's life, his adopted
Roman Catholicism - perhaps too close to it. Any man with
his heart in his mouth must either blurt the whole thing
out or be content to say almost nothing at all. In 'Helena,'
Waugh says almost nothing at all about his own feelings,

about his characters, or about the religious motives that compelled their lives. Not even St. Helena herself is much more than a dignified old lady of purpose.

Waugh makes no great claims for his new book; he calls it 'just something to be read; in fact a legend.' Yet there can be little doubt, especially when page after page of Waugh's sky-blue prose goes purple with emotion, that the author intended his legend to be literature - a lovingly wrought story that would take its place in the Christian Apocrypha.

Several times in his writing life - in his study of Jesuit Edmund Campion, in 'Brideshead Revisited,' and now in 'Helena' - Author Waugh has tried to clear the satiric brambles out of his literary field, and to plant in their stead the herb of grace. He has had no very impressive crop so far, but most Waugh readers don't mind. They can be pretty sure another season will bring forth a bucketful of raspberries on the old Waugh briers.

Notes

* Slivers of this wood are still preserved and venerated in shrines throughout Christendom. In the Middle Ages, the hawking of spurious slivers became a scandal, and it was largely to reassure the faithful that a 19th Century Frenchman, Rohault de Fleury, devoted years to measuring the certified pieces still in existence. Their volume, according to De Fleury, was only 4,000 cubic centimeters, or about 2% of the probable volume of the cross.

† Waugh follows a 12th Century legend in having Helena born a British princess. The more accepted view: she was born a commoner in Bithynia.

130.   FREDERICK J. STOPP, 'MONTH'

August 1953, 69-84

Dr Frederick John Stopp (1911-79) was a scholar of Renaissance German and Fellow of Gonville and Caius College, Cambridge. He was the author of 'A Manual of Modern German' (1957) and 'Evelyn Waugh. Portrait of an Artist' (1958), arguably the subtlest critique of Waugh's work. Waugh delighted in this review and subsequently encouraged Dr Stopp to expand his ideas in his 'Portrait'.

Now that Mr. Waugh has, in his latest work, 'Men at Arms,'
returned to the setting of twentieth-century England before
and during the Second World War made familiar to us by his
earlier novels, it is possible that his retelling of the
legend of St. Helena will be regarded as a momentary episode, an aberration even, in the work of this sharp deline-
ator of the modern social scene - an episode indeed of
peculiar entertainment value by reason of the apparent incongruity between the venerable Christian story and the
familiar, racy modern idiom in which it is retold. Such
apparent incongruity between theme and medium may be felt,
according to the taste of the reader, either as an entertaining levity ... or as a rather shocking incursion into
the pious field on the part of a writer who would be much
better advised to stick to flippant and esoteric social
satire. The disproportionate bother caused by the character
in 'Men at Arms' who referred to Confession as 'scrape'
(see a recent exchange of incivilities in the 'European')
is symptomatic of such confusion of critical standards. For
it is a critical confusion, since there are not two Mr.
Waughs - the serious and the frivolous - but one, and this
one writer has in 'Helena' achieved a work which is
entirely of one piece. The alleged incongruity is in fact a
congruity, that between the supernatural and the natural;
and ... this is a problem which will always face the
'Catholic' novel.... 'Brideshead Revisited' [was] his
immediately preceding work, and his first post-war work in
which the problem was specifically faced. 'Technically this
is the most ambitious work of a writer who is devoted to
the niceties of his trade,' said the dust-cover of 'Helena,'
but when the work appeared the eminently critical task of
developing this statement was perhaps rather obscured, both
for those who approved of the work and those who did not,
by a feeling of discomfort resulting from the apparent incongruity between theme and technique. Further reflection
at a distance of time may succeed in revealing this incongruity as the key to Mr. Waugh's greatest success....
    It is a far cry from the England of the twentieth cen-
tury [as seen in 'Brideshead'] to Roman Britain, Rome and
Jerusalem in the third and fourth, the time and place of
Mr. Waugh's next novel, 'Helena.' And yet there are strong
points of similarity in the treatment of the impact of the
supernatural on the natural. This has in fact become the
central theme of the work. In an essay elsewhere on St.
Helena, Empress (the 'Month,' January 1952 [7-11]), Mr.
Waugh gives us some valuable pointers to his intentions in
writing the novel. Helena, he says, belongs eminently to
that special class of saints 'who are remembered for a
single act,' in this case the discovery of the timber since

venerated throughout Christendom as part of the true
Cross. Apart from this journey, undertaken at an advanced
age, she would have no fame. Once made, this act of
supreme sanctity was made for all time, and could not be
repeated. Nor was the historical turning point which saw
and accompanied this one personal act, the final victory of
Christianity in the Mediterranean world, less unique. For
Mr. Waugh, therefore, any book about St. Helena (and this
one is described both as a legend and a novel), must show
the intimate fusion of the historical and the personal in a
unique act in time, and the no less intimate consonance of
the supernatural and the natural which made of this act a
miraculous and saintly one.

The common root of these four aspects of the act known
ever since as the Finding of the True Cross, Mr. Waugh sees
in the fundamental reality of solid material fact itself.
Historically and supernaturally, by this discovery,

> she was asserting in sensational form a dogma which was
> in danger of neglect. In the academies of the Eastern
> and South-Eastern Mediterranean, sharp, sly minds were
> everywhere looking for phrases and analogies to recon-
> cile the new, blunt creed for which men had died, with
> the ancient speculations which had beguiled their minds,
> and with the occult rites which had for generations
> spiced their logic.... Everything about the new religion
> was capable of interpretation, could be refined and
> diminished; everything except the unreasonable assertion
> that God became man and died on the Cross; not a myth or
> an allegory; true God, truly incarnate, tortured to
> death at a particular moment in time, at a particular
> geographical place, as a matter of plain historical fact.
> This was the stumbling block in Carthage, Alexandria,
> Ephesus and Athens, and at this all the talents of the
> time went to work, to reduce, hide and eliminate.... And
> at that crisis suddenly emerged God-sent from luxurious
> retirement in the far north, a lonely, resolute old
> woman with a single concrete, practical task clear
> before her; to turn the eyes of the world back to the
> planks of wood on which their salvation hung.

Personally and naturally, therefore, Mr. Waugh sees
Helena's whole life as a preparation for, and prefiguration of this one supreme supernatural and historical act.
'She might claim, like that other, less prudent queen: "In
my end is my beginning."' In a sense any major choice in
the supernatural field is both an end *and* a beginning. So
the whole framework of recollection in 'Brideshead Revisited' emphasizes that the end of Charles Ryder's human

struggle is the beginning of his supernatural life; the long
awaited avalanche creates the possibility of a fresh start.
Helena's discovery of the True Cross is the avalanche which
has been impending all her life. But the special interest
of this book is that, by choosing as the central character
one about whose life almost nothing else is known but this
one supreme, final and yet constitutive act, the author has
a clear field in which to build up the total rounded picture of a life and a social and historical setting whose
every line of development converges on to that point.
Legendary in its beginning and its end, historical in its
middle course, the book is a striking representation in
artistic form of that living and inherited historicity
which is known as the tradition of the Church.

...Mr. Waugh gives Helena two fundamental qualities of
mind: an innate and unshakeable realism, and a childlike
questing for some half-perceived ideal. Innocent of all
aesthetic or social exclusiveness, she hobnobs when young
with Roman soldiers in the stables, with sailors over their
fishmeal, just as when old she, as first lady in the civilized world, went to live with the nuns of Mount Zion
'where she did her own housework and took her turn in waiting at table.' Whether faced in Ratisbon with the intri-
cacies of initiation into Eastern cults, or in Jerusalem
with the subtleties of scholars concerning the probable
composition of the True Cross, Helena's favourite word is
'Bosh.'

...Helena ... always ... inquires; throughout the book
all who come into contact with her are subjected to the same
persistent, sometimes wide-eyed, sometimes impatient questioning ... [including] ... Pope Sylvester on the whereabouts of the Cross. Her questions gradually narrow down
and become more explicit, until at last, on the threshold
of Holy Week in Jerusalem, 'she had come to the end of all
her questions,' until on the night of Good Friday, 'she lay
quite relaxed at last, like the body in the tomb,' and the
answer was vouchsafed to her in another mode: through
revelation in a dream. Truly the discovery lay already in
a sense in the power of grace and in the personal humility
which told Helena what question to ask. When it is first
put to Pope Sylvester he answers 'I don't think anyone has
ever asked before,' and thus sums up the situation of the
whole book. And it is not just a specious effect of frivolous modernity which Mr. Waugh achieves when he makes
Helena answer: 'Just at this moment when everyone is forgetting it and chattering about the hypostatic union,
there's a solid chunk of wood waiting for them to have
their silly heads knocked against.'

Against this central core of inspired and questing
common sense represented by Helena, almost all the other
characters and situations are in some degree foils and
contrasts. The supernatural and immensely practical wisdom
of Helena is seen against the practical but wholly secular
wisdom of Constantius, her husband - Constantius, who is
also an indefatigable asker of questions, but only of those
directed to the knowledge of men and the acquisition of
power, who even in religious practice only went as far as
one of the earlier degrees of Mithraism, 'seeking neither
plain truth nor ecstasy.' *His* talents also 'comprised all
that was needed, no more.' *His* basic need also 'was simple;
... sometimes before he grew too old to make proper use of
it, Constantius wanted the World.' It is seen further
against the false supernaturalism of Marcias, her tutor and
the later Gnostic, who also dreams of the City, of freedom
and immortality; but it is the freedom of the City of Troy
seen as a poetic universe, an invisible Republic of Letters, or of a spurious mysticism avoiding all commitment
in the world of reality. It is seen against the characteristic situation of Constantine, poised between the old
world and the new, the unredeemed and the redeemed. On the
one hand he takes after his father - 'Power without Grace'
is Helena's summing up - on the other hand after his mother,
as when he dismissed the new-fangled sculptors who have
lost contact with the world of naturalist representation,
and orders that the carvings of the Arch of Trajan should
be removed for his Triumphal Arch - 'Spoken like a man, my
son,' is Helena's comment. It is seen against the inadequate piety of Pope Sylvester, who has not understood that
the supernatural is most adequately conveyed and revealed
in the natural, the whole sense of 'Epiphany,' with which
Mr. Waugh entitles a later chapter. To Helena's remonstrance that 'it stands to reason' that God expects us to
find the Cross, he can only give the answer of religious
quietism: 'Nothing "stands to reason" with God. If he had
wanted us to have it, no doubt he would have given it to
us. But he hasn't chosen to. He gives us enough.' And
lastly, Helena's later act in its supreme natural honesty
is set in subtle contrast to the unnature and duplicity
which has undermined the life and thought of pagan Rome.
Consider the description by Constantius of the wonders of
the Imperial City when he returns from Aurelian's Triumph:

'The Triumph was something I shall never forget,
something I could never have imagined.'
'Elephants?'
'Twenty of them and four tigers. Aurelian's chariot
had a four-in-hand of stags; there were ostriches and

giraffes and animals there isn't a name for, who've
never been seen before.... Sixteen hundred gladiators....
We had parties every night. All the biggest senators
opened their palaces to us ... they gave us some staggering dinners. Everything was got up to look like something else, partridges made of sugar, peaches of mince-
meat; you couldn't tell what you were eating....'

The keynotes of this description are the size of everything, the concentration at Rome of the plundered resources
of the civilized world, and the debased taste which finds a
sensation in things which are not as they appear. Against
this is set by anticipation Helena's act, _her_ final Triumph, which consisted in the finding of just six baulks of
timber, for which in all humility she left Rome and brought
her homage to an Eastern site, and the fundamental solidity
of that mind which never cared to forget that wood was wood
and nothing else. Helena, whose dream since childhood has
been to go to Rome, who begged to be taken with Constantius
on this occasion, but stayed behind to bear his child, the
future Constantine, realizes at this significant moment
that she has lost forever her husband, and with it the
larger ideal which had caused her to leave the shores of
Britain.

> Rome, where all the treasure of the world flowed and
> was squandered, had despoiled Constantius ... that large
> shadow of him which Helena had glimpsed, pursued,
> briefly enjoyed, was lost forever.... Helena saw all
> this in the first days of his return and accepted it.

Constantius and pagan Rome were for Helena the 'forerunners' in the language of 'Brideshead Revisited.' She has
lost both, has measured their inadequacy against the half-
formulated ideal in her mind, she has stayed behind to bear
the first Christian Emperor.

Constantius and pagan Rome are indeed for Helena but
'forerunners,' prefiguration of the City and its _civitas_,
which she has desired from early youth. Born of the chieftain Coel, equally proud of his Roman citizenship and of
his descent from the more remote Aeneas and Troy, she is
filled with the conviction of belonging to a wider citizenship than that represented by the area of Colchester.
Symptomatic of this are her desire to see the Eternal City
in her lifetime, and her equal determination to find the
historical site of her Trojan origin: thus her questioning
of the unwilling Marcias, who for himself is quite satisfied that 'of Troy itself there is nothing left but poetry.'
Helena does not agree that a city like Troy could ever have

been destroyed, or for that matter that the other City of
Rome could ever in the future be destroyed. 'Why don't
people dig? Some of Troy's bound to be there ... when I am
educated I shall go and find the real Troy - Helen's.'
Which is just what she does. If, in the natural course of
Helena's life, culminating in the discovery of the Cross,
she could say, in Mr. Waugh's words: 'In my end is my
beginning,' in the spiritual significance of her determination to find and return to her ancestral home of Troy, she
could also say: 'In my beginning is my end.'

Meanwhile, however, and through the greater part of her
life, it is the more immediate presence of Rome which
occupies her thoughts. But even before the final loss of
her illusion - her faith in Constantius and the pagan
metropolis of power which he represents - her thoughts have
taken a wider sweep. Even when travelling down the Limes as
a young bride, to her first station at Ratisbon, she asks:
'Must there always be a wall? ... I mean couldn't the wall
be at the limits of the world and all men, civilized and
barbarian, have a share in the City?' The question is
answered at the end, when, after concluding her task, 'she
sailed away, out of authentic history,' leaving legends
among the fishermen of Cyprus and the Adriatic, relics of
the True Cross from Constantinople to Cologne, and a
Christian Britain....

...In the Labarum, which the half-crazed Constantine
shows his mother as a special favour, we have another
admirable foil to the unique act of Helena. This superb
and sumptuous product of the jeweller's art, with medallion
portraits of the Emperor's children, is the epitome of that
falsification of the past in the spirit of myth which is
the mark of pseudo-religions. To Constantine's bland assertion that this was the emblem which the vision bade him
make, and in which he conquered, Helena answers:

> 'But it must have taken months to make.'
> 'Two or three hours, I assure you. The jewellers were
> inspired. Everything was miraculous that day.'
> 'And whose are the portraits?'
> 'My own and my children's.'
> 'But my dear boy, they weren't all born then.'
> 'I tell you it was a miracle,' said Constantine
> huffily.

The miracle of the finding of the True Cross is in every
respect an antithesis to this episode, born as it is from
a humble and believing acceptance of the true and unaltered
facts of past history.... For Constantine the Cross is an
attractive and useful myth, which, enjoying power without

grace, he can create or fashion at will. For Marcias the
slave, with neither power nor grace, Troy is also a beautiful myth, a world of poetry. For Helena, with both power
and grace, the Cross and the City of God are realities; and
her task is to show their solidity by knocking silly
people's heads against them.

But to find the City of God, to undertake the quest for
the larger and deeper loyalty, local loyalties must be
relinquished. Under the guise of Rome, it is of this city
that Helena and her father Coel are talking when Constantius asks for her hand in marriage....

That other Helen, in whose involvement with Paris the
British princess took such intense and rollicking interest
when the immortal story was read to her by Marcias, also
chose exile and left all for love. When Menelaus challenged
Paris to mortal combat, but Aphrodite plucked him up in a
cloud of darkness and bore him to his chamber, and brought
also fair Helen to lie with him, then Menelaus raged
through the camp but failed to find Paris, so Agamemnon
proclaimed Menelaus the victor and 'fair Helen forfeit.'
Fair Helen of Colchester is also forfeit, when Mr. Waugh
uses this phrase as the title of Chapter II. No wonder that
Marcias considers it as 'an incident quite inconsistent
with the heroic virtues' or that 'For that reason the
Great Longinus considers it the interpolation of a later
hand.' (It is in fact an interpolation by the later hand of
Mr. Waugh.) For what did Marcias, or for that matter the
Great Longinus, know of the supernatural aspect of heroic
virtue? And how can it be an act of heroic virtue to slip
away with divine assistance from father and husband and to
lie with one's lover? And yet it is so in the case of
Helena, the British princess. The innocent Helena has
grown up with two heroic myths: from Marcias she has
imbibed the myth of the wisdom and omniscience of the
Great Longinus, from her nurse she has heard stories of the
valour and integrity of her nurse's father, a valiant
'sapper-sergeant slain by the Picts.' Representing natural
wisdom and natural valour, the heroism of truth and of
action, 'these dissimilar paragons were the twin deities of
her adolescence; she had a homely, humorous intimacy with
them, but also awe.' Neither of these ideals survived the
brutal contact through Constantius with pagan Roman realities: the sapper-sergeant died within her at the news of
the unsoldierly treachery of Tetricus and the butchery
which ensued; the Great Longinus has his 'block chopped
off' during the Roman Eastern campaign. But these figures
were powerful forerunners in the mind of Helena whose
crowning achievement was one which combined in equal measure wisdom and action, both supernaturally illuminated.

It is significant that Helena, who became homeless in
answer to a wider loyalty, who uprooted herself from her
ageing routine to travel through the Mediterranean East
questing for the Cross, should receive the miraculous news
of its whereabouts from that other homeless figure: the
wandering Jew. The Jew who had stood outside and reviled
Christ when He stumbled under the weight of the Cross, had
had the words addressed to him: 'Tarry till I come.'
Helena had also tarried long, perhaps beyond the natural
span of years, with no apparent major aim in life; but it
was not an endless wait through the ages of the world, but
only till she could come to Christ in finding His Cross,
lying in the ground waiting to be found like the ruins of
Troy which Helena had so decidedly intended to dig for.
'Aphrodite ... sought Helen where she stood among her
women ... plucked her perfumed gown and said: "Come, Paris
is waiting on his carved bed, radiantly, delicately clad as
though he were resting from the dance."' That call to the
carved bed of the Cross took a lifetime to answer, but the
answer, that act of heroic virtue which neither Marcias nor
Longinus, in their world of pagan nature, could understand,
was prefigured in her life from the beginning. Marcias
knows perfectly well that the memory of Troy lives on in
the present world, as the reality of Troy sleeps on below
the modern town: 'The guides will show you anything you ask
for - the tomb of Achilles, Paris's carved bed, the wooden
leg of the great horse. But of Troy itself there is nothing
left but poetry.' That is, the showmen of the world like
Constantine will assent to and exploit the myth as far as
it is profitable to them, and the learned men, like Marcias
and the Christian divines of third century Rome and the
East, may exploit and refine on its inherent poetic beauty:
'It is generally believed,' a Coptic elder assured her,
'that the Cross was compounded of every species of wood so
that all the vegetable world could participate in the act
of redemption.' But only Helena was prepared to take the
alleged wooden leg of the great horse in its solid and
repugnant reality: as an invitation to enter through the
tomb of Achilles, through complete submission to a supernatural purpose, into the chamber where Christ was waiting
on His carved bed of the Cross.

When Aphrodite first plucked at Helena's gown, it was in
the guise of her natural love for Constantius. But the
invitation to the mystical marriage of the soul was not for
long able to disguise itself under the 'steadfast and
bruised passion' of which Helena thought that Constantius
was the only object. But one natural fantasy of the supernatural life does accompany Helena throughout her life and
is never shown wanting: the horse and its bridle. The

passage in which Helena, during the epic recital in
Coel's banqueting hall, indulges in the exhilarating fantasy of being a horse which is ridden, and the moment in
which hers and Constantine's glances meet, leading to love
at first sight, is a magnificent symbol of erotic struggle
and surrender, of the integration of two natures and two
wills in intimate fusion. But it does not end there.
Throughout her youth and maturity the horse theme keeps
cropping up, and we can be certain that Constantius's
insensate ride for Rome and power, after thirteen years'
absence in the East, having all the post-horses ham-
strung behind him to escape from pursuit and violence,
offends something very deep in Helena.... Constantius
nicknamed Helena 'Stabularia,' the ostler, when he found
her the day after their first meeting in the stables with
a bit in her mouth, and this name had remained with her.
Towards the end, the True Cross and the Nails having been
discovered, the motif is taken up again when Constantine
puts one of the nails to the idiosyncratic use of having
it forged into a snaffle for his horse. 'When Helena
heard this she was at first a little taken aback. But
presently she smiled, giggled and was heard to utter the
single, enigmatic word "stabularia."' In spite of the grotesque way in which it was done, her son has thus re-
affirmed this intimacy of association between the human and
the divine, which for Helena was the absolute submission of
her own aristocratic and vitally assertive nature to the
beloved and divine will. In his conclusion Mr. Waugh falls
back into the hunting theme. The divine huntsman has used
her to put humanity and the human hunt on to its right
course: 'Hounds are checked, hunting wild. A horn calls
clear through the covert. Helena casts them back on the
scent.'
   'Brideshead Revisited' is a social novel, while 'Helena'
is described by its author as both a novel and a legend.
In either case, as in other recent Catholic novels, the
dimension in which they take place is a poetic one, even
if the setting is one admitting or even based on theological implications. Lord Marchmain's change of heart and
Charles Ryder's conversion, Helena's heroic virtue and her
discovery of the fragments of the True Cross ... are all
matters which are the appropriate subjects of aesthetic
delineation. But they are not problems for solution, since
the novel is not a spiritual case-history. It is enough for
the novelist that such things are humanly possible; his
task is limited to making them humanly and poetically probable. But the delineation with human sympathy and artistic
tact, of that impact of the supernatural on the natural
which is inescapable in any realistic appreciation of the

situation of man, is the achievement of the post-war work
of our two leading Catholic novelists. As such they aim at
neither conversion nor explanation, but rather at the 'hint
of an explanation,' a perception of the workings in human
life of a kind of cosmic analogy never to be fully resolved
in this life. This sense of cosmic analogy comes from the
consciousness that natural motives, reactions and events
have always a supernatural resonance, that the human game
is played out against a gigantic backcloth on which
shadowy figures can be descried, both dictating and reflecting human action, and yet leaving intact human responsibility and the economy of salvation by one's own efforts.
The exploration of this dimension of poetry and analogy is
pre-eminently the task of the critic.

131.   CHRISTOPHER DERRICK, 'THE TIMES'

20 April 1974, 14

Christopher Derrick (b. 1921), critic and writer of books
on contemporary problems in Catholic theology, was once a
close friend of Muriel Spark. He is author of 'Trimming the
Ark' (1969), 'Reader's Report on the Writing of Novels'
(1969) and 'The Delicate Creation' (1972).

Towards the end of ... 'Helena', the old Empress is in
Jerusalem, hunting in practical fashion for the True Cross,
which (she believes) must exist somewhere; and she asks
around, seeking advice on what such an object might be like,
and how one might hope to find it.

People are helpful, ready with theories. 'It is
generally believed', a Coptic elder assures her, 'that the
cross was compounded of every species of wood, so that all
the vegetable world could participate in the act of redemption.' Alternatively, it is suggested to her that the four
arms of the cross were made of four different woods - box-
wood, cypress, cedar, and pine - for an unspecified symbolic reason or that it was made of aspen wood, for which
reason the aspen tree now shivers continually with shame;
or that a unique tree was used, richly mythological in its
origin and nature.

'Nonsense, rot, and bosh', replies Helena; and from all
that head-in-the-clouds pursuit of symbolism and significance, she turns to brisk factuality [sic], to questions of

human probability, of regimental carpentry and Jewish
observance, and this different approach gets its concrete
reward: not without divine assistance, she finds what she's
looking for.

It is the most theological of Waugh's novels, this story
of a cheerful horsey girl out of Debrett who is slowly
broken and matured into sainthood, while English empiricism
keeps her feet on the ground, her attention upon fact when
the whole world seems obsessed with subtle meaning. Waugh
himself was clearly and even aggressively a Catholic; but
as a novelist, he was mostly concerned to use the Catholic
faith for imaginative purposes rather than to assert or
analyse its substance. Like his recurring image of the
Great House, it provided him with a useful symbolism of
order and goodness, as against the besieging forces of
chaos and the irrational; in the war trilogy, for example,
such a contrast is pointed by repeated allusions to the
quiet sanity of the liturgical year and its serene ritual,
still continuing there in the background as the world progressively consummates its own monstrous death-wish. Many
another symbolism - not necessarily Christian, not necessarily religious at all - might have served very much the
same imaginative purpose.

But in 'Helena', he turned to consider the central
Christian assertion in itself: incarnation, the Word made
flesh, the one intersection of myth and history of meaning
and fact. His heroine lived, as we live now, in a time
marked by the disintegration and collapse of a great civilization, by a despairing of mere power and politics, and
by a consequent proliferation of mystical cults, broadly
Gnostic in tendency.

Into the fevered atmosphere of such a time, Helena
brought a breath of fresh air. Once she had listened to
the mythologically meaningful narratives of a fashionable
Gnostic preacher, and had offended him by asking bluntly:
'When and where did all this happen? How do you know?' A
childish question, they told her; but when she put the same
question to a Christian, in connexion with narratives
which seemed comparably mythological, she received a
straight answer: 'I should say that as a man he died two
hundred and seventy-eight years ago in the town now called
Aelia Capitolina in Palestine.'

It was the kind of answer she wanted: she had an
appetite for objectivity, for plain fact, but when she
asked elsewhere for that bread, she was given only the
precious stones of symbolism, the gilt and filigree'd
tortuosities of pure meaning. Getting the message and duly
grateful, she resolved after baptism to make her own contribution, to find a concrete object that would help to

keep the Church's feet on the ground. Those head-in-the-clouds mystagogues chattered away; but all the time there was 'a solid chunk of wood waiting for them to have their silly heads knocked against. I'm going off to find it.'

However you state it, the central balancing-task of the Christian mind is a difficult one: for individuals and for whole cultures, it is too easy to drift off into either the Arian or the Docetist one-sidedness, to forget either the divinity or the humanity, the Word or the flesh, myth or history, meaning or fact. At any time, the half-forgotten side of the matter will need to be remembered and re-emphasized; and in our time as in Helena's, it seems that there is need for a renewed emphasis upon Christianity as *fact* - so powerful and one-sided is the current appetite for *gnosis*, insight, and subjectively-conceived 'meaning', so sharply diminished the appetite for mere truth, for objective reality.

Waugh was a novelist, not a theologian; and it could be argued that those two great images, the Great House and the Ancient Faith, dominated his mind too obsessively. He might have been an even better novelist if he had devoted a smaller proportion of his creative energies to punishing the human counterparts of those images - actual aristo-crats, actual priests - for their failure to come up to expectations. But in 'Helena' at least he laid the obses-sion aside and became a positively religious writer and a topical one too.

'Men at Arms'

1952

132.   CYRIL CONNOLLY, 'SUNDAY TIMES'

7 September 1952, 5

Mr. Waugh is now off on the first volume of his long
wartime novel. 'Men at Arms' describes what he has called
the 'honeymoon period of his love-affair with the Army'.
It is unlike his other books for two reasons. Since it is
a honeymoon he is unexpectedly gentle and good-tempered,
but it is also a religious novel, and I should guess one of
its themes to be the particularly Catholic way in which a
holy medal preserves the hero from sin. For the hero is not
a convert, as in tumultuous 'Brideshead', but a Maurice
Baring type, (1) resident in Italy, heir of an old but impoverished English Catholic family with a saintly father
and a life blighted by an unhappy marriage. At thirty-five
he joins a fighting regiment named the 'Halberdiers' with
another thirty-five-year-old called Atwater. Presumably the
'Atwater' (2) of 'Work Suspended', who had got to Rhodesia
after all.

   Novels of Army life are difficult to write. After an
admirable hundred pages Mr. Waugh slips into a vein highly
reminiscent of 'The First Hundred Thousand'(3) with touches
of 'Stalky and Co.',(4) and the P.G. Wodehouse of 'Ukridge'.
Atwater is not so much a comic character (unless it is
comic to have two aunts and say 'old man') but a private
joke, and for the first time I found myself bored by the
central section of a Waugh novel. The 'Stalkified' ending
is exciting but scarcely credible. The atmosphere of 1940
is better recovered in 'Put Out More Flags'. One raises the
silver loving cup expecting champagne and receives a wallop
of ale.

   Once we accept that it is beer, a chronicle rather than

a novel, it is of its kind perfect; admirably written,
humorous rather than witty, genial, courteous, consistently
delightful in texture, with none of the lumps and snags of
'Brideshead'; it imparts much fascinating information of a
theological and military nature. Characters like the
saintly father are wisely and convincingly drawn, and there
are flashes of the old diamond on the pane....

Where I feel Mr. Waugh has gone wrong - and he can put
this right in remaining volumes - is in failing to build up
relationships between his military characters, who do not
exist in the round but only in their reality to the narrator. He must quicken the pace of events and be more on his
guard against the perishable nature of gregarious clowning,
and the hero should be tuned up to the point at which he
influences others and is more than an elderly version of
Ian Hay's 'Little of the Loamshires'. The calm and established serenity of the religious element as provided by the
narrator and his father is wholly desirable, but inclined
to bottle up the impetuous glancing ferocity of Mr. Waugh's
genius. There is a discord here between love and aggression
which Mr. Hemingway's Old Man has resolved into a harmony.
(5)

Notes

1 Maurice Baring (1874-1945) was a novelist, critic and
   writer of historical tales.
2 A misreading for 'Apthorpe'.
3 Ian Hay, 'The First Hundred Thousand' (1915).
4 Rudyard Kipling, 'Stalky and Co.' (1899).
5 Ernest Hemingway, 'The Old Man And the Sea' (1952),
   was also reviewed.

133.   JOHN RAYMOND, 'NEW STATESMAN'

20 September 1952, 326-7

Mr. Waugh is the most English of satirists. However contrary, however much below form, any new novel from his pen
is bound to add immeasurably to the gaiety of his own
nation. His new book fulfils all Chalky White's expectations. We can imagine those old eyes watering gleefully
as Mr. Gutteridge describes each salty character and incident. As a novel, 'Men at Arms' is not nearly as good as

'Put Our More Flags'. As a 'novel of military life', is is
uproariously and unflaggingly funny.

Though they have been heavily curtailed, most of the
writer's newer and more irritating mannerisms are here
fleetingly in one form or another. There is the huge prep
school conspiracy of the faithful, that seeming wish to
depict Mother Church as one Big Dorm and her mysteries as
so much sacred larking. We know from his Life of Edmund
Campion that Mr. Waugh's real convictions are held on a
very different level. Why, then, must his characters be
forever splashing each other with holy water?

> 'Mass is at eight,' said Angela....
> 'Oh I say, isn't there something later? I was looking
>   forward to a long lie.'
> 'I thought we might all go to communion tomorrow. Do
>   come, Tony.'
> 'All right, Mum, of course I will. Only make it twenty-
>   five-to in that case. I shall have to go to scrape
>   after weeks of wickedness.'

And there are flashes of the old *saeva indignatio*. The
Ensa party contains a 'neuter beast of indeterminate origin' and there are three pre-arranged blackballs waiting
for the unpukka Air Vice-Marshal when his name goes up on
the club notice-board. Towards the end of the book there is
more than a hint of the physical cruelty with which Mr.
Waugh inevitably hunts down his favourite characters.

Yet, on the whole, 'Men at Arms' is good-tempered
Waugh - and therefore Waugh at his second best. Compared
with 'Scott-King's Modern Europe' or with 'The Loved One',
it might have been written by the Cheeryble Brothers. (1)
Like every satirist at a loss for prey, the writer has made
a temporary excursus into Myth. Mr. Waugh's myth (he could
have, and has, chosen a great many worse ones) is the English regimental tradition in 1940. Guy Crouchback, a
middle-aged exile, returning to England and joining a crack
regiment, the Halberdiers, is quick to sense the professional leaven working in the voluntary lump.

> Guy's companions ... had been chosen ... from more
> than two thousand applicants. He wondered, sometimes,
> what system of selection had produced so nondescript
> a squad. Later he realized that they typified the pecu-
> liar pride of the Corps, which did not expect distin-
> guished raw materials but confided instead in its age-
> old methods of transformation. The discipline of the
> square, the traditions of the mess, would work their
> magic and the *esprit de corps* would fall like blessed
> unction from above.

We are back on the box seat of the holiday brake,
'takin' time,' from Uncle Stalky.... How alike, despite
their divergent loyalties, Kipling and Mr. Waugh are! Their
great gifts spring from a common fountain-head of anger.
Kipling the non-sahib glorifying the sahibs and trouncing
the lesser breeds because of a dark unhappy childhood, Mr.
Waugh playing the Catholic Bayard and breaking his neuter
beasts' backs with pack-drill on the barrack-square because of - what? Perhaps because the lush Arcadia that was
once Brideshead has 'become submerged and obliterated,
irrecoverable as Lyoness, so quickly have the waters come
flooding in.' Though the reasons for their anger and
ferocious self-pity may escape us, it is these traits that
have made both men great, though uneven, writers. Their
common impulse springs not from James's 'madness of art'
but from the madness of the great artist who is also a
great hater.

Here, for the space of one book at least, Mr. Waugh has
his hates on a leash. He is content to give us the humours
of military training, ringing the changes on P.T., King's
Regulations, rifle-practice and the rest. The 'biffing'
one-eyed Brigadier, the preposterous Apthorpe and his more
preposterous 'thunder-box,' the tough platoon sergeants
and fatherly adjutant - all have been conceived with affection and understanding. At only one point - the chapter
describing Guy's attempt to win back his divorced wife
during a week-end at Claridge's - does Mr. Waugh strike a
false note. He has realised, better and more bitterly than
any of his contemporaries, the grey predicament of secular
marriage in the twentieth century. Yet in this book all
that was poignant in 'A Handful of Dust' has turned to
rhodomontade. The episode reads like a scene from some
shabby and tasteless bedroom farce.

For the rest, I can only say I have enjoyed Mr. Waugh's
new book as richly as I have enjoyed all his others. At
his worst, he writes ten times as amusingly as anyone else
and his affectations, whether they take the form of priest-
holes or Bollinger, mess silver or medal ribbons, are
matched by his gifts. As Edmund Wilson declared, 'his
snobbery carries us with it.'(2)

Notes

1   Charles and Edwin, the philanthropic, affectionate
    twins in Dickens's 'Nicholas Nickleby'.
2   Edmund Wilson, 'Classics and Commercials', p. 145.

134.   UNSIGNED REVIEW, 'TIME'

27 October 1952, 58-9

Good satirists get so hot under the choler that they are
always in danger of breaking out in a sentimental sweat -
which is why many of them cling tightly to cold ferocity
and suppress the feeblest spasms of affection. Satirist
Evelyn Waugh has been no exception, but he is one of the
few of his kind who has found the conflict between satirical art and goodness of heart a nagging, challenging problem. His ideal is the simple, honest 'Christian gentleman'; Waugh cherishes things romantic, patriotic and
traditional. Moreover, he is a religious man, whose
irrepressible satirical arrogance is at variance with his
sense of Christian humility.

In some of his novels Waugh has got around his problem
by succumbing wholly either to ferocity (as in 'The Loved
One') or heartburn (as in 'A Handful of Dust'). More often,
he has kept his anger uppermost and merely hinted at a
grumpy sympathy with mankind. But in 'Brideshead Revisited'
he made his first major effort to express fully both sides
of his divided self - to give poison only where poison was
due, to cool boiling oil with holy water.

In his new novel ... Waugh broadens and deepens the
scope of this experiment. Reading 'Men at Arms' is like
hearing a full keyboard used by a pianist who has hitherto
confined himself to a single octave. Waugh is fully alive
to the fact that no modern war is just a soldier's war.
The drawing rooms, kitchens and clubs of the home front
interest him just as much as the barracks and the tents.
Furthermore, his interest in the battles is tightly linked
with his interest in the cause for which they were (or were
not) fought. His war is simultaneously against Hitler and
against 'a public quite indifferent to those trains of
locked vans ... rolling East and West from Poland and the
Baltic, that were to roll on year after year bearing their
innocent loads to ghastly unknown destinations.'

Hero Guy Crouchback is a familiar Waugh character in
that, dramatically speaking, he is not a hero at all. Like
Waugh himself, Guy is a Roman Catholic romantic, but for
the rest he is an older version of those earlier Waugh
stooge-heroes whose very decency caused them to be trampled
underfoot by he-men, clawed apart by harpies, robbed of
their rights by double-dealers - and then trounced by
Evelyn Waugh into the bargain. World War II finds Guy a
dispossessed man in every sense, abandoned by a feckless
wife, deprived of spiritual zest by isolation. Waugh is

frank to admit that to a man like Guy, World War II was a
matter for 'jubilation.'

Guy joins ... the Halberdiers, to be trained as an
officer. To him, as to Waugh (who was himself a captain in
the Royal Horse Guards), the Halberdiers are a dream come
true. They embody all the sentiments of which Guy was
starved in the prewar world. Tradition, *esprit de corps*,
ritual and courtesy are combined with high efficiency and
discipline. The Halberdiers still loyally toast their
Colonel-in Chief, the Grand Duchess Elena of Russia, who
lives 'in a bed-sitting-room at Nice.' They take 'peculiar
pride' in accepting whatever recruits are sent to them,
confident that their 'age-old methods of transformation'
can make a good fighting man out of the poorest mouse. In
Guy's eyes they are both monks and soldiers – in short,
Crusaders.

One of the most surprising feats in 'Men at Arms' is
the way Waugh, too, throws open the sacred doors of the
Halberdier mess to all sorts and conditions of men, making
the regiment a symbol of the church militant in which he
believes. Apart from Guy, none of the newer offiers is a
devout man, and most of them are intellectual mediocrities
at best. But to Waugh – and to the reader, after Waugh has
waved his magic wand of characterization – mediocrity seems
not only a human condition but a fascinating one. The only
trouble with it is that it is incapable of leading a Crusade – a job which Waugh turns over to one of his most
scintillating creations, Brigadier Ben Ritchie-Hook.

Ritchie-Hook is anything but a saint. Like many a Crusader, he fights simply because he loves 'blood and gun-
powder.' Hand-to-hand scrapping is his ideal: 'Everything
else [in war],' he assures Guy, 'is just bumf and tele-
phones.' His pursuit of his ideal has left him with 'a
single, terrible eye ... black as the patch which hung on
the other side of the lean, skew nose.' His smile is a
grim baring of carnivorous teeth; he grasps his cocktail
glass in 'a black claw' consisting of 'two surviving fingers and half a thumb.' He is fond of discoursing on the
proper use of infantry. 'You must use them when they're on
their toes.... Use them ... spend them. It's like slowly
collecting a pile of chips and then plonking them all
down.... It's the most fascinating thing in life.'

Brigadier Ritchie-Hook, brute symbol of ferocity and
military leadership, stands at one extreme of 'Men at
Arms.' At the other is Captain Apthorpe, who stands for all
that is most ridiculous, most pompous, most bumbling and
yet most sympathetic in human nature. He has spent most of
his life in Bechuanaland, and he joins the Halberdiers with
a 'vast accumulation of ant-proof boxes, water-proof

bundles, strangely shaped, heavily initialed tin trunks and
leather cases.' As an antiseptic precaution he has his
'Thunder Box' - a portable chemical toilet built of oak and
brass.

Boastful, untruthful, utterly incompetent, Apthorpe dies
of fever in a West African hospital. But it is only when he
is on his deathbed, 'staring at the sun-blinds with his
hands empty on the counterpane,' that the reader grasps the
true nature of Waugh's creation. Captain Apthorpe is
Shakespeare's Falstaff, perfectly brought up-to-date, but
with his roots set firmly in the historic past. And it is
Brigadier Ritchie-Hook who drives him to his death, much as
King Henry V impatiently rid his army of 'that stuff'd
cloakbag of guts.'

It is this blending of history and modernity, of changing and changeless things, that gives 'Men at Arms' its
weight and vision. By the end of the volume the Halberdiers
have not done much more than finish their training, but
Waugh has already completed them as individual representatives of an ancient nation turning a new page of its history. Sometimes the load is too much for his stature and he
reverts (particularly where the 'Thunder Box' is concerned)
to scatological burlesque. Sometimes his passion for blood-
shed and his awe of warriors like Ritchie-Hook so dull his
intelligence that he becomes absurd. But such collapses
have always been a part of Waugh. Sometimes they have
seemed to be a major part, but 'Men at Arms' argues that
they are not. If his trilogy continues as well as it has
begun, it will be the best British novel of World War II.

135. UNSIGNED REVIEW, 'NEW YORKER'

1 November 1952, 117

The hero of this uneven novel ... is a youngish Englishman
named Guy Crouchback, the scion of one of those august
pre-Reformation Catholic families on which the author
increasingly dotes. The time is the first year of the
recent war, and Crouchback, who has never got over his
wife's having left him eight years earlier, enlists in the
Royal Corps of Halberdiers, with the hope of finding in
battle a means of mending his damaged spiritual faculties.
Most of the novel is given over to Crouchback's training in
the Corps. Mr. Waugh has been one of the funniest writers
alive, and it is fitfully evident here that his eye for the

outrageous is as keen as ever, but he appears to have lost
interest in the happy seductions of farce. The raffish note
of the barracks, which enlivens the middle portion of the
book, yields to the note of Newman, and under the circumstances the reader can't help feeling disappointed. Perhaps
in the succeeding novels Crouchback's difficulties of flesh
and spirit will prove more interesting - or, at any rate,
more real. So far, the author has echoed, though with
diminished force and virtuosity, some of the great themes
developed in Ford Madox Ford's superb failure, 'Parade's
End.'

136.   DELMORE SCHWARTZ, 'PARTISAN REVIEW'

3 November 1952, 703-4

Delmore Schwartz (1913-66), American poet, short-story
writer and critic, editor of 'Partisan Review', 1943-7,
and poetry editor of 'New Republic', 1955-7, was the author
of 'Genesis, Book 1' (1943) and 'Summer Knowledge' (1959).

...If one had no other information on the subject, the
beginning of Evelyn Waugh's 'Men at Arms' would convince
one that the Second World War occurred solely to rescue
Englishmen from boredom and decadence. But if one happens
to read next Angus Wilson's 'Hemlock and After', one begins
to see what Waugh has in mind, and one begins to be afraid
that so far as any redemption of England was at stake, the
war may well have been waged in vain. And it is only when
one reads Patrick O'Brian's 'Testimonies' (1) that it becomes apparent how Waugh and Wilson have permitted their
subject matter to cripple their point of view and sensibility.
    Waugh's ... hero, moved by a noble patriotism, has
returned from a life of expatriate idleness in Italy to
fight for England. His patriotism is as foreign and
strange to virtually everyone he encounters as a formula in
relativity physics, and the view that the war is a lark or
a racket prevails. When, after great difficulty, he succeeds in getting into an ancient and famous regiment, his
fellow soldiers turn out to be disoriented eccentrics who
behave in the course of their training as if they were
elder statesmen in a lunatic asylum. The point of the
satire, if there is a point, is that everyone but the hero

is silly, inane and asinine. The hero, by virtue of his
nobility, is also silly in that he is naive, always at a
loss and utterly ineffectual. Waugh appears to be saying
to the reader: I see the stupidity, foolishness and triviality of human beings just as much as you do, but I draw
a different conclusion; human beings are ridiculous without religious belief and they are just as ridiculous when
they are possessed by religious belief, but at least when
they are truly religious, they have a touching, pathetic,
bewildered quality which makes possible a little compassion amid one's overwhelming contempt. If this is all that
Catholicism means to Waugh, then any old religion and any
old myth would serve as well and as vainly; and since it is
all the meaning it has in his recent novels, no great fantasy is required to read them as the fiction of an *agent
provocateur* in the pay of a society for the propagation of
atheism. And apart from one scene in which the hero seeks
to seduce his former wife, the wonderful bounce and *brio*,
the daring and the gaiety of the books which made Waugh
justly famous, have been succeeded by what can only be
described as a bored titter....

Note

1   Published in England as 'Three Bear Witness' (Secker &
    Warburg, 1952).

137.   JOSEPH FRANK, 'NEW REPUBLIC'

10 November 1952, 19-20

Evelyn Waugh's latest novel illustrates the unhappy predicament of a satirist who has fallen in love with his
subject. The best of Waugh's earlier books - 'Decline and
Fall,' 'Vile Bodies,' 'Put Out More Flags' - were the creations of a caustic, though by no means pitiless, observer
of the eccentricities of English upper-class society. He
recorded its bored disintegration with inimitable wit, considerable comic invention, and an unrivaled gift for turning English small talk into revelatory dialogue. But then
the Second World War came along, and Waugh, like everybody
else, has never been quite the same since. The war turned
his weaklings and wastrels into heroic fighting men; it
gave a focus to their lives and a meaning to their actions;

somehow, it re-established their contact with all that was
vital in their ancestral traditions.

Up to the present, this theme of war-time reinvigora-
tion has appeared only fitfully in Waugh's pages (for
example at the end of 'Put Out More Flags' or, somewhat
more boldly, in 'Brideshead Revisited'.... 'Men at Arms'
... is a curiously hybrid affair. The claws of the satirist
are so well sheathed that nobody really gets scratched; and
the crispness of the Waugh manner cannot conceal a spiritual affinity with the more maudlin aspects of Kipling,
G.A. Henty (1) - and the movie version of the 'Lives of a
Bengal Lancer.' (2)

Waugh's hero, Guy Crouchback, is what the French would
call a *pauvre type* and the Americans a sad sack. Nothing
had ever gone right for Guy: his family had lost most of
its money, he had never been much at school, his wife had
inexplicably gone off with another man, and even the uncritical Italians among whom he lived did not think him *sim-
patico*. It is typical that when Guy refrains from sin, like
a good Catholic, it should be 'a habit of dry and negative
chastity which even the priests felt to be unedifying.'
The war, however, gives Guy a shot in the arm, and after
some false starts he becomes an officer-candidate in the
... Halberdiers....

Regimental tradition, Guy finds, suits him.... Nothing
makes him quite so ecstatic as the sacred and solemn ritual
of an officers' mess; and he feels only shame, if not contempt, for those cheeky sons of the middle classes who
would much prefer to stay at home with their wives. Reflecting on his sudden access to bliss, Guy realizes 'that in
the last few weeks he had been experiencing something he
had missed in boyhood, a happy adolescence.'

This last phrase is exactly right: nor has it, as one
might suspect, an ironical edge. From time to time, Guy
remembers with some amusement the stories of Army life he
had read as a boy - but Waugh does not use these flashbacks for satirical effect. Guy's experiences in the Halberdiers do not diverge from, indeed they reinforce, his
boyhood idealizations. All one really needs is a stiff
upper lip: no other scale of values is even fleetingly tolerated. Happily, there still *are* occasions when the old,
irreverent Waugh peeps out behind the regimental full-dress.
But these are few and far between, and, for the most part,
the book may be described as a discreet orgy of adolescent
sentiment.

At the close, Guy is winging back to home and court-
martial for several offenses of which he is entirely innocent. No doubt he will get his promotion and command, and
acquit himself nobly (but modestly) as befits an English

officer and gentleman. But what is the hapless Waugh reader
to do while all of this is going on? Guy, too, paraphrases
the book slightly [when he] asks at one point whether God
really concerns Himself with the well-being of the English
Catholic aristocracy. God probably does because, as Heine
once remarked of forgiveness, 'c'est son métier.' But it is
not, I think, the métier of Evelyn Waugh. I should like,
therefore, to propose a judicious division of labor. Let
God look after the well-being of the Anglo-Catholic aristocracy, and let Evelyn Waugh, to the continuing delight of
his readers, return to their follies and their foibles.

Notes

1 Henty (1832-1902) wrote historical novels for boys.
2 Francis Yeats Brown(1886-1944), 'Bengal Lancer' (1930).

'The Holy Places'

1952 (US edition, 1953)

138.   UNSIGNED REVIEW, 'TIMES LITERARY SUPPLEMENT'

23 January 1953, 52

In 1951 Mr. Waugh was invited by the magazine 'Life' to
revisit Jerusalem and to write an article on his impressions. The article is now republished, with the addition of
a short preface and a chapter on St. Helena and the Holy
Cross. This last gives a charming, if historically dubious,
picture of a simple and virtuous old Empress, whose finding
of the Cross revolutionized not only the religious thought
but even, it seems, the artistic achievements of the age.
    The main chapter, called The Defence of the Holy Places,
is an able piece of Catholic journalism. Mr. Waugh has many
wise and sad comments to make on the present state of the
Holy Places, on Zionism, on the United Nations and on
modern scepticism. But he sees some hope for Christendom so
long as all the chapels and buildings round the Holy Sepulchre remain under one roof.... He suggests that the United
Nations should honour its undertaking to internationalize
Jerusalem and should itself see to the urgent task of
repairing the Holy Sepulchre, restoring it as far as possible to its condition before the fire of 1808. Mr. Waugh's
history is at times oversimplified and a little facile,
especially with regard to the Great Schism and the Eastern
Churches, and he underrates the Byzantine restoration of
the eleventh century, which was responsible for the Rotunda
and the Tomb. His style, though smooth and easy to read,
has one or two tiresome tricks, especially in his use of
the pronoun 'one'. The sentence 'One has been at the core
of one's religion' sums up neither elegantly nor convincingly a genuine religious experience. But the whole essay
leaves a vivid impression of the tragedy of the Holy City.

The book is beautifully produced. The wood-engravings by
Mr. Reynolds Stone are pleasant but unimpressive.

139.   D[OUGLAS] W[OODRUFF], 'TABLET'

7 February 1953, 110-11

John Douglas Woodruff (1897-1978), Catholic journalist,
publisher and historian, was on the editorial staff of 'The
Times', 1926-38; Editor of the 'Tablet', 1936-67; Chairman
of Associated Catholic Newspapers from 1953; and Deputy
Chairman of Burns and Oates (publishers), 1948-62. He was
author of 'Plato's American Republic' (1926), 'The Tich-
borne Claimant' (1957) and 'Church and State in History'
(1961). Woodruff was a powerful friend in the world of
Catholic letters. It was he who first introduced Waugh to
the Oxford Union in 1922 and secured him the post of
'Times' correspondent in Abyssinia in 1930. He replaced the
irascible Ernest Oldmeadow (see headnote to No. 44) as
Editor of the 'Tablet'. Waugh and he remained friends
although they saw little of one another in later life.

This slender volume is an example of the fine printing, in
14-point Pilgrim type, of the Queen Anne Press. It contains, in less than forty pages, much more matter than
could be expected if the writer were anyone else. Few men
can say more in a short space than Mr. Waugh, and his
exceptional gift for the concise and illuminating epithet,
his feeling for shades of expression, is here displayed to
the full, in writing informed by the deep feeling to which
the fate of the Holy Places moves him.
    At the outset, under the heading Work Abandoned, he
tells us how, some twenty years ago, he entertained the
idea of a great literary life's work, successive volumes
illustrating England's connection with the Holy Land, told
through the strangely diverse lives of the Empress Helena,
Richard Lion-Heart, Stratford Canning, and Gordon. These
volumes will not be written. The record of England towards
the Holy Land and the Holy Places in the last twenty years
makes the theme a bitter one. But the idea kept its hold
through all the vicissitudes of the war, and it did result,
two years ago, in the remarkable imaginative reconstruction
of the strange story of St. Helena, mother of Constantine.
This work was generally acclaimed, but the author feels

that he 'failed in most cases to communicate' his
enthusiasm.

In the past a great many churches, up and down Christendom, were dedicated to St. Helena - she even has a somewhat notable island - but she is not inside the very small
circle of the saints to whom there is any living Catholic
devotion, for such saints are few indeed, beyond the Holy
Family; St. Francis, St. Teresa, and hardly any others,
in a generation with an exceptionally impoverished idea of
the Communion of Saints and caring so little about the members of the glorious company whom the Church herself never
forgets through the liturgical year. There is also today a
revulsion against the older hagiology, with all the liberties it took, which extends to all imaginative reconstruction, even where, as with most of the early saints, they can
only be known imaginatively. The strangeness of the vocation of Constantine's mother, the fidelity with which she
fulfilled it, her life as an example that there is some
unique individual thing which each Christian soul is created and called to do, captured Mr. Waugh's imagination. He
reprints here, as the first of the two essays that make up
this volume, that written to explain the dramatized broadcast version of 'Helena', (1) setting out candidly how very
few the known facts are. It was not altogether surprising
that some critics found the pagan setting over-elaborated,
by comparison with the spiritual development. (On one occasion a much regretted injustice was done to the work in
this journal). But the lack of appeal of St. Helena as a
saint in the twentieth century comes also because she was
the great saint of relics, of the major relics of the passion. The Church is profoundly relic-minded, but that is
not the spirit of the age, and since the beginning of the
Reformation honour to relics has been far removed from the
spirit of Protestant Christianity. Hence it is that neither
Protestant America nor Protestant Britain, in the last
thirty years where they have held the power over Palestine,
has really cared at all about the fate of the greatest
relics of all, the Holy Sepulchre and the other Holy Places.

Mr. Waugh, like Mr. Chesterton before him, saw beyond
the poverty and acrimony of the Christians there, and was
impressed in particular by the fidelity with which, century
after difficult century, the Franciscans, 'with absolute
singleness of purpose since 1291', have kept the Custody of
the Holy Places. Mr. Waugh writes of the Franciscans:

They have learnt to avoid attachment to their own
transient structures. Indeed, they seem positively to
relish the demolition of buildings which anywhere else
would be patiehtly preserved. Give them the chance to

put up something brand new, strong and convenient, and
the Franciscans of the Custody jump at it. They have no
sentiment except the highest. No association later than
the Apostles interests them. There is only one period
for them, the years of Our Lord. It is not for us to
look askance. They have had small help from art connoisseurs during their age-long, lonely sentry-duty.

Mr. Waugh is definite about what should be done with the
church of the Holy Sepulchre: the building should be recon-
structed as it was in 1800. He is against the grandiose
plan sponsored by the Apostle Delegate [sic] in Jerusalem
for an ambitious scheme of town clearance which would involve the destruction of two Mosques to make a Christian
centre where all existing bodies would have their churches.
About this he drily remarks: 'No one, I think, regards this
undertaking as practicable; few as desirable. Apart from
any aesthetic objection - and there are many - there is the
supreme objection that this immense erection would be in
effect a monument to the divisions of the Church.' The
Franciscan may take such divisions for permanent, 'but
there is still all the difference between a quarrelsome
family who still share one home and jostle one another on
the stairs and one which has coldly split up into separate,
inaccessible households.'
  Meanwhile, only the Holy See continues to call for the
internationalization of the Holy Places; and they lie on a
frontier which runs through Jerusalem, while the Government of Israel, although it may awaken to the tourist possibilities, at present makes Israel one of the costliest
and least comfortable of countries, where pilgrimage is
really pilgrimage in the old, hard sense. No English Christian whose heart was lifted up when Allenby entered the
sacred city on foot in 1917 imagined that the later story
was to be such a wretched business, or so inglorious a
chapter in our history.

Note

1 Broadcast in December 1951; see Sykes, pp. 344-5.

'Love Among the Ruins'

1953 (no US edition)

140. CYRIL CONNOLLY, 'SUNDAY TIMES'

31 May 1953, 5

One of the oldest plots in the world is the story of the
two lovers who are persecuted by the State. In the past the
Caliph and the King were reactionary; an element of satire
is introduced when the State is progressive. Mr. Huxley's
'Brave New World' was one of the first novels in which the
old-fashioned, old-world lovers rebel against the new type
of authority. Orwell's '1984' is another and Mr. Waugh's
'The Loved One' a third. The Welfare State provides most
writers with an indispensable Aunt Sally. 'The Loved One',
however, really was about love and contained just enough
genuine passion to illuminate the theme of death and so
constitute a rather cold and formal, yet still genuine work
of art. 'Love Among the Ruins' has no erotic content; it is
pure slapstick, and depends for its success on the neatness
of its paradox and the brilliance of its timing. One must
judge such a book as if it were a film sequence or a scene
in a revue.

Now in order to achieve this timing and sustain this
paradox (in a Welfare State only prisoners are happy,
people queue for euthanasia, abstract art is official art
and so on) an author must digest his own stomach so completely that his anger and loyalties, indigation and regrets, are invisible to the naked eye. One trace of emotion
and the illusion will vanish, the magician in his tails is
gone and an embittered old schoolmaster is in his place. On
the whole, by great verbal elegance, Mr. Waugh has succeeded; he whirls a malacca sword-stick and beheads one
with a back-hander:

> The director was an elderly man called Dr. Beamish,
> a man whose character had been formed in the nervous
> thirties, now much embittered, like many of his contem-
> poraries, by the fulfilment of his early hopes.

Or like this:

> All her possessions had come from her mother, nearly
> enough of them to furnish the little room - a looking
> glass framed in porcelain flowers, a gilt, irregular
> clock. She and Miles drank their sad, officially com-
> pounded coffee out of brilliant, riveted cups.
>   'It reminds me of prison,' said Miles when he was
> first admitted there.
>   It was the highest praise he knew.

Or again:

> 'My father and mother hanged themselves in their own
> backyard with their own clothes-line. Now no one will
> lift a finger to help himself. There is something wrong
> in the system. Plastic. There are still rivers to drown
> in, trains - every now and then - to put your head
> under; gas-fires in some of the huts. The country is
> full of the natural resources of death, but everyone
> has to come to us.'

Waugh the satirist hates politicians (Eden and Bevan
are in coalition when his story opens), he hates bureaucracy, model prisons, psycho-analysis, abstract art, func-
tional architecture and *avant garde* poets, and seems never
so happy - believe it or not - as when writing a drawing
by Mr. Osbert Lancaster.

He does, however, reveal two unexpected interests, in
pyromania and in bearded ladies. It is the heroine's beard
which lures Miles Plastic into the classical past and en-
franchises him from his compulsory freedom. This is very
odd because a bearded lady is also a central figure in Mr.
Auden's libretto, 'The Rake's Progress', and Messrs. Auden
and Isherwood are connected in my mind with Mr. Waugh's
characters Parsnip and Pimpernel, who are resuscitated for
a parting thrust in 'Love Among the Ruins'.

Now bearded ladies belong to the world of pre-adolesc-
ence; those who find them funny find murder and lunacy
even funnier, and in this respect Mr. Waugh and Mr. Auden
have failed to grow up. Yet they also find them rather
disquieting. In this novelette Mr. Waugh is the little boy
flinging half an old Roman brick at the new policeman.

Reading time: half an hour. Sensation: delight and pleasure - after a while tinged with concern. What a waste of
his time - though not of ours - this elusive pastiche of
himself, this science-hater's science fiction.

141.   UNSIGNED REVIEW, 'TIMES LITERARY SUPPLEMENT'

5 June 1953, 361

Mr. Evelyn Waugh has frequently astonished his large following by his choice of form and subject. Not many of his
closest observers could have prophesied his explorations
into the large-scale novel of sentiment, his later experiment with Christian legend, or his present commitment to
a war trilogy. Between major undertakings, meanwhile, this
avowed disbeliever in the inevitable beneficence of progress has mounted the Time Machine and rocketed off on a
brief excursion into the terrestrial world to come. The
excursion is very brief in literary extent, occupying only
51 pages, and in distance taking us to a future so near
our own day that we are told of one character, 'an elderly
man called Dr. Beamish', that in his hot youth 'he had
raised his fist in Barcelona and had painted abstractedly
for "Horizon"; he had stood beside Spender at great con-
courses of Youth, and written "publicity" for the Last Vice-
roy.' Dr. Beamish is the director of an Euthanasia Centre,
whither the recording demon of Whispering Glades instinctively steers his flight. But though death takes a prominent
place in this story, his dance is not essentially macabre.
    It is hardly necessary to record that Mr. Waugh's vision
of the shape of things to come is very different from that
of H.G. Wells, though he does seem to have borrowed from
that last of the great optimists the useful discovery that
the rate of progress can be safely accelerated, to almost
any speed that may suit the novelist, without the illusion
breaking up. Thus here, within the lifetime of a contributor to 'Horizon', the Christian religion has become a distant memory, and the State has acquired that complete dom-
inion which Mr. Aldous Huxley contemplated as the work of
centuries. With this author's brave new world Mr. Waugh's
'Satellite City' has more things in common, notably a high
significance accorded to community singing, but (though
the Euthanasia Centre itself is paralleled in Bernard
Shaw's Methuselan paradise) the closest ancestor of this
'romance of the near future' is to be found in George
Orwell's '1984'. The later contrivers of Utopia have had
to take note of a lesson of practical Utopia-making which
was not foreseen by pioneers of the Wells and Huxley
schools, namely, that when translated into material existence these idealistic societies tend to break down. The
loathsome 'airstrip' of Orwell's tragic imagination was a
place of makeshift repair and short-term distraction. In
Satellite City the great overall plan is in a similar state
of constant failure, yet Mr. Waugh's township could not

have been harmoniously situated in Orwell territory because
of a certain irresistible jollity surrounding the ghastly
life conducted within its walls. We are not in the world of
the Loved One, but of Mr. Pennyfeather's decline and fall.

In his first period Mr. Waugh captured the good will of
his readers by tackling subjects of much complexity, notably prison conditions, with the aid of imagination alone.
Certain of his admirers have recklessly wanted him to continue the invention of such daydreams free of the con-
structions of experience, even after he has achieved things
far surpassing his youthful success. Yet for all their
narrowness these admirers have some sense on their side:
the enchantments in which greatly gifted youth finds expression are worth recapturing at the expense of almost any
trouble, providing the recapture is authentic, although, in
the nature of things, this can hardly be. But here the miracle has happened, if only for a moment, in this flight to a
Not-Yet-Perhaps-Never Land. The wings of the imagination are
freed; the observation of experience is only used to streng-
then fantasy. A short quotation may prove the point:

> There had been a strike among the coal-miners and Eu-
> thanasia had been at a standstill. Now the necessary
> capitulations had been signed, the ovens glowed again,
> and the queue at the patients' entrance stretched half-
> way round the dome. Dr. Beamish squinted at the waiting
> crowd through the periscope and said with some satisfac-
> tion: 'It will take months to catch up on the waiting-
> list now. We shall have to start making a charge for the
> service. It's the only way to keep down the demand.'...

Many adventures into the future have come to grief through
the wish to combine non-existent worlds with literary creation of character. Nothing so unlikely to succeed is attempted by this practised hand. The hero-villain, the worthy Dr.
Beamish, and even the abominable Minister of Rest and Culture, are drawn in two dimensions. There is a love affair,
but not such as to make impossible appeals to sympathy, and
there are terrible acts of incendiarism and murder at which
we laugh helplessly. It should be mentioned, perhaps, that
the heroine has 'a long, silken, corn-gold beard'.

142.   CHRISTOPHER HOLLIS, 'TABLET'

27 June 1953, 563

Maurice Christopher Hollis (1902-77) was a Catholic publisher, historian, biographer, critic, writer on politics

and Conservative M.P. for Devizes, 1945-55. He was author
of 'Dr. Johnson' (1928), 'Thomas Moore' (1934), 'A Study
of George Orwell' (1956), 'The Mind of Chesterton' (1969)
and 'Oxford in the Twenties' (1976). Hollis was a close
friend of Waugh from their time at Oxford together and was
a West Country neighbour later in life at Mells, near
Frome. His autobiography 'The Seven Ages' (1974) and
'Oxford in the Twenties' recall his early memories of the
novelist. He also wrote the 'Evelyn Waugh' booklet in the
British Council series (1954).

There are two types of character to be found in Mr. Waugh's
books - what may be called the two-dimensional and three-
dimensional. There are the characters of whom Mr. Waugh
does not pretend to give us a full picture. They are
brought into the story in order that they may say something or may do something, and there is no attempt to build
up a rounded picture of them, to make them seem like real
people for whose sufferings we can have sympathy. Thus none
of us can be expected to shed tears for the death of Mr.
Prendergast or of Agatha Runcible, as we might shed them
for that of John Last in 'A Handful of Dust'. Mr. Waugh
has put his explanation and defence of this kind of creation into the mouth of John Plant, the detective-story writer of 'Work Suspended':

   The algebra of fiction must reduce its problems to
   symbols if they are to be soluble at all. I am shy of a
   book commended to me on the grounds that the 'characters are alive.' There is no place in literature for a
   live man, solid and active. At best the author may
   maintain a kind of Dickensian menagerie, where his
   characters live behind bars, in darkness, to be liberated twice nightly for a brief gambol under the arc
   lamps; in they come to the whip crack, dazzled, deaf-
   ened and doped, tumble through their tricks and scamper
   out again, to the cages behind, in which the real business of life, eating and mating, is carried on out of
   sight of the audience. 'Are the lions really alive?'
   'Yes, lovey.' 'Will they eat us up?' 'No, lovey, the
   man won't let them' - that is all the reviewers mean as
   a rule when they talk of 'life.' The alternative, classical expedient is to take the whole man and reduce him
   to a manageable abstraction. Set up your picture plain,
   fix your point of vision, make your figure twenty foot
   high or the size of a thumb-nail, he will be life-size
   on your canvas; hang your picture in the darkest corner,
   your heaven will still be its one sound source of light.
   Beyond these limits lie only the real trouser buttons

and the crepe hair with which the futurists used to
adorn their paintings.

Elsewhere, as in 'Brideshead Revisited' and 'Helena', he
has given us rounded three-dimensional characters, whom we
can consider and judge as persons, and perhaps sometimes
there are characters who fall betwixt and between, of whom
we are not quite certain into which class they come, and of
whom those unfamiliar with the milieu of which Mr. Waugh is
writing ask in bewilderment, 'Are people really like that?'
    In any event, in this little *jeu d'esprit* of which even
the publishers' advertisements proclaim that Mr. Waugh
turned aside from his more serious novel to write it, the
characters are certainly two-dimensional. It is an account
of the experiences of Miles Plastic, a modern man, brought
up in the England of the near future in the total ignorance, which our educational system imposes, of the traditions and morals from which we have sprung....
    There is nothing new about writing histories of the
future. The Victorians were always at it. But, of course,
the great difference here between the nineteenth and the
twentieth centuries was that the nineteenth-century authors - William Morris, Tennyson, Bellamy - always imagined
that the future would be better than the present. None of
the authors of the twentieth century imagines that, and Mr.
Waugh is only one of a considerable company in foreseeing
it as dreary and inhumane. Yet he has his own vision. He is
looking to a much nearer future than George Orwell or Mr.
Aldous Huxley. They look to a future that comes after drastic revolution - atomic destruction or the victory of 'the
Party.' Mr. Waugh asks us to accept no more than a Coalition between the two existing political parties, the Eden-
Bevan Coalition, and the triumph which he forsees as dominant is not the triumph of the Marxian revolution but only
that of the Welfare State.
    This leads to a very important contrast between Mr.
Waugh's future and that of other authors. Whereas they all
look forward to a future in which the nation's new masters
are far more savage than those of today in the physical
sufferings which they inflict, in Mr. Waugh's future criminals receive every comfort and the physical suffering of
society is the suffering which the unrebuked criminals
impose on their fellow citizens....
    So, if it be true that we are moving towards a society
in which all memory of our religion and our traditions has
perished, I think that that is more likely to be a world of
'1984' and 'Ape and Essence' and [C.S. Lewis's] 'That Hideous Strength' than of 'Love Among the Ruins'. The society
of 'Love Among the Ruins' has upon it all the marks of a
society in transition. It is not to be believed that the

Minister of Welfare and the Minister of Rest and Culture
would prefer their theories to their love of power, when
they found their power threatened. Such men are not like
that....

The illustrations are admirable, in their ironic recall
of the classical culture which we have lost.

143.   CHRISTOPHER SYKES, FROM 'EVELYN WAUGH. A BIOGRAPHY'

1975, 355

Christopher Sykes (b. 1907) - novelist, short-story writer,
biographer and BBC executive, 1948-68 - is author of 'Innocence and Design' (1936), 'Four Studies in Loyalty' (1946),
'Orde Wingate' (1959), 'Nancy' (1972) and 'Evelyn Waugh. A
Biography' (1975). Mr Sykes was Waugh's friend from the
1930s and accompanied him on the visit to the Holy Land
which resulted in 'The Holy Places'. When working for the
BBC he negotiated the deal securing 'Helena' as a radio
play and other similar 'scoops'.

'In the spring of 1953 Chapman and Hall produced a new book
by Evelyn, 'Love Among the Ruins'. It is a fantasy of the
future, a short nightmare on the subject of the perfected
Socialist state, with the Euthanasia centre as the main
scene of the story. It has had its admirers, but they are
only to be found among the uncritically dedicated or those
who see a depth of meaning in all Evelyn's writings. I see
it as the least book of Evelyn's maturity. Of course there
are some of his inimitable touches, but there [sic] are not
more than touches. It lacks originality, a very rare fault
with Evelyn. It is manifestly based in part on Max Beerbohm's parody of H.G. Wells in 'A Christmas Garland', in
part on his friend George Orwell's '1984', and (if one
can plagiarize oneself) in part on 'The Loved One'. The
central joke is that the heroine has a 'long, silken,
corn-gold beard', and it cannot be maintained that bearded
women are an unused subject for jesting. The poet Parsnip
(vaguely identifiable as W.H. Auden) reappears from 'Put
Out More Flags'. Evelyn derived from this book none of the
artist's satisfaction in accomplishment. '" Love Among the
Ruins"', he wrote to Graham Greene, 'was a bit of nonsense
begun 3 years ago & hastily finished & injudiciously published. But I don't think it quite as bad as most reviewers
do.' The reviewer pack was out and baying for the blood of
Evelyn who seemed for once to be cornered. But if the book
was not quite as bad as the reviewers said, it was nearly.

'Tactical Exercise'

1954 (US edition only)

144. FRANK O'CONNOR, 'NEW YORK HERALD TRIBUNE BOOK REVIEW'

7 November 1954, 10

Frank O'Connor (pseudonym of Michael O'Donovan, 1903-66) was an Irish short-story writer, poet and theatre critic once associated with the Abbey Theatre, Dublin. He was author of 'Bones of Contention' (1936), 'Crab Apple Jelly' (1944), 'Art of the Theatre' (1947), 'More Short Stories' (1954) and his autobiography 'My Father's Son' (unfinished, 1968).

Mr. Evelyn Waugh is one of a group of writers who may, without offense, be described as 'specialized.' His master-pieces deal with the last great binge of European society between the wars, and this society had a certain fruiti-ness which needed only a touch of Mr. Waugh's poetry and wit to blossom into fantasy. One story only in his new col-lection reminds us of Mr. Waugh and his world. That is the long Work Suspended, and already it begins to read like ancient history.

> 'I don't take those political opinions of his too
> seriously, and anyway it's all right to be Communist
> nowadays. Everyone is.'
> 'I'm not.'
> 'Well, I mean all the clever young people.'

The short story was never a form in which Mr. Waugh ex-celled. Apart from Work Suspended, the rest of the book consists of tales rather than stories, and the rigidity of the formula almost suggests that the author had taken a

correspondence course in story-telling with the Metroland
School of Journalism. Bella Fleace Gave a Party and Mr.
Loveday's Little Outing are excellent magazine stories
which commit suicide by falling on their own gimmicks. The
least contrived is Excursion in Reality which deals with
the fate of a writer for films and the Annual Metroland
Award for Tortuousness goes to the title story. In this, a
husband and wife who hate one another see a film in which
a wife who hates her husband spreads the rumor that he is a
somnambulist and then chucks him off a cliff. When the real
wife chooses a cottage on a cliff for their next holiday,
the real husband suspects nothing. On the contrary, he
thinks it very convenient and begins to spread the rumour
that his wife is a somnambulist, only to discover that she
has spread the same story about him. The implacable logic
of the correspondence course requires the still unsuspect-
ing husband to return to the cottage, and the reader can
only feel that he richly deserves his fate when we leave
him, drugged and ready for the final gimmick. Perhaps Mr.
John Collier (1) could have treated such nonsense without
any loss of literary grace, but it returns from its outing
with Mr. Waugh without hide, hair or flesh on it.

Note

1 John Collier is a poet and short story writer (b. 1901),
   and the author of 'No Traveller Returns' (1931) and
   'Fancies and Good Nights' (1951).

145. LOUIS O. COXE, 'NEW REPUBLIC'

8 November 1954, 20-1

Louis Osborne Coxe (b. 1918), American poet, playwright and
critic, is author of 'The Wilderness and Other Poems'
(1958), 'Edward Arlington Robinson' (1962) and 'Passage.
Selected Poems 1943-1978' (1979). His review was entitled
A Protracted Sneer.

This exhibition, in part retrospective, of Mr. Waugh's
short fiction will do little to alter or enhance his reputation. Most of the pieces are reasonably familiar to readers of Mr. Waugh, and the later ones exhibit no startling

developments or departures in theme and mode. It is Waugh,
more or less pure and for the most part fairly simple. If
one were to characterize the stories in general, one might
plump for the heading, Satire.

Yet, is it after all satire as we look to find it in the
work of such writers as Swift, Pope or Fielding? After all
allowances for differences of time, place and action are
duly made, the question persists: what has Mr. Waugh been
writing about all these years, and out of what feelings,
what attitudes, does the fiction come? Curiously, we never
seem to ask such questions as we read say, 'Gulliver's
Travels' or 'Joseph Andrews'; behind every line, informing
the whole, pulsate the rhythms of the authors' hatred or
contempt or scorn, and from the vitality of such feeling
we can catch the sense of love, sometimes perhaps thwarted
or deformed, that gave rise to the invective and the irony.
What do we look for in satire, after the first sneers and
laughter, but some reassurance that the time is indeed
flagitious (like all times) and that here is an author who
in castigating vice knows and clings to virtue - not the
virtue of mankind as it could never be, but as it by nature
was meant to be and can be. The most devastating ironies of
the great satirists come from hatred, surely, yet from a
hatred that for its very vitality must tap the source of
all vitality; namely, love. Vicissitudes of fame and fashion apart, this always, it seems to me, separates the men
from the boys, the writers of satire from the journalists;
Jonson from Fletcher, Congreve from Sheridan, Shaw from Van
Druten. (1) A high moral purpose, working in the fury and
mire of human veins, and the low shifts men stoop to: this
is the double theme of classic comedy and of satire, and
it is just here, I believe that Mr. Waugh fails, for all
his real virtues of wit and style.

When one has said this much, one has in a sense said all,
for certainly satire without moral center is not satire but
at best the protracted sneer, often effective and invariably destructive, if not of its object, at least of its
presumptive aim. Significantly, Work Suspended, the longest
and best of the pieces in this collection, ends in irreso-
lution - it is abandoned, not in the Wildean sense. Though
Mr. Waugh may tell us that this represents a fragment of a
novel he did not care to complete, most of us who have read
the earlier novels would guess that there can be no com-
pletion for such work, only the dissolution of, say,
'Brideshead Revisited' or 'Put Out More Flags.' It would
seem that when Mr. Waugh cannot manage to end his stories
with absurd accidents, as in 'A Handful of Dust,' he must
simply let them go - and for reasons that are, I think,
implicit in the moral view of the writer and the attitudes

he takes towards humanity and individual human beings.

It is all accident, whatever happens. The characters
in the novels are beset by the demon of the absurd; rarely
wholly vicious, they are never credibly decent, nor do
their fates have relevance to anything but the designs of
the demon, who, in Mr. Waugh's eyes, seems to rule affairs
as shabbily as a bureaucrat. Under the very laughter he
provokes, Mr. Waugh seems to provide a current of self-
congratulation that it is not thus with him nor with us -
these people have no business with you and with me. They
may be as contemptible as we wish to make them and none of
the contempt can turn back on us, for it has no real moral
measure, no specific object save that of an amusement we
may hate ourselves for feeling and a disgust that is too
cool to fire a purpose.

The stories included in 'Tactical Exercise' go along
with the novels with due appropriateness. Only the last,
'Love Among the Ruins,' suggests a turn, a new excursion,
on Mr. Waugh's part, and it is the most considerable failure in the volume. The reasons for such failure are various, but what strikes one most vehemently is the inescab-
able inference that the author's subject has passed away
with his world; since the death of Agatha Runcible and the
London of *l'entre deux guerres*, a new society with which
the author neither can cope nor sympathize has arisen, with
the result that such a story as 'Love Among the Ruins' must
fall back on Aldous Huxley and the George Orwell of '1984'
to attain to some sort of point of view. Lacking the somber
fury of Orwell and the levity of Huxley, Mr. Waugh can only
depress us, if that, with his sketch of Miles Plastic and
his world. What oft was thought but usually better expressed, in fine. Perhaps such a story is the logical conclusion of the path Mr. Waugh found himself on at the end
of 'Brideshead Revisited', unlike another humorist, Mr.
P.G. Wodehouse, Mr. Waugh could not let well enough alone,
could not stick to putting out what he could do and taking
his chances of becoming dated or repetitious.

The religious intrusion that so embarrassingly destroys
'Brideshead Revisited' does not recur in 'Love Among the
Ruins' yet for the reader acquainted with the novel some of
its shadow falls across the pages of the story. What, one
wants to ask, does the author want? what does he like? Must
we all, to avoid the society the author says must be ours
if we pursue present sources, join his secret society of
pure English Roman Catholics, a club that reminds one more
of some sort of cross between the Knights of Columbus and
Skull and Bones than it does of an ecumenical church? What
bothers Mr. Waugh about the society of contemporary England
is, quite frankly, the people. He does not like them. I

dare say Swift did not like the people about Queen Anne's
court nor Pope the dunces that filled his world, yet these
latter two had a firm moral base from which to rear their
satiric structures; their hatred of the licentious and
depraved serves even today to remind us of how far short
we fall - not of the ideal but of the appropriate. Mr.
Waugh has no power so to remind because he has neither love
for life nor attachment to places and persons, only a vague
hagiology, a hankering after some lost innocence, a time
when everyone loved Beethoven quartets and could tell good
cognac from cheap brandy. The often-flung accusation of
snobbery falls short of the mark, I think; snobbery is
often a vital quality in a writer; it literally forces him
to be on the make. But in Mr. Waugh's stories, as in the
novels, one feels mostly weariness and the frail lamenta-
tion of the poor in spirit.

This is, of course, largely Mr. Waugh's chosen subject,
yet what can he resort to finally to *show* this but expressive form? The brilliance of style is with these stories
still (it is notably absent in 'Love Among the Ruins'),
the power to make of a bald narrative something depres-
singly vivid, as in the title story - a spare idiom that
hits unerringly on details that suggest the theme of ruin,
waste and dispossession. Yet now, after the war, the author
finds little that is funny in all this. It comes too close
to home; the exposure of a ruined society becomes an exposure of the self, real or imagined, and the comfort of
ironic understatement rings coldly in the ear. What can a
man do but look for someone or something to blame?
Unfortunately, Mr. Waugh allots the blame exclusively to
'modern' ways - bureaucracy, centralization, psychologizing.
The plight of Miles Plastic in 'Love Among the Ruins' may
well be an example of the author's prescience, but it has
all been done before and for the reader it is simply not
enough to be told that all these things are bad; he wants
to be moved to feel their essential badness. To do this
Mr. Waugh would have to abandon that weary, cynical style
and put passion on. The expressive form eventually defeats
itself, and though we recognize the truth in much that the
author has to say, it has become very nearly a matter of
indifference.

Perhaps of all disappointments this book brings, the
chief may lie in our sense that there seems to be nowhere
for Mr. Waugh to go. The stories represent work done over
a period of twenty-one years, and it is curious how little
the focus widens or sharpens. Always the same good ear for
dialogue, the same sharp eye for revealing detail, the same
sensitivity to the pompous and the fake. Such gifts are
rare and Mr. Waugh employs them fully in many cases. Who

nowadays can see the type so clearly under the singular? As a writer of a certain kind of comedy, Mr. Waugh belongs to an eminent English tradition - Jonson, Wycherley, Congreve, Shaw - but he has had the misfortune to live in an age hostile to artifice and style. The theater would have been the proper home for his characters and plots, but fiction is today's literature. An aristocratic society would have patronized such comedy but we are all middle-class. No work is harder to write than comedy of manners and none more difficult to apply to life, particularly in periods remote from that of the author. If Mr. Waugh's work has already begun to obsolesce, not manners but what manners reveal is at fault. For comedy of manners, like satire, has a moral base and without that there is nothing but humor, then quaintness, and finally nothing.

Note

1   John Van Druten (1901-57), lawyer turned playwright, was the author of 'Bell, Book and Candle' (1951) and 'I am a Camera' (1952, based on Christopher Isherwood's Berlin stories).

'Officers and Gentlemen'

1955

146. NORMAN SHRAPNEL, 'MANCHESTER GUARDIAN'

1 July 1955, 4

Norman Shrapnel (b. 1912), journalist and author, has been
reporter, theatre critic and book reviewer for the Guardian
since 1947 and the paper's Parliamentary Correspondent,
1958-75. He is author of 'A View of the Thames' (1977) and
'The Performer: Politics as Theatre' (1978).

The set-piece of blazing London with which 'Officers and
Gentlemen' opens has a fierce gaiety that could have come
from no other pen now at work; it is merry as the night is
long, and as funny as hell. 'On the pavement opposite
Turtle's a group of progressive novelists in fireman's uniform were squirting a little jet of water into the morning-
room.' Turtle's is doomed; its whisky store is running down
the gutters of St James's; but it was never, as somebody
consolingly remarks, much of a club. Not by the measure of
Mr Evelyn Waugh's characters, a private army in which a
lieutenant (though not necessarily an air-marshal) may be
run home by the commander-in-chief, or taken to lunch by a
casually met young woman with oceanic eyes and find the
table glittering with eminent nicknames.
 The early high spirits fade into the mist of a Scottish
island where commandos are training, and the rest of the
book plunges us into the chaos of Crete. By that time Mr
Waugh's severest critics will have ceased to call him a
snob, unless it is to be defined as something between a
snarl and a sob. His fictional war aims are serious. Physical and moral confusion go hand in boot, or foot in glove.
Mr Waugh is angrily deploring what he sees as the phase of

ambiguity and confused loyalties. In the day of the Russo-
German alliance we knew, presumably, where we were. The
blur on the scutcheon is something he finds it hard to
tolerate; he laments the passing of the world where the
demands of honour were clear, however deadly, under blue
skies. Disorganisation is more than merely a subject for
his fierce brand of farce; it is an expression of spiritual
perversity. Who but Mr Waugh would observe that the military catch-phrase about putting someone 'in the picture'
had come into vogue just at the time 'when all the painters of the world had finally abandoned lucidity'? Certainly it is something that he himself has never abandoned.
There is no blur or blot in this writing. Its clarity must
be taken as a sermon in itself.

Those who read Mr Waugh purely for his comic qualities
will find these working, like the hoses of the progressive
novelists, in spurts rather than a steady flow. He has
sacrificed the two memorable characters of 'Men at Arms',
the companion volume which this book completes; the dedicated Apthorpe is a memory and the ferocious Ritchie-Hook
a shadow. We are driven back upon the hero. The essentials
about Guy Crouchback are Roman Catholicism, innocence, and
well-bred unsuccess. In order, presumably, to achieve the
maximum deflation he had to enter the war at an improbable
pitch of unworldly enthusiasm. He is a 1914 rather than a
1939 figure. A middle-aged man tilting into that far more
sober conflict so unstained by the world, and buoyed by
so romantic an expectation, is automatically a special
case. A writer must build himself the hero he needs; but if
it were any part of Mr Waugh's aim to win sympathy as well
as admiration, he might seek his key material in less exclusive circles.

147.   CHRISTOPHER SYKES, 'TIME AND TIDE'

2 July 1955, 871-2

Critics are more at ease with reliable churners than with
masters of variety and surprise such as Mr Evelyn Waugh. As
a result, when the author of 'Decline and Fall' and 'Vile
Bodies' evolved into the more serious novelist of 'A Handful of Dust' many literary judges found themselves disconcerted. (Some of them got their own back in the Hundred
Best Books Exhibition.) (1) When Mr Waugh returned to the
'Vile Bodies' manner in 'Put Out More Flags', they moaned

that he was not following up his more solid achievement, and when he surprised his admirers with a long book, written without his usual economy but with almost Thackerayean profusion, many leaders of thought accused him of debasement and sentimentalism. When he wrote a historical novel about St Helena, they wrung their hands. He cannot fit easily into any critical measure, and by taking his superb literary gifts a giddy dance, he does not give critics time to pin him down. Few would deny that he is among the half-dozen best living English authors, nor that he is one of the most grumbled against.

The present book is the second and concluding part of the war saga which opened in 'Men at Arms', but it can be enjoyed without reference to the first part from which it shows considerable divergence in mood and to which it is only lightly attached. 'Men at Arms' was in large part a consciously restrained and realistic picture of army life, which might have been even dull at times without the outrageous central figure of Apthorpe, one of Mr Waugh's finest inventions. In contrast 'Officers and Gentlemen' is one enormous firework; a wild extravaganza on the most fantastic side of military life, that of the 'private armies'. This is recognizably the work of the man who wrote 'Black Mischief', but for comedy, enormity and success in ambitious effect, it leaves the Abyssinian saga far behind.

As befits extravaganza, the plot is elaborate and, except for the hero, there are no normal characters among the principals. There are moments when the violence and remorselessness of continual farce must leave every reader momentarily fogged, and there are audacities which must make many even of the friendliest critics take in their breath. Of these audacities the most hazardous is the way the story opens in farce, and then sets out in the spirit of farce towards the horrors and tragedy of battle and defeat. The final subject is our disastrous attempt to defend Crete, and the British rout in that island. A primary rule of style is broken: farce is mixed with comedy, with tragi-comedy, and even with tragedy. Well, the only question worth asking is whether this matters. It does not matter a bit. The result is abundantly successful.

The book will probably strike many readers as being fantasy absolute, but in fact this caricature of life in the private armies is closer to its model than is easily suspected. All war is dreamlike but freebooter warfare is like nothing else on earth. A charge which can be brought against 'Officers and Gentlemen' is that by making the civilian background fantastic, especially in the Scots castle whose interior 'owed its decoration more to the taxidermist than to the sculptor or painter', the author

gives his reader no hint of where something of reliable
record begins. Who cares in the midst of so much entertainment? Another charge which is often levelled against
Mr Waugh is that he is excessively partial to the upper
classes, treating them with tolerant humour while reserving
his flail [for] what are now prudishly called the 'lower income brackets'. In this book he is merciless to all his
models, turning the comic muse to her proper duty of all-
devouring assault, and only Mr Waugh's own personal regiment, 'the Halberdiers', escapes all harshness of ridicule.
The book ends on a Kipling note as the hero returns to his
unit from his Cretan ordeal and submits with a joyful heart
to being resmartened on the square.

Unlike 'Men at Arms' there is no great dominating figure
such as was provided by Apthorpe. Instead there is a team
of wild men who dominate different parts of the book by
turn. Captain Ivor Claire who is discovered

> reclined upon a sofa, his head enveloped in a turban of
> lint, his feet shod in narrow velvet slippers embroi-
> dered in gold thread with his monogram. He was nursing
> a white pekingese; beside him stood a glass of white
> liqueur;

the hairdresser Mactavish, alias Gustave, alias Trimmer,
who obtains an MC under a total misapprehension and becomes
the hero of the nation, so that men say 'We've got no
Junker class in this country, thank God'; the Laird of Mugg
and his Nazified daughter whose subversive pamphlets set
Colonel Marchpole the official spy-catcher (all too briefly
glimpsed) on to an ingenious false trail. In this memorable
fellowship perhaps no figure is more rewarding than that of
the orderly room clerk Major-Corporal Ludovic who is great
with literary genius. His *pensées* are frequently quoted,
and the measure of Mr Waugh's stature as a comedian is that
these jottings really are somewhat impressive for all their
absurdity. You feel here, and in other places, that the
novelist's inventions have been given the power to take on
independent life.

Note

1   Waugh broadcast a talk, 'A Progressive Game' (Third Pro-
    gramme, 17 May 1951), in which he had great fun with the
    National Book League's exhibition, then open in Albe-
    marle Street, London. He complained of the unrepresenta-
    tive nature of the selection as a reflection of the
    authors' talents and interests. Mr Sykes is presumably

making the same point here with regard to the selection
from Waugh's opus: only 'Decline and Fall' was chosen.
The talk was published in the 'Listener', 31 May 1951,
872-3; cf. Sykes, pp. 346-7.

148.   CYRIL CONNOLLY, 'SUNDAY TIMES'

3 July 1955, 5

'Men at Arms' was announced as the first work of a trilogy,
but now Mr. Waugh tells us that his new novel completes the
cycle: 'The two books constitute a whole.' I was not a great
admirer of 'Men at Arms' and I had been looking forward to
its successor in order to make amends.

I am disappointed. Except for the last hundred pages,
which are a magnificent description of modern warfare (in
this case the fiasco in Crete) and the opening account of
the Blitz, it suffers from a benign lethargy which renders
it very slow reading, and which affects both treatment and
subject.

The subject is one of considerable difficulty; officers without men. We do not witness the great battles and
deployment of armies which enliven war novels; we see only
training camps and the officers' mess and one blurred and
mapless conflict; everything depends on human relationships. It is these relationships which seem to me the chief
weakness of the book. They are too superficial to sustain
the structure.

I am not suggesting that the officers of a Commando unit
should be a Kafkaesque nest of enthralling neurotics who
merit a deeper analysis; the point is that they are a group
of efficient and adventurous young men whose real life
stems from their peace-time activities. We see only one
side of them in relation to the war-effort. Thus part of
Mr. Waugh's problem is to describe a glamorous aristocrat
who at the testing point disobeys orders and runs for
safety, symbolising the silver-spoon element of the English
upper-class which has lost the traditional instinct to die
obeying orders. This character, whose disobedience has had
a profound effect on Mr. Waugh, is not drawn fully enough
to make his fall dramatic. It seems not much more than a
bit of gossip to the average reader. We should really
require to have a picture of the whole submerged peace-
time personality to understand this dereliction of duty in
what appears to be an exquisite military machine.

The dashing colonel is hardly more than a sketch, and
the most stimulating character, Corporal Ludovic, is also
produced against an insufficient background. Friendship
and envy, the two poles of the military life, exist in the
novel but fade against the drabness of the training routine. We need warriors like Pierre and Prince Andrey of
'War and Peace' to animate such stories, men with strong
personalities and a philosophical insight into the processes of war. The general effect in 'Officers and Gentlemen' is of a series of amiable cartoons in which the characters become easily distinguishable but seldom real,
comedians in a series of humorous sketches, actors who
have studied their parts but not read the play.

This brings us to another difficulty: the problem of
humour. Mr. Waugh used to be a satirist, the possessor of
a ferocious private weapon which he did not hesitate to
use. With middle-age his character has changed, mellowing
rather than increasing in bitterness; and in this novel a
new element of amiability, even of what might be called
Christian charity, informs the pages. This I find absolutely delightful but not conducive to satire. The Stoics
were right to condemn pity, if satirists are what is
needed.

We are therefore left with Mr. Waugh's humour, which is
gentle and anecdotal, depending largely on a simple use of
exaggeration, schoolboyish jokes and military paradoxes.
There is even a Scottish fun section. The writing is always
crisp and agreeable; this is one of Mr. Waugh's best-
written books - but goodness, how slow!

The last section is an account of a 'shambles,' the
evacuation of Crete. For this I have nothing but praise.
We are led inexorably forward from comedy to disaster,
order to chaos, and in a few pages, on the tiny canvas of
the Cretan hills and the road to Sphakia, we witness the
change of heart which the rest of Europe experienced at
Dunkirk or Sedan or the Battle of the Bulge. Even as in
the visitors' book of the hotel at Vourtsi, off Nauplia,
the honeymooners' couplets give way to crude drawings of
'Tommy' fleeing from a rain of bombs as the German para-
troopers arrive, so the 'phoney war' expires under the
Stukas. This and the Blitz on St. James's Street with
which the book opens are equal to the best Mr. Waugh has
done.

What of the future? It does not now look as if Mr. Waugh
is likely to change back. In Guy Crouchback he has drawn a
charming and simple narrator, a member of an old Catholic
family impervious to the charm of wealth and whiggery and
never likely to succeed in any profession to the point of
arousing the reader's envy. He is a milder version of Ford

Madox Ford's Tietjens.... (1)
   I suppose Mr. Waugh will develop along the lines of
Maurice Baring and, of course, being so gifted, surpass
him, as this new grace of feeling which animates his prose
takes firmer possession and finds at last a subject worthy
of it.

Note

1 Christopher Tietjens is the central character in Ford's
   trilogy 'Parade's End' ('Some Do Not' (1924), 'No More
   Parades' (1925), 'A Man Could Stand Up' (1926); he epi-
   tomizes the decline of the English gentleman during and
   after the Great War.

149. KINGSLEY AMIS, 'SPECTATOR'

8 July 1955, 56-9

Kingsley Amis (b. 1922) is a novelist, poet and critic. He
has written 'A Frame of Mind' (1953), 'Lucky Jim' (1954),
'Take a Girl Like You' (1960), 'One Fat Englishman' (1963),
'What Became of Jane Austen?' (1970), and is editor of
'Tennyson' (1972) and 'The New Oxford Book of Light Verse'
(1978).

Mr. Evelyn Waugh is continuing to check that farcical vein
which founded his reputation, and upon which, even now, his
status as a novelist may well seem to depend. It is true
that his other, more serious, vein produced his best novel,
'A Handful of Dust', and was going to produce an even
better one, as can be seen from the fragments published as
'Work Suspended'; it also produced his worst, 'Brideshead
Revisited'. Here there were symptoms of radical decline so
numerous and appalling that prognosis almost broke down:
could the author of 'Decline and Fall' really be going to
turn into a kind of storm-trooper from the Sixth at Downside (1) with nothing to offer his audience but a universal
grudge and invocations of a fanciful past? The story 'Love
Among the Ruins' upheld this reading with a fidelity which,
in such small space, put a strain on belief. With the publication of 'Officers and Gentlemen', in spite of the ominous overtones of the title, it is clear that that danger

has passed. The angry bitterness, at any rate, has cooled; the tones of denunciation, though still to be heard, are sad rather than hectoring; a great deal of the baronial wrought-iron, on which one was always barking one's shins at Brideshead, has been torn down. Even farce, in the shape of a ludicrous commando raid which succeeds for every possible wrong reason, is given a mild outing....

If the [elements of the plot seem] discursive and episodic, then they have been truly rendered. (2) The continuation of this saga promised us by Mr. Waugh may perhaps pull them together, but it seems more likely that his plan, like most large-scale plans, countenances a good deal of irrelevance, of including matters which are to justify themselves. I hardly think that this is decisively achieved here. A great deal of what is obviously offered as comedy is not quite funny enough to be that, however promising it may sound in summary. Even during life, Apthorpe was a bit of a bore with his silly field latrine and his aunts, and his shade hangs heavily over the early stages of this volume: the mystery of his 'gear' is not worth solving. The other eccentrics we meet are like him in being models of dull conformity, or alternatively models of cardboard and paste, compared with someone like Colonel Blount of 'Vile Bodies'. And the war scenes in Crete, though rendered vividly and sympathetically enough, are no better, and in places a good deal less passionately realised, than the war scenes of quite a few younger novelists who have not yet hit the headlines of the Sunday book-pages: Mr. Alexander Baron (3) is the obvious example. At one point - the beginning of Fido Hound's crack-up - it does look as if we are in for a dose of that disconcerting blend of the funny, the horrific and the pitiful which is Mr. Waugh's distinctive contribution to the repertory of literary effects. But this episode is typical of the rest of this book, and its predecessor, in that the humour is purely decorative, a stray effect, not something which embodies the author's whole intention.

A ruder way of putting this would be to say that Mr. Waugh is unwilling - I cannot believe that he is unable - to chance his arm and have a go and lay us in the aisles. The reason is not far to seek. If one is really going to satirise army life, in all its confusion and arbitrariness, then sooner or later one has got to start satirising the army itself, which contains in its nature confusion and arbitrariness just as much as order and custom. Mr. Waugh's attitude to the army is much too serious to permit that. Although it is often risky to assume that a novelist shares his hero's feelings, Mr. Waugh participates in Guy Crouchback's cause with an intensity which recalls the effect of

complete fusion in 'Brideshead Revisited'. If Guy's
standards are too high for the modern world, they share
this feature, it is implied, with every other kind of traditional (i.e., real) standard, and these days a lack of
worldly wisdom, even a degree of naivety, can only be
admirable. The two volumes are certainly packed with infer-
ential approval for every kind of regimental usage, ceremonial and idiosyncrasy: the almost fanatically exclusive
Corps of Halberdiers seem to spend most of their working
day showing how differently they do things from other
units. Some of all this will draw an embarrassed grin, as
when we hear of new subalterns being sconced for mis-
management of the snuff-engine after dinner in Mess; others
will arouse mild incredulity, such as the discovery that
the frightful Brigadier Ritchie-Hook, with his taste for
decapitating enemy sentries, is not to be taken as the
caricature of the 'mad major' type he seemed at first, but
is a figure we are expected to admire. Admirable as a soldier he may perhaps be, though he conspicuously lacks that
consideration for subordinates which, so I was taught, is
an indispensable mark of the good officer; admirable as a
person he certainly is not.

Reverence for the army is to be expected from a Waugh
hero who derives from Tony Last and Captain Ryder rather
than from Basil Seal. At odds with the modern world, long-
ing for the certainties of a past age which are preserved
chiefly in the public school, bitterly romantic or, in Mr.
Donat O'Donnell's expressive phrase, neo-Jacobite, (4) the
Crouchbacks and Ryders find in the army not only the sta-
bility they crave but a macrocosm of the world of school
and a church-militant as well. Both by image and by direct
parallel the traditional, ritualistic and hierarchical
aspects of army life and organisation get rubbed in. It is
again no more than natural that actual combat, which dis-
turbs this stasis, should be the field in which Guy's disillusionment is worked out, and that his crusading zeal,
his feeling of having taken up arms against the Modern Age
- all this is urged with complete literariness - should
wither before the harsh and inconvenient realities of war-
time diplomacy. A man to whom Italian Fascism was merely
'a rough improvisation,' for whom it was Nazi participation
that 'dishonoured the cause of Spain,' who was much more
angry at the Russian invasion of Poland than the German, is
going to take some knocks when June 22, 1941, comes along
and England is 'led blundering into dishonour.' He is also
a man with whom few, I hope, will want to identify themselves.

Crouchback is really a terrible fellow. He has none of
the unpleasant vigour of Ryder, and compared with Tony Last

his dream is a pipe-dream, his sufferings would be deserved
if they were not so unreal. I suppose he may pull round a
bit in later volumes, but he will have to pull round a lot
to efface the memory of that scene in 'Men at Arms', as
remarkable in its way as anything in recent fiction, where
he tries to seduce his ex-wife in the flush of the discovery
that theologically he would be committing no sin. If Mr.
Waugh had set out with the intention of discrediting him
for good and all, he could not have done it more skilfully.
The wife says, on discovering the set-up: 'I thought you'd
chosen me specially, and by God you had. Because I was the
only woman in the whole world your priests would let you go
to bed with,' and she adds with truth and finality: 'You
wet, smug, obscene, pompous, sexless lunatic pig.' The next
day Guy looks to Apthorpe to 'bear him away to the far gardens of fantasy,' as well he might. They are the only place
where he can live.

I implied earlier that an important difference between
these two books and what preceded them lies in a toning-
down or cutting-out of elements previously present. The
trouble is that the new elements are, in comparison, thin,
neutral and private. The next novel in the series will show
whether Mr. Waugh's invention is really impaired. When I
think of 'Decline and Fall', 'Vile Bodies', 'A Handful of
Dust' and 'Work Suspended' I cannot believe that it is.

Notes

1   A famous Catholic public school.
2   Mr Amis's résumé immediately preceded this statement.
3   Alexander Baron (b. 1917) is author of 'From the Plough'
    (1948), 'Rosie Hogarth' (1951) and 'The In-Between Time'
    (1971).
4   See No. 102 above.

150.   GEOFFREY MOORE, 'NEW YORK TIMES BOOK REVIEW'

10 July 1955, 7, 18

Geoffrey Moore (b. 1920) is Professor of American Studies
at the University of Hull, and a poet, anthologist and
critic. He is author of 'American Literature and the American Imagination' (1964) and editor of 'Poetry from Cam-

Cambridge in Wartime' (1946), and 'The Penguin Book of
Modern American Verse' (1977).

Some novelists deal with life as it is; others caricature
it in comedy and satire. Evelyn Waugh started out a novelist of the second type, but increasingly over the past
twenty years – that is, ever since the portrait of Tony
Last in 'A Handful of Dust' – he has been allowing signs of
developing into a more serious and realistic writer. He
has never quite made it, however, so that his latest novel,
'Officers and Gentlemen,' is something of a mixture. In
style, it forsakes the flowing periods of 'Brideshead
Revisited' for the more casual, crisper manner of the pre-
war novels, and yet its scope, despite two or three hilarious incidents ... is plainly larger than that of the earlier satirical fantasies....

Guy's adventures are surely not intended to be merely
picaresque; it cannot be for nothing that he has been made
both Catholic and anciently upper-class – although, of
course, Mr. Waugh's heroes rarely escape one or other of
these distinctions. Should we take Guy's response to the
war as having been misguided? Will Ivor Claire turn out not
to have been a coward after all? The book ends in such a
tangle of loose threads that it is difficult to agree with
Mr. Waugh that it and 'Men at Arms' 'form a whole.' The
several too-convenient coincidences would have been toler-
able, even unnoticeable in the wild fun of the delightfully improbable earlier books, but these and the loose
ends of the plot give one the impression of slightly shoddy
workmanship in the more serious atmosphere of the Crouchback and Halberdier saga.

There is, too, the matter of the snobbery. One cannot
explain it away, as some have tried to do. Mr. Waugh loves
a lord and is unremiss about it. It is all bound up with
his view of life, which seems to be sentimental nostalgia
for the days of privilege and order – a view which was incipient even in 'Decline and Fall' when Paul Pennyfeather
meekly accepted Mrs. Beste-Chetwynde's caddishness because
'there was, in fact, and should be, one law for her and
another for himself.' Social snobbery can be mildly funny,
but it now looms so large in Mr. Waugh's novels and is so
seldom relieved by humor that it gives his work the edge of
bigotry. There is so much attention to scoring off non-
gentlemanly characters that Mr. Waugh reads at times like
the Frances Parkinson Keyes of the intellectuals.

It is not merely that the picture presented lacks
perspective and chiaroscuro, it is that it is lopsided as
well. Mr. Crouchback Senior, for example, is a dear old

gentleman, but his every appearance is the excuse for another act of unrelieved and fulsome goodness, and his
lower-class foils are made as black as he is white. The
grasping and common hotel-keepers, who are outwitted by his
determined innocence, are even made to say to one another:
'Somehow his mind seems to work different than yours or
mine.'

There you have it. Mr. Waugh seems to believe that with
the passing of the old way of life, which he idealizes and
white-washes, all principles and values passed from the
earth too. Fortunately it is not so, and until Mr. Waugh
recognizes this his serious work, for all his great talents,
will seem, to an ever-younger, more hopeful and more realistic audience, without either wholeness or humanity.

151. CURTIS BRADFORD, 'NEW REPUBLIC'

11 July 1955, 19-20

Curtis Bradford (b. 1934), an American academic who has
specialized in contemporary British and Academic poetry
and fiction, is the author of 'Yeats at Work' (1965).

Many, perhaps most war novels fail because sooner or later
they affront the reader-veteran's sense of reality; he
begins to talk back; it wasn't like that. The usual reason
for this back-talk is, I think, that most writers split
war's tragedy from war's comedy. Either they heap horror on
horror, eventually overwhelming the reader with mere turgid-
ity - even a book so fine in parts as [Mailer's] 'The Naked
and the Dead' seemed ultimately to do that, or they reduce
the whole thing to a gagging minstrel line with a comic
noncom as end man. It is a special merit of Mr. Evelyn
Waugh's war novels, of 'Men at Arms' and now of 'Officers
and Gentlemen,' that they avoid this split; in them war's
tragedy is wholly informed by and involved in war's inef-
fable comedy. Both books are remarkable pieces of realism;
they arouse the memory. As the reader closes 'Men at Arms'
he says, 'yes, improbably, impossible the "sitzkrieg," the
"phony war" was like that'; as he closes 'Officers and
Gentlemen' he is aware of having lived again through the
emotional roller coaster ride of 1940-1941, a world tragedy unrelieved by catharsis.

'Officers and Gentlemen' completes the story of Guy
Crouchback begun in 'Men at Arms.' It is not merely a

sequel; the two books are a single unit. Mr. Waugh repeats
none of his exposition, so the reader of 'Officers and
Gentlemen' must first review the earlier part of the story.
Guy Crouchback, in his middle thirties, a member of a distinguished English Catholic family, is a typical inhabitant
of the Waste Land. All his ventures have failed - marriage,
colonial farming, expatriate life in Italy, religion. He
sees in the Nazi-Soviet pact of 1939 the preparations for
Armageddon, with Anti-Christ for once aligned against the
feeble and divided forces of good. By chance he gets into
an ancient regiment as an officer-volunteer. The farce of
the civilian being turned into a soldier is told again for
the thousandth time with full attention to its burlesque
possibilities, but in contrast to this burlesque is another
story that has seldom been told. Guy Crouchback finds the
military ritual curiously sustaining, more sustaining even
than the round of his religious duties, practiced for so
long without enthusiasm....

The neo-classic tone of much of the second novel,
'Officers and Gentlemen,' is established at the outset by
the ceremonies Guy goes through to placate the shade of
Apthorpe. He accomplishes Apthorpe's informal testamentary
wish that a ton or so of miscellaneous tropical gear be
collected and turned over to one 'Chatty' Corner.... He is
at the end of the book utterly deflated, not only by the
failure of his personal adventures, but by the emergence
(after the German invasion) of the USSR as Britain's com-
rade-in-arms. He is to an extent sustained by the complementary rituals of his religion and his regiment....

This simple story is set forth with a technical brilliance few living writers could match. It begins with a
series of burlesque episodes done with Mr. Waugh's customary bravura; he intertwines with this burlesque long
passages of nearly unaccented realism, which not only set
off the burlesque but serve also as a kind of middle
ground between it and the long account of the tragedy in
Crete which follows. This account is surely one of the
finest pieces of sustained tragic narrative to be found in
recent fiction. Ghostly classic associations with Crete
haunt it and give it universal implications. Guy is a
modern Theseus, lost without an Ariadne's thread in the
new labyrinth of war-torn Crete, threatened by forces more
destructive than Minotaur and Talus. His Daedalean wings
of escape are a wretched, bug-infested, open fishing boat.
Fatigue, hunger, thirst change the physical world into a
phantasmagoria that has its counterpart in the mind and
soul. Guy's last illusions about himself and his fellows
disappear when priests turn out to be spies; when Major
Hound - 'Fido' - an embodiment or function of military

routine collapses with the collapse of that routine; when his
Athenian Prince, Ivor Claire, rats. The experience of war
transvalues all values. Though Waugh's intention is clear
enough - the rapid shifts of tone remind one of Elizabethan
tragedy - I am not sure he altogether succeeds with it. Like
many other recent writers, he no doubt finds the heroic mood
difficult to sustain in an unheroic age, so chose this way
out of a possible embarrassment.

His Catholic apologetics are so quiet, so undemanding
that the non-Catholic reader is quite willing to accept
them. Catholicism is a traditional and humane way of life.
Belief in its authority, practice of its rituals, will save
a man from the collapse that usually follows deflation. The
spiritual and moral vacuum is filled, so to speak, by the
practice of traditional modes of thought and feeling. There
is much in 'Officers and Gentlemen' that on the surface is
unfamiliar to the American reader. But though the initials
of command and operations are strange and the details of
military routine different, those who have served in the
various American military forces will close the book
reminded again that the more it changes the more it's the
same. Compared with the fare that has been served up as
serious prose fiction in recent years, this is a very good
novel indeed.

152.   ROBERT LINDLEY, 'MONTH'

September 1955, 182-3

Let us be clear about Mr. Evelyn Waugh. He is one of the
greatest of living English novelists, one of a select set
indeed. To class his new book, in (say) a review, with two
or three of the hundreds of new novels spewed forth
annually by a diminishing number of publishers, is an
insult more or less deliberate according to the prejudices
of the reviewer. The fact that 'Brideshead Revisited' is
widely thought to be (a) his best book, and (b) his worst
book is some indication of his following. The reasons for
this eminence are obvious; one is that he is readable to
the point of magic - compelling, uproariously readable even
on the rare occasions when his material is unpromising, -
and the other is that he writes from a point of view. His
point of view, moreover, is not an exclusively personal one,
certainly not the flaccid sensitivity commonly prevailing,
which does no good, if little harm, either to reader or

writer. Mr. Waugh's point of view is drawn from two curiously diverse sources - White's Club and the Catholic
Church, both of which institutions undergo a slight, but
somehow menacing transformation under his (ultimately)
loving hands. For it seems to be his personal misfortune
that he must, at intervals, present the objects of his
devotion - or at any rate the human beings who are taken to
share his faiths - in the coldest and least flattering possible light, as one who should say 'There you are. That is
how these people behave. Now, do you still believe?' Many
of his readers yelp protestingly at this treatment, and
ally themselves with Mr. Waugh's villains, thereby missing
the point. Both in 'Men at Arms' and in his latest work,
'Officers and Gentlemen,' these passages of extreme disillusion aim, as it were, at the heart of the book, but do
not kill it.

'Officers and Gentlemen' reverses the usual fate of a
sequel by being a good deal better than its predecessor.
The fortunes of the melancholy Guy Crouchback are followed
downhill from a blitz in London ... into the disasters of
Crete. The book is episodic and full of wild improbabili-
ties. It is also marvellously funny, satirical and tragic
by turns. Mr. Waugh's view of the English aristocracy might
appear to be the principal casualty. 'Captain Crouchback,'
writes one of the more detached characters, 'is pleased
because General Miltiades is a gentleman. He would like to
believe that the war is being fought by such people. But
all gentlemen are now very old.' And '"This is a People's
War," said Ian prophetically, "and the People won't have
poetry and they won't have flowers. Flowers stink. The
upper classes are on the secret list. We want heroes of the
people, to or for the people, by, with, or from the
people".' But, while one of the gentlemen conspicuously
fails, the 'people's hero,' inflated for the occasion, is
wholly a sham. Mr. Waugh's savagery, both in attack and
defence (and in the latter the savagery is reserved for
that which he is defending), comes, it seems, from a kind
of ruthless regard for truth - a regard which, be it said
to their discredit, arises otherwise than from contact with
his English co-religionists. But the *reductio* is never
carried fully *ad absurdum*. He is rather like the man in
Boccaccio's story, who became a Catholic because he was
so shocked and astounded at what went on in Rome that he
felt there must be a great deal in a religion which could
simultaneously sustain such wickedness and retain such
support. It is a comfortless kind of attitude. But in so
far as it is Mr. Waugh's, it has helped rather than hin-
dered him from writing a brilliant book.

'The Ordeal of Gilbert Pinfold'

1957

153. DONAT O'DONNELL, 'SPECTATOR'

19 July 1957, 112

Mr. Waugh, so his publishers tell us, suffered three years
ago from a brief attack of hallucinations. He has now,
according to the same source, made these 'the theme of a
light novel which should delight all those who live on the
border lines of sanity - rather more than half the inhabitants of the kingdom according to medical figures.'

It seems doubtful whether a novel about delusions of
persecution - which is what Mr. Pinfold's hallucinations
mainly are - will bring unalloyed pleasure to those whose
reason is tottering on its throne. The present reviewer,
who has no claim to speak for the British lunatic, found
'The Ordeal' moderately interesting, almost entirely
unfunny, and a little embarrassing. The first, and probably the best, chapter in this short book is called
Portrait of the Artist in Middle Age. The portrait it
presents of Mr. Pinfold seems to be in fact a portrait of
Mr. Waugh, painted by no satiric or malevolent hand.
'Affectionate, high-spirited and busy in childhood; dis-
sipated and often despairing in youth; sturdy and prosperous in early manhood; he had in middle age degenerated less
than many of his contemporaries. He attributed this superiority to his long, lonely, tranquil days at Lychpole, a
secluded village some hundred miles from London.' He had
been a good soldier, is a Catholic - with the prefix
'Roman' - professes an 'idiosyncratic Toryism; and has a
short way with intruders into his personal life. (Why, if
literate, they need to intrude is not made clear.) He has
become physically lazy and 'corpulent,' eats less, drinks
more, sleeps less, becomes 'decidedly seedy' and is ordered

to go on a sea voyage. In his cabin on the ship he begins
to hear, through some defect in the wiring as he believes,
various strange conversations, at first unrelated - a Bible
class, a jazz session - then beginning to take the form of
a conspiracy directed at him: he is threatened with a beating, there is a plot to kidnap him. He tries to relate this
conspiracy to his fellow passengers - then he begins to
hear these passengers talking about him:

> '...He'll commit suicide one of these days, you'll
> see.'
> 'I thought he was a Catholic. They aren't allowed to
> commit suicide, are they?'
> 'That wouldn't stop Pinfold. He doesn't really
> *believe* in his religion, you know. He just pretends to
> because he thinks it aristocratic. It goes with being
> Lord of the Manor.'
> 'There's only one Lychpole in the world, he told the
> wireless man.'
> 'Only one Lychpole and Pinfold is its Lord....'
> 'Here he is, drunk again. He looks ghastly.'
> 'A dying man, if ever I saw one.'
> 'Why doesn't he kill himself?'
> 'Give him time. He's doing his best. Drink and drugs.
> He daren't go to a doctor, of course, for fear he'd be
> put in a home.'
> 'Best place for him, I should have thought.'
> 'Best place for him would be over the side.'

For anyone who finds that kind of dialogue funny 'The
Ordeal of Gilbert Pinfold' will be a feast indeed. Some of
Mr. Waugh's admirers will regret that he has chosen to make
'a light novel' out of material fundamentally unsuited to
such treatment. It may be said that the comic treatment of
the grimmest themes - as in 'The Loved One' - is precisely
where Mr. Waugh excels. That is true when as a satirist he
allows himself a free hand - dealing, for example, with
the proletariat, Americans, or other beings beyond the
range of human sympathy - but not when he is treating
sacred subjects, such as himself. Then the mellowness of
'Brideshead' blurs the vision and the tone of the satirist,
and impairs the cruelty which alone could turn delusions of
persecution into comedy. The Waugh of before 'Brideshead
Revisited' seldom wrote about himself; the Waugh of after
'Brideshead' seldom writes about anything else.

154. UNSIGNED REVIEW, 'TIMES LITERARY SUPPLEMENT'

19 July 1957, 437

Mr. Waugh's publishers make it clear that this 'light novel'
is based on personal experience; the narrator is sufficiently like Mr. Waugh for it to be taken as fantasticated
autobiography rather than fiction. A grumpy, middle-aged
novelist becomes addicted to chloral and bromide. On a
cruise to the East he begins to hear voices. At first he
imagines he is eavesdropping on some plot but the voices
soon attack him directly, taking the stock accusations
against him, like snobbery, and adding preposterous details.
He flees home and his wife, who has been alarmed by his
letters, tells him she has consulted a priest who is a student of paranormal psychology. The priest says firmly that
long-range persecution by means of 'waves' is impossible
and that what he has heard has all been said by himself.
The voices cease and the novelist feels that he has won a
victory over them in his running fight, for he is not quite
convinced that cutting off the drugs which have been poison-
ing him has cured his hallucinations. A free man, he sits
down eagerly to write an account of it all, 'a hamper to be
unpacked of fresh, rich experience - perishable goods.'
    The thin little tale does not throw much light on states
in which, to quote the publishers again, 'the reason
remains strenuously active but the information on which it
acts is delusory.' Its real interest is that it is an
experiment in self-examination. Mr. Waugh stands just outside himself and describes what he sees as simply and
accurately as he describes a building. The opening chapter,
much the best thing that has ever been written about him,
implicitly discountenances some of the claims that have
been made on his behalf.
    It is time people stopped treating Mr. Waugh as a failed
Mauriac. He is a lightweight who has suffered from being
bracketed with completely different writers like Mr. Graham
Greene. The trouble began in the period when only biographies were allowed to aim at a laugh. Leading reviewers
felt guilty at being amused by him and refused to face the
fact that he had nothing much to say. They insisted on
treating any reference to Eternity, any expression of cosmic disquiet, as evidence of a profundity that justified
their enjoyment. In 'The Creative Element', (1) Mr. Stephen
Spender was reduced to claiming that Mr. Waugh was primarily a comic writer because he was unable to project his own
spiritual struggle into a character, which suggests an odd
definition of comedy. Mr. Donat O'Donnell, in 'Maria

Cross', (2) has fun at his expense, saying that in his theology the love of money is not only the root of all evil but is a preliminary form of the love of God. Yet after pages of gay denunciation he calls him a great Catholic writer, a judgment that bears no relation to anything that has gone before.

Like Sheridan or FitzGerald or Max Beerbohm, Mr. Waugh has a freak talent and he is entitled to be judged on what he writes without any attempt to relate him to trends or other writers or anything else. If he is taken as the author of a number of obstinately vital minor classics he is seen to be, what Dr. Edwin Muir called Mr. Wodehouse, the most consistently successful novelist of his time and a comic writer of immense talent. The comparison with Mr. Wodehouse is usually intended as a sneer; it is an inept one. Mr. Waugh is obviously far more observant and his prose is, of course, a finer instrument than Mr. Wodehouse's. But he shares his complete originality and he shares his freshets of wonderful new jokes, of humour that is as pure as the horror in a Border Ballad or the devotion in a carol. His Toryism resembles Mr. Wodehouse's tendency to snuggle down into memories of his youth, though his attitude to peers is more awestruck, nearer, perhaps, to Mr. Wodehouse's attitude to the American girl. (3)

Mr. Waugh's wartime series has not, so far, attained more than an amiable readability. Is his future, and his best work, to be autobiographical? His brilliant little description of Sir George Sitwell in Sir Osbert's 'Left Hand, Right Hand!' (4) showed a wonderful diarist's eye. If he does not pursue the experiments foreshadowed in 'The Ordeal of Gilbert Pinfold' he has, at least, set a problem in form for other autobiographers. After all, many years ago, in a casual sort of way, he invented the contemporary novel.

Notes

1   The World of Evelyn Waugh in 'The Creative Element: A Study of Vision, Despair and Orthodoxy among Some Modern Writers' (Hamish Hamilton, 1953), pp. 159-74.
2   The Pieties of Evelyn Waugh in 'Maria Cross: Imaginative Patterns in a Group of Modern Catholic Writers' (OUP, 1952), pp. 119-34. The essay first appeared in the 'Bell' (December 1946); see No. 102.
3   Waugh defended Wodehouse's reputation vigorously; cf. his review of 'Laughing Gas' and a short essay, An Angelic Doctor. The Work of P.G. Wodehouse ('Spectator', 17 October 1936, 532-3, and 17 June 1939, 786-7). Waugh

also went to great lengths publicly to refute allega-
tions made against Wodehouse during the war. To celebrate The Master's eightieth birthday Waugh broadcast a
talk, 'P.G. Wodehouse. An Act of Homage and Reparation',
on the Home Service, 15 July 1961, twenty years to the
day after the slander which condemned the man as a
quisling for his broadcasts from Germany.

4   'Left Hand, Right Hand!' is Sir Osbert Sitwell's massive,
Proustian autobiography (five volumes, 1944-50); Waugh
contributed Appendix B to the fourth volume, 'Laughter
in the Next Room' (Macmillan, 1949), p. 349. This is a
sketch of Sir George Sitwell, Osbert's eccentric father,
and is dated 20 June 1942.

155.   JOHN RAYMOND, 'NEW STATESMAN'

20 July 1957, 88

In the crazy mixed-up world in which we live - as the
reader conjectures I have been reading the Sunday newspapers - Mr Evelyn Waugh sometimes seems to me our maddest
and safest interpreter, the poet of the diminishing England
that Hilaire Belloc called our 'crumbling stye'. Secular
and despairing, he is a satirist and a romantic. The two,
as always, go together and our age, which cries out for
satire and romanticism, is badly understaffed with either.
He is also possessed of a unique type of moral vision. (Has
he not, in 'A Handful of Dust', written the most powerful
twentieth-century sermon on the break-up of a Christian
marriage?) In addition he happens to be the only major
writer in English whose work reveals any genuine signs of
development. It is possible to predict a new novel by Mr
Graham Greene say, a new Compton Burnett, a Henry Green
even, in a way that is impossible in the case of Mr Waugh.
He has had four manners to date and in at least three of
them, by the general consent of enjoyment, he has triumphed completely. In the present volume - it runs to just
over 200 pages - he has reverted to his earliest manner and
given us one of his wittiest, most humane entertainments.
   The book appears to be largely autobiographical, probably the nearest thing to a self-revelation this writer will
will ever vouchsafe us. Testy, vinous, conservative, an
'old soul' who abhors 'plastics, Picasso, sun bathing and
jazz - everything, in fact, that had happened in his own
lifetime', Mr Pinfold is very much as one imagines Mr.
Waugh:

He wished no one ill, but he looked at the world *sub
specie aeternitatis* and he found it flat as a map;
except when, rather often, personal annoyance intruded.
Then he would come tumbling from his exalted point of
observation.

Shocked by a bad bottle of wine, an impertinent
stranger or a fault in syntax, his mind like a cine-
camera trucked furiously forward to confront the
offending object close-up with glaring lens; with the
eyes of a drill sergeant inspecting an awkward squad,
bulging with wrath that was half-facetious.

He was neither a scholar nor a regular soldier; the
part for which he cast himself was a combination of
eccentric don and testy colonel and he acted it strenuously, before his children and his cronies, until it
came to dominate his whole outward personality....

Three years ago, as his book's blurb relates, Mr Waugh
(alias Pinfold) suffered from a brief attack of hallucinations (as he later heard 'this was not nearly as rare as
he supposed ... the reason remains strenuously active but
the information on which it acts is delusory'). During a
cruise to Ceylon he finds himself inhabited by voices –
basically a threesome, but two powerfully ventriloquist,
mimicking the skipper, the chaplain, the first mate, the
ship's surgeon, a couple of majors-general and sundry passengers. When he first hears them Mr. Pinfold thinks them
due to a fault in the war-time Intercomm. His cabin, he
believes, has been transformed into a kind of command-post
into which all the ship's tensions and intimacies are being
scrambled. Gradually, the voices turn persecutory. Mr Pinfold, they declare, is a Communist, a homosexual, a Jew
('Hark-ark-ark. Come out Peinfeld. We know where you are.
We've got you.'). Fuddled by drink and sleeping-draughts,
tormented by his voices – which must have been hell for
Mr Waugh, but which are pure joy for the reader – Mr Pinfold leaves the ship at Port Said. He flies to Colombo,
takes a plane home, is restored to Mrs Pinfold (a model of
cool and tranquil affection, one of Mr Waugh's happiest
side-line characterisations) and cured. Cured, that is to
say, in the sense that the voices 'trail away, sink to a
whisper, a sigh, the rustle of a pillow', and are then
silent. Nothing as funny – or as stylised – as this book
has been written this year or last, and the fact that for
once Mr Waugh is being cruel about himself will give his
admirers an extra fillip. To read anything he writes has
always been, for this reviewer, an almost physical pleasure, and it is good to see him in his true and best form
on the present occasion. My only criticism is that the book

lacks a satisfactory denouement. This, however, is the
fault of all case-histories. Also, the reader has laughed
so much by the time the book ends, that the lack of a climax goes almost unnoticed. Several readers of the 'Observer' to whom I talked over the week-end objected to the
published first chapter of the book on the grounds that it
was 'stuffy', and I think Mr Waugh has done a serious dis-
service to his novel by allowing a section of it to be
printed out of context in this way. The chapter forms, in
fact, an ideal introductory norm, the *grande entrée* to this
near-perfect farce of bromide, chloral and champagne.

156.   PHILIP TOYNBEE, 'OBSERVER'

21 July 1957, 13

Philip Toynbee (1916-81) was novelist, critic and foreign
correspondent (on the 'Observer's' editorial staff from
1950). He was author of 'Savage Days' (1937), 'Tea with Mrs
Goodman' (1947) and 'Friends Apart' (1954). Mr Toynbee
gained a reputation as an 'experimental' novelist. His
father was Arnold Toynbee, the historian, and his daughter,
Polly, writes for the 'Guardian'.

Mr Waugh has written many different kinds of novels: farce
('Decline and Fall'); satire ('The Loved One'); romance
('Brideshead Revisited'); satirical romance ('A Handful of
Dust'); farcical-romantic sociology ('Men at Arms' and
'Officers and Gentlemen'). He has never written a book in
the least like this one before. Fictionalised autobiography? Nightmare? An essay in the macabre?...
    The book is extremely deft. It was a *tour de force* to
tell the story entirely from the hero's point of view and
yet to keep the reader constantly aware of the line which
divides reality from hallucination. I was tempted to write
the word reality in inverted commas, for the hallucinations
are described with a dreadful vividness which wholly persuades us that they are no less real than the normal events
of the voyage.
    I confess that I have never been a great admirer of Mr
Waugh as a stylist, although it is clear that he takes very
great pains to write as he intends to write. This book was
marred for me by the mannered precision of its writing.
Indeed I find it very hard to say whether it is a good book

or not. But it is certainly an interesting and a moving
one. And one reason why it is so moving is that Mr Waugh
has not a trace of self-pity in his character. Pinfold's
ordeal is a truly shocking one, and it would be an odd
reader who did not find himself deeply involved in it. But
the hero and his creator retain their courage throughout,
and retain as well an ironical detachment which is very
rare in books of this kind.

What interests me most about the book is that the hero's
imaginary persecutors are not, as one might have expected,
parlour pinks, pacifists, non-believers with the wrong
accent or any of the other stage villains of Mr Waugh's
mythology. They are colonels, public school men, upper-
class thugs, anti-Semites, Fascists and bullies - just the
kind of people, in fact, to whom Mr Waugh has sometimes
seemed to be a little over-indulgent in the past. It is
deeply interesting that the ultimate horror in the recesses
of Mr Waugh's mind is the same horror which has obsessed so
many of us who experienced the normal torments of public
school life. For the bully, of course, is an enemy not only
of weakness, not only of sensitivity, not only of loving
kindness, but also of intelligence. It is the appalling,
nagging, shrewd *stupidity* of the imaginary persecutors
which is best brought out and which will haunt my own
imagination for many days.

These are the self-revelations of a remarkably honest
and brace man who has also allowed us to see that he is a
likeable one. It is a book which seems to suggest that Mr
Waugh has shifted gear and has begun to explore depths of
experience which were previously beyond his reach - or at
least beyond his desire. Whatever will he do next?

157. J.B. PRIESTLEY, 'NEW STATESMAN'

31 August 1957, 224

Mr Priestley's article was entitled What was Wrong with
Pinfold. Waugh's response, Anything Wrong with Priestley?,
appeared in the 'Spectator', 13 September 1957, 328-9, and
is reproduced in ALO, pp. 136-9.

Mr Evelyn Waugh's semi-autobiographical novel, 'The Ordeal
of Gilbert Pinfold', has been both sharply attacked and
enthusiastically praised. Literary criticism is not our

concern here, but perhaps I ought to add that I liked the
beginning of the story, was prepared to admire the general
plan of it, but found the hallucination scenes aboard ship
rather crude and tedious, quite without the nightmare
quality I had expected to find in them. This surprised me
in a writer I have long admired - and indeed I was one of
the very first to shout his praises (1) - a novelist of
originality, great technical skill, and personal distinction. I came to the conclusion that in these scenes he had
got himself bogged down somewhere between reality and invention: reality, because he was describing more or less
what had happened to himself; invention, because he had
decided, perhaps hastily at the last moment, to substitute
imaginary imaginary voices for the imaginary voices he himself seemed to hear; and that this would explain why, being
hasty substitutions, they seem far below his usual level of
creation and invention. But all this is guesswork. And it
is not Mr Waugh but Gilbert Pinfold who is the subject of
this essay.

Pinfold, we are told, is a middle-aged novelist of some
distinction. He is well known abroad, where foreign students write theses on his work. He lives in an old house in
the country, where his wife, who is younger than he is,
farms their property. He has a large young family. He no
longer travels widely as he used to do, and now pays only
infrequent visits to London, though he is still a member
of 'Bellamy's Club'.

> Since the end of the war his life had been strictly
> private. In his own village he took very lightly the
> duties which he might have thought incumbent on him.
> He contributed adequate sums to local causes but he had
> no interest in sport or in local government, no ambition
> to lead or to command. He had never voted in a parlia-
> mentary election, maintaining an idiosyncratic toryism
> which was quite unrepresented in the political parties
> of his time....

His wife is a born Catholic and he is a convert. His days,
we are told, are passed in writing, reading and managing
his own small affairs. He lives as he wants to live and,
unlike most people nowadays, is perfectly contented with
his lot.

Nevertheless, he drinks a good deal, indeed rather too
much. And because he sleeps badly he finds himself taking
larger and larger doses of an opiate or sedative that he
keeps mixed with Crème de Menthe, a remedy, based on an old
prescription. So it is a boozy and half-doped Pinfold who
finds his way, not without difficulty, to the cabin he has

booked for a three-week voyage to the East. It is in this
cabin that he begins to hear the voices that torment him,
belonging to persecutors who have no existence, who are
creations of his own unconscious. For the benefit of Jung-
ians, it may be added that both the Shadow and the Anima
are busily engaged in these spectral intrigues. Poor Pinfold
finds himself in a kind of waking nightmare, out of which
he does not emerge until he returns home. The local doctor
tells him he has been the victim of the bromide and chloral
he has been swigging so heartily. We leave him, safe and
cosy again in his study, ready to start work, but preferring to his unfinished novel a more urgent piece: 'The
Ordeal of Gilbert Pinfold'.

But if Pinfold imagines his troubles are over, he is a
fool. He has been warned. Because the voices talked a lot
of rubbish, making the most ridiculous accusations, he is
ignoring the underlying truth uniting them all, the idea
that he is not what he thinks he is, that he is busy deceiv-
ing both himself and other people. Consciously he has rejected this idea for some time; he has drowned it in alcohol, bromide and chloral; and now it can only batter its
way through to him by staging a crude drama of lunatic
voices. And though they are a long way from the truth in
their detailed charges, they are right, these voices, when
they tell him that he is a fake. It is of course Pinfold
remonstrating with Pinfold; the fundamental self telling
the ego not to be a mountebank. What is on trial here is
the Pinfold *persona*. This *persona* is inadequate: the drink
hinted at it; the dope more than suggested it; the voices
proved it.

The style of life deliberately adopted by Pinfold is
that of those old Catholic landed families, whose women
live for the children and the home farm and whose men,
except in wartime when, like Pinfold, they are ready to
defend their country, detach themselves from the national
life, behaving from choice as their ancestors were compelled to do from necessity, because of their religion.
Everything we learn about Pinfold fits this style of life -
with one supremely important exception, the fact, the
obstinate fact, that he is by profession a writer, an
artist. And this is the central truth about Pinfold, who
could never have achieved any distinction as a novelist if
he had not been essentially an artist. He is not a Catholic landed gentleman pretending to be an author. He is an
author pretending to be a Catholic landed gentleman. But
why, you may ask, should he not be both? Because they are
not compatible. And this is not merely my opinion. It is
really Pinfold's opinion too.

Though Pinfold may imagine he has achieved a style of

life that suits him perfectly, his behaviour shows that he
is wrong. Take the heavy drinking. Some men drink a lot because their work demands that they should appear to be easy
and affable with persons they rather dislike; other men do
it because they are natually gregarious and like to lap it
up with the boys; others again, like some politicians,
journalists, actors, take to booze because their days and
nights are a difficult mixture of boring waits and sudden
crises. But Pinfold belongs to none of these groups. He is
a solitary soaker, hoping to deaden his mind against reality. This explains too his reckless traffic with opiates
and sedatives. Anything is better than lying awake at three
in the morning, when the *persona* is transparent and brittle.
So in the end the voices arrive. Their accusations are
absurd, monstrous; he is an alien who has changed his name,
a homosexual, a traitor, a would-be-murderer; always they
miss the mark, perhaps deliberately overshooting at it, as
if there could be a deception even in these attempts to end
deception; nevertheless, they are telling him he is not
what he pretends to be. And if they stopped clowning and,
perhaps with his consent, spoke plainly, they would say:
'Pinfold, you are a professional writer, a novelist, an
artist, so stop pretending you represent some obscure but
arrogant landed family that never had an idea in its head.'
   Pinfold has to do some writing, from time to time,
otherwise he could not earn a living. And when he is in the
middle of a book he behaves like an artist, breaking the
country gentleman pattern; but such times –

   were a small part of his year. On most nights he was
   neither fretful nor apprehensive. He was merely bored.
   After even the idlest day he demanded six or seven hours
   of insensibility. With them behind him, with them to
   look forward to, he could face another idle day with
   something approaching jauntiness; and these his doses
   unfailingly provided....

This is very revealing. When he is not working, Pinfold is
bored because his *persona* is inadequate, because the role
he has condemned himself to play is too sketchy and empty,
because the intellectual and artist in him feel frustrated
and starved. An author is not an author only when he is
writing. Genuine authorship, to which Pinfold, who is no
hack, is committed, is just as much a way of life as farming or soldiering. It is one of the vocations. This is why,
at a time when most people are demanding more and more for
their goods and services, the author can safely be offered
less, for it is an open secret, no matter what he may say,
that he is in love with his trade. If the worst came to the

worst, he would take a clerkship at the gasworks and pay
out of his savings to be printed.

What we may call *Pinfolding* - the artist elaborately
pretending not to be an artist - is an old trick here in
England, thanks to our aristocratic tradition and our
public suspicion of intellect and the arts. Congreve was
pinfolding when Voltaire visited him, only to be told that
Congreve considered himself to be a gentleman of leisure,
not a writer of plays; which drew from Voltaire the retort
that he would not have wasted his time calling upon a
gentleman, only upon the writer of plays. The English are
born pinfolders. (Think of Elgar, his mind brooding over
the heartbreak of his Cello Concerto, doing his best to
look and behave like a retired colonel with a passion for
horse-racing.) It saves us from the solemn posturing we
have observed among our foreign colleagues, who are more
portentous about a short review than we could be about an
epic creation. We avoid the *Cher Maître* touch. Yet I think
the Continental attitude, for all its pomposity, extravagance, incitement to charlatanry, is saner, healthier,
better for both the arts and the nation, than ours is. If
authors and artists in this country are not only officially
regarded without favour but even singled out for unjust
treatment - as I for one believe - then the Pinfolds are
partly to blame. They not only do not support their profession: they go over to the enemy. Congreve may have
shrugged away his reputation as a poet and dramatist, but
at least he identified himself with a class from which were
drawn the chief patrons of poetry and the drama, whereas
the Pinfolds are hiding themselves among fox-hunters,
pheasant slaughterers, horse and cattle breeders.

Let Pinfold take warning. He will break down again, and
next time may never find a way back to his study. The central self he is trying to deny, that self which grew up
among books and authors and not among partridges and hunters, that self which even now desperately seeks expression
in ideas and words, will crack if it is walled up again
wtihin a false style of life. Whatever Mrs Pinfold and the
family and the neighbours may think and say, Pinfold must
step out of his role as the Cotswold gentleman quietly re-
gretting the Reform Bill of 1832, and if he cannot discover
an accepted role as English man of letters - and I admit
this is not easy - he must create one, hoping it will be
recognisable. He must be at all times the man of ideas, the
intellectual, the artist, even if he is asked to resign
from Bellamy's Club. If not; if he settles down again to
sulk and soak behind that inadequate *persona*, waiting for a
message from Bonnie Prince Charlie; (2) then not poppy, nor
mandragora, nor all the drowsy syrups of the world, shall
ever medicine him.

Notes

1 See No. 15.
2 Presumably an oblique reference to Donat O'Donnell's
   criticism of Waugh as a 'neo-Jacobite' (No. 102);
   Kingsley Amis also picked up the phrase in No. 149.

'The World of Evelyn Waugh'

1958

158.   GERALD SYKES, 'NEW YORK TIMES BOOK REVIEW'

13 April 1958, 5

Gerald Sykes, American novelist and academic, is the author
of 'The Center of the Stage' (1952), 'The Children of
Light' (1955), 'The Perennial Avant Garde' (1971) and
'Foresights: Self-Evolution and Survival' (1975). Mr Sykes
regularly reviewed contemporary British fiction in the 'New
York Times'.

At last Evelyn Waugh has had the anthology that his extraordinary comic gifts deserve. It is adroitly edited, brilliantly introduced, and it covers his whole career. An
image of the man - and of the changing world that he
refused to change with - emerges.

   Aside from a typically violent (and amusing) story written at the age of 7, the book begins with the first chapter
of his first novel, 'Decline and Fall' (1928), where we are
abruptly introduced to the Evelyn Waugh 'world.' It is
first of all a world without justice....

   This acceptance of cruelty appears again and again
throughout the volume. The elementary decencies are hooted
at, and if we are to make any sense of a brutal spectacle,
or get any fun out of it, we had better begin with joyful
complicity. This is the way the world is; it is never going
to change. If you happen to be born into a few privileges,
make the most of them. If someone else is climbing up the
ladder after you, there is only one thing to do: jump on
his fingers....

   Hemmed in as we are by the manifold efficiencies of our
day and hectored by the ever-increasing demand for more

'maturity,' we cannot help being delighted by a mind that
seems to have come to a halt, in many ways, at the level of
putting a pin on the teacher's seat. We love gags, and when
the gag is tough, as tough as its predecessor, bullbaiting,
and has moreover the gloss of an Oxford education, not to
mention an extremely expert literary craftsmanship, we are
given a chance to get back at the uplifters. Thus Mr. Waugh
has contrived a genuine niche for himself in an over-
reasonable society. He is our carefree clown in an Eton
collar.

Some professional children on our side of the pond have
also tried to do the same thing. We have only to compare
their efforts with those of Waugh to appreciate the inroads
of orange juice and piety upon our smiling land. For an
authentic return to the Dark Ages of Beelzebub minor, beware of substitutes. There is only Evelyn Waugh.

159.   UNSIGNED REVIEW, 'TIME'

21 April 1958, 66, 68

Aldous Huxley, 63, is now so venerable a figure of modern
letters that a middle-aged critic - the 'Atlantic Monthly's'
Charles J. Rolo - owns a poodle named Aldous. Evelyn Waugh,
54, never reached the same status of a chic literary household pet. But, unlike poodles, both writers - two of the
century's most gifted entertainers - are no longer quite
fashionable. Both have had the premature burial of collec-
tions in their lifetime, Huxley's latest prepared by an
anonymous Harper editor, Waugh's by Rolo.

Huxley and Waugh share many things apart from talent and
an interest in drugs and religion (in Huxley's case mesca-
line and Vedanta, in Waugh's wine and Roman Catholicism).
Each has a deep artistic integrity and an interest in odd
characters - almost, unlike modern young men, to the exclusion of his own. If the '20s and '30s are remembered as
nothing more than a dismal tract of history leading to
present discontents, it will be partly because two wondrously articulate Fools were wiser than the lugubrious
Lear of the tottering old order, whose motley they wore.
Each disdains modern life. Huxley presents one character
who might well speak for both authors when he recalls
'Oxford in the remote days towards the beginning of our
monstrous century.'

Each took his time and made a horror comic of it. The

characters are British middle and upper class of the great
inter-bellum years - but Huxley's are drawn with a
Daumier-like fascination and disgust. Waugh's by the lunatic but precise line of a Ronald Searle.... (1)

The Waugh sampler takes in more territory than the
Huxley collection, but it is scrappy. Waugh is the most
economical of writers, and Editor Rolo has performed a
doubtful service by cutting his little dancing paper figures into even smaller ones. But those who encounter Waugh
for the first time will still enjoy the old combination
of black-face comedian and commando: face darkened for his
curiously combined operations, surrounding atmosphere
crackling and popping with the sound of snapping bones. And
Waugh veterans will be glad to meet again some of the more
outrageous characters....

It is clear that Waugh is on the side of Lady Circumference. He satirizes the British nobility not because they
behave as aristocrats but because they do not. Whimsically,
Editor Rolo has included Waugh's first known work, 'The
Curse of the Horse Race,' written when the author was
seven. It is about a betting man named Rupert, with 'a
dark bushy mistarsh and flashing eyes,' who is hanged for
killing a 'puliesman.' Adds Master Waugh darkly: 'I hope
the story will be a leson to you never to bet.' Forty-
eight years later, Waugh, now a self-made conservative
Catholic country gentleman, is in business at the same
stand: comic policeman and characters in guardsman mus-
taches still take their pratfalls. All is gaiety on the
shiny, brilliant stage - only the author-manager in the
darkened wings fails to laugh; he is a moralist.

In his introduction Editor Rolo has used the best
phrase for Waugh - 'funny as hell.' Huxley, as the title
of one of his books suggests, deals with a place where
there are fewer fireworks - Limbo. (2)

Notes

1   The cartoonist.
2   A volume of short stories, 'Limbo' (1920). Huxley's
    'Collected Short Stories' (Harper, 1958) was also
    reviewed.

'Ronald Knox'

1959 (US title: 'Monsignor Ronald Knox', 1959)

160. UNSIGNED REVIEW, 'TIMES LITERARY SUPPLEMENT'

9 October 1959, 569-70

...It is an extremely good biography: beautifully clear,
tersely written, matter-of-fact about friendships and
money, never uncritical, never dull. In a sense, obviously,
it is prejudiced, but with a good kind of prejudice: a
combination of personal liking and religious sympathy which
gives the story force without preventing the reader from
making his own interpretation. 'He was well aware of the
limitations of our friendship,' says the short, self-
explanatory preface.

> I knew him primarily as a man of letters rather than as
> a priest; that is to say, I never went to confession to
> him or asked him for spiritual or moral advice. He knew,
> also, my curiosity and lack of discretion. He knew the
> kind of book I was likely to write....

It is a moving and, in some ways, profoundly tragic story.
It will certainly stick in men's minds.

The thesis of the book is evident from its plan. Mr.
Waugh has divided it into three parts: Laughter and the
Love of Friends (up to 1914); Keeping an Armageddon (the
war, with its personal separations and losses, its subor-
dination of all dogmatic disputes to the bald question:
R.C. or C. of E.?); finally The Hidden Stream. The hidden
stream is that tributary of the Isis which flows beneath
the Old Palace, the Catholic Chaplain's house at Oxford,
and it stands here for the pervasive influence which Knox
had on his charges and on his friends, and ultimately on
the Church which he had joined.

396

He had been very mistaken – though perhaps understand-
ably so, in view of the powerful dominance of the Church of
England in the society where he was brought up – in thinking that conversion would make him 'a more important person – but in a less important show,' for he never became
effectively geared into the Roman hierarchy; he never had
a parish, let alone any larger responsibility; and he remained until his death what Mr. Waugh calls 'still essentially a private person.' For this, in a variety of polite
and less polite terms (from 'anomalies in the economics
of Grace' to 'men who were notoriously deficient in taste
and manners') Mr. Waugh blames Knox's ecclesiastical superiors, and in particular Cardinal Bourne. Deliberately he
stresses his 'tribulations,' whether at the uncongenial
Catholic school where Bourne put him to teach, or at the
hands of Bishops who failed to appreciate his long work
of translation and revision. For 'genius and sanctity,'
he argues, 'do not thrive except by suffering.' The suffering he makes plain, and it was certainly no less bitter for
being slightly neurotic. The genius and the sanctity he
asks us to take largely on trust.

Does Mr. Waugh really feel that Knox was a genius? That
he had genius at his command is another matter, and the
Greek, Latin and English verses of 'In Three Tongues'
must convince us that this was so.... But he never widened
the frontiers of humour as the great humorous writers have
done, and as for Mr. Waugh's judgment that 'all his life
he found it easiest to express his thoughts in parody and
needed special exertion and discipline to write *in propria
persona*': must not something vital be missing in a writer
of whom that can be said?...

The snag of Mr. Waugh as a biographer is that his add-
icts are bound to be reminded at times of his novels: to
spot in real people and situations echoes of characters to
whom they have long ago determined their attitude, and to
be on the look-out for idiosyncrasies which, for better or
worse, they already know. Thus Pinfold now leaps to mind,
who likewise saw his world *sub specie aeternitatis*, and
found it

> flat as a map, except when, rather often, personal
> annoyance intruded. Then he would come tumbling from
> his exalted point of observation....

There is no denying that Ronald Knox, too, takes rather
frequent tumbles in this book, in directions often favoured by Mr. Pinfold and his creator, so that the reader
sometimes suspects Mr. Waugh of projecting on him his own
discontents. 'Peace in Europe and the Socialist régime in

England brought him little comfort'; 'the drab and sour
period of victory', 'a debilitating rancour' (this of the
mood that sent pre-war undergraduates to fight in Spain)
'that sprang from private fear rather than from any generous indignation...': sweeping verdicts like these are as
much proclamations of the author's slightly synthetic
grumpiness as evidence of his subject's views. None the
less some of this rather double-edged sourness and rancour
seems inseparable from the figure of Knox, who plainly disliked the post-1914 age and is shown as suffering from
'slight peevishness' in 1915, 'rather crochety' in the
1920s, 'unable to make a continual show of cheerfulness' in
the Second World War, and finally 'sulky and querulous'
with the return of peace.

It is also perhaps unfortunate for the three generous
women friends with whose families he made his successive
homes that they fall so smoothly into the framework of
'Brideshead Revisited': into that small upper-class Catholic world whose houses, pursuits and wartime difficulties
('absurd servants came and went') have vividly figured in
Mr. Waugh's novels. It makes it difficult to look at them
in an entirely natural light. But it is certain that Knox
felt closer to these people (who were apparently converts
like himself), and through them to the old world of his
lost friends, than to any other class of modern society,
including perhaps his fellow priests....

161.   D[OUGLAS] W[OODRUFF], 'TABLET'

10 October 1959, 857-8

When it was announced that Ronald Knox's biography was to
be written by Mr. Evelyn Waugh, a good many doubts were
expressed, particularly by Knox's fellow-priests to whom
his name and fame as a spiritual writer were dear. Mr.
Waugh's own laurels had been gathered in a markedly different field from that which the preacher and retreat-giver
cultivates. But it was Ronald Knox himself who chose Mr.
Waugh to be his literary executor, and approved him as his
biographer. A friendship dating back to Mr. Waugh's own
reception into the Church nearly thirty years ago had
deepened in the post-war years in the West of England.
One of its strong strands was a mutual recognition of
literary and critical quality, which included on Mr.
Waugh's side whole-hearted public tributes to his friend's

pre-eminence as a master of English, and these were most
grateful to a man prone to grow discouraged. Ronald Knox,
knowing that his life would inevitably be written by somebody, set as literary guardian a friend whom he knew to
share all his own distaste for hagiology or sentiment or
any form of literary excess.

Mr. Waugh has done his work with *gravitas* as well as
pietas; with that continual and generally successful choice
of the single exact epithet, in economical and restrained
prose which may easily conceal how great are the pains
which have been taken. The long prefatory list of persons
thanked for information bears its own witness. They have
mostly been interrogated to establish the exact why and
wherefore of events; to establish, as has been done, the
true record; and either they did not provide or Mr. Waugh
did not choose to use much in the way of anecdote and
remembered remarks and quotations from letters. There is
some of all this, but not very much for the life of a man
whom 'The Times' when he died called the wittiest clergyman since Sydney Smith....

This is a life written in the classical and not in the
Victorian discursive tradition, and the novelist's imagination and humour have been kept under complete control,
although there is the crackling of a dry ironic wit, and
there are a few asperities which would have been better
away in the life of a man so distinguished for his courtesy.
Mr. Waugh had three autobiographical documents to help him
for the three main events of Ronald Knox's life: 'The
Spiritual Aeneid' for the conversion to Rome, the treatise
on 'The Whole Art of Chaplaincraft' for the Oxford Chaplaincy, and the writings collected in 'On Englishing the
Bible' for the *magnum opus*. Armed with these, and the
chronological record and well-arranged papers of a very
methodical man, many writers could have produced a good
external account, and most of them would have given more
place to notable occasions to which Knox made his notable
contribution. Mr. Waugh has set out to do something more.
Ronald Knox knew that his biographer would never let himself be tempted to the crudely impertinent psychological
probings now fashionable in biography, but he must have
recognised that the novelist by *métier* is not going to
underestimate or ignore, as another only interested in the
public priest might have done, Ronald Knox's dependence
on the delicate inter-action of human relationships; and
human affection is brought fully into the portrait, with
impeccable good taste and regard for the living....

162.   GRAHAM GREENE, 'OBSERVER'

11 October 1959, 23

A priest presents even more difficulties to his biographer
than a writer. As with an iceberg, little shows compared
with what lies beneath: we have to dive for depth, but if
we so dive we have the sense of breaking into a life far
more private and exclusive than a bedroom. We need not
hesitate much over a man's love affairs; they are in a
sense public, for they are shared with another human being,
if not with waiters, chambermaids, that intimate friend;
but when a man prays he is quite alone. His biographer -
except when controversy, persecution, sanctity or disgrace
lend to the story a spurious drama - must write a life of
his hero which excludes the hero's chief activity.

   This Mr. Waugh does with a sense of style which would
have delighted his subject and an exquisite tact which
Father Knox had obviously foreseen in asking him to be his
biographer. It is no fault of Mr. Waugh that the story lags
a little in the middle: during the years of the Oxford
chaplaincy, the years of the satirical essayist and the
detective writer, the years of popularity, the years of
'Ronnie.' Every Catholic, I suppose, has his favourite type
of priest. The Knox of Oxford, the Knox of the rather precious style and of the Latin verses, the chaplain and the
translator, had his apostolate in a region which I have
always found uninteresting and even at moments repellent.
Writing an obituary of Father John Talbot, of the Oratory,
Knox describes this world with a, to me, terrible precision. He knew it to the last drain of the glass of dry
sherry:

   He was always there if you wanted him; and perhaps
   from long acquaintance you marked yourself as the sort
   of young man one meets in John Talbot's room.... If the
   comparison may still be used, the simplest thing to say
   of him is that he was the opposite number, in London,
   of Sligger at Oxford; his rooms had their characteristic
   clientele, on Sunday mornings especially, which irresistibly carried your mind back to a don's rooms in the
   garden quad at Balliol; and indeed there were many there
   who drifted on, as if predestined, from one salon to
   the other.... He had indisputably St. Philip's own
   knack of making people come to see him by always being
   at home when they came; and his clients, like those of
   the Santo, were in great measure the young men of
   fashion who are commonly reproached with shunning cleri-
   cal society.

These priests are as necessary to the Church as the
apostles of the darker, poorer, more violent world - the
priest we may have encountered on the borders of a battlefield in Vietnam, in the region of the Mau Mau or in the
dying white world of the Congo, but it is Mr. Waugh's very
great achievement that he holds the interest even of the
unsympathetic. He is no blind hero worshipper and long
friendship has not made him indifferent to the tiny warts.
He quotes Knox's extraordinary entry in that list of pros
and cons which he drew up before his conversion: 'You'll
be a more important person - but in a less important show,'
and Mr. Waugh adds:

> He was complacently insular, and in many respects
> remained so all his life. His travels were meagre and
> superficial; he had a gently humorous distrust of every-
> thing foreign; he had been brought up in an age when
> 'Land of Hope and Glory' had no undertone of irony, and
> the stability and expansion of the British Empire and
> with it the Church of England, seemed to follow a law
> of nature. Even so, when all these limitations are con-
> sidered, the two propositions still seem preposterous.

To me the beginning and the end of Mr. Waugh's biography
are outstanding: the end where Mr. Waugh has his 'villain'
and can show Knox meeting the meanness, jealousies and misunderstandings of the hierarchy without complaint, and the
early pages which include, besides the troubled years of
the conversion, a hero of extraordinary interest, Knox's
grandfather, the Anglican Bishop of Lahore. This old man,
after his retirement, set out 'unpaid and alone' for the
Muslim strongholds of North Africa and Muscat and died in
solitude attended at the last by a family of Goanese Catholics whom he had never consciously known. Only a writer
like Mr. Waugh, who has travelled in a hard poor fashion,
could have picked out so accurately the illuminating
details, 'the waxing incandescent wind of summer' and 'the
dirty upper room of a Goanese grog shop,' which is so far
psychologically from the Old Palace at Oxford.

He will, I hope, forgive me if I prefer as a character
the Bishop of Lahore. He may have been no more a mystic
than his grandson, but would he have wished to substitute
for the passage of St. John translated at Douai: 'He was
in the world and the world was made by him and the world
knew him not,' Father Knox's smooth and ambiguous version,
'He through whom the world was made, was in the world and
the world treated him as a stranger,' which seems to echo
the Oxford common-room rather than the hut of wattle and
thatched leaves where the grandfather began his last agony?

163.   C.M. BOWRA, 'LONDON MAGAZINE'

December 1959, 63-5

When, not long before his death on August 24th, 1957,
Ronald Knox expressed his approval of the suggestion that
Mr Evelyn Waugh should write his biography, he could not
have made a wiser decision. Though Mr Waugh is neither a
practising theologian nor a professional scholar, and
might for either of these reasons be thought unfitted to
deal with a prominent apologist of the Roman Catholic
Church, his other qualifications outweigh any possible
defects. He knew and admired and loved Knox not as a confessor but as a friend: he enjoyed his jokes and his re-
creations, appreciated his command of a subtle and elegant
English, moved and felt at ease in the same circle of well-
situated Catholics who were usually converts. Above all Mr
Waugh writes our language with a mastery in which he has
few, if any, living equals. He combines precision with
grace: ease and clarity with a rich variety of tones and
rhythms; skilful insinuation and ironical under-statement
with an ability to rise fully and freely to a high occasion. He differs from some academic practitioners of English in the respect which he pays to syntax and his avoidance of overworked phrases and colloquial vulgarities.
Even his generous portion of prejudices adds colour and
drama to his story, and we always know where we stand with
him, though his more savage critics will be disappointed at
his generous treatment of those members of the Church of
England, whether High or Low, who pass through his pages.
   In his Preface Mr Waugh gives a brilliant sketch of
Knox as his public saw him, but he goes on to say that
'genius and sanctity do not thrive except by suffering',
and warns us that he intends to speak of Knox's tribulations. He has skilfully composed his book so that we see
Knox both from without and from within, through the appearance which he presented to the world and through his own
hesitations and disappointments and defeats. What might
otherwise have been the story of a highly gifted man who in
the end found the full range of his talents gains greatly
in depth and in power from the inner drama of his struggles
and from the contrast between the common view of him and
what Mr Waugh reveals of his private life. There have been
those who, knowing Knox only from his public manner, have
thought him frivolous or narrow or even hard-hearted. Mr
Waugh dispels this view and presents a human being who
may have found it hard to make his final decisions but in
the end made them; who had friends to whom he was deeply

devoted and whose death, too often in war, left an
enduring wound; who even in the jaunty frolics of the
Society of SS Peter and Paul was an unrelenting moralist,
true to a code of behaviour which he inherited from his
evangelical, episcopal father and to which he adhered
faithfully to the end of his life.

To those who do not share the religious faith of Knox
and his biographer this book presents at least an absorbing account of a human being, but we may doubt whether it
will mean quite so much to them as Mr Waugh might wish. In
ascribing sanctity to Knox he speaks of what he knows, and
we must take his word for it, but he does not strain himself to make clear what he means by it or even to illustrate it at all fully. No doubt the evidence for it may be
found in Knox's religious works and still more in the
memories of those who came under his spiritual guidance.
But others, less intimately acquainted with him, may feel
that between them and Knox there is a veil which they cannot penetrate. This is not because they do not know or do
not care what sanctity is, but because they are given very
few opportunities of seeing it at work in him. His inner
struggles before he took the final step of being received
into the Roman Church are indeed moving in the strain
which they put on his loyalties and his affections no less
than in his natural hesitation to commit himself irrevocably, but other men have passed through similar struggles
and not been regarded as saints. Compared with other
priests of his faith, Knox in his public utterances seems
sometimes to lack charity and compassion, and his sheltered,
regular life denied him the splendours granted to more apos-
tolic spirits. Even his sufferings look small in the scale
of what other men in like positions have endured. No doubt
his years at St Edmund's Old Hall were drab and unfruitful,
and the opposition in certain circles to his translation of
the Bible may well have been a bitter disappointment when
he had put so much of his best work into it. But Knox was
transferred from St Edmund's to a congenial post at Oxford,
which left him with six months of every year to do what he
liked in, and his translation was before long approved and
welcomed with the warmth it deserved. In absorbing so
unusual a convert the Roman Catholic hierarchy displayed
far more insight and good nature than it had to either
Newman or Hopkins.

In the say way we must also take on trust Mr Waugh's
attribution of genius to Knox. He was an extremely gifted,
versatile, and scholarly writer. He wrote English, Latin
and Greek with equal ease, and nothing that he wrote is
dull or feeble. Yet in the last analysis he was not truly
creative. He excelled at parody and pastiche, and the little

volume of his *obiter scripta*, collected by his friend Mr
L.E. Eyres, (1) shows how unusual his gift was. Even 'Let
Dons Delight', which is a serious criticism of academic
life, is hardly written in his own voice, and his version
of the Bible remains, with all its ingenuity and eloquence,
a translation. His most impressive and least popular book
is 'God and the Atom'. In it we can see how strong his
moral convictions were and how deeply he felt the fallen
state of man when he resorted to his latest and most
ghastly means of destruction. In this Knox expressed something that meant a very great deal to him, and it is on
this side of his nature that we should have liked to hear
more. We cannot complain that Mr. Waugh has not attempted
to combine literary criticism with biography, and we must
take his book as it is - a remarkable work of letters which
contains a living and touching portrait of an uncommon man,
even if for many readers the central mysteries are still
hidden.

Note

1   'In Three Tongues' (Chapman & Hall, 1959).

164.   CHARLES A. BRADY, 'NEW YORK TIMES BOOK REVIEW'

24 January 1960, 6, 14

Charles Andrew Brady (b. 1912) is an American poet, novelist and critic, the author of 'Wings over Patmos' (1951)
and 'Stage of Fools' (1953). In 1960 he was Professor of
English at Canisius College and Saturday book critic for
the 'Buffalo Evening News'.

Before Evelyn Waugh fixed the public image of that essentially 'private person,' Ronald Arbuthnott Knox, in this
splendid first biography of the celebrated monsignor,
one still was at liberty to view Knox as a cross between a
Gilbertian curate and a kind of P.G. Wodehouse clergyman
whose idea of a pastoral cure was a perpetual long week-end
punctuated, at canonical intervals, by the highest of high
teas. Mr. Waugh has seen fit to choose a different fashion
of remembering his friend of thirty years - one that, if it
will not altogether please, will surely surprise the

reading world, Catholic as well as Protestant.

Neither affirming nor denying his subject's personal winsomeness, Waugh views him as an ineluctably shy personality continuously growing in holiness, touched, on at least one occasion, by what Waugh is inclined to accept as genuine mystical experience. The straightforward narrative account is set down with old-fashioned punctilio in prose of classic distinction, singularly free from bravura, and marked by the hard clarity of outline that is one of Waugh's several manners.

This does not mean that Waugh overlooks entirely the side of Knox which made him seem at times a kind of Peter Pan in a biretta whose wire-drawn flights of wit were not invariably attended by ecclesiastical imprimatur. It does mean that he eschews retailing the staple Knoxisms, leaving any real Boswellizing to lesser hands, in order to concentrate on the paradox that the most distinguished Anglican convert to Roman Catholicism since Newman was destined to suffer Newman's fate of 'the official frustration of his talents.'...

165. ANGUS WILSON, 'ENCOUNTER'

January 1960, 78-80

Sir Angus Wilson (b. 1913), Professor of English Literature at the University of East Anglia , 1966-78 (now Emeritus), is a novelist, playwright, short-story writer and critic. He is author of 'The Wrong Set' (1949), 'Such Darling Dodos' (1950), 'Emile Zola' (1950), 'Hemlock and After' (1952), 'Anglo-Saxon Attitudes' (1956), 'The Old Men at the Zoo' (1961), 'As if by Magic' (1973) and 'Setting the World on Fire' (1980).

Reviewers do not generally care for established authors to change their style, mood, or purpose. The prejudice is easily understandable, born of a laudable affection for familiar virtues, yet largely detrimental to the development of literature. To be told 'the same again,' again and again, is for many writers an insultingly obtuse compliment which large sales can only very moderately palliate. It is a sort of death-sentence. Something of this sort, I have long thought, happened to Mr. Evelyn Waugh when the clever, but not clever enough critics lined up against

'Brideshead Revisited' and later 'Helena'. That some of
their objections had substance, that our best novelist by
changing his mood and his form ran the risk of impairing
the near perfection he had achieved from 'A Handful of
Dust' onwards - none of this, I think, should have prevented them from awaiting the new developments in Mr.
Waugh's work with excitement and some measure of trust;
they chose rather to be clever about the obvious.

Mr. Waugh is tough; I do not imagine that criticism in
general nor the hostile critics of 'Brideshead Revisited'
and 'Helena' in particular alone would have deflected him
from his literary purposes; nevertheless, they may have
done much to confirm internal doubts which always assail a
considerable writer when he is moving towards new things.
The critics had tried by their acclaim of 'The Loved One'
to type-cast Mr. Waugh for the mordant court jester; he
retreated from their demand into the shadowy desert world
of Crouchback. The exuberance of 'Brideshead' and the originality of 'Helena' had been refused, so now he gave us
'the same again' but thinned, chilled, and soured. Mr.
Waugh's war novels, in fact, follow the pattern of his
great pre-war novels, but they are deprived of light, dry
and brittle, near to desiccation; even so, because he is so
masterly an artist, they are never less than good. Had he
travelled along the road suggested by 'Brideshead' he
might, as the critics were quick to point out, have fallen
into many lapses of taste, but the road would not surely
have led across quite such a desert tract. For a brilliant
moment, of course, he emerged into the crazy lights of
'Gilbert Pinfold' and told us the English Kafka tale of
how it had all happened; but now it seems to me with this
life of Ronald Knox, so competently, even lovingly carried
out, Mr. Waugh has returned to the desert.

All this preface is a little to appease my own disquiet, for it has long been my wish to review a work of Mr.
Waugh whom I admire above all contemporary novelists; and
now I find myself committed to the review of a book, that
for all its competence and high intention, seems to me
dull, at times even empty.(1)

Why is this biography of Ronald Knox so grey in tone,
why does it impart a sense of wet afternoons, soggy, ill-
prepared meals, vague aches and pains too feeble to locate,
yet nagging enough to destroy all pleasure or serenity?
Does the fault lie with the subject? There are times when
Mr. Waugh seems to suggest that Knox was temperamentally
depressive. I remember my only glimpses of him, an isolated
figure walking around Christ Church Meadow on cheerless,
leaf-strewn, windy October afternoons, and I can believe it.
Yet his less serious published works, for all that they are

so much of the day before yesterday, for all the sort of
scholar's humour that to later generations seems to suggest
some immaturity of vision, have a real gaiety and a sense
of delight in form that comes through even to readers who,
like myself, are prejudiced against their whole tradition.

It is clear, of course, that Knox's scholarship promised
so much more than the pleasant trivia he published; that
only the last years of his life allowed him any real intellectual fulfilment. It is this that Mr. Waugh makes the
line of his tragedy, for despite the spiritual blessing of
his conversion, it is as a tragedy of unfulfilment that he
portrays Knox's life. The Roman Catholic hierarchy - for
all Knox's and Mr. Waugh's ultimate submission - appears
as the villain - a lower middle-class, semi-educated, un-
cultivated villain, often not even English, but Irish or
even in one case a Gibraltarian. We may accept this picture, I think, without qualms, where it describes the first
years of Knox's service after his conversion. However
Cardinal Bourne may have hoped to create a Catholic Eton or
Harrow out of St. Edmund's College, Mr. Waugh does persuade
us that Ronald Knox was not the man to do it. His life at
Ware with its background of bickering, its narrow cultural
standards, and his own hopeless task, must have been
exceedingly dispiriting; although even here some part of
the disgust we feel as we read of it is, I suspect, conveyed by Mr. Waugh's own feelings rather than those of Knox.
The Chaplaincy at Oxford is surely another matter. Mr.
Waugh's picture of life at the Old Palace is one of his
triumphs of evocation, a splendid set piece, yet I am not
wholly convinced by it. The fact that Knox played so full a
part in the intellectual life of the pre-1914 Oxford of his
own youth was no guarantee of success with the Oxford youth
of the late 'twenties and 'thirties. Mr. Waugh rightly insists on this changed world. Yet I still find a colouring
of his own prejudices here. Mr. Waugh shrinks from the Left
Wing atmosphere of those days. That it was predominant I
can attest, for I was a typical Left Wing undergraduate of
that time; but it was by no means universal. Certainly
among Catholic undergraduates whom I knew the most part
rejected the current progressivism. Many of these I remember speaking of Knox not only with affection but with
admiration as a witty and fascinating host. It is more
than likely that Knox himself may have been often bored by
them; but can the picture of such a dispirited, failed
career be quite exact? The fact is that Mr. Waugh seems
determined to give us a downward curve whichever way we
look. If we take the picture back before Knox's conversion
to the days of his Anglican *jeunesse dorée* at Balliol Mr.
Waugh suggests that the happiness was corroded by growing

religious doubt; if we look forward to the years of the
translation of the Bible they are clouded by war, while
the happy promise of civilised living and scholarly work
at Mells was cut short by cancer.

It's a dismal story wherever you pick it up; but can it
really have been *felt* so dismally by Knox? - that is what I
find hard to believe. There is no reason at all why his
vocation as a priest should preclude him from the tastes
Mr. Waugh suggests were his true way of life - scholarship
in dignified, comfortable surroundings, a certain sort of
very English good talk and good living, not perhaps the
don's life so much as that of the chaplain of the great
aristocratic household. It is sad to see him baulked of
this so often, but can he really have been so sad and fretful under the discomforts of rationing and billeting as Mr.
Waugh makes him seem? It is not the English scholar and
gentleman born out of his time that is suggested, but too
often Mr. Wodehouse complaining of the draughts and the
noise.

It is so strange that such a picture should emerge when
Mr. Waugh was clearly so fond of the original. If one suggested that surely Knox's conversion and more still his
priestly vocation must have brought him more joy than is
shown in this book, Mr. Waugh would no doubt dismiss this
as the sentimental naïveté of a latter-day pagan. Faith
and vocation may, for all I know, be accompanied by the
sadness Mr. Waugh suggests; but not, I believe, the sort
of goodness which Mr. Waugh convinces me Knox possessed.
The portrait he gives in fact is that of a humane, loving,
good man who inexplicably can make no human contacts,
whose love of the created world is forever clouded by
melancholy, whose goodness shines through a damp mist of
disappointment. It is a portrait uncomfortably in tune
with the mood of 'Men at Arms' and 'Officers and Gentlemen'; perhaps Mr. Waugh has not permitted himself enough
anger at what he feels to have been the waste of a good
deal of Knox's life, and without anger he has sought
refuge in this dismal acceptance.

Note

1   Waugh had reviewed 'Hemlock and After' favourably
    ('Month', October 1952, 338-40) and Sir Angus no doubt
    wished to repay his generosity. Despite his inability to
    do so here, however, Waugh again came to his defence a
    little later, supporting 'The Old Men at the Zoo'
    against a review by John Mortimer in the 'Spectator'.
    Waugh did not simply write a letter but an alternative
    review ('Spectator', 29 September 1961, 431).

'A Tourist in Africa'

1960

166. DAN JACOBSON, 'SPECTATOR'

23 September 1960, 448

Dan Jacobson (b. 1929), an expatriate South African novelist,
is the author of 'A Dance in the Sun' (1956), 'The Evidence
of Love' (1960) and 'The Beginners' (1966).

Readers of the 'Spectator' will know (1) that 'A Tourist in
Africa' is Mr. Waugh's brief and unemphatic account of 'a
happy two months' he spent travelling through parts of East
and Central Africa. Mr. Waugh went to Africa in search of
warmth, and found it; he found too some pleasant company,
some aesthetic satisfaction, and much entertainment in
observing the appearance and manners of the people around
him. He can hardly be said to have exerted himself in
putting together this little volume; but his travel-diary
is continuously interesting, and does make a more forceful
impression, read between hard covers, than it did when published serially.
    As a tourist, Mr. Waugh 'eschewed politics'; neverthe-
less, some of his insights into the true political condition of Africa are valuable - not least because liberals
in Africa have long been spoilt by having inarticulate
hearties or crackpot racialists as their only opponents.
Mr. Waugh, it need hardly be said, is no liberal. But he
is no racialist either, and in 'A Tourist in Africa', as
in his earlier works set in Africa, he makes it a little
less easy for liberals to avert their eyes from the
shabbiness, the pathos, the human dislocation and inco-
herence which are so much a part of the African 'awaken-
ing.' One does not need to sympathise with Mr. Waugh's own

political views to share his distaste for the intellectual
pride and false charity which too often pass for thought
on the problems of Africa. And one goes to other writers
to read of the eagerness, curiosity and hope to be found
among the peoples of the continent.

'A Tourist in Africa' seems to illustrate a development
from the earlier books which must arouse the interest of
any admirer of Mr. Waugh's novels. These novels were all,
among other things, exercises in nostalgia; even, in certain instances, indulgences in nostalgia. In the present
case the reader is struck by the fact that, travelling
through territories in which the power of Great Britain is
in swift decline, Mr. Waugh seems to feel no discernible
nostalgia for the glories, the miseries, the heroic absurdities of the imperial achievement. Considering the way he
has expressed himself in the past, this seems to me surprising. He has never been a jingo; but one would have
thought that his imagination would have seized upon the
passing of the Empire as an occasion for the expression of
pride, regret and scorn. Once [in 'Vile Bodies'] Mr. Waugh
celebrated those 'pious and honourable people'.

> ...who had represented their country in foreign places
> and sent their sons to die for her in battle, people
> of decent and temperate life ... of independent judg-
> ment and marked eccentricities, kind people who cared
> for animals and the deserving poor, brave and rather
> unreasonable people, that fine phalanx of the passing
> order....

Not even the ghosts of this phalanx are evident in the
present book: no melancholy cadences lament their absence.
Instead we are offered a bleak aphorism: 'The foundations
of Empire are often occasions of woe; their dismemberment,
always.'

Mr. Waugh has for many years been England's finest practising novelist, and in my opinion his last two full-
length novels, 'Men at Arms' and 'Officers and Gentlemen',
were his best: they managed to be at once as funny as the
early novels and more convincingly serious than 'Brideshead
Revisited'. What, one wonders, does his present bleakness
or severity of spirit presage? Certainly, the absence of
nostalgia in the latest book is not all loss; one feels in
it a measure of charity and self-restraint which seems to
arise directly out of its severity. But Mr. Waugh has some
words of reproof which can be applied to speculations of
this sort. 'It is the fault of the modern eye,' he writes,
'to be forever goggling ahead, of the modern mind to concern itself only with "influences" and "movements,"

instead of accepting with gratitude the tangible gifts
of the past and present.'

Note

1 Six excerpts from 'A Tourist in Africa' appeared first in
   the 'Spectator' between 15 July and 19 August 1960.

167.   ANTONY ALLOTT, 'TABLET'

24 September 1960, 870

Antony Allott (b. 1924) became Professor of African Law
at the University of London in 1964. He has written 'New
Essays in African Law' (1970).

Of the making of books about Africa there is no end. Every
month a fresh wave of literature on the politics, peoples,
cultures and wild life of the continent submerges us.
Many of these works are either technical and not intended
for the general reader, or else ephemeral popular journalism. One must therefore be selective in one's reading
about Africa. It says much for the character of Mr. Waugh's
writing and observation that his slim and unpretentious
record of a recent journey to East and Central Africa
ought to find a place on everyone's short list.
    This was not Mr. Waugh's first visit to Africa, and
indeed his 'Black Mischief' is now recognised as an
authoritative early guide to African self-government;
nevertheless, he is free from the blindnesses which cloud
the vision of those who have Africa perpetually before
their eyes, whether as inhabitant, politican, or - word of
dread - 'Africanist.' To a professional student of Africa,
such as myself, it is a fascinating and illuminating
experience to see again familiar places and problems reflected in the mirror of Mr. Waugh's sensibility. He has an
acute eye for human types and human weaknesses, and also
the charity to refrain from judging them.
    Every journey to Africa is a voyage of discovery, often
of self-discovery; the persona that Mr. Waugh discloses in
his diary, as it expresses itself in an African context, is
an attractive one. His ability to surmount the hardships
and unexpected trials of African travel is remarkable. But

this is very much more than a mere travel-diary for bedside reading, as the blurb (as idiotic as any of its kind)
characterises it; implicit in the whole narrative is a
moral criticism of the so-called civilisation that Europe
has introduced into Africa. As Mr. Waugh says at [sic]
page 151:

> It is hard to realise now that at the time of the
> Diamond Jubilee many men of goodwill and intelligence
> thought the Pax Victoriana a reality. The bloody little
> forays of the Matabele seemed to them a shocking ana-
> chronism. Even now you will find people of some good-
> will and some intelligence who speak of Europeans as
> having 'pacified' Africa. Tribal wars and slavery were
> endemic before they came; no doubt they will break out
> again when they leave. Meantime, under European rule
> in the first forty years of this century there have been
> three long wars in Africa on a far larger scale than
> anything perpetrated by marauding spearmen, waged by
> white men against white, and a generation which has seen
> the Nazi regime in the heart of Europe had best stand
> silent when civilised and uncivilised nations are
> contrasted.

To say that this book shows a well-balanced and objective
appreciation of some of the problems of East and Central
Africa is perhaps merely to say that the reviewer shares
the prejudices of Mr. Waugh; there is little, either of
fact or interpretation, with which one can disagree. The
author's loathing of the flying padded cell known as the
commercial aeroplane will be readily understood by other
experienced travellers; and one can sympathise with his
distaste for English hotel-keeping, verbal avoidances
(especially in the naming of races), the treatment of
Lobengula, racialism, and the Englishman's tendency to exaggerated self-condemnation for the faults of others.
    It would be hard to find a more stimulating or congenial
travelling companion in Africa than Mr. Waugh, with his
curiosity, his erudition, and his wit; but, failing the
author in person, there is at least his diary to take
along.

168.   BASIL DAVIDSON, 'NEW STATESMAN'

24 September 1960, 439-40

Basil Davidson (b. 1914) is a journalist, historian, novel-
ist, and writer on African affairs. He is the author of
'Partisan Picture' (1946), 'The African Past' (1964), 'The
Andrassy Affair' (1966) and 'Can Africa Survive?' (1975).

This is Waugh, once again, of the Middle-Late Mood: more in
sorrow, for the most part, than in wit. Meeting this Stout
Party from the Western Shires is even a slightly embarrassing experience in Africa - a little, say, like having to
share a third-class sleeper with a member of the Upper
Classes. He cannot really bear the company; his political
opinions (uttered, of course, after a forthright declaration of ignorance of all politics) are often silly and
nearly always out of touch with reality; needlessly many of
the facts he gives you are wrong. Yet Mr Waugh has cast
himself cunningly, delightfully, in tolerant and expansive
mien: the old boy behaves splendidly. Through it all he
smiles with patient puzzled fortitude, meets the most curious people with a proper respect for social propriety, and
generally carries off the venture with a modesty and charm
that will please admirers and shame any would-be critic
into silence.
     The journey was by train to Genoa and then by boat to
East Africa. Personally, I would have settled for Mr
Waugh's staying in Genoa.... Here we get the very best of
Waugh....
     Afterwards, about three weeks in Tanganyika and two in the
Rhodesias. That is really the sum of Squire Waugh's travels
on this occasion. Not much: not often memorable: not seldom
foolish; and yet enough for a book that will be read and
liked, I should think, by people of the most various kinds.
Above all, a book that is meant to be enjoyed - from the
superbly civilised use of the semicolon to the gentle whip
of ironical understatement that is wielded now and then.
     It is - we know it well by now - a rather odd world that
Mr Waugh lives and travels in. That is part of the great
Victorian play (or do I mean ploy?) that he has built around
around himself. Before leaving he has to be inoculated
against Yellow Fever, but he knows so little about 'the new
medical organisation' that instead of getting his inocula-
tion for nothing at the Hospital for Tropical Diseases he
goes to the trouble of searching out a nurse in London who
'was giving, it seemed, some thirty shots an hour at a

guinea a time', and buys one from her. The same antiquated
attitude continues through Mr Waugh's inquiries into the
historical site's of Africa. It would be ungraciously pedan-
tic to drop on all of his historical mistakes; but perhaps
he might have read a modern book or two on the subject? As
it is, the dear old Zimba, 'a ferocious cannibal tribe',
turn up in full array; and the medieval civilisation of the
East Coast is duly written off as Persian or Arab - just as
though archaeologists like Mathew (not Matthew) had never
worked or written there.

All that is perhaps to be expected. But it is a little
much to present the origins of Zimbabwe as 'a mystery'
when every responsible investigator for the last 55 years
has found them medieval and Bantu. Moreover it is surprising that someone as widely travelled as Mr Waugh should not
have seen or heard of the Kushite ruins of Meroe or the
pre-Amharic ruins of Axum, and should thus allow himself to
call the Zimbabwe ruins 'the most remarkable in Africa
south of the Sahara'. Still, one must be grateful to Mr
Waugh for recognising African history and visiting, for
example, the remote island of Kilwa. At this stage of the
argument, almost anything about African history is better
than nothing.

Conclusions? Mr Waugh is on the side of the angels.
Indeed, his awareness of religion gives him some of his
best insights into an Africa that is still firmly linked,
in this way as in others, with the past. For the new
settlers of Rhodesia and the old settlers of South Africa
he has some charitably tough things to record. 'Racialism
is dotty, and rather modern....' And he sticks to his chosen character no matter the company. Placed at a Salisbury
dinner next to 'a local cultivated bigwig', he is lectured
on the 'great progress and potentialities' of Southern
Rhodesia.

> I said: 'I think you are a bachelor. I should
> not care to bring up children here.'
> 'Why not?' rather sharply scenting politics.
> 'The Accent'.

169. CYRIL CONNOLLY, 'SUNDAY TIMES'

25 September 1960, 27

When we are young we travel to see the world, afterwards to

make sure it is still there. In 'A Tourist in Africa' Mr
Waugh makes a routine check-up on various places which had
delighted him as a youth. Aden? 'Here Sir.' Zanzibar? 'Here
Sir.' Mombasa? 'Here Sir.' Dar-es-Salaam? 'Here Sir.' Happy
Valley? Silence - and the blue pencil strikes it off the
roll. I know the obsession by which re-visiting places
where one has once felt becomes a substitute for feeling,
but it does not make for the best kind of travel book. In
fact 'A Tourist in Africa' is quite the thinnest piece of
book-making which Mr. Waugh has undertaken and must be
viewed in relation to the labours on Father Ronald Knox
which preceded it.

It is not that Mr. Waugh has seen so much already,
although many of these places he seems to have visited only
the year before, but that the particular pose he affects -
of an elderly, infirm and irritable old buffer, quite out
of touch with the times - is hardly suited to enthusiasm,
a prerequisite of travel-writing. His book is full of
little bread-and-butter letters, but, on the whole, his
motto seems to be like Yeats's lines:

> On life, on death
> Cast a cold eye.

The fact must be faced, however, that there are people
who are interested in every single word Mr. Waugh writes,
and I am one of them. While deploring the perfunctory and
blasé handling of his material, the rows of short sentences,
the occasional carelessness, such as misquoting Tennyson,
using words like 'insomnious,' together with his indifference to scenery, and all forms of wild-life (so unlike the
descriptions of Kenya in 'Remote People'), I can still
assert that the magnetism of his extraordinary personality
breaks through and that one is loth to part from it, even
when he is on the level of:

> Mrs. Newman forbade one to go to this hotel and very
> kindly put me up for the night in her own cheerful
> villa. That evening she collected some of her neigh-
> bours for cocktails.... All were most welcoming to a
> rather travel-worn stranger.

He is really at his best in Europe, in his description
of Genoa, and I wish he could have included his articles
for the 'Daily Mail' on European cities, for he has
reached the age when one writes much better if one is comfortable and not too hot or too cold. There is one exception; when kindled by his faith, his pen surmounts other
obstacles, and he describes Father Groeber's school of
native wood-carvers at the Serima mission in Southern

Rhodesia with vivacity. Emin Pasha also kindles his interest.

What would we learn of (1) Africa (2) Mr. Waugh - if we
had only this book to go by? That we must travel by sea,
not air, that the coast towns are too hot, that Mombasa is
the best of them, that we must avoid British-owned hotels,
that the hospitality of the landed gentry of the White
Highlands has been replaced by that of government officials,
that there is some jealousy among them, that the Eastern
Highlands of Southern Rhodesia round Umtali are an unspoilt
paradise ('Perhaps the development of this district may
provide the elderly and well-to-do with a more dignified
resort than the beaches where they now exhibit themselves.
The craze for sunburn has lasted long enough').

On racialism, nationalism, the colour bar, even the
ground-nuts scheme, Mr. Waugh is without prejudice. He dis-
approves, but will not let them spoil his holiday. He
defends the Aden smells:

> It is always a wonder to me that the English - who
> cheerfully endure the reek of cabbages, diesel fumes,
> deodorisers, fish and chips, gaspers, ice-cream - fight
> shy of 'native streets'.

'Paris at the cocktail hour. How gaily I used to jump
into a taxi and visit the bars while the train crawled
round the ceinture. Nowadays, hard of hearing and stiff in
the limb, I sit glumly in my compartment.' That really is
a bad sign, especially with a good restaurant in the Place
D'Aligre close to the Gare de Lyon. About planes and boats
he is rather unfair. The menus on boats are good, but the
food is often deadly dull, and nothing on a plane is as bad
as having to share a cabin or even a table in the restaurant with the same people for a week.

To travel first class, on the other hand, on a Comet or
a Caravelle from London to Rome, Madrid, Athens or Tripoli
compared to any other means of getting to such places is
absolute bliss. But I have made a mental reservation on
the Pendennis Castle, noted the excellent library on the
Rhodesia Castle (for the East Coast Route) and not forgotten the German hotel at Kibo. 'A very pleasant bedside
book,' the blurb says of 'A Tourist in Africa,' and so it
is. But what a drubbing I should get if I had written it.

170. ALAN SILLITOE, 'TIME AND TIDE'

15 October 1960, 1226

Alan Sillitoe (b. 1928) is a novelist, playwright, poet,
essayist and short-story and travel writer whose portrayal
of the relentless hardships of working-class life accelerated him to fame in the late 1950s. He is the author of
'Saturday Night and Sunday Morning' (1958, filmed 1960,
play 1964), 'The Loneliness of the Long Distance Runner'
(1959), 'The Rats and Other Poems' (1960), 'This Foreign
Field' (1970) and 'The Story Teller' (1979).

It is the way of the ignorant, perhaps, to judge a book by
its opening. Evelyn Waugh begins 'A Tourist in Africa':

> 28th December 1958. On the third day after Christmas
> we commemorate the massacre of the Holy Innocents. Few
> candid fathers, I suppose, can regard that central
> figure of slate in Breughel's painting in Antwerp with-
> out being touched by sympathy. After the holly and
> sticky sweetmeats, cold steel.

And D.H. Lawrence:

> Comes over one an absolute necessity to move. And
> what is more, to move in some particular direction. A
> double necessity then: to get on the move, and to know
> whither.

It is strange how these first paragraphs sum up the
pace and content of both travel books so completely. Lawrence at 38, in his trip to Sardinia, gets us by the
scruff of the neck and pushes us before him, arrogantly
pointing out in dizzy and colourful prose what his vision
wishes us to see; Waugh at 55 tells us about his journey
to Africa as if we were walking beside him and just able to
catch his quiet and civilised observations on those sights
and sounds that get through to the well-padded core of
upper-class English values. To me his prose is a bit too
smooth, gives off an aura of lifelessness reinforced in
the beginning by constant flashbacks to the more sanguine
atmosphere of his earlier books. The first fifty pages
of this one could be called 'The Travel Diary of a Chun-
terer.'
  ...Each chapter is well-laced with the same old digs
against the long-dead Labour Government. What a traumatic

shock that was to a lot of people! We have a couple of
scorching pages on the misguided Fabian idealism of the
Groundnuts Scheme (in which forty million quid went like
a blue streak down the drain), unconsciously (though not
unfairly) compared later to the patient and gentle efforts
of Father Groeber's teaching at Serima which explores the
temperament of his African pupils for evidence of artistic
leanings not contaminated by European influences. 'The
savage African art of the eighteenth and nineteenth centuries which delighted the European and American connoisseurs of the 1920s seems as dead as the civilised art of
Europe.'

Waugh's account of his journey to Africa is full of that
curious, falsely attractive sense of tolerance of a caste-
bound mind. It is easy to read because it demands nothing
from you. His defence mechanism is near to perfect, in that
little he says is really slateable, either because it isn't
fully enough explained, or because he has no firm opinions
to stand on.

'Few people anywhere, I suppose, deserve the government
they get. Too many English voices are at the moment raised
to reproach the South Africans for me to join in the
clamour.' And 'acts of violence are also widespread everywhere in the world. It would be interesting to know how
often during the last five years the Indian police have
(quite properly) opened fire on rioters and charged them
with *lathis*.'

If you are familiar with the world Mr. Waugh lives in,
this sort of prose may be faultless, but if you find his
values too alien you will see it lacks just that bit of
explanatory padding in which inspiration and uncertainty
may have broken loose. The best section in the book is
that describing the decline and fall of the Matabele
chieftain Lobengula - victim of a war of attrition in
which his manhood was eaten away by the corrupting gifts
of his white 'friends'. This is a solid episode out of the
past, and marvellously handled, and is the only thing
which makes me doubt the accuracy of the last sentence of
the blurb which says that this 'travel diary makes a very
pleasant bedside book (which should induce sleep in all but
the most stubborn insomniacs).'

'Unconditional Surrender'

1961 (US title: 'The End of the Battle', 1961)

171. KINGSLEY AMIS, 'SPECTATOR'

27 October 1961, 581-2

The major theme of all Mr. Evelyn Waugh's novels has been
disintegration, social and moral, and he has often made
good use of structural devices to reflect this theme. Thus
in the earlier books long stretches of narrative, heavily
populated with variegated characters, would give place to
tiny fragmentary snapshots of the same people singly or in
pairs, held for the instant that enabled us to infer their
destiny. The result is a looser but more widely ranging
kind of unity than that which most narratives afford, and
it is here, in this apparently quite casual attitude to
matters of coherence and direction, that Mr. Waugh's
celebrated airiness of manner is largely to be traced. His
style, an elegant instrument based on scrupulous attention
to syntax and word-order, is perhaps secondary.

With all its virtues of economy, mobility and breadth
of coverage, the dangers of the open-ranch method of
character-farming, as opposed to the enclosed-pasture
technique of more cautious practitioners, are obvious
enough: parts of the herd will wander off and set up on
their own. Mr. Waugh can be relied on to see to it that
they are brought back in time for slaughtering - being a
Waugh minor character is still almost as hazardous as being
a Graham Greene hero - but their cavortings meanwhile, however spectacular, may bear little relation to even the
freest overall plan. Tony Last's dash up the Amazon had
better have been left in its original short-story form instead of furnishing an out-of-key, and unnecessary, coda
to 'A Handful of Dust'. And there are few parallels to the
headlong vigour with which the author of 'Work Suspended'

rides off in two contrary directions.

Now that its third and final volume has appeared, a similar centrifugal tendency can be seen in the 'Men at Arms' sequence. The figure of Apthorpe, brother-officer of the hero, Guy Crouchback, in the Royal Corps of Halberdiers, seemed at the time to bulk unduly large in the first volume, not only in that he suffered his predictable demise at the end of that volume and was forgotten altogether soon after the start of the next, but also by reason of his lowly status in Mr. Waugh's grotesques' gallery. When the Apthorpe portable latrine came up for the eleventh time, one had the unexpected feeling that comic material was being spread out thin. It is curious that, after giving his name to all three main sections of 'Men at Arms', he gets only one passing mention in the four-page authorial synopsis prefixed to 'Unconditional Surrender', and that as merely 'another officer.'

The second instalment, 'Officers and Gentlemen', promised more in the way of emergent unity among apparent diversity. It seemed to offer a firm but unstated contrast between types doing well out of the war and the social changes accompanying it (Trimmer ... Ludovic ...) and types meeting or evidently heading for various levels of disaster (Ivor Claire ... Crouchback himself ... Fido Hound ...). If additional room had been found for Fido earlier, among the transients who thronged the pages devoted to training and preparation, his reappearance might have lent continuity, but one readily conceded that discontinuity and randomness better befit an account of the Cretan debacle.

'Unconditional Surrender' disappoints most of these hopes of final coherence. Trimmer vanishes, even though the fact that before doing so he has rendered pregnant Virginia Troy, Crouchback's ex-wife, does something to keep his memory green. Claire, whose dereliction of duty before innumerable witnesses might have preluded an interesting conflict of values, is let off by everybody including Crouchback, the Army, Bellamy's Club and Mr. Waugh, who extends to him that indulgence for the ruthless egotist which he normally reserves for women of this type, from Margot Metroland to, in the present volume, Julia Stitch (described in the synopsis simply as 'a beauty' - that's enough, you see. She's a beauty all right, mate). And to take a small but significant example of the defeat of expectation, Grace-Groundling-Marchpole's counter-espionage department, whose mounting but baseless suspicions of Crouchback looked like issuing in a frenzy of injustice, fades quietly from the scene half-way through - I will suggest why in a moment.

What does tie the book to its two predecessors, and
what abundantly justifies it in itself, is the continued
history of Ludovic, now a major in Intelligence. While
holding the post of commandant of a parachute training
school he is terrorised by the arrival of Crouchback,
whom he supposes to know about certain events in Crete.
Unaware that shock and privation have removed these from
Crouchback's memory, visualising imminent exposure as the
murderer of Hound and another officer, Ludovic retreats
into a sort of somnambulism, from which he emerges only to
play with his poodle (which he names 'Fido,' of course),
plunge the Mess into leaden gloom and tinker with the
volume of *pensées* he is compiling. Equally in this last
role - that of a rather more sensitive and adult Palinurus (1) - in his final appearance as a successful trashy
novelist, and in his earlier career as valet-cum-secretary-
cum-what-may to a diplomat of specialised tastes, Ludovic
is a creature of the airiest fantasy.

This means that he and his doings score heavily over
much else in the book, especially Crouchback and his. Even
the latter's decent actions have a way of arousing suspicion, as when he tries hard to save a party of Jewish
refugees from miserable internment in the Balkans: Greeks
or Turks, presumably, would not give him such a signal
opportunity of showing how he can put duty above prejudice. But the real trouble with Crouchback is his failure
to act, his great and varied inabilities. He feels this
himself, and his creator claims sympathy for him as a man
trying in vain to find a place for himself in a great
battle of our time. This would be acceptable if he seemed
to be really trying, but he never looks back from that
stage, early in 'Men at Arms,' when he appears in England
in the first weeks of the war 'looking for a job' by
buttonholing powerful friends at Bellamy's and writing to
Cabinet Ministers' wives. What about all those jobs in the
ranks of, say, Signals or the RASC? Unthinkable, naturally.

This, again, would be acceptable if Crouchback were
another kind of Waugh hero, the sort to whom cruel and
unjust things are always happening. But to be a Paul Pennyfeather of 1939-45 is inconceivable for the heir of a
landed recusant family, a member of Bellamy's, an officer
of the Halberdiers who *enjoys guest nights*. And so Grace-
Groundling-Marchpole's bomb fizzes away into harmlessness.
Apthorpe and Ludovic draw the laughs Crouchback cannot be
allowed to draw, Hound and Trimmer meet the serio-comic
humiliations reserved for persons who have no dignity to
start with. The lopsided construction of the sequence
faithfully reflects the predicament of a hero - and the
difficulty of using a hero - who is surrounded by activity

he cannot share, who can barely remain on his feet, prop-
ping himself up on Catholicism and peace-time regimental
tradition. No wonder he is always hurting his knee.

It is tempting to believe that Mr. Waugh, à la Pinfold,
sees this more clearly than anybody else. Certainly there
is a strong hint of self-consciousness about some of those
top-people-isms with which his later work is encrusted:
things like

> When Guy rose to leave, all his little house-hold,
> twenty strong, assembled to see him go ,

and (the time is September, 1939)

> Everywhere houses were being closed, furniture stored,
> children transported, servants dismissed, lawns
> ploughed, dower-houses and shooting-lodges crammed to
> capacity; mothers-in-law and nannies were everywhere
> gaining control.

You know, everywhere from South Shields to Llanelly. (See
page 7 of the present book for the latest.) These are
almost certainly put in specially to annoy the Labour
Party, etc. But it would be too fanciful to say the same
of the souped-up traditionalism with which, for instance,
the funeral of Crouchback senior is recounted. That
'baronial wrought-iron on which one was always barking
one's shins at Brideshead,' and which one reviewer (2) saw
as having been largely 'torn down' in 'Officers and Gentlemen', is back in full profusion.

We might note here the small detail that we are invited
to think it is all right for the Crouchbacks to call the
local church 'the chapel' although it is not a chapel, but
not all right for Box-Bender, Crouchback's brother-in-law,
to call his den 'the business-room' because it is not a
business-room. The Crouchback motto is *It's all right when
my family have always done it*, or more shortly, *It's all
right when I do it*, whether 'it' is studiously maintained
uncharitableness for six years of war service or dining
at a black-market restaurant. And conversely, of course,
it's not all right when they do it, and this 'it' and
'they' have now multiplied exceedingly. Crouchback's original enemy, 'the Modern Age in Arms,' has come to have less
to do with Germany and Russia than with jazz-lovers, diners
on expenses, hirers of evening dress, Americans, pilferers
on the railways. Trimmers of all sorts, holders of temporary commissions. (Crouchback had one of those, too, but it
was all right when he did it.)

These would be valid targets if clearly seen. But

Trimmer cannot be made the key figure he might have become, because the task of finding out about him would be
too distasteful; his liaison with Virginia can only be
alluded to and he must be dropped from the story. Ludovic
must remain insulated from probability. An American officer
can be introduced, but is not worth the effort of close
observation: the result is the dullest and least differen-
tiated character Mr. Waugh has ever created. As for
American enlisted men - well, Coca-Cola and peanuts and
gum and whores will do for them, won't it? No, it won't,
not even on TV. Guy Crouchback has maintained his integrity at the cost of keeping his eyes shut and his fingers
in his ears.

Notes

1   The pseudonym used by Cyril Connolly for his volume of
    pensées, 'The Unquiet Grave'; see No. 16.
2   Mr Amis is quoting himself; see No. 149.

172.   BERNARD BERGONZI, 'GUARDIAN'

27 October 1961, 7

...The quality of the writing is, throughout, superb, and
confirms my belief that Mr Waugh is the best living writer
of English prose. And in spite of a fair degree of complexity in the story the book is admirably plotted and organised - much more so than the earlier volumes. Yet above all
this is, I think, an intensely personal book; not necessarily in any autobiographical or Pinfoldian sense -
though the highly successful Yugoslav chapters obviously
draw on Mr Waugh's own experiences - but because Guy
Crouchback embodies the nostalgic myth of so much of Mr
Waugh's writing: the notion that true value lies in a combination of Catholicism and the aristocratic virtues. To
anyone brought up as a Catholic Mr Waugh's image of Catholicism is, to say the least, peculiar; and the same thing
may well be true of his picture of the gentry. But that is
beside the point; it is enough that Mr Waugh has found the
myth creatively valuable. And in this book the defeat and
disillusion of Guy Crouchback seems to indicate the total
collapse of Mr Waugh's dominating myth; the modern world
has triumphed, and the implications of the book's title are

everywhere apparent. Yet the myth has never been stronger
than at its moment of extinction; the novel is permeated by
a disdain and bitterness that gives great strength to the
prose. The off-hand violence that in the early farces was
merely an element in an eccentric personal vision, here
becomes part of the texture of reality. As in the casual
remark about a British officer engaged in forcibly repatri-
ating refugees to Yugoslavia just after the war: 'This man
was in fact dispatching royalist officers - though he did
not know it - to certain execution.'

There are many excellent things in the novel. Mr Waugh is
coldly savage about the pro-Stalin hysteria that the Russian alliance generated in England in 1941-45. The book
opens with the Sword of Stalingrad being exhibited like a
precious relic in Westminster Abbey; this grotesque and
ironic symbol casts its shadow across the whole book. Nor,
fortunately, are elements of low comedy altogether missing;
the absurdities of military and bureaucratic life are constantly exposed, and there is one splendid character in
Major Ludovic, queer in more ways than one, whose burning
literary ambitions are triumphantly realised.

'Unconditional Surrender' seems to me Mr Waugh's best
book since 'The Loved One'. It is exciting, too, because
it makes much more sense of the first two volumes of the
military trilogy; the whole work now looks a substantial
achievement, and one which may alter our total picture of
Mr Waugh's writings.

173. V.S. PRITCHETT, 'NEW STATESMAN'

27 October 1961, 603-4

...At the beginning of the third and final volume of the
story, Crouchback's apathy is complete; but his capacity
for pain has been noted by the gods.... Crouchback's
apathy breaks when he realises that a sense of the futility
of life is not enough, for life has culminated in the monstrous. It is perhaps the final mortifying irony of the
book that Crouchback survives and prospers. He even has the
pleasure of seeing Box-Bender, his extremely unlikeable
Protestant brother-in-law, having trouble with his son.
The boy talks of becoming a monk.

Evelyn Waugh is our present master of the hardened
school of English comedy, the heir of Firbank's slashing
grace. He has a genius for very specialised social

effrontery and its delight in outrage. It required a nerve
to treat the war as a sordid social jamboree of smart and
semi-smart sets, who are mainly engaged in self-inflation
and in climbing up the ladder, to present it as a collection of bankrupt sideshows. But Mr Waugh has more nerve
than any English writer now living, and large portions of
the last war were exactly as he describes them.

The war is not, of course, presented as anything more
than heightened (or deflated) personal experience; the
trilogy is a memoir rather than a novel. Other books about
the war have gone straight for the conventional - the
battle. He, too, can negligently turn out a battle, but his
interest is, fundamentally, the moralist's. His eye is
trained on the flat detail of human folly, vanity and
hypocrisy; and although he can be rightly called a wounded
Romantic, he is a most patient and accurate observer. His
glances at London life during the period are laconic and
just. The last war saw the birth of the organisation man
and Mr Waugh was in, all eyes and ears, at the dreadful
accouchement.

There are, we know, two Evelyn Waughs: the satirical
blessing who wrote 'The Loved One' and the appeasing, even
tender comic moralist, the accomplished, testy, courteous,
epigrammatic man of letters who wrote 'A Handful of Dust'.
(Crouchback characteristically takes Anstey's 'Vice Versa'
(1) to read on his campaigns.) The trilogy is in his humane
and perfectly finished manner. His scorn is modulated, his
sentences are distillations. Most comic writers like to
think they could play it straight if only their public
would let them. Waugh is able to be grave without difficulty for he has always been comic for serious reasons. He
has his own well-understood conventional bent, an almost
romantic sense of propriety. His snobbery, when he is in
this mood, is an amusing and acceptable mixture of High
Romance, Puritan decorum and tartness and has a professional sense of the rules of the English class game. To
object to his snobbery is as futile as objecting to cricket,
for every summer the damn game comes round again whether
you like it or not.

Only one kind of snobbery is affronting in Mr Waugh: the
violent. It is ugly, theatrical and falsely generalised.
Even if we accept that ranker-officers are envious, calculating, unsure showmen and on the make, must we add cowardice, lack of nerve and - as in the case of the minutely
observed Ludovic - crime? Is the envy of the lower classes
any more likely to lead to dishonesty and cowardice than
the conceit of the uppers? It is here that Mr Waugh's High
Romance becomes vulgar sentimentality. In this book he
throws Ludovic away as a recognisable human being and an

original type rarely attempted: the solemn, climbing, half-sinister, half-hurt queer with shattering gifts as a bad writer. I do not deny that Mr Waugh uses him with malign masochistic skill when he shows him writing a novel that falsifies a good deal of Crouchback's experience, for Ludovic has watched Crouchback like a cat.

Amid the antics of brigadiers, generals, politicians, socialites, partisans, wives and mistresses, the dry and stoical Crouchback is a frosty figure. His apathy makes him a perfect focus. He is given a nullity that, on the one hand, may represent the gentlemanly ideal: the whole of life will be vulgar to him. On the other hand, he is subtly endowed with the reticence and decency that suggest a life profoundly satisfied by the pains that have been inflicted on it, and by the one or two affections that remain.

Virginia, the faithless wife and good-time girl, is beautifully understood. The comedy of her conversation, full of four letter words, with the almost virginal Uncle Peregrine is exquisite. He had never heard a lady use such language; it astounds rather than displeases; it also misleads, for he has the flattering illusion that she is making a pass at him and is piqued when he finds she is not. What she is after is re-marriage to her ex-husband who has come into money, for she is at the end of her tether. It is the measure of Mr Waugh's sympathy that he lets out no savage laugh at the cynical proposition and yet is not sentimental about it. The war has, at any rate, taught Crouchback to recognise a 'displaced person' when he sees one. He does not love her. She does not love Trimmer's child when it is born: she calls it 'that baby'. Crouchback does not weep when she is killed in an air raid, which lets him off some of the awkward consequences of playing so straight a bat in the sex Test. And when, at the end of the novel, his awful brother-in-law complains that things have turned very conveniently for Guy, we muse happily on the richness of Mr Waugh's point. His comedy has always been hard, perverse and shocking; but that in no way prevents it from reproducing the human heart with delicacy, or at any rate, that portion of the heart that, however shallow, can still feel wrong and pain.

Only two episodes in this final volume strike me as being tame: the strange, dull, set-piece when Ludovic files past the sword of Stalingrad in Westminster Abbey. As symbolism, irony, fragment of war chronicle, whatever it is, this scene is in the way. Later on, Ludovic goes to a party given by the editor of a literary monthly whose grubby camel-hair coat and sharp Sultanic orders to the girls will bring back sentimental memories to some readers; but again, this is a tame jest. The vanities of the military

and social servitudes are Mr Waugh's subject; it is good,
of course, of Mr Waugh to call and all that on his Bohemian
friends, but somehow the visit falls flat. No literary figure can compete with an Apthorpe, a Trimmer, an Uncle Peregrine, or any of the huge list of exquisitely touched-in
characters who fought the war with chits, passes and top
secret reports, in Mr Waugh's terse 'Who's Who' of the
National Peril.

St George Crouchback ends by reassessing his views on
the dragon. Mme Kanyi, a Hungarian Jewess, says to him:

> 'Is there any place that is free from evil? It is too
> simple to say that the Nazis wanted war. These commu-
> nists wanted it too. It was the only way in which they
> could come to power. Many of my people wanted it, to be
> revenged on the Germans, to hasten to the creation of
> the national state. It seems to me there was a will to
> war, a death wish, everywhere. Even good men thought
> their private honour would be satisfied by war. They
> could assert their manhood by killing and being killed.
> They would accept hardships in recompense for having
> been selfish and lazy. Danger justified privilege. I
> knew Italians - not very many perhaps - who felt this.
> Were there none in England?'

'God forgive me', said Guy, 'I was one of them'. It was
after being told, by an enthusiastic little bureaucrat, of
her arrest, that Crouchback was tempted to strike an
officer.

Note

1   Thomas Anstey (pseudonym of Thomas Anstey Guthrie,
     1856-1934) was a comic novelist; 'Vice Versa' (1882),
     his greatest success, describes how a father and son
     interchange ages and personalities.

174.   CHRISTOPHER DERRICK, 'TABLET'

28 October 1961, 1024, 1026

A sword is shaped rather like a cross, and it used to be
kissed accordingly by great men at noble moments. Guy
Crouchback's story began, in 'Men at Arms', with him

leaving his Italian home in 1939 to take up the sword for
Christendom and his king; and he paused on the way for a
moment of perspective and dedication, running his finger
along the effigy-sword of another knight, a crusader who
made the supreme sacrifice and died *in causa Christi* far
from his English home.

Looked at from the outside, Sir Roger de Waybroke's
sacrifice fell rather flat: he died not at paynim hands
before Jerusalem, but in the course of a dirty bit of local
power-politics in Italy, into which accident and the pressure of events had deflected him. The Crusades being what
they were, this anti-climax and waste represents no great
loss to Sir Roger's conscience, no great betrayal of his
own moment of dedication; perhaps his confessor advised
him to think 'not of the harvest, but only of proper sow-
ing,' and warned him of the booby-trap which Heaven lays
before good men when they make great gestures of offering
and sacrifice but still try to stipulate the terms. At any
rate, the Italian peasants canonised the English knight,
and we can provisionally make a kind of saint out of Guy,
whom we leave at the end of the trilogy restored like Job
to something better than his former condition, the heavenly
visitation over and done with, the sacrifice accepted in
tongues of fire, the books balanced, the past still there
to be lived with.

The sacrifice cuts deep, of course, 'costing not less
than everything.' There are two issues, two loves to be
mortified, lineage and the sword; and in each case the
mortification is necessarily a gruesome business, a mirror-
reversal or photographic negative of something that seemed
innocuous enough when it first appeared. In a key passage
of 'Men at Arms', Mr. Goodall the mild genealogist recounted an episode of gentle casuistry, its outcome being that
'under another and quite uninteresting name a great family
has been preserved,' and Guy made a fine fool of himself in
consequence, noting the application but mistaking its
terms; now, his unconditional surrender to the nightmarish
mirror-reversal of this arrangement is his making and
deliverance, and Virginia's as well. She dies in the odour
of sanctity; Guy is left, to rear an unwanted and ignomini-
ously begotten bastard to his own name and inheritance.

Sir Roger's Christian blade has dwindled meanwhile into
commando daggers ('mostly given away to tarts') and the
monstrous incongruity of the Stalingrad Sword, worshipped
in the Abbey by grey crowds. Behind the scenes and with its
own kind of efficiency, the new religion starts to take
over, its few active apostles finding it all too easy to
lead by the nose a nation and especially an intelligentsia
hopelessly fuddled by the old dichotomy of left and right

and the simple identification of right with enemy. The wide boys climb on to the band-waggon, notably de Souza, the fretful and rootless intellectual from Cambridge: for a time he finds the social and personal modes of subversion enough to ease his venom and fret, but not for long; he moves on to higher things in Jugoslavia, among the partisans, and there helps expertly to steer policy in the right direction, while Guy stands helplessly by. That betrayal is neatly completed, and the war's own death-wish consummated; in a final forlorn biff, the mirror-image of Trimmer's commando assault (and similarly laid on strictly as a propaganda deception) the great Ritchie-Hook is fortunate enough to go to his own fine Halberdier Valhalla. Guy is compelled in the wrath of God once again to survive, and to hear from a refugee Jewess the last hard words about those who run their fingers in noble sentiment along the cutting edges of swords.

This novel is not quite the pacifist tract it will be taken for in some quarters; Guy's brooding about 'the antithesis between the acceptance of sacrifice and the will to win' does not quite exclude a limited synthesis, possible even to those wholly committed to a religion of sacrifice. Once the will to win this particular war against the Germans had been erected into a national absolute and tied to unconditional surrender (as if armies could be used to defeat evil once and for all at its source), then Guy's original war, the one worth fighting, was already lost past recovery: the Communists needed not to win, but only to step firmly into the emptiness we made for them when we decreed from on high that the only question to be asked in Jugoslavia was the one about which side was able and willing to hurt the Germans most. But there was a point up to which the will to win could be meaningfully treated as a vehicle for sacrifice; the identification of sword and cross is never quite the hundred-per-cent folly it seems, and the idea of the Holy War is not necessarily and entirely a blasphemous oxymoron. Guy's great sin was against the virtue of prudence; it was not sensible, not scientific to expect any public good to come of that huge blind banging of public power. Ideally, he should have noticed earlier what was happening, and pulled out. At one point, while languishing in the military doldrums, he was offered a post as almoner to a civilian hospital: he should have laid his sword on the altar and accepted the offer. But nobody saw things like that at the time.

'Unconditional Surrender' is not a perfect book: in a number of small ways, Mr. Waugh's pen seems rustier than before. It was a particularly sad mistake to exhume Corporal-Major Ludovic - a frightful image of hell where he

first appeared, in 'Officers and Gentlemen' - for the sake
of heavy satire about 'Horizon' and the wartime cultural
scene, and there is a curiously boring quiet American: we
have never had cause before to suspect Mr. Waugh of padding. But he is writing more deeply than ever before, and
much more gently: the acid seems to have gone out of him
since Guy's fear and hatred of 'the Modern Age in arms'
ceased to be an eccentricity and became common form. The
armies have changed direction, the perspectives have
altered. There will be fine old diehards, crusty reactionaries, to cry snobbery and romanticism at the account of
old Crouchback's funeral, to dissent from these unpatriotic
misgivings about the war, to utter sad regrets that the
Festival of Britain should appear as a final image of the
jungle closing in; what they emphasise in fact will be Mr.
Waugh's own present position, an *avant-garde* position, a
very serious and responsible one in the front rank of the
contemporary movement.

175. CYRIL CONNOLLY, 'SUNDAY TIMES'

29 October 1961, 31

Mr. Waugh writes: 'In 1950 I wrote of "Officers and Gentlemen", "I thought at first the story would run into three
volumes. I find that two will do the trick." This was not
quite candid. I knew that a third volume was needed.'...
    The first novel, 'Men at Arms', was published in 1952;
'Officers and Gentlemen' in 1955 (it was then, not in 1950,
that he announced there would be no further novels) so that,
with 'Unconditional Surrender' in 1961, nearly ten years
separates the first and last volume. Three other novels
also deal with Mr. Waugh's disillusionment: 'Put Out More
Flags' (optimistic); 'Brideshead Revisited' (starting with
the conclusions of his 'love-affair with the army'), and
'Scott-King's Modern Europe'. It must have been a grand
passion.
    I found it so difficult to recapture the values of
'Unconditional Surrender' owing to the long interval from
its predecessor that I read the whole trilogy again. I
strongly urge the publisher to issue all three books in
one volume immediately; the cumulative effect is most impressive, and it seems to me unquestionably the finest
novel to have come out of the war. Mr. Waugh has the
maniac's power of carrying the reader along with him but

without the mania, and in Guy Crouchback he has created a
deeply sympathetic character. One is reminded of Tietjens,
the country gentleman hero of Ford's four novels of the
1914 war; (1) but Ford is a wildly romantic mythomane,
Waugh a most accurate reporter.

In his novels eye and ear pick up everything essential,
and the style seems effortlessly to incorporate his observations into a compact, fast-flowing narrative with seldom
a word out of place. Like Kipling, Wodehouse, perhaps
Hemingway, and certain other novelists, he is at heart a
private schoolboy, full of *esprit de corps*, gang jokes,
sometimes over-done, tribal shibboleths and healthy hero-
worhip.

In all his novels, especially these army ones, there are
a group of 'bloods,' usually members of a club once called
Bratts, and now Bellamy's, which is the home of all the
gallantry and good fellowship that remains in the world,
while, outside, jabber the 'lesser breeds without the law'
- climbers, schemers, crypto-Communists, planners, business-
men and politicians: the civilian *canaille*. Sometimes one
of these strays into the bloods' sanctum and gets cut down
to size.

Each of the three novels shows a different form of hero-
worship and consequent disillusion. Politically the two
disasters which upset Crouchback's simple faith are the
acceptance of Russia as an ally, and (though this is not
stressed) the arrival of Americans in Europe to organise
'the final dismemberment of Christendom.'

In 'Men at Arms' Crouchback is in love, quite simply,
with the army; more especially with the Halberdiers, his
first regiment, and with Apthorpe, who is not a 'blood'
but the other new boy, the chum who becomes a symbol of
the hopes and delights promised by the great love-affair.
The 'bloods' are Colonel Tickeridge and Ritchie-Hook....
Personally, I am allergic to Apthorpe and am bored by the
elaborate rags and teasing which surround this rose-
coloured character; nevertheless, there is a happy glow
about this first volume which is not found in the others.

'Officers and Gentlemen' (I think the title implies an
ironical contrast) shows Crouchback taken up by the
'bloods,' with Bellamy's very much in the picture. His
esprit de corps is now transferred to the Commandos.
Tommy Blackhouse replaces Ritchie-Hook, and Ivor Claire,
the languid dandy, flower of our *ancien régime*, takes the
place of the unfortunate Apthorpe; and the mock-hero,
Trimmer, becomes the butt.

'Officers and Gentlemen' is a magnificent novel, containing all the arduous excitements of commando training
and ending with the 'shambles' of Crete, one of the most

effective accounts of defeat in which the rapid, light-
machine-gun fire of Mr. Waugh's prose produces an overtone
of tragic horror. Here Ivor Claire reveals feet of clay, a
shock from which Crouchback's esteem for the Commandos
never recovers, and from which even Bellamy's rocks; and
here emerges the 'new man,' the ruthless, enigmatic ranker,
Corporal-Major Ludovic, who seems to prefigure the army
novels of Mr. Simon Raven.

In 'Unconditional Surrender' we are shown the eclipse of
Ludovic in his turn, pursued by the Furies, though successful as a writer; and the final disillusionment of Crouchback, a Laocoon festooned with crypto-Communists, among
the Partisans in Jugoslavia.

'One Man's War' might be a working title for all three
volumes, for Mr. Waugh reports nothing of which he has not
had acquaintance (except perhaps Dakar) (2) and this is a
strength and a weakness. For he is cut off from the main
conduct of the war, from all the great battles from Alamein
to the Rhine; even as he is cut off from the people and
their war-aim.

I have left out what is perhaps Mr. Waugh's major theme:
the recovery of Crouchback's faith, of the sense of joy and
purpose in life which he had lost when his marriage broke
up, and which had invalidated his scrupulous orthodoxy.
This Catholic world of ancient landed gentry (some of them,
fortunately, members of Bellamy's) never forfeits Mr.
Waugh's loyalty. But I wish I took more interest in Crouchback's ex-wife, Virginia; this important character seems to
me so artificial and shallow that I cannot react to her
predicament as I should.

This brings me to what I think is wrong with the novel
as a whole. Where Mr. Waugh's enthusiasm is engaged everything glows; but it is much colder among the minor characters outside the camp-fire.

Here the essential biliousness of Mr. Waugh's gaze is
at fault. He makes them too dreary to hold the reader's
attention, they become humours or caricatures. This distaste blinds him to their quality as human beings; thus
Box-Bender, like all Mr. Waugh's politicians, is a scheming
windbag, but one never gets the impression that he enjoys
politics; Ian Kilbannock, a journalist peer, receives a
little more animation but a baleful eye is cast, too, on
him; and Trimmer, the fake-hero, is too ridiculous. Intellectuals generate a surreptitious leer at the audience as
the prep-schoolboy goes into the old routine for their dis-
comfiture.

In a saga of 'disillusion' one must expect plenty of
bitterness, but in such a crisp and sparkling writer as
Mr. Waugh it should never be allowed to give way to weari-

ness of which there are signs in some of the dialogue of
this last volume. Although more jaundiced, 'Unconditional
Surrender' is nearly as readable as the other two novels,
and the effort entailed was well worth making.

Notes

1 The 'Parade's End' trilogy (see No. 148, n. 1) and 'The
   Last Post' (1928).
2 Waugh had been involved in the Dakar expedition and in a
   Commando raid on Bardia, Libya, details of which he published (much to his superiors' anger) in various newspapers including the 'Evening Standard' (15 November
   1941, 2).

176. PHILIP TOYNBEE, 'OBSERVER'

29 October 1961, 21

In modern times, satire and farce have always been in close
but uneasy alliance. Juvenal was not funny, and he never
meant to be, for the classical satirist saw himself first
and foremost as a moralist, a scourger of social abuses.
     But there is much to laugh at in 'Gulliver's Travels'
and 'The Tale of a Tub', and 'Candide', at its most
extravagant moments, makes us laugh without the least
overtone of indignation. For the method of modern satire is
to exaggerate an evil, to inflate it like some vast and
multicoloured balloon. And the moment of greatest satirical
effect is not the final moment of inflation but somewhere
on the way to it. Somewhere on the way the emotion of the
reader becomes an indefinable combination of violent indignation and violent amusement. It seems that this moment
can seldom be prolonged and that the true satirical experience is bound to be a rare one.
     There are many ways of approaching Mr. Waugh, fewer ways
of keeping a grip on him throughout his devious progress. I
shall use the notion of Mr. Waugh as satirist to provide
some sort of handrail - no more than that - to cling to
when he becomes most recalcitrant. He is, of course, not
only a satirist but also a famous *farceur* and a claimant to
be regarded as a straight and serious novelist. His singular elusiveness springs from the protean mingling of these
roles and our difficulty in deciding which of them, at a
given moment, he supposes himself to have adopted. And all

this is still further confused by Mr. Waugh the *enfant
terrible*, a snook-cocking urchin who inserts an aside, or
even a whole passage, simply to make us go purple in the
face and shake our fists at him.

His latest book, 'Unconditional Surrender', is the last
volume of a trilogy ... and in the whole work we find a
more baffling interchange of roles than ever before. It is
worth trying to trace how he arrived at his present ambiguous and, I believe, deeply unsatisfactory position.

'Decline and Fall' was a work of purest farce. It has
been interpreted otherwise; Llanabba Abbey (1) has been
seen as a satire on the English educational system, and
Mrs. Beste-Chetwynde's traffic in girls has been interpreted as an assault on the morals of the upper classes.
This is solemn rubbish, and it is Captain Grimes who
exposes it as such. He is an immortal figure of farce and
his garish light illuminates the whole book. It remains one
of the four or five really funny English books of the
century.

'Vile Bodies' and 'Black Mischief' are also best seen as
funny books, though by now a clear satirical intention has
begun to show itself. The awkward turning-point, the
beginning of real confusion, comes in the middle of 'A
Handful of Dust'. Much of this book is in the old manner,
funny-preposterous laced with funny-bitter, but the whole
tone and atmosphere are violently changed when the little
boy is killed.

We have gone in a single sickening stride beyond the
reach of satire and are suddenly asked to undergo the
direct experience of a tragic, or at least a pathetic,
emotion. It is like being kicked in the stomach just as one
is sharing a good joke with an acquaintance. And after that
point in the book farce and a cutting satire are most uneasily combined with a straight and serious demand on our
emotions. We are meant to feel that Tony's final fate on
the Amazon is a symbol of the inevitable destruction of the
decent man in a world of selfish and vulgar maniacs. It is
a measure of Mr. Waugh's technical skill that he almost
persuades us to adjust our emotions in this way.

'Scoop' and 'Put Out More Flags' returned more or less
to the manner of 'Black Mischief'. Farce alternated with
satire. The combination was a happy one; the books make us
laugh with an edge of perfectly appropriate discomfort.
The next violent change came, of course, with 'Brideshead
Revisited'. For here at last Mr. Waugh's romantic nostalgia
was allowed free rein, to gallop away at a headlong pace
dragging strange trails of farce and satire behind it. It
was an incautious book, for Mr. Waugh had lowered his
defensive mask and revealed behind the grin a deep

schwärmerei for the golden dignities of a mythical upper class.

A critic should be cautious, too. I thought the book a vulgar one and I can only hope that I did not think this because I differ so strongly from the author's social views and tastes. Like most reviewers, I am on a conventionally liberal turn of mind; and the problem with which Mr. Waugh increasingly confronts us, is how to do him justice in spite of his views. No; the problem is, of course, far more daunting than that. We know that in the end we shall be unable to separate these later books from the importunate attitude to life that they purvey. And what we must try to do is to judge the quality of his heart and mind within the accepted terms of extreme conservatism. His cause has inspired great books: has it inspired Mr. Waugh to any such achievement?

'The Loved One' was the most perfect of Waugh's books since 'Decline and Fall', and also his nearest approach to pure satire.

'The Ordeal of Gilbert Pinfold' was a fascinating sport, a work of introspection which suggested that the unmasked Waugh might easily have another and more endearing side to his real face. And this brings us, perfunctorily enough, to the wartime trilogy and its present conclusion in 'Unconditional Surrender.'

The present volume opens with a synopsis of the earlier ones, and it is surely of great significance that there is no mention of Apthorpe in this résumé. Three of the four sections of 'Men at Arms' bore the name of Apthorpe in their titles, and his farcical history was the most memorable element in the book. We may feel that an old friend, the last in the line of Captain Grimes, has been cruelly dropped in deference to the author's ever more 'serious' intentions. It is certainly true that the trilogy has become progressively less funny, and it is clear that this was an intentional development. Is it the case, then, that Mr. Waugh has at last declared himself, made himself, as it were, directly accessible to the baffled and simple-minded critic?

A record of the book's events is not much to my present purpose.... I am concerned with the book's texture rather than its shape, with the mind and attitudes that it partially discloses rather than with the craftsmanlike conduct of the narrative. Has Mr. Waugh got something true or useful or impressive or good or beautiful to tell us?

We must try to disentangle the elements which he has so carefully tangled up for us. We must try to see where the urchin ends and the writer of farce begins; where the satirist intervenes and where we may legitimately assume that Mr. Waugh is confronting us directly. 'Bachelors, unless dedicated to some religious function or deluded by vice, are said to be unknown among the lower races and classes.' No mistake about that; Mr. Waugh is being naughty, and he knows it.

'Mrs. Scrope-Weld in Staffordshire meant by "normality" having her husband at home and the house to themselves; also certain, to her, rudimentary comforts to which she had always been used; nothing sumptuous; a full larder and cellar; a lady's maid (but one who did her bedroom and darned and sewed for the whole family), a butler, a foot-man (but one who chopped and carried fire-logs), a reliable mediocre cook training a kitchen-maid to succeed her in her simple skills, self-effacing house-maids to dust and tidy; one man in the stables, two in the garden; things she would never know again.' It is made very plain indeed that this Catholic lady is not being satirised. There is no doubt, either, that Mr. Waugh knows how preposterous this passage will seem to nearly all of us. But the urchin is surely mingled here with the lunatic romantic who believes that there is true pathos in the spectacle of such an in-decent deprivation. There is a joke here, but heaven knows on whom it falls.

'For [the] comfort [of the American soldiers] there swarmed out of the slums and across the bridges multi-tudes of drab, ill-favoured adolescent girls and their aunts and mothers, never before seen in the squares of Mayfair and Belgravia.' In this case the urchin has got dangerously out of hand, for this is no innocent squib like the two above but the heartless reduction of people to things. Mr. Waugh meant, of course, to shock us, but the shock that we receive cannot be quite of the kind he inten-ded. There is no joke here, and the no-joke is on the author.

And this leads on, of course, to the deep misanthropy of the whole book, and to the question of its relationship to Mr. Waugh's satirical intentions. Juvenal and Swift were misanthropic in the extreme, and we find this acceptable in them because they were writing pure satire, because the hated figures seem to us to deserve hatred, and because, above all, there is a powerful but unstated ideal which these creatures are so signally betraying. In Mr. Waugh's present book almost everyone is odious except for a few members of old and dignified Catholic families. (A decent Jewess is rather surprisingly thrown in as a belated corrective to this.) But it is not the case that all these figures are satirically intended. The ubiquitous and socially success-ful American 'Loot,' for example, is closely modelled, in his outside properties, on a real person. The caricature is

blatant; the satirical intention is obvious enough. (Though
it seems hard that Mr. Waugh should ascribe to this, in
real life amiable and decent, man a fictional enormity of
which the original would have been quite incapable.)

But what are we to make of all the high officers and
others who appear to be involved in a widespread Communist
conspiracy? Satire, or some kind of lunatic McCarthyism?
What are we to make of the 'respectable' English doctor who
casually prescribes an abortion for his patient? His con-
frère, the African witch-doctor who is employed by a
Ministry to cast spells on the Nazi leaders, is plainly
a figure of farce. And though it is clear that we are
meant to dislike the Yugoslav partisans very much indeed,
are we also meant to dislike all Americans, the Royal Air
Force, the London poor and, to do Mr. Waugh a kind of justice, most Protestant members of the upper class as well?
The Loot is a pasteboard figure, yet he associates with
others who are clearly meant to be the rounded portrayals
of possible human beings. Farce, satire and plain hatred
are most uneasily thrown together, and in addition to these
we are called upon, as we were in 'Brideshead Revisited,'
to accord our concern, sympathy and admiration to a small
group of characters who are seen through the golden
lenses of romance.

For, unlike the true satirist, Mr. Waugh has again been
rash enough to give us a loving picture of what, by contrast, *ought* to be admired. The burden of this role has
been borne throughout these three books by Mr. Crouchback
senior, an innocent, sweet, almost saintly old gentleman
whose pride of family is too deep ever to be divulged.
And the high contrast of this book is provided by the
country funeral of Mr. Crouchback, which is described in
straightforward high-romantic terms.

I can only say that I found this passage painfully
gushing and ... yes, alas *vulgar*. For here we have that
deep snobbery of the Insider, the man who knows a good
brandy (see 'Brideshead') (2) in the same terms as he
knows a good funeral. How much I preferred the disposal of
Miss Thanatogenos in the animal cemetery at Whispering
Glades!

The other, closely-allied ideal which Mr. Waugh quite
explicitly presents is that of national honour, patriotism,
the glory of regimental tradition and of death on the
battlefield. It would be a foolish and misguided man who
sneered at any of these. But the weakness of their presentation is that they seem to hang in the air, divorced from
any tangible or intelligible application. The hero imagines himself to be a patriot, yet he loathes modern England
and most of its inhabitants. His patriotic emotions are not

merely for an England that has passed away, but for an England that could never have existed. These Golden Age emotions are real, and they have real aesthetic value. But Mr. Waugh, this fantastic confuser of issues, also confuses the moral with the aesthetic emotions. The man who knows a good brandy is a *better* man than the man who does not.

Mr. Waugh is a clever man and an able craftsman. But I am not sure that his immense popularity is a very happy portent of our times. In a very sophisticated form he appeals to us in the same way as the 'Queen' magazine. But satire, farce and savage misanthropy are ill-accompanied by that soft glow of brandy and chandeliers which illuminates the tiny group of the Saved as they look down at us from their magic dinner-table in the sky.

Notes

1 Llanabba Castle.
2 A reference to the scene between Rex Mottram and Charles Ryder at Paillards restaurant, Book Two, Chapter One (Penguin, p. 171).

177. GORE VIDAL, 'NEW YORK TIMES BOOK REVIEW'

7 January 1962, 1, 28

Gore Vidal (b. 1925) is an American novelist, playwright and critic; he is author of 'Williwaw' (1946), 'Myra Breckenridge' (1968), 'An Evening with Richard Nixon' (1972), 'Burr' (1973) and 'Matters of Fact and Fiction' (1977).

A satirist is a man profoundly revolted by the society in which he lives. His rage takes the form of wit, ridicule, mockery. Aldous Huxley puts satire somewhat far down the scale of literary esthetics making the good point that 'the pure comic genius must be a great inventor' on the order, say, of Arisophanes, who created worlds, as opposed to the 'mere satirist,' who necessarily is rooted in·this world. Almost by definition, the satirist does not create; he reacts to what exists with caricature and burlesque, two skills Max Beerbohm described: 'Burlesque consists in the application of incongruity. Caricature consists merely in exaggeration. To burlesque a statue of Hermes, you need but put a top hat on his head. To caricature it you must exaggerate its every limb and feature.' A satirist may do anything he likes to that Hermes, except carve it originally from the stone. Someone must do that for him. In the nicest sense, he is critic.

Our time's first satirist is Evelyn Waugh. For thirty years his savagery and wit have given pleasure and alarm. His mixed dish is celebrated: the Bright Young People of the Twenties, the popular press, Africa's political pretensions, death in Hollywood ... all set down in a prose so chaste that at times one longs for a violation of syntax to suggest that its creator is fallible, or at least part American.

Though the bright cold line never falters, Waugh is not a comic genius in Huxley's sense. His characters are taken from life, sometimes still struggling as he pins them to the page. He makes no new worlds. He simply turns this one inside out. He tends to look to the past for what was good rather than to the future for what might be. He is a reactionary.

Politically, he is a Tory; in religion, a Roman Catholic convert. To deal properly with the sins of the present, the satirist needs an alternative view of the way life should be. He does not need to stress it. Few satirists mean to be taken seriously as political or even moral reformers, but the alternative way must exist for them, if only as a contrast. In Waugh's case that alternative is old Catholic England, where one's place was one's place and to protest it was to quarrel with God's appointment.

Ordinarily, one would do no more than note Waugh's private preferences and move on to the pleasures of his destructive art, but in recent years he will not let us off so easily. Since 'Brideshead Revisited' (1945) Waugh has tended to extol his dream world at the expense of satirizing that world's implacable enemy, the twentieth century. Unfortunately, when he turns from vice to virtue, he disarms himself. His great precursor, Juvenal, preferred the old Roman Republic to the parvenu Empire, but he was too shrewd an artist to write books celebrating the political continence of Sulla or the fine austerity of Cato. He stuck to the sins of the dreadful, usable present.

Waugh, however, in the military trilogy, which 'The End of the Battle' completes, indulges himself in romantic daydreams which are not only quite as unpleasant as the things he satirizes, but tend in their silliness to undermine his authority as critic. Juvenal would not have made that mistake.

...Guy Crouchback belongs to one of the ancient Catholic families of England, whose seat is an old house called Broome.

When the trilogy begins, Guy is leading a solitary's
existence near Genoa.... He suffers, one would suspect,
from a malady Catholics term 'the arid heart.' Or as Waugh
puts it, 'Guy had no wish to persuade or convince or to
share his opinions with anyone. Even in his religion he
felt no brotherhood. Often he wished that he lived in penal
times when Broome had been a solitary outpost of the Faith,
surrounded by aliens. Sometimes he imagined himself serving
the last Mass for the last Pope in a catacomb at the end of
the world.'

This reader found himself daydreaming: Evelyn Waugh and
Pope John XXIII are together in the basement of an English
country house. The Bomb has fallen. The human race is destroyed. Waugh is rapturous. The Holy Father looks at him
with despair. They celebrate Mass: it is *huis clos*.

Of the three volumes, 'Men at Arms' is the best. Crouchback is in training. The mood of the day is caught. Despite
the studied dimness of his role as Catholic gentleman,
Waugh is still capable of splendid acts of destruction.
Referring to Winston Churchill's broadcasts: 'Guy had found
them painfully boastful and they had, most of them, been
immediately followed by the news of some disaster, as
though in retribution from the God of Kipling's Reces-
sional. Guy knew of Mr. Churchill only as a professional
politician, a master of sham-Augustan prose, a Zionist, an
advocate of the popular front in Europe, an associate of
the Press Lords and of Lloyd George.' Juvenal was amiable
to Domitian by comparison.

'Men at Arms' is also remarkable for one of Waugh's
finer creations, Apthorpe. He is Guy's fellow officer; a
fabulist, a monomaniac – and monomania is the secret of
comedic invention. Unswervingly dedicated to absurd ends,
each of Apthorpe's stern consistencies adds to the comedy.
His passion for his 'thunder-box' and his defeat at the
hands of an equally monomaniacal character, Brigadier
Ritchie-Hook, display the master at his best.

'Officers and Gentlemen' continues the narrative from
England to Alexandria to the débacle at Crete. Accounts of
military action did not suit Waugh's manner, possibly because he realizes that one man's war is another man's
bore. Despite its relentless clarity, the prose often becomes perfunctory, and one starts to notice the Waugh
tricks. Not since the Victorians has a writer so used mistaken identity ('Scoop' was based brilliantly on one) and
coincidence. I found myself wondering if Trimmer ... would
actually meet Guy's ex-wife so neatly in Edinburgh. The
British island is not that small.

One also notes a new pessimism in Waugh. Out of charity,
Guy gives Apthorpe whisky in the hospital, and kills him.

Though Waugh regards a virtuous act as its own reward, he
seems also to suggest that no good act may have a good
result in this bleak world. Like so many Catholic converts in the British literary establishment, Waugh comes
perilously close to the Manichean heresy.

'The End of the Battle' completes the saga.... Waugh's
account of the British Communists' successful conspiracy
to establish Tito is fascinating; admirers of Robert
Welch's 'Blue Book' will be gratified that their worst
suspicions are confirmed. The Left-Wing intellectuals,
Waugh's *bêtes noires* since the Thirties, get a thorough
going-over. He also has some genially malicious things to
say about Americans, whose speech he does not deign to
record accurately (though they are from the Middle Atlantic States, they all say 'I reckon').

Another target is the lower middle class. They are
Waugh's Snopeses. (1) They are everywhere, conniving,
social climbing, inheriting the earth, with their terrible
accents and disastrous hair. One of his characters remarks
that the hair alone makes a certain plebeian insufferable.
When someone remarks that the hair might be cut differently, the outraged exclaims that it is not the way the
hair is cut, it is the way it '*grows!*'

In 'The End of the Battle' Waugh manages to round out
one final creation: Ludovic, an officer come up through
the ranks; he is self-educated, enamored of words. He becomes, first, a highbrow author of 'Pensées,' then a lurid
best-selling novelist, mad as a hatter, talking baby talk
to the Pekingese he has bought 'for love.' By the end of
the trilogy, most of the characters are dead, briskly
killed off. The few who do survive are allowed happy end-
ings. Guy Crouchback marries a Catholic girl of ancient
lineage and they live happily ever after at Broome, the
future clouded only by his tendency to put on more weight.

Satirists seldom end well. The rage that fills them and
makes possible their irritable art is apt to turn on themselves. Dean Swift's madness is instructive. Waugh's own
experiences, recorded in his extraordinary novel 'The
Ordeal of Gilbert Pinfold' (1957), are in that dark tradition. For Waugh's art, the difficulties inevitably increase
as he turns from present horrors to his private vision of
the good life. His religious and social preferences are his
own business, but when he tries to make a serious case for
them in his work, he is on shaky ground.

Even the prose - so precise in its malice when he is on
the attack - grows solemn and hollow when he tries to celebrate goodness and love and right action. One might say of
him, to paraphrase James on Meredith, that he does the best
things worst. Also, the snobbism, the passionate love of a

lord (who can forget the dying speech of the peer in 'Brideshead Revisited' as he recites his own titles to the ravishment of the Waugh protagonist?), the mean dislike of the less fortunate, tend to set one's teeth on edge.

Yet there are odd surprises and new insights. One startling turn to the screw occurs at the very end of the trilogy. Ludovic's popular novel is called 'The Death Wish,' a work described by Waugh as a turning 'from drab alleys of the Thirties into the odorous gardens of a recent past transformed and illuminated by disordered memory and imagination.' He describes the plot. He mocks it. Why? Because the dreadful Ludovic has written 'Brideshead Revisited' and Waugh has turned the full glare of his cold eye upon himself. The effect is startling, even to the comment of a literary-minded character.

'"It is an interesting thing," said Spruce, "but very few of the great masters of trash aimed low to start with. Most of them wrote sonnet sequences in youth. Look at Hall Caine – the protege of Rossetti – and the young Hugh Walpole emulating Henry James. Practically no one ever sets out to write trash. Those that do don't get very far."'

A satirist capable of self-scrutiny breaks new ground. Fortunately, Waugh is never trashy, and his military trilogy has much to recommend it. The wit endures; at full strength, wit is rage made bearable, and useful.

Note

1 Presumably a reference to the various unsavoury characters called 'Snopes' in William Faulkner's fiction.

178. JOSEPH HELLER, 'NATION'

20 January 1962, 62-3

Joseph Heller (b. 1923), an American novelist and playwright, is the author of 'Catch 22' (1961), 'We Bombed New Haven' (1969), 'Clevinger's Trial' (1974), 'Something Happened' (1974) and 'Good as Gold' (1979).

To get the most pleasure out of Evelyn Waugh, it's been said, one must take his humorous novels seriously and approach his serious novels with a sense of humor. In the

category of his serious novels belongs 'The End of the
Battle.'... This new work, in fact, is so much a part of
something larger that it is almost pointless to consider
it alone. It begins with a prologue and is preceded by a
synopsis. The synopsis relates in swift and sketchy fashion
the principal events of the first two volumes, while the
prologue attempts to account for the activities of the
central character in the two years intervening between the
end of the action in the second volume and the beginning of
events in this same one. Much of the writing that follows is of
exactly this same kind: the work often reads less like a
novel than a chronicle closing out the lives of people who
are brought into the book for no better purpose than to be
eliminated.

...At the end of the battle, both England and Guy have
survived, although neither seems particularly elated by
that result. Guy has found a proper Catholic wife and is
the father of two sons. Earlier, he had remarried his first
wife, the frankly libidinous Virginia, who was destitute
and pregnant with another man's child, and who was killed
shortly afterward in a London air raid.

The author writes of these events with an emotionless
precision that borders on indifference. England, Crouchback and the war seem to be utterly unimportant to Waugh –
and so, in fact, does his own novel. He tells his story
without excitement and organizes his incidents without any
feeling for the dramatic or tragic. His special accomplishment in these pages is to treat matters that were of great
significance to everyone as though they were of no significance to anyone. Even more disappointing, there is almost
none of that wicked humor that has always been his most
precious talent. In Guy Crouchback, Waugh has given to
literature one of its biggest bores since J. Alfred Pru-
frock. The difference is that while Eliot knew his man
thoroughly from the beginning – and made such brilliant use
of him – Waugh seems to have discovered the shortcomings of
his creation too late, certainly long after almost everybody in these novels who is acquainted with him.

Guy Crouchback is incurably a creature of inaction and
ineptitude, a person of large sensibility and no will. He
is used, abused and manipulated by almost every person he
meets, a victimization that comes, after a while, to seem
only just, since he does not appear capable of making any
better use of himself. His only virtue is that he lacks
vice. In the Waugh allegory he personifies middle-aged
innocence, emasculated and bewildered in a world teeming
with petty ambitious and small and nasty conspiracies. Yet,
innocence in a man of forty is no longer innocence but
stupidity. It was not innocence but stupidity that led

Crouchback to cause the death of an invalid friend with a well-intentioned gift of whiskey in an earlier volume, just as it is stupidity in this volume that leads to the execution by the Communists of a Jewish refugee he has attempted to aid while on assignment to Yugoslavia. And it is not innocence but apathy – although he tells himself otherwise – that leads him to remarry his first wife when she is so desperately in need of help, just as it is apathy with which he learns by letter of her death, and of the death of his uncle and his uncle's housekeeper by the same bomb: 'The news did not affect Guy greatly.' One has only to compare this report of a death with the one in 'Handful of Dust' to see how much less concerned Waugh now is with the potential of his material. In the earlier scene Brenda Last reacts with terror when informed that 'John' is dead, thinking that her lover is meant, and sighs with relief on learning that it is only her son. The difference is that Brenda is capable of loving someone, while Crouchback is not.

The net result is that Crouchback is a pitiful, rather than sympathetic, figure, and that Waugh makes a mockery of those causes he seems to be espousing so zealously. It is doubtful, for example, that a more unflattering portrait of Roman Catholics will soon appear in literature than the one Waugh draws of his favorite people in these novels. Were he not himself a Catholic, there would probably be a strong protest accusing him of malicious bias. And were this a more effective novel, it would outrage many of his countrymen, for even the best of the loyal and courageous Englishmen he presents do not fare well in comparison with all those seedy and lower-class figures involved in the Communist conspiracy. It is not that these scheming commoners are as good as their social superiors in Waugh's view of English society, but simply that their social superiors are no longer any better. And if the character of these Communists is no higher, their ambitions certainly are. Crouchback's brother-in-law cavils over a minor part of an inheritance, but the Communists are after Yugoslavia!

It is a dangerous thing to write a novel about a character as dry and unimaginative as Crouchback; Waugh has written three. Because so much more of 'The End of the Battle' centers on its hero, it is, I believe, the weakest member of a trilogy whose first two members have not made a very deep impression in this country. For someone who has never read Evelyn Waugh, this would be a poor place to begin. For many who always read him, this may, unfortunately, seem a good place to stop.

179. FRANK KERMODE, 'PARTISAN REVIEW'

20 August 1962, 466-71

Class - how it conditions morality and even how it binds
or dissolves national communities - continues to pre-
occupy English novelists; the more serious and ambitious
they feel, the franker their expressions on this topic....
Class, indeed, might seem to be as crippling a self-
imposed limitation on English writers as Intelligence is on
French; but the truth is that it is less of an impediment
than might be supposed, especially since the generation of
powerful myths expressive of the emotional force of the
topic. For instance, class in actual life seems merely a
more or less odious weapon in the universal struggle for
prestige and money, but it does not feel like that to the
people who possess it; they like to think of it as belonging, like some ancestral sword, to a lost epoch when
everybody knew his place and all the talk was of the
obligations, not the privileges of nobility. History is a
record of the decay of this happy arrangement, and to
understand our present miseries one needs to study history
in this light. And that is why there are at present in
progress, or recently completed, so surprising a number of
many-volumed novels by serious writers, all variously pre-
occupied with class and the history of England in this
century. [Anthony] Powell in 'The Music of Time', [C.P.]
Snow in 'Strangers and Brothers', Waugh in his now completed trilogy, all need history to explain the decline and
rise of classes; and now Richard Hughes has published the
first part ['The Fox in the Attic'] of a three- or four-
volume novel to be called 'The Human Predicament', assuming
- and why not? - that a study of the English and German
upper classes between the wars can add something to what we
know of that subject....
    Mr. Waugh's trilogy is now complete.... The resemblances
to 'Brideshead Revisited' are limited to the kind of family
in question, and to the general theme - present, in various
forms, almost throughout Waugh's work - of the Catholic
gentry and aristocracy as garrison of England, that 'most
devoted child of the see of St. Peter;' the chivalrous defenders of Catholic faith and reason in difficult times,
when hierarchy is threatened and most of their cousins
apostate. The norm of conduct is a simple, un-clever
gentlemanly piety; without the Faith this type is Tony Last
in 'A Handful of Dust', within it the boring Brideshead or,
in this sequence, the boring Uncle Peregrine; but it must
be added that Guy's father, humbly confident in his charity,

his abstinence, and his view that there are really only
two kinds of people, his kind and everybody else, is present almost throughout as a representative of this peculiar *noblesse oblige*....

...[The] first episode [of the new volume] represents
the final degradation of England; the unconditional surrender. By the King's order there was made a sword, not
for an English crusader but for Stalingrad; and the
people stand in an enormous line to inspect it where it is
on show in Westminster Abbey, 'hard by the shrine of
Edward the Confessor and the sacring place of the Kings of
England.' All around Guy sees the total abasement and
ugliness of England at war - universal treachery, false
heroes, crafty American lootenants; his father's words,
'quantitative judgments don't apply' no longer appear to
apply. But in a world where Corporal Ludovic's *pensées*
succeed, and in which, torn by guilt, he writes a great mad
trashy novel called 'The Death Wish'; where flying bombs
hover over London, and British officers work uselessly with
atheist partisans in Yugoslavia - even in that world there
are movements of grace, as when Uncle Peregrine, without
trying, brings Guy's errant wife to the Faith. Guy's total
disillusion is not despair; he had merely misunderstood the
way of a fallen world. Like Alastair Digby-Vane-Trumping-
ton in 'Put Out More Flags', he had supposed that 'danger
justified privilege,' and that he could 'accept hardships
in recompense for having been selfish and lazy.' A Jewish
displaced person corrects him; the world is otherwise. In
a word, it is Hooper's world (he was the base officer-
fellow in 'Brideshead'); in another, it is a world of derision in which the Faith survives precariously, though of
course it must triumph. This trilogy has nearly a thousand
pages, all written with that chaste precision with which
Waugh catalogues truth and enormity alike. If Apthorpe is
the funniest thing, and the evacuation of Crete the most
splendidly sustained thing, there are nevertheless a dozen
features to be remembered as possible only to a writer of
very great talent. The autobiographical preliminaries in
'The Ordeal of Gilbert Pinfold' claim only a high competence; Waugh is in fact a novelist who has got into his
books a whole self-subsistent vision. That this is to some
implausible, to some repulsive, may matter only in the very
long run; perhaps the aristocratic myth, however extreme
and bizarre, corresponds to a society which, seen under
this aspect, offers possibilities for what James called
'saturation,' which may be denied to those who see it as
amorphous, lacking the formal restrictions of caste and
religion....

180.   SIMON RAVEN, 'SPECTATOR'

12 June 1964, 798

Simon Raven (b. 1927) is a novelist, playwright and
critic. He has written 'The Feathers of Death' (1959) and
the 'Alms for Oblivion' sequence of novels (ten volumes
from 'The Rich Pay Late' (1964) to 'The Survivors' (1976).

In 1961, when the publication of 'Unconditional Surrender'
at long last completed Evelyn Waugh's trilogy about the
Second World War, it seemed to me that the following comments were called for. First, this was the story of a pilgrimage: the hero, Guy Crouchback, answered the call to
arms with high hopes for himself and his country (in that
order); he later came, at the time when Crete fell and
seeming champions were revealed as men of straw, to disillusionment and even despair; and he finally hauled himself out of the Slough of Despond by his own bootlaces,
having discovered that honour might be in good part
retrieved by private acts of mercy or of grace. Secondly
(I should have said in 1961), all three volumes were
immaculately written and constructed. Thirdly, the understanding of martial custom and procedure was such as to
encompass, with irony, brio or dignity as appropriate, any
eventuality from wholesale catastrophe to barrack-room
farce. Lastly, and in sum, this was a major work of fiction, disfigured only by certain wilful eccentricities
which had to do with politics and the Church of Rome.
      Three years have now passed since I formed these judg-
ments, (1) and the appearance of a Penguin edition of the
trilogy (an edition remarkable especially at the beginning
of the third volume for vile misprints) invites one to
read, and to think, again. Having done so, I find that my
original assessment still stands, but stands shakily; what
before seemed only minor complaints have now become
serious and sometimes fundamental objections.
      Take the beginning of the whole work. We are given, in a
few pages, a shrewd insight into Crouchback and his discontent, a glowing impression of the old order to which he
belongs, and a very funny description of the Italian village to which he has exiled himself; we are also shown how
the trumpet call which summons him to battle turns his discontent to aspiration, and we see him going to ask a farewell blessing on his pilgrimage at the tomb of Roger of
Waybroke, an English Crusader who had been killed in the
service of the local robber-baron:

> The Count gave [Sir Roger] honourable burial and
> there he had lain through the centuries, while the
> church crumbled and was rebuilt above him, far from
> Jerusalem, far from Waybroke, a man with a great jour-
> ney still all before him and a great vow unfulfilled;
> but the people of Santa Dulcina delle Rocce ... adopted
> Sir Roger and despite all clerical remonstrance canon-
> ised him, brought him their troubles and touched his
> sword for luck, so that its edge was always bright....
> [Crouchback] ran his finger, as the fishermen did, along
> the knight's sword. 'Sir Roger, pray for me,' he said,
> 'and for our endangered kingdom.'

So, shriven and dedicated, Crouchback starts his journey,
has an amusing argument with a fascist but unbellicose
taxi-driver, and arrives in London to be greeted by wary
friends, who are busy calculating what's in the war for
them.

The perfect prologue, one would have said. Rich,
funny, lyrical, but always with an uneasy element of warning, it introduces the hero and his situation with economy
and ease. And yet even here, even before Crouchback has
left Italy, there are strong hints of the sheer *silliness*
which is to recur so often and mar so much. There is the
impertinent, the grotesque presumption which proclaims on
the very first page the superior quality and virtues of
the old recusant families; there is an indication that Sir
Roger is something more than a symbol, that he is indeed in
a position, somewhere, somehow, to grant petitions, to influence events; there is more than a suggestion that what
Crouchback will righteously resist is not merely Nazism but
the whole apparatus of modern and secular progress as pro-
moting religious apostasy and social change - two calami-
ties which Mr. Waugh does not, it is true, equate but sees
as intimately connected.

And when we reach England with Crouchback, such absurdities obtrude themselves even more grossly. Leave aside further factious pedantry about the old Catholic families (as
represented, this time, by Crouchback's saintly and senile
father) and yet further officious preachment about the
efficacy of the Roman Faith, we find a peevish disregard,
sometimes an outright discourtesy, displayed whenever anyone is mentioned, citizen or soldier, who is not of gentle
or armigerous rank. (An exception, I should add, is made in
favour of faithful servants.) The lowest social stratum to
be treated with serious attention is that comprising the
middle-class officers of the Halberdiers, the unsmart but
valorous regiment into which Crouchback is commissioned;
beneath that level, except for a few loyal warrant officers,

the nation apparently consists at best of mindless cannon-
fodder, at worst of whining and mutinous malingerers.
    Now, heaven knows that some of the 'democratic' atti-
tudes current during the war were quite insufferable and
that Mr. Waugh had good cause to be irritated by them: but
it is futile to counter nonsense with another brand of nonsense, to react with dogma or violence. The people of England fought and fought bravely - a proposition which, in
the abstract, Mr. Waugh would certainly allow, but which he
cannot seem to apply to any 'common' person within his own
or his novel's immediate compass. He abjures sweet reason
for personal rancour, and the result is that, in so far as
he proceeds outside the ranks of gentility, his picture is
false.
    What is worse, even when Mr. Waugh is operating on his
chosen ground, that of 'officers and gentlemen,' he often
has recourse to sleight of hand or caricature. The former he
he uses to assist the plot or, as one sees now, to camou-
flage some highly implausible twists of military machina-
tion; for one of the things revealed by re-reading these
books is that Mr. Waugh's grasp of the Army's methods is by
no means as sound as one had thought. The tricks he plays,
which are ingenious and exceedingly funny (e.g. Jumbo
Trotter's excursion, or the apotheosis of Trimmer), would
be very acceptable as occasional light relief; the trouble
is that they are so frequent as almost to form a staple of
the narrative, a state of affairs undesirable in what pur-
ports to be - what is - a serious *oeuvre*. As for the other
suspect technique, that of caricature, this is used in part
unconsciously, as when Mr. Waugh is inflating the excellence of Catholics and gentlemen, in part quite shame-
lessly, as when he seeks to discredit their Communist and
American foes.
    Once again, of course, one sees what Mr. Waugh is at.
So much tedious propaganda once exalted the gallantry of
the partisan, the sterling simplicity of the GI, that it is
a relief to be reminded of the brutal inanities of the one,
the boasts, shifts and crapulence of the other. But there
is, after all, a happy mean. As a quick slick piece of
malice, to label three American journalists 'Scab, Bum and
Joe' is apt; but to deal with the entire American war
effort in such terms is misleading. As for the Communists,
we know well enough the extent of their war-time achievement for our own good and our own ill; in no case can we
just write off Russia, as Mr. Waugh would like to, as an
evil, slobbering and rather ridiculous bear.
    When all this is said, however, now as three years ago
it still seems to me that Mr. Waugh brings Crouchback's
pilgrimage to a legitimate goal: private salvation through

private good faith. Despite the silliness, the convent
chatter, the militant snobberies; despite the unconcealed
ill-will towards nine-tenths of mankind, the mistrust of
intellect and progress, the ludicrous *ex cathedra* pronouncements; despite the tricks, the distortions, the un-
abashed insolence of the entire display - despite all
this Mr. Waugh asserts, through 700 pages of pithy English
and matchless story-telling, that in a naughty world there
is hope to be had from personal honour. If the structure
which he has reared to enshrine this truth now reveals
widening cracks in its fabric; it says so much the more
for his skill that the whole defies gravity and stands
[sic].

Note

1   See Mr Raven's review of 'Unconditional Surrender' for
    the 'London Magazine' (November 1961, 72-5).

'Basil Seal Rides Again'

1963

181. JOCELYN BROOKE, 'LISTENER'

7 November 1963, 764

Jocelyn Brooke (1908–66), a poet, critic, novelist and
amateur botanist, was the author of 'December Springs'
(1946), 'The Military Orchid' (1948), 'Ronald Firbank'
(1951), 'The Elements of Death' (1952) and 'Private View'
(1954).

'Basil Seal Rides Again' is published in an expensive
limited edition of 750 copies, not because it is unfit to
be read by our servants (as a certain Q.C. once so strikingly put it), nor, goodness knows, because its public is
likely to be a small one, but for the benefit, presumably,
of people who collect expensive limited editions. It is
hardly more than a short story, bulked out by large print
and thick paper, and charmingly produced. In his preface
Mr Waugh calls it a 'senile attempt' to recapture his
earlier manner, but there are no signs of senility here,
and one only wishes he had made a full-length novel out of
it. The story itself is a mere anecdote, typically outrageous in the Seal tradition, but we catch tantalizing
glimpses of a number of old friends: Ambrose Silk has become an O.M. (why?), Margot Metroland is permanently glued
to television (oh dear), Parsnip and Pimpernell are both
professors at American universities (predictable). As for
Basil himself, he is respectably married to Angela Lyne,
has a nearly grown-up daughter, and is now fat, reactionary,
and gratifyingly rich. One can only hope that Mr Waugh will
some day write his 'Temps Retrouvé', of which this fragment
seems an appetizing foretaste.

It is possible to disagree violently with Mr Waugh's
opinions, and to deplore his romantic snobbery (I myself
remain strictly neutral in the matter), but no literate
person can fail to detect, beneath the public *persona*, the
dedicated artist for whom the art of writing consists in
putting the right words in precisely the right order. Here
his prose is as impeccable as ever, and after all the Jack
Murdochs and Iris Kerouacs I have been reviewing lately,
this book seemed like a glass of sound claret after an
enforced regime of Coca-cham or Baby-Cola....

182.   V.S. PRITCHETT, 'NEW STATESMAN'

15 November 1963, 706-7

Cronies, toadies and friends of friends of Basil Seal,
fellows who knew him at Bellamy's, African tribesmen who,
in the Thirties, watched him inadvertently eat a British
diplomat's daughter at a tribal dance, generals who had
been insulted by him, relations and mistresses who were
often £10 short when he left - many of these will have it
in for Evelyn Waugh when they read this little postscript
to one of the most enjoyable disgraceful careers of their
youth. Sequels rob fictions of their immortality and re-
introduce them to the vulgar stream of time. The cannibal
and trafficker in evacuees has aged. The ordinary meats
and vintages that turn us into respectable fat stock have
empurpled him also. He is known to cloakroom attendants as
Florid. He is short of breath. He goes to public dinners.
He has married into paralysing wealth. He romps with his
18-year-old daughter - Dad's girl - who calls him Pobble.
Her boyfriend steals his champagne and proposes that
Pobble shall keep them in the splendour to which - chroni-
cally unwashed - they are accustomed. In his late fifties
and on the point of apoplexy, the plague of Mayfair and
Gloucestershire asks himself what went wrong. At what
instant in his past did his happy bent for decline and fall
turn into the corpulence of rise and shine. It must have
been just after the war when coming back from California
with loads of scarce consumer goods, he declared the lot at
the Customs and paid up in a burst of patriotic remorse for
having dodged the currency regulations in a rather large
way. Now in his daughter's awful boyfriend he meets his own
awful youth. In fact the boy is merely rude.
    The question is whether Basil will be able to recover

his old form for once and commit one more discreet outrage.
Here, we become more interested: the art of going one worse
has always been Waugh's gift. How can Basil destroy the
impossible young man? The happy idea of suggesting that
there would be more than a whiff of incest about the marriage does the trick. Very sad, because neither the young
man nor the darling daughter fight back. A mere say-so has
robbed a deb of her delight. It was not like that when we
were young, before Lady Metroland got glued to her television, before we started groping for our spectacles or our
sleeping pills and taking the turnip-water cure at £50 a
day: a rumour of incest would have made us jump to it and
set the joy bells ringing round Berkeley Square. There is
something flat in Basil's diplomatic success: in the past
his unfailing nerve led him to unfailing disaster. No one
ever believed a word he said. Now he is believed.

Mr Waugh has lately become a self-indulgent moralist
where once he was as hair-raising as Savonarola. Since he
is as clever as they come one can admire where the expert
in the young of one decade takes on the young of the
next; the few lines of their talk show his ear for folly
does not fail. And as the most accomplished comic of his
period he has his privileges, for he is never slapdash. He
may do wrong but he's never incompetent. I wish he had not
exposed his immortals to the thin and deadly air of time.
The real Basil Seal can never be in his fifties. His place
is on that beautifully cock-eyed old Grecian urn where age
never wearies and the chase is never up. Comics have the
right and, eventually, the duty to be resolutely out of
date.

'A Little Learning'

1964

183. WILLIAM PLOMER, 'LISTENER'

10 September 1964, 397

Those of us who happen to have been born in 1903 are likely
to have at least two things in common - a clear memory of
life in Edwardian England and our formation by persons
evolved in Victorian England. We must be allowed to have
had, besides luck, some powers of readaptation, though they
may not be infinite. We need no excuse for having enjoyed
certain lost graces or for preferring them to some present
ugliness. And it would be intolerant to blame us for stick-
ing to some of the things we were taught, even if we sometimes show it too plainly. Early Latin may help a writer to
think what he is saying and may guide him in the direction
of such unfashionable virtues as order and moderation, but
Mr Waugh's vocabulary and syntax do now and then have an
old-world air, like a well-dressed sexagenarian wearing
spats. He is liable to use words like 'eschew', phrases
like 'the precipitancy of my dispatch', and occasionally a
sentence of eighteenth-century stateliness:

> The intermittent but frequent presence of a dissi-
> pated and not always respectful spendthrift disturbed
> the tranquillity of the home to which he always looked
> for refuge.

But let nobody suppose that Mr Waugh is an anachronism, or
that he does not have a good reason for what he does, or
that he does not do it as well as ever.

To this first volume of his autobiography he brings the
weight of his experience of the world and of human nature,
his clear head, his wit, and the equipment of a brilliant

social satirist whose prose is never careless and almost
always entertaining. The supposed motive for reading autobiography being 'understanding of the immediate past', he
sets out to provide it, but not before examining his heredity. If only more autobiographers would take more trouble
over their origins! The various professional men in Mr
Waugh's family tree seem to throw light upon himself and
give a sense of mingling roots, lively intelligence, vigorous idiosyncrasy, and the continuity of certain strains
in our civilization.

After a happy childhood in Hampstead with a father who
was a publisher and ought perhaps to have been an actor,
and without isolation in one of those sometimes odious pre-
paratory schools of the time, he had to live through what
he thinks may have been 'the most dismal period in history
for an English schoolboy'. Lancing, by his account,
sounds bleaker than, for example, Rugby during the 1914-18
war. Muscular Christianity, in the absence in the hellish
trenches in France of the best younger men and schoolmasters of their generation, seems to have exacerbated the
shortage of food and physical comfort and even decency by
a gruesome lack of spiritual and social warmth. His time
there was redeemed a little by the attentions of a solitary old aesthete (1) outside the school, and by contact
with the energetic personality of J.F. Roxburgh, the creator of Stowe. Roxburgh, who helped to form the young
Waugh's prose style, wrote to him in 1921: 'If you use
what the gods have given you, you will do as much as any
single person I can think of to shape the course of your
own generation'. Mr Waugh disclaims any such achievement,
but how can a man estimate his own influence?

About his time at Oxford ('especially fortunate in my
generation') he is on the expansive side: it is one of the
problems of an autobiographer to estimate how far what has
been and still seems important to him can seem so to
others - and to what others. There is always a danger of
approaching the point where recollection may be nearer self-
indulgence than entertainment. But zest is the important
thing, and Mr Waugh recognizes it in his youthful self,
'a zest for the variety and absurdity of the life opening
to us', and with it 'a veneration for ... artists, a scorn
for the bogus'. One would expect to find, and one does
find, in this first volume plenty of life-like and skilful
character-drawing of kinsmen, friends, and acquaintances,
as well as self-portraiture, and one ends it with an appetite for its continuation.

Note

1 Francis Crease.

184. MALCOLM BRADBURY, 'SPECTATOR'

11 September 1964, 347

Malcolm Bradbury (b. 1932), Professor of American Studies
at the University of East Anglia since 1970, is a critic
and novelist; he is the author of 'Eating People is Wrong'
(1959), 'Evelyn Waugh' (1962), 'The Social Context of
Modern English Literature' (1972), 'The History Man' (1975)
and 'The Novel Today' (1977).

Much of the literary criticism that has been written on the
fiction of Evelyn Waugh has complained, in one way or
another, about the author's snobbery or his distrust of
total democracy. One of the sharpest of these attacks
occurs in 'Donat O'Donnell's' (Conor Cruise O'Brien's)
'Maria Cross', in which book Waugh is attacked for linking
the history of the Catholic faith in England with a fixed
and intolerant mythology about the English upper classes.
More recently, Frank Kermode has taken that line of argument a step further, discerning in Waugh's work a view of
the world and its history centred upon a notion of a
Catholic-aristocratic saving remnant. Other critics - like
Philip Toynbee, and more latterly Simon Raven, writing in
the pages of this journal - have quite simply felt that
Waugh draws too readily on the snobbish instincts of his
readers, and have attacked his 'idiosyncratic Toryism.' (1)
And it's probably true to say that, in the insistently
egalitarian atmosphere of the post-war period - which has
remarkably succeeded in severing itself intellectually
from the class-bound orientations of the preceding years -
Waugh's critical reputation has diminished, and largely for
this single reason.
    It took a profile article in the 'New Statesman' to
point out that Waugh uses his snobbery very obliquely in
his fiction, and that his pronouncements on public matters
are vastly comic and ambiguous in tone. For Waugh is, after
all, a comic writer, one of the best we have; what is more,
he is, I think, a man with a deep conception of the comic,
and a place for it in his conception of living. He deals in

a world of ironies. Clearly his novels are set largely in
an upper-middle-class world, verging on the aristocratic;
they are much concerned with hereditary distinctions, great
estates, and high style in living. Waugh can invest the
loss of these things with great pathos; but the novels are
usually *about* their loss, and he can perceive these dis-
possessions largely from outside. The early and the late
novels don't differ much in this respect; in the Second
World War trilogy, for instance, Crouchback is not vindi-
cated. He lives in a world of heroic delusions and false
quests, and must finally compromise and surrender, as Tony
Last surrendered. Waugh's novels aren't concerned with
retreat into the safe Catholic citadel; he is deeply concerned, as a comic visionary, in the forces of comic
anarchy which threaten and destroy. In Pinfold the anarchy
is turned inward, and it virtually engulfs the stylised
dandyish self that Pinfold-Waugh has adopted to protect,
remember, his modesty.

It is, I think, because Waugh can give so much to the
notion of a contingent and debased world in which comic
anarchy operates that he is so important a twentieth-
century writer. Certainly, too, he has been a vast influence upon the form of comic fiction, which has been a much
more important form in this century than in almost any
other, precisely because this sense of contingency and
anarchy is so familiar to our experience. Critics often try
to distinguish between the early and the late Waugh - the
early Waugh being the comic writer who sees, with great
objectivity, a comic modern world, that of the Twenties,
and the late Waugh being the Catholic snob. It is an in-
efficient division; it is possible to discern the snobbery
(if that is one's primary critical business) in 'Decline
and Fall', possible to discern Waugh's remarkable atten-
tiveness to the modern and fashionable in his most recent
fiction. Always Waugh has been fascinated, in his fiction,
by the past *and* by the manifestations of the present; upon
such conflicts, to different extents, all his novels are
based.

And now that Waugh has undertaken an extensive autobiography, the first volume of which has just appeared,
the culture out of which these conflicts emerged should
grow more apparent. 'A Little Learning', which takes
Waugh's life as far as his unhappy ventures in schoolmastering after leaving Oxford, is a fully reminiscent,
rather reticent, low-keyed volume. The publishers draw
the comparison with Waugh's biography of Ronald Knox, and
rightly; it is written with high elegance and a good deal
of self-irony, but apart from the passage in which Waugh
gives a delightful account of his schoolmastering

experience, it isn't a book to remind us that Waugh is one
of the great comic writers. Rather it shows him living in
the context of a culture to which his comedy must be seen
as a perplexed response.

Waugh lived through his early years in an atmosphere of
fairly well-endowed, but not elegant, upper-middle-class
suburban London life. Arthur Waugh, his father, was a man
of letters, a lover of cricket, an essayist, and managing
director of the publishing firm of Chapman and Hall. In the
family were literary connections (Gosse was related),
ecclesiastical connections (various clergymen), and distant
aristocratic connections (the Cockburn family); but what
here seems to predominate was a vaguely agrarian aesthetic
atmosphere common among the well-rooted intelligentsia of
the day, the atmosphere of Pre-Raphaelitism plus cricket.
Arthur Waugh found his sons 'modern' and disturbing, but
Evelyn Waugh clearly assimilated much of this culture.
Because of his religious interests he was sent to Lancing,
a Woodard foundation; but what was fostered was rather
dilettantism and aestheticism. He had a great interest in
art, penmanship, and the development of great personal
style; and these interests continued at Oxford. Oxford was
undergoing a period in which the idea of the aesthete was
again much in currency.

The ideal of the dandy had by no means died out, however, and Waugh's fascination with both the modern and the
reactionary takes much of its tone from this situation.
Waugh was politically relatively unaware; he professed
Conservatism, but, as Harold Acton points out, he was close
in many ways to the spirit of William Morris. Aestheticism
and dandyism afford a style of prejudice and narrowed
artistic commitment in periods of confusion; and a conspicuous avoidance of the intellectual and the political
seems to characterise Waugh's later schooldays and his
undergraduate career. Craftsmanship takes on a positive
value. But the world tends to be without system and meaning, to be, rather, full of ironies; after the loss of his
strong religious interests, Waugh would appear to have
lived in a passive agnosticism until, after the close of
this volume, he became a Catholic, when faith assuaged but
did not relieve his sense of the contingent nature of the
world.(2)

About the work that derives from this, Waugh says very
little. Presumably the next volume will concern his decision to become a writer; all he does is to point the way by
suggesting that it was the one thing for which his education fitted him. But to remind us of what these days of
little learning brought about, his publishers have brought
out a new edition of 'Scoop'. This is the latest in a

number of re-issues of the novels; Waugh's work has suffered considerably from misprints, and the new editions
have revised - and in some cases altered - texts. One
might add that 'A Little Learning' is not without a fair
share of misprints.

Notes

1 For O'Donnell see No. 102, for Kermode No. 109, for
   Toynbee No. 156 and for Raven No. 180.
2 In the 'Face to Face' interview (1960) Waugh was asked
   what his religious position was at the time of and
   before writing 'Vile Bodies'; he replied: 'I was as near
   an atheist as one could be ... at that time I
   should think from the age of sixteen to the age of
   twenty-eight I didn't go to church at all....'

185. V.S. PRITCHETT, 'NEW STATESMAN'

25 September 1964, 445-6

Many good writers live on their nerves and can turn to anything. Clever, they have only one self. This is not the
case with Evelyn Waugh; he has many selves, deeply embedded,
on which to draw. He might have settled down with Lady
Metroland and tippled away at a mixture of the 'Bab Ballads', (1) the cautionary tale and Firbank; but his real
line was the prose, not the poetry, of outrage. The wild,
feathered feminine scream of that last master was not for
him. His temperament was sober. He moved to the hard-
headed traditions of English satirical comedy; one glance
at the English upper classes, imposing their private fantasies on whatever is going on, treating everything from
war downwards as if it were all happening in one of their
country houses, has been enough to provide comedians with
material for a lifetime. Mr Waugh went on next to be in-
convenienced by his Sir Galahad and Saint George complexes;
but after 'Brideshead' and a brief return to the outrageous
in 'The Loved One', the gentleman moralist appeared, a club-
bish writer assiduously polishing his malign sentences,
drily persisting with the stings of mortifying circumlocu-
tion. His early books spring from the liberating notion
that human beings are mad; the war trilogy, a work of maturity, draws on the meatier notion that the horrible

thing about human beings it that they are sane.

Since I prefer the earlier to the later Miss Brophy, I can hardly blame her, in turn, for failing to understand the mellowing of a brilliant novelist, as she does, I notice, on a later page. (2) For better or worse, there is a masculine vein in English comedy, a vein which is sociable and not intellectual, sensible rather than sensitive. It shows us willingly paying the price of misanthropy for the pleasure of making a go of life in clubs - day and night - parsonages, public schools, villas, furnished apartments and other privacies of the national masochism. It required a nerve on Mr Waugh's part to treat the war as something which could or could not be known socially in these terms. It also required the accomplishment of a lifetime to bring off those three volumes. It is true that they have the formal melancholy of a memoir, and that Sir Galahad strikes a few unattractive poses; but the comic invention is strong; and there is an advance towards a compassionate study of human nature. Crouchback's bad wife would once have been seen as a vile body; she is now discerned as a displaced person.

The melancholy note persists in the first volume of Mr Waugh's autobiography. In his dire way he has done what he can to pass himself off as a fossil. Like his father - as he appears in this volume - the son is a considerable impersonator. His prose is set to the felicities of misleading. This book is of great importance to students of his novels - though he does not yet discuss them - for it shows how long-established his preoccupations as a man and writer have been. An outstanding quality of his work has been its care for cadence in English prose and his regard for craftsmanship as a moral duty; he comes of a line of clergy and doctors, some of whom were minor writers; his background is literary and unassumingly sedate. The youthful taste for working at medieval script is another sign of the craftsman to come and a sign too of that feeling for Romance which has been the less successfully manifested aspect of his work. (His father was also romantic; he would refer to the 'stout timbers' of the villa he built for himself as if it were some galleon anchored in the North End Road and never forgave the local authorities for incorporating his then rustic part of Hampstead into the ugly and socially ambiguous brashness of new Golders Green.)

As for religion, Mr Waugh was always interested in theology and never at all bored by church. There is nothing to suggest that his later conversion to Catholicism was Romantic; everything to suggest that theological ingenuity was an important appeal. A relative in the Bengal Lancers brought in the St George touch and the nostalgia for swords and regalias. The designs of the nursery wallpaper were medieval: it was a taste of the period. The boy's up-bringing was quiet, instructed, entirely happy. No Oedipal struggles appear. There was nothing to provoke the later sense of outrage, nothing - apparently - to titillate the psychiatrist except the mildness of it all. Even at the end of the volume, when he plans to drown himself after coming down from Oxford, full of debts and depressed about lost fun, Mr Waugh takes the view that this was a normal adolescent gesture, abandoned at once when he swam into some jellyfish.

What provoked the taste for outrage? Mr Waugh is a thoughtful rather than intimate autobiographer, in this volume. He keeps the lid on. His aim appears to be the desire to conform, no doubt ironically, to a carefully prepared conventional pattern and to repose, almost maso-chistically, upon a belief in the Unremarkable. Clearly this, in so brilliant a man, suggests a conflict. His mar-vellous feel for the disreputable comes from a man with a family addiction to the neutral and unaspiring. But one thing *did* go wrong. There was no woodshed. But home was so happy that to leave it for school made him 'nastier' (on the general principle that all schoolboys are 'nasty'?). And then there was the despoiling of England.

As one who belongs to his generation, though coming from a very different background, I understand something of what Mr Waugh means when he writes of the shock caused by the ruin of rural England. It would seem all the worse to a literary suburban:

> This is part of the grim cyclorama of spoliation which surrounded all English experience in this century and my understanding of the immediate past (which presum-ably is the motive for reading a book such as this) must be incomplete unless this huge deprivation of the quiet pleasure of the eye is accepted as a dominant condition, sometimes making for impotent resentment, sometimes for mere sentimental apathy, sometimes poisoning love of country and of neighbours. To have been born into a world of beauty, to die amid ugliness, is the common fate of all us exiles.

The evil, then, was the sense of exile. Most, indeed I would say all writers have this sense anyway. It was ex-acerbated for him, as for many schoolboys, by the frus-tration of 'being out of the war'. It was Alec Waugh, not Evelyn, who would be the hero. One was reduced to dreamy, hungry, insubordinate futility. In some respects Mr Waugh's

exile is snobbish. Mr Waugh, senior, was an industrious
and kindly reviewer of the old school who hated the new
thing in the best jocose tradition of elderly criticism;
Mr Waugh, junior, turns rancorous: 'There are the State-
trained professional critics with their harsh jargon and
narrow tastes.' Mr Waugh senior has his jargon too. Of
D.H. Lawrence's art he wrote: 'his fancy is half asleep
upon a foetid hot-bed of moods.' But, as his son truly
says, as a critic the elder Waugh was no snob. His limitation was the 'common enough inability to recognise the
qualities he loved unless they were presented in familiar
forms.' Mr Waugh's own 'State-educated' reveals a parallel
inability.

Prep school, public school, university: these now tedious influences standardise English autobiography, giving
the educated Englishman the sad if fascinating appearance
of a stuffed bird of sly and beady eye in some odd seaside
museum. The fixation on school has become a class trait.
It manifests itself as a mixture of incurious piety and
parlour game. (Some of Mr Waugh's contemporaries are now
writing or have written their autobiographies and are
watching each other like chess-players. What was Rugby
doing when Sherborne saw Waugh go to Lancing and did Eton
care?)

Cautious, lonely, observant at first at Oxford, Mr
Waugh eventually kicked out, did the right thing by drinking a lot and coming down deep in debt, and was ready for
a far more interesting life than appears in this opening
volume. One must hope that his feeling for impersonality
will not become so subtle as to make the irony too sober.
The best things in the present volume are those that recover the detail of a period. One recognises this room:

> The dining-room was dark and full of oil-paintings. The
> drawing-room was much cluttered with small tables, dra-
> peries, screens and ornaments on carved brackets. It
> contained two cabinets full of 'curiosities' - fans,
> snuff-boxes, carved nuts, old coins and medals; some of
> them unremarkable, such as, carefully wadded, encased
> and labelled, the charred tip of a walking-stick with
> which some relation had climbed Mount Vesuvius and a
> lock (unauthenticated) of Wordsworth's hair.(3)

There was even a phial containing a specimen of 'White
Blood' from a patient dying of anaemia. Tourists' trophies
had not yet become standardised.

Mr Waugh is a master also of the compressed portrait.
There are three maiden aunts - an extinct genus now, as Mr
Waugh points out:

My Aunt Connie sat on the bench when women became eli-
gible as magistrates and was much distressed by the
iniquities there revealed to her. All three had the
prudishness proper to maiden aunts, though Aunt Elsie
in old age developed a tolerance of very slightly indelicate fiction.

The portrait is good, the prose embroidered here with the
facetious parlance - is that the word? - of clubs. This is
the trouble with club Mandarin - it becomes flunkeyish.
Better write like Wooster than like Jeeves. The crisp manner used in describing W.W. Jacobs (4) is preferable:

In person he was wan, skinny, sharp-faced, with watery
eyes. Like many humorists he gave scant evidence of
humour in private intercourse. In losing the accents of
Wapping he lost most of his voice and spoke through the
side of his thin lips in furtive, almost criminal tones,
disconcerting in a man of transcendant, indeed of
tedious respectability. He was a secular puritan, one of
those who 'have not got the Faith and will not have the
fun'....

Except for the last sentence, the portrait is exact. The
little man was skipping up and down, as merry as popcorn,
when I once caught sight of him at a suburban 'hop'. It
must be remembered that all humorists suffer from overwork.
   The gentle portrait of the author's father is the longest in the book. It is interesting for many reasons,
chiefly as an example of a quality that is generally overlooked by admirers of the son's comic originality. The
wit, the hilarious transitions, the pace and savagery of
his comedies, deceive us into seeing Mr Waugh as a writer
who jumps with inspired carelessness from one fantasy to
the next. The dialogue alone, his early forte, should un-
deceive us. Its quality is accuracy; in fact a grave ex-
actitude has been the ground of his comic genius as it is
of his serious writing in travel and biography. He can be
accurate to the point of testiness. Indeed he is only bad
when he is not accurate, that's to say when St George,
panache etc. come in and make him slur.
   Mr Waugh's eye for the fact enables him to catch the
changing impressions so important to the faithful memorial-
ist. Until he was 16, he had supposed that his father was
simple and prosaic; then a friend (5) came down and said:
'Charming, entirely charming, and acting all the time'. He
was. Between bouts of coughing he would cheerfully call to
death for release; declare in the middle of signing a
cheque he was being driven to a pauper's grave. He talked

aloud to imaginary people continuously. He assumed, without knowing it, Dickensian roles. Before the 'ingratitude'
of his sons, he became Lear. His sighs could be heard
across a theatre. He had talent as an amateur actor and,
on the evidence of the son's prose, on the confessions of
Pinfold and the anecdotes that trickle down from the West
Country about his histrionic mischief, one would guess
that Evelyn Waugh's sobriety is a genuine impersonation.
It is unsafe to trust the elegiac tone of this volume; he
may also be trying out his own funeral in advance, to see
what a literary demise could look like. Autobiography is a
way of dressing up the past.

So far we have been reading about the unknown Evelyn
Waugh. In the last chapter the frosts of youth vanish; the
young sparkler appears. We see contemporaries who were
later to become famous or notorious, among them Gerald
Gardiner, Harold Acton, Robert Byron and Brian Howard.
Of the last two we have striking, not to say pungent preliminary sketches. Brian Howard, particularly, was one
of those dangerous, brilliant and seminal nuisances, a
plaguing character of wasted talent who begins to barge
about in the corridors of Mr Waugh's early fancy. Grimes
turns up in Wales, an effusively homosexual schoolmaster.
We have reached the verge of 'Decline and Fall', when Mr
Waugh began to rise and shine.

Notes

1 W.S. Gilbert, 'Bab Ballads; (1869); 'More Bab Ballads'
   (1873).
2 See No. 58.
3 A description of Waugh's grandfather's house.
4 The short-story writer, a family friend in London.
5 Harold Acton.

186. STANLEY KAUFFMANN, 'NEW REPUBLIC'

21 November 1964, 23-5

Stanley Kauffmann (b. 1916) is an American novelist, playwright and publisher, and was literary and film critic for
the 'New Republic' from 1958. He is the author of 'Altogether Reformed' (1936), 'A Change of Climate' (1955) and
'Living Images: Film Comment and Criticism' (1975).

This is only an interim report because it deals only with
the first volume of an as-yet incomplete autobiography.
Worse, much of the first volume is about the least interesting part of any subject's life - his childhood, when he
is more like everyone else than he is likely to be again.
But for those already engaged by Waugh, particularly those
(like me) who consider him a genius, his autobiography is
irresistible and the first volume unavoidable.

About the prose itself, little more needs to be said
than that his essay style has never been more Handelian.
Waugh - not all that old, actually, only 61 - has decided
to write his life story because he has reached what he
thinks is the proper age. ('Only when one has lost all
curiosity about the future has one reached the age to
write an autobiography.') In this book he takes us from his
pre-history up to a youthful moment of despair, after he
had quit his first post-Oxford teaching job, when he more
or less attempted to drown himself in the sea.... The last
line: 'Then I climbed the sharp hill that led to all the
years ahead.' He was not yet a published writer, a husband,
or a Roman Catholic.

He tells us at just bearable length about his forebears,
who were neither eccentric nor attractive enough for much
discussion - a rather usual bunch of professional men and
clergymen. The only really striking portrait is that of his
father, a prominent editor and minor *litterateur*, a quietly
beneficial influence on contemporary writers, whose firm
distinctions between private and professional life seem
quaintly archaic in the light of current British-American
publishers' practices. Waugh anatomizes the characters of
his great-grandparents and grandparents to discover the
strains that, he believes, have combined in him.

> Such, then, are the materials of which I am made. The
> body, which includes the mind and nerves, is a link in a
> heterogeneous concatenation; the soul is a separate
> creation.

Anti-rationalist still, he discards science to compare
heredity with poker.... Psychology, even more than biology,
gets short and sharp shrift. Waugh *vs* the 20th Century,
sometimes a grave and important battle, is here a moderately amusing joust.

His early boyhood was spent in Hampstead, which was then
much more rural than suburban (and is now more urban).
But he makes no sentimental caterwauling about the topo-
graphical·changes in England. He simply clarifies that it
is 'impossible for the young, difficult for the elderly' to
see the world as it was. Even the latter can be misled by

the continuity of a place-name into thinking that the place is the same.... His treatment of this matter is typical of one of his modes: affection underscored by brusque flourishes of concentration on the facts, rather than on the feelings created by the facts.

His early schooling reveals only a few matters of note. Among them: he was bright but, before he finished public school, fashionably bored; he was fascinated by calligraphy and studied it with a pudgy eccentric who lived near his school; he had an early interest in the authenticities of religion and tradition. His behavior, his boyhood diaries, his comments on those daries, substantiate implicitly some of the psychological theory he disputes explicitly.

His Oxford life, which he clearly loved, reveals a change of key. His previous schooldays showed him reasonably industrious and serious; in his Oxford days he took the social life as a prime part of his education: the parties, jokes, special clubs, relatively heavy drinking. It all seems a bit 'mad twenties' now and seems to have been considerably modified in the next Oxford decade; but it cannot be claimed that this life was ruinous. Some of his friends were Anthony Powell, Claud Cockburn, Peter Quennell, Alfred Duggan, Christopher Hollis, Harold Acton, and the present Lord Gardiner.

The reader of a novelist's autobiography cannot avoid playing the game of sources, wondering whether this or that was the original of a setting or character. Waugh is aware of this and sometimes sets us straight by denial or hint.

In a novel ('Brideshead Revisited') which portrays some aspects of my Oxford life I gave a description of two undergraduates made free of a fine cellar and exulting in their acquaintance with wine. That was never my happy experience.... In fact we drank copiously but indiscriminately....

A very surprising man ... had come to take the place ... as second-master.... He later provided certain certain features for the character, 'Captain Grimes', in my first novel.

After Oxford he spent some months in art school, before he went on to the teaching post that he later immortalized - not too strong a word - in 'Decline and Fall'. Reproductions of some of his drawings and woodcuts display a competent devotion to the 'moderne' but show that he did not mistake his true vocation.

In the last chapter there is a brief account of an early love, discreetly stated and moving. The girl did not

requite it; in fact, she died a spinster in early middle
age. His description of her is one of the masterly
touches:

> A book, a play, a film, a ballet, a new, and usually
> deleterious friend, a public injustice, generally known
> and generally accepted, but suddenly discovered by
> Olivia, [1] would totally engage her for a time;
> these crazes were mitigated by a peculiar fastidious-
> ness, which did not prevent her from saying and doing
> outrageous things, but preserved her essential delicacy
> quite intact; also by shyness which made her unwilling
> to make any friends save those who were attracted by her
> and forced their way into her confidence. She nagged and
> bullied at times, she suffered from morbid self-
> consciousness, she was incapable of the ordinary arts
> and efforts of pleasing and was generally incapable of
> any kind of ostentation; a little crazy; truth-loving
> and in the end holy.

But that is enough from and about this book - which is
not a book, only a separately bound portion of a work in
progress. The author doubtless had his reasons for issuing
it by itself, not all of which are apparent. It is a compliment to this (presumably) least interesting part to say
that it does nothing to diminish eagerness for the rest.

Note

1   Olivia Plunket Greene (1907-55), an important influence
    on Waugh's conversion to Roman Catholicism.

187. ALEC WAUGH, 'COSMOPOLITAN'

November 1964, 26-7

It is a curious experience to read the autobiography of a
brother - so much is familiar, yet so much is strange; I
had the sense of seeing a large part of my own life -
little though I figure in the narrative - from another
angle.
    Evelyn is rather more than five years younger than my-
self and that, in early years, is a considerable disparity,
particularly in view of the fact that from the age of nine

I was away from home at a boarding school for eight months
of the year. We are also temperamentally very different.
In discussing our family tree, he says of four of our
great-great grandfathers, 'There is an element of fantasy
in these four totally dissimilar men, quite unknown to one
another, entering into a partnership to manufacture my brother and myself who, apart from a common aptitude for
storytelling, are antithetical though not antipathetical.'

In nothing is the difference between us more marked than
in our relations with our parents. Evelyn was the mother's
favorite, I the father's. He was, indeed, so absorbed in
his mother that he regarded his father's return from the
office in the evening as an intrusion; it took his mother
away from the nursery. For me, on the other hand, the click
of my father's latchkey in the lock would mark the beginning of my day.

'A Little Learning' is the first volume of a trilogy.
Evelyn was born in October, 1903; the narrative closes in
the summer of 1925 - three years before the publication of
his first novel 'Decline and Fall'.... His was a happy
childhood, as was mine. In both of us was inculcated by our
father a deep love of poetry. 'He read aloud,' Evelyn
writes, 'with precision of tone, authority and variety that
I have heard excelled only by Sir John Gielgud.' Both sets
of our grandparents lived in Somerset. We spent our summer
holidays with them. This part of our childhood, too, is
warmly and charmingly described.

Twenty-five years ago, Evelyn was labeled 'the Mouth-
piece of the Bright Young People': and I think it will be
of particular interest to Americans, in view of the amount
that has been written about Scott Fitzgerald, to compare
the different atmospheres of the English and American
1920s. For both, it was a period of fast and brittle living, but the roads which led to it were very different.
Evelyn was ten years old when the First War began. He cannot have expected to be actively involved in it. Yet it
clouded his boyhood. In the First War in England, when
recruiting for the first twenty months was on a voluntary
basis and landlocked trench warfare kept the 'high brass'
in relative immunity, it was a point of honor for young
men to get as near to no-man's-land as possible. Men like
Rupert Brooke and Raymond Asquith (the son of the Prime
Minister) refused staff appointments because they wanted
to be 'with their men.' In consequence, all the best young
schoolmasters went to the war, and boys like my brother
were put under feeble and ineffectual teachers.

Several generations have described themselves as 'lost.'
My brother's generation was lost in that they were, and
knew themselves to be, neglected between the years of ten

and fifteen. If they complained, they were contemptuously
admonished to 'remember their seniors in the trenches.'
'These were,' Evelyn writes, 'dismal years for half the
world. I believe it was the most dismal period in history
for an English schoolboy.' This suppression in their teens
was largely responsible for their flouting of authority
when they reached the universities.

Many critics consider that the Oxford section of
'Brideshead Revisited' is the high peak of Evelyn's writing. I think that the Oxford chapter in 'A Little Learning' will be the most admired. He went up with a scholarship in January, 1922, and came down in the autumn of
1924. It was a halcyon period with the young men who had
been submerged at their public schools during the war, at
last free to spread their wings. It was also a wild period.
Evelyn wrote in 'Brideshead': 'All the wickedness of that
time was like the spirit they mix with the pure grape of
the Dours, heady stuff full of dark ingredients; it at
once enriched and retarded the whole process of adolescence as the spirit checks the fermentation of the wine,
rendering it undrinkable, so that it must lie in the dark,
year in, year out, until it is brought up at last fit for
the table.' And indeed most of the young men, who in 1925
seemed hell-bent for perdition, are now prosperous and
influential citizens.

The last chapter is entitled 'In Which Our Hero Finds
Himself in Very Low Water.' Indeed he did! He took a bad
degree - a third - which disqualified him for the recognized professions. He had neither capital nor influence
in the big world. He went to a London art school, but his
heart was not in it. He was idle, he drank too much, he
got into debt. He seemed to be headed nowhere. I remember
an occasion when one of his checks bounced and his father
was called to honor it. 'I don't know what to do with him.
Can't you do anything?' A prescient caution prompted me to
say, 'Father, he may turn out to be a genius. You and I
might be made to look rather silly.' Does not this episode
prove a salutary warning to those who are put in charge of
youth? Within thirty months the object of so much family
concern had written one of the greatest comic novels of all
time.

To me, naturally, this book is of absorbing interest. I
am confident that it will prove so for many others. Evelyn
has a unique gift for dialogue. The narrative is constantly
lighted with humor. There are a number of vivid character
sketches. The atmosphere of a vanished day is skilfully and
tenderly evoked. The story that it tells is undramatic.
There are no sensational confessions, no scandals, no
revelations. There is no deep love affair. But it is an

important book because it presents and interprets the seed-
time of one of the most important writers of our day. What
would we not give for a similar book from Balzac, Turgenev,
or Thomas Hardy? I do not see how it could have been better
done.

188.   ANTHONY BURGESS, 'ENCOUNTER'

December 1964, 64, 66, 68

Anthony Burgess (b. 1917), novelist, composer, translator
and critic, is the author of 'Time for a Tiger' (1956),
'The Enemy in the Blanket' (1958), 'Beds in the East'
(1959) (the three published as 'The Malayan Trilogy',
1972), 'A Clockwork Orange' (1962), 'The Novel Now'
(1967), 'Beard's Roman Women' (1976) and 'Earthly Powers'
(1980). Mr Burgess has established himself as a senior
Catholic 'apologist'.

We need no cybernetic word-count to demonstrate how
frequently the verb 'repine,' in its negative conjugation,
occurs in the works of Mr. Evelyn Waugh. None of his later
heroes - Scott-King, Gilbert Pinfold, Guy Crouchback, the
author himself - ever repines, in spite of the march of
barbarism, the failure of the vintage, and the decay of
classical syntax. The pose is robed and stoic. In the last
imperial outpost the doomed values of language and chivalry
are upheld, though always with a certain discreet self-
mockery. Indeed, Scott-King takes a definite masochistic
pleasure (not uncommon here, we are told, though unknown to
the New World) in the rise of horrible Modern Europe. The
red-eyed scavenger is creeping in. Mr. Waugh goes so far as
to open the gates of Hampstead to him, cooing about its
peace:

> Oh, but I have done an unselfish thing in telling him
> this! For I know he will yearn to be about the business
> of Balbus, and, as likely as not, he will plant himself
> upon the meadow with the willows, that looks so spring-
> like from my book-room door today. Nevertheless one must
> not repine. My work in this line is done. Balbus has
> built his wall.

The style, and the slippered epoch it so well expresses,

will tell the reader which Mr. Waugh this is - not the comic-stoic mock-Augustan novelist but the whimsical man-of-letters, managing director of Chapman & Hall, friend of the great fraud Gosse. But the 'one must not repine' is a significant link, a shared nose or villainous trick of the eye. The father, despite all the differences in the world, prepares us for the son.

And, of course, in reading this first volume of Mr. Waugh's autobiography, we are most interested in the genesis of a vocation, a temperament, and a style. We can ignore the remoter heredity, though Mr. Waugh makes it very entertaining; what we cannot ignore is the father, with his continual 'flamboyant declamation to imaginary audiences', his despondent waltz-song ('*Nobody cares for me in the least. Everyone thinks I am a horrible beast*'), his mercuriality and his dramatic asthma, but, most of all, the limitations of his literary taste. 'Mr. Rupert Brooke,' he wrote, 'has the itch to say a thing in such an arresting fashion as to shock the literary purist into attention even against his will.' The art of D.H. Lawrence needs 'a shower bath of vital ideas.' T.S. Eliot is the drunken slave who, in the classic custom, was exhibited at the height of a feast to the sons of the household, 'to the end that they, being ashamed at the ignominious folly of his gesticulations, might determine never to be tempted into such a pitiable condition themselves.' Well, the son's best novel takes its title from 'The Waste Land,' but, with some inevitable advancing of the frontier of taste, the limitations have been passed on. Does not Mr. Pinfold abhor jazz and Picasso? Did not his creator affirm on television that James Joyce went mad to please the Americans? (1)

The Gibbonian classicism of 'A Little Learning' is a great joy, but it is an act, a posture, and it derives from the father's more Dickensian histrionics as much as the fictional gift itself. It is no more a 'natural' style than the Elianism of Mr. Waugh's father's bookish contemporaries, though it evokes an England of firmer tastes and more powerful convictions than were known to E.V. Lucas (2) (whom Mr. Waugh cites as his father's peer), Jack Squire, or W.W. Jacobs. The perfect mastery of the exact conceptual locution, often implying - as in Gibbon's own 'Autobiography' - a moral judgment that is not really there, is the source of all of Mr. Waugh's humour and irony, as well as his carefully outmoded elegance. But when he falls from his own high standards - as when he uses the ghastly neologism 'undergraduette' in the Oxford part of the book - we are shocked as we are shocked by no other author. In Mr. Waugh style is a kind of morality, and a solecism strikes with the force of an act of delinquency. But such lapses are

very rare. Stylistically this is a consummate achievement,
yet (and this is no paradox) the beauty of the writing
draws away our concern with the subject-matter as recorded
fact. Was Mr. Waugh's Oxford, for instance, really as he
describes it? It reads, with the Arcadia of 'Brideshead
Revisited', like some world of idyll far older than anything Mr. Waugh could have known. Still, we do not care
much, and though Mr. Waugh's three delightful maiden aunts
undoubtedly have historical referents, he is as welcome
as is Apthorpe to invent them so long as we continue to be
beguiled by the wonder of form and language. The professional fiction writer seeks the suspension of our disbelief when he writes a novel; it is hard to break the
habit of credulity when we read his autobiography. Credulity, though, is a different condition from the ineluctable
need to accept fact as fact.

The youth who emerges from this book is neither forward
nor, as Mr. Waugh himself is only too ready to admit, particularly likeable. At Lancing he and his cronies chris-
tened a boy, for no good reason, 'Dungy.' 'Once this large,
desperate youth approached me in the cloisters and said:
"If you'll stop calling me 'Dungy' I'll do anything you
like. I'll publicly kick *anyone* in another House." I
replied: "Oh, go and kick yourself, Dungy."' Along with the
'malice and calculation' went a gulosity that was to re-
appear in 'Brideshead Revisited', though later (and I
believe wrongly) expunged:

> [We] began with crumpets, eight or more a head,
> dripping with butter. From there we swiftly passed to
> cake, pastry and, in season, strawberries and cream,
> until at six we tottered into chapel taut and stupefied
> with eating.... Little pots of *foie gras* and caviar
> occasionally came from London and we were as nice in
> the brewing of tea as a circle of maiden ladies.

And so on. Lust is the only deadly sin not to appear, and
Mr. Waugh's youth, after a phase of mutual exhibition with
a little girl, is innocent of sexuality. (3) Indeed, the
only sexual revelation in the entire book comes at the end,
and the prototype of Captain Grimes - Mr. Waugh's colleague
at a school not much like Llanabba - makes it. There had
been a vast outing in honour of the headmaster's birthday:

> When it was all over and the boys in bed we sat in
> the common-room deploring the miseries of the day.
> Grimes alone sat with the complacent smile of an Etrus-
> can funerary effigy.
> 'I confess *I* enjoyed myself greatly,' he said as we
> groused.

We regarded him incredulously. '*Enjoyed* yourself,
Grimes? What did you find to enjoy?'
    'Knox minor,' he said with radiant simplicity. 'I
felt the games a little too boisterous, so I took Knox
minor away behind some rocks. I removed his boots and
stockings, opened my trousers, put his dear little foot
there and experienced a most satisfying emission.'

There are pederasts of more distinction in the book, but
no other podorasts.
    As for the young artist, we are reminded that Mr. Waugh,
though he bloomed as a novelist early, started with the
ambition to be a calligrapher and illustrator - an ambition
as modest as that of the father in the field destined for
the son. We have met Mr. Waugh's illustrations to his own
novels and, with the indulgence appropriate to the *violon
d'Ingres*, admired. There are other examples of his first
and secondary art here and the technique is, I should
think, faultless. The aim is cognate with that of the
prose stylist - to achieve ironic effects (I am thinking
particularly of 'The Tragical Death of Mr. Will. Huskisson')
through a severely classical, almost sculptural, line, but
the flavour is of a mere hobby - like the flavour of the
essays of Lucas and the senior Waugh. And, even in the
author's attitude to the art that became his profession,
there is something amateur and hobbyish: we need the discipline of Latin and Greek in order to write good English
prose: 'the old-fashioned test of an English sentence -
will it translate? - still stands after we have lost the
trick of translation.' That excludes a great deal of modern
English literature, much of it valuable, and it fixes the
writer at an immovable frontier, administering the laws of
a dead empire. But Mr. Waugh is probably disingenuous
here, as he is in his very opening sentence: 'Only when one
has lost all curiosity about the future has one reached the
age to write an autobiography.' It is that charming television act again - the old man in a dry month. Mr. Waugh
is writing for the future.
    The reader will be surprised at the lack of any literary
passion in this first phase of Mr. Waugh's development - no
books set him on fire, unless they are about the pre-
Raphaelites. The young man who reads History and leaves
Oxford with a bad third betrays no concern with scholarship. Mr. Waugh, an ironic statue in a toga, practitioner
of perfect prose, has always tended to frighten us as Gibbon or Johnson or Junius frightens us - with the hint of a
formidable library, much of it in his brain. We need not be
frightened any more, nor need we cringe, with an underdog
whine, in the presence of the accents of aristocracy.

Mr. Waugh's father worked in an office, worried about
money, and went to Lord's or the cinema before going home
to Hampstead. At Oxford the contacts with the ruling class
begin, and there is a sufficiency of name-dropping. The
'Brideshead Revisited' postures are a legitimate indulgence for a novelist unrid of his father's romanticism, but
the dream of a great Catholic aristocracy has a faint whiff
of the sentimental about it. That there is no sentimentality in the harking back to Augustan solidity - temperamentally, if not historically, cognate - is a tribute to Mr.
Waugh's perfect artistry, though artistry itself is all
poses.

Mr. Waugh's conversion to Catholicism will appear, one
presumes, in the next volume. A cradle-Catholic myself,
and hence one of a long line of underdogs, I tend both to
despise (always unjustly) and envy (sometimes justly) a
man like Mr. Waugh who, with calm 18th-century logic, can
sail into the Church after the sort of *echt* English up-
bringing presented in 'A Little Learning'. It is the best
of both worlds. Mr. Waugh gives us what he calls 'A Brief
History of My Religious Opinions', and the cradle-Catholic
is aware of the great social, as well as theological, gulf
fixed. In an earlier chapter we look in wonder on St.
Jude's, Hampstead Garden Suburb, and its eccentric incum-
bent:

> Mr. Bourchier was a totally preposterous parson.
> When he felt festal he declared a feast, whatever the
> season or occasion marked on the calendar. He dressed
> up, he paraded about, lights and incense were carried
> before him. When the mood took him he improvised his
> own peculiar ceremonies. Once he presented himself on
> the chancel steps, vested in a cope and bearing from
> his own breakfast table a large silver salt-cellar.
> 'My people,' he announced, 'you are the salt of the
> earth,' and scattered a spoonful on the carpet before
> us.... Despite all Mr. Bourchier's extravagant display
> I had some glimpse of higher mysteries.

Well, this was the England of Mr. Waugh's boyhood and it is
perhaps no more difficult for the Old Catholic to understand than the world of the minor public school with its
'good Church traditions.' The curious reader will take
delight in pincering out from the brew the gobbets and
slivers of genuine influence - the medieval illuminations,
the comedy of bourgeois life, the individualists of Oxford
and, above all, the paternal devotion to tradition.

This first volume, like Mr. Waugh's first novel, records
a decline and fall. An academic failure, indecisive in his

choice of vocation, inclined, like St. Augustine himself,
to debauchery, in need of a greater solidity than Anglican
Hampstead could provide, young Evelyn Waugh looked at the
successes of his friends and tried to escape from his
loneliness and dejection. Less resilient than Paul Pennyfeather, his wounds unpalliated by the large confidence of
'Grimes,' he sought a sempiternal quietus in the waters of
the North Wales coast. The jellyfish stung him and sent
him back to the future; the sea proved lustral, not lethal.
Naturally, we rejoice. We look forward to reading about
the larger learning, a lifetime's lessons on how not to
repine.

Notes

1 No, he did not. The reference is presumably to the
   'Face to Face' interview again, and no mention was made
   of Joyce or the Americans. Mr Burgess is perhaps confusing this with two other interviews: one for the BBC Home
   Service series 'Frankly Speaking' (16 November 1953)
   where he spoke slightingly of 'a little cosmopolitan
   group in Paris that collected round Gertrude Stein' and
   'tried to introduce gibberish into literature'; the
   other with Julian Jebb in April 1962 in which he said:
   'Experiment! God forbid! Look at the results of experiment in the case of a writer like Joyce. He started off
   writing very well, then you can watch him going mad
   with vanity. He ends up a lunatic' ('Writers', pp. 110-11).
2 The critic.
3 Since the publication of the 'Diaries' (1976) we now
   know that this is incorrect; during this period Waugh
   was passing through an active homosexual phase.

'Sword of Honour'

1965 (rescension of trilogy; US edition, 1966)

189. UNSIGNED REVIEW, 'TIMES LITERARY SUPPLEMENT'

17 March 1966, 216

As part of the revised edition of his novels Mr. Waugh has
edited the trilogy of 'Men at Arms', 'Officers and Gentlemen' and 'Unconditional Surrender' to make a single book.
Nothing now indicates the breaks between the original volumes; the two or three 'books' into which each was divided
have (roughly speaking) been demoted to the status of
Chapter; the original chapters have become numbered sections within them; a good few of the lesser divisions -
spaces between paragraphs - have been eliminated. The
result is above all a change of pace, suitably adjusted to
the longer distance. At the end of 800 pages the reader
feels that he has read a large and very fine novel, whose
scale and seriousness are offset by a remarkable lightness
of texture.

The trilogy had its flaws, and these have not been set
right. The hiatus before the start of 'Unconditional Surrender' becomes less conspicuous now that the synopsis
('The story so far ...') has been dropped; but those two
years remain puzzling, and the explicit suggestions that
Ludovic murdered both Major Hound and the sapper captain
have gone with the synopsis. Ludovic himself remains far-
fetched in his subsequent appearances; these and the quite
unnecessary air crash in Yugoslavia still stick out as the
weak points of the last third of the book. The one thread
of the whole intricate web that led absolutely nowhere
still does so, though the end has been tied with a fresh
knot, the fizzling out of the security authorities' interest in Guy being feebly excused by a dozen interpolated
lines consigning Colonel Grace-Groundling-Marchpole to

insignificance and confusion. There has only been a single
major change, and that is effected by a tiny amendment on
the last page of the book. In 'Unconditional Surrender' Guy
and his new (Catholic) wife had 'two boys of their own' as
well as the cuckoo planted by Trimmer. This has been cut,
and now Box-Bender says, 'Pity they haven't any children of
their own'. The happy, lucky ending is for some reason no
longer acceptable. Mr. Waugh's picture of divine provi-
dence has been seriously altered.

A number of small episodes or descriptions have been
cut, running to between one and four pages each, and this,
so the preface suggests, is because they struck the author
as tedious. In one or two cases he may be right; thus it is
not unreasonable to curtail the account of the trip out to
the Middle East and the hospitality of Cape Town, while the
fishy Haw-Haw-type lieutenant-colonel encountered in Crete
seemed improbable and led nowhere. But in the main the
excisions seem a great pity. We have now lost the delightful account of Mr. Crouchback's reactions to the auctioning
of his own furniture; we have lost Guy's memories of the
house after his death; Brigadier Ritchie-Hook's descent
into the jollities of Bingo has gone; so has the description of Sergeant Soames and the penetrating account of
relations between officers and N.C.O.s; so has everything
to do with the flight of the Greek General Militiades; so
has the lunatic but all-too-true incident of the bathers
and the Bren gun towards the end of 'Men at Arms'. None
of these was at all tedious to the reader. If the real idea
(as one must suspect after the admitted disingenuity of
other of Mr. Waugh's prefatory notes) was to keep the book
to 800 pages and fifty shillings it was a short-sighted
piece of economy.

What is more interesting to connoisseurs is the many
much smaller cuts and changes, sometimes two or three to a
page, right through the book. These are very seldom
designed to reduce 'repetitions and discrepancies' (the
other pretext given by the preface); indeed, fresh discrepancies have arisen as a result; the proof-reading has
also been less successful than before. In a number of
cases the amendments are obviously meant to thin out the
minor characters, or at least to expunge those characters'
surnames; thus Roots, Slimbridge and Smiley of Hookforce
H.Q. are all disidentified; the mad commando colonel Pren-
tice is more or less eliminated (which seems a pity), and
the otiose Welsh conductor from the Yugoslav episode is
rightly thrown out, except for one quite unnecessary and
now double puzzling appearance on page 762. There is a considerable reduction in the use of the overworked phrase
'in the picture', but otherwise it hardly seems that

Mr. Waugh is doing what he claims.

For the effect of the great majority of such alterations is slightly to tilt characters, opinions or apparent
judgments. With Guy, for instance, the references to his
having been at Downside and at university are removed; so
is more than one mention of his relative poverty (which was
always hard to believe); so is the solicitor's computation
that his father's estate will bring in an income of some
£7,000 a year. Four separate mentions of his romantic,
almost schoolboyish attitude to war have gone; so has a
good part of Mr. Goodall's disquisitions on Catholic
genealogy, together with the author's implied ridicule.
Ian Kilbannock's former job turns out to have been gossip-
writer, not sporting journalist as before; the phrase is
cut in which he admits to having been 'pretty red ever
since the Spanish Civil War'. The air-marshal's vulgar
rhyme about Elinor Glyn is omitted; so is the mention of
'some nonsense of Brendan's' and the reference to
Churchill's 'sham-Augustan prose'.

The most important of these retouchings affects Ivor
Claire, the gentleman rider who to Guy represented quin-
tessential England but disobeyed orders and abandoned his
men in Crete. Though he is still the pivot on which the
whole story swings, the shock originally represented by his
action has been toned down; it is no longer said that he
'behaved abominably', or that Tommy Blackhouse would bar
him from any responsible job and might even be less
friendly to him at the Club. On the contrary it is suggested that Guy, now, resigned 'an immeasurable piece of
his manhood' on the same 'fatal morning', and although it
is far from clear what this means - Blackhouse has no such
criticisms of Guy as he originally had of Claire - profound
significance is presumably intended by the fact that Guy
now loses his brother's Lourdes medal during his escape.
It is much simpler with the Yugoslav incidents, where three
or four minor changes ('betrayal' for 'intrigue' as a term
for our break with Mihailovic) indicate the author's stif-
fening disapproval, and the communist Frank de Souza is no
longer allowed an M.C.

Nothing is too trivial for amendment. The allocation of
capital letters, for instance, now favours the church
rather than the military, so that instead of 'mass at the
Castle' we have 'Mass at the castle'. The members of the
Auxiliary Fire Service operating outside Bellamy's are no
longer 'progressive novelists' but 'experimental novelists'.
Mr. Crouchback brushes up his classics from a pale blue
'Xenophon' only; the North and Hillard's Latin Prose he was
previously also holding has now for some baffling reason
been cut. Whether such decisions in any way improve the

novel is a moot point, but no doubt they will make it more interesting to academic students.

The book remains what it set out to be: 'a description of the Second World War as it was seen and experienced by a single uncharacteristic Englishman', and the view remains less uncharacteristic than Mr. Waugh thinks, for the aspects covered - the initial stagnation, the raising (and publicizing) of the Commandos, the defeat in Crete and the irregular campaign in Yugoslavia - are all fairly representative of the war we waged, so that a surprisingly wide swath of history is illuminated, as well as the individuals on all levels who made it. Perhaps Guy is not quite so uncharacteristic as his author, for certainly the view of the book which Mr. Waugh himself now takes is one that would hardly occur to anybody else:

> On reading the book I realised that I had done something quite outside my original intention. I had written an obituary of the Roman Catholic Church in England as it had existed for many centuries.... When I wrote 'Brideshead Revisited' I was consciously writing an obituary of the doomed English upper class. It never occurred to me, writing 'Sword of Honour', that the Church was susceptible to change....

It would hardly be more far-fetched to call it a study of the servant question. After all, we start with a hotel kept by former Crouchback servants, where the staff's failure to fetch Guy's luggage is remedied by the servant of a Halberdier major. Guy joins the Halberdiers, and the service in barracks (the wine butler, the 'toiling old Halberdiers' who stoke the fires) is part of his initial love affair with that regiment. Then comes the disillusionment of Kut-al-Imara House ('it won't kill you to hump your own gear for once') where all men are equal and 'the whole hierarchic structure of army life was offended'; it becomes a symbol of 'that new world' which Guy had enlisted to fight. Worse still, the barracks themselves are undermined; 'they've taken my servant away', the embittered Adjutant tells Guy on his return from Crete, while in the officer's mess - ichabod - 'an A.T. came in from the serving door whistling....' Yet here as in so many other respects the experience of Crete seems to transform all values. The lady who, at one of the crucial points of 'Unconditional Surrender', is cited as believing that the 'normality' to be restored by peace will include a full staff of a dozen servants is plainly being ridiculed. At the beginning of the book a household of twenty sees Guy off from Italy; at the end he is in The Lesser House.

And the name of this study? 'Active Service'? 'Divine
Service'? Never mind. For it is not the book that Mr. Waugh
has in fact written, any more than is the 'document of
Catholic usage of my youth' which he now feels that he has
produced. All the same, the test of a first-rate work of
fiction (or drama, for that matter) is that each re-reading
should reveal fresh aspects, undetected threads, new
implications. This the trilogy fulfils, in both the original and the revised versions. It says more than it was consciously meant to say; more than any single reading can
reveal it as saying. Admittedly the author's amendments are
often to be mildly regretted. But if they encourage more
people to read it as a whole then they will have added both
to our literature and to our knowledge of what we were
really up to between 1939 and 1945.

190.   JOHN P. McKENNA, LETTER TO 'TIMES LITERARY SUPPLEMENT'

7 April 1966, 314

I can find no trace of Mr McKenna in reference works concerning American scholars, writers or celebrities. He gave
his address as Twin Oaks, 78 Bay Drive, Massapequa, New
York 11758.

Your reviewer's perceptive account (Wartime Revisited,
March 17) of Evelyn Waugh's minor but significant revisions
in the trilogy about Guy Crouchback, now entitled 'Sword of
Honour', does not contain any explicit suggestions about
the motives or events responsible for the changes. Surely,
however, readers aware of Mr. Waugh's hostility to the
enactments of Vatican II can understand the author's subtle
recasting of his work. If, as Mr. Waugh notes in the introduction to the volume under discussion, 'Brideshead Revisited' was a deliberate 'obituary of the doomed English
upper class' it is equally clear that 'Sword of Honour' is
the death notice of what Ford Madox Ford calls 'the Old
Faith in the Old Way' in that delightful swansong of the
historical novel, 'The Fifth Queen'. Mr. Waugh, who claims
in the introduction that he did not know 'the Roman Catholic Church was susceptible to change' when he was writing
the Crouchback novels, was nervous about the Council well
in advance of its decisions. American readers will recall,
for example, his article in the conservative secular

journal of opinion, the 'National Review', entitled The
Same Again, Please: A Layman's Hopes of the Vatican Council
(December 4, 1962). The author saw the handwriting on the
wall, but it wasn't in Latin so he refused to read it.

Although it is true that the many minor changes taken
collectively affect the tone of the entire work, the
'single major change' your reviewer notes is the key to
the radical redirection Mr. Waugh's textual recensions produce. In this pessimistic variation on Forster's symbolic
pattern of inheritance in 'Howard's End', Guy and his second wife, the landed Catholic Domenica, forfeit their two
sons by erasure leaving the 'cuckoo' born of the cowardly
Trimmer and Guy's providentially blasted heretical first
wife Virginia to inherit England. Thus is 'Mary's Dowry'
lost to the creedless masses. How could God long survive
the Marchmains once the Papacy itself undercut the Ultra-
montanes? Unless, as Anthony Burgess wrote about 'Sword of
Honour' in the recent religious books issue (The Manicheans, March 3), (1) 'a decayed order of chivalry has ...
little to do with religion...'.

Note

1   Anthony Burgess, The Manicheans, 'TLS', 3 March 1966,
    153-4.

Christopher Sykes, 'Evelyn Waugh.
A Biography'

1975

191. ANGUS WILSON, 'TIMES LITERARY SUPPLEMENT'

3 October 1975, 1116-17

'I describe this book as a not the biography of Evelyn
Waugh because the great quantity of documentary material on
which it is based suggests to me that other biographical
studies could and perhaps should be written.' Thus Christopher Sykes in the first sentence of his preface to 'Evelyn
Waugh', and I suppose that he is right. Nor is it only on
account of the abundance of material that the way remains
open for future biographers. There are other reasons, too:
the complex character of Waugh, the close relation of Mr
Sykes to his subject not only as a friend but in creed and,
to some extent, in social sympathies as well. Yet if subsequent biographies are bound to take a different approach,
it is unlikley that they will be better, and they will certainly not have the particular virtues and faults that
arise from the author's being one of the characters in the
Evelyn Waugh Play and at the same time a writer - and, I
should guess, a man - strongly averse by temperament to
appearing on the boards. Generally speaking this combination makes for a successful narrative, though of a rather
special kind.
But before I discuss Mr Sykes's book, I must say that
surely what we would most like to have would be Evelyn
Waugh's Life of Evelyn Waugh. Not his autobiography. We
had the first volume of that; and, although it has many
rather dull merits, in relation to this biography, as I
shall suggest, it is a serious stumbling-block. No, what
we want is a book about the creator of an absurd, sad and
touching world, Evelyn Waugh, by that famous creator of an
absurd, sad and touching world, Evelyn Waugh. But, alas,
death has intervened; and, in any case, as we know from

482

'Rossetti', 'Edmund Campion', and 'Ronald Knox' (books published at wide intervals in his writing career), when Evelyn
Waugh celebrated the lives of other men, he left the stage not
for the privacies of backstage, for greater intimacy, but
for the auditorium, the public arena where he presented
orations, decorous, conscientious and balanced but a trifle
absurdly 'lettered', almost genteel, as though the ghost of
his father had returned to possess him and force him to
mend his literary ways. Waugh the biographer would never
have done justice to a personality as splendid as his own.

Yet the decorum had its whimsical side, and the whimsy
reminds one of how Evelyn Waugh stood in relation to all
but the most private areas of his life. He was one of those
men who transform everything they do, every place they see,
every conversation they overhear, every person they meet,
into part of their own special play. Such men are nearly
always clowns (with pity and fury in the wings of their
clowning, as they are traditionally in the circus), and
they number among them many of the best comic writers.

On the other hand they need not necessarily turn to
authorship, and if Evelyn Waugh was a writer it was because of a deep need for aesthetic perfection and a lifelong devotion to excellence of craft. As a result, his re-
shaping of experience has a logic of exaggeration in colour
and in form that frequently makes him a master novelist.
But he also played out his fiction in his life (as have
many other comic writers) as constantly and delightfully
and frighteningly as any of his inventions like Grimes or
Atwater.

The price that such great histrionic masters pay for the
masking of their tears by the creation of havoc and absurdity is large; above all, in its actual transformation of
the seeming substantial world around them into something
quite different. Rejecting the so-called real world from
boredom or loneliness or disappointment, the clown-creator
wrenches and forces everything into his own comic, twisted
patterns through mimicry and exaggeration and invention.
He is able to laugh and the world laughs with him. But his
gift leaves the world distrustful: 'Waugh was magnificent
about B. last night, but then - awful thought - how funny
and unfair will he be about me today?' Out of hilarity is
born hysteria, out of companionship a sense of conspiracy.

We can see this process again and again in this life of
Waugh, building up and building up, turning entertainer
into victim, leading in the last years to his most heroic
achievement (and, if not his best book, a very good one),
'The Ordeal of Gilbert Pinfold' - Mr Maskelyne (1) or Mr
Devant nailing down his own magical devices and making a
work of art of the revelation. But then in some degree

(though less consciously) Waugh introduced his own acting
self not only into 'Pinfold' but into most of the fictions
he made of life, and this had an effect upon the whole pattern of his artistic career.

I shall return to Waugh as victim-hero of his own novels
in a moment. First I must suggest the effect that being
part of Waugh's theatre of life, as he was for thirty
years, has upon Mr Sykes as Waugh's biographer. Mr Sykes
was one of Waugh's Horatios, one, it would seem, who,
though he was often cast as 'exasperated friend' or the
straight man who receives a custard pie slap in the kisser,
nevertheless did not become the object of Waugh's conspira-
torial suspicion, but remained a constant, loving and loved
friend, loyal and loyally treated. Yet the effect of their
relationship on the book is a very complicated one, and not
just a matter of maintaining a balance between loyalty and
admiration for a friend, a proper severity, and the objectivity that Mr Sykes would wish to give to the compilation
of a researched biography. There were times, particularly
when I had just been delighted by one of the hundred ludicrous anecdotes of Waugh's life, especially one in which
Mr Sykes is an embarrassed bystander or even a butt, when I
was not quite sure how much Mr Sykes himself is aware of
how deeply involved he is in Waugh's scenario. I even
found myself wondering - for without doubt Waugh, like
other creators of black comedy, exacted an unconscious contribution to the action from everyone around him - how much
of the effect of these stories was added by Mr Sykes's
unwitting contribution to their making.

The relationship here between story and teller is an
uneasy one. Yet, in general, the pull between Mr Sykes as
friend and participant and as objective biographer works
for a splendid narrative, especially as his natural urbanity and flow are punctuated by extraordinary violence of
opinion, as considerable as Waugh's though far less constant, violences of religious and social attitude and of
literary judgment - so that Aldous Huxley's claims to be a
novelist are as totally, suddenly and peremptorily dismissed as those of Graham Greene are accepted. This makes
for a beautiful flowing book which is interrupted at intervals by sudden convulsive outbursts: a form of narrative
that carries the reader along but does not allow him to
slumber.

So much for the effect of Waugh's theatrical view of
life upon Mr Sykes in his double role of participant and
author. What of the effect of Waugh's own role-playing on
his novels? It was, I think, as Mr Sykes suggests, harmful.
The heroes of the novels from Pennyfeather to Crouchback
are comic hero-victims, and, fearing to lose the balance

between asking for affection, for ridicule, for admiration
or for pity, Waugh ends by settling for a certain boring
nullity.

The heroes are all honourable men, as he was, but they
are none of them appalling, alarming and magical men as he
was - *those* characteristics he gives to other characters.
The only hero whose painful predicament, especially because
of its terrible, ludicrous climax, seems to me truly to
touch one's heart is Tony Last, the hero of 'A Handful of
Dust', and it is this which makes me place that novel above
all Waugh's others as a work of art.

What was it that led Waugh to assign this particular
role to himself in life (again, I must emphasize, perhaps
not in his most private life) and to his heroes in life-
made-art? Mr Sykes's diagnosis is self-hatred, and I feel
sure that he is right. And perhaps this view of the matter
specially commends itself to a devout Catholic like Mr
Sykes by helping to explain what must surely trouble him
most of all - Waugh's growing fear at the end of his life
that, in the face of the victories of Catholic modernism,
he might lose his faith. I cannot but think that this self-
hatred sprang from a certain self-pity, a certain contempt
for himself for being self-pitying, for wanting a love
that, if he ever received it, came too late. But Mr Sykes
is reluctant to pursue the investigation this far, possibly
because it might involve too extended a consideration of
the fitful sentimentality which, together with his cruelty,
is undoubtedly the major blemish of Waugh's work and his
life.

Yet once self-hatred has been diagnosed, we are bound
to ask what it was in Waugh's life that it sprang from.
And this Mr Sykes does not seek to answer. The blurb (for
which the author cannot of course be held responsible)
says that 'no portrait of so complex and contradictory a
man could or should explain him'. This is governessy nonsense. It should try even if it cannot succeed. And I'm
afraid that at this point Mr Sykes hides behind the published volume of Waugh's autobiography. He seeks to add
little to the story of his subject's childhood and boyhood as though Waugh had told it all; but needless to say
he hadn't. Why did Waugh come at a certain time so to dislike his father? What were the full effects of his brother
Alec's great popular success as a novelist? Why did he
neglect his mother in her last years? One feels compelled
to ask whether here do not lie some of the causes of the
disease that Mr Sykes diagnoses.

Inevitably such excursions into the foundations of
character run the risk of silliness and of vulgarity, but
that can hardly excuse evading them. I suspect that

Mr Sykes reposes on the false excuse of the autobiography
to avoid such inquiries for more respectable reasons: an
innate concern for privacy, and the fact that Catholic
metaphysics make psychological speculation a very secondary,
even an arrogant approach to the qualities of a human soul.

Yet it does seem a pity, for the one letter quoted from
Evelyn Waugh to his wife, the few remarks of his son
Auberon, and, above all, the brief memoirs of his daughter
Margaret which appear as an appendix open up glimpses of a
private second world - not the unhappy 'private' country
gentleman's life that degenerated into gin and staring out
of the window, but a very real world of private affections
and concerns that is absolutely integral to the magic of
his best novels. It is just because we glimpse this more
gentle comedy of life behind the violent comedy of his invention - and it was a world that perhaps he himself only
glimpsed - that so many of his novels have that extra
dimension of Paradise half-lost (nothing to do with the
cruder social and historical aspects of 'Brideshead
Revisited'), and we feel, throughout 'A Handful of Dust'
and in certain passages of some of the other novels, that
we have moved beyond the realm of great talent into that of
genius. This is the poetry of his novels.

As it is, with family privacy respected (and one half of
me respects Mr Sykes for respecting it) we are left with
Waugh the occasional monster, and the frequent honourable
good friend of the club or the mess room; or, at a deeper
level, Waugh, half *arbiter elegantarium*, half little boy
lost, as he shows himself in his relation with his elegant,
intelligent women friends - Nancy Mitford, Diana Cooper,
Diana Guinness (as she was), Ann Fleming - who made the
outer world bearable for him.

The existence of the autobiography, indeed, throws out
the balance of Mr Sykes's book. I should not claim for
'Decline and Fall' or 'Vile Bodies' (central to my own
early adolescence as I feel them to be and love them for
being) the superiority which too many people of older
years automatically attribute to the first works of
favourite authors. Yet they are surely small post-
Firbankian masterpieces, and Mr Sykes, I feel, gives them
too little notice, perhaps because they are works which
antedate Waugh's Catholicism. (2)

This neglect of the early days, however, has its com-
pensation in the wealth of wonderful anecdotes of the later
ones, especially the war and post-war years. Mr Sykes is
very close to his subject by then, and not only personally
but in matters of faith and of social philosophy. True, his
Catholicism is more strictly rational; he reprehends with a
certain amusement his friend's flight into superstition....

As to Waugh's distaste for the liberalism of the Church since John XXIII (or indeed earlier), Mr Sykes's voice is that of Mr Crouchback urging a wider historical vision of the vagaries in papal secular policy.

But there is one sense in which his sharing of Waugh's faith seems to make for a lack of vision. He speaks of his sense of the difficulty that a non-Catholic reader must feel in understanding 'Brideshead Revisited'. I have never felt this myself, perhaps because two of my elder brothers were converted to Catholicism in the late 1920s with the same aura of conversion that Waugh knew, and they came to have social views little different from his. Under their influence, at sixteen, I was nearly converted myself. For this reason I do not find 'Brideshead Revisited' (a fine novel, surely) difficult to comprehend. But I suspect Mr Sykes does not see how far away those 1920s and 1930s days are for most modern English readers. That Catholic conversion was, then, 'in the air' and that Christianity, let alone Catholicism, is not very significant for most English readers today must inevitably be a matter of historical interest only, though also of sadness for believers; yet it does militate against Waugh's novels now. Their social-religious flavour is no longer, as it was, a relevant eccentricity, but rather an irrelevant one.

Nor does it help that he came to associate his religious faith so closely with his extravagant social views. Mr Sykes rightly regards Waugh's snobbery as unimportant. Snobbery is endemic in England and often an endearing trait. Nor was Waugh ashamedly snobbish. The best of the few conversations I had with him was about my father's memories of Lancing in late 1879. I had always heard that Waugh was ashamed of having been at Lancing rather than at Eton, and I ventured upon the topic very cautiously. As it turned out, he was delighted. Indeed his only reproof was characteristic. I told him of my father's having won a modern history prize in many years of education almost entirely classical. What was the prize, he asked, how did it originate? And when I could not inform him, he said sternly: 'You should have asked your father more about that.'

What Mr Sykes reprehends in his friend is not his looking up but his looking down. Dislike of the age of the common man should surely not have led him into such savage lack of charity towards the uneducated or the self-educated. Mr Sykes deplores this in his life but takes insufficient notice, I think, of its bad effect in his books. The deplorable treatment of the evacuees in 'Put Out More Flags' is the most unpleasantly vulgar and heart-less example. But more important is the way that Waugh's social sympathies could defeat his deeper purposes.

This, it seems to me, is the real trouble with 'Helena'. Waugh magnificently conveys in that book (and unexpectedly, too) the horror of the cruelties of the pagan world, especially of slavery, in the smallest, most delicate aspects of what the pagan characters take for granted. Yet the portrayal of Helena herself is very self-indulgent. There is no reason why (translated into modern idiom) Helena, the daughter of a British chieftain, should not appear as Miss Hunter-Dunn (the book is dedicated to Penelope Betjeman). But the belittling, the seemingly arrogant social coterie effect that this has on the deeper religious meaning that Waugh wished to establish is disastrous to his purpose. And it springs, I think, directly from a wish to *épater* the bourgeois, to snarl at the common reader. Here Waugh's tired, familiar theatrical props are allowed to spoil the true play....

Perhaps there was a deeply suppressed sadism in Waugh that caused [his] horrible outbursts. The one story of his homosexual period suggests this. Visiting a Paris male brothel, his wish was that a strong negro should fuck a youth dressed as an Egyptian princess. Luckily he hadn't the cash to command the realization of his imaginings.

Yet, in the long run, religious demands, social extravagances, sadistic feelings distort his novels very little when set beside their consummate art. This is surely because he was, above all, an aesthete deriving from his beloved Pre-Raphaelites through the 1890s and Firbank. Craftsmanship counted more than anything else for him. Artistic values, in this world, were the highest.

I have written elsewhere of my lasting gratitude for the encouragement he gave me in my early days of publication and later - an encouragement I knew from no other writer in England. And, although we could never have been congenial companions, his liking for my work led him, as I remember, to act with courtesy and kindness to me as a very shy newcomer on the literary scene the few times I met him - notably at a party for the Catholic journal the 'Month', where he took great pains to introduce me and make me feel at ease.

This generosity came to my mind whenever I read the shocking brutalities that crop up in Mr Sykes's book. It sprang, I think, from his respect for anyone whose work he admired in any degree, however small. It is beautifully illustrated by the way he accepted the transgression of all his social rules by Henry Green during a weekend visit, because, as he rightly thought, Green was a novelist of genius. They were surely the two best English novelists of their generation, and, if Green had the edge over Waugh,

it was because of his exceptionally wide social sympathies.
Perhaps we may hope that Mr Sykes will now give us a biography of Henry Green, the most shamefully neglected of
all English novelists. It would be a good companion piece
to this very entertaining, sympathetic, wise, but not un-
flawed book.

Notes

1   A British Intelligence officer in Laurence Durrell's
    'The Alexandria Quartet' (1957-61).
2   Mr Sykes responded:

> Angus Wilson ... has devoted a long and thoughtful
> article to my biography.... I cannot be expected to
> agree with all his propositions, but one calls for
> refutation. Mr Wilson alleges that I give too little
> space to Evelyn Waugh's first two novels. I may have
> done, but not, as Mr. Wilson suggests, 'perhaps be-
> cause they are works which antedate Waugh's Catholi-
> cism'. This can only be described as bosh.
>   Mr. Wilson has plentiful criticism of my book but
> I am grateful to him for not drawing attention to my
> gross misquotation from Tacitus on p. 156. I fool-
> ishly forgot Dr Routh and relied on memory. (TLS,
> 17 October 1975, 1237)

'The Diaries of Evelyn Waugh',

ed. Michael Davie

1976

192. MARTIN STANNARD, 'NEW REVIEW'

December 1976, 52-4

Martin Stannard (b. 1947), Lecturer in English at the University of Leicester, is author of essays on Waugh including Work Suspended: Waugh's Climacteric, (Essays in Criticism, October 1978) and Debunking the Jungle in 'The Art of Travel' ed. Philip Dodd (Cass, 1982).

In September Michael Davie's long-awaited edition of 'The Diaries of Evelyn Waugh' was published. It was heralded by the publisher as a 'major literary event'. Most reviewers, however, were more cautious. Margaret Drabble (1) found it depressing; Frederic Raphael (2) saw it as 'a portrait of the artist as a bad man'; Perry Anderson (3) considered that it lacked 'the true note of soliloquy' (whatever that may be); Auberon Waugh (4) thought it a stick with which to belabour poor Christopher Sykes's biography and the trends of British socialism.

But behind much of the commentary, and even the adulation, there lies the unspoken assumption that Mr Davie has rather embarrassingly heaped moral refuse between the amiable reader and Waugh's work. The diary is an astringent we must swallow while holding courageously to our critical assumption that distaste for an author's personality must never interfere with an assessment of his writings. 'Without his art', says Mr Raphael, 'he would have emerged as merely the bellicose, vindictive and bullying clown he seemed to imagine impersonated all that was best in British life.' It is a common enough view. One reviewer feared that the 'Diaries' might set back Waugh's literary reputation by ten years.

Certain criticisms of Davie's editorship have arisen directly out of this. Couldn't we have had less of the Lancing entries and social engagements? The Preface rather feebly forestalls the argument with the claim that the editor has 'become increasingly aware of the interest of certain entries that may, at first sight, appear boring'. But it surely goes without saying that, in the case of an important author only recently dead, the severe reduction of the text of private papers would prove premature. We are too close to it. Mr Davie has not provided us with an entertainment but a lamp - and a good one - with which to investigate the shadows of Waugh's mind.

The text is almost free of error, perhaps one word in ten pages being open to dispute. Yet reviewers have referred rather patronisingly to the editor as 'an excellent journalist'. Let there be no mistake. The transcription, editing, and background research represent a considerable work of scholarship. Waugh's hand is difficult in his later years and the MS is studded with near-illegible phrases, idiosyncratic contractions and nicknames. It was a private record not intended for publication. Dating is often only by days of the week and on occasions is wildly inaccurate. This mass of jottings (300,000 words) Mr Davie has successfully ordered, standardised and annotated. Unfortunately the index is lazy (using *et passim* for obscure references, omitting too many names) and the footnoting inconsistent. It is this which will prevent its being accepted as a scholarly work. But it was a conscious and sensible editorial decision to leave the bulk of the text untouched. In order to cut the adult diaries (1924 onwards) Mr Davie would have needed, as a working hypothesis, a balanced judgment of Waugh's scale of values. Too many reviewers readily assume that these values were rooted in philistinism. Mr Davie, more modestly, leaves generalisations to posterity.

It seems a great mistake indeed to take the 'Diaries' at face value. In one entry (p. 726) we see Waugh reporting an interview with American television:

The impresario kept producing notes from his pocket. 'Mr Waugh, it says here that you are irascible and reactionary. Will you please say something offensive?' So I said: 'The man who has brought this apparatus to my house has asked me to be offensive. I am sorry to disappoint him.'

His attacks in later life were defensive rather than offensive, and he erected a pasteboard persona - the

combination of 'eccentric don and testy colonel' so
accurately analysed in 'Pinfold' - for protection. But
what was he defending?

'I believe', says Mr Raphael, 'most of the causes he
supported to be wicked or wrong.' What were these causes?
A Bellocan hybrid fascism? The Catholic aristocracy? Conservatism? Certainly none of these. The 'Diaries' reflect
nothing more than his complete inability to associate with
groups or causes. He suffered slanderous attacks from
Earnest Oldmeadow in the 'Tablet' about the irreligious
nature of 'Black Mischief' but consistently refused, until
1945, to be a proselytising 'Catholic author'. Later, he even
came to see 'Brideshead' as a mistake and completely revised it in 1959. It was not causes, but principles, individuals, and aesthetics that interested Waugh, a view
neatly summarised in the 'Diaries' as 'Liberty, Diversity,
and Privacy' (p. 662). A lifelong friend, John Sutro, was
Jewish; Claud Cockburn and Tom Driberg were communists; the
aristocratic households he frequented were often not Catholic.

The interview quoted above shows how careful we must be
about generalisations. He was never sorry to disappoint.
In fact he went out of his way to obscure the truth about
himself. But his obstruction took different forms at different periods. The 'Diaries' for instance, reveal a complete change of tone between the third and fourth sections.
The gap (November 1928 to May 1930) almost certainly represents the destruction of those entries dealing with the
most painful incident in his life - the collapse of his
first marriage. From 1930 onwards the writing is brusque
and impersonal, and reflects the mind of a man who expects
little but pain from the world and is rather proud of his
pragmatism. Before this there is a pugnacious exuberance
broken by periods of despair. He wrote of Pinfold: 'He gave
nothing away'. But before 1930 he gave everything away.

At Lancing he furiously espoused lost causes, ragging
the Corps, writing subversive editorials for the school
magazine, and gaining a reputation as an unhealthy influence. At Oxford he espoused Conservatism because the
Socialists formed the new intellectual establishment. He
grew up in a 'literary' family with soirées at the Rhys's
and a sophisticated novelist for an elder brother reading
'Ulysses' and Havelock Ellis. Yet the last thing he wanted
to become was a writer. He could not bear following the
crowd yet, simultaneously, he wanted to be popular.

The 'Diaries' go some way towards providing an answer to
this paradox. In the very first entry we see him speaking
of the need to keep his life in 'water-tight compartments'.
Towards the end the entries frequently refer to the

interference (usually by his children) with the 'rational',
the controlled life. Behind the early need to compartmen-
talise emotions lay the fear of failure; behind the later,
a fear that he had become emotionally sterile. To be
'rational', of course, did not mean to Waugh to be Godless;
he had passed through that phase and discarded it between
1921 and 1930. It meant to accept absolutely the teachings of
of the Church and to struggle with the absurdities of idol-
atry he saw beyond its doors. In Addis Ababa he describes
the Church as 'an island [of] sanity in a raving town' (p.
332). The graven images changed and solidified with age.
In the thirties, the lonely and unhappy man scouring the
world for entertainment and illumination had time for
Picasso. But looking back from the drab routine of premature old-age he rather sadly remarks: 'It was fun thirty-
five years ago to travel far and in great discomfort to
meet people whose entire conception of life and manner of
expression were alien. Now one only has to leave one's
gates' (p. 791).

It is not simply a question of the encroachment of the
'lower classes' on the ground of privilege. This was an
effect rather than a cause. All stemmed from the premise
that a world which denied Catholicism, the tactile fabric
of Helena's cross, was egocentric and necessarily intro-
verted and self-destructive. The principal sign of this
was to him the decay of the arts beneath the onslaught of
subjectivity. The 'grey lice' of socialism he reviewed more
from a philosophical, an aesthetic, position than a political one. The new power reduced his ability, as an artist
and as a man before his God, to control his environment by
taking his profits and invading his privacy. The possibility of the rational (not 'rationalist') life grew dimmer as
the individual became part of the bureaucratic machinery.
In addition, the objectivity of the artist was clouded by
questions of 'social conscience' and the aesthetic taste of
the century debased by the euphoria of self-expression, a
consequent emphasis on mass production and a fall in standards of workmanship. It seemed the height of intellectual
depravity to him when it took two men (Auden and Isherwood)
to write a book.

In the now infamous 'Face to Face' interview John Freeman mentioned that at Oxford Waugh had moved in 'the aesthetic set' and presumed that he must have forsaken it at
some stage. 'Have you been conscious', he asked, 'of any
revulsion against that particular set of people or has this
been a gradual development?' Waugh quickly replied, 'Oh no,
I'm still a pure aesthete.' Perry Anderson remarks that,
'There is no trace of any book in the diaries that had a
major impact on him; indeed reading would seem, from this

evidence alone, to have played a very small part in his
life.'

I can only suggest that Mr Anderson first re-reads the
book he is supposed to have reviewed and then pays a visit
to Waugh's library in Texas. Waugh read avidly. References
to Bergson, Kant, I.A. Richards, the Pre-Raphaelites,
Aldous Huxley, and Virginia Woolf are to be found in the
early entries alone. He engaged in large amounts of reviewing, usually contemporary novels, in the thirties. He was
at one time on the board of Chapman & Hall. True, his
interests were not confined to literature. Perhaps the
most detailed accounts are of his frequent visits to gal-
leries. He is quoted as saying that if it had not been for
his faith he would have been daemonic. A similar restora-
tive power can be granted to his aesthetic interest. He
took art very seriously indeed.

Waugh envied the Pre-Raphaelites their inter-disciplin-
ary approach as painters, scribes, decorators, architects
and printers; above all, as craftsmen modestly eschewing
individual indulgence for the reputation of 'The Shop'.
But he (like the Pre-Raphaelites) was disappointed.
Attending Heatherley's Art School he realised that he would
never be more than an illustrator; the Press he wanted to
work for used modern photographic methods; the carpentry
lessons had to be abandoned so that he could write a novel
to make enough money to marry Evelyn Gardner. He was quite
literally forced to use the gift his friends knew he
possessed but which he found irksome to exercise. Writing
was hard work and he was by nature a dilettante.

Behind all, lurks the figure of Rossetti, the subject of
his first book. Erratic, mysterious, with no respect for
the establishment and without a sense of perspective, he
represented to Waugh the rogue-elephant figure in any Great
Tradition of pictorial art such as Roger Fry and the advo-
cates of 'significant form' wished to propagate. 'It is not
so much that as a man he was a bad man', Waugh wrote,
'- mere lawless wickedness is frequently the concomitant
of the highest genius - but that there was fatally lacking
in him that *essential rectitude* that underlies the serenity
of all great art' ('Rossetti', pp. 226-7). In the 'Diaries'
we see:

> Q[uennell] imputes debauchery to Hogarth on the slight-
> est evidence. His huge, efficient output alone proclaims
> him a temperate man. (p. 726)

It is this struggle for 'rectitude', against all the
natural leanings of his temperament towards the violent
expression of emotion, that is consistently documented by

the 'Diaries'.

The reviewers fail to notice that he rejects Belloc as
an amusing but redundant eccentric 'proclaiming the griev-
ances of forty years ago' and Robert Byron for his
[extreme] views. He grieves over Greene's 'A Burnt-Out Case'
as an irreligious novel but delights in him as 'very sweet
and modest. Always judging people by kindness' (p. 721).
His own major emotional problem in later life appears to
have been an inability imaginatively to project himself
into the world of those who did not share his tastes. 'My
children weary me', he writes, 'I can only see them as
defective adults; feckless, destructive, frivolous, sensual, humourless' (p. 640). But surely the reader who fails
to register the pain involved in such an admission is himself guilty of a lack of imaginative sympathy?

'Those who reprobate and ridicule their fellows - e.g.
Samuel Butler and Osbert Sitwell - were not fathers themselves' (p. 790). An extraordinary comment in such a diary?
Butler and Sitwell were both formative influences on
Waugh's early writings, in his childless, reckless days.
But perhaps the most pathetic of the later entries refer to
his relationship with his eldest son. 'Randolph made a bon-
fire and Auberon fell into it' (p. 632) and, when the boy
was arrested for drunkenness, 'We ... found him white and
dirty and eating a bun' (p. 732). Waugh suffered from an
aesthetic sensibility so acute that it bordered on para-
noia. Speaking of Lord Longford's biography he recorded:
'It might be the work of a second-year undergraduate at
BNC. I had in the preceding days taken a physical revulsion
to the MS. and couldn't bring myself to touch it' (p. 704).

In the long, tedious days after the 1939-45 war, in
which he had once again been forced to recognise that he
was generally disliked and incapable of being a 'man of
action', he resorted to an eccentric seclusion, like Wem-
mick in 'Great Expectations', in which he sought to create
his own aesthetic and religious order. 'I live in the
country', he told Freeman, 'because I like to be alone.'
He had no interest in the 'squirearchic' life of cattle
shows and magistrates' benches. The library was his haven
as it had been at Lancing. (Mr Davie rather unfortunately
cuts one passage expressing this on Sun. June 6th, 1920:
'Today the library was closed for stocktaking and I was
consequently rather homeless.') But he had been born
amongst bricks and buses and he used frequently to travel
to London, ostensibly to get his hair cut but really to
find someone to talk to. At home the days suppurated in
petty routine:

By the time I have written my letters the papers come

and when I have read them it is nearly noon so I do
little work before luncheon and then don't get out after
luncheon and then have tired eyes by 8 o'clock and don't
want to sit up reading and not sleepy so take drugs at
11. A flaw somewhere. (p. 714)

Another entry, more concise: 'Clocks barely moving. Has
half an hour past? no five minutes' (p. 722). (Why did Mr
Davie retain Waugh's spelling here?)

None of the normal comforts of family life seemed open
to him. His tastes hardened into real prejudices he could
not control and interfered with the desired 'rectitude'.
He became acutely conscious of his inability to sympathise:
'In spite of my earnest prayers I was delighted to see
Bron go' (p. 737) and 'Communion, praying again for charity
towards Bron' (p. 739). His aesthetic and ascetic senses
were at odds and his Catholicism idiosyncratic:

When I first came into the Church I was drawn, not by
the splendid ceremonies but by the spectacle of the
priest as craftsman. He had an important job to do
which none but he was qualified for. He and his appren-
tice stumped up to the altar with their tools and set
to work without a glance to those behind them, still
less with any intention of making a personal impression
on them. (pp. 792-3)

This is how he reviewed his own art, as something 'quite
external to himself to be used and judged by others'
('Pinfold', p. 2). His sympathy and humility are there, but
through a long experience of refusal and disappointment, he
kept them safely sealed in water-tight compartments until,
eventually, the eccentric don and testy colonel became himself and went mad.

What then, did the diary represent to Waugh? It is
noticeable that in the most exciting periods of his life
of exotic foreign travel, it tends more to the factual
notation of day-to-day detail. Here, during the war and in
later life, it is certainly, as Mr Davie suggests, an *aide-
mémoire*, a writer's notebook. What it is not, except in the
schooldays, is an exploration of personal motivation.

In the drabbest periods - as a schoolboy, a schoolmaster,
as a bored recluse - it is spiced with scandal and over-
stated prejudice. If an event is not unusual he makes it
so, if bizarre he makes nothing of it. It is the old comic
trick of inversion he had used in the early novels and we
might suspect that this vast collection of writings was
Waugh's private entertainment, the novel of his life, with
Captain - or is it Dr? - Waugh as the central character

voicing the heartless bombast everyone else believed to be the real thing. It is of course much more than this. It is an unonscious confessional. It contains the thoughts he dared not speak (except to Randolph Churchill) and was (usually) too intelligent to publish. It records his temptation and persecution because he could see his boorishness but still believed what he was saying to be true.

The final entries reflect not only a man attempting to live in an alien world, but one who longs to exorcise his own bilious spirit. His boredom and his inability to sympathise were as much a burden to himself as to others. Ultimately he came to see that the isolation, the spiritual and aesthetic exile he had suffered throughout, could only be embraced with prayers for humility:

> Resolved: to regard humanity with benevolence and detachment, like an elderly host whose young and indulged wife has asked a lot of people to the house whose names he does not know. (p. 747)

Notes

1   Margaret Drabble, 'Listener', 2 September 1976, 283-4.
2   Frederic Raphael, 'ST', 5 September, 1976, 27.
3   Perry Anderson, 'Guardian', 2 September 1976, 7.
4   Auberon Waugh, 'Spectator', 4 September 1976, 13-14.

'A Little Order' (Waugh's journalism), ed. Donat Gallagher

1978

193. PAUL JOHNSON, 'PUNCH'

11 January 1978, 73

Paul Johnson (b. 1928), Catholic literary journalist and commentator on foreign affairs, is the author of 'The Suez War' (1957) and 'Left of Centre' (1959); he abandoned his early socialist views to support those of right-wing politics.

A good test of a serious writer is the degree to which his control of the language survives the experience of journalism. Can he still write well when he is writing to order, against a deadline, on a subject not of his choosing, for readers he does not respect and for an editor who is both demanding and gruesomely uncivilised? Evelyn Waugh was well aware of this test and took a sombre satisfaction in his ability to survive it. It was, I should think, the only pride he took in his journalism, which was done for money. He would not have approved of this collection, except in so far as it testifies to the almost insatiable demand for his work, itself springing from a reluctant acknowledgement, most marked among his ideological enemies, that he was the great prose master of his age.

Professional writers, especially if they work in the mandarin tradition, can learn a great deal from Waugh; and this book is particularly valuable because it shows him engaged on journeyman prose in a variety of styles. And it is clear that Waugh thought deeply about writing even when engaged on such stuff. There is a sharp autobiographical touch at the end of an article on Literary Style in England and America. 'One thing I hold as certain,' Waugh

498

writes, 'is that a writer, if he is to develop, must concern himself more and more with Style.' The progress of
the writer's mind was rarely of interest to the reader. But
is was vital that the writer's own interest should be sustained, and 'Style alone can keep him from being bored with
his own work.' Is not Waugh here clearly speaking of himself? He goes on:

> In youth high spirits carry one over a book or two. The
> world is full of discoveries that demand expression.
> Later a writer must face the choice of becoming an
> artist or a prophet. He can shut himself up at his desk
> and selfishly seek pleasure in the perfecting of his own
> skill or he can pace about, dictating dooms and exhorta-
> tions on the topics of the day. The recluse at the desk
> has a bare chance of giving abiding pleasure to others;
> the publicist has none at all.

This analysis reflects Waugh's own progress. In the
Thirties he became a writer primarily to make a living.
'Brideshead Revisited' (1945) sold over 600,000 and offered
Waugh the opportunity to emerge as a public figure in the
Catholic cause - or, as he put it, a prophet. The offer was
toyed with, then rejected, and for the remainder of his
life he 'shut himself up at his desk', concentrating on his
wonderfully pure yet elaborate English, and the nuggets of
anarchic humour and nostalgic sadness it enshrined.
  Waugh's craftsman-like devotion to his art, so characteristic of his last years, was often carefully concealed
behind an elaborate facade of gentrification, which
deceived many. Among the dupes was J.B. Priestley, who
criticised Waugh for his social posture, and was mockingly
rebuffed in one of the most striking pieces in this book
(Anything Wrong with Priestley?).(1) Waugh also used the
gentry pose (No Admittance on Business) to keep at bay bra-
zen intruders such as the late Nancy Spain, even or rather
especially when accompanied by peers of vulnerable lineage.(2) Waugh's contest with Lord Noel-Buxton ('I'm not on
business. I'm a Member of the House of Lords') which culminated in a brilliant article in the 'Spectator' (Awake
My Soul! It is a Lord) probably gave him more pleasure
than any other professional episode towards the end of his
life, not excluding his majestic confrontations with the
BBC over TV interviews. The article, I should add, was rejected by 'Punch', to its everlasting shame!
  What emerges strongly from this collection is Waugh's
adamantine concern with quality and with honesty of
artistic intention. He felt that English writers were
specially privileged: 'English is incomparably the richest

of languages, dead or living. One can devote one's life to learning it and die without achieving mastery. No two words are identical in meaning, sound and connotation.' Those made free of this privilege had, therefore, to be severely castigated if they abused it. There is a cruel review of Stephen Spender's autobiography: 'to see him fumbling with our rich and delicate language is to experience all the horror of seeing a Sèvres vase in the hands of a chimpanzee.'(3) Cyril Connolly also came under Waugh's lash, though here the blows were administered with more mixed feelings. Waugh admired Connolly's wit and sense of style, but deplored his grammatical lapses, political views and lack of logic: his demolition of 'Horizon's' social blue-print (Palinurus in Never-Never Land) (4) is merciless. As always with Waugh, a neat sense of order, of hierarchical distinctions, is conveyed: Spender was a literary nonentity but Connolly a lost soul. Or again, in dealing with literary dons, not a tribe for which Waugh had much sympathy: 'Sir Maurice Bowra is learned and lucid, but dull; Lord David Cecil has grace but no grammar; Mr Isiah Berlin is diffuse and voluble; Mr Trevor-Roper vulgar.'

Though seen, and seeing himself, in a curmudgeonly mask, Waugh in fact fell into error more often by praising than excoriating. The fulsome praise of Ronald Knox now strikes us as embarrassing ('His "Enthusiasm" should be recognised as the greatest work of literary art of the century'), though it is fair to say that Waugh came nearest a just estimate in his elegant biography of Knox. Occasionally, out of sheer *pietas*, he was kinder than was just or right: thus his absurd over-estimation of Alfred Duggan, an old crony and in part the model for Sebastian Flyte.(5) But friendship alone might not ensure Waugh's approval: the writing of the much-loved Nancy Mitford is dismissed as 'babbling down the telephone, often very prettily'. Once or twice, a Waugh judgment is inexplicable. Odd to find him, of all people, praising the grievously mannered Hemingway as 'lucid and individual and euphonious. He has imposed limits on his powers which only a master can survive. He has won mastery....' As a rule, however, Waugh's idols are straightforward and predictable: Wodehouse, Beerbohm, Firbank, Compton-Burnett, Henry Green, Anthony Powell and (with theological reservations) Graham Greene.

There is of course much more in this book besides literary criticism. But there are not enough travel-pieces. Waugh, like D.H. Lawrence, was a great travel-writer, carrying around with him his own elaborate penumbra, within which the passing scenery and natives were arranged with elaborate artistry, but not above the occasional penetrating shaft of pure, visual observation. Some of the best passages of his novels - a paragraph, often only a sentence or two - hauntingly evoke places. One would be glad to have, in book form, the raw material from which they were distilled.

Notes

1 See No. 157.
2 See No. 197.
3 Two Unquiet Lives, 'Tablet', 5 May 1951, 356-7.
4 Palinurus in Never-Never Land or The 'Horizon' Blueprint for Chaos, 'Tablet', 27 July 1946, 46. This was a response to Editor's Comment, 'Horizon', June 1946, 365-6.
5 It is much more likely that Alastair Graham was the 'model' for Sebastian although elements of Duggan's character have clearly been incorporated.

'The Letters of Evelyn Waugh',

ed. Mark Amory

1980

194. PHILIP LARKIN, 'GUARDIAN'

4 September 1980, 14

Philip Larkin (b. 1922) is a poet, novelist and critic. He
is the author of 'The North Ship' (1945), 'Jill' (1946),
'A Girl in Winter' (1947), 'The Whitsun Weddings' (1964)
and 'High Windows' (1974), and the editor of the 'Oxford
Book of Twentieth Century Verse' (1973).

It is impossible to imagine getting a letter from Evelyn
Waugh, unless it were of the 'Mr Waugh deeply regrets that
he is unable to do what is so kindly proposed' sort. In
the first place, one would have to have a nursery nickname
and be a member of White's, a Roman Catholic, a high-born
lady or an Old Etonian novelist; but even if that difficulty were overcome one would need to know about two hundred similar persons who were continually chucking or being
chucked by their life partners, going bankrupt or mad, and
becoming incapacitated for days by heavy eating or drinking, and have a consuming interest in their goings-on. For
Waugh was an avid gossip; 'please tell me any *English* gossip you hear,' he implores Nancy Mitford in Paris; and to
Cyril Connolly in London, 'do dictate a page of social
gossip. I have no idea what my friends or enemies are
doing.' Connolly's high-minded refusal ('I don't find
other people's misfortunes uproariously funny') was prudent:

> After the first course Boots ['Smarty-Boots,' i.e.
> Connolly] had a seizure, fell off his chair frothing
> and gasping, was carried straight to a waiting van and

whisked off to Tring where he spent the first fortnight of married life in a padded cell.

The degree to which these letters are readable depends on how far Waugh can convert the gossip into his own kind of black comedy. His patient and thorough editor cautions us against assuming anything Waugh writes to be 'true'; when he says of a dinner acquaintance 'Her new daughter is a negress,' the footnote stolidly comments 'Not a negress'. 'Quennell had a seizure brought on by sexual excess,' Waugh writes; the footnote says 'Hangover.' Comparable conventions abound, particularly to [sic] his letters to Nancy Mitford, such as his horribleness to his second wife ('The only servant in the house is my pre-war valet. Laura makes his bed and cooks his meals'). But what of his assurance to her, written from the Hyde Park Hotel, that he is 'looking eagerly' in 'The Times' each day for news of the arrival of their next child, before going on to say 'The Court Ball was wholly delightful'?

A writer's letters stand midway between literature and biography. Since Waugh's biographer Christopher Sykes has already used much of this material, it is not likely to tell us much about Waugh we did not know already, but they remind us what a self-contradictory man he was. His constant travelling before the War (between his marriages he never had a home of his own) seems unaccompanied by any interest in or liking for the countries he visited, but even after 1945, when he was settled in Gloucestershire, he continued to regard such trips as part of a writer's life.

He was a brave man who joined the Army with alacrity in 1939, only to be told in 1943 that he was 'so unpopular as to be unemployable'. He was a major writer, but his mentions of literature are sparse and terse: 'the worst book in the world' ('Dombey and Son'); 'nothing any character thinks or says or does has any relation to human nature as I know it ('La Chartreuse de Parme'); 'Well the chap was plain barmy' (Proust). At the same time, his own artistic commitment remained absolute: 'while I have any vestige of imagination left, I must write novels.'

None of this caused him any heart-searching: his nature was impenetrably indivisble. There are no letters about his conversion to Roman Catholicism (and nothing in the 'Diaries' either) yet it was fundamental to his life. The most remarkable letters in the book are those urging John Betjeman (whose wife was turning to the Catholic Church) to undergo instruction likewise. Waugh writes urgently in black-and-white terms ('(1) We may both be wrong (2) We can't both be right,' etc) that typifies the unsentimental nature of his devotion remembered by Father D'Arcy.

Betjeman, though distressed, stood firm ('it is not so much a matter of which church, as of loving God'), and Waugh later apologised for being 'a bully and a scold.' Later, however, he was writing to Edith Sitwell 'Is it exorbitant to hope that your example and prayers may bring Osbert to the Faith?'

His piety, that divided the world into 'Papists & heathens,' did little for his charity. There is a shocking sentence to the Marchioness of Bath saying that 'Mr Masaryk defenestrating himself would make a good subject for a picture,' and there is a constant barrage of remarks such as 'Alfred Duggan kicked the bucket,' 'Two [dance] bands, one of niggers and one of buggers,' and 'There are 2 jews in this club.' They may be part of Waugh's epistolary irony, and understood as such by his correspodents, but they support Claire Luce's quick judgment that he had 'no heart.' Yet against them can be set his letters to his wife and family, nearly always affectionate, sometimes charming, as if a totally different person had held the pen.

'Beware of writing to me,' his last letter begins. 'I always answer.' Even so, the collection hardly sustains its editor's claim that Waugh was the last of the great letter-writers. The world his gossip evokes has none of the appeal of Horace Walpole's, for instance: it is curt, cheap, brutal. Its humour lacks the rich lunacy of the novels; its observations, despite their impeccable language, have no charity. Towards the end, when his infirmities ('carrying too much weight ... no teeth' seemed an outward expression of inner accidie, some sentences take on a greater resonance: 'He takes away all zest in human affairs to give us the chance of seeing our immortal destiny.' None has quite the poignancy of Pinfold's 'Why does everyone expect me to find it so easy to be nice?'

195.   GEOFFREY WHEATCROFT, 'SPECTATOR'

11 October 1980, 18-19

Fourteen years after his death Evelyn Waugh retains the power to captivate and to enrage. He was more than just the first English novelist of his age - the verdict by happy coincidence of two contemporaries presently appearing in our pages, Mr Graham Greene and Mr A.J.P. Taylor. Mr Greene complains in his new book 'Ways of Escape' that 'Evelyn's

diaries have been joyfully exploited by the media, a word
that has come to mean bad journalism. Journalists have
always been intent on transforming a fine writer into a
"character".'

The point is well made. And yet Waugh *was* a larger-
than-life personality, and the reviewers of these letters
whether or not they pay tribute to the writer unfailingly
react to the man. Some have reacted warmly. Mr Anthony
Quinton in the 'Listener' writes of the 'force of his intelligence ... a style [which] is a clear indication of
mental power on its own.' Mr Philip Toynbee in the 'Observer' praises Waugh as 'a loving husband, a wise and affectionate father', adding that he does not himself come well
out of Waugh's Letters (though he does not quote the passage: 'P. Toynbee spoke for 20 minutes - absolute balls. I
had never seen him sober before and greatly preferred him
being sick in Ann Rothermere's lap.')

Others have risen straight to the fly, resentful and
vengeful: Mr Jonathan Raban in the 'Sunday Times,' Mr
Philip Larkin, alas, in the 'Guardian' - 'curt, cheap and
brutal' - and Mr Rayner Heppenstall in the 'New Statesman': Waugh was 'a fat popinjay', his 'wit being mirth-
less'; that he 'was one of the great letter-writers will
not, I fancy, be said....' (Mr Heppenstall did not hit it
off with Waugh, who 'repeated the story' of their meeting,
'with trimmings, to Christopher Sykes, in whose biography
of Waugh I am maligned under a false name....' He is in
fact described there as 'a disappointed novelist, a deeply
class-conscious man whose self-esteem bordered on mania
and who regarded Evelyn's work as decidedly inferior to
his own.')

The public's and the media's fascination has been
fuelled by an expanding Waugh industry, not always a model
of managerial efficiency. We have had the 'Diaries', rather
poorly edited; Mr Sykes's unsatisfactory biography which
quite apart from its odd prose manages to be coyly reticent
and intrusive at the same time; a particularly inadequate
selection from Waugh's journalism; and many another memoir
and picture book. Apart from the varying editorial standards it would surely have made more sense to publish
'Diaries,' 'Letters' and a much larger selection of occasional writings before the biography.

Mr Amory thinks that the 'Letters' show Waugh 'to his
best advantage so far.' It is not hard to see why this
should be. They are not a compendium of intermittent self-
loathing like the Diaries; and the letter-writer does not
describe his most odious behaviour, as his biography did
('to the naturally weak he was as merciless as he had
been in his bullying school days. I witnessed the spectacle

many times and it always utterly disgusted me.')...

The most impressive letters are those to other writers;
the most remarkable those about religion; the happiest
those to (or about) his children. With fellow writers -
Mr Graham Greene or Mr Anthony Powell, Henry Green or
Orwell - discussing their, his own or others' works he is
at his very best. The letter of 17 July 1949 to Orwell is
a model of intelligence and honesty, even if he missed the
essential point, that '1984' is - surely - a specific
attack on, inter alia, Christianity.

Others are not treated with such conspicuous deference.
He enjoyed a 'long but precarious friendship' with Cyril
Connolly which Mr Sykes caught well. Waugh felt a justified
contempt for most of Connolly's literary pretensions; but
after 'a recent article by Cyril was mentioned', 'Evelyn as
usualy demolished it, adding with a reflective sigh,
"Heavens, how I love that man!"'

The letters here are exquisitely needling. 'Dear Cyril,
I thought your review of "Men at Arms"(1) excellent. It is a
pity you called "Apthorpe" "Atwater" throughout and credited him with two aunts (whereas it was one of my humdrum
comic effects that he had only one) because it will make
your readers think you did not give full attention to the
book. You plainly did.' 'Dear Cyril, I am sorry to learn
that the wording on my gift gave you pain - "Keep the home
fires burning" to me plainly meant what you clearly expressed in a "Horizon" Comment ... saying very justly that
the civilians had had the worst of the war and further
thanking you for making a delightful salon for men on
leave....' By contrast to this unkind teasing when Waugh
descried real ability - a Wilson or a Spark - he was un-
stinting with praise and encouragement.

If his religion is the key to his character it is also
the side least understood, even by other Catholics. He was
not merely a fundamentalist. He was, as Belloc once said,
possessed; a man for whom the Four Last Things (especially
Hell) vividly existed. The extraordinary letters to Sir
John Betjeman and Lady Avon (as they then weren't) are not
to be compared with the busy-bodying in friends' lives in
which everyone sometimes indulges. He believed that two
dear friends were in imminent danger of damnation, of condemning themselves to eternal torment. The belief may have
been right or wrong or simply deranged; believe it he did.

The first letter to Betjeman is remarkable also for the
intensity and force of its ecclesiastical argument, quite
demolishing the Anglo-Catholic position which 'is entirely
without reason. You cannot be right. Marxist-Atheists may
be. Zealous protestants may be.... What is inconceivable is
that Christ was made flesh in order to found a Church, that

he canalised his Grace in the sacraments ... that he saw
the Church as a human corporation, part of his Mystical
Body, one with the Saints triumphant - and then to point to
a handful of homosexual curates and say: "That is the true
Church."'

We see how Waugh's religion set him apart from the beau
monde in which he otherwise delighted. There is a harrowing
account of the death in 1949 of Peter Beatty, who lost his
sight, sank into impenetrable depression, and killed himself. Almost the worst of it, Waugh told Nancy Mitford, was
that 'In White's he is talked of as a kind of Captain
Oates: "Good old Peter ... he took the best way out". In
fact, of course, he was stark mad. The world is full of
radiantly happy blind men.'

There are fewer letters about politics. Mr Pinfold maintained 'an idiosyncratic toryism which was quite unrepre-
sented in the political parties and was regarded by his
neighbours as being almost as sinister as socialism'.
Waugh's politics are still thought of as tomfoolery. But
see the scene in White's after the 1948 Budget: 'all the
men who to my certain knowledge have not £100 in the world
yelling themselves hoarse ... that they are being ruined
and the dozen or so really rich men smoking quietly in corners have made themselves registered companies in Costa
Rica years ago'; after the 1951 General Election: 'Now
that there is a tiny Conservative Majority the persecution
of the rich by the politicians will be greatly intensified
so that they can display class impartiality'.

Better still is the analysis of Suez: 'it cannot be justified on moral or legal grounds ... any troup of Boy
Scouts can defeat the Egyptian army ... no-one can govern
Egypt now that Nasser has armed the school children ...
[if Eden] really wants to increase the traffic in this
country by importing more petrol through the canal, he
must depopulate Egypt. This can very simply be done by
destroying the Nile barrages ... a more human solution is
to stop motor traffic - particularly buses and charabancs
in England.' And although Waugh's attitude to Yugoslavia
was highly prejudiced, this, written at the time of Tito's
visit in 1953 - 'What is wrong is not Russia but Communism.... Great Empires never seek war; all their energies
are taken up in administration.... The one certain way to
start Third War is to establish half a dozen independent
atheist police states, full of fatuous nationalism & power
hunger' - looks remarkably prescient nearly three decades
later.

Waugh once wrote that he saw his children once a day
'for ten, I hope awe-inspiring, minutes'. Perhaps the phrase
suggests what Mr Larkin means by a want of charity. Yet the

letters to his children are delightful and if he describes
them to others with ironic resignation there is also a
gleaming humorous affection. Meg is 'very pretty, very
stupid, with abounding charm'; 'My dud daughter Hatty
divides her time rather oddly - by day she works in the
College of Arms, by night she is lavatory attendant at an
expensive homosexual restaurant ... in happier days she
would have been sent to Malta to marry a sailor'; 'My
youngest son [Septimus] is a jewel but I suspect he will
grow up homosexual' (the editor might have added here one
of his notes: 'He didn't').

Bron is reported in 1946 (aged six) as having 'told his
headmaster that I had separated from Laura and "lived
purely in Africa"'....

Mr Amory has put in a vast effort of work ... [but in-
evitably] ... there are mistakes. 'Randolph Churchill
failed to get elected at Preston [in 1945] and did not try
again' is wrong if it means that he did not stand again for
Parliament. The election address to which Waugh refers in a
letter to Margaret on 2 October 1959 is not for the election of the Chancellor of Oxford University but the general
election: the address appeared as Aspirations of a Mugwump
in the 'Spectator.' The Laski who had reviewed Nancy Mitford's 'The Water Beetle' unfavourably in the 'New Statesman' in 1962 was probably Miss Marghanita, rather than
Professor Harold who died in 1950.

The letter about Mr Muggeridge and Mr Macmillan was
obviously published in the 'New Statesman', where Mr Muggeridge's revelations had been made, rather than, as un-
accountably here headed, in the 'Spectator'. Around p. 587
the letters appear to be out of order. And although Mr
Amory explains the most abstruse points of nicknames and
private language, he puts '[?]' after 'spinal' in the letters to Lady Acton. He might have known from Waugh's life
of Ronald Knox that 'spinal' was a word by which Knox
meant 'something which gave him "the creeps"'. 'But', as
Evelyn Waugh once said in a review, 'it is a dreary critic
who treats a book as a school exercise to be corrected
instead of as an object to be possessed and enjoyed'.

Not everyone has enjoyed these 'Letters' as much as I
have, and not everyone will. There is evidence here of what
made and still makes people loathe Waugh. Even for those
who don't there is evidence here of his saturnine melancholy and misanthropy. But those who find no charity have
chosen not to look for it. Catherine Walston writes to ask
(presumably, her letter is not quoted) whether Waugh minds
her and Mr Greene staying in his house as an adulterous
couple. The reply is a letter of great sweetness. 'I met
you first as a friend of Graham but I hope I can now look

on you as a friend in my own right.... Please believe that
I am far too depressed by my own odious, if unromantic,
sins to have any concern for other people's.' The last
sentence should be an aide memoire for some one can think
of. And it can stand as token of the charity of this brilliant, complicated, tormented man.

Note

1   See No. 132.

Miscellaneous

196. WYNDHAM LEWIS, FROM 'THE DOOM OF YOUTH'

1932, 106-8

Percy Wyndham Lewis (1884-1957), novelist, artist, critic
and popular philosopher, was the leader of the Vorticist
movement and co-editor (with Ezra Pound) of its magazine
'Blast' (1914-15). He was the author of 'Tarr' (1918),
'Time and Western Man' (1928), 'The Apes of God' (1930),
'Filibusters in Barbary' (1932) and two volumes of autobiography, 'Blasting and Bombadiering' (1937) and 'Rude
Assignment' (1950). Waugh reviewed 'Filibusters' (Spectator', 6 August 1932) and admired Lewis's 'unique ability
to grope down into common speech and bring up, muddy-
handed, fine nuggets of diction'.

The function of the revolutionary agent is to stir up
trouble and set some population by the ears, by the time-
honoured means of arousing the envy and hatred of everybody for everybody else. But such work as Mr. Winn's (1)
is directed to similar ends - within the family circle,
instead of outside, in the streets. The facetious and gos-
sipy technique of *Youngergenerationconsciousness* is merely
a mask for something not at all 'young' or especially
attractive (not more than other political gadgets): it is
the form in which, in Anglo-saxony, a revolutionary purpose is bound to clothe itself. You may say that that gives
Mr. Winn too sinister an air altogether, and that in fact
he is merely a money-maker, who has been up-and-coming
enough to perceive that by saying with an arch lisp, over
and over again, 'I am just of Age!' he can put money in
his pocket. But it is not so much a question of what

Mr. Winn feels about it, or how much Mr. Winn is able to
gauge the true sources of his prosperity: it is the why
and wherefore of this particular portent, and the nature of
the political interests whose ends are served by the
spectacle of Mr. Winn, that we are attempting to lay bare.

Now Mr. Waugh is not a Mr. Winn. Only as a journalist
(in a quite separate capacity from that of the author of
'Decline and Fall') he does a bit of agitation of the same
order as Mr. Winn - to turn an honest penny doubtless, too.
Yet Mr. Waugh makes too good a 'class'-warrior, and plays
his 'Youth' trumps with too much unction and delighted
bluff, not to be a bit of a born revolutionary agent, and
not to be perhaps a little *too* like Mr. Winn, as well.

I need only quote from his Matter-of-fact Mothers of the
New Age ('Evening Standard', April 8, 1929) to show you how
this must be, and what a confirmed 'class'-warrior he is -
and how his particular sort of Western Marxism causes him
to community-sing in chorus with Mr. Winn.

The Attitude of Mind of the Younger Generation was the
subject of a former article of Mr. Waugh's - in response to
which it seems whole Brigades of red-faced Old Colonels
wrote threatening letters - with minatory gestures of great
horsewhips in the direction of his naughty *Youngergenera-
tionconscious* b.t.m. And then, he says, as regards this
'younger generation,' whose views he voices, 'Loyalty to
one's own age is the only really significant loyalty remaining to us.'

So the 'Mysticism of Youth' provides a kind of *temporal*
substitute for the old *geographical* one of 'England, Home,
and Beauty.' 'Youth,' in Mr. Waugh's view, is in fact a
sort of *temporal Fatherland*. All merely racial aggregates
have become shadowy and meaningless. There is no *esprit de
corps* left in our civilization, because there is no *corps*
left - a corpse if you like, but no living body. The only
reality is a chronological reality. Time is Waugh's god.
The 'philosophy of Time,' as I have called it elsewhere, is
here revealed in full dogmatic operation.

An Elizabethan (upon this partisan chronologic ground)
would shoot at sight (or run through with his sword), as a
mortal enemy, a Victorian. They would be *Time-foes*, as it
were. The fact that they were both Englishmen would mean
nothing at all beside this all-important *temporal* fact.
This is, of course, the chronological dogma *in excelsis*.

Similarly a Father and his child, or a Mother and her
child, of necessity they are enemies - Time-foes: the child
only owes allegiance, and 'loyalty,' to other Children.
The fact that his Parent and himself inherit the same traditions, belong to the same race, are the closest blood-
relations, is immaterial to a properly *generation-conscious*

Child. Time is the great fact for the Time-philosopher.

I have exposed this 'chronological' dogma enough in other essays, and need not again, in these pages, state its pros and cons. I will content myself with referring the reader to 'Time and Western Man' (pp. 218 etc. and pp. 434 etc.). And with that I must leave Messrs. Winn and Waugh - those militant 'Youths' engaged in a crusade not dissimilar to that of the Suffragette. Indeed their movement is so like the Suffragist Movement, that some months ago 'a young man in full evening dress' introduced himself at speech-time into the Guildhall while a banquet was in progress (the Prince of Wales was, I believe, the guest of honour), and having, unremarked, tied himself to a chair, he began vociferating 'Will you hear me! I am only Twenty-One! Will you listen to me or won't you! I am only Twenty-One!' until he was untied and removed from the banqueting hall and taken away to the Infirmary. Apparently all he was heard to shout was that - just that he was 'Only Twenty-One.' A weak-minded victim, it must be supposed, of the propaganda of the Winns and Waughs!

Note

1   Godfrey Winn (1906-71), popular, 'smart' writer and broadcaster linked by Wyndham Lewis with Waugh as a promoter of the cause of 'youth'; he was the author of 'Dreams Fade' (1928) and 'The Infirm Glory' (autobiography, 1967).

197.   UNSIGNED REPORT, 'DAILY TELEGRAPH'

20 February 1957, 9

One of Waugh's less serious ventures for raising tax-free money was to scan the papers for possible libel and vigorously to pursue any likely quarry in the courts. The suit against Nancy Spain is now famous; this is an account of the first day's proceedings. The next day Waugh was awarded £2,000 damages and Miss Spain's counter-claim was dismissed. On 5 April 1957 'The Times' reported another successful suit which claimed a further £3,000 from 'Beaverbrook Newspapers and Another' for a defamatory article comparing Waugh unfavourably with Rebecca West.

Mr. Evelyn Waugh, the author, said by his counsel to have
the 'rather old-fashioned idea that an Englishman's home
is his castle,' claimed damages in the High Court yesterday
from Beaverbrook Newspapers and Miss Nancy Spain, book
critic and authoress.

Mr. Gerald Gardiner, Q.C., for Mr. Waugh, suggested that
the words complained of were written when Miss Spain was
smarting under the fact that Mr. Waugh had declined to see
her when she called at his home in Gloucestershire. She
later described this visit as 'an attempt to gate-crash my
favourite idol.'

Mr. Waugh alleged that he was libelled in an article by
Miss Spain in the 'Daily Express' on March 17, 1956. Miss
Spain and Beaverbrook Newspapers denied that the words were
defamatory.

Miss Spain counter-claimed for damages for libel in an
article written by Mr. Waugh in the 'Spectator' on Feb. 24,
1956, headed Dr. Wodehouse and Mr. Wain. In his reply Mr.
Waugh denied that the words referred to Miss Spain or that
they were defamatory of her in their natural and ordinary
meaning.

Opening the case before Mr. Justice Stable and a jury,
Mr. Gardiner said Mr. Waugh had a high reputation as an
author. He had published some 23-24 books which had been
translated into many languages.

He lived in Gloucestershire with his wife and children.
He wrote at home but did not bring his professional life
into his home. If he wanted to do business he went to London. On the gate of his home was a notice: 'No admittance
on business.'

In June, 1955, the 'Daily Express' announced a new
series of articles and it became apparent that the articles
would attack well-known people. Among the names mentioned
were Mr. Waugh and Sir Malcolm Sargent. The first article
was a particularly vicious attack on Sir Laurence Olivier
and his wife.

Some days later Miss Spain, who was the 'Daily Express'
book critic, telephoned Mr. Waugh's home and asked if she
could interview him. Mrs. Waugh, who answered the telephone, said it would be no use coming because her husband
would not see reporters at home.

That evening she saw Miss Spain and a man, who was
introduced to her as Lord Noel-Buxton, on the front door
step. Miss Spain asked if she could persuade her husband
to see her. Mrs. Waugh said it would not be any good, but
asked her husband, who said they should go away.

They would not go away, said Mr. Gardiner. The man was
rather truculent, so Mr. Waugh went out and shut the door.
That evening he wrote to the editor of the 'Daily Express'

complaining and saying he hoped the 'delinquents' would
be punished. Later he learned that Lord Noel-Buxton was
not employed by the paper.

Shortly afterwards the 'Daily Express' published an
article by Miss Spain entitled My Pilgrimage to See Mr.
Waugh. This was not the subject of the action. Its purpose
was to contrast the courtesy and hospitality of Mr. John
Masefield, the Poet Laureate, with that of Mr. Waugh.

Meanwhile, Mr. Waugh's brother, Alec, had written a
book called 'Island in the Sun' which it was clear was
going to be an enormous success in America. Miss Spain
interviewed Mr. Alec Waugh and foretold that the book would
be a success in Britain.

On March 17, 1956, the article complained of appeared
headed: Does a Good Word from Me Sell a Book? It read:

> There is a war between Evelyn Waugh and me. He said
> some weeks ago in a literary weekly that the 'Express'
> has no influence on the book trade.
>
> The 'Express' he complains, sold only 300 of his
> novels. He once had a book chosen by the Book Society
> that sold well. But the total first edition sales of all
> his other titles are dwarfed by brother Alec.
>
> 'Island in the Sun' (Cassells, 16s) foretold by me
> as this year's run-away best-seller, has now topped
> 50,000 copies as a direct result of my 'Daily Express'
> notice. So the publishers told me yesterday. Now read
> what I say about this week's books....

Mr. Gardiner said the general effect of the article was
that Mr. Evelyn Waugh was a failure and it suggested that
he was embittered by his brother's success. The brothers
were good friends and no one was more delighted by the
success of 'Island in the Sun' than Mr. Evelyn Waugh.

The sales of Mr. Evelyn Waugh's books amounted to
4,228,125, quite apart from translations. First edition
sales amounted to 180,000.

'It is an article which in my submission is plainly
malicious in every sentence. It must have been written in
a flaming temper when she was still annoyed at not being
asked to dinner when she called.'

Referring to Miss Spain's counter-claim, Mr. Gardiner
said the article of which she complained read:

> An investigation has lately been made in the book trade
> to determine which literary critics have most influence
> on sales. I remember the time when the 'Evening Stan-
> dard' was undisputed leader.
>
> A good review there by Arnold Bennett was believed

to sell an edition in 24 hours. The claim was exaggerated as I learned to my disappointment when he kindly
noticed my first novel.

The ensuing demand was, I think, something between
200 and 300, but I wonder whether any critic to-day has
so large and immediate an influence.

At the same period his colleague on the 'Daily
Express' was D.H. Lawrence, then at the height of his
powers. Things have changed. The Beaverbrook Press is no
longer listed as having any influence at all.

Mr. Evelyn Waugh, who gave his address as Piers Court,
Stinchcombe, Glos, said in evidence that after he told his
wife to tell Miss Spain and Lord Noel-Buxton to go away he
heard 'confused sounds of a male voice wrangling.'

'I became extremely angry, went out and said, "Clear off
both of you," or words to that effect, and slammed the door
on them.' He went outside and secured an iron gate so that
they would not come back.

Cross-examining for both defendants, Sir Hartley Shaw-
cross, Q.C., quoted from reviews of Miss Spain's autobiography which, he said, described her as a friendly, warm-
hearted person. One review quoted was by Mr. Gilbert Harding in the 'Evening Standard.'

Mr. Waugh did not reply when Sir Hartley asked: 'Perhaps you do not approve of him?'

Sir Hartley: No, I though you would not. (Laughter.)
I must not express my view of these matters. Do you think
that it's just possible that like so many of us you sometimes take yourself just a shade too seriously? - No.

Mr. Waugh thought a remark by Lord Noel-Buxton saying
'I am not on business, I am a member of the House of
Lords,' seemed to show him as 'an extremely ridiculous
person.' He was not so much annoyed with Miss Spain as with
Lord Noel-Buxton.

Questioned about the 'Spectator' article, Mr. Waugh
agreed he knew Miss Spain was the leading literary critic
of Beaverbrook Newspapers. The purpose of the article was
to defend Mr. P.G. Wodehouse who he thought had been unfairly attacked.

Mr. Alec Waugh said he had come from Tangier to give
evidence for his brother. He had written 40 books.

'I have supported myself by my pen - except when I was
in the Army - and I made more in a month with my last book,
"Island in the Sun," than with the other books in 40
years,' he added.

Nothing could have prevented 'Island in the Sun' being
an enormous success in England except a war.

Mr. Gardiner: Spelt 'W.A.R.'? Mr. Waugh: Yes, 'W.A.R..'

Asked whether he was familiar, as a test of literary quality, with the quantity of first-edition sales, he said he thought it a misleading term.

He remembered at one time authors were anxious to be able to advertise the seventh or eighth impressions. He used to have small impressions printed so that his publisher could announce 'seventh impression' before publication. That was when his father was a publisher.

Opening the case for Miss Spain and Beaverbrook Newspapers, Mr. H.P. Milmo said a reasonable person would not think one tittle the worse of Mr. Waugh because of what Miss Spain had written. She had brought the counter-claim only because she was being attacked in the action.

Mr. Waugh's article in the 'Spectator' could mean only that the 'Daily Express' critic had no influence at all. That was plainly defamatory.

Miss Spain, in evidence, said she read all Mr. Waugh's works. She thought the first books 'simply brilliant' and enjoyed them all enormously.

Mr. Waugh was probably one of the greatest living English writers. In her opinion he was probably the only one who would be thought of in 40 or 50 years' time.

Mr. Milmo: Do you regard yourself as having any influence at all? - I believe I have influence. I am sure I hope so.

Miss Spain said she thought Mr. Waugh was referring to her in his article in the 'Spectator.' What she wrote in the 'Daily Express' was a reply.

Mr. Milmo: Were you actuated in any way by dislike of Mr. Waugh in writing this? - Goodness, no. What I know of Mr. Waugh I like enormously.

Mr. Gardiner: Is it your view that a 'Daily Express' reporter can go on anyone else's property whether he has a right to or not? - A reporter's function is to do his best to get a story.

Miss Spain said she admired Mr. Waugh for expelling her from his house. 'I never smarted as a result of being expelled.'

She agreed that there were 'discrepancies' in the article Mr. Waugh complained about. She now knew he had had four books chosen by the Book Society and she was delighted about it. She agreed that she had not taken any steps before the article was published to ascertain whether it was true or not.

Mr. Gardiner: Have you ever discussed Mr. Evelyn Waugh with Lord Beaverbrook?

Miss Spain: No.

Did not Lord Beaverbrook tell you that Mr. Evelyn Waugh was very jealous of his brother? - No, certainly not.

In your book you say you love Lord Beaverbrook. - Yes.
He doesn't like Mr. Evelyn Waugh, does he? - I have no
idea....
Mr. Leonard Frederick Russell, literary editor of the
'Sunday Times,' said that when he read Mr. Waugh's article
in the 'Spectator' he thought it referred to 'my friend'
Nancy Spain.
The hearing was adjourned until to-day.

198. UNSIGNED ARTICLE, 'DAILY TELEGRAPH'

27 June 1960, 14

Evelyn Waugh was seen on television last night in the
B.B.C.'s 'Face to Face'. He admitted publicly for the first
time that in his novel, 'The Ordeal of [Gilbert] Pinfold',
the ordeal was largely his own. (1)
Mr John Freeman reminded him of the sinister voices.
'The most odious said that Pinfold was a homosexual, a
Communist Jew, a parvenu. Were these the kind of hallucinations that you yourself felt?'
Mr Waugh replied: 'Oh yes. Those were the voices
exactly.' He said he had been rationalising the experience
all the time. It was not like losing one's reason; it was
the reason working hard on wrong premises.
The novelist was asked why he had changed from mixing
in society and writing books about it to a life of absolute
solitude in the country. 'Were you conscious of a sudden
decision to do that?' Mr Freeman asked.
'It happened about eight years ago,' said Mr Waugh, who
is fifty-nine. (2) 'I gradually got bored with society,
largely I think through deafness ... if there's a crowd I
get dazed. I don't hear because I'm bored: it's not that
I'm bored because I can't hear.'
Mr Freeman asked him if his country life was not a kind
of charade. Mr Waugh answered: 'It's quite true that I
haven't the smallest interest in the country in the agri-
cultural or local government sense. The country to me is a
place where I can be silent.' He denied that he ever
brooded on what might appear to be unjust criticism of his
work. The best he could hope for was for the critics to
take no notice of him.
Mr Freeman: Then why are you appearing in this pro-
gramme?
Mr Waugh: Poverty. We have both been hired to talk in

this deliriously happy way.

Mr Freeman later asked Mr Waugh, a Roman Catholic convert, about his behaviour to those he came into contact
with. 'How high in your scale of values do you put the
Christian duty of service to others?' Mr Waugh replied:
'It isn't for me to make these scales. My service is simply
to bring up one family.'

Notes

1   Inaccurate; cf. the opening paragraph of Waugh's reply
    to Priestley's attack (cited in headnote to No. 157)
    which appeared on 13 September 1957. Waugh had also
    admitted that 'the central character is to a large
    extent a portrait of myself' in a speech at a Foyle's
    lunch on 19 July, 1957 (DT, 20 July 1957).
2   Inaccurate; he was fifty-six.

Select Bibliography

ACTON, HAROLD, 'Memoirs of an Aesthete' (Methuen, 1948).
ACTON, HAROLD, 'More Memoirs of an Aesthete' (Methuen, 1970).
AMORY, MARK (ed.), 'The Letters of Evelyn Waugh' (Weidenfeld & Nicolson, 1980).
BRADBURY, MALCOLM, 'Evelyn Waugh' (Oliver & Boyd, 1964), Writers and Critics series.
CARENS, JAMES F., 'The Satiric Art of Evelyn Waugh' (Seattle and London, University of Washington Press, 1966).
CAREW, DUDLEY, 'A Fragment of Friendship. Evelyn Waugh as a Young Man' (Everest Books, 1974).
COOK, WILLIAM J., Jr, 'Masks, Modes and Morals: The Art of Evelyn Waugh' (Cranbury, NJ; Fairleigh Dickinson University Press, 1971).
DAVIE, MICHAEL (ed.), 'The Diaries of Evelyn Waugh' (Weidenfeld & Nicolson, 1976).
DAVIS, ROBERT MURRAY, 'A Catalogue of the Evelyn Waugh Collection at The Humanities Research Center, The University of Texas at Austin' (New York, Whitson Publishing Co., 1981).
DAVIS, ROBERT MURRAY, 'Evelyn Waugh, Writer' (Oklahoma, Pilgrim Books, 1981).
DAVIS, ROBERT MURRAY, DOYLE, PAUL A., KOSOK, HEINZ, and LINCK, CHARLES E., Jr, 'Evelyn Waugh: A Checklist of Primary and Secondary Material' (New York, Whitson Publishing Co., 1972).
DE VITIS, A.A., 'Roman Holiday. The Catholic Novels of Evelyn Waugh' (Vision Press, 1958).
DONALDSON, FRANCES, 'Evelyn Waugh. Portrait of a Country Neighbour' (Weidenfeld & Nicolson, 1967).
DYSON, A.E., Evelyn Waugh and the Mysteriously Disappearing Hero, 'Critical Quarterly', 2 (Spring 1960), 72-9; revised and reprinted in 'The Crazy Fabric' (Macmillan, 1965).

519

EAGLETON, TERRY, 'Exiles and Émigrés' (Chatto & Windus, 1970).

FUSSELL, PAUL, 'Abroad' (Oxford University Press, 1980).

GALLAGHER, DONAT (ed.), 'A Little Order' (Eyre Methuen, 1978) (selection of Waugh's journalism).

GREENBLATT, STEPHEN JAY, 'Three Modern Satirists: Waugh, Orwell and Huxley' (Yale University Press, 1965).

HEATH, JEFFREY, 'The Picturesque Prison' (Weidenfeld & Nicolson, 1982).

HOLLIS, CHRISTOPHER, 'Evelyn Waugh' (Longmans for British Council, 1966), Writers and their Work series.

HOLLIS, CHRISTOPHER, 'Oxford in the Twenties: Recollections of Five Friends' (Heinemann, 1976).

JOHNSTONE, RICHARD, 'The Will to Believe: Novelists of the Thirties' (Oxford University Press, 1982).

KERMODE, FRANK, 'Puzzles and Epiphanies: Essays and Reviews 1958-61' (London, 1962); reprints Mr Waugh's Cities.

LITTLEWOOD, IAN, 'The Writings of Evelyn Waugh' (Oxford, Basil Blackwell, 1983).

LODGE, DAVID, 'Evelyn Waugh' (Columbia University Press, 1971), Columbia Essays on Modern Writers series.

O'DONNELL, DONAT, 'Maria Cross: Imaginative Patterns in a Group of Modern Catholic Writers' (London, 1954); reprints No. 102.

O'FAOLAIN, SEAN, 'The Vanishing Hero: Studies in the Novelists of the Twenties' (Eyre & Spottiswoode, 1957).

PHILLIPS, GENE D., 'Evelyn Waugh's Officers, Gentlemen and Rogues: The Fact Behind the Fiction' (Chicago, Nelson-Hall, 1975).

POWELL, ANTHONY, 'Messengers of Day' (Heinemann, 1978).

PRYCE-JONES, DAVID, 'Evelyn Waugh and his World' (Weidenfeld & Nicolson, 1973).

SPENDER, STEPHEN, The World of Evelyn Waugh, in 'The Creative Element: A Study of Vision, Despair and Orthodoxy Among Some Modern Writers' (Hamish Hamilton, 1953).

ST JOHN, JOHN, 'To the War with Waugh' (Leo Cooper, 1973).

STOPP, FREDERICK J., 'Evelyn Waugh. Portrait of an Artist' (Chapman & Hall, 1958).

SYKES, CHRISTOPHER, 'Evelyn Waugh. A Biography' (Collins, 1975).

WAUGH, ALEC, 'My Brother Evelyn and Other Profiles' (Cassell, 1967).

WAUGH, ALEC, 'The Early Years of Alec Waugh' (Cassell, 1962).

WAUGH, ALEC, 'The Fatal Gift' (W.H. Allen, 1973).

WAUGH, ARTHUR, 'One Man's Road' (Chapman & Hall, 1931).

WAUGH, EVELYN, 'A Little Learning, the First Volume of an Autobiography' (Chapman & Hall, 1964).

WILSON, EDMUND, 'Classics and Commercials: A Literary Chronicle of the Forties' (W.H. Allen, 1951).

Index

The index is divided into three parts: I Works by Evelyn
Waugh; II The Critics on Evelyn Waugh; III General Index.

I WORKS BY EVELYN WAUGH

II   THE CRITICS ON EVELYN WAUGH

III   GENERAL INDEX

DATE DUE

261-2500			Printed in USA

THE CRITICAL HERITAGE SERIES

GENERAL EDITOR: B. C. SOUTHAM

Volumes published and forthcoming